MW00775989

Price Management

Hermann Simon • Martin Fassnacht

Price Management

Strategy, Analysis, Decision,
Implementation

 Springer

Hermann Simon
Simon-Kucher & Partners Strategy
and Marketing Consultants
Bonn, Germany

Martin Fassnacht
WHU – Otto Beisheim School of Management
Chair of Marketing and Commerce
Düsseldorf, Germany

ISBN 978-3-319-99455-0   ISBN 978-3-319-99456-7   (eBook)
https://doi.org/10.1007/978-3-319-99456-7

Library of Congress Control Number: 2018959416

This Springer imprint is published by the registered company Springer Nature Switzerland AG
The registered company address is: Gewerbestrasse 11, 6330 Cham, Switzerland

Testimonials

"This book is truly state of the art and the most comprehensive work in price management."

—Prof. Philip Kotler
Kellogg School of Management, Northwestern University

"This very important book builds an outstanding bridge between science and practice."

—Kasper Rorsted
CEO, Adidas

"This book provides practical guidelines on value creation, communication and management, which is an imperative for businesses to survive in the coming era of uncertainty."

—Dr. Chang-Gyu Hwang
Chairman and CEO, KT Corporation (Korea Telecom)

Preface

The title *Price Management* expresses our ambition to produce a book which is both grounded in theory and relevant in practice. The author team—an academic (Fassnacht) and a practitioner (Simon)—guarantees the desired integration of theory and practice.

State of the Art

This book is state of the art yet also looks into the future. Digitalization is penetrating all phases of the pricing process, from strategy and analysis to decision-making and implementation. The Internet and other new technologies (sensors, measurement, etc.) have led to a wealth of price management innovations which this book explores in detail. These include flat rates, freemium, pay-per-use, pay-what-you-want, new price metrics, two-sided price systems, negative prices, sharing economy, Big Data, artificial intelligence, and machine learning. Innovative payment systems and even cryptocurrencies are also having effects on price management.

The Integration of Theory and Practice Using Case Examples

We use real-world cases throughout the book to ensure the link between theoretical rigor and practical relevance. That is possible because we could draw on the vast and diverse experience of Simon-Kucher and Partners, the global market leader in price consulting. We have anonymized these examples whenever necessary to protect confidentiality.

Industry Orientation

It is easy to see price management as a basic discipline, similar to accounting or controlling and generally applicable across all sectors. But our decades of involvement in price management have taught us that the ways of framing and solving pricing problems are often industry-specific. Consumer goods, for example, are sold primarily through intermediaries (retailers), while industrial products are predominantly sold directly. The resulting pricing issues, strategies, and tactics in these sectors are very different. For this reason, we devote separate chapters to the respective price management issues in the consumer goods, industrial goods, service, and retail sectors.

Global Approach

This is *the* global book on pricing! We committed ourselves to a global approach throughout the book. Global competition means that companies around the world are confronted with similar price management challenges. In line with this global approach, we selected representative case studies and practical examples from around the world.

Target Audience

The integration of theory and practice makes this book equally relevant for students and academics as for entrepreneurs and managers. Price management is becoming more and more professionalized in companies around the world, with stronger engagement from senior management, all the way up to the CEO. We not only cover the role of price as a short-term profit driver but also show how companies can use price as a means to drive sustained increases in shareholder value.

Price management is taking up a larger portion of business studies. This is due in part to the Internet, which has massively increased price transparency, intensified price competition, and triggered more price wars. But at the same time, the Internet also increases value transparency. This dichotomy results in some surprising and highly asymmetric effects for the marketing instrument "price."

We have many people to thank for their contributions to this book, and we call attention to them individually in the acknowledgments. But we are especially thankful to Anna-Karina Schmitz for her outstanding work as our project leader and to the associates of Simon-Kucher and Partners for their valuable support.

The preoccupation with price management dates all the way back to Ancient Rome. The Latin language uses the identical word for "price" and "value," namely, the word "pretium."

Pretium = Price = Value

That is the core equation of price management!

Hermann Simon

Bonn, Germany
Düsseldorf, Germany

Martin Fassnacht

Hermann Simon
Martin Fassnacht

Contents

About the Authors

Hermann Simon is the founder and honorary chairman of Simon-Kucher and Partners, the world's leading price consultancy. Ranked on the Thinkers 50 list of the most influential international management thinkers, he is considered the world's leading authority on pricing. Simon has published over 35 books in 27 languages, including the worldwide bestsellers *Hidden Champions, Confessions of the Pricing Man, Power Pricing*, and *Manage for Profit, Not for Market Share*. From 1995 to 2009, he served as CEO of Simon-Kucher and Partners. He has advised many of the world's leading companies and has served as a board member of foundations and corporations. Before committing himself entirely to management consulting, Simon was a professor of business administration and marketing at the Universities of Mainz (1989–1995) and Bielefeld (1979–1989). His visiting professorships include Harvard Business School, Stanford University, London Business School, INSEAD, Keio University in Tokyo, and the Massachusetts Institute of Technology. He has served on the editorial boards of numerous business journals, including the *International Journal of Research in Marketing, Management Science, Recherche et Applications en Marketing, Décisions Marketing*, and *European Management Journal*. He was also president of the European Marketing Academy (EMAC). Simon studied economics and business administration at the Universities of Cologne and Bonn, where he received degrees in economics and earned his Ph.D. in management science. He has received many international awards and three honorary doctorates. He is honorary professor at the University of International Business and Economics in Beijing, and the Hermann Simon Business School in China has been named in his honor.

Martin Fassnacht is the Otto Beisheim chaired professor of marketing and commerce at the WHU—Otto Beisheim School of Management in Düsseldorf, Germany. He ranks as one of Germany's most influential economists. Under the motto "We Inspire Marketing," he and his team at WHU generate fresh ideas for research, practice, and teaching in price management, retail marketing, and brand management. He serves as a strategic advisor to consumer goods manufacturers and retailers, and he and his team conduct projects in cooperation with partners from industry and trade. He is also the author of numerous publications in international peer-reviewed journals and magazines. Fassnacht is the scientific director of the Center for Market-Oriented Corporate Management at WHU and the academic director of WHU's MBA program. He is the chairman of the Advisory Board of the Henkel Center for Consumer Goods (HCCG) at WHU. Fassnacht completed his postdoctoral work at the University of Mannheim and at the WHU with Prof. Christian Homburg. He received his Ph.D. in business administration from the University of Mainz under the direction of Prof. Hermann Simon, co-author of this book. Fassnacht was a visiting scholar at the Owen Graduate School of Management at Vanderbilt University and at the McCombs School of Business at the University of Texas at Austin.

Fundamentals of Price Management

1

Abstract

In this fundamental chapter, we will identify price as the strongest driver of profit and explore the relevant aspects of price management. Despite its significance, price is often not well managed in practice. Sharp profit declines are not uncommon because of poor price management. The consequences of pricing are not fully understood for many reasons, including gaps in how theory is applied to practice, the multidimensionality of prices, complex chains of effects, psychological price phenomena, and implementation barriers. We should view price management as a process which encompasses strategy, analysis, decision-making, and implementation and which draws on insights from different scientific fields. In general, price mechanisms are increasingly penetrating parts of society beyond traditional business. More and more, fields such as education, traffic, and health care are controlled through price mechanisms. Price management is coming under an increasingly comprehensive regulatory framework, so that one always needs to make the appropriate checks before implementing a price measure.

1.1 Profit and Price

This book is fundamentally about profit and price. Price is the most effective profit driver. The definition of profit is as follows:

$$\text{Profit} = (\text{Price} \times \text{Volume}) - \text{Costs} \tag{1.1}$$

The profit formula shows that there are ultimately only three drivers of profit: price, volume, and costs. Costs, in turn, have fixed and variable components. To demonstrate the influence of each of these drivers, consider the following simple example of a typical price structure for many products and services. Imagine a

© Springer Nature Switzerland AG 2019
H. Simon, M. Fassnacht, *Price Management*,
https://doi.org/10.1007/978-3-319-99456-7_1

An improvement of five percent ...   ... increases profit by ...

	Profit driver		Profit		
	old	new	old	new	
Price	$100	$105	$10 mill.	$15 mill.	50%
Unit costs	$60	$57	$10 mill.	$13 mill.	30%
Sales volume	$1 mill.	$1.05 mill.	$10 mill.	$12 mill.	20%
Fixed costs	$30 mill.	$28.5 mill.	$10 mill.	$11.5 mill.	15%

Fig. 1.1 Effect on profit from improvements in profit drivers

company sells 1 million units of a product priced at $100 per unit. The company has $30 million in fixed costs, plus $60 in variable costs per unit. This results in sales revenues of $100 million and a profit of $10 million. The return on sales is 10%. What effect would an isolated change (*ceteris paribus*) of 5% in one of the profit drivers have on profit? Figure 1.1 shows the answer. A 5% increase in price means the price is now $105. Holding all other factors constant, the revenue would increase to $105 million. The profit rises from $10 to $15 million, an improvement of 50%. For the other profit drivers, the percentage changes in profit from a 5% improvement in the respective factor (again, *ceteris paribus*) are 30%, 20%, and 15%. Under these circumstances, price is by far the strongest profit driver.

No less interesting is the reverse perspective, examining the consequences of a decline of 5% in an individual profit driver. Figure 1.2 shows what happens. The consequences are the mirror image. In the same way that a price increase has the strongest positive influence on profit, a price decrease has the strongest negative influence.

The comparison of price and volume as profit drivers is particularly revealing. Whether we increase or decrease price or volume (in isolation), we get the same revenue ($105 million for an increase; $95 million for a decrease). But whereas the entire $5 million revenue increase drops to the bottom line when we increase the price, the majority of the revenue increase from an improvement in volume ($3 million of the $5 million) gets absorbed by the resulting increase in variable costs. The opposite effect holds true for a price decrease, as the revenue decrease reduces profit by the same amount. If volume declines by 5%, in contrast, variable costs fall correspondingly by $3 million, which means profit declines only by $2 million. As we can see, changing the price has a far greater impact – positive *or* negative – on profit than changing the volume.

A decline of five percent ...   ... reduces profit by ...

	Profit driver old	Profit driver new	Profit old	Profit new		
Price	$100	$95	$10 mill.	$5 mill.	-50%	
Unit costs	$60	$63	$10 mill.	$7 mill.	-30%	
Sales volume	1 mill.	0.95 mill.	$10 mill.	$8 mill.	-20%	
Fixed costs	$30 mill.	$31.5 mill.	$10 mill.	$8.5 mill.	-15%	

Fig. 1.2 Effect on profit from declines in profit drivers

From this example, we can conclude that it is more advantageous for profit to grow through price increases than through volume increases. Conversely, it is better from a profit perspective to accept lower volumes than lower prices.

Confront managers with these statements as they need to choose between alternatives A and B below, and you get an explosive debate.

Alternative A: Accept a price cut of 5% (e.g., in the form of a rebate) and volume remains constant.

Alternative B: Accept a volume reduction of 5% and price remains constant.

We have discussed these alternatives with hundreds of managers in seminars and workshops. Almost all of them lean toward Alternative A, which means they defend volume at the expense of price, even though profit is $3 million lower (using our earlier numbers) than in Alternative B. Even in the case of improved profit drivers, many practitioners prefer volume growth, usually making the argument that market share is higher under that alternative. One could cite the mobile telecommunications operator T-Mobile US as an example. In 2014, the company endured high losses in order to expand its share of the US market [1]. We take a more in-depth look at the conflict between profit and market share in Chap. 2.

In the simplest possible way, this example demonstrates the interdependence between profit and its drivers. The assumption, however, that one can change only one profit driver without affecting the others is not commonly borne out in reality. A price increase of 5% often leads to a decline in volume. That applies analogously to changes in volume. In a stable market, volume would normally not rise by 5% unless there is a decline in price. At the same time, in our practice we have experienced many cases in which volume did not change despite a substantial increase in price. That happens frequently for price changes in the range of 1%, 2%, or 3%. Such

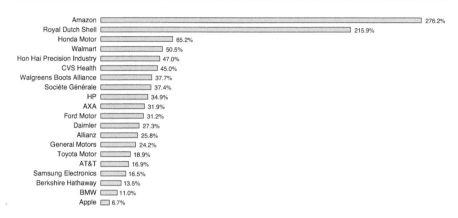

Fig. 1.3 Leverage effect of a 2% price increase (based on profits for selected Fortune 500 companies in 2015)

changes can be implemented in real life with little or no effect on the other profit drivers, i.e., without any noticeable violation of our ceteris paribus assumption.

If we apply this simple thought process to selected companies of the Global Fortune 500, we can see what would happen if these companies realized a price increase of 2%. Figure 1.3 shows the percentage change in pre-tax profit as a result of such a price increase. (The pre-tax return on sales is the pre-tax profit divided by the revenue. Dividing 2% by this calculated return on sales results in the profit increase (in percentage terms) which would result from a price increase of 2%, assuming no loss of volume.)

The effects on profit from such a seemingly small price increase of 2% are very strong for most companies. If Amazon succeeded in raising its prices by 2% without any loss in volume, its profit would increase by 276.2%. For HP, the profit increase would be 34.9%. Even companies which are already highly profitable benefit from such a slight price increase. Apple has the highest return on sales (29.7%) of the companies listed in Fig. 1.3, but even in Apple's case, profit would rise by 6.7%, which is still more than three times the price increase on a percentage basis. On average, a price increase of 2% would raise the profits of the companies shown in Fig. 1.3 by 52.2%! This calculation shows the enormous leverage that price has on profit. It pays to optimize prices.

The lower a company's margins, the greater this leverage effect from a price change will be. If a company has a net profit margin of only 2% (which is typical for many retailers), a price increase of 2% would double the company's profits, assuming no volume loss. Moreover, the profit margins of companies tend to be much smaller than people would generally assume. The average after-tax profit margin for the 500 largest companies in the world was 6.3% in 2013 [2]. If we assume a tax rate of 30%, then the pre-tax margin amounts to around 8%. Figure 1.4 shows the return on sales for industrial companies from different countries for the years 2007–2011.

American companies achieved an average return on sales of 5.1% in the 5 years from 2007 to 2011. On an international basis, this return is relatively low. The average

Fig. 1.4 Average after-tax return on sales for industrial companies (international comparison for 2007–2011) [3]

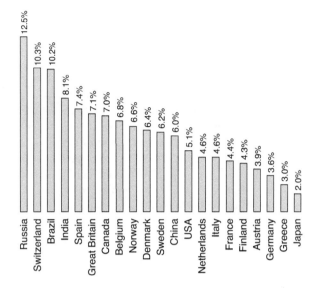

for the other countries was 6.1%. Companies in Russia achieved 12.5%. Returns were 8.1% and 7.1%, respectively, in India and Great Britain. Companies in France realized an after-tax return of only 4.4%, but this was still above their German counterparts' (3.6%). Companies in Greece (3%) and Japan (2%) achieved the lowest returns. Amid such weak yields, every tenth of a price point makes a difference.

1.2   Definition of Price

The *price* is the number of monetary units which a buyer must hand over for one unit of a product. This definition is simple and clear. Indeed, many of the prices we encounter on a daily basis have this one-dimensional character. Think of a pound of coffee at the supermarket, a gallon of gasoline, or a magazine at the kiosk. However, prices often come in forms which are much more complex. Prices or price systems can comprise several parameters, even a large number of them. Here is a selection of complex price parameters and structures:

- Base price
- Discounts, bonuses, rebates, conditions, and special offers
- Differentiated prices by package size or product variant
- Differentiated prices based on customer segment, time of day, location, or phase of the product life cycle
- Prices for complementary or substitutive products
- Prices for special or additional services
- Prices with two or more dimensions (e.g., upfront charge and a usage fee)
- Bundles and prices for individual components

- Prices based on personal negotiations
- Manufacturer and end consumer prices

This list of price parameters and structures is by no means complete, but it illustrates that prices are often complex constructs, and not one-dimensional. Companies can have hundreds or even thousands of prices, all of which must be determined. The price list of a bank usually contains several hundred line items. In trade, assortments with tens of thousands of articles are common. The range of replacement parts for the manufacturers of cars or heavy machinery can comprise several hundred thousand items and price points. Airlines make millions of price changes over the course of a year. Important questions in this context are: how do customers deal with this large number of prices, price parameters, and price changes? What is the level of price transparency? And what are the effects on volume and profit [4]? The complex and multidimensional nature of prices holds significant potential for optimization.

1.3   Price and Management

1.3.1   Price as a Marketing Instrument

If prices were predetermined by the market, management would not need to devote much attention to them. We encounter this situation with pure commodities which are traded on exchanges. The only things that matter with such goods are cost efficiency and volume adjustments. However, even within commodity markets, there are still ways to use price movements to one's own advantage. With better price forecasts, for example, one can improve the timing of price and delivery agreements.

In modern product and service markets, price is typically a parameter whose management, flexibility, and effects offer very interesting opportunities:

- Price has a strong influence on volume and market share. For consumer goods, the price elasticity is on average 10–20 times as high as the advertising elasticity and roughly eight times as high as the sales force elasticity [5]. That means that the effect of a price change, on a percentage basis, is 10–20 times stronger than the effect of a similar percentage increase in the advertising budget and 8 times stronger than the effect of a comparable percentage change in the sales budget. Sethuraman et al. [6, p. 467] have even determined that advertising budgets would need to increase by 30% in order to match the effect of a price decrease of 1%. The level of price elasticity varies by product category and product [7, p. 82].
- Price is an instrument known for its fast applicability. In contrast to changes to a product (innovation), an advertising campaign, or a cost-cutting program, prices can be readily adjusted on short notice as new situations arise, apart from

long-term contractual agreements or catalog periods. The Internet has only increased the speed of these adjustments. A company can change prices in a matter of seconds. The same applies to retailers whose scanner systems have electronic displays at the shelf. Such changes have also been a topic for gas stations. Germany has a price registration database in operation, which consumers can access via an app to find up-to-the-minute fuel prices at around 14,500 filling stations [8]. On the one hand, this increases price transparency for consumers, but at the same time, it also reveals price differences for competitors [9]. In order to reduce the number of price changes, the Australian government limits price changes to one per day. The concept of dynamic pricing takes advantage of the ability to change prices quickly by adjusting prices to the prevailing supply and demand situation.

- The effects of price manifest themselves quickly on the demand side. If a gas station changes its prices and the local competition does not follow, market shares can shift significantly in a matter of minutes. The same goes for the Internet, which has created unprecedented price transparency. With one tap or keystroke, a consumer can call up the current prices for a vast number of suppliers and can make an immediate purchase decision. This has advanced to the point where a consumer can scan the barcode of a product in one store and find out instantly what the product costs online or in nearby stores. In the case of other marketing actions such as advertising campaigns or new product introductions, the response from the demand side often comes with a considerable time lag.
- The flipside of quick price actions with rapid demand responses is that competitors can act just as swiftly with their own prices. Such price reactions often happen quickly and can come with such an intensity that they may ignite a price war. Because competitors can respond to price changes almost instantaneously, it is hard to achieve a sustainable competitive advantage purely through price measures. That would require a cost advantage which prevents competitors from maintaining low(er) prices for very long. A Big Data analysis by Feedvisor [10] tracked 10 million Amazon products over a period of 10 months. It found that over 60,000 price wars occur every day. On average, 92% of those price wars happened between two competitors, and 72% lasted less than 6 h. Usually the price wars follow predefined rules; however, the level of knowledge about competitive behavior is low.
- Price is the only marketing instrument which does not require upfront expenditures or investments. This makes it possible even for cash-strapped companies (start-ups or companies launching a new product) to implement the optimal price. In comparison, it is rarely possible to optimize instruments such as advertising, sales, or research and development – which require upfront investments before they earn a return – when a company has limited financial resources.
- Cost reductions and rationalization are vitally important goals for many companies. These efforts are always ongoing, but in many companies, the residual cost savings potential is limited, if not already exhausted. Furthermore, in mature markets it is difficult to capitalize on the third profit driver, which is

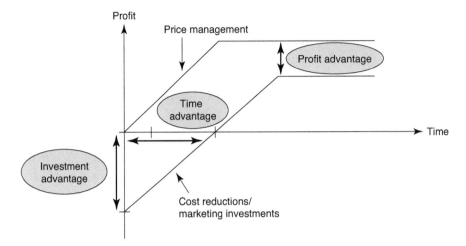

Fig. 1.5 The three advantages of price management compared to cost reductions and marketing investments

volume. Mature markets are generally characterized by a zero-sum game, which means any volume increases must come at the expense of competitors, who will defend their market shares. The improvement potential in price management, however, is not even close to being exhausted in many cases.

Figure 1.5 shows the advantages which pricing offers as a marketing tool compared to cost reductions or to investments in other marketing instruments such as advertising or sales. The investment advantage means that price optimization requires little upfront capital, unlike cost reductions or marketing investments. The time advantage implies that pricing has a positive effect on profit sooner than the other measures. And the profit advantage expresses the fact that price measures often lead to higher profit increases.

Pricing plays a standout role as a marketing instrument, but it also has an important meaning to customers. The price is the "sacrifice" which the customers must accept when they acquire a product. The higher the price is, the greater this sacrifice. Figure 1.6 shows how consumers in different countries (130,000 respondents) reacted to anticipated price increases.

According to this study, German and Chinese consumers tend to react to a price increase by buying a less expensive product at the same store or switching to a store which offers lower prices. American consumers respond less strongly to price increases.

In light of the outstanding role of price as a profit driver and the notable ways it affects a business, one should expect that managers and even top executives would devote a lot of attention to pricing. But in practice, this is often not the case. Instead, management continues to commit the greatest attention and energy to another profit driver, namely, to costs.

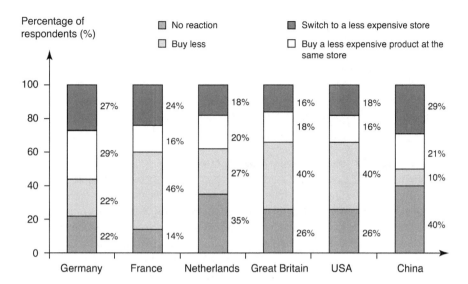

Fig. 1.6 Reactions of consumers to anticipated price increases [11]

"As a manager, it is easier to work on the cost side than on the revenue side," said the CEO of an airline [12]. Companies also tend to spend more time and energy on increasing volume (e.g., through investments in sales and advertising) than they do on price management. Many companies give pricing neither the professionalism nor the seriousness it warrants.

Take, for example, the response of a large engineering group to a question about how the company arrives at its actual transaction prices: "Essentially we proceed like this: we apply a factor of 2.5 to the manufacturing costs, and leave the rest to the sales force." Such a process makes no sense. A closer look at this company's performance uncovered that it was sacrificing a large amount of profits, or "leaving a lot of money on the table," as the business cliché goes. The following statement from a board member of one of the world's 100 largest banks is also eye opening in this context: "This bank is 125 years old. To my knowledge, this project marks the first time the bank looks at pricing in a professional manner."

In the recent past, especially since the Great Recession, however, we observe that top management shows increasing interest in price management. A large number of CEOs have spoken openly about pricing in recent years. Their comments have come in interviews and road shows, at shareholder meetings, and during conferences with analysts. Our impression is that such comments come predominantly from companies with above-average profits [13]. That leads to the conclusion that these companies, or more precisely their leaders, have understood – better and sooner than companies with lower profits – the critical role that price plays as a driver of both profit and shareholder value.

Why do many companies still neglect or play down the importance of price management? We see several reasons.

1.3.2   Understanding the Role of Price

People from all parts of the economy – from businesspeople and managers to consumers to regulators, investors, and analysts – have difficulties understanding at a deeper level the role of price. Granted, many of these same people have an intuitive feel for how pricing works and why it matters. But this is insufficient as the basis of solid price decisions. Why is it so hard to "get" pricing at a deeper level?

1.3.2.1 Gaps Between Theory and Practice

Although many managers have studied economics and received exposure to pricing during their academic studies, they struggle to take what they have learned about price theory and apply it to their business. Many young entrepreneurs are asking themselves what the right price is for their offer [14]. Universities treat concepts such as price-response functions, price elasticity, and price differentiation theoretically, supported by mathematical models. When the university graduates enter the business world, they encounter very different processes such as cost-plus calculations or experience-based pricing. The theory from their studies does not seem relevant to real-life business decisions. Thus, it falls into disuse and gradually fades from memory. This leads to situations where managers talk about concepts such as "price elasticity," but do not know precisely what "elasticity" means or the extent to which it even applies to the problem at hand. They are often unable to empirically quantify the effects of price measures. This failure to transfer and apply theoretical knowledge to real-life business problems has two root causes. First, the teaching of pricing is too abstract. Second, many companies still have a broad-based resistance to academic concepts. Having said that, we do notice sharp differences across industries. The leader in the application of highly sophisticated price systems is the pharmaceutical industry. We also see relatively high levels of pricing competence at premium carmakers, telecommunications companies, leading Internet companies, and airlines.

1.3.2.2 The Multidimensional Effects of Price

The multidimensional effects of price contribute to the lack of understanding. Revenue is the product of price and volume. Thus, it corresponds geometrically to a rectangle. The same applies to profit, which is the product of unit contribution margin (price minus variable unit cost) and volume minus fixed costs. While it is easy to make one-dimensional comparisons, it is more difficult to compare two-dimensional surfaces. Such comparisons become really challenging when there are multiple price parameters, which means managers need to consider multi-dimensional structures. It is no surprise that intuition reaches its limits amid such complexity.

To illustrate this, we recall our previous example with the price of $100, variable unit cost of $60, fixed costs of $30 million, and a sales volume of 1 million units. In this initial situation, revenue is $100 million and profit is $10 million. Now we pose the following question: "If the company cuts the price by 20%, how much more does the company need to sell, in order to achieve the same profit?" Ask this question in a real-world business setting, and most of the spontaneous answers to the question are wrong. The most common such answer is "20%." A volume increase of 20% would indeed result in roughly the same revenue as before. We would have sales of 1.2 million units (20% volume increase) at a price of $80 (reflecting the 20% price cut), which leads to revenue of $96 million. But in this situation, the company would lose $6 million.

The correct answer is that a volume increase of 100% is required. Yes, the company would need to double its sales volume in order to maintain profit at $10 million. Due to the price decrease of 20%, the unit contribution margin (i.e., the difference between price and variable unit cost) falls by half from $40 to $20. Therefore, the company would need to sell twice as many units in order to keep profit constant.

We witness similar responses when we pose the question in another way: "What volume decline could a company accept in order to keep profit constant after a price increase of 20%?" Despite the relatively simple calculations required, we rarely receive correct spontaneous answers to this question. The company could accept a volume decline of as much as one third before profit would fall below the original level. Due to the price increase, the unit contribution margin rises from $40 to $60, so even when we cut volume to 666,666 units, we generate revenue of $80 million. Subtracting the variable costs ($40 million) and fixed costs ($30 million) leaves us with a profit of $10 million, identical to the original amount. This calculation underscores the difficulties of intuitive problem-solving when we need to compare different two-dimensional profit structures.

1.3.2.3 Complex Chains of Effects

We present our examples with the utmost simplicity. In reality, the interdependencies and the resulting chains of effects are much more complex. Price effects are not only multidimensional but also interdependent and in some cases countervailing. Figure 1.7 clarifies that many paths lead from price to what we are ultimately interested in, which is profit. The dashed arrows identify defining equations, e.g., revenue as the product of price and volume and profit as the difference between revenue and costs.

The core relationships of this system are the so-called behavioral equations symbolized by the thick solid arrows. These are the price-response function and the cost function. The price-response function gives us the sales volume as a function of price. As the figure demonstrates, knowledge of the price-response function is an indispensable prerequisite for making a rational price decision. The cost function yields the cost as a function of volume. The feedback loop shown by the thin solid arrow illustrates the profit effects of a particular price measure.

Price-response and cost functions determine the different junctures where price influences profit. In this system there are precisely three paths along which price exerts its influence:

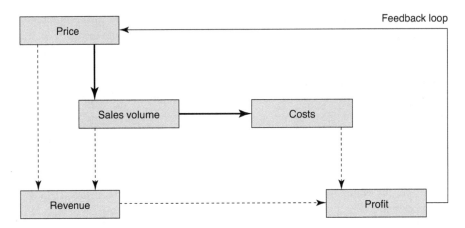

Fig. 1.7 Interdependencies and chains of effect in price management

Price → Revenue → Profit
Price → Volume → Revenue → Profit
Price → Volume → Cost → Profit

Figure 1.7 considers the simplest case, with only one supplier (monopoly) and one period. When we consider several competitors (e.g., oligopoly), several periods, or multistage sales, paths of effects become more complex:

Price → Competitors' price → Market Share → Volume → Revenue → Profit
Price (current) → Volume (future) → Revenue (future) and Profit (future)
Price (current) → Volume → Costs (future) → Profit (future)
Price (manufacturer) → Price (retailer) → Volume → Revenue → Profit

Those are only the most important and most obvious paths. We will explore them in detail in various chapters of this book. Because of the complexity and the difficulty in quantifying these chains of effect, many practitioners tend to prefer experience-based price decisions and rely on rules of thumb. It is rather unlikely that these intuitive approaches result in optimal prices.

1.3.2.4 Psychology

The volume-, revenue-, and profit-related price effects can be more readily understood, in part because we can quantify them. In addition to these effects, though, there are a variety of psychological effects to account for, some of which seem to defy rational economics. These phenomena include price thresholds and price anchors and the snob or Veblen effect (associating high quality or prestige with high prices). The field of behavioral economics has yielded many new insights which call some of the tenets of classical economics into question. In some cases, these revolutionary insights have refuted traditional theories. While behavioral economics has contributed valuable new insights, it has also caused confusion and made the challenge of understanding pricing even more difficult. What is noteworthy is that some experienced businesspeople have implicitly and intuitively understood many of these insights for years and have applied them to their pricing tactics. Such examples include the use of price anchors and the prevalence of tricks such as cash-back programs. These tactics defy explanation through classical economics, which assumes complete information and utility-maximizing behavior from economic actors.

1.3.2.5 Implementation Barriers

Implementation barriers and weak implementation are two more reasons why companies can fail to realize their full profit potential through price management. Even when a company does careful analysis and makes sound price decisions, the price measure can still fail due to poor or inadequate implementation. The root causes for this failure include wrong goals, unclear roles and responsibilities, ineffective incentives, conscious attempts by sales people to undermine discount guidelines, misleading price communication, and careless price controlling. In his empirical study of consumer goods companies, Nelius [15, p. 172] showed that organizational parameters such as specialization and coordination have a direct and significantly positive effect on the economic success of a company. If companies applied the same thinking to pricing, by institutionalizing their own pricing departments, they could develop core competencies and provide support for more objective and more nuanced price decisions [16]. Typically, however, price implementation does not receive the attention it deserves, especially considering how relevant it is to profits. At the end of the day, the price that counts is the closing transaction price.

1.3.2.6 Industry Specifics

The basic laws of economics, such as the inverse relationship between price and volume, apply broadly and generally across all industries. Nonetheless, individual industries exhibit very different circumstances and, as a result, different pricing practices. These depend on the market structure (monopoly, oligopoly, perfect competition); the type of product (homogeneous vs. differentiated); the prevailing nature of competition (peaceful vs. aggressive); the habits of customers (more or less price sensitive); the cost structure (ratio of fixed vs. variable costs); trade or retailer price practices (own determination vs. compliance with recommended prices); and the role of the Internet.

These differences demand that practitioners become familiar with the circumstances and nuances peculiar to their industry before making price decisions. These differences, habits, and industry-specific conventional wisdom often stand in the way of efforts to transplant a successful price system from one industry to another. According to the motto "it doesn't work that way in our industry," there is often little willingness to even consider adopting a new system or model from another industry. Price management has its own history in every sector, which makes change difficult. Having said that, we feel that many industries could learn from others in how to improve their pricing. The different characteristics often explain why some industries remain profitable year after year, while others are notorious for their persistently low margins.

1.3.3   Price Management as a Process

When it comes to price, textbooks traditionally focus on price decisions, or more specifically, on price optimization. Our definition of the price management process is more comprehensive and, at the same time, more concrete. We define it as follows:

The price management process is a system of rules and procedures to determine and implement prices. It covers the following aspects:

- Information, models, rules for decision-making, and optimization
- Organization, responsibilities, and incentives
- Competencies, qualifications, training, and negotiation
- IT support

Under the process perspective, we think in terms of the following sequence: "Strategy → Analysis → Decision → Implementation."

Price decisions and price optimization can be perceived as parts of a comprehensive price management process. While price optimization normally stands at the forefront of the academic literature, other sub-processes of price management are equally important. The introduction of a new car model or a new pharmaceutical product is largely a price optimization challenge. But price setting for the automaker's spare parts requires taking the entire process into account. Optimizing individual prices for thousands of parts is out of the question. The situation can be heterogeneous in a similar way for a pharmaceutical company. Sales through pharmacies and through hospitals present the drug maker with fundamentally different situations. Any company confronted with a range of different situations needs to develop systematic processes for price management.

One interesting question is whether the optimization perspective or the process perspective dominates in practice. We have discussed both perspectives in a large number of companies. A significant majority (71%) claimed that the process perspective is the more relevant theme. The remaining 29%, in contrast, see price decisions and price optimization as the dominant topic. Figure 1.8 shows this breakdown.

Of course, such a result depends on the selection of the respondent companies and the industries they are in. In the automotive industry, the description of price processes already plays a prominent role. Riekhof and Lohaus [17, p. 6] found in their study that more than 70% of companies have a detailed description of these processes. All in all, price management processes play an outstanding role in practice, and the process perspective is moving forward [18].

The treatment of price management processes in the literature is not in line with its applications in practice. For several years now, scientific research has focused increasingly on price management processes [19, 20]. But empirical studies of these

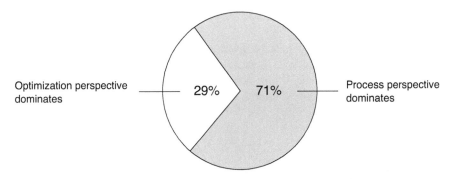

Fig. 1.8 The relevance in practice of price decision/optimization vs. price management process (Simon-Kucher & Partners)

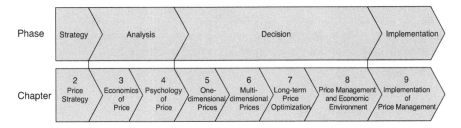

Fig. 1.9 Process perspective of price management and the structure of this book

processes have proven difficult for several reasons. First, many companies fail to understand price management as a process [21, p. 4]. Second, investigating such processes, which are often neither transparent nor documented, requires a deep internal and industry examination which takes considerable time and ties down a lot of personnel. Third, in most organizations, price management processes are highly confidential. Automotive industry suppliers and food/grocery retailers, among others, do not want to give their customers even the slightest impression that they devote much time and resources to prices. In short, the academic study of price management processes faces significant roadblocks.

The resource-based view of price management fits into the context of the process perspective. In strategy, there are two schools of thought. One defines strategy based on market opportunities, the other uses internal competencies, or resources, as its basis. In this sense, competence in price management is being classified as an increasingly important resource [22]. There is empirical evidence that companies which have a high level of competence in price management perform better over the long term [21, p. 150, 23].

In putting this book together, we follow the process perspective shown in Fig. 1.9.

1.4   Knowledge Sources for Price Management

Modern price management benefits from a wide variety of knowledge sources. These include academic as well as practice-oriented subdisciplines. The academic sources comprise macro- and microeconomics, marketing, behavioral economics, and brain research. Sources from the practitioner side include specialized consultants, software developers, innovative companies, and popular authors.

1.4.1   Macroeconomic Price Theory

This research area explores the interaction of supply and demand, the overall economic efficiency of the price system, and questions of market equilibria. This subdiscipline is vitally important for economic policy and, for labor, competition, antitrust, and other regulatory activities. It contributes to our understanding of markets and their mechanisms but provides only limited insights for price decision-making and price management at the business level.

1.4.2   Microeconomics

Under the neoclassical paradigm, researchers developed models characterized by theoretical rigor, highly precise assumptions, and normative statements. The classic price optimization model, which says that the optimal price is defined by the equality of marginal revenue and marginal cost, is one of the typical results of this research area. Microeconomic models foster theoretical understanding, the importance of which we cannot emphasize enough. Microeconomics makes an important contribution to price management.

1.4.3   Marketing Science

Since the 1970s, this discipline has focused primarily on empirical research into the effects of price and the advancement of measurement techniques. Marketing science has made essential contributions to our knowledge and to the understanding of innovative price structures such as nonlinear pricing, price bundling, flat rates, freemium concepts, or multi-person pricing. One measurement technique, conjoint measurement, deserves special mention. It enables the simultaneous quantification of customer utility and willingness to pay. Over the last two decades, process-related or organizational aspects have moved to the forefront.

1.4.4 Behavioral Economics

Behavioral economics is a more recent and increasingly important field. It is based primarily on experimental research rather than theory. Many of the phenomena revealed through these experiments are relevant for price management. They call the information and rationality assumptions of classical economics into question. However, some issues remain unresolved. The extent to which we can generalize from the experimental findings is often unclear. Likewise, it is not completely clear under what circumstances the findings apply and when they do not apply. Behavioral economics has an interdisciplinary nature. Economists, psychologists, and sociologists are all seeking to uncover the arcane phenomena of price. This innovative discipline is adding valuable new explanations and hints for the development of business models and price structures.

1.4.5 Brain Research

The newest research area relevant for price management is brain research. It can be seen as a subdiscipline of behavioral sciences. Using the latest devices available, researchers observe and measure the impact of price or other marketing stimuli on the human brain. There is already an abundance of results with potential implications for price management, but how these insights will apply in practice is hard to say [24].

1.4.6 Price Consulting

As far as we know, the late Dan Nimer was the first to name himself a "price consultant" [25]. That was in the 1970s, and Nimer worked on his own. Since then, we have seen the rise of several consulting firms which focus on price management. The firm Simon-Kucher & Partners, founded in Germany in 1985, is considered to be both the pioneer and the global market leader in the field. The firm currently has more than 1200 employees and 37 offices, spread across 25 countries. Beyond Simon-Kucher & Partners, there exists a host of other smaller, specialized consulting firms, particularly in the United States and Europe. The Professional Pricing Society (PPS), based in Atlanta, also belongs to this sphere. The PPS regularly holds conferences in the United States, Europe, and Asia on topics of price management, publishes several magazines devoted to pricing topics, and offers educational and training programs as well as formal certifications. In contrast to academic researchers, price consultants are application- and practice-oriented. They take concepts developed in research and apply them to real-life business problems. This transfer of knowledge from theory to practice has enabled the spread of new pricing techniques around the world.

1.4.7 Software for Price Management

As information technology has penetrated deeper into management, companies have turned over more and more operational functions to enterprise or specialized software. This trend has led to the development of software packages and software suppliers devoted to price management. This evolution began with revenue management systems, which rose to prominence with airlines and have now spread to other sectors such as hotels, car rental companies, and parking garages. Modern software for price management is used today for many products and services. In the context of Big Data, these applications will become ever more important. Artificial intelligence and machine learning also contribute to advancing our pricing competencies. With their help, companies can partially or completely automate pricing decisions.

1.4.8 Pricing Innovators

In the recent past, there has been a wave of innovations in price management. The majority, but not all of them, come from Internet-based companies. A notable example is the freemium model, which includes a basic version of a product or service at a price of zero (free) and a premium version which has a positive price. Other forms include pay-per-use, new price metrics, flat rates, prepaid systems, "pay what you want" or "name your own price" models, and behavior-based pricing such as "pay as you drive" insurance. In that last case, the premium is based on the driver's actual behavior and performance, which an installed device tracks. The wave of innovative price models has shown no signs of cresting. We expect more innovations in the coming years, especially from the online sector.

1.4.9 Popular Literature

The fact that price is a very effective marketing instrument, and should therefore be applied more consciously, has not escaped the public. So it does not come as a surprise that popular authors have devoted themselves to this topic. One of the best-known contributions is the book *Priceless* by the American author William Poundstone [26], who has written numerous works on other "hot" topics. The book *Why Popcorn Costs So Much at the Movies – And Other Pricing Principles* by Richard McKenzie [27] also belongs in this category. These books are not aimed primarily at price decision-makers but rather at consumers. Taking the consumer's perspective, they cast a critical eye on all kinds of pricing tactics and tricks. The media is also looking more and more critically on how businesses manage price. When the rumor percolated that Amazon varies its prices by time of day, the media quickly filled with a flood of articles. In Japan, Coca-Cola allegedly backed away from an effort to vary prices in vending machines according to temperature amid negative press and a public backlash once plans became known. Newspapers and magazines report regularly on controversial price strategies. In 2016, Evian, which is part of Danone and one of the world's leading brands in water, reduced the volume of a popular bottle in Germany from 1.5 to 1.25 L and, at the same time, raised the price. Evian was chosen as the "deceptive packaging of 2016" by Germany's most prestigious national daily newspaper [28]. Because of the greater price transparency due to the Internet, we expect that authors and the media will increase their critical monitoring and "supervision" of price behavior. But the news is not entirely negative. The media also reports on innovative, original approaches to pricing which provide context and ideas for price management – not only to practitioners but to academics as well. We will explore these in greater depth in Chap. 14.

1.5   The Legal Framework of Price Management

Price management is subject to a multitude of legal regulations designed to keep businesses from restraining competition or abusing their pricing power. These regulations limit the freedom companies have in their pricing, in order to preserve competition and safeguard consumers. They are based on domestic and international (e.g., European) law and form a relatively confusing mass of rules and guidelines. In addition, antitrust, competition, and consumer protection laws are in a constant state of flux. Not only are legislatures and regulators continually enacting new rules, we also see the oversight agencies (competition, antitrust) intervening in price management. Finally, the courts are setting precedents through landmark decisions based on these laws and regulations.

Particularly relevant for price management are the following sets of laws and regulations:

1.5.1   United States

In the United States, antitrust violations, price cartels, etc. are criminal offenses and can result in prison sentences of up to 10 years. Price discrimination is explicitly forbidden for all companies, not only for market leaders or dominant suppliers. According to *§2 of the Clayton Act*: "It shall be unlawful [. . .] to discriminate in price between different purchasers of commodities of like grade and quality." The prices can, however, reflect differences in manufacturing or other costs. Even the recipient of a more favorable price could technically be breaking the law: "It shall be unlawful for any person [. . .] to induce or receive a discrimination in price which is prohibited." In New York and California, it is against the law to offer men and women different prices for the same or similar service, e.g., for a haircut.

1.5.2   European Union

Conduct or actions which have the potential to constrain trade among EU member nations and suppress competition are forbidden in the European Union

(EU) according to *Article 101 of the Treaty on the Functioning of the EU*. This covers agreements such as fixing price and trade conditions, dividing markets along geographic or other lines, limiting production or sales volumes, or implementing different conditions for the same level of performance in a way that puts trade partners at a disadvantage.

Article 102 of the Treaty on the Functioning of the EU forbids the abuse of a dominant market position. A business has a dominant market position if it essentially faces no current or potential competition in a product or geographic market, which means it can act independently without consideration for competitors, buyers, or suppliers in that defined market.

1.5.3 Worldwide

Violations of antitrust guidelines pose considerable risks. If, for example, one set of supplier conditions or one price component within a contract is held in violation of antitrust law, it can invalidate the entire contract. The victims of discrimination by a market-dominant business can demand an injunction against the practices and claim monetary damages. Antitrust violations are also viewed as criminal acts in many jurisdictions, with penalties including harsh fines or even prison sentences. Most jurisdictions do not exempt or approve price-fixing and similar actions. In other words, businesses need to assess their legal risks.

In addition to laws and regulations, individual countries have a large number of court decisions and precedents relevant for price management. This body of legal guidance and references is continually growing, deepening, and becoming more concrete. Therefore, rather than devoting a separate and more in-depth chapter on certain laws and regulations, we limit discussion to this brief overview.

1.5.4 Activities of the Antitrust Agencies

In nearly every country, there is an agency charged with uncovering price cartels. The activities of these agencies have increased over the last several years. In the United States, the Department of Justice and the Federal Trade Commission have this watchdog role. In Europe, the responsibility falls to national antitrust agencies and the European Commission. In 2016, the European Commission fined four truck makers a total of nearly €2.93 billion. That was the largest such fine ever imposed to date in the European Union. The largest fine against an individual company in Europe was the fine of €1.09 billion against Daimler for its participation in that cartel [29]. In the United States, Apple was found liable for conspiring with five publishers to increase e-book prices in 2015 and had to pay $450 million as part of a settlement [30].

Violations of US antitrust laws and regulations can lead to prison sentences. In the "largest price-fixing investigation ever" to date, launched against leading (and predominantly Japanese) automotive suppliers, 12 defendants were found guilty, sentenced to prison, and fined a collective $1 billion. In 2015, the longest prison sentence to date was handed down. Because of price-fixing on the route between the United States and Puerto Rico, the former CEO of the cargo company Sea Star Line received a sentence of 5 years [31].

Individuals or companies who turn state's evidence can play an important role in uncovering cartels. Companies which help the authorities uncover a cartel face either reduced penalties or no penalties at all. The economic consequences for companies which participate in cartels extend beyond the government fines they must pay. Affected customers can sue for damages, and more and more parties are doing exactly that. The immunity granted to state's witnesses does not extend to such damage claims.

We expressly advise every single company to examine the legality and conformity of price moves very carefully. This examination must happen prior to implementation and ideally takes place in the early planning stages. In most cases it is necessary to bring in specialized legal counsel. This advice applies in particular to companies holding dominant market positions. Price cartels have become increasingly risky, and as part of their compliance programs, companies have introduced internal codes of conduct designed to prevent their employees and management from undertaking unlawful pricing activities.

1.6 Current Trends in Price Management

1.6.1 Prices Are Penetrating Management Thinking

The primary focus of this book is on price management for products and services. This involves the business model, the price structure, and how the company sets and implements individual prices. We assume that the seller – be it a manufacturer, reseller, or service provider – has a certain amount of leeway to set and implement prices. Price is the central lever in a market economy. There are many sectors whose pricing we do not cover in this book. These include pricing of stock and commodity exchanges, price-fixing for gold, corporate or other asset valuations, the setting of wages in labor markets, bidding for government contracts, pricing of real estate, pricing of art, and tactics and behavior in tender processes. The fundamental laws of supply and demand apply in all of those markets, but the concrete nature and nuances of the respective price systems are very different. We recommend that interested readers consult the available specialty literature on these markets.

We observe an increasing penetration of price into areas of our lives where questions of supply and demand historically followed norms and rules other than pricing. Some of these are services traditionally provided free of charge by government, religious, or charity organizations. In days gone by, it was considered morally questionable to contemplate charging for these services. Usage of public highways was free, school attendance cost nothing, and other services have traditionally been inseparable parts of all-inclusive bundles. And in some areas, the sheer idea of asking a price was taboo.

This is changing rapidly. As the American philosopher Michael J. Sandel [32] asserts in his book *What Money Can't Buy: The Moral Limits of the Markets*, prices have begun to penetrate many sectors of our personal lives. For a price of $85 for a 5-year membership, travelers can join Pre-Check, a program of the "Transportation Security Administration" (TSA) in the United States, and take advantage of an "expedited security line" at airports [33]. Today more than 5 million people have registered, more than 200 US airports and 42 airlines participate, and 94% of the TSA Pre-Check waiting times are less than 5 min [34]. Entering the United States from abroad costs $14, the fee for an entry into ESTA (Electronic System for Travel Authorization). In some places in the United States, drivers can pay for access to special highway lanes during rush hour, with prices varying according to the traffic flow. Market design specialists suggest a much more general traffic pricing system which would apply to all roads. They estimate the costs of current worldwide traffic congestion at $1 trillion. Modern technology allows road use to be monitored and priced based on real-time scarcity. The authors see efficient usage-based pricing as "the inevitable future of roads" [35].

For $1500 per year, some doctors in the United States provide their cell phone numbers with a promise of 24/7 availability. In Afghanistan, mercenaries from private firms earn between $250 and $1000 per day to fight. The price depends on the person's qualifications, experience, and citizenship. In Iraq and Afghanistan, there were at times more active personnel from private security companies than soldiers from the US Army [36]. For $6250, one can hire a surrogate mother from India to carry an embryo. A flat rate for unlimited surrogate mothers in India plus extra arrangements for twins or triplets would cost $60,000 [37]. One can purchase the right to immigrate to the United States for $500,000. There is also talk of auctioning enrollment at prestigious universities to the highest bidders.

Smoking is forbidden in most places in US hotels and motels. But some charge a fine of $200 or more for violating this rule. One can consider that fine as the price a guest must pay to buy the "privilege" to smoke in the room.

More and more we are seeing price stickers on everything, as market and price mechanisms reach deeper into our day-to-day lives. This invasion of pricing into areas historically organized outside of market norms is one of the remarkable changes of our times. Sandel [32] comments on this trend: "When we decide that certain goods may be bought and sold, then we decide—at least implicitly—that it is appropriate to treat them as commodities, as instruments of profit and use. But not all goods are properly valued in this way. The most obvious example is human beings."

While we call attention to this trend, we will not explore it further here. In this book, we limit ourselves to business price management. We will make the effort to provide relevant insights from as many subdisciplines as possible. This holistic perspective is intended to illuminate the multifaceted nature of the phenomenon we call "price."

1.6.2   Price and Power

Competition does not only play out between companies who offer substitutes. It also plays out along the value chain, where firms compete for their sliver of the overall economic pie. These fights are intensifying up and down the entire value chain. Pricing power is becoming increasingly important. It represents the extent to which a supplier is in a position to extract the desired value from customers, despite competition. The flipside of pricing power is purchasing power, i.e., the ability of a buyer to impose prices on its suppliers. To what extent does pricing power exist? It is claimed that automobile manufacturers have high pricing power vis-à-vis their customers and substantial purchasing power over their suppliers. Purchasing power can be very strong in concentrated industries or among large retailers. In most highly developed markets, four or five grocery chains account for 80% or more of sales. The legendary investor Warren Buffett [38] considers pricing power to be the most important criterion when evaluating the value of a business. The value of a brand is also ultimately determined by the extent to which it can achieve a price premium.

An interpretation of price, which puts the power aspect of price at the forefront, goes back to the French sociologist Gabriel Tarde (1843–1904) [39]. He considered every agreement on a price, wage, or interest rate to be equivalent to a military truce. This view is corroborated when one looks at wage negotiations between unions and employers. The peace lasts only until the next round of fighting begins and strikes loom. Setting and implementing a price is a form of power struggle between the seller and the buyer. It is not a zero-sum game, but the way the pie is divided among seller and buyer is primarily determined through the price.

In reality, most firms view their pricing power as quite limited. In its "Global Pricing Study," Simon-Kucher & Partners [40] surveyed 2713 managers in 50 countries. Only one third of the respondents ascribed high pricing power to their own company. The remaining 67% believed that their company is unable to realize the prices it needs in order to achieve appropriate profit margins.

The practices for exercising pricing power are getting rougher. In this regard, the conflict between Volkswagen (VW) and its supplier Prevent garnered a lot of high-profile attention. VW needed to shut down its assembly lines for several days because Prevent suspended its deliveries of components. One view described the battle as a "war in the automotive industry. Suppliers and carmakers cannot live without each other, but the power is unevenly distributed. The suppliers complain time and again that they are at the mercy of the manufacturers" [41].

"Higher prices through Acts of God" was the title of an article which described how the chemical industry was shutting down plant after plant, claiming *force majeure*, and then made massive increases in prices [42]. There are also bitter price battles between major publishers and libraries. "A university is breaking off negotiations with Elsevier," according to reports. The director of the university's library system accused Elsevier of "greed" and "profiteering" [43]. The suppliers of innovative pharmaceutical products face similar attacks. The firm Gilead set a price of \$94,500 for a 12-week treatment regime of its hepatitis C product, which translates to \$1125 per pill. This price level put the company under extreme pressure from insurance companies, physicians, and politicians [44]. Even consumers are becoming active and increasingly trying to exercise their own power over prices. More than 10,000 French car drivers brought a class-action suit against highway operators for charging tolls that they considered too high [45]. Such battles over pricing power will become more frequent and more intense, accelerated by the power of the Internet. Pricing power will become even more important in the future.

1.6.3   Price and Top Management

Another important current trend is the rising level of attention which top management is paying to price. In the Global Pricing Study by Simon-Kucher & Partners [40], some 82% of respondents from around the world said that top management is taking a more active role in pricing. There are several reasons for this. First, top managers and executives realize that their companies have either exhausted their cost-cutting potential or will have great difficulty in achieving further gains. At the same time, they are becoming aware that they have neglected the professionalization of price management. The awareness of price's central role as profit driver has most certainly increased among top managers and CEOs. This thinking does not stop at short-term profits, though. It extends to shareholder value. Several studies show that missteps in price management can quickly destroy a company's market value. Other case studies prove that companies can boost their market capitalization through smart pricing.

When top management gets involved in pricing, we observe a significant impact on the company's performance. Table 1.1 shows the effects this participation has on pricing power, success rates at implementing price increases, and the improvement of margins and EBITDA.

There is strong improvement across all indicators when top managers get involved in price management. Their inclusion obviously pays off. This does not mean that top managers should be responsible for individual price decisions but rather that they establish the right framework for pricing. We will take a closer look at this topic in Chap. 9.

Like top managers, investors are also paying more attention to pricing. This was partially triggered by Warren Buffett's comment that pricing power is the most important factor in determining enterprise value. Price topics are addressed more frequently now at shareholder annual meetings and road shows, in investment analyst reports, and in corporate filings.

Table 1.1 The effects of top management involvement on selected KPI's [40]

	Involvement of top management		
	Without (%)	With (%)	Difference (%)
High pricing power	26	35	+35
Successful implementation of price increases	50	59	+18
Margin improvement after price increases	57	72	+26
EBITDA improvement after price increases	37	48	+30

Conclusion

We summarize this fundamental chapter:

- There are only three profit drivers: price, volume, and costs. Price has a particularly strong effect on profit.
- Under ceteris paribus assumptions, price increases lead to massive improvements in profit, while price cuts effect very sharp profit declines. It is often more advantageous to grow through higher prices than higher volumes, or conversely, to accept volume declines instead of making price cuts.
- American, German, Japanese, and French companies have underperformed for years in an international comparison of profits. Inadequate price management may be a primary root cause for this underperformance.
- The very simple, fundamental definition of price – the number of monetary units that a buyer has to pay for one unit of a product – belies the fact that real prices are often multidimensional and complex.
- Price has several special characteristics relative to other marketing instruments. These include the speed and the strength of its efficacy, the negligible upfront investment required to use it, and the possibility to respond immediately to competitors' moves.
- In practice, managers' understanding of the role of price leaves much to be desired. Causes for this discrepancy include the theory-versus-practice gap, the multidimensionality of price, complex chains of effects, psychological phenomena, and implementation barriers.
- Price management should not only be viewed as optimization but as a process which comprises strategy, analysis, decision, and implementation.
- Price management draws on influences and impulses from different scientific fields. These include macro- and microeconomics, marketing, behavioral science, and brain research. Additional inspiration comes from the practice side through consultants, software developers, innovative companies, and popular literature.
- Price management is subject to legal frameworks, which are becoming both increasingly stricter and more confusing due the sheer number of regulations. More and more price cartels are being uncovered. Companies should conduct a thorough legal review before implementing price measures that could be construed as collusion.
- Price mechanisms are increasingly penetrating into sectors such as education, traffic, and health care.
- Pricing power receives more attention as fights over the distribution and sharing of value break out across the value chain. Pricing power is a very important determinant of enterprise value.

(continued)

- We observe ever greater involvement of top managers in price management. Their participation leads to gains in pricing power and financial performance.
- We anticipate that these last two trends will continue and expect investors to show more interest in price management issues.

This chapter briefly shined spotlights on the most important aspects of price management. In the coming chapters, we will embark on a thorough exploration of these diverse facets of price management, keeping the goal of profit in mind.

References

1. Crow, D. (2015, January 08). T-Mobile US Emerges as Biggest Winner in Price War. *Financial Times*, p. 16.
2. Mehta, S. N. (2014, July 21). Global 500. The World's Largest Cooperations. *Fortune*, p. 95.
3. Annual data published by the Instituts der Deutschen Wirtschaft (German Economic Institute), Cologne 2005 till 2011. This statistic has not been continued since 2011.
4. Gladkikh, I. (2013). *Pricing Strategy. Consumer Orientation*. St. Petersburg: Graduate School of Management.
5. Albers, S., Mantrala, M. K. & Sridhar, S. (2010). Personal Selling Elasticities: A Meta-Analysis. *Journal of Marketing Research, 47*(5), 840–853.
6. Sethuraman, R., Tellis, G. J. & Briesch, R. A. (2011). How Well Does Advertising Work? Generalizations from Meta-analysis of Brand Advertising Elasticities. *Journal of Marketing Research, 48*(3), 457–471.
7. Friedel, E. (2014). *Price Elasticity: Research on Magnitude and Determinants*. Frankfurt am Main: Peter Lang.
8. Anonymous. (2014, November 28). Frühabends ist Benzin günstig. Kartellamt: Nach 20 Uhr steigen die Preise kräftig. *Frankfurter Allgemeine Zeitung*, p. 20.
9. Anonymous. (2012). Beschluss des Bundesrats: Benzinpreise kommen bald in Echtzeit. http://www.handelsblatt.com/politik/deutschland/beschluss-des-bundesrats-benzinpreise-kommen-bald-in-echtzeit/7430708.html. Accessed 10 December 2014.
10. Feedvisor (2017). Price Wars: Overtaking Your Competition on Amazon. http://rsdoades.com/img/portfolio/price_wars_web.pdf. Accessed 16 March 2018.
11. OC&C (2012). Reaktion der Konsumenten auf Preiserhöhungen in ausgewählten Ländern weltweit. http://de.statista.com/statistik/daten/studie/222384/umfrage/umfrage-zu-reaktion-der-konsumenten-auf-preiserhoehungen. Accessed 16 December 2014.
12. Anonymous. (2015, March 28). Air Berlin macht einen Rekordverlust. *Frankfurter Allgemeine Zeitung*, p. 28.
13. Simon, H. (2015). *Pricing and the CEO*. Lecture. Spring Conference of the Professional Pricing Society. Dallas. 7 May.
14. Müller, H. C. (2014, December 15). Digitalisierung der Betriebswirtschaft. *Handelsblatt*, p. 14.
15. Nelius, Y. (2013). *Organisation des Preismanagements von Konsumgüterherstellern: Eine empirische Untersuchung*. Frankfurt am Main: Peter Lang.
16. Fassnacht, M., Nelius, Y. & Szajna, M. (2013). Preismanagement ist nicht immer ein Top-Thema bei Konsumgüterherstellern. *Sales Management Review*. 9 October, pp. 58–69.

17. Riekhof, H.-C. & Lohaus, B. (2009). Wertschöpfende Pricing Prozesse: Eine empirische Untersuchung der Pricing-Praxis. *PFH Forschungspapiere/Research Papers. Private Fachhochschule Göttingen.* No. 2009/08.
18. Riekhof, H.-C. & Werner, F. (2010). Pricing Prozesse bei Herstellern von Fast Moving Consumer Goods. *PFH Forschungspapiere/Research Papers. Private Fachhochschule Göttingen.* No. 2010/01.
19. Wiltinger, K. (1998): *Preismanagement in der unternehmerischen Praxis: Probleme der organisatorischen Implementierung.* Wiesbaden: Gabler.
20. Simon, H., Bilstein, F. & Luby, F. (2006). *Manage for Profit, Not for Market Share.* Boston: Harvard Business School Press.
21. Breitschwerdt, F. (2011). *Preismanagement von Konsumgüterherstellern.* Frankfurt am Main: Peter Lang.
22. Dutta, S., Zbaracki, M. J. & Bergen, M. (2003). Pricing Process as a Capability: A Case Study. *Strategic Management Journal,* 24(7), 615–630.
23. Liozu, S. M. & Hinterhuber, A. (2013). CEO Championing of Pricing, Pricing Capabilities and Firm Performance in Industrial Firms. *Industrial Marketing Management,* 42(4), 633–643.
24. Müller, K.-M. (2012). *Underpricing: Wie Kunden über Preise denken.* Freiburg: Haufe-Lexware.
25. Simon, H. (2012). How Price Consulting is Coming of Age. In G. E. Smith (Ed.), *Visionary Pricing: Reflections and Advances in Honor of Dan Nimer* (pp. 61–79). London: Emerald.
26. Poundstone, W. (2010). *Priceless: The Myth of Fair Value (and How to Take Advantage of It).* New York: Hill and Wang.
27. McKenzie, R. (2008). *Why Popcorn Costs So Much at the Movies – And other Pricing Principles.* New York: Springer Copernicus.
28. Anonymous. (2017, January 21). Evian ist Mogelpackung des Jahres. *Frankfurter Allgemeine Zeitung,* p. 18.
29. Menzel, S. (2016). Milliardenstrafe für Lkw-Kartell. http://www.handelsblatt.com/ unternehmen/industrie/eu-bestraft-daimler-und-co-milliardenstrafe-fuer-lkw-kartell/13896088. html. Accessed 17 November 2016.
30. Anonymous. (2016). Apple to pay $450m settlement over US eBook price fixing. https://www. theguardian.com/technology/2016/mar/07/apple-450-million-settlement-e-book-price-fixing-supreme-court. Accessed 17 November 2016.
31. Connolly, R. E. (2014). US record 5-year jail price-fixing sentence imposed. http://www. lexology.com/library/detail.aspx?g=4dff9956-dacf-4072-8353-ca76efd13efc. Accessed 17 November 2016.
32. Sandel, M. J. (2012). *What Money Can't Buy: The Moral Limits of Markets.* New York: Farrar, Straus and Giroux.
33. Sharkey, J. (2014, December 02). A Look Back at the Year in Air Travel. *International New York Times,* p. 24.
34. Transportation Security Administration (2018). TSA Pre&check. https://www.tsa.gov/ precheck. Accessed 22 January 2018.
35. Cramton, P., Geddes R. R. & Ockenfels, A. (2018). *Markets for Road Use – Eliminating Congestion through Scheduling, Routing, and Real-Time Road Pricing.* Working Paper. Cologne: University of Cologne.
36. Peters, H. M., Schwartz, M. & Kapp, L. (2016). *Department of Defense Contractor and Troop Levels in Iraq and Afghanistan: 2007–2016.* Congressional Research Service.
37. Lenzen-Schulte, M. (2015, April 10). Deine Zwillinge gehören mir. *Frankfurter Allgemeine Zeitung,* p. 9.
38. From a transcript of an interview with Warren Buffett at the Financial Crisis Inquiry Commission (FCIC). 26 May 2010.
39. Tarde, G. (1902). *La Psychologie Économique.* Paris: Alcan.
40. Simon-Kucher & Partners (2012). *Global Pricing Study 2012.* Bonn.

41. Kollenbroich, B. & Kwasniewski, N. (2016). Zulieferer gegen Volkswagen – Die Machtprobe. http://www.spiegel.de/wirtschaft/unternehmen/volkswagen-gegen-zulieferer-prevent-die-machtprobe-a-1108924.html. Accessed 17 November 2016.
42. Freytag, B. (2015, May 23). Mit höherer Gewalt zu höheren Preisen. *Frankfurter Allgemeine Zeitung*, p. 30.
43. Anonymous. (2015, February 11). Es gibt keine andere Erklärung als Gier. *Frankfurter Allgemeine Zeitung*, p. N4.
44. Anonymous. (2015, February 11). The Race to Cure Rising Drug Costs. *Financial Times*, p. 7.
45. Anonymous. (2015, February 14). Frankreichs Autofahrer verklagen Autobahnbetreiber. *Frankfurter Allgemeine Zeitung*, p. 22.

Price Strategy

2

Abstract

The business strategy defines the framework for price management. This starts with articulating the set of goals the business is pursuing. In general, these goals have many dimensions and are often to some extent contradictory, so that it is necessary to prioritize the goals when setting prices. The price strategy of a company has an enormous influence on shareholder value. The right strategies contribute to sustained growth of the value of the enterprise. Pursuing the wrong strategies can quickly destroy enterprise value, in some cases permanently. The most fundamental decisions concern price positioning. We distinguish among five typical price positions: luxury, premium, medium, low, and ultra-low. We will explore each of these positions, looking in particular at their respective bases, the associated marketing instruments, and the opportunities and risks. Markets are dynamic, which means that a price position should change in line with changes in market conditions. Yet the process of making such changes can take a long time to unfold, and the results are not easy to correct.

2.1 Goals

Strategy is the art and science of developing and deploying all of a company's resources so as to achieve the most profitable long-term survival of the company. Strategy is all-encompassing and affects all functions. A company's strategy must embody a high-level vision for the firm, but it must also be concrete and practical. Developing strategy starts with the company's goals, from which specific objectives for managing each aspect of its business, including price, can be derived. Having clear, unequivocal goals and targets is an indispensable prerequisite for professional price management. While this may sound simple, developing such clear strategic goals can be difficult in practice. Objectives for price policies are not always clearly formulated and may occasionally give greater weight to unspoken goals than to explicit ones.

Common corporate goals include:

- *Profitability goals* (profit, return on sales, return on investment, shareholder value): Most companies pursue profitability goals in a more or less well-defined form. While short-term profitability goals often differ, ultimately, the most important long-term goal is to increase shareholder value.
- *Volume and growth goals* (volume, market share, revenue, or revenue growth): Volume and growth goals are alternative goals or proxies for long-term profit maximization or growth in shareholder value. Since its founding in 1994, Amazon has focused almost exclusively on growth and, as a result, has not made any significant profit in its first two decades. In 2015, the company achieved an after-tax profit of $596 million on revenue of $107 billion, which corresponds to a margin of 0.56%. In 2016 Amazon's revenue increased to $136 billion and its after-tax profit to $2.37 billion, corresponding to a margin of 1.7%. By the beginning of 2018, Amazon's market capitalization had almost doubled in 3 years to $669 billion, an immense increase in shareholder value.
- *Financial goals* (liquidity, creditworthiness, debt-to-equity ratio): These goals come to the fore in particular for new companies short on capital or for any company facing a crisis.
- *Power goals* (market leadership, market dominance, social or political influence): Volkswagen sets itself a singular goal: outsell Toyota. It is often said that Google wants to dominate the markets it enters. Peter Thiel's bestseller "Zero to One" encourages companies to find niches they can monopolize. Fighting and beating the competition is a very common goal of managers.
- *Social goals* (creating/preserving jobs, employee satisfaction, fulfilling a grander social purpose): In line with such goals, a company will sometimes accept orders at prices which do not cover costs, in order to avoid cutting jobs. Companies may also cross-subsidize products or services in order to make them accessible to target segments who otherwise might not be able to afford them—for instance, providing student or senior citizen discounts. For Patagonia, the maker of outdoor and athletic gear, environmental sustainability is a core part of the mission. Patagonia donates employee time, services, and at least 1% of sales to grassroots environmental groups all over the world in service of its social goal.

Almost all goals have an effect on price management, though price is certainly not the only instrument companies use to achieve their goals. In the pursuit of growth goals, a company might rely on innovation, or it could set aggressive low prices. Companies can meet profit and financial goals through cost-cutting, or they could raise their prices. To fulfill their power goals, companies might wage a price war or take control of a distribution channel. In most cases, price makes an important contribution to achieving a company's strategic goals.

In practice, companies pursue several goals simultaneously, even though some goals can conflict with or even contradict each other. For instance, profitability goals

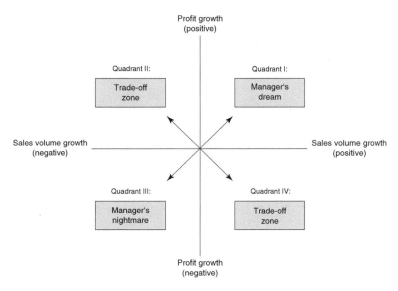

Fig. 2.1   Goal conflict: Profit growth, volume growth, or both?

often conflict with volume, revenue, or market share goals. Such competing priorities are a day-to-day reality in companies. Figure 2.1 illustrates this problem. Profit growth is depicted on the vertical axis and volume growth on the horizontal axis. The intersection of the two axes represents the status quo.

Quadrant I shows the "manager's dream"—profit and volume are both growing simultaneously, a situation most frequently encountered in expanding markets or with new products just achieving economies of scale. For a mature market that is no longer growing, the manager's dream can only occur when a company's prices are too high and are cut as a result. In that case, the lower prices lead to a significant increase in volume, overcompensating for the lower margin, and generating a higher profit.

In practice, we observe the situations in quadrants II and IV quite often. A company achieves either profit or volume growth, but not both. Quadrant II represents rising profit and declining volumes. In this case, the company's prevailing prices were below the optimal level. Increasing the prices leads to a volume decline, but the higher contribution margin more than offsets that decline and results in a higher profit. In Quadrant IV the profit decreases, but the volume grows. This situation occurs when a company's prices were either at or below their optimum and then get cut. In Quadrant II as well as in Quadrant IV, management must choose between the countervailing profit and volume changes. No matter what, managers should avoid Quadrant III, which we refer to as the "manager's nightmare." If prices are already too high and are then increased even more, the result may be a decline in both profit and volume.

Table 2.1 Contradictory
goals among senior leaders

Senior leader	Profit	Growth	Market share
Chief executive officer	1	3	2
Chief financial officer	2	1	3
Head of sales	1	2	3
Head of marketing	2	3	1
Product manager	3	1	2

Priorities range from high (1) to low (3) (Simon-Kucher & Partners project)

Table 2.1 shows a case in which the goals of individual managers are poorly aligned. While the CEO and the head of sales agree that profit is more important than growth or market share, the CFO puts the highest priority on growth. For the head of marketing, market share is the most important goal. In our experience, few managers explicitly make profit their top goal, despite what Table 2.1 suggests. This table reflects their actual behavior and not necessarily what they aver in official statements at investor conferences or at annual shareholder meetings. Fundamental goals such as margin, return/yield, or absolute profit often fall short. A board member of a well-known carmaker captures this sentiment very well: "If our market share falls by 0.1%, heads will roll. But if our profit falls by 20%, no one really cares." While this statement may be exaggerated at face value, it does get to the core of a pervasive problem in business: revenue, volume, and market share goals—not profitability goals—often determine day-to-day actions.

What explains the predominance of these goals, and where does this fascination with volume and market share goals come from? The reasons are myriad. The best-known source and justification for those who favor market share is the PIMS study (Profit Impact of Market Strategy), whose most important finding is shown in Fig. 2.2. Regardless of how we define market share (rank or percentage), there is a highly significant positive correlation between market share and returns. The market leader achieves a pre-tax return on investment (ROI) which is almost three times as high as the ROI of the fifth-largest competitor. The strategic conclusion is thus self-evident: maximize your market share and become the market leader with the highest profits!

A second and somewhat older justification for the pursuit of high market shares is the concept of the experience curve, which states that the cost position of a company is a function of its relative market share. The relative market share is defined as one's own market share divided by the market share of the strongest competitor. According to the experience curve hypothesis, the larger a company's relative market share is, the lower its unit cost will be [2]. The market leader has the lowest costs in the market and thus—assuming the same prices across competitors—the highest returns.

The experience curve concept and the PIMS study are the grandparents of all market share philosophies. Jack Welch, CEO of General Electric from 1981 to 2001, became their most famous proponent. At the beginning of his tenure, he declared that

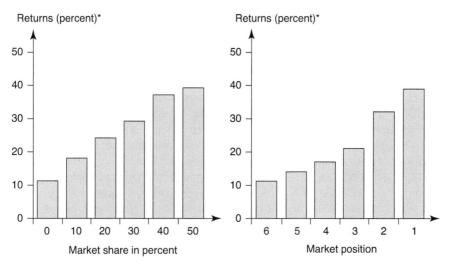

*Return on Investment (pre-tax) in percent

Fig. 2.2 Results of the PIMS study [1]

General Electric would withdraw from all sectors in which it could not attain the number one or number two position in terms of market share.

The central question is whether the link between market share and returns reveals a true causal relationship or merely represents a correlation. Numerous studies have called into question whether a causal relationship actually exists. The results in fact show a much weaker link between market shares and returns than what the authors of the PIMS study postulated. Farris and Moore [3] provide an overview of the insights. Analytical methods which filter out so-called "unobservable" factors lead to the following conclusion: "Once the impact of unobserved factors is econometrically removed, the remaining effect of market share on profitability is quite small." These "unobserved" factors include the capabilities of a company's management, the corporate culture, or a sustained competitive advantage. Ailawadi et al. [4, p. 31] conclude: "Although high market share, by itself, does not increase profitability, it does enable high-share firms to take certain profitable actions that may not be feasible for low-share firms." A study by Lee [5] likewise comes to the conclusion that not more than 50% of a company's profitability can be explained by absolute size and that other factors play the decisive role for return on investment. "While a typical firm's absolute size matters for its profit experience, perhaps some other factors matter even more" [5, p. 200].

The most comprehensive meta-analysis on this topic to date comes from Edeling and Himme [6]. They examined 635 empirically calculated elasticities for market share and profit which reflect the percentage change in profit when market share increases by 1%. Here we note that these calculations measure changes in the starting values in percent and not percentage points. The authors found that the average elasticity for market share and profit is very low, at 0.159, but statistically significant.

The following example demonstrates the findings of their study. Let us assume a company has a market share of 50% and a profit margin of 10%. If the market share rises by 1–50.5%, the profit margin rises only to 10.0159%. If the market share rises by 10–55%, the profit margin would increase to 10.159%. In a further step, Edeling and Himme [6] eliminated the skewing induced by his analytical methods and arrived at a slightly negative adjusted average market-share-profit elasticity of -0.052, which was not statistically significant. These results more than call into question the validity of the "market share is everything" philosophy.

Older studies considered the effects of competition-oriented corporate goals (such as market share or market position) more thoroughly. Lanzillotti [7] conducted a well-known study of this kind. It revealed a negative correlation between the pursuit of competition-oriented goals and a company's return on investment. Armstrong and Green [8, p. 2] concluded that: "Competitor-oriented objectives are harmful. However, this evidence has had only a modest impact on academic research and it seems to be largely ignored by managers." We find additional empirical evidence for a negative link between the pursuit of market share and the success of a company in a study from Rego et al. [9]. Using data from 200 US companies, the authors identified a trade-off between the pursuit of higher market share and higher customer satisfaction, which itself is seen as an important driver of long-term profitability [10]. The authors explain this through the heterogeneity of consumer preferences: the larger a company becomes, the harder it is for the company to meet consumer preferences. These are only a few studies among many which have explored the effects of market share goals, the experience curve, or portfolio management based on the "Boston Matrix." For many other arguments against the "market share myth," we refer the reader to the book "The Myth of Market Share" by Miniter [11]. In summary, the pursuit of volume and market share goals—especially in mature or highly competitive markets—is problematic and in many cases prevents a company from earning higher profits.

A company's size can make it difficult to increase revenue. A growth goal of 50% for a company with $10 million in revenue means an increase of only $5 million. For a company with revenue of $150 million, the same goal would call for a revenue increase of $75 million. Once a company reaches a certain size, there may not be a sufficient number of customers or suppliers to enable further rapid growth.

Albert M. Baehny, the non-executive chairman and former CEO of Geberit, also disagrees with the supposed importance of market share: "I am not interested in market share. In my career, I hardly ever looked at market share. If the price-value relationship is good, the demand will follow" [12]. Geberit is the global market leader for so-called behind-the-wall sanitation products and has a market capitalization which is roughly five times its annual sales. Baehny emphasized that when his company decides whether to introduce a new product, it does not look at the product's market potential or achievable market share. According to him, such forecasts are too unreliable. Instead, Geberit identifies the product's value to the end users and uses that metric to ensure a sufficient willingness to pay for the product.

In our view, what matters is not the absolute level of the market share but how a company achieves its market share. If that market share comes through aggressive prices without a correspondingly low-cost base, then a company has "bought" that market share at the expense of its profit margins. This is true for many start-ups, which spend exorbitantly to acquire customers in the hope that they will one day be profitable at scale. However, it means per se that in most cases, the company will not earn much profit. If the company achieves its high market share through innovation and quality at appropriate prices, then margins and profits are healthy and aligned. The high profit in turn allows the company to make additional investments in innovation and product quality. Recent studies, such as one from Chu et al. [13], examine the link between market share and profitability in a homogeneous sector (insurance) and confirm this strategy: a company can improve its profitability by developing new services or technologies or by growing market share through acquisitions.

It is clear that balancing profit and volume goals is necessary for price management. In the early stages of a market or a life cycle, it can make sense to give greater weight to volume, revenue, or market share goals. In the latter phases of the product life cycle, a company should put higher priority on profit goals. Ultimately, management should orient itself toward long-term profitability.

2.2 Price Management and Shareholder Value

Profit and growth drive shareholder value. Because price exerts a strong and decisive influence on both profit and growth, price is a crucial determinant of shareholder value. More and more managers have begun to recognize this connection. They have incorporated it into their strategic planning as well as into their communication to the capital markets [14]. Investor Warren Buffet's claim that pricing power is the most important criterion for determining the value of a firm has boosted this trend. Well-known Silicon Valley investor Peter Thiel likewise stresses the connection between price and shareholder value, as he is decidedly in favor of using pricing power to expand a market position [15].

As we will see, price management can dramatically impact shareholder value, both positively and negatively. Good price management fosters a significant increase in enterprise value. Mistakes in price management can destroy enterprise value. The following cases prove that the destructive effects take hold much more rapidly than positive (long-term) growth in enterprise value.

The first case involves a B2B telecommunications company, i.e., one which sells its capacity to other telecom companies, not to consumers. This market is infamous for its price wars. Once the network cable is buried, a company has very few ongoing variable costs, tempting companies to attract customers by using aggressive prices. This practice contributed to a 67% decline in this company's enterprise value over a 2-year period. In a subsequent consulting project, we developed a comprehensive program for price stabilization and imposed strict price discipline on the sales force. When the company revealed this strategy's initial successes at a quarterly earnings

Share price ($)

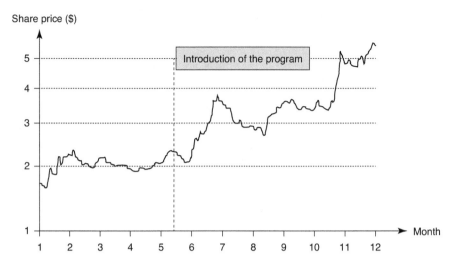

Fig. 2.3 Price discipline and share price of a telecommunications company [16]

press conference, its stock price rose sharply that same day. Some of the company's competitors then followed suit and implemented their own forms of price discipline. The end result is a textbook example of a company practicing price leadership. The company's share price doubled in 6 months. Figure 2.3 shows the share price movements after the launch of the price discipline program [16].

The company's CEO greeted the stock market's positive response by saying: "We are very satisfied with our disciplined approach to pricing. The results reflect a positive dynamic in our industry, which includes diminished price pressures." Investment analysts also praised the newfound price discipline. "The rise in whole-sale prices reflects the trend toward reduced price pressures, a very healthy development. More stable prices should help all market participants," said one report.

Another case involves a group of private equity investors who owned a large operator of parking garages. The investors planned to use price management to increase the value of that operating company prior to divesting it. They succeeded in implementing price increases and built the new prices into the contracts with the local garage lessors, thereby locking in an additional profit of $10 million per year. Shortly after this price action, the investors sold that company at a multiple of 12 times profit. The price increases led directly to an increase of $120 million in enterprise value.

A third case looks at the market for luxury goods. The French company Hermès is known for its strict commitment to high prices and the avoidance of price erosion in any form. *The Wall Street Journal* writes that: "Hermès bets on higher prices while others even cut their prices" [17]. In contrast to other luxury goods companies, Hermès sticks to this strategy even in economic downturns and crises. While the JBEF Luxury Brands Index did not move from 2015 through March 2017, the share

Share price (€)

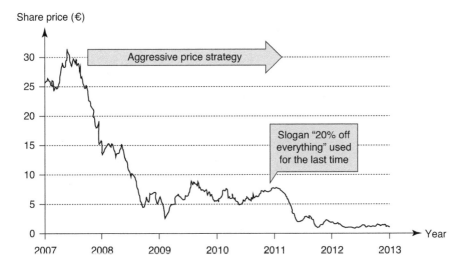

Fig. 2.4   Share price of Praktiker [19]

price of Hermès almost doubled in the same period. The company's consistent price strategy made a decisive contribution to that increase.

In contrast, mistakes in price management can cause the destruction of enterprise value on a gigantic scale, as in the case of Praktiker, a large German-based chain of home improvement stores. In mid-2007, Praktiker's share price was at €30. It had experienced rapid growth on the back of its slogan "20% off everything," which had run for several years. Later on, Praktiker began offering discounts of 25% for certain product groups, such as "25% off of everything with a plug" [18]. Praktiker positioned itself as a hard discounter among home improvement chains and eventually defined itself solely through its low prices. One slogan was "This is the price talking." This aggressive price strategy ended in disaster. By the end of 2008, the share price had fallen below €10 per share. The discount policy had led the company astray. But when Praktiker finally tried to change course in 2010 (the slogan "20% off everything" ran for the last time at the end of 2010), the share price fell sharply again. Figure 2.4 shows Praktiker's share price trend from 2007 to 2013 [19].

What is interesting is that during that same time period, other home improvement chains flourished and were able to increase their revenues. The Praktiker case shows that a company should carefully consider the potential consequences of building a market positioning exclusively around low prices. This strategy and the subsequent attempt to overcome its consequences both ended badly for Praktiker. Praktiker went bankrupt in the fall of 2013 and no longer exists.

Value destruction can also occur when a company abandons a previously peaceful price strategy in favor of an aggressive one. We can look at the global market for potash (potassium compounds) as an example. This market is an oligopoly predominantly under control of four companies, one each from Russia, Belarus, Canada, and Germany. In mid-2013, the Russian firm, Uralkali, announced that it would end its

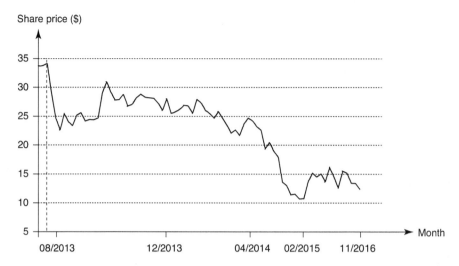

Fig. 2.5 Share price of Uralkali [20]

sales cooperation agreement with its Belarussian counterpart and, at the same time, significantly expand its production. Aggressive market share goals and price cuts usually go hand in hand. Figure 2.5 shows the effects of these decisions on Uralkali's share price. The share prices for its competitors followed similar paths [20].

But price cuts aren't the only decision which can lead to the destruction of shareholder value. Price increases can sometimes have the same effect, as the example of the US retailer J.C. Penney shows. In June 2011, the company announced that Ron Johnson would take over as CEO. Johnson, no ordinary manager, was the man behind the spectacularly successful Apple stores, which he had opened and developed since 2000. Without doing any advance testing, he undertook radical changes in the J.C. Penney price strategy. When faced with criticism that the new strategy was untested, he reacted by saying that "We didn't test at Apple" [21]. Prior to his taking over at J.C. Penney, around a quarter of all products were sold at discounts of 50% or more. Johnson eliminated almost all special promotions and at the same time launched a massive trading-up campaign focused on expensive brands sold in more than 1200 separate boutiques. In the 2012 fiscal year, revenue declined by 3%, while procurement costs rose because of the trading-up to more expensive brands. These two effects combined to flip the company's after-tax result from a profit of $378 million in fiscal 2011 to a loss of $152 million in 2012. While the equity markets had responded positively to the announcement of Johnson's taking over as CEO, the share price plummeted once Johnson set the new price strategy in motion, as Fig. 2.6 shows. Johnson was

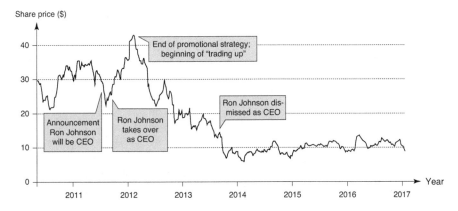

Fig. 2.6 Share price of J.C. Penney [22]

dismissed in April 2013. On January 30, 2012, J.C. Penney had a share price of $41.81. By the end of 2017, the share price had fallen below $3. Over the same period, the Dow Jones Industrial Average (DJIA) had almost doubled from 12,623 to over 23,000.

Marketing science has historically conducted scant investigation into the relationship between marketing instruments and shareholder value. In recent years however, this has begun to change for the better. In a meta-analysis of 83 studies, Edeling and Fischer [10] found that advertising has a slight positive effect and that so-called marketing-asset variables (which include brand and strong customer relationships) have a significantly stronger effect on shareholder value. The median elasticity was 0.04 for advertising and 0.54 for the marketing-asset variables. In other words, a 1% improvement in marketing generates an increase of 0.54% in enterprise value. Price was not explicitly studied in the meta-analysis, so it is not possible to say anything about the price vs. shareholder value elasticity. Two additional studies looked at how price actions and innovation affect shareholder value. Pauwels et al. [23, p. 142] came to the following conclusion: "New product introductions increase firm value, but promotions do not." The findings from the study conducted by Srinivasan et al. [14] point in the same direction. Innovations and marketing support for them drive higher enterprise value, but price actions (i.e., discounts or aggressive price moves) have a negative effect. Our own experience leads us to support these findings emphatically.

These elaborations and empirical insights prove the strategic relevance of price management for the value of an enterprise. With the help of the right price strategy, a company can increase the enterprise value. At the same time, the wrong price positioning can reduce shareholder value and can even—as the case of Praktiker shows—destroy it completely and forever.

2.3   Value and Price

The core questions of strategic price management concern value and price positioning. We are asked again and again what the most important aspect of price management is. We always give the same answer: "value-to-customer." The price a customer is willing to pay, and thus the price the seller can achieve, is always a reflection of the customer's perceived value of the product or service. If customers place a higher value on the product, then they are prepared to pay more. If the perceived value is lower than that of a competing product, they will only buy the product if the price is also lower (relative to the competitive product). This unwavering market view was best expressed by Peter Drucker, who urged managers to "see the entire business through the eyes of the customer" [24, p. 85]. When it comes to the price that a seller can achieve, the most relevant parameter is the customer's subjective perception of value.

In Ancient Rome, the fundamental relationship between value and price was already well understood. The Latin language uses the same word, "pretium," for both value and price. Interpreted literally, this means that price and value are two sides of the same coin. As a guideline for addressing price problems, this view suggests that we should start by looking at value through the eyes of the customer, giving rise to three important tasks for the supplier or seller:

Create value: Innovation, product quality, the standards and nature of a product's materials and components, design, etc., all contribute to value creation. The choice of customer segments also influences value creation, because customers have different requirements and different perceptions.

Communicate value: Statements about the product, its position, and last but not least about its brand all communicate value. Value communication includes packaging, product presentation, and placement at shelf or online.

Retain value: The degree to which a product retains its value will influence first-time willingness to pay for consumer durables. For luxury goods and automobiles, value retention—resale value—can even constitute a deciding factor for initial willingness to pay.

Only when a seller has clarity on the value of the product or service can the seller approach the specifics of price setting. When establishing value—which in practice spans a very wide range from highest to lowest quality—the seller or supplier must be mindful of the achievable price from the very beginning. Ramanujam and Tacke [25] insist in their book "Monetizing Innovation" that companies should design a product around a price. In other words, they should start with the price range and then begin with research and development, designing a product with the appropriate features and quality for that price range. Putting effort into understanding value is likewise important for the buyer. The only way for buyers to avoid overpaying is to understand the value of what they are buying. This knowledge of value protects the potential customer from buying a product which looks like a bargain at first glance but upon use or consumption turns out to be a lemon [26]. The Spanish philosopher

Baltasar Gracian (1601–1658) stated this sentiment eloquently and succinctly: "It is better to be cheated in the price than in the quality of goods" [27]. Ripping off a customer by charging too high a price is infuriating for the customer—but this anger is often only temporary. Selling a buyer goods of poor quality, however, causes the anger and frustration to linger until the customer grows tired of the product and disposes of it. The moral of this story is that when negotiating and making a purchase, the buyer should pay more attention to the quality of the product or service than to its price. Admittedly, that is not so simple in practice. It is generally easier to judge whether a price is advantageous than to judge the full merits of a product or service.

A French saying echoes this sentiment: "Le prix s'oublie, la qualité reste," which essentially means that quality endures long after you have forgotten the price. It is not uncommon for prices to be ephemeral and quickly forgotten, while impressions of value and quality last much longer. Who has not hastily celebrated capturing a bargain or paying a low price, only to find out later that quality was poor and the bargain an illusion? Conversely, who has not at least once complained about paying a high price and then been pleasantly surprised when the quality turned out to be excellent? The English social reformer John Ruskin (1819–1900) described this insight succinctly: "It is unwise to pay too much, but it is worse to pay too little. When you pay too much, you lose a little money—that is all. When you pay too little, you sometimes lose everything because the thing you bought was incapable of doing the thing you bought it to do. The common law of business balance prohibits paying a little and getting a lot—it cannot be done. If you deal with the lowest bidder, it is well to add something for the risk you run, and if you do that you will have enough to pay for something better" [28]. Buyers who choose the lowest-priced suppliers may not be aware of or heeding Ruskin's wisdom.

2.4   Positioning

Marketing science visualizes a market as a cognitive map, on which every product takes up a position. This is why we speak of positioning, which we define as "the endeavor of a company to craft its offer in such a way that it takes on a special, appreciated, and differentiated place in the awareness of the customer" [29, p. 423]. Figure 2.7 shows the positioning of products. Positioning is thus the arrangement of value, performance, and price elements in such a way that the product achieves the desired perception in the mind of the customers. In many markets we observe a differentiation across five value and price categories. At the upper end of the price scale is the luxury price position. At the lower end is the ultra-low price range. This spread gives rise to enormous price differences. For automobiles, prices range from a few thousand dollars up to more than $2 million. For watches, the spread is even larger. The least expensive watch costs less than $10, while the most expensive ones cost $2 million or more. Consumer goods such as cosmetics and fashion can also have enormous price spreads.

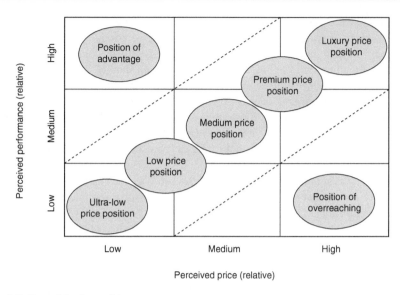

Fig. 2.7 Potential price positions

A product's positioning should never be based solely on price but should rather reflect the underlying basis of the product's or service's value, including its brand. Positioning, in this sense, is synonymous with "price-value positioning" or "price-performance positioning." A product's positioning provides the fundamental orientation and leeway for price decisions. The positioning can apply to the entire firm, to a particular brand, to a product group, or even to an individual product.

The value the customer perceives is derived from tangible and intangible features, both of which provide benefits to the customer and thus satisfy needs. We segment these value and performance attributes into four categories:

- Functional
- Emotional
- Symbolic
- Ethical

Functional attributes apply to each performance element of the product or service with respect to its ability and suitability to satisfy the customer's needs [30]. The functional attributes enable the customer to solve a specific core problem or mission, i.e., for an airline the problem of transporting passengers from point A to point B. Functional performance would also encompass the resources and infrastructure necessary to meet these transportation needs. For a smartphone, attributes such as screen size and battery life comprise the functional performance. For a laptop computer, functional attributes include the processor speed and the amount of memory.

Emotional attributes refer to the value that the customer derives from the product because of positive feelings the product elicits. Needs such as the desire for change or escape, excitement, sensory pleasure, sensual experiences, or beauty are fulfilled by emotional attributes [30]. For a car, this can mean the fun of driving a sports car or the pleasure from appreciating the car's aesthetics and design. Customers feel pleasure or even excitement when they spend a night at a luxury hotel, and these count as emotional benefits. A product's or service's ability to stimulate emotions can have a pronounced effect on the willingness to pay.

Symbolic attributes refer to the value a customer gains from a boost in confidence or self-esteem from the product or service. These attributes allow customers to associate themselves with a group or person, express their belonging (actual or desired) to a particular group, or conversely, to separate or distinguish themselves from a group. They also fulfill the need for social recognition or serve as a form of self-expression [30]. Brands play a very important role as symbolic attributes. A very expensive watch, say from Rolex, or an exclusive suit from Zegna, confers social prestige and creates the impression that one belongs to a certain social class. This symbolic performance, in the sense that it signals membership in a certain group, is a powerful driver of willingness to pay. Similarly, driving a Porsche vs. driving a Toyota Prius sharply conveys different symbolic attributes.

Ethical attributes include those which foster the positive feeling that one has done something beneficial for others, for society, or for the environment. These attributes are the focus of mission-driven brands. This feeling likewise provides customer value, as the other three categories of performance attributes do. Through these attributes, one expresses and fulfills one's desire to help others in a specific way or manifests the general desire to act morally or altruistically [30]. Examples of ethical performance include Procter & Gamble's "One-Pack = One Vaccine" campaign, under which the company pledged to provide UNICEF with funding for one lifesaving tetanus vaccine to protect a mother and her newborn in the developing world for every package of Pampers diapers purchased in the United States or Canada. Other such examples are the drinking water initiative from the Volvic water brand and the Breast Cancer Awareness Campaign sponsored by Estée Lauder. These companies attract customers through a commitment to support charitable initiatives or serve a larger social cause. This commitment can influence the willingness to pay.

Overview
Each of these four types of performance attributes is capable of fulfilling customer needs and thus of generating willingness to pay. This means that the nature or extent of a product's performance must always be incorporated in its positioning. All marketing instruments and other corporate activities such as R&D, procurement, and even the selection of personnel should be consistent with the price position for which the company is striving. A company

(continued)

needs a fundamentally different showroom and a different caliber of salesperson for luxury cars than it does for low-price models. In addition to this consistency, a company also needs endurance, because it can take years to establish the desired price position.

2.5 Approach

Price and value should always be seen relative to each other. As Fig. 2.7 shows, one must interpret the price position from the perspective of the price-performance or price-value relationship. The consistency band in Fig. 2.7 illustrates the ultra-low, low, medium, premium, and luxury price positions. The dimensions of price and performance are at different levels for each position, but in balance with each other. The perception of the customer is the factor which counts.

Deviations from the consistency band may be viewed as fair or unfair in the eyes of the customer. A fair or advantageous position (again, in the eyes of the customer) reflects a favorable price-performance relationship. The customer perceives a surplus of performance relative to price. The unfair position results when the seller demands a high price which is not aligned with the perceived value or performance. A Dutch customer's comment on a German engineering firm illustrates this: "Your price is 1.2 million euros. The price from a Chinese supplier is 750,000 euros. I realize that your product is better, but it is not 60% better. So I will not pay 60% more." The Dutch customer bought the Chinese equipment.

In 2016, Sprint began to use that same kind of quantification and logic to its advantage in its advertising campaigns. Under the slogan "Don't let a 1% difference cost you twice as much," Sprint presented data which show that its network reliability is within 1% of the performance of competitors such as AT&T and Verizon, but its plans are 50% less expensive. Some companies, meanwhile, are criticized that their price-performance relationship is out of whack, even in the absence of numbers for comparison. McDonald's is one example, as one observer remarks. "Nowadays the Big Mac in America costs $4.80. The price-value relationship is completely off" [31].

To develop solid price positions for a product or service, we recommend a three-step approach. First, a company should make a rough segmentation of its market from a price-performance perspective. Start by delineating the market, including an analysis of customers and competitors. A valid market segmentation is an indispensable prerequisite for successful price positioning. Within the framework of the company's strategic direction, the company then selects one or more target segments and the appropriate price position for each one. Related to this task, the company must also decide whether it will use one brand or multiple brands to cover the different price positions. When Apple launched its smart watch in 2015, the "Apple Watch" brand served several segments across an extreme price range from $349 all the way to $18,000 per watch [32]. Later the watches were available between $249 and $1399. Apple removed the "luxury" edition from the assortment.

In saturated markets or markets where market fragmentation is increasing, a rough segmentation is usually not sufficient. Within a chosen price range, one must further differentiate from the competition. A premium supplier can examine whether it has enough price leeway to extend into the luxury segment. In a similar way, at the lower end of the price scale, there may be additional demand at prices below the current price levels. No-frills airlines and hotels have greatly expanded the overall travel market with low-price positions.

In the low-price segment, the functional attributes tend to dominate. Customers in these segments are interested in basic products and services, such as economical transportation. Additional performance attributes such as a powerful engine, comfort, sportiness, aesthetic design, or prestige play a secondary role. In the premium segment, customers demand not only a higher level of performance on the functional attributes; they also give increasingly greater weight to emotional, symbolic, and ethical attributes. Buyers of electric cars put symbolic and ethical attributes at the forefront of their decision-making. Such customers will only develop the appropriate willingness to pay when these attributes fulfill or exceed their expectations.

Price positioning must be regarded as a strategic decision because of the inherent risks involved. Because price positioning is established for the long term, it is very difficult to correct mistakes. Despite this, improper positionings are not uncommon in practice. The so-called "Personal Transporter" Segway, a revolutionary innovation and cult product, was introduced in 2001 at a price of $4950. Nowadays, the least expensive model i2 SE costs $6694, which one can confidently declare to be a luxury positioning for that kind of vehicle. Sales projections called for 50,000 units in the first year and average annual sales of 40,000 units in the first 5 years. In reality, the company sold only 4800 units per year in the first 5 years after launch. They fell short of the original volume target by 88%. The primary cause for this shortfall was probably the product's misaligned price positioning [33].

In 2014, Amazon introduced the "Fire" smartphone at a price of $200. This launch price reflected a medium-price positioning between basic Android phones and the more expensive iPhone. Yet no one bought the "Fire" at that price. Amazon responded by cutting the price to just $1, but even this radical move could not save the product. Amazon wrote off $170 million as a result. Apparently, Amazon was way off in its estimates of consumers' willingness to pay [34].

Similarly, the luxury goods brand Gucci failed to assess its potential customers correctly when it assumed that a higher price would automatically make the brand even more luxurious and sought after. The attempt to raise handbag prices by then-CEO Patricio di Marco proved to be unsuccessful due to a miscalculation regarding customers and their preferences. The case shows that a price increase alone does not create or improve a luxury brand [35]. Successive price increases by the British leather goods maker Mulberry brought sales to a virtual standstill. Customers found one price increase of several hundred pounds particularly unjustified. The image of the brand simply did not live up to the prices the company was charging. Declining revenue and frustrated customers prove that a price repositioning cannot be effected over a brief period. The positioning must unfold as a long-term process both within the company and in the eyes of the customers [36].

We have also witnessed numerous cases in which a company chose a price position which was too low. Playmobil priced its new "Noah's Ark" set at €69.90. The product soon sold on eBay for €84.09, a clear indication that the product's price position was too low. In 2014, Microsoft launched the hybrid tablet Surface Pro 3, which could completely replace a laptop. The tablet sold out immediately. The primary reason was a price position which was too low relative to competitors such as Apple and Samsung. The British firm Newnet introduced an "uncapped service" for £21.95 per month, but the first 600 customers immediately used up all available capacity. As a result, the company raised the price by 60% to £34.95. The Taiwanese computer maker Asus launched the mini-notebook "Eee PC" at €299, and similar to Microsoft's tablet, this product sold out within a few days. During the launch phase, the company could only satisfy 10% of the actual demand.

The Audi Q7 was also positioned too low, entering the market at €55,000. The company received 80,000 orders against an annual production capacity of only 70,000 units. Procter & Gamble overhauled the pricing for its Olay "Total Effect Creme," raising the price by 375% from $3.99 to $18.99. The creme sold even better than before at the much higher price. Subsequent products received the same positioning in this higher price segment. Procter & Gamble succeeded in boosting the Olay brand from a low-price to a medium-price position [37]. These cases illustrate the enormous significance of finding the optimal price positioning when launching a new product.

2.6   Price Positions

In this section we will elaborate on the five basic options for price positioning. We will look at the following categories: luxury, premium, medium, low, and ultra-low. We start with the luxury segment.

2.6.1   Luxury Price Position

2.6.1.1   Basics

A luxury price position implies that a company offers an extremely high level of quality or service (relative to the market average) at a sustained extremely high price. In terms of price management, and marketing in general, luxury goods exhibit a range of conspicuous characteristics. In order to protect the image of high prestige, rarity, and the finest quality, the price of the product or service should remain very high and stable [38]. Thus, the price of luxury goods is often a multiple of already-expensive premium prices. Table 2.2 compares the prices of selected luxury products with the prices of premium brands. The luxury goods are several times more expensive than the premium products.

Table 2.2 Examples of luxury and premium price positions, Status: February 2018

Product	Premium price position	Luxury price position
Wristwatch	Michael Kors Ceramic MK5190, $348	A. Lange & Söhne, Lange 1 Tourbillon Platinum, $403,000
Car	BMW 7 Series, base price $83,100	Ferrari 458 Italia, base price $264,000
Hotel	Hilton New York Midtown, $269	Burj Al Arab Dubai, Royal Suite, $13,058
Flight	Lufthansa Business Class, Frankfurt to Moscow $1031	Lufthansa Private Jet, Frankfurt to Moscow, $20,794
T-shirt	Ralph Lauren, $79	Prada, $740

Another distinction for luxury goods is their unit sales. Among true luxury goods, annual global unit sales often total only a few hundred, perhaps a few thousand, while premium products can generate volumes in the hundreds of thousands or even millions of units. Rolls-Royce sold only 4011 cars in 2016. Ferrari limited its sales volume in 2016 to 8014 units. In contrast, Porsche shipped 237,800 new vehicles in 2016. Although all three brands belong to the luxury segment, their sales volumes vary dramatically. Luxury goods markets have seen strong growth over the last several years and show high returns. There are more millionaires and billionaires in the world today than ever before. The price trend for luxury goods over the last 25 years is interesting. The average price of exported Swiss watches has increased by around 250% since 1990 [39]. Some luxury goods makers such as Bentley are trying to take advantage of this trend and improve their sales numbers. Bentley had already boosted its volume in 2013 by 19% to 10,120 units and maintained that level in the ensuing years. In 2016 Bentley sold 11,023 cars.

The world's largest luxury products group, LVMH, posted an EBIT margin of 19.5% in 2017, and its revenue has grown by around 10% per year since 2007. The Swiss luxury goods firm Richemont, the number two in the world, had an EBIT margin of 16.6% in the fiscal year 2017. Its average annual revenue growth since 2007 is around 9.2%. Profit and growth are the drivers of shareholder value [40]. The market capitalizations of these two firms reflect this. LVMH's sales of $52 billion and a pre-tax profit of $10.2 billion in 2017 helped sustain a market capitalization of $144.89 billion (as of February 2018), which is four times the firm's 2007 market cap of $35 billion [40]. Richemont had a market cap of $51 billion on sales of $13 billion and a pre-tax profit of $2.2 billion [41]. That is likewise more than three times its value in 2007. Despite their attractiveness with regard to profit and growth, luxury goods remain a niche market, albeit an extremely lucrative one.

2.6.1.2 Management

Product

Luxury goods must offer the highest performance and the best quality across all attributes. That applies to functional, emotional, and symbolic attributes. Johann Rupert, the chairman of Richemont, says: "We understand that we have to produce exciting and innovative products combined with excellent service to meet the demand of an ever more discerning clientele" [42]. They combine perfection in detail and opulence with excess in many facets. Burmester, which makes luxury audio systems, has developed and patented a device which can "clean" electricity. The "power conditioner" preserves and improves sound quality by filtering out the slight residual DC current mixed with the AC current from the power mains. Luxury goods do not necessarily differ from premium products in terms of functional performance. An international study of 28 leading manufacturers of luxury goods revealed that brand image, quality, and design are the main differentiation criteria, not higher functional performance [43].

Personalized service is an integral part of the luxury goods experience. At Burj Al Arab, guests staying in suites have their own butler team available 24 h a day. Leica manufactured gold-plated cameras for the Sultan of Brunei. Each year, Louis Vuitton produces around 300 custom-made special editions for prominent or exclusive customers. The process takes between 2 and 4 months for each piece. Such products include cases for two champagne flutes or for a collection of valuable batons. Things which would be considered extras for premium products are standard for luxury goods.

Luxury goods can actually have some conflicts when it comes to ethical attributes. The Bugatti Chiron, whose 16-cylinder engine delivers 1500 horsepower, has a price tag of $2.7 million. But similar to a private jet, the Chiron is certainly not considered an environmentally friendly vehicle.

Handmade is another hallmark of luxury goods. By nature, hand manufacturing limits production volume but gives the product a personal and individual character. In order to maintain full control over quality and the production process, luxury goods manufacturers tend to be highly vertically integrated and avoid outsourcing. They seek to apply strict controls of their supply chain. Hermès even has its own cattle farms and stitching departments. When Montblanc decided to enter the market for luxury watches, it added its own handcrafting facility in Switzerland. Some customers become so devoted that they make pilgrimages to such facilities. This intensive focus on handmade production and unique pieces offers small firms an opportunity in the luxury segment when they would have little chance of success in the mass market. One example is the Welter Manufaktur in Berlin, which specializes in wall decor. For their customized work, they charge between €1000 and €3000 per square meter. Despite these high prices for wall decor, the German firm has established itself in the international luxury market. It did the walls for the department store Harrods in London as well as the World Trade Center in Dubai [44].

Luxury goods makers rely on dedicated product life cycle management to ensure that their products retain their value. Ideally, a luxury product will appreciate in value over time. Limited editions and collectors' editions enhance this effect and help provide the desired exclusivity. In 2011, a Hermès Birkin Bag fetched a price of $150,000 at one auction. The original prices for the bags were between $5300 and $16,000.

Price

"Nothing is too beautiful, nothing is too expensive" is the tagline for Bugatti. Nick Hayek, the head of the Swatch Group, says that "there are no limits for luxury goods" [45]. One would imagine, therefore, that pricing of luxury goods could not be simpler: set the price as high as possible. But this simplicity is an illusion. In reality, price management for luxury goods demands very deep knowledge of the customers and the market as well as a delicate balancing act between volume and price.

The price itself is an outstanding indicator of quality and exclusivity for luxury goods. The so-called snob and Veblen effects result in a price-response function with a positive slope over some price intervals [46]. In other words, price increases lead to higher, not lower volumes. Profit rises due to the simultaneous effects of higher unit margins and higher volumes. Such cases really do occur. Delvaux, a Belgian manufacturer of exclusive bags, undertook a massive price increase as part of its repositioning. As a result, sales volumes rose sharply because customers began to view the products as relevant alternatives to Louis Vuitton bags. The effects of a luxury positioning are not limited to consumer goods. The effects can happen for industrial goods as well. The "Hidden Champion" Lightweight, which produces luxury carbon wheels, sells them in sets which cost between €4000 and €5000. These are not meant for the consumer market but rather for professionals. Lightweight does not grant any discounts. Yet demand for the wheels continues to rise [47]. Similar performance attributes played a decisive role in Porsche's price setting for its innovative line of carbon brakes. Within the company, the price of $8520 as an option for the Porsche 911 model was initially viewed as too high. But the market accepted the price, exhibiting high demand for these yellow brakes. Relative to the usual red brake discs, the yellow ones signaled the status of the car owner and thus served as a symbolic attribute. Despite the considerable price premium, the carbon brake sets became a "must have" for many Porsche 911 owners [48].

The part of the price-response function with the positive slope, however, is not relevant for price setting. The optimal price always lies along the negatively sloped portion of the curve. Luxury goods manufacturers need to know their price-response functions if they want to reach that optimal zone for price setting. Without this knowledge, they are stumbling around in the dark.

In order to support the very high price levels, companies usually limit production. This decision is made up front and communicated to the market. The limiting of an edition therefore becomes binding. Violating this self-imposed limit, for instance, in the case of unexpectedly high demand, can be a severe breach of consumers' trust. Thus, Bugatti plans to make no more than 500 Chiron vehicles. Montblanc restricts its series of fountain pens dedicated to US presidents to 50 pens per president. Depending on the design, such pens cost $25,000 and up. Very expensive watch models are often limited to 100 pieces or fewer. A. Lange & Söhne made only six units of the most expensive watch at the 2013 Geneva Watch Salon. The price tag was just under €2 million apiece.

Long waiting lists and delivery times enhance the impression of both scarcity and enduring value. Patrick Thomas, the former CEO of Hermès, described the phenomenon: "Indeed we have to deal with a paradox in our branch: the more desirable you are, the more you sell. And the more you sell, the less desirable you are. That is why at times we stop the production of a tie once it becomes too successful. Simply because success may denote triteness" [49]. Some luxury goods manufacturers carefully select their customers in order to prevent the wrong customers (e.g., seedy guests at a luxury hotel) from harming the brand's image.

The joint setting of prices and volumes for luxury goods is fundamentally different from the approach taken in other markets. In raw commodity markets, suppliers must accept the prevailing price and can only decide how much volume to put on the market. In non-commodity markets, the supplier sets the price, and the market decides how much volume it is willing to absorb. In luxury goods markets, suppliers set both the price and the volume. This combination requires a very high level of information and carries considerable risks. The following real-world case illustrates this. A luxury watchmaker presented a new watch at the watch trade fair in Basel (the world's largest) and limited volume to 800 pieces. Because the preceding model was highly coveted, the watchmaker raised the price for the new model by 50% from €16,000 to €24,000. At the trade fair, the company received 1500 orders for the new model. At a price of €24,000 and a total run of 800 timepieces, the company would have generated €19.2 million in revenue. If it could fulfill all 1500 orders placed, revenue would be €36 million. If the company had set the price at €36,000 instead of €24,000 and still sold out the originally planned run of 800 units, revenue would have been €28.8 million. The difference between €28.8 million and €19.2 million is pure foregone profit. That means the company missed a profit opportunity of €9.6 million. The moral is that poor estimates of volume and/or price can cost a manufacturer a fortune.

It is equally problematic for luxury goods manufacturers to overestimate demand and thus to produce too many units. Such a precarious situation risks price erosion, especially on secondary markets. It is difficult to reconcile strict production limits with volatile demand. Manufacturers use certain approaches to strike a balance. One is bundling. De Beers has done that for years with diamonds. Customers are offered a mix of higher quality and lower quality diamonds at a set price. The customer must then make an all-or-nothing decision on the bundle. They cannot cherry-pick. Watchmakers take a similar approach. Let us assume that Model A is in high demand and Model B less so. The manufacturer has rigid production capacity for each model. One dealer orders 20 Model A watches, but does not want to buy any of Model B. The watchmaker offers ten units of Model A, but only on the condition that the dealer also buys five units of Model B. The prices are nonnegotiable. From the manufacturer's perspective, this approach is understandable, but has a downside: the Model B watches will probably end up in secondary channels, where sales can jeopardize the consistent price levels the watchmaker works so hard to establish and protect. The ultimate cause of such price declines and inconsistencies is the miscalculation of supply and demand. This situation is very problematic for luxury goods manufacturers. First, price erosion can lead to massive frustration among customers who have paid full price. Second, these effects damage the brand image. Price stability, continuity, and consistency are indispensable for luxury goods. The myth of luxury goods is that they are everlasting and that is incompatible with price volatility. Ideally, prices for secondhand luxuries rise over time. Some customers therefore view luxury goods as investments. The prices of luxury goods usually reflect all performance attributes. Comprehensive service and other performance attributes (e.g., lifelong guarantees, club memberships) are built into the price. In other words, prices for luxury goods are usually "all inclusive."

Distribution

A key aspect of distributing luxury goods is selectivity. Luxury goods companies often have only a small number of carefully chosen outlets or dealers per country. The watchmaker A. Lange & Söhne has only 25 dealers in the United States and 15 in Japan. In Germany, there are only four cities where you can purchase a Rolls-Royce. The exclusivity in the sales channel reflects the exclusivity of the product. This applies not only to the number of stores or outlets but also to a brand's quality standards in terms of design and appearance of the sales floor, as well as the competence and discretion of the sales staff. To maintain these quality standards, manufacturers must exercise strict supervision and quality control.

The striving for high-quality standards and price enforcement have led luxury goods manufacturers to rely more and more on their own stores. Groups such as LVMH or Richemont already generate a large share of their business through their own stores. Luxury brands benefit more from their own retail stores and sales networks than from wholesale distribution. Although wholesale overall still accounts for 64% of sales of luxury brands, sales in retail (at current exchange rates) is growing more than twice as fast as sales in wholesale [50]. Revenue at the Italian luxury fashion group Prada shows a similar breakdown. The group currently generates 82% of its total revenues through its 613 self-managed stores [51]. Shifting to company-owned or company-managed stores is very important for companies which want to make the leap from premium to luxury. Luxury goods makers also use the agent model, under which, similar to the gas station business, the dealer acts as an agent representing the manufacturer. Under both systems, the manufacturer maintains complete control over all parameters, including price.

For a long time, luxury goods companies shunned the Internet as a sales channel. Personalized service and the shopping experience in an exclusive store seemed too important. Most companies have therefore limited themselves to the presentation of their products online. Only recently have some established online stores. The growth of online sellers such as net-a-porter.com or mytheresa.com has shown, however, that luxury goods buyers do make purchases online. The Internet and social media are becoming increasingly important for the luxury goods industry, even as brands wrestle with how to maintain the allure and exclusivity of "luxury" in a digital world. E-commerce in luxury grew to 9% of the market in 2017, more than doubling its share 5 years ago [50, 52].

Communication

Luxury goods require sophisticated and superior advertising, selective media usage, and collaboration with the best ad designers and photographers to maintain their brand image and convey their value to potential customers. Manufacturers often allocate up to a quarter of overall revenue to communication budgets. Public interest in luxury goods is generally high. Marketing makes strong efforts to reach out to customers through editorial content and background stories. The attractiveness of luxury products depends to a certain extent on their inaccessibility—while they are highly desirable to many, most people cannot afford or do not have access to them. The companies consciously cultivate this aspirational tension. Public relations and sponsoring therefore play a more prominent role than classical forms of advertising. The communication is often supported by spectacular actions or events.

Tradition is an important facet of a luxury good's image and communication. A brand's image is refined and solidified over time, and current advertising cannot replace a rich brand history. The Richemont and LVMH groups demonstrate the power of tradition in lending gravitas to their luxury brands. The average age of Richemont's brands is 120 years, while those of LVMH are on average 110 years old. Classic may mean old, but not obsolete.

Price almost never appears in communications about luxury products, at least not explicitly. Rarely do luxury brands list price points in brochures, on homepages, or in stores. Prices are only available on request. This quasi-secrecy surrounding prices is a further signal that luxury goods are about pure value; price is not displayed as a point of interest. Implicit in this behavior is the idea that anyone who needs to ask for the price is not a "real" luxury goods customer. Charles Rolls, the founder of Rolls-Royce, put it this way: "If you have to ask what it costs, you cannot afford it" [53, p. 229].

In Table 2.3 we summarize our insights into how luxury goods manufacturers configure their marketing instruments.

2.6.1.3 Opportunities and Risks

Increasing wealth around the world and strong growth in emerging markets are driving the expansion of luxury goods markets. This creates interesting opportunities but also pronounced risks:

Table 2.3 Configuration of marketing instruments for luxury price positioning

Product	Price	Distribution	Communication
• Extreme in quality and performance, especially on emotional and symbolic attributes • Comprehensive, personalized service • Highest exclusivity • Own manufacturing, often handmade or customized (very little outsourcing)	• Very high • Consistent across channels to retain value • No discounts whatsoever • Limited editions; price and volume planned concurrently	• Extremely selective distribution • Strict control of sales channels • Trend toward company stores or agent systems • Rather low but increasingly significant online sales	• Sophisticated advertising • Selective media usage • Heavy use of print (>60% of the ad budget) • Emphasis on PR, editorial content, reports, sponsoring, and special events • Emphasis on tradition • No active/explicit price communication

- Luxury goods markets are extraordinarily attractive because they combine high growth and high profitability. But conquering these markets is anything but easy. In the luxury sector, one finds primarily French, Italian, and Swiss firms. For luxury cars, the German and British brands are well represented. New players often struggle to establish the prestige and demand of true luxury brands.
- Top performance on functional attributes is table stakes, but in and of itself not sufficient for success. The products must also deliver very high emotional and symbolic value.
- In order for luxury goods to be profitable, they need to reach sufficient volumes—without producing such high quantities that they cheapen the brands. One risk is that the production volumes remain too small to be profitable ("curse of the small volumes").
- On the other hand, loss of exclusivity poses a threat. Luxury goods are by their very nature elitist. Exclusivity plays a key role. Growth strategies and expansion plans which dilute a brand's exclusivity must be avoided. This applies to horizontal expansion into new product categories (brand extensions) as well as vertical extensions, i.e., down-market line extensions. Watering down the brand is extremely dangerous for luxury products. The expansion may pay off in the short run, but long term it can lead to the trivialization of the brand.
- More and more, luxury goods makers are opening their own stores in order to maintain control over prices and the quality of the sales experience. This opens up growth opportunities but requires a massive capital investment and the assumption of additional risk.

2.6.2 Premium Price Position

2.6.2.1 Basics

A premium price position means that a product or service is offered at a price which is noticeably and sustainably above the market average. There are premium products and services in almost every sector. On the consumer side, these include Mercedes-Benz and Lexus (cars), Miele (washing machines), Nespresso (coffee), Starbucks (coffee shops), Clinique (cosmetics), and Apple (consumer electronics and computers). Premium services include Singapore Airlines and Lufthansa, private banks, and hotel chains such as InterContinental and Four Seasons.

But premium products are by no means limited to prestigious consumer products. There are also many premium offerings in B2B industries. We often hear the expression "We are the Mercedes-Benz of our industry" in connection with industrial goods. Midsized world market leaders, the so-called Hidden Champions, usually have a price level of 10–15% above the market average and still rank as global market leaders [54].

For a premium price position, the quality, competence, or uniqueness of the supplier is at the forefront of the customer's interest. Price is not. The cost differences between competing offers are typically smaller than the differences in the perceived value and the resulting willingness to pay. The latter is systematically

Table 2.4 Price difference between market average and premium prices, Status: January 2018

Product	Medium-price position	Premium-price position
Chocolate (3.5 oz)	Cadbury: $1.93	Scharffen Berger: $4.99 (+159%)
Ice cream (35 oz)	Breyers: $2.18	Ben & Jerry's: $8.68 (+298%)
Pencils (each)	General's Kimberly Graphite Pencil: $0.95	Faber-Castell 9000 Pencil: $2 (+110%)
Men's dress shirt (white)	Alfani: $52.50	Hugo Boss: $95 (+81%)
Smartphone	Huawei P10 (64 GB): $449	iPhone X (64 GB): $999 (+123%)
HDTV (55 in.)	Toshiba: $449.99	Samsung: $1099.99 (+144%)
Midsized car (base model)	VW Passat: $22,995	Mercedes-Benz E-Class: $52,950 (+130%)
Hotel, Miami (one night, classic room)	Hilton Miami South Beach: $217	Four Seasons $478 (+120%)

exploited through the premium price. A board member of a premium automotive company explained the premium position: "Our prices should be 12–16% above the market average, but our costs should only be 6–8% higher. This difference is where the music plays."

The differences between a medium-price position and a premium one can be considerable, as the selected examples in Table 2.4 show. There is no general rule of thumb for how large a price premium should be. For consumer goods in particular, the gap can amount to several hundred percent. The border between premium and luxury is fluid.

Premium products are not only superior in terms of functional performance; they should perform strongly across emotional, symbolic, and ethical attributes as well. They are characterized by high quality and an outstanding service package. Innovation is often the basis for their superiority. The high price itself can become a positive attribute. This effect can come from price serving as an indicator of quality as well as from the social signals (Snob or Veblen effect) it sends. Through the purchase and use of a premium product, customers consciously separate themselves from the crowd, but without fully removing themselves from mainstream society (as might happen with luxury goods).

2.6.2.2 Management

Product

Given the quality expectations, the product itself plays a central role in premium price positioning. Superior competencies along the entire value chain are indispensable, from innovation to the procurement of raw materials. It also covers stable production processes and above-average capabilities of the sales and service organizations. In no other product category—not even for luxury goods—is innovation more important than for premium products. This is because the unique selling proposition (USP) of premium products is often first established through innovation.

In the smartphone industry, groundbreaking innovations (front camera, retina display, HD camera with optical zoom, stereo speakers, 3-D touch) are generally introduced in premium models (such as the iPhone) and then spread to the average and lower price ranges. As a result, the competitive advantage derived from any given innovation is only temporary, so premium suppliers face constant pressure to innovate. Some brands stress this emphasis on constant innovation in their advertising claim. The premium household appliance manufacturer Miele has used the slogan "forever better" since its founding in 1899. This slogan represents the firm's guiding philosophy. Miele has always strived to be better than its competitors and continually improves its products.

Nonetheless, innovation isn't the only successful premium strategy—a company can also focus on remaining true to what has worked well. One calls this variant the "semper idem" (always the same) strategy. "Semper idem" is actually the motto of Underberg, a digestive famous in German-speaking countries. The USP of such products, such as Chivas Regal, derives from the fact that the product never changes. Constancy is an advantage. But this applies only to the product itself. The company has to adjust and adapt its marketing methods and its production processes. Premium products also require a level of service which is both comprehensive and of a similar quality as the product itself. To deliver this, companies require highly qualified employees both internally and at its sales and distribution partners.

Price
The comparatively high price is an integral feature of a premium product. The price cannot become a ping-pong ball for discount actions, special offers, or similar price-driven measures. Premium suppliers must place a high value on continuity, price discipline, and price maintenance. Wendelin Wiedeking, the former CEO of Porsche, explains: "Our policy is to keep our prices stable, in order to protect our brand and avoid a decline in the residual value for used Porsches. If demand falls, we cut our production, not our prices." The current marketing decision-makers at Porsche, Bernhard Meier and Kjell Gruner, have a clear philosophy on this point: "We always want to sell one vehicle fewer than the market can absorb, in order to remain true to our brand promise of high exclusivity and high retained value. We are not volume driven, but rather obligated to an enduring business" [55].

This policy works well for several reasons:

- Sharp variations in price are not compatible with the sustained high-value image of a premium product.
- Temporary price reductions will frustrate or anger customers who purchased the product at its normal (high) price.
- For durable goods, price actions can jeopardize prices for used products. The residual value is an important purchase criterion for these kinds of products. A decline in residual value can diminish willingness to pay for new products.

Recommended prices for resellers are appropriate for premium products and should be enforced. The manufacturers of premium products should be resolute in preventing the use of their products as loss leaders, even though this may not be easy to achieve for legal reasons. Retailers and resellers continually try to circumvent the efforts of manufacturers to maintain resale price discipline.

Above all, manufacturers should resist the temptation to lower their prices. It could certainly be the case that the price elasticity for a premium product is very high when the price cut is massive, leading to a sharp rise in sales volume. After repeated use of this tactic, however, the product could lose its premium status and become a mass-market product. An example of this is the clothing brand Lacoste. The French professional tennis player René Lacoste founded the company in 1933 to sell sports shirts he designed. The recognizable crocodile emblem stood for exclusive prestige, and the Lacoste shirts achieved high prices and margins. US President Dwight Eisenhower and other celebrities wore Lacoste shirts in public. For 50 years, Lacoste was a brand associated with high social class. Over time, though, Lacoste became a mass product. The prices fell. As a consequence, sales volume declined, triggering more price reductions and ultimately lower profits. This case sheds light on why price discipline for premium products is so important.

Distribution

Premium product distribution rests on exclusivity and selectivity, beginning with control over how the product is presented. This goes beyond the visual presentation to include the qualifications and appearance of sales personnel. Implementing this maxim in practice often proves difficult. In industries such as clothing or consumer electronics, it is not uncommon for premium products to be sold in an environment dominated by medium or even low-priced products, even though that is unlikely to be in the best interests of the premium manufacturers. Increasingly, premium suppliers are setting up stand-alone "shop-in-shop" spaces within department stores to separate their products from the medium-priced ones. This concept has proven itself and is fitting for a premium price position.

According to Lasslop [56], one should split the distribution hierarchy for premium products into three levels. At the highest level are the flagship stores, whose primary purpose is to "celebrate and worship" the premium brand. Examples of such stores are those of Apple, Nike, or the coffee brand Nespresso. Achieving high revenue is not the main purpose of these stores. Rather, they showcase the brand, as the term "flagship" implies. They should create a destination for consumers to immerse themselves in the brand and its aspirational, premium nature. The second level is franchised stand-alone stores in which the manufacturer still maintains control overall key parameters. The third level of the distribution hierarchy is comprised of specialty retailers and upscale stores, such as Nespresso boutiques in Sur La Table or Macy's in the United States. The trend toward the "shop-in-shop" has taken hold in particular in upscale stores. Because of the demands placed on these intermediaries, their selection follows very strict criteria. In exchange for complying with the manufacturer's demands for a high-quality presentation of the product, a sophisticated ambience, and highly qualified personnel, the selected intermediary receives a certain level of territorial exclusivity. In some cases, the manufacturer adopts an exclusive distribution system.

The distribution of premium products through a national network of factory outlet centers (FOCs) should be viewed critically. True stand-alone factory sales stores, which operate only locally, expose the image and price of premium products to less risk. In sectors where customers don't tend to have strong loyalties to a retailer (e.g., textiles, furniture, and household appliances), factory outlet centers can be an interesting distribution option. These centers tip the balance of power in retail, which often favors the store, slightly in favor of the manufacturer. Manufacturers prefer to offer goods from the previous season at FOCs rather than the latest models.

While the luxury price segment still has a limited online sales presence, due to its inaccessibility and exclusivity, the premium segment is increasingly using alternative distribution channels. Online sales now account for around 17% of the revenue for premium brands [57]. When they buy premium products or premium brands, customers still expect outstanding service, customer orientation, and customer care [58], which are prerequisites for a high willingness to pay in this segment. But these service aspects are often very hard to fulfill online. Thus, the opportunities for success in online distribution channels depend on the sector and on how explanation-intensive the product is. For example, consumers are rather willing to purchase an iPhone upgrade online than a new washing machine or furniture.

Communication

Due to the relevance of branding for premium products, it goes without saying that communication is very important. The content of the communication focuses primarily on exclusivity, prestige, and continuity. In addition to classical advertising, premium products are increasingly relying on "below-the-line" activities. These include public relations, event marketing, and product placement. James Bond drives a BMW 750iL in "Tomorrow Never Dies." BMW marketed the launch of its i8 hybrid electric vehicle in conjunction with the Mission Impossible film "Ghost Protocol" by having Tom Cruise drive the car. The slogan "Mission to drive" connects the reputation of the film to the automobile. Apple products also appear prominently in many films.

The communication of premium products derives from performance, emotion, and social prestige. Price stays in the background. If a company succeeds in establishing a premium image, the price plays a secondary role in the purchase decision.

Table 2.5 provides an overview of the configuration of the marketing instruments for premium price positioning.

2.6.2.3 Opportunities and Risks

The logic of a premium price position is as follows: high margins together with reasonable unit volume lead to high profits. This logic only works, however, when demand remains sufficiently strong in spite of the high price. The higher the price is, the smaller the accessible segment becomes. A host of empirical findings indicate

Table 2.5 Configuration of marketing instruments for premium price positioning

Product	Price	Distribution	Communication
• Outstanding functional performance and quality • Comprehensive service package • High importance of emotional, symbolic, and ethical attributes	• Sustaining a high relative price • Uncompromising on discounts and promotions • Price discipline and maintenance are particularly important • Clearance sales only for fashion products	• High exclusivity and selectivity • Establishing control over the presentation of the product; high demands placed on the seller/retailer • Selective, but increasing level of online sales	• Emphasizes non-price factors • Continuity of the message • Use of below-the-line activities (e.g., product placement)

that premium suppliers enjoy above-average profitability [1, 59]. The following opportunities and risks are associated with a premium price position:

- Relatively low-price elasticities in the upper price ranges allow for higher premiums.
- Because customers in the premium segment place higher value on performance attributes, there are more opportunities for product differentiation than in mass markets. Every performance attribute is a potential competitive advantage. Canoy and Peitz [60, p. 307] assess these opportunities from the customer perspective: "Customers' evaluations are more dispersed in the high-quality range than in the low-quality range."
- The frequency and the danger of price wars are lower in the premium segment than in the lower price ranges. A "price warrior" in this segment risks ruining its brand image.
- Rising wealth and rising incomes are driving growth in the premium segment. Customers are trading up from the medium segment to the premium segment.
- Financial crises can cause shifts in demand from the luxury segment to the premium segment.
- A greater emotional awareness among customers can be observed. The demographic transformation—or more specifically, the aging of society—leans in that direction. According to an Accenture-GfK study, many older consumers prefer expensive products and sales channels [61].
- A particular challenge lies in achieving and maintaining a high level of quality and innovation. A purely image-based differentiation will not endure if the product or service does not deliver the quality to back it up. Quelch [62, p. 45] states: "Mere exclusivity without quality leadership is a recipe for failure."
- The brand faces similar risks. If a company fails to position or maintain its brand at the level that premium customers expect, it is headed for trouble. The VW Phaeton could serve as the poster child for this. The VW brand proved too weak in competing against BMW or Mercedes in the premium segment.

- Products upgraded from medium pricing also pose risks to existing premium products. If the aspiring company improves both the product's quality and its image, that product can attack premium products from below. Such trade-ups occur in many markets. Toyota's Lexus is a telling example.
- Managers of premium products must resist the "temptation of large volumes" and the growth they promise. One of the most effective and quickest ways to destroy a premium price position is to cut prices in order to reach the mass market, i.e., to hit higher volume numbers and achieve wider distribution.
- For consumer durables, the secondhand market can pose risks. Premium products enjoy a high level of popularity on secondhand markets. The Internet has aggravated this problem. This is well-known in the market for cars. A flourishing secondary market can suppress demand for new products and exert downward pressure on the prices for new products. Premium manufacturers should keep a close eye on the secondary market and intervene if necessary.
- The premium position implies higher complexity and higher costs. A high level of performance does not come at low costs. Thus, there is the risk that costs get out of control. For premium products, one must always make sure that higher prices overcompensate for additional costs. Costs which do not contribute to an increase in customers' willingness to pay should be avoided.

2.6.3 Medium-Price Position

2.6.3.1 Basics

A medium-price position means that from the customers' point of view, a product or service has a middling level of performance and a consistently midrange price, relative to the market average. A medium price falls within the customers' perceived market average. The same applies to the level of performance. Products with a medium-price position typically include classic branded products which have often helped to set standards in their respective markets. Examples include Buick, the household goods manufacturer Whirlpool, or retailers such as Kroger and Tesco. Products and brands in the medium-price range have been and remain very significant. Characteristic aspects comprise brand, the promise of quality, image, becoming synonymous with an entire category (Kleenex, Q-Tip), and ubiquity.

As discounters penetrate further into markets, the medium-price position has come under attack, but in the recent past, there has been a countertrend—the medium-price position is getting stronger again. In terms of overall volume and value, the medium-price range still forms the largest segment in many markets. Brands such as Gap or American Eagle achieved success with a medium-price position. Importantly, their level of quality distinguishes medium-priced retailers from low-priced competitors such as H&M, Forever 21, or Primark, combined with current, up-to-date designs. The medium-priced retailers do not offer top cuts or materials such as Hugo Boss or Ralph Lauren do, and the symbolic performance does not stand out as much, but the price is also noticeably lower than for premium products. Within fast-moving consumer goods, there are numerous product categories in which the medium-price position is dominant. Some 60% of the market for noodles falls in the medium-price range [63].

2.6.3.2 Management

Product
Good and constant quality is the predominant characteristic of medium-priced products. In comparison to low-priced products, a supplier should pay attention to establishing customer preferences based on performance. This affects primarily the components of the functional attributes, such as technology, the degree of innovation, and reliability or durability. Medium-priced products should also differentiate themselves in terms of packaging and design (emotional performance) as well as at a rudimentary level along symbolic attributes. This applies above all to consumer products. The management of the brand therefore is highly important. While medium-priced products are less differentiated than premium products, they offer more variants and models than low-priced products.

If variable unit costs fall due to scale and experience curve effects, the company needs to decide whether to reduce prices or improve performance. In many cases, the company with a medium-price position opts for improved performance in such a situation, whereas a manufacturer of low-priced products would react by lowering the price. This is done in order to further expand the competitive advantage of "superior performance." For this reason, prices in the medium-priced segment of the computer industry generally do not fall but instead offer more performance and more accessories from generation to generation for the same price. A committed low-priced supplier would instead tend to cut prices in order to reinforce the "low-price" competitive advantage.

Price
Consistent with the brand image and stable quality, many suppliers of medium-priced products try to maintain a steady price level as much as possible. They are trying to keep price competition at the retail level in check. In order to stem the frequency and the extent of special offers or discounts, medium-priced suppliers practice active price maintenance. The goal is to harmonize end consumer prices within a certain range (price corridor). Because vertical price-fixing is forbidden, it is not possible to steer end consumer prices directly when the products are sold through distributors or retailers. Nonetheless, the manufacturers definitely exert some influence over end-customer prices. The associated measures include identifying loss leaders, tracking the flow of goods in order to prevent gray imports, buying up reduced price goods, appealing to the trade partners, limiting on deliveries, or incentivizing channel partners to maintain and enforce recommended prices. Legally, this is a gray area in which the power of the manufacturer has been declining.

Special offers play a bigger role for medium-priced products than they do for low-priced ones. First, the wider price spans across competitors give a company more leeway to make temporary price reductions. Second, the effects of special offers or price promotions on sales volumes are typically strong. A volume increase of five to ten times normal sales can occur during promotional periods. Special offers are also employed to win back customers who have switched to bargain or low-priced products. But one must be careful not to use such price tactics too frequently, run promotions for too long, or offer a reduced price that is too far below the normal price level. When one fails to follow these maxims, the customers get accustomed to the lower prices and start to buy only when they see them. This erodes the brand image. Banana Republic, Ann Taylor, and J. Crew have all fallen into this trap, offering as many as 18–20 promotion days per month in recent years to keep their sales volumes consistent. In reality, the position slips into the low-price category, but without being armed with the corresponding low-cost structures.

Price differentiation according to different package sizes or feature sets is important for medium-priced products. While bargain products are often only available in fixed configurations, customers in the medium-priced segment have many options to choose from. In contrast to the discounter stores, the assortment in medium-priced stores tends to be broader and show greater price differentiation. Of course, the customer also expects competent advice, better service, and more goodwill than they would from low-priced products. This creates opportunities for tactics such as price bundling or charging for certain services separately (unbundling).

Distribution

A classic characteristic of medium-priced branded products is their ubiquity, but we observe some differentiation in distribution channels. Some discounters only offer limited quantities of branded products, if they offer them at all. Nonetheless, medium-priced products enjoy the larger sales reach. They are sold through many channels and by many intermediaries. That holds true even in new sectors.

In harmony with the quality claim of medium-priced branded products, manufacturers must exercise quality control over the sales channels. This is especially important for products which may create liability risks or require extensive consultation. These are areas where the specialty trade still dominates. The more important the performance of the reseller is, the greater the markups in the respective channel. Here we need to distinguish between push and pull products. A "push" situation occurs when the reseller serves the customer and can recommend the product, such as when someone buys an over-the-counter medication at a drugstore. In such cases, the reseller often has a decisive influence over which product the customer buys. And the reseller wants appropriate compensation for this service. In a "pull" situation the customers determine on their own which product to buy. Self-service is a good example. The manufacturer must then use its advertising in order to ensure that an end customer has a sufficiently strong preference for its brand. The reseller fulfills only a logistical role in this case.

Online sales are becoming increasingly important for medium-priced products. Many well-known brands use the Internet and online shops for direct sales or sales through third parties. But the use of online sales varies significantly by sector. The food and grocery industry has not made much use of this channel so far, but the emergence in the United States of Instacart, Amazon Fresh, and Google Express alongside older forms such as PeaPod shows this may be changing. Nowadays, though, it is hard to imagine software, electronics, or travel industries without the online channel. Customers use the Internet for research as well as for price comparisons. It is also normal to purchase electronic devices or shoes online. The digital competition is putting the survival of many brick-and-mortar stores at risk, as they have difficulties in keeping up with what the online stores offer. Mainstream music and video stores have been almost extinguished entirely by online channels such as the streaming services Spotify and Netflix.

Communication

For the medium-price position, communication plays a different and more important role than for low-priced products. There are many reasons for this. First, performance and quality advantages across many dimensions demand more intensive communication than the one-dimensional price advantage does. Second, brand recognition and brand image—created largely through communication—have a greater significance. Medium-price suppliers therefore invest a lot more in communication than low-price suppliers. In order to reach a broad target audience, they mainly use mass media (television, popular magazines, etc.). Increasingly the Internet is serving as a supplementary communications medium to TV. This holds true in particular for younger target groups with a high Internet affinity. That is how digital, cloud-based services often market themselves, predominantly through advertising and banners. Such firms include Spotify, Amazon, and online boutiques. Online communication in this regard is no longer limited to banner ads or video clips; it is largely driven through the use of social media and branded content instead of traditional advertising. It is customary for medium-priced brands to use Facebook, Twitter, Instagram, or Pinterest to communicate with fans and followers directly.

In terms of advertising content and design, the performance and quality matter most. The price itself is rarely an object of communication, and when it is, it's usually in terms of the price-value relationship. Depending on the product group, the advertising often emphasizes an emotional component. Companies attempt to associate the product with feelings and experiences which foster a connection to the product and create willingness to pay. One peculiar aspect of medium-priced products is their socially neutral image. Low-priced products, in contrast, tend to be associated with a lower social status. Premium and especially luxury products confer a higher level of social prestige. Of course it goes without saying that these effects influence willingness to pay.

Table 2.6 summarizes the configuration of the marketing instruments for medium-price positioning.

2.6.3.3 Opportunities and Risks

For a long time, it was common to proclaim the imminent demise of the medium-price position. These forecasts did not come true. The medium-price range continues, as it long has to account for a large majority of the demand in many markets, and in some it has even grown stronger. The medium-price position faces the following opportunities and risks:

Table 2.6 Configuration of the marketing instruments for medium-price positioning

Product	Price	Distribution	Communication
• Good functional performance • Continuous performance improvement • Emotionally charged; occasionally symbolic and ethical • Many variants • Brand is very important	• Consistent prices, but functional improvement from version to version • Monitoring and maintenance • Use of special offers • Price differentiation based on moderate/slight performance differences • Opportunities for complex price structures (bundling and unbundling)	• Ubiquity • Many sales channels • Online sales are significant • Some quality control over the channels • Specialty trade (for products requiring extensive explanation)	• Relatively high investment • Relatively high share of classical advertising (mass media such as TV and print) • Emphasis on performance and quality, not on price • Social neutrality • Increasing use of online sales and social media

- Classic branded products in the medium-price range are not only well-known but also positively charged. They are associated with attributes such as fair, honest/genuine, and reliable.
- They avoid in equal measure being "cheap" or "pretentious." This aversion to extremes helps medium-priced products. They are not as polarizing as products in the upper or lower ends of the price scale.
- Medium-priced products minimize search costs and perceived risks for consumers. When customers are not well-informed about a product, they often opt for something from the medium-price range. Hayward [64, p. 66] remarks: "Consumers are seeking options that perform satisfactorily, are simple and easy to understand and find, require little research to select, carry little risk either emotionally or economically, and are reliable and trustworthy."
- On the other hand, the medium position can contribute to the lack of a well-defined profile. "They are significantly more expensive than the lower-priced products, but not as good as the premium products—a lousy compromise" captures the essence of what consumers might think.
- The medium-price range is subject to attacks from above and below. From above, premium competitors may want to carve out their own piece of the medium segment. From below, low-priced competitors attack with products whose quality continues to improve. In food and grocery, the discounters are attacking the midrange retailers with improved selections at consistently lower prices.
- Companies also face internal risks. Cost pressures can lead a company to reduce its traditional performance advantage or give it up entirely. This so-called "salami-slicing" tactic might escape the customers' notice in the short term, but long term, it can destroy a medium-price position. In order to avoid this, one must understand very precisely what attributes or performance levels are indispensable for customers and for which they are willing to pay a bit more.

- Medium-priced products often have a long tradition. Thus, they face the risk that they appear old-fashioned as their core consumers age. They may lose their attractiveness to younger buyers. One must work directly and resolutely against this trend and keep the image up to date. Using discounts to compensate for an outdated image is ineffective.

It is controversial as to whether "the middle" is getting weaker or stronger. On the one hand, the polarization of markets poses a serious challenge to the medium-price position. On the other hand, one would think there will always be a market for offering a reasonable level of performance at a fair price. Some studies show that the middle is getting stronger, while others reveal the opposite. Low-priced and premium-priced products are both moving toward the middle. The low-priced suppliers do this by continually improving their quality, while the premium suppliers try to offer slimmed-down or scaled-back versions of their products at more favorable prices. Both trends are apparent, depending on the market. The medium-price position is also not necessarily a "stuck in the middle" with poor returns. Cronshaw et al. [65, p. 25] have found that medium-priced companies perform better than low-priced ones. Sharp and Dawes [66, p. 749] note that many medium-priced companies and brands have shown sustained, above-average success. One could mention examples here such as Toyota (automobiles), LG (electronics), Dove (cosmetics), Best Western (hotels), Pepsi (beverages and snacks), and Kellogg (breakfast foods).

2.6.4 Low-Price Position

2.6.4.1 Basics

A low-price position means that relative to the market average, a company offers a lower level of performance at a sustained lower price. The low-price positioning has grown in importance over the last few decades. Among Germany's food and grocery retailers, discounters have been able to grow their market share to around 45%. The hard discounters ALDI and LIDL are penetrating other countries successfully, including the United Kingdom and the United States. Low-price companies have penetrated other sectors as well. They include electronics (Best Buy, Dell), clothing (Forever 21, Primark, H&M), beer (Keystone), motels (Motel 6, Red Roof Inn, Microtel), or furniture (IKEA). In air transportation, there are many inexpensive alternatives nowadays (Southwest Airlines, Ryanair, EasyJet), just as there are in car rental (Enterprise, Budget).

The same applies to banks which take advantage of the Internet and pass the cost advantages on to their customers. They include Bank of Internet USA and Capital One 360. Even in sectors where intensive pre-purchase consultation is required, low-priced suppliers have established market-leading positions. One example is prescription eyewear, where Fielmann is the European market leader. Fielmann's prices are significantly lower than those of traditional eyewear retailers. In the United

States, Costco offers low-priced eyeglasses and contact lenses through its own Costco Optical department, whereas Warby Parker primarily sells eyeglasses online.

A special low-priced segment which has shown strong growth is the factory outlet center (FOC). These centers offer an additional sales channel for branded products and are predominantly used by clothing and fashion companies. True to the name, companies market unsold branded merchandise at marked down prices at these outlets. In some cases, retailers create outlet-specific lines with lower quality and lower cost but still branded. The FOC removes the retailer markup and cuts shipping costs. These savings are passed on to consumers in the form of lower prices. This is similar to the method carmakers use when they sell vehicles to their employees, car rental companies, or other fleet operators at reduced prices. For some car brands, almost half of the volume goes through this "second price track," which brings weaker margins.

Companies with low-price positions have been broadly successful in seizing large market shares. But the results are mixed when we look at their profitability. The majority of low-priced companies do not survive over the long term. The German home improvement chain Praktiker AG, which used the slogan "20% off everything" for years, ultimately shut its doors. When these companies survive over the long haul, though, they often have both growth rates and returns which are significantly above those of comparable companies with higher price positions. Such companies include ALDI, IKEA, Ryanair, and Southwest Airlines. The market capitalization of Ryanair, at around $23 billion, is higher than that of Lufthansa at around $15 billion. Price transparency, which the Internet has amplified, and the trend toward keeping the basic service as low-priced as possible have combined to increase price sensitivity and lure new customers to these companies.

These successful examples show that a low-price strategy only makes sense when it is based on a low-cost position: "There is no such thing as a low price strategy. The only way to win is to have lower costs than your competition" [37, p. 13]. A low price on its own will not lead to success unless the company also keeps its costs low. The principles of a low-cost strategy come into play even for complex products, such as investment funds. A comparison of the investment firms Fidelity and Vanguard illustrates this. While Fidelity focuses on active portfolio management, Vanguard offers lower-cost investments in index funds (ETFs). This is how Vanguard succeeds in maintaining the lowest costs in the industry [66].

2.6.4.2 Management
In the spirit of Michael Porter, a low-price position is tightly linked to cost leadership [67, pp. 11–22]. In order to survive long term with low prices and generate adequate returns, companies must have sustainable cost advantages. They need to exploit the economies of scale and the experience curve. Constant monitoring and the minimization of costs along the entire value chain are indispensable for low-price positioning. Product/service simplification is closely tied to cost leadership. This simplification requires limiting product and service offerings to the essentials—aiming for the most basic level of functional performance which sufficiently satisfies the customers' needs. Low-cost sellers shy away from offering anything in excess of

that. They avoid over-delivering on functional attributes and refrain from addressing additional emotional, symbolic, or ethical needs, especially when doing so would result in additional costs or complexity.

Product

The demands of cost leadership imply that a company needs to offer standardized products and services. Economies of scale and experience curve effects only take hold at large volumes. The costs of unnecessary complexity must be avoided. Therefore, low-price companies place strict limits on their assortments. For example, ALDI stocks only 57 types of juice, while the classic supermarket would have 165 juice varieties on the shelves. A classic supermarket would offer 223 different coffee products; ALDI offers 49.

This has a massive effect on inventory turnover. ALDI turns its capital over 2.6 times per year, whereas a supermarket achieves about one time [68]. In order to offer a relatively large number of end-product variants despite a small number of base modules or versions, some companies turn to a so-called platform strategy. Different variants result from the combination of standardized modules. This approach is widespread in the automotive industry, in computers, and increasingly in heavy equipment and engineering.

Product simplification, however, remains the most important factor in saving costs. It is always a question of "what level of performance adequately solves the customer's problem?" The mobile telecom company Congstar ("you want it, you got it") offers no service. It does not subsidize phone purchases, provide 24 h service, or even have any physical stores. All it does is sell prepaid phone cards (with no extras) online. In other words, what Congstar offers is rudimentary and purely functional.

In a similar way, low-cost airlines leave out many of the services passengers came to expect from classic airlines. The low-cost competitors usually do not offer seat reservations, lounges, status cards, programs, or magazines. When they offer food and drink or checked baggage, they collect a surcharge. In 2006, Ryanair pioneered carving out the previously sacrosanct passenger baggage allowances and started charging separately for them. Other airlines followed suit.

As part of its aggressive price repositioning, HanseMerkur Insurance drastically simplified its product and service portfolio. By offering entry-level rates for policies which eliminated everything (e.g., ambulant psychotherapy) which does not involve an existential risk, the company successfully established itself in the low-price segment of the health insurance market. The simplification of its offering not only spares the customers from high insurance premiums; it also boosts the insurance group's income from premiums [69]. A strong focus on functional performance is typical for low-price resellers.

The principle of simplified performance also manifests itself in a company's branding. A low-priced position is often seen as synonymous with "no name" brands, "me too" products, or store brands. Building up a strong product brand requires high investment and is incompatible with cost leadership. Minimal or basic branding goes hand in hand with sensible packaging. Products which have a limited range of options but whose quality is highly transparent (such as basic foodstuffs) lend themselves well to low-price positioning. In addition, such products should be more or less self-explanatory, rather than require extensive consultation or an in-depth sales pitch.

Price

The USP (unique selling proposition) and the competitive advantage of the low-price position is the price itself. In retail this translates into the prevailing practice of "every day low prices" (EDLP). All other marketing instruments are aligned with the goal of maintaining and supporting the low price. Using a "Hi-lo" approach—i.e., offering temporary low prices on a recurring basis—is atypical for low-price suppliers. IKEA provides a success case. For years, the Swedish furniture maker has mastered the challenge of achieving high product volumes at consistently low prices across diverse markets, languages, and cultures. The IKEA model is based on the volume of the assortments and the production of the exact same products, year after year. This helps IKEA lock in low prices from its suppliers and pass some of these savings on to consumers. The more stores IKEA opens, the more volume it can generate. That means that IKEA can implement further price reductions. Another important aspect of IKEA's price strategy is the selection of so-called breathtaking items. These iconic, very familiar products with very low prices (such as Billy shelves) exert a halo effect on the entire assortment [70].

In order to maintain an attractive price image, it can be advantageous to cut prices on a regular basis. Low-priced suppliers are usually quick to pass cost savings on to their customers. This is not necessarily driven by altruism, but rather by the goal of preventing competitors from undercutting them on price. "At the end of the day, ALDI needs to re-establish its good reputation over and over by making fresh price cuts," said one expert [71]. ALDI's corporate philosophy is expressed as follows: "Every aspect of our operations has been rethought and reinvented to maximize the quality of our products and savings for our customers." The German website is more specific: "Whenever we have the opportunity, such as when commodity prices decline, we pass on those savings to our customers and lower our retail prices right away" [72]. When raw materials costs rise, however, even the discounters cannot avoid price increases. When configuring a price or conditions structure, simplicity rules. Complicated price structures require too much time-consuming explanation. Such factors include payment terms and discounts.

Distribution

Sales management contributes to cost leadership by using efficient distribution structures and a limited number of channels. Online sales play a very important role for low-cost suppliers, especially in the service sector. Tickets from low-cost airlines are available online or by telephone, but not through travel agents. Dell sells almost all of its computers directly to end customers. Such distribution channels do not require a large sales force. In the physical trade, low-cost suppliers look for less expensive locations which are easily accessible by car. Nonetheless, even discounters have begun to follow a trend toward more expensive locations in city centers. The overarching focus on simplicity extends not only to store locations but to the rather spartan appearance of the stores themselves and to the standardization of internal processes. For example, it is advantageous to always place the same product at the same location in the store, often on palettes or in the original shipping cartons.

Communication

The communication of low-priced suppliers faces contradictory demands. On the one hand, low prices do not leave room for large advertising budgets. Strict control and minimization of communication costs are imperative. At the same time, the company needs to effectively communicate the low prices to their target audience in order to achieve the correspondingly high volumes and market shares.

Some low-priced suppliers forgo advertising entirely and rely instead on the pull of the distribution channels they use. When they do advertise, it is primarily done to communicate the price advantage and done through inexpensive media. For example, Europe's leader in prescription eyewear, Fielmann, relies on radio and newspaper ads. The advertising budgets of low-priced companies are usually below the industry average. Nonetheless, companies –especially retailers—sometimes wage fierce communications battle for the "low-price" mantle. Walmart and Best Buy come to mind in this regard.

An additional tactic of the low-price suppliers is the use of spectacular actions or provocative statements, in the hope of garnering wide media exposure. That is free advertising. Michael O'Leary, the CEO of Ryanair, is famous for such actions. These include, for example, his announcement that Ryanair may start charging passengers to use the bathroom in flight (something the company never actually implemented). Ryanair even wants to offer price comparisons for all airlines on its own homepage. With his characteristic cockiness, O'Leary proclaimed that Ryanair would "always be the cheapest anyway" [73].

Successful low-price positioning is about using aggressive advertising to convince as many customers as possible with the low-price argument. Once the low-price image is anchored firmly in the customers' minds, the company can perhaps scale back its ad spend. The Internet is a particularly good fit for communicating a low-price position. Price comparison sites reach a large audience and favor the low-priced suppliers.

The price is the central message and selling argument number one for a low-price position. Other performance aspects are relegated to the background. Price advertising tends to be very aggressive. In print media, the price often appears larger than the product itself. In radio and television, the ads hammer home the same, price-based slogan over and over again.

Table 2.7 provides an overview of the configuration of the marketing instruments for a low-price position. Such a positioning demands that the entire value chain is built around low costs and the highest efficiency. This applies to procurement, to internal processes, and to personnel. Labor costs can total 12–14% of revenue for a classic supermarket, while hard discounters keep these costs down to 5–7% of sales [74]. Dedication to these principles, and their consistent application, is essential for success in the low-price segment.

Table 2.7 Configuration of the marketing instruments for a low-price positioning

Product	Price	Distribution	Communication
• Focus on essential functional attributes (core performance) • Low emotional, symbolic, and/or ethical performance • Limited assortment	• Sustained low prices (EDLP) • Few special offers • No complex price systems • No discounts	• Hardly any product support services • Limited sales channels • Inexpensive locations and sales methods • Very high importance of online sales	• Emphasis on price (price advertising) • Limited, affordable media • Simple slogans which run for a long time

2.6.4.3 Opportunities and Risks

As the cases have demonstrated, some but in no way all low-price suppliers are successful in practice. Success in these segments requires fulfilling a lot of prerequisites:

- The low-price segment must be sufficiently large. This applies not only to the willingness to pay but also to the acceptance of less value. The low-price segment can draw demand from above (decline in social status), from below (increasing incomes, which applies in particular to emerging countries), or by tapping into latent demand ("products are getting more affordable"). All three pools of demand play a role. Stagnating real incomes are causing some consumers to trade down to less expensive products. In emerging markets, in contrast, many consumers are now earning enough money to afford low-priced products for the first time. The radical low prices of the budget airlines opened up new layers of demand for air travel.
- Low-priced suppliers need to achieve and maintain significantly lower costs. These cost advantages can be achieved through new business models (e.g., IKEA, Dell, Ryanair, Amazon) and/or scale advantages, which result from high volumes or high capacity utilization. But this means that in most markets only a small number of bargain suppliers can survive and succeed over the long term.
- Quality still must be acceptable for a sufficiently large number of customers. Low-price suppliers don't succeed because they are "cheaper" but because they combine low prices with acceptable (but not high!) quality. ALDI is a prominent example for this strategy. Its consistent quality is an important reason why customers who have traditionally shopped in higher price ranges increasingly find ALDI's low-price offers acceptable.
- Traditionally higher-priced manufacturers face structural barriers which make it very difficult for them to respond to the market entry of low-price competitors. These structural constraints can be existing price contracts, investments they have made, locations, technology, or corporate culture.
- Low-price suppliers require special marketing competencies. They need to understand precisely what they can remove from their offerings—in terms of

performance and cost savings—without doing much harm to the customers' perceived value. It is a misconception that marketing for a low-price positioning is easy. In fact, the opposite is true.

- Despite their low costs, low-priced suppliers are still dependent on a mix of businesses. That means that they need a certain number of customers who are willing to pay a bit more for some products in the assortment. That applies to bargain airlines, who charge more for late or last-minute bookings and for business travelers. It also applies to retail. Fielmann, for example, offers its basic models at very affordable prices, but it also sells more expensive eyewear and does offer a wide range of additional features (e.g., special lenses, anti-reflection, insurance) for which the customer pays extra.
- Low-priced companies face considerable risks. The biggest one is that their costs get out of control. This can happen when the company's cost consciousness weakens (perhaps they want to become a more sophisticated or finer supplier) or if certain cost drivers get out of control. When fuel costs spike, bargain airlines are affected disproportionately relative to traditional airlines, because fuel makes up a larger share of their costs. Many Chinese competitors have suffered from wage increases which they could not pass on to their customers, because their market positions and their brands were too weak. The social milieu can also be a risk factor. If the core customers or the locations of a low-priced supplier fall down the social ladder, it can turn off the customers at the higher end of the price range. If that happens, the low-cost supplier cannot make the math work anymore.

2.6.5 Ultra-Low Price Position

2.6.5.1 Basics

An ultra-low price positioning represents a radically minimalist product offered at an extremely low price. In the developed, industrialized countries, the low-price segment we described in the previous section forms the low end of the price scale. In emerging markets, an entirely new segment has come into existence over the last several years. Prices in this ultra-low price segment are sometimes up to 50% below those in the low-priced segment.

Two Indian-American professors called out the emergence of this new segment years ago. With his book "The Fortune at the Bottom of the Pyramid," the late C.K. Prahalad, a strategy expert, was the first to point out the opportunities in the rapidly growing bottom price segments in emerging countries [75]. The steady growth in China, India, and comparable countries means that every year, many millions of consumers gain sufficient purchasing power to afford industrially produced goods, albeit in the lowest price ranges.

In his book "The 86% Solution" Vijay Mahajan identifies this segment as the "biggest market opportunity of the 21st century" [76]. The 86% in the book's title refers to the fact that the annual income of 86% of mankind is below $10,000. People in this income tier cannot afford products which are common in highly developed countries, such as automobiles or personal care products. But they will buy products which are much less expensive. With the ultra-low price range, a new and very large segment comes into existence. Every company must decide whether and most importantly how it can participate in this segment. This will only work with a radically different strategy if the company wants to still make money despite the ultra-low prices.

These developments are taking place not only in Asia but in Eastern Europe as well. Renault has been very successful with the Dacia Logan model, which it manufactures in Romania. The prices for the car start at €7990 and through 2017, Renault has sold more than 3 million cars [77]. The price for a typical Volkswagen Golf is more than double the price of the Dacia Logan. The prices for ultra-low price cars in emerging markets are even far below those of the Dacia Logan. The small Nano vehicle from the Indian manufacturer Tata has attracted a lot of attention around the world. The car costs just under $3000, but the Nano has faced major difficulties and has yet to achieve a big breakthrough in the market. Altogether, the ultra-low price segment comprises a very wide variety of small cars, and around 10 million of them have already been sold around the world. This segment is growing twice as fast as the overall automotive market.

Ultra-low price products are spreading rapidly in emerging countries. Consumer product giants such as Nestlé and Procter & Gamble sell very small pack sizes for a few cents apiece so that consumers with very low incomes can occasionally afford to use such products (e.g., a single-use pack of shampoo). In India, Gillette introduced a razor blade for $0.11, which is 75% below the price for established products. Ultra-low prices are also becoming more common in markets for industrial goods. This applies to medical devices and machine tools. Such products have already carved out substantial market shares.

An interesting question is whether the ultra-low price products from emerging markets can penetrate the high-income countries. There are already examples of this happening. The Dacia Logan, originally conceived for markets in Eastern Europe, has been a success in Western Europe as well. Siemens, Philips, and General Electric have developed simple medical devices meant for sale in Asian markets, but these ultra-low price devices are now being sold in the United States and Europe. They are not necessarily cannibalizing the market for much more expensive devices used in hospitals and specialized practices. To some extent, they are giving segments such as general medical practices access to these kinds of devices, which they can use to make some basic diagnoses on their own [78], expanding the overall market for medical devices.

2.6.5.2 Management

Product
Ultra-low price strategies have only one dominant aspect: extremely low costs. Everything else is subjugated to this criterion. It follows, then, that the product must be limited to only those functional attributes which are absolutely indispensable. Everything which is not a "must have" for the customer is left out. The entire process chain from development to procurement to production, sales, and service

must be designed for the highest cost efficiency and simplicity. "The product concepts of machine tool and plant equipment manufacturers need to undergo a radical simplification if they want to conquer growth markets such as China and India," one study says [79].

A company cannot develop ultra-low price products with engineers from high-income countries [80]. That means that one must not only establish production capability in emerging markets but research and development as well. Setting up the entire value chain within an emerging market is the only way to compete in the radically low-price ranges. The book "Reverse Innovation: Create Far From Home, Win Everywhere" analyzes this process and caused quite a stir [81]. For the Nano car in India, Bosch developed a radically simplified, extremely inexpensive common rail technology. The question of whether ultra-low price products can generate profits, and not only revenue, remains open.

An alternative to doing it alone is to acquire local companies which are active in the ultra-low price segment. The Swiss company Bühler, the global market leader in milling technology, took over Chinese manufacturers in order to keep up in the low-price ranges in China. According to CEO Calvin Grieder, this allows the company to achieve a better harmonization between product and customer expectations than would have been possible with their original higher-priced and more complex products from Switzerland. The world market leading manufacturer of industrial lasers, Trumpf, purchased a Chinese company as well. From 2014 to 2017, 32 Chinese companies have been acquired by German firms, typically with the goal to get access to the ultra-low price segment.

Karl Mayer, which has a 75% share of the global market for tricot machines, has been pursuing a two-pronged strategy. The goal is to secure a position not only in the premium segment but also in the lower-priced market segments. CEO Fritz Mayer tasked his development teams to develop products for the lower segment which have the same performance at 25% lower costs, and in the premium segment, to deliver 25% more performance at the same price. And the teams achieved these extremely ambitious goals. In doing so, Karl Mayer expanded its price and performance ranges both upward and downward, winning back market share in China.

Radical simplification makes a satisfactory level of functional performance at extremely low costs and prices possible. This definitely creates opportunities in developed countries. In this regard, the decision on an ultra-low price positioning is not only about the attractiveness of this segment in emerging markets but also about the potential backflow effect on industrialized countries with higher price ranges.

Price

The price is the overwhelming—one could argue the only—selling argument with an ultra-low price strategy. Roughly speaking, the prices for such products are 50–70% below the prices in the low-price range. As incomes rise, hundreds of millions of consumers in developing markets can afford industrially produced consumer and durable goods for the very first time. The following case from Vietnam is illustrative.

Honda is the world market leader in motorcycles. It is also the number one global manufacturer of small gas-powered engines, producing over 20 million units per year. Honda used to dominate the motorbike market in Vietnam, with a share of 90%. Its best-selling model, the Honda Dream, sold for the equivalent of $2100. As long as it faced no competition, it got along well with that price. Chinese competitors then entered the market with ultra-low price products. Their bikes sold for prices between $550 and $700 or between a quarter and a third of the price of the Honda Dream. These extremely aggressive prices turned market shares upside down. The Chinese manufacturers moved over 1 million bikes per year, while Honda's volume dwindled from about 1 million to 170,000.

Most companies would have thrown in the towel at this point or withdrawn into the premium segment of the market, but not Honda. Its initial short-term response was to cut the price of the Dream to $1300 from $2100. But Honda knew it could not make money with this low price over the long term. And this price was still roughly twice the price of Chinese motorbikes. Honda developed a much simpler, extremely inexpensive new model which it called the Honda Wave. The new bike combined acceptable quality with the lowest possible manufacturing costs. "The Honda Wave has achieved low price, yet high quality and dependability, through using cost-reduced locally made parts as well as parts obtained through Honda's global purchasing network," the company said. The new product entered the market with an ultra-low price of $732, which is 65% less than the former price of the Honda Dream. Honda reconquered the Vietnamese motorcycle market so successfully that most of the Chinese manufacturers eventually withdrew.

This case offers or reinforces several important lessons:

- The price range of 50–70% below previous price levels is typical for ultra-low price products.
- In developing countries with low incomes, a company can only use ultra-low prices to defend itself against extremely price-aggressive newcomers.
- Companies such as Honda, which come from the industrialized world and are normally positioned in the medium-price range, are able to compete against ultra-low price competitors in emerging markets. But they cannot succeed with their customary products. Instead, success demands radical reorientation and redesign, massive simplification, local production, and extreme cost consciousness.

Distribution

What we have said about production efficiency applies equally to distribution. Ultra-low prices only allow for tiny margins for third-party sellers/intermediaries, so they must be able to sell high volumes. There is no room for offering time-intensive consulting or generous levels of service or for indulging special customer requests. The Internet, with its high sales efficiency, is ideally suited for an ultra-low price strategy. One can expect that e-commerce will become an essential pillar of success in this segment. These products' very limited complexity places few demands on sales and service personnel, which manifests itself in lower sales costs. In emerging markets, the service providers who offer repair and maintenance typically have only primitive tools. Auto repairs are often made on the side of the road. The ultra-low price products must take these conditions into account. Parts must be easy to remove and replace, in the simplest way possible.

Communication

The ultra-low price is the central communication message. There are no sizable advertising budgets available. The product needs to be so inexpensive that the media reports about it and thus provides free advertising. The Tata Nano is the classic example for this communication strategy. Because of its radical approach, the model achieved considerable attention in a short period of time. In Europe, the media reported on the Dacia Logan multiple times. Although ultra-low price products offer only the absolute bare minimum in functionality, they still need to deliver on quality. If this is the case, the chances for effective word-of-mouth advertising are good. Naturally, the Internet is a useful communications channel for these products, in particular the low-cost social networks. Models such as the Tata Nano or Dacia Logan receive an additional "pioneer" bonus, because they were the first products to crack the ultra-low price segment open. On its own, this does not build a reputation, but it does drive awareness. According to the AIDA model (attention—interest—desire—action), attention or awareness is the first step to market success.

Table 2.8 summarizes the configuration of the marketing instruments for the ultra-low price positioning.

As one sees, many elements of a traditional marketing strategy fall by the wayside when a company offers ultra-low price products. Extremely low costs and prices permeate the entire strategy.

2.6.5.3 Opportunities and Risks

As we have already said, the question of whether one can earn sufficient returns with ultra-low price products has yet to be resolved. As always, there are opportunities and risks which one must weigh when deciding on such a strategy:

Table 2.8 Configuration of the marketing instruments of the ultra-low price positioning

Product	Price	Distribution	Communication
• Only the most essential performance, forgoing anything which is not absolutely necessary • The simplest product design and use • Essentially no emotional, symbolic, or ethical performance • Few variants, in some cases only one	• Extremely low price, around 50–70% below market levels • No discounts or rebates, because there is no room to go down on price • Only one price; no price complexity	• Extremely low-cost distribution • The lowest possible level of consulting and service, to the extent it is offered at all • Online sales	• The price does the communicating • No paid communication efforts if possible • Free PR from "pioneer" status • Word-of-mouth advertising, also online over social networks

- The ultra-low price segments have the greatest growth potential. Professors Prahalad and Mahajan cited this years ago. With the growth in developing and emerging markets, hundreds of millions of consumers are going to have incomes which will allow them to afford industrially produced products for the very first time.
- The reduction of the product to the absolute bare necessities is a prerequisite for success. Robust simplicity is what matters. At the same time, the products cannot be too primitive. It could be that the Tato Nano falls short on that last aspect, while the Dacia Logan has surpassed that hurdle.
- The product development must take place in the emerging countries; that is the only way to develop suitable solutions for this segment. Building up an R&D department in these countries as well as an innovation process carries considerable risks.
- Securing the lowest manufacturing costs with the appropriate design and producing the products in lowest-wage plants carry an equal portion of opportunities and risks.
- This lowest-cost mentality extends to marketing and sales methods, as well as the service approach. The products must be easy to use and easy to maintain, in line with the low education level of the users and the limited range of tools available to service providers.
- The extreme cost pressure can put quality at risk. To ensure sustained success, the quality of ultra-low price products must be both acceptable and consistent.

The core challenge of an ultra-low price strategy lies in establishing the value-to-customer in a way that will be accepted by a sufficient number of customers and allow for the associated radical minimization of costs.

2.6.6 The Dynamics of Price Positioning

The positioning of a product, a brand, or a company requires a clear and steady long-term orientation. Image and price position cannot be changed quickly or at will. But markets are dynamic. Technology, costs, consumer behavior, and competition are in constant flux. Regular review and examination, and, if needed, an adjustment of the performance profile and the price position, are therefore warranted.

Various developments, such as a shift in customer preferences, could precipitate changing a product's price range, entering a previously unserved price segment or exiting certain price segments. Over the last 20 years, in some markets the medium-price segment has thinned out to the benefit of both the premium and the low-price segments. Coffee exemplifies this trend—while McDonald's sells a small coffee for only $1, a Starbucks specialty coffee drink can cost more than $5. One retailer noted that "consumers almost always buy products on sale" presumably at the expense of the medium-price products. Another complains about the flood of discount prices and says that "the customers draw down their supplies until their brand is on sale again, which happens more or less every 4 weeks" [82]. On the other hand, consumers are preferring new methods of preparing coffee such as Nespresso at prices which are many times higher per cup. A recent study revealed supermarket pod or cup sales—including brands such as Nespresso, Tassimo, and Dolce Gusto—could overtake standard roast and ground coffee [83]. When such shifts occur, a company must put its established price position under review.

A typical trigger for repositioning is a new technology, which comes with increasing performance and/or lower costs. This can lead to corresponding consequences for the price positioning of established products. For example, traditional telecommunications companies have come under price pressure due to the Internet, cable companies, or entirely new models such as Skype, WhatsApp, or WeChat and had to significantly lower their prices as a result. In other cases, a price repositioning is not warranted. It would not make much sense for postal companies to cut the price of stamps in response to the introduction of e-mail, even though e-mail has largely taken the place of traditional "snail mail." The marginal cost of an e-mail is practically zero, so any realistic price for postage would still be too high in comparison. Furthermore, these two forms of communication are not complete substitutes. For example, many invoices, checks, and similar documents are still sent by traditional mail.

Another trigger for price repositioning is a competitive entry. When the patent for a pharmaceutical expires, for example, one can expect the rapid market entry of knock-offs and generics. These new competitors enter the market at price points far below those of the original product. The incumbent must consider potential price adjustments early on. Should the incumbent continue to sell the original product at its prevailing high price level? Should it cut the price sharply, thus entering a new and lower price range? Or should it offer its own generic form?

The global shaving and personal hygiene giant Gillette offers a classic example of premium pricing. For years it followed a strategy of continually raising prices as it introduced innovations (e.g., better design, more blades). The price for the Gillette Fusion ProGlide razor in the United States was more than twice as high as the price of its predecessor, the Mach 3 model. But resistance to Gillette's high prices has grown in recent years. Online competitors have sensed an attractive opportunity, and several start-ups have begun to attack Gillette from below. Traditional consumer goods giants have recognized the potential and have responded accordingly. Unilever improved its ability to compete against Gillette by purchasing Dollar Shave Club for $1 billion in 2016. As a result, Gillette's market share declined from 70% to 54%. Gillette, in turn, lowered wholesale prices to retailers by up to 20%, depending on the product and package size. This marks a significant departure from its original strategy of continually implementing higher prices in the premium segment.

A price repositioning in response to new competition can be impractical if the value or cost differences are too large. This has allowed high-speed train connections to replace air travel on some routes (e.g., in China, France, Spain, and Germany). Airlines cannot compete with these new offerings in terms of travel time or price. Thus, it would serve no purpose for the airlines to cut their prices. They either discontinue the route or accept a smaller number of passengers who continue to fly (e.g., business travelers).

In markets such as fashion, consumer goods, retail, and services, we see similar dynamics of market and price positions. For a time, one French clothing maker struggled with its price positioning in the premium segment. Our analysis revealed that the brand actually belonged in the medium segment. A price reduction of 15% on average caused a 45% increase in sales volume. Profit rose sharply, though, even at the lower prices, because the margin was still satisfactory. The brand Hugo Boss went the other direction, systematically working itself up into the premium segment. The same applies to Lufthansa, which used to be a state-owned company and now holds a top position in the global air travel market. But there are also repositioning attempts which failed or backfired. Walmart, which is a very successful retailer in the United States and in other markets, entered the German market by acquiring stores and repositioning them significantly lower in terms of price, in order to become profitable. The attempt failed and Walmart withdrew. It has also retreated from the South Korean market.

The long-term character of a price position grows out of the fact that it becomes binding. Once chosen and implemented, a price position cannot be changed at will and especially not in the short term. This applies even more acutely to an upward repositioning. J.C. Penney is a prime example of the dangers of rapid upward repositioning. The main cause of the binding effect lies in the inertia of customer perceptions and preferences. A repositioning from higher to lower would seem to be easier. When a premium brand enters into a lower price segment, this can lead to short-term volume growth. But at the same time, the profit situation of the company can deteriorate because the company's processes, costs, sales, infrastructure, and culture—designed for a higher price position—are rarely competitive in lower segments. Successful low-price companies such as ALDI, Ryanair, Dell, or IKEA pursue fundamentally different strategies than classic medium- or premium-priced suppliers. These internal "givens" are difficult to change, if they are changeable at all. In this sense, a price position has a strong binding effect from both an external and an internal perspective.

From these cases of price positioning dynamics, we can derive the following conclusions:

- Due to market, customer, or competitive dynamics, it can be necessary or sensible to fundamentally change an existing price position.
- The challenges and risks associated with such a repositioning move are often underestimated. This is true for the fundamental feasibility as well as the time requirements. Such changes should therefore be undertaken with extreme care. Even after rigorous analysis, a high level of uncertainty will remain as to whether the repositioning will succeed.
- A downward price repositioning can take place comparatively quickly, because a higher price image has a positive radiance in the market. Shifting to a lower price positioning, however, will often erode that image—a brand's position in a higher market segment may be endangered if prices are extended too far downward

("overstretching"). The downward positioning may generate volume and revenue growth, but the effect on profits is dubious. Entry into a lower price segment must be accompanied by associated cost reductions. All levels of the value chain need to be prepared for higher cost efficiency and cost consciousness. For that reason, a downward repositioning requires an internal cultural transformation.

- The upward repositioning of an existing brand proves even more difficult and protracted. Many functions (R&D, quality, design, sales) must be upgraded to deliver higher value. Before undertaking an upward repositioning, any company must ask itself whether it has the corresponding competencies or can develop them. The higher price positioning is by no means merely a challenge for marketing, price management, and communication. It gets into the internal fabric of a company. One of the biggest barriers lies in having the necessary patience and endurance. Such repositionings can take decades, as the case of Audi shows.

- Creating a new brand is a serious alternative to a price repositioning of an existing product or brand. Companies do this in the form of second brands, multiple brands, or "fighting brands." Separating oneself from the established price position and its associated image is normally less problematic and faster through a new brand. On the other hand, this is often a significantly more expensive approach, both short and long term. To make a clear separation work and stick, one generally needs stand-alone products, plants, designs, and sales channels. These additional expenditures only pay off when the new brand achieves sufficient volumes and margins.

- An additional option is the acquisition of brands or firms already positioned in the desired price range. This approach can be advantageous due to its speed and the ability to limit risk. Luxury goods groups such as LVMH or Richemont have used acquisitions to build up and expand their highly attractive portfolios of brands. BMW pursued this path with Mini and Rolls-Royce. In the mass market, Volkswagen has added the Seat and Skoda brands while also adding Audi and Porsche and in the luxury segment Bentley, Bugatti, and Lamborghini.

- But even with this alternative, the acquiring firm must have the competencies to lead the acquired brands successfully and sustainably in the corresponding price segment. These competencies are not a given, even when the acquiring firm is in the same industry, as the example of General Motors showed when it bought Saab. The same holds true for Ford when it acquired brands such as Volvo and Land Rover with the hope to establish itself in the premium segment or for Walmart's attempt to enter the German market via acquisitions. The leadership demands on a premium manufacturer, never mind a luxury one, are totally different from the challenges a low-price supplier commands. Cultural barriers can cause the integration to fail. All of these factors should be considered when contemplating a price repositioning or entry into a new price segment.

Conclusion

This chapter has focused on the fundamental strategic questions of price management, including a company's goals, value drivers, and price positioning, i.e., the choice of the performance profile and price range the company wants to serve. We conclude with the following summary points:

- Clearly defined goals are a prerequisite for professional price management. In practice, there is often a conflict potential between profit goals and revenue, volume, or market share goals. Achieving both categories of goals at the same time is difficult, especially in mature markets. Setting priorities is therefore essential.
- Managers have traditionally assumed that market share has a strong influence on profit. More recent research, however, has raised skepticism about such a causal link. The impact on profit depends on how the market share is acquired. If it comes via low prices without corresponding low costs, one must question whether a positive profit effect exists. In contrast, if high market share is achieved through innovation and quality at a reasonable cost, causation is liable to exist.
- Price is an important determinant of shareholder value. A company can create sustained shareholder value through the right price strategy. In the same vein, mistaken price strategies can destroy shareholder value and can do so quickly and permanently.
- A company needs to make a conscious decision regarding the price range (s) in which it will conduct its business. We distinguish among five price ranges: luxury, premium, medium, low, and ultra-low. These segments are not sharply demarcated, nor do all of them necessarily exist in all markets.
- Price segments are not static—they undergo changes. Hybrid customers shop in different price segments depending on the product category or the occasion. In some sectors, we observe that the medium segment is shrinking. The ultra-low price segment is most common in developing or emerging countries.
- Price positioning is not confined to a product's price. Behind it is value, which in turn consists of functional, emotional, symbolic, and ethical components. Each of these components must be designed to meet specific customers' needs and thus generate willingness to pay.
- The positioning determines the entire direction of the company in terms of R&D, design, technology, production, and marketing competencies. All marketing instruments must be aimed at supporting the desired position.
- Luxury price segments are small but very lucrative in terms of growth and profitability. Luxury products differ significantly from the rest of the market. They are often manufactured by hand or in small production runs and typically have a long brand history. Price itself becomes a decisive

(continued)

status and prestige attribute, so that some parts of the price-response function actually slope upward. Manufacturers limit production volumes of luxury goods in order to keep the supply tight and the price high. Exclusivity in distribution, communication, personalization, and comprehensive service is part of the luxury offering. Top performance, if not perfection, in all facets is an absolute must.

- Premium products offer high functional performance and distinguish themselves from medium-price products in terms of emotional, symbolic, and ethical performance. The high relative price signals lasting value and continuity. Premium products should avoid special offers as well as discount-driven compromises as much as possible. One should also pay attention to price maintenance. Distribution is selective and directed more toward quality than reach. Advertising emphasizes the emotional, symbolic, and ethical aspects.
- For a medium-price position, both functional performance and price are at or around the market average. Emotional aspects and brand have a moderate importance. Product and price differentiation come into play. Controlled special offers and promotions can make sense. Multichannel approaches are used in order to achieve wide distribution. The communication focuses on performance or on the price-value relationship, but not on price alone.
- The low-price position is based on a favorable price combined with sufficient functional performance. Here the challenge for the supplier is to understand what features to leave out without jeopardizing customer acceptance. Sales costs should be minimized, and the company should forgo offering additional services. Communications center on the low price.
- The ultra-low price positioning is entirely about extremely low costs and prices. Anything that is not absolutely essential to the product is left out. Radical simplification along the entire value chain is required. This low-cost maxim applies to distribution and communication as well. The Internet plays a key role. This segment is likely to become very large in emerging countries. How far the ultra-low price products penetrate the developed world remains to be seen.
- Market, customer, or competitive dynamics can necessitate the repositioning of a product, i.e., to change the price range. A downward repositioning has a good chance of success due to the positive resonance. But it can put the original established position in upper segments at risk and impede profitability if costs are not reduced accordingly. An upward repositioning in contrast is difficult and time-consuming. Either change would require a redesign of many functions (R&D, production, quality, design, sales) in order to be competitive cost-wise in lower segments or performance-wise in higher segments. As an alternative to repositioning an

(continued)

established product or brand, a company could consider creating new brands or acquiring existing brands in the targeted price range.

The price strategy sets the framework for tactical price decisions. It encompasses the establishment of goals, price positions, and how the company deals with changes in market structure. Operational price management can only be successful when these fundamental decisions are in harmony.

References

1. Buzzell, R. D., & Bradley, T. I. (1987). *The PIMS Principles-Linking Strategy to Performance.* New York: The Free Press.
2. Henderson, B. (1968). *Perspectives on Experience.* Boston: The Boston Consulting Group.
3. Farris, P., & Moore, M. J. (Eds.) (2004). *The Profit Impact of Marketing Strategy Project: Retrospect and Prospects.* Cambridge: Cambridge University Press.
4. Ailawadi, K. L., Farris, P. W., & Parry, M. E. (1999). Market Share and ROI: Observing the Effect of Unobserved Variables. *International Journal of Research in Marketing*, 16(1), 17–33.
5. Lee, J. (2009). Does Size Matter in Firm Performance? Evidence from US Public Firms. *International Journal of the Economics of Business*, 16(2), 189–203.
6. Edeling, A., & Himme A. (2018). When Does Market Share Matter? New Empirical Generalizations from a Meta-Analysis of the Market Share-Performance Relationship. *Journal of Marketing*, 82(3), 1–24.
7. Lanzillotti, R. F. (1958). Pricing Objectives in Large Companies. *The American Economic Review*, 48(5), 921–940.
8. Armstrong, J., & Green, K. (2005). *Competitor-Oriented Objectives: The Myth of Market Share.* Working Paper, 17(05). Victoria: Monash University.
9. Rego, L. L., Morgan, N. A., & Fornell, C. (2013). Reexamining the Market Share-Customer Satisfaction Relationship. *Journal of Marketing*, 77(5), 1–20.
10. Edeling, A., & Fischer, M. (2016). Marketing's Impact on Firm Value – Generalizations from a Meta-Analysis. *Journal of Marketing*, 53(4), 515–534.
11. Miniter, R. (2002). *The Myth of Market Share.* New York: Crown Business.
12. Baehny, A. M. (2015). Wachstum vs. Gewinn – Perspektive eines Schweizer Hidden Champions. Lecture on the occasion of the conference on Simon-Kucher's 30th anniversary, Frankfurt am Main, September 17.
13. Chu, W., Chen, C. N., & Wang, C. H. (2008). The Market Share – Profitability Relationships in the Securities Industry. *The Service Industries Journal*, 28(6), 813–826.
14. Srinivasan, S., Pauwels, K., Silva-Risso, J., & Hanssens, D. M. (2009). Product Innovations, Advertising, and Stock Returns. *Journal of Marketing*, 73(1), 24–43.
15. Thiel, P. (2014). *Zero to One – Notes on Startups or How to Build the Future.* New York: Crown Publishing Group.
16. Share price of a telecommunications company (2015). http://www.finance.yahoo.com. Accessed 11 November 2015.
17. Anonymous. (2015, March 25). *The Wall Street Journal*, p. 16.
18. Anonymous. (2009, March 18). *Frankfurter Allgemeine Zeitung*, p. 15.
19. Share price of Praktiker (2016). http://www.onvista.de. Accessed 01 December 2016.
20. Share price of Uralkali (2016). http://www.onvista.de. Accessed 01 December 2016.

21. Mattioli, D. (2013, February 25). For Penney's Heralded Boss, the Shine is Off the Apple. *The Wall Street Journal*, p. A1.
22. Share price of J.C. Penney (2016). http://www.onvista.de. Accessed 01 December 2016.
23. Pauwels, K., Silva-Risso, J., Srinivasan, S., & Hanssens, D. M. (2004). New Products, Sales Promotions, and Firm Value: The Case of the Automotive Industry. *Journal of Marketing*, 68 (4), 142–156.
24. Simon, H. (2009). *Think – Strategische Unternehmensführung statt Kurzfrist-Denke* (p. 85). Frankfurt am Main: Campus. Original quote by Peter F. Drucker: "Marketing means seeing the whole business through the eyes of the customer."
25. Ramanujam, M. & Tacke, G. (2016). *Monetizing Innovation: How Smart Companies Design the Product Around the Price*. Hoboken: Wiley.
26. Akerlof, G. A. (1970). The Market for "Lemons": Quality Uncertainty and the Market Mechanism. *The Quarterly Journal of Economics*, 84(3), 488–500. In this article Akerlof used the expression "lemon" for a bad product, based on his study of the market for used cars and the signals which prices give. He received the Nobel Prize in 2001.
27. Gracián, B. (1601–1658). Spanish Jesuit, moral philosopher and writer. http://www.aphorismen.de/zitat/6535. Accessed 03 March 2015. Original quote: "It is better to be cheated in the price than in the quality of goods."
28. Ruskin, J. (1819–1900). Gesetz der Wirtschaft. http://www.iposs.de/1/gesetz-der-witschaft/. Accessed 10 February 2015.
29. Kotler, P., Keller, K. L., & Bliemel, F. (2007). *Marketing-Management: Strategien für wertschaffendes Handeln*. Halbergmoos: Pearson Studium.
30. Wiegner, C. M. (2010). *Preis-Leistungs-Positionierung: Konzeption und Umsetzung*. Frankfurt am Main: Peter Lang.
31. Kowitt, B. (2014). Fallen Arches: Can McDonald's Get its Mojo Back? Fortune. http://fortune.com/2014/11/12/can-mcdonalds-get-its-mojo-back/. Accessed 10 February 2015.
32. Linder, R., & Heeg, T. (2015, March 10). Eine Uhr so teuer wie ein Auto. *Frankfurter Allgemeine Zeitung*, p. 22.
33. Valentino-Devries, J. (2010). From Hype to Disaster: The Segway's Timeline, The Wall Street Journal. http://blogs.wsj.com/digits/2010/09/27/from-hype-to-disaster-segways-timeline/. Accessed 10 February 2015.
34. Lashinsky, A. (2014). Amazon Goes to War Again (and Again), Fortune. http://fortune.com/2014/11/13/amazon-jeff-bezos-retail-disruptor/. Accessed 10 February 2015.
35. Mesco, M. (2014, December 15). Struggling Gucci Reshoes Top Ranks. The Wall Street Journal. http://www.wsj.com/articles/SB2250190000108398376580458033232335819210 4. Accessed 10 February 2015.
36. Löhr, J. (2014, December 23). Auf den Hund gekommen. *Frankfurter Allgemeine Zeitung*, p. 23.
37. Martin, R. L., & Lafley, A. G. (2013). *Playing to Win: How Strategy Really Works*. Jackson: Perseus Distribution.
38. Fassnacht, M., Kluge, P. N., & Mohr, H. (2013). Pricing Luxury Brands: Specificities, Conceptualization, and Performance Impact. *Marketing ZFP – Journal of Research and Management*, 35(2), 104–117.
39. Preisentwicklung der Schweizer Uhrenexporte (2013, October 5). *Finanzwirtschaft*, p. 15.
40. LVMH (2017). Annual Report. https://r.lvmh-static.com/uploads/2017/11/2017-financial-documents.pdf. Accessed 13 February 2018.
41. Richemont (2017). Annual Report. https://www.richemont.com/images/investor_relations/reports/annual_report/2017/ar_fy2017_f73jdsf82s64r2.pdf. Accessed 13 February 2018.
42. Richemont (2007). Annual Report. https://www.richemont.com/investor-relations/reports/report-archive.html. Accessed 10 February 2015.
43. von der Gathen, A., & Gersch, B. (2008). *Global Industry Study: Profit Excellence in the Luxury Goods Industry*. Bonn: Simon-Kucher & Partners.

44. Wüstefeld, E. (2014, December 19). Sie stehen nicht mit dem Rücken zur Wand. *Frankfurter Allgemeine Zeitung*, p. 23.
45. Stock, O. (2006, April 07). Sechs Fragen an Nick Hayek. *Handelsblatt*, p. 16.
46. Fassnacht, M., & Dahm, J. M. (2018). The Veblen Effect and (In)Conspicuous Consumption: A State of the Art Article, *Luxury Research Journal*. 1(4), 343–371.
47. Braun, S. (2015, January 20). Die Kunst, Atome richtig anzuordnen. *Frankfurter Allgemeine Zeitung*, p. 2.
48. Feth, G. G. (2005). Die Keramikbremse ist auf dem Weg in die Großserie. Frankfurter Allgemeine Zeitung. http://www.faz.net/aktuell/technik-motor/auto-verkehr/porsche-die-keramik-bremse-ist-auf-dem-weg-in-die-grossserie-1114868.html. Accessed 10 February 2015.
49. Tuma, T. (2012). Wir sind Handwerker. Spiegel Gespräch mit Patrick Thomas, Hermès. Der Spiegel. http://www.spiegel.de/spiegel/print/d-90254957.html. Accessed 10 February 2015.
50. Bain & Company (2017). Luxury Goods Worldwide Market Study, Fall-Winter 2017. http://www.bain.de/Images/BAIN_REPORT_Global_Luxury_Report_2017.pdf. Accessed 13 February 2018.
51. Prada Group (2017). H1 2017 Results. https://www.pradagroup.com/en/investors/investor-relations/results-presentations.html. Accessed 14 February 2018.
52. Wilken, M. (2013). Prada mit Rekordzahlen. Fabeau. Fashion Business News, http://www.fabeau.de/news/prada-mit-rekordzahlen/. Accessed 10 February 2015.
53. Kapferer, J. N. (2012). *The Luxury Strategy: Break the Rules of Marketing to Build Luxury Brands*. London: Kogan Page Publishers.
54. Simon, H. (2009). *Hidden Champions of the 21st Century*. New York: Springer.
55. Reidel, M. (2014, December 11). Hintergrund. Wir kaufen keine Freunde. *Horizont*, No. 50, p. 16.
56. Lasslop, I. (2002). Identitätsorientierte Führung von Luxusmarken. In H. Meffert, C. Burmann, & M. Koers (Eds.), *Markenmanagement* (pp.327–351). Heidelberg: Gabler.
57. Anonymous. (2014). Erfolgreiche Marken nutzen alle Vertriebswege. Auch die Discounter. http://www.absatzwirtschaft.de/erfolgreiche-marken-nutzen-alle-vertriebswege-auch-die-dis counter-2747/. Accessed 10 February 2015.
58. Anonymous. (2010). Erwartungshaltung bei Premiumprodukten hört nicht beim Produkt auf. http://www.absatzwirtschaft.de/erwartungshaltung-an-premiummarken-hoert-nicht-beim-produkt-auf-9387. Accessed 10 February 2015.
59. Little, A. D. (1992). *Management von Spitzenqualität*. Wiesbaden: Gabler.
60. Canoy, M., & Peitz, M. (1997). The Differentiation Triangle. *The Journal of Industrial Economics*, 45(3), 305–328.
61. Anonymous. (2008, June 24). *Frankfurter Allgemeine Zeitung*, p. 14.
62. Quelch, J. A. (1987). Marketing the Premium Product. *Business Horizons*, 30(3), 38–45.
63. Gruner & Jahr (2003, December 29). Nudeln, Kartoffelprodukte und Reis. *Märkte+Tendenzen*, pp. 1–4.
64. Hayward, S. (1990). Opportunities in the Middle Market. *Marketing Research*, 2(3), 65–67.
65. Cronshaw, M., Davis, E., & Kay, J. (1994). On Being Stuck in the Middle or Good Food Costs Less at Sainsbury's. *British Journal of Management*, 5(1), 19–32.
66. Sharp, B., & Dawes, J. (2001). What is Differentiation and how Does it Work? *Journal of Marketing Management*, 17(7–8), 739–759.
67. Porter, M. E. (1985). *Competitive Advantage: Creating and Sustaining Superior Performance*. New York: The Free Press.
68. Anonymous. (2014, December). *Lebensmittelzeitung*, p. 31.
69. Krohn, P. (2015, January 19). Das Enfant terrible unter den Versicherern. *Frankfurter Allgemeine Zeitung*, p. 19.
70. Kowitt, B. (2015, March 15). It's IKEA's World. *Fortune*, pp. 74–83.

71. Anonymous. (2014). Deutschlands Discounter sind angriffslustig wie lange nicht mehr. http://
    www.faz.net/aktuell/finanzen/meine-finanzen/geld-ausgeben/aldi-und-lidl-deutschlands-dis
    counter-sind-angriffslustig-wie-lange-nicht-mehr-13297814.html. Accessed 10 February 2015.
72. Aldi Süd (2015). ALDI SÜD oder: Die Konzentration auf das Wesentliche. https://
    unternehmen.aldi-sued.de/de/ueber-aldi-sued/philosophie/. Accessed 19 February 2015.
73. Anonymous. (2014, November 11). Ryanair will das Amazon der Lüfte werden. *Frankfurter
    Allgemeine Zeitung.*
74. Laudenbach, P. (2011). Schwerpunkt Großorganisation, Geiz ist geil. Service ist geiler. http://
    www.brandeins.de/archiv/2011/grossorganisation/geiz-ist-geil-service-ist-geiler/. Accessed
    10 February 2015.
75. Prahalad, C. K. (2010). *The Fortune at the Bottom of the Pyramid.* New Jersey: Financial Times
    Press.
76. Mahajan, V., & Banga, K. (2006). *The 86% Solution: How to Succeed in the Biggest Market
    Opportunity of the 21st Century.* New Jersey: FT Press.
77. Renault (2017). Annual Financial Report 2016. https://group.renault.com/wp-content/uploads/
    2017/05/dr-2016-version-anglaise.pdf. Accessed 14 February 2018.
78. Interview with former Siemens CEO Peter Löscher at the Asia-Pacific Conference in Singapore
    on May 14, 2010.
79. Anonymous. (2007, March 30). VDI-Nachrichten, p. 19.
80. Ernst, H., Dubiel, A., & Fischer, M. (2009). *Industrielle Forschung und Entwicklung in
    Emerging Markets. Motive, Erfolgsfaktoren, Best-Practice Beispiele.* Wiesbaden: Gabler.
81. Govindarajan, V., & Trimble, C. (2013). *Reverse Innovation: Create far from Home, Win
    Everywhere.* Boston: Harvard Business Press.
82. Hanke, G. (2014, March 21). Essay Pfeile im Köcher Aldis. Pressenkungen zeigen Wirkung.
    Lebensmittelzeitung, No. 12, p. 32.
83. Alexander, S. (2016). The Clooney Effect? Pods Set to Overtake Instant and Ground Coffee,
    The Telegraph. http://www.telegraph.co.uk/food-and-drink/news/the-clooney-effect-pods-set-
    to-overtake-instant-and-ground-coffe/. Accessed 01 December 2016.

Analysis: The Economics of Price

3

Abstract

Value-to-customer, costs, and competing offers are the economic determinants of price. This chapter will examine these three determinants and their interrelationships. Viewed in isolation, costs only represent the lower limit for price. The most important determining factor for the price is value-to-customer, from which we derive customers' willingness to pay, the price-response function, and the price elasticity. The offers and the prices of competitors typically also influence the sales volume of a product. The primary focus of this chapter is the understanding and explication of price's effects on volume. The applicable methods—expert judgment, customer surveys, experiments, and market observations—will be explored in depth and illustrated by cases from practice.

3.1   Introduction

In this chapter we will discuss the economic determinants of price management, which essentially are costs, value-to-customer, and competitors' prices. In the ensuing Chap. 4, our focus will be on the psychological aspects of price management. Naturally these also have an effect on volume, market share, revenue, and profit. For now, though, we will look at the economic side.

When we ask managers how they set prices, or what information they base their price decisions on, they typically give one or more of the following answers:

- Our prices come from our history in the market.
- We figure out our costs and apply the typical markup for our industry.
- We orient ourselves to what the competition is doing.
- The market determines the price.
- We try to estimate value-to-customer, but that is difficult.

© Springer Nature Switzerland AG 2019   85
H. Simon, M. Fassnacht, *Price Management*,
https://doi.org/10.1007/978-3-319-99456-7_3

All of these price rationales can be relevant. But they are not signs of truly professional price management. In most cases, the companies lack solid information about customers' needs and their willingness to pay. The effects of different prices on volume are rarely quantified. In other words, the company forgoes the explicit determination of a price-response function. The management either feels that the concept is too theoretical or is unsure about it. In the end, decision-makers need information about all the factors which influence the optimal price.

In the following section, we will describe the information which is necessary for the analysis phase of price management. Then we explain the price-response function as the central concept of price management and show how this function can be determined in practice.

3.2   Analysis of Price-Relevant Information

Figure 3.1 illustrates the factors which influence how much leeway a company has for setting a price. Value-to-customer and competitors' prices define the upper limit for the price, and in practical terms the sharper of the two limits is the one which counts. In both cases (except in the case of a pure commodity), we are not talking about sharply defined borders or limits but rather about boundary zones. A company's costs determine the lower limit for the price. In the short term, these are the variable unit costs or the marginal costs, but long-term they are the fully loaded unit costs (total unit costs). Corporate objectives and legal/regulatory restrictions can shift the upper and lower limits for price in either direction. For example, if a company sets a minimum margin goal, the price leeway shifts upward, while a minimum market share goal shifts it downward.

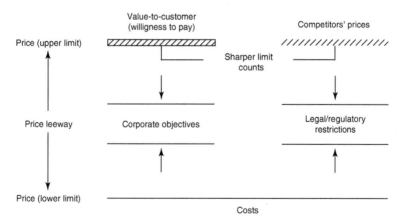

Fig. 3.1 Factors which influence price leeway

3.2.1 Cost-Plus Pricing

Companies must consider their corporate goals as well as their costs when setting prices. Thus, we will now focus on the cost information, which is significant both for setting the lower limit for price as well as for ensuring the company's profitability. It's worth noting in this context that some historical theories considered costs as the sole determinant of price. The most famous of these is Karl Marx's labor theory of value, according to which the value of a product is solely determined by the labor needed to manufacture the product. Thus, Marx sees the value of labor as the sole determinant of price. In 1865 he wrote: "The prices of goods are determined or regulated by the wages" [1]. Today, this theory is outdated and still upheld, if at all, only by hard-core Marxists. On their own, costs are not sufficient for setting an optimal price. But a thorough understanding of costs, especially of marginal costs, is fundamental for any price decision. Unless marginal costs are zero, a new phenomenon which we will discuss later on, we cannot fully neglect Karl Marx.

For the price decision, the most important aspect of the cost analysis is the clear distinction between fixed and variable costs. Fixed costs by definition do not depend on the volume produced, while variable costs change depending on production volume. In contrast to the price-response function, the cost function is simpler to determine, because the necessary information comes from within the company. Cost functions can be classified according to the behavior of marginal costs. The marginal costs express how costs change when production volume increases or decreases by one unit, i.e., changes incrementally. In practice, we most commonly see two forms: the linear cost function with constant marginal costs and the monotone increasing, concave cost function with declining marginal costs. Figure 3.2 shows sample cost functions with constant and with declining marginal costs.

With the help of cost information, a company can determine a lower limit for price as well as the effects on profit as a function of volume. The lower limit corresponds to the lowest price at which a product would be offered for sale or at which the company would accept an order.

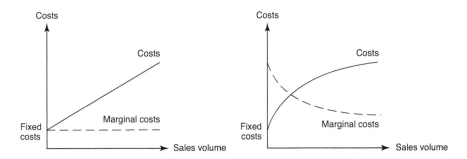

Fig. 3.2 Important cost functions and their marginal costs

In determining the lower limit for price, we need to distinguish between the long and the short term. Over the long term, one would only offer a product for sale when the price covers both the variable and the fixed costs. The long-term lower price limit is therefore determined by the fully loaded unit costs.

The situation is different when we look at the short term. By definition, a company cannot reduce its fixed costs in the short term, which means they should be covered to the greatest extent possible. A contribution margin, i.e., a contribution to covering this block of fixed costs, is earned whenever the price exceeds the variable unit costs. The short-term lower limit for price is therefore equal to the variable unit costs. The difference between price and variable unit costs is the unit contribution margin. One can also say that it makes sense to offer a product (from a short-term perspective) when the sale generates a positive unit contribution margin.

If it is possible to set differentiated prices for individual product units, i.e., for build-to-order, then the marginal cost, not the variable unit cost, is the lower limit for price. In such a case—assuming sufficient capacity and independence among orders—a company would accept an additional order as long as the price is above the marginal cost. If a company produces multiple products and the acceptance of an incremental order for one product is possible only at the expense of producing less of another product or products, then we need to add the forgone profits from the latter product (the so-called opportunity costs) to the marginal cost of the first product. In other words, in such a case, the lower limit for price is the sum of the marginal and opportunity costs.

Opportunity costs in the broader sense can arise from a whole range of dynamic relationships on the production (supply) as well as the sales (demand) side. As a result, the lower limits for price have a complex structure and defy generalization.

The most important insights for lower price limits, in short, are as follows:

- Long-term lower price limit: fully loaded unit costs
- Short-term lower price limit:
    - With uniform prices: variable unit costs
    - With differentiated prices: marginal costs
    - With capacity constraints/bottlenecks: marginal costs plus opportunity costs

3.2.2 Customers

The core piece of customer information is the customer's *willingness to pay*. It reflects the customer's perceived value ("value-to-customer"). At the individual customer level, the question is what individual willingness to pay exists for a product and what the distribution of that willingness of different customers looks like. At the aggregated market level, we have to ask what effect different prices have on sales volume, i.e., what does the price-response function look like. For now, we will adopt the microeconomic perspective, i.e., consider value-to-customer, willingness to pay, and price-response relationships. These factors form the basis of price decisions. We will supplement them with the psychological perspective in Chap. 4.

Value-to-customer and the resulting willingness to pay should already have been taken into account before and during the product development stage. The starting point is not solely the entire product, but rather the individual performance attributes it comprises. The value-to-customer and the resulting willingness to pay arise from these attributes. If done right, the product will fulfill customer needs and can be sold profitably.

Companies traditionally take an "inside-out" perspective toward product development. Products are conceived, developed, and then priced on a cost-plus basis. One can describe this sequence as "design-build-price." Even today this approach is in widespread use, though it can lead to over-engineering. As a consequence of this "inside-out" approach, some products are developed but not launched or flop when they are launched. Ideally, companies should flip this flow around, i.e., follow with the sequence "price-design-build" [2]. The question "what should the product we just developed cost?" gets replaced by the question "how much should the product we plan to develop cost?" based on what buyers are willing to pay for it. This approach is referred to as target pricing.

Target pricing starts with the willingness to pay. The product and price design derives strictly from the customer perspective. The customers' demands and willingness to pay are incorporated in the design and development process from the very beginning. A modern term for this approach is called "design thinking" [3]. This concept acknowledges the idea that customers are not interested in technical product components as such, but rather in value-to-customer. In other words, they are interested in value, not features. Product features which contribute less value than their costs are excluded from consideration. Product development processes do not start with the performance attributes of the product and then derive the price; instead the development starts with an idea for the price, and the product will be designed and built to fit that target price. This puts customer research at the very beginning of the R&D process. It reveals information about customers' future needs.

Product requirements are likely to vary across individual customers. This leads to different levels of value-to-customer and willingness to pay. At the outset of the target pricing process, the company should identify customers with the same or similar requirements and willingness to pay and group them into customer segments. The company must then formulate product ideas, so-called performance bundles, for these target segments. The sum of the willingness to pay for each of the value-generating features results in the target price for the product. The company should be able to achieve the target price in the market, assuming the initial market research yielded valid results. If we deduct the required profit margin from the target price, we get the target costs [4, 5]. These target costs serve as a guideline for the costs for individual product attributes. The goal of target pricing is to ensure that the cost of each individual product feature is below the corresponding willingness to pay of the customer for the respective attribute. With the help of target pricing, the company can eliminate or modify product features whose costs exceed the associated willingness to pay. In this manner, companies can concentrate on performance they can deliver profitably.

Similar to the model from Herzberg, which distinguishes between hygiene factors and motivators, one can categorize performance attributes according to their effect on value-to-customer [6]. Based on Herzberg's two-factor model [7], Kano developed the so-called Kano model. This represents an application of Herzberg's thinking to the level of customer requirements for a product in terms of basic attributes (Herzberg, hygiene factors) and attraction attributes (Herzberg, motivation factors). For the basic requirements, the customer will not recognize (i.e., pay for) any level of performance above what is expected. At the same time, the company must avoid customer dissatisfaction with basic attributes. One example from the automotive industry: the brakes of a normal passenger car need to work, but they do not need to have the same level of performance as the brakes on race cars. Not fulfilling these basic requirements, however, puts the customer relationship at risk. Too much performance can jeopardize profits because of unnecessarily higher costs. Meeting basic customer needs is a "conditio sine qua non," but does not generate additional willingness to pay.

For the performance requirements, the formula "money for value" applies. The value-to-customer rises more or less in proportion to the performance level of the attribute. This applies, for example, to the fuel efficiency of a car. Less fuel consumption leads to higher willingness to pay, which can be monetized in the form of higher prices. However, innovating the performance of a product has its limits. Improvements, especially incremental ones, need to convince customers that they are clearly superior compared with the effects of a predecessor. The Danish pharmaceutical company Novo Nordisk, for example, could not enforce a price premium with slight improvements of its insulin. Charging more for each improvement simply resulted in "overstretching" customers' willingness to pay [8].

For attraction attributes, customer satisfaction increases overproportionally when the performance level improves. For cars, the brand, the design, and breakthrough innovations come to mind. These attraction attributes can turn into very effective profit drivers. Introducing a higher level of performance, which does not necessarily need to cost much to produce, will be rewarded by customers through an overproportional increase in willingness to pay.

Collecting this kind of information can be accomplished with conjoint measurement, which quantifies willingness to pay across individual product attributes. To sum up, value-to-customer and willingness to pay are the central pieces of customer information for price management.

3.2.3 Competition

Companies must take competition into account in price decisions primarily for three reasons:

- In many markets, competitors' prices exert a strong influence on a company's sales volume. In other words, the so-called cross-price elasticity is significantly different from zero.
- If competitors feel threatened by price measures, they tend to react, i.e., their reaction elasticity is likewise significant.
- A company can implement its own price actions quickly, but competitors can usually respond just as fast.

The interdependent reactions and their effects create some of the most complex problems in price management. We strongly advise companies to monitor their competition systematically by undertaking these three tasks:

- Identifying the relevant competitors
- Analyzing the current prices of the competitors
- Anticipating their potential future price behavior

The first step is to identify the relevant competitors. This task may seem simple at first glance. Almost everyone knows that Coca-Cola competes against Pepsi or that BMW is viewed as a competitor of Mercedes-Benz. But these simple views are not always sufficient. If we broaden our definition of competition to all companies which are after money from the same customers, it follows that different spheres of competition exist. These in turn need to be considered separately for price decisions [9, p. 529]. Fassnacht and Köse [10] distinguish among three *spheres of competition*:

- Narrow sphere of competition (similar/identical products)
- Broader sphere of competition (same types of products)
- Outer sphere of competition (products which provide similar/related kinds of value)

When airlines set prices, they must not only take other airlines into account (narrow sphere) but also companies which provide the same kinds of service such as railroads and buses (broader sphere) and competitors which meet the same customer needs with different kinds of services, e.g., video conferences (outer sphere). Price decisions should also take potential new competitors into account, not only the current ones.

Moreover, it is advisable to analyze competitors' current and future situations. Information which describes the current situation includes the performance attributes and prices for their products, their revenue and market share, their customer structure, and the perceived value of their products from the customers' perspective. Information one can use to assess a competitors' future potential includes cost structure, capital structure, financial strength, capacity, manufacturing technology, patents, and sales organization. A company should anticipate the actions and reactions of competitors and take these into account in its own pricing considerations. Competitive monitoring can take up considerable time and financial resources. On the other hand, it can be even more costly to make price decisions without solid information on competitors.

While data on the past pricing behavior of competitors is relatively easy to collect, information on their future plans is not readily accessible. This is true in part because this kind of information is internal in nature (investments, new or modified products, price measures) and is often considered top secret. Competitors are reluctant to take part in surveys or experiments which may directly or indirectly reveal such secrets.

One method to determine the cost of competitor products is reverse engineering. A company buys a competing product and deconstructs it, or it tests the competitor's services in order to understand the process and the outcomes meticulously. With this process, a company can succeed in replicating costs, discovering differences in the manufacturing or service processes, and identifying cost differences.

The weight a company gives to such competitive information depends first and foremost on the market structure (e.g., monopoly, competition) and the homogeneity of the products. A monopolist has no direct competitors, but such companies should still take potential competitors into account in their price decisions. Even a monopolist needs to consider whether a price decision (e.g., a high-price strategy) might motivate other companies to enter its market.

In the case of a competitive market, the influence of price depends on how homogeneous the products are. Homogeneous, easily substitutable products severely limit a company's leeway to price. If customers don't have clear preferences for a particular supplier, the sales volume of a product is highly dependent on its competitors' price levels. This substitutability implies that a unilateral price increase can trigger a strong decline in sales volume. Price cuts, in turn, can touch off a ruinous downward price spiral. In heterogeneous markets with differentiated products, there is less dependence on competitive prices. Companies have a certain level of "monopolistic" price leeway [11, p. 243]. Isolated small price increases result only in slight declines in volume, while price cuts generate only a limited risk of competitive reactions.

3.3   The Price-Response Function

3.3.1 Classification of Price-Response Functions

The demand curve, also called the price-response function, describes the functional relationship between the price p and the sales volume or quantity q:

$$q = q(p) \tag{3.1}$$

The price is the independent variable and the sales volume is the dependent variable. In economic textbooks, one sees in most cases the mirror-image function $p = p(q)$ with volume as the independent variable and price as the dependent variable. This demand function is based on the idea that a supplier offers a certain quantity and the market determines the price. For modern, heterogeneous markets, a function of the form (3.1) is more realistic.

The price-response function is a prerequisite for price optimization. In practice, the knowledge of one's price-response function is often limited and subject to a high margin of error. Price-response functions can be classified according to the following criteria:

- Aggregation level: Individual vs. aggregated price-response functions. The individual function describes how the demand of an individual customer varies by price. The aggregated form consolidates how the demand across all customers varies as a function of price.
- Market form: Here one distinguishes between monopoly and competitive markets. In a monopoly, the level of demand depends solely on the price of the monopolist. In a competitive market, competitors' prices have an influence on a company's sales volume and must therefore be included as independent variables in the price response function.
- Form: Price-response functions can be expressed in tabular or graphical form or as a mathematical formula.
- Data sources: The data used to determine a price-response function can come from expert judgment, customer surveys, experiments, or market data.

3.3.2 Price-Response Functions and Price Elasticity

3.3.2.1 Individual and Aggregated Price-Response Functions

We begin by considering the individual price-response function. We then derive aggregated price-response functions.

For *individual demand* we need to distinguish between two cases:

- Durables: The demand curve reflects a yes-no decision by each individual customer. We refer to this as the "yes-no" case. People buy one washing machine, one smartphone, one camera, or one notebook. Or they don't buy at all.
- Consumables: In this case, buyers often purchase several units at a time, depending on the price. We call this the "variable-quantity" case. Foods such as yogurt and soft drinks fall into this category, as do services such as going to a movie. If the price is lower, the individual customer buys more and consumes more often.

The left side of Fig. 3.3 illustrates the "yes-no" case. A customer buys if the price is less than the (perceived) value of the product. The highest price which a customer is willing to pay for a product corresponds to the perceived value of the product and is referred to as the maximum price (in the economic literature it is also called the "reservation price" or "prohibitive price").

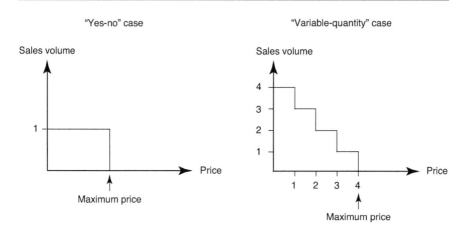

Fig. 3.3 Individual price-response functions for the "yes-no" case and the "variable-quantity" case

In the "variable-quantity" case, analogously, the customer compares price and value for each unit of the product. As we see on the right side of Fig. 3.3, the customer is prepared to spend $4 for the first unit of the product but only $3 for the second unit. This declining willingness to pay reflects Gossen's second law [12], which says that marginal utility (or "marginal value-to-customer") declines with increasing consumption of the product. The second, third, and fourth unit of a product bring less additional utility than the previous ones. The consequence for the "variable-quantity" case: the higher the price, the lower the quantity the individual customer buys. The best way to think of the "variable-quantity" case is to consider it as a series of "yes-no" cases. For each successive unit, the customer makes a "yes-no" decision based on the perceived value of an additional unit.

When prices are set on an individual basis, implications for the two cases are different. In the "yes-no" case, the seller should strive to find out the maximum price of the individual buyer and demand exactly that price. That is the primary problem in pricing when prices are negotiated individually with each customer. In the "variable-quantity" case, one has two options. One can either set a uniform price per unit regardless of the volume purchased or differentiate the price by purchase volume. The latter option is called non-linear pricing. In the "variable-quantity" case, the marginal utility for each unit of the product must be known, in order to be able to determine the individual price response functions.

3.3.2.2 The Aggregated Price-Response Function

The aggregated price-response function results from the addition of the volumes for each price across all customers. The customers can be homogenous or heterogeneous. In reality, they are almost always heterogeneous, which means they have different maximum prices. In Fig. 3.4 we assume heterogeneity and show the

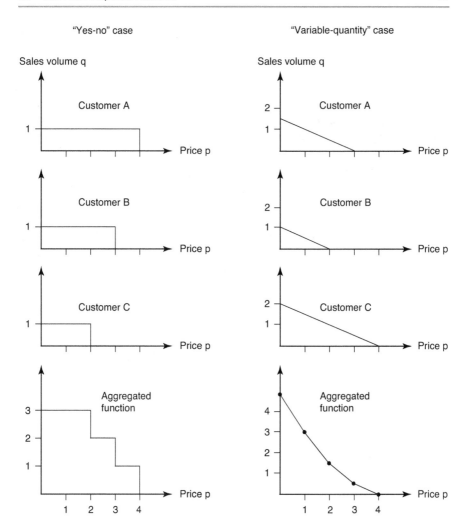

Fig. 3.4 Aggregation of individual price-response functions for three different customers

aggregation across three customers for the "yes-no" case and the "variable-quantity" case.

In both cases, the aggregated price-response function has a negative slope, i.e., fewer units are purchased at higher prices. If we incorporate a larger number of customers, the function shape approaches that of a continuous curve.

3.3.2.3 Definition of Price Elasticity

The influence of price on sales volume is measured by the price elasticity. An elasticity is the ratio of the percentage change in one variable to the percentage change in the variable causing the change. The elasticity is dimensionless. The price elasticity is defined as:

$$\varepsilon = \frac{\text{sales change in percent}}{\text{price change in percent}} \tag{3.2}$$

If a price decrease of 10% results in volume expansion of 20%, the price elasticity has a value of -2. The negative sign indicates that volume and price changes move in opposite directions. The price elasticity of -2 says that the percentage change in sales volume is twice the percentage change in price. For infinitesimal changes the price elasticity is defined mathematically as:

$$\varepsilon = \frac{\partial q}{\partial p} \times \frac{p}{q} \tag{3.3}$$

where $\frac{\partial q}{\partial p}$ is the first derivative of the price-response function $q = q(p)$, q is the volume, and p is the price.

3.3.2.4 Linear Price-Response Functions and Price Elasticity in a Monopoly

The linear dependence of the volume q on the price p is the simplest hypothesis:

$$q = a - bp \quad a > 0, \quad b > 0. \tag{3.4}$$

Figure 3.5 represents the linear price-response function in a monopoly. The parameter a is the intercept on the volume axis and thus shows the maximum volume (at a price of zero). The quotient a/b determines the price at which volume would be zero. This price corresponds to the intercept with the price axis. It is the (aggregated) maximum price.

The parameter b is the slope of the price-response function. In other words, it shows the volume change caused by a price change of one unit. The larger b is, the more sensitive volume reacts to changes in price. Because the slope of a linear function is a constant, the volume change occurring for a certain price change is the same everywhere. It is independent of the previous price level. The price elasticity for the linear function is $\varepsilon = -bp/(a - bp)$. It is a negative number, but when price elasticity comes up in discussions, it is often expressed in terms of its absolute value. For a linear price-response function, the price elasticity follows the pattern shown in Fig. 3.5. Its absolute value gets very high when prices are high and approaching the maximum price.

The biggest advantage of the linear price-response function is its simplicity and its ease of interpretation. To determine the function, one needs to estimate only the two parameters a and b. We will show later that this function leads to simple rules for price decisions. On the other hand, the linear function lacks a theoretical basis. It originated in a theoretical void, as the following statement implies: "It may be just as correct to draw a straight line as to use any other form" [13, p. 49]. Despite its

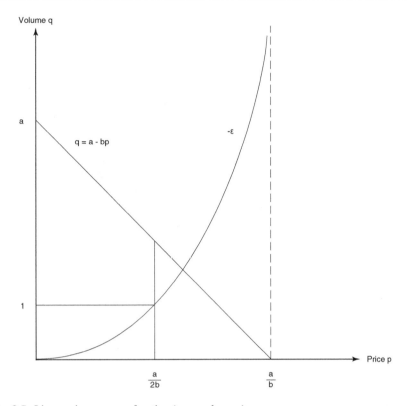

Fig. 3.5 Linear price-response function (monopoly case)

simplicity, the linear function often has a satisfactory fit to empirical data. Based on our experience, we advise using it only in situations where the price interval under consideration does not deviate too much from the range of existing or previous prices. For large price changes, the linear model can lead to erroneous conclusions. Within reasonable intervals, however, chances are good that it will not perform any worse than more complex models. The maxim of "when in doubt, keep it simple" applies.

3.3.2.5 Linear Price-Response Functions and Price Elasticity with Competition

In a competitive market, variables such as market share, relative price, or price difference should be incorporated into the price-response function.

The Independent Variables

In addition to one's own price p_i, we need to take the competitors' prices into account as independent variables. Table 3.1 provides some options on how this can be done.

Table 3.1 Alternative operationalizations of the independent variables in the price-response function with competition

Dependent variable	No.	Independent variable
Volume q_i or market share m_i	1	Own price p_i and each individual competitor's price p_j
	2	p_i and the average price $\bar{p}$ for competitors' products
	3	Absolute price difference between p_i and $\bar{p}$
	4	Relative price $p_i/\bar{p}$

Alternative 1 requires very intensive analysis and is generally excluded from consideration because of problems with multicollinearity, i.e., the effect of each individual price cannot be isolated. Variants 2 through 4 require a definition of the average price $\bar{p}$. One can do this unweighted or using market shares as weighting factors. Kucher [14] demonstrated that average prices weighted by market share lead to better explanatory quality, statistical significance, and economic plausibility.

The effect of competitors' prices on one's own volume is measured by the cross-price elasticity. The cross-price elasticity quantifies the effects of competitors' prices on one's own volume:

$$\varepsilon_{AB} = \frac{\text{Sales change of product A in percent}}{\text{Price change of product B in percent}} \tag{3.5}$$

Or in the infinitesimal case:

$$\varepsilon_{AB} = \frac{\partial q_A}{\partial p_B} \times \frac{p_B}{q_A} \tag{3.6}$$

The cross-price elasticity expresses the percentage change in volume q_A of product A, when the price p_B of product B changes by 1%. If A and B are substitutes, i.e., products which are direct competitors (such as the Ford Focus and the Honda Civic), the cross-price elasticity is positive. If the competitor cuts its price by 10% and one's own volume drops by 5%, the cross-price elasticity is +0.5. The sign is positive because both changes (the competitor's price cut and one's own sales decline) move in the same direction. If both products are complements (e.g., copy machines and cartridges), the cross-price elasticity—like the direct price elasticity in formula (3.2)—is negative.

There are several ways to define the dependent variable in a competitive situation. The dependent variable could be either volume q_i or market share m_i of product i. If we let Q be the total volume for the chosen market, the two variables have the following relationship:

$$m_i = \frac{q_i}{Q}, \quad \text{respectively,} \quad q_i = m_i \times Q. \tag{3.7}$$

For the price elasticity of volume q_i and market share m_i, we get the following equation:

$$\varepsilon_{q_i} = \text{Price elasticity of total demand } Q$$
$$+ \text{ price elasticity of market share } m_i \qquad (3.8)$$

We can use volume q_i or market share m_i interchangeably as dependent variables only if the price elasticity for the total demand Q equals zero. If Q is in in fact dependent on price, we need two price-response functions (one for the total demand Q and one for the market share m_i). Both sub-models can be treated separately or integrated into one model which captures the influence of price on volume q_i. When determining the dependent variables, one should look carefully to see which variables are influenced by price. A general recommendation for determining the independent variables does not make sense. In each individual case, one should analyze various alternatives. That is the best way to build a valid price-response function.

3.3.3 Additional Forms of the Price-Response Function

In addition to the linear model, there are three other forms of price-response functions which apply in a competitive situation: the multiplicative, the attraction, and the Gutenberg model, as shown in Table 3.2.

3.3.3.1 The Multiplicative Model

The rationale for the multiplicative form is its simplicity and the fact that the coefficient b can be interpreted as a constant price or cross-price elasticity. In the multiplicative price-response function shown in Fig. 3.6, the relative price (own price/competitive price) serves as the independent variable. The exponent b measures the price elasticity, which is independent of the price level. This model has a constant price elasticity which is also equal to the cross-price elasticity. The main advantage of the multiplicative model is its simplicity. The constant price elasticity makes discussions easier in practice. But just as with the linear price-response function, there is no theoretical basis.

The constant price elasticity of the multiplicative model, however, is not very reflective of reality. That the volume does not fall to zero even at very high prices seems unrealistic. Unlike in the linear model, a maximum price does not exist. One should thus be skeptical when a multiplicative model indicates considerable leeway for raising prices. There is a strong suspicion that the model generally

Table 3.2 Formulas for price-response functions (with competition)

Model	Dependent variable	Formula
Linear	q_i or m_i	$a - bp_i + c\bar{p}$
Multiplicative	q_i or m_i	$a\left(p_i/\bar{p}\right)^b$
Attraction	m_i	$a_0 + a_i p_j^{b_i} / \sum\limits_j a_j p_j^{b_j}$
Gutenberg	q_i or m_i	$a - bp_i + c_1 \sin \mathrm{h}\left(c_2\left(\bar{p} - p_i\right)\right)$

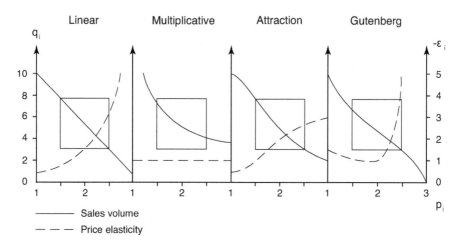

Fig. 3.6 Price-response functions in competitive markets

underestimates price elasticity, at least in the higher price ranges. Indeed, in empirical estimates of the multiplicative model, there are often (constant) price elasticities with an absolute value of less than one, which makes no sense from a price optimization perspective. Such a situation would mean that every price increase would result in higher profits. Based on our experience, we consider the multiplicative model to be less robust than the linear model. It should only be used in narrow intervals around the existing price.

3.3.3.2 The Attraction Model

Unlike the previous two models, the attraction model has explicit roots in behavioral theory. The hypothesis is that the market share m_i of product i is determined by the product's relative attraction. In order to explain the market share m_i, one uses the ratio of the attraction of product i to the sum of the attractions of all competing products:

$$\text{Market share } m_i = \frac{\text{Attraction of product } i}{\text{Sum of attractions of all products}} \qquad (3.9)$$

"Attraction" derives from the fact that this model was originally conceived to describe the attraction effect of quality attributes, advertising, etc. We can interpret attraction as utility or preference. The price is obviously an attribute with a negative effect on attraction. An advantage of the attraction model is its logical consistency: all market shares m_i lie between 0 and 100% and add up to 100%.

Independent of the concrete specification, models of the attraction type are recommended when additional product attributes besides the price are included, and one measures them at the utility or preference level. This applies, for example, to conjoint measurement. The attraction model allows using utility as the basis for calculating volume, revenue, and profit for alternative prices.

Regarding the price effects, the attraction model should be viewed with skepticism at its extremes. As one can see in Fig. 3.6, the effect of a price change or price difference near a competitor's price is comparatively strong and decreases as the distance to the competitor's price increases. This hypothesis is diametrically opposed to the Gutenberg model, which as we will see in the next section has a solid empirical validity. Combining this finding with our own experience, we recommend to use the attraction model with great caution, when one is considering to set prices which deviate strongly from existing price levels. There is a risk of error at the extreme ends of the function. But if looking only at a narrow price range, the attraction model is acceptable.

Here is another empirical observation, although we admit that there is not a sufficient basis for generalization. In our experience, the market leader often achieves a market share which is higher than what the attraction model predicts. There is apparently a "market leader bonus." To compensate for this, very small competitors tend to have lower market shares than the model forecasts.

3.3.3.3 The Gutenberg Model
The Gutenberg model is best known in the form of a double-kinked price-response function. Gutenberg [11, 15], however, viewed a version with more gradual transitions as equivalent to the double-kinked curve. Both versions are shown in Fig. 3.7, where $\bar{p}_i$ represents the average price of the products which compete with product i.

Small price changes or price differences prompt only slight customer shifts from one product to another. The middle, flat part of the price-response function is called the "monopolistic interval," because this part resembles the price-response function of a monopolist. However, the model posits that in the case of a price cut "with

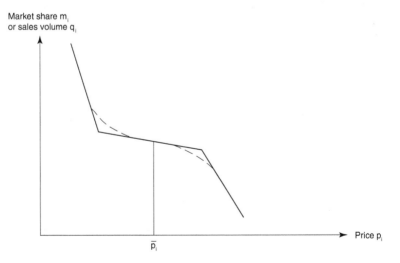

Fig. 3.7 Gutenberg model in double-kinked and continuous form

increasing distance between one's own selling price and the average competitive price, progressively more buyers who formerly bought from a competitor are attracted." In the case of an upward price change, "the degree of fluctuation progressively increases the further the price increase deviates from the initial price" [11, p. 221].

When we ask experts to estimate sales volumes across a sufficiently large price range, the results typically resemble the Gutenberg curve. The managers or experts usually note a price threshold beyond which the volume changes get noticeably sharper. This experience confirms that practitioners think in the structure of the Gutenberg model. The Gutenberg model is confirmed less often when one performs econometric analysis on market data. This may be due to the fact that the range of empirically observed price fluctuations is too small. Prices which lie outside the "monopolistic interval" usually do not last in the market for very long.

3.3.4 Empirical Findings on Price Elasticity

Because of the central importance of price elasticity in price management, a large number of scientific studies have examined the concept. Although comparisons of price elasticities are problematic for a number of reasons, a meta-analysis by Bijmolt et al. [16] provides interesting insights. Their study covered 1851 price elasticity estimates based on actual B2C purchase data. In his book *Empirical Generalizations about Marketing Impact*, Hanssens [17] portrays these estimates as representative for consumer packaged goods. The distribution of the 1851 price elasticity values is shown in Fig. 3.8.

The average of the absolute value of the estimates is 2.62 and the median is 2.22. The median in this context is more meaningful, because it is not influenced by outliers. Figure 3.8 illustrates that price elasticities show considerable differences.

Fig. 3.8 Distribution of econometrically estimated price elasticities [16]

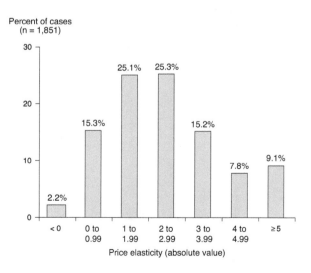

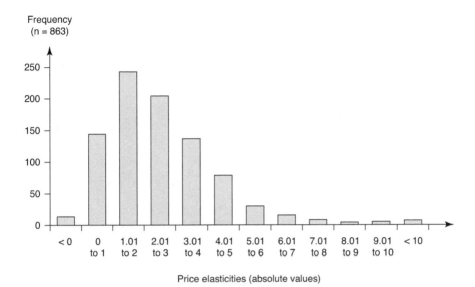

Fig. 3.9 Distribution of econometrically estimated price elasticities (from academic publications) [18, p. 49]

While the price elasticities collected by Bijmolt et al. [16] come from the period between 1961 and 2005, the ones shown in Fig. 3.9 are based on a more recent meta-analysis by Friedel [18], whose work represents the most comprehensive evaluation of empirical price elasticities to date. In a first study, Friedel examined 863 empirical price elasticities from academic journals published between 1981 and 2006. The price elasticities from this part of Friedel's meta-analysis show an average of 2.51 and a median of 2.21. The consistency between Friedel's analysis and the findings of Bijmolt et al. [16] is high.

In a second sample, Friedel used data from consulting. The distribution of price elasticities shown in Fig. 3.10 is based on consulting projects of Simon-Kucher & Partners [18]. The project data are from the period 2003 to 2007 and include 386 price elasticities. The average of the absolute values came to 1.73 and the median to 1.29 [18, p. 68]. These elasticity values are very different from the values reported in the literature.

The Simon-Kucher & Partners data covers a very wide spectrum of products and services such as automobiles, pharmaceuticals, electrodes, industrial tools, insurance, cosmetics, kitchen appliances, etc., while the meta-analysis by Bijmolt et al. [16] was essentially confined to fast-moving consumer goods (FMCG). The price elasticities were calculated by looking at price increases and price decreases of 10%, and the average of the respective elasticities was taken. One could assume that the elasticities from discounts and promotions make up a majority of the dataset of Bijmolt et al. [16]. These tend to be higher than long-term price elasticities estimated in the consulting projects, a finding also confirmed by Hanssens [17].

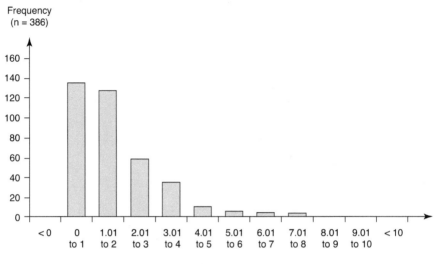

Fig. 3.10 Distribution of price elasticities (based on consulting projects) [17]

Table 3.3 Comparison of price elasticities for price increases and price decreases

Direction of price change	Average	Median
Price decrease	−1.62	−1.07
Price increase	−1.84	−1.50

Overall, one can see that the diverse goods considered in the Simon-Kucher & Partners consulting projects have lower price elasticities on average than fast-moving consumer goods do. This can be explained by the fact that the Simon-Kucher & Partners dataset, among other products and services, included specialized industrial goods, occupational health and safety products, innovative medications, and luxury goods, all with relatively low price elasticities.

Finally, Friedel's work [18, p. 83] provided further insights on the effects of price increases and price decreases, using the Simon-Kucher & Partners dataset. In Table 3.3 we see the averages and the medians of 386 price elasticities for price decreases and increases. The average price elasticity for price decreases was −1.62 and for price increases −1.84. The median price elasticity was −1.07 for price decreases, compared to −1.50 for price increases. These findings suggest that sales volumes respond more strongly to price increases than price decreases. Differences in competitive reaction patterns may explain this discrepancy.

Table 3.4 provides an overview of empirical price elasticities for various product categories. This selection is not meant to be either representative or complete, but rather provides an impression of the large range of empirical values of price

Table 3.4 Selected empirically calibrated price elasticities (Simon-Kucher & Partners)

Product category	Price elasticity (absolute value)
Consumer goods	
Consumables	Mostly >2
Durables	Large variation
Pharmaceuticals	
Innovative products	0.2–0.7
Me-too products	0.5–1.5
Generics	0.7–2.5
Over-the-counter medications	0.5–1.5
Industrial goods	
Standard products	2.0–100
Specialty products	0.3–2.0
Automobiles	
Premium segment	1.0–3.0
Midsize and compact	2.5–5.0
Tires	1.3–4.3
Services	
Air travel	1–5
Rail travel	<1.0
Logistical services	
Letter/mail	0.2–0.9
Package/parcel	1.0–3.0
Freight	0.5–2.0
Banking services	
Personal account fees	0.2–1.4
Investment account fees	0.05–0.5
Mortgages/home loans	0.8–1.9
Mobile telecom plans (voice)	
Monthly base prices	0.5–0.9
Price per minute	0.3–1.1
Additional services	
Computer/IT services	0.5–1.5
Online games	0.6–3.5
Advertising	0.8–2.1

elasticities. In some cases we see very high price elasticity values. An example is a cigarette brand for which a price cut of 13.2% led to market share growth of 1300%. This corresponds to an absolute price elasticity of almost 100. For industrial goods, the range can also be wide. In a survey of machinery manufacturers, respondents estimated their price elasticity to be significantly lower than one. In an expert survey at a supplier of a commodity, the respondents expected a price increase of 2% to cause sales volume to fall by 50%. That translates into an absolute price elasticity of 25.

In the following case, we found an extremely low price elasticity. It concerns the membership dues for the ADAC, which is the German-based counterpart to the American Automobile Association (AAA). The ADAC has 19 million members, making it Europe's largest automotive club. After a decade of price stability, the ADAC had to raise its membership dues [19]. The price for the classic membership rose by 10.1% from €44.50 to €49. The fee for the "Plus" membership rose by 13% from €79.50 to €89.50. The average price increase across all membership classes was 12%. Only 0.1% of the members—or 18,956 people out of a total membership base of 18.92 million—cancelled their membership in the ensuing year [20]. The price elasticity based on these numbers was $-0.01 = (-0.1\%/12\%)$ which is effectively zero. One study used data from a large taxi company to estimate price elasticities. The dataset includes almost 50 million individual observations. The price elasticities range from -1.5 to -2 [21]. This example shows how Big Data (transactional and web demand data) can be used to estimate price elasticities.

The academic literature often attempts to identify the conditions under which price elasticities are either high or low. Most of the empirical experiments do not yield any clear results. We warn of generalizations on price elasticities because they depend to a great extent on the product attributes and the specific competitive context. One assumes, for example, that a high-quality product has a comparatively low price elasticity. This hypothesis seems to be intuitively plausible. But the empirical analysis conducted by Friedel [18] does not support that hypothesis. In fact, the results of the analysis indicate instead that products of high quality exhibit high price elasticities. In Friedel's study, this effect was seen for price increases as well as for price decreases, with the price decreases showing higher elasticities [18, p. 121].

The brand of a product is another driver of price elasticity. The response to discounts of leading brands is much stronger than the response observed with less desirable brands on promotion. Fong et al. [22] assert that store brands have a lower price elasticity than manufacturers' national brands. Bijmolt et al. [16], however, did not detect any significant effect of brand (manufacturer vs. store brand) on price elasticity. Krishnamurthi and Raj [23] concluded that customers loyal to a certain brand have a lower price elasticity than non-loyal customers when it comes to selecting a product. But with regard to the decision of how many units to buy, brand-loyal consumers demonstrate a higher price elasticity. In addition to the quality and the volume of a product, the duration of a price action has an influence. Olbrich et al. [24, p. 282] conducted an empirical analysis of the effectiveness of price actions of food and grocery products over time. Their analysis revealed that the effects of the price actions tend to decrease over time.

Supplementing these findings, Friedel [18] reports that a product's degree of differentiation has a significant effect on its price elasticity. The greater a product's perceived differences across key attributes vs. the competition, the lower that product's substitutability is and the lower its price elasticity [18, p. 110]. Friedel's study indicates that this holds for price decreases as well as price increases [18, p. 129].

Regarding a product's perceived complexity as a determinant of price elasticity, Friedel [18] offers similar results for price increases and decreases. In both cases, the study supports the hypothesis that a higher degree of complexity reduces price elasticity [18, p. 129]. The explanation is that price plays a secondary role in the buying decision for complex products, and customers pay relatively less attention to price than they pay to the other product attributes [18, p. 114].

The direction of a price change influences the effect of customer satisfaction on price elasticity. Koschate [25, p. 165] found that more satisfied customers are less sensitive to price increases than customers with lower satisfaction. It is unclear, though, whether customer satisfaction also has a moderating effect for price decreases.

Overview

Based on the literature and the large project database of Simon-Kucher & Partners, we conclude that the following attributes tend to raise price elasticity:

Product characteristics:

- High similarity and substitutability among competing products; little differentiation.
- High purchase frequency.
- Mass-market quality, positioning, and distribution.
- High share of the product's price in the total cost.
- Frequent use of the product for discounts; heavy price advertising.
- Low level of product complexity.
- Single units (in contrast to product bundles or solutions).
- Product is a traffic driver for retailers.
- High share of the product in promotions.

Market characteristics:

- High competitive pressure on the selling side
- High price transparency
- Industry/sector with low return on sales
- Heavy price pressure from customers (procurement/purchasing)
- High concentration at the customer level
- High e-commerce share

Customer characteristics:

- High price awareness
- High willingness to accept risk
- Good product knowledge: ability to evaluate products objectively

(continued)

- Low/underdeveloped brand awareness
- Low importance of image and prestige
- Low brand loyalty
- Low quality awareness
- Low importance of convenience and of one-stop shopping

Ultimately, price elasticity must be determined on a case-by-case basis. Academic literature has some findings on price elasticity, but these are often inconclusive or even contradictory. Although the results from Friedel [18] support our statements on empirically estimated price elasticities and their influencing factors, we suggest you treat these statements as starting points or guidance, not as generalizations or universally applicable rules.

3.4   Empirical Determination of the Price-Response Function

Surveys and observations are two fundamental options for collecting the data needed to determine a price-response function. Among surveys we distinguish between expert judgment and various forms of customer surveys. We divide observations into experiments and market observations. Table 3.5 provides an overview.

3.4.1   Surveys

3.4.1.1 Expert Judgment
The expert judgment method involves surveying specialists or experts who have deep knowledge of markets, individual market segments, or specialized price knowledge. Such experts who could estimate a price-response function include:

- Company employees: executives, managers, sales and marketing team members
- Management consultants with expertise on the market or market segments, products, or price management in general

Table 3.5 Methods to determine the price-response function

Surveys		Observations			
Expert judgment	Customer surveys	Experiments		Market observations	
	Direct	Indirect	Price experiments	Experimental auctions	Market data	Data from online auctions

- Specialists from market research institutes
- Dealers/distributors or customer advisory panels/councils

Expert judgments are appropriate when a survey of customers is too expensive, too time-consuming, or too difficult to conduct. In the case of true innovations or new situations (e.g., the impending market entry of a new competitor), expert judgment may be the only practical option. Because of its affordability and speed, expert judgment is frequently used to supplement other methods. The surveys can be conducted in an unstructured form (open interviews) or in a structured form with the help of a questionnaire or in a workshop format. The free, unstructured form may help uncover new aspects relevant to pricing. The structured format makes it easier to prepare and analyze the data. For such formats, the use of computer-aided surveys and analysis tools is recommended. Expert surveys conducted as structured individual interviews lend themselves to investigations of market trends, customer reactions, and product/performance evaluations. Workshops enable simultaneous questioning and an in-depth discussion among several experts.

For expert interviews we provide the following recommendations:

- One should survey no fewer than five to ten experts. It is not unusual for estimates to vary sharply from expert to expert. Including more experts increases the validity.
- The experts should represent a range of functions and positions in the hierarchy (e.g., both managers and salespeople) and have relevant knowledge about the market in question (e.g., price sensitivity, market size, competition, etc.).
- The survey should be conducted by a neutral (outside) party (e.g., a consultant).

An expert judgment survey should follow three steps. In the first step, the experts jointly discuss the basic data, including a detailed analysis of the competitive and market environment. Individual customer segments, competitors, competitive products, and the industry environment are identified and analyzed. The experts must achieve alignment around key assumptions on prevailing prices and their associated sales volumes. In the case of a new product, they must be aligned on the presumed base prices and estimated sales volumes.

The actual survey takes place in the second step. First, the experts determine the volume at one specific price. Using that as a basis, each expert then estimates the expected sales volume at different prices. If one wants to incorporate competitive reactions, one has to assess how competitors would respond at each price point and revise the original estimate on sales volume at that price point accordingly. Ideally, one would use a program (such as PRICESTRAT from Simon-Kucher & Partners) to compile the data, analyze it, and plot the results.

In the third and final step, the experts should reconvene to have a joint discussion. Such a discussion is easier if the experts can view the survey results—in particular the price-volume relationships – together in graphical form. A plausibility check on the results is to investigate outliers or any extreme estimates made by individual

Change in sales volume

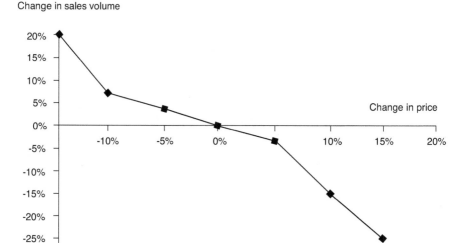

Fig. 3.11 Price-response function derived from expert judgment (tourism industry) (Simon-Kucher & Partners)

experts. Discussing the thought process and logic behind the estimates helps put them in context and makes them understandable.

Figure 3.11 illustrates the use of an expert judgment approach for a vacation resort. The experts examined price changes in a range of −15% to +15% and estimated their effects on sales volume.

The volume response is weak in the ranges where price changes are slight. But there is a threshold for price increases at 5%. If the price increase goes beyond that threshold, it triggers a significant loss of volume. According to the experts' estimates, a price increase of 15% would cause 26% of the customers to leave. The price elasticity is −1.73 (=−26%/+15%). For price decreases, the price elasticity is smaller in absolute terms. For a price decrease of 15%, it is 1.33 (=+20%/−15%). The curve of the price-response function has a Gutenberg form. This form is typical for expert judgment.

The expert judgment method has several advantages and disadvantages.

Advantages:

• The expert judgment process is simpler and easier to use than customer surveys. In general, the results are available sooner and the method is relatively inexpensive.
• Structuring the expert judgment questions using a systematic model (e.g., PRICESTRAT) yields good results. The quantitative approach helps to structure the problem and to extract market knowledge and experience from within the company. It also takes emotions out of the discussion.

- One can anticipate and incorporate competitive reactions and new situations.
- The process can accommodate large price intervals, although the risk of error grows as the price changes become larger than what customers are used to.

Disadvantages:

- The estimates come from "internal" experts, not from customers.
- The experts can respond under false assumptions or fall into the trap of groupthink.
- Individual estimates sometimes vary by a factor of 10 or 20. In such situations, even an average is of little help. An additional danger is that those who are higher in the hierarchy use their clout to force through their own estimates, even when they do not necessarily have the best market knowledge.

3.4.1.2 Customer Surveys

Direct Customer Surveys

The questions in a direct customer survey come straight to the point. One determines price elasticities, for example, by asking customers directly what they are willing to pay for the product or service in question and how they would respond to price changes. There are numerous options, including open questions such as:

- How much are you willing to pay for this product?
- What is the highest price at which you would still be buying this product?
- How much of this product would you purchase at a price of $X?
- How large would the price difference need to be for you to switch from product A to product B?

The questions vary according to whether we are dealing with a "yes-no" case or a "variable-quantity" case. From the answers to these or similar questions, we can derive price-response functions.

Figure 3.12 shows the use of direct questions for an industrial product. The customers of a supplier were asked at which price increase they would switch to another supplier, assuming other competitors hold their prices constant. At a price increase of 5%, 9% of the current customers would switch (price elasticity -1.80). At a 10% increase, 31% of existing customers would switch (price elasticity -3.10). The larger the price increase, the greater the price elasticity is in absolute terms. At a price increase of 20%, no customers would remain loyal to the supplier. The price-response function corresponds to the right-hand portion of a Gutenberg model.

The next case looks at the calibration of a price-response function for a notebook. The question posed to buyers was: "how much would you be willing to spend on this product?" The respondents were asked to provide only their maximum willingness to pay, the so-called maximum price. Figure 3.13 shows the results. There is a distinct price threshold at $750.

Customers (Index)

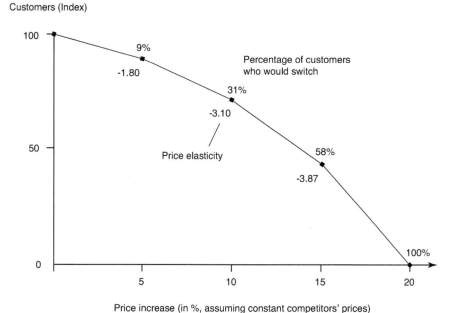

Price increase (in %, assuming constant competitors' prices)

Fig. 3.12 Price-response functions based on direct questions (industrial product)

Percentage of customers who would buy

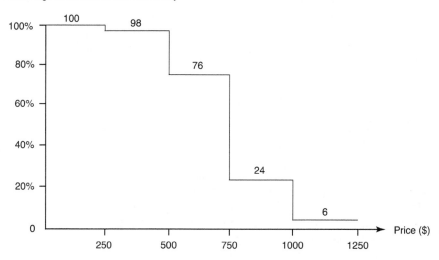

Fig. 3.13 Price-response functions calibrated using direct questions (notebook)

An alternative is to ask respondents whether they would purchase the product at certain prices. The respondents provide a series of yes-no answers. It is unclear which yields the more valid results: yes-no questions to predetermined prices or letting the respondents name a price.

Direct customer surveys have several advantages and disadvantages.

Advantages:

- Using direct customer surveys allows one to explore the desired price issue in a focused, targeted way.
- In contrast to expert interviews, the estimates come directly from the customers.
- In our experience, the direct questioning method has higher validity for industrial products than for consumer goods. We always recommend using direct methods in combination with other methods—in the spirit of a multi-method analysis—in order to cross-check validity.

Direct questioning methods do have their limitations regarding validity and reliability. In particular, we see the following disadvantages.

Disadvantages:

- The price is considered in isolation, while in reality the customer always weighs price and value aspects against each other. The direct approach may put too much emphasis on the price and thus overestimate the price effect.
- Questions about price behavior risk reveal a discrepancy between what customers say in the survey and how they actually behave. This can be due to the prestige effect. The possibility that the respondents' answers are distorted by social desirability can jeopardize the validity of the survey. Empirical comparisons between direct questions and observed market behavior lend support to this skeptical assessment [26–29].
- The use of direct questions is especially problematic in the "variable-quantity" case because customers generally have a hard time quantifying the marginal utility of an additional unit.

The van Westendorp Method

The van Westendorp method is a special form of the direct customer survey. It is based on the fundamental assumption that the willingness to pay of a customer can be expressed both as a maximum price ("I will pay at most $400 for a smartphone") and a price range ("I am willing to spend between $200 and $400 on a smartphone"). According to this assumption, the willingness to pay does not necessarily imply a specific price point or reference price. It can alternatively be considered as a price range construct, in the spirit of the Assimilation-Contrast Theory (see Chap. 4). Thus, a customer buys neither when the price is too high nor when the price is too low.

In the first step of the van Westendorp method, the respondent is asked four questions:

Question A:

"At what price would the product be too expensive, so that you would not buy it?"

Question B:

"At what price would you consider the product to be expensive, but you would still be inclined to buy it?"

Question C:

"What price would you consider to be acceptable or a bargain, so that the product is good value for money?"

Question D:

"What price would be too cheap, so that you would doubt the quality of the product and would not buy it?"

Out of these answers, we get four price points for each respondent, and from these we can compile a cumulative frequency distribution. The resulting curves are shown in Fig. 3.14.

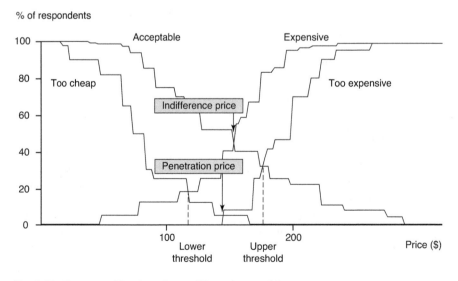

Fig. 3.14 Curves resulting from the van Westendorp model

The various curves and their intersections can be interpreted as follows:

- Questions B (expensive) and C (acceptable): This intersection indicates the so-called indifference price, the price at which the same number of respondents describes the product as "expensive" and "acceptable." The indifference price is the price at which 50% of the respondents perceive the product to have a balanced price image (not too cheap, not too expensive). From the perspective of price image, the indifference price represents a kind of optimal compromise.
- Questions A (too expensive) and D (too cheap): This intersection is referred to as "penetration price," the price at which the respondents consider the product to be acceptable. It is the price at which the smallest number of respondents refuses to buy the product because it is too inexpensive. The sales volume is highest at the penetration price.
- The intersection of the curves to Questions B and D defines a price threshold. Below this barrier, the purchase likelihood falls off rapidly due to the impression of poor quality. This threshold forms the lower limit of the relevant price interval.
- The intersection of the curves to Questions A and C marks the upper threshold. Above this price threshold, the purchase likelihood drops off quickly because of the high price.

One takes the curves to Questions B and C into account to determine the implementable price. These curves describe the expensive and the acceptable prices. The optimal price should fall within that price range.

The *van Westendorp method* does not define a price-response function, but rather reveals a range in which many customers accept the price and decide to make a purchase [28]. The willingness to pay measured in this manner cannot be transformed into precise sales volume forecasts. Indeed, one can assume that the volume will usually be higher at a lower price, but this cannot be generalized on the basis of the data and definitely not quantified. A product could be perceived as expensive and still be preferred over less expensive alternative. Nonetheless, at a price beyond the "too expensive" price point, one has to expect a sharp drop in sales volume.

The van Westendorp method has the following advantages and disadvantages.

Advantages:

- Simple to set up, conduct, and analyze
- Appropriate for determining price thresholds
- Helps to define the price ranges where a product is too expensive or too inexpensive
- Provides information on the penetration and indifference prices

Disadvantages:

- Risk of overemphasis on price, because price is considered in isolation.

- The sales volumes associated with specific price points cannot be quantified, i.e., it is not possible to determine the revenue-maximizing or profit-maximizing price.
- Competition is at best implicitly taken into account.

Overview
The van Westendorp method helps to get an idea of the range of prices achievable in the market. The method has gained in importance in market research in recent years. Because its results are not sufficient for forecasting sales volumes, the van Westendorp methods should not be used as the sole approach, but rather to validate the results from other methods (e.g., conjoint measurement).

Indirect Customer Surveys

Indirect customer surveys avoid treating price in isolation. The goal of these methods is to come as close as possible to replicating a real buying situation. Customers do not pay for a product or a service as such, but rather for the fulfillment of their needs. In a real buying situation, the customer does not base the purchase decision solely on price, but rather makes trade-offs across perceived utilities for different product attributes. The conjoint measurement method helps to quantify these trade-offs. Conjoint measurement is the most successful and most frequently used analysis method in marketing. It permits the simultaneous estimation of the utility of product attributes and price effects. The method can be applied to a wide spectrum of problems in product and price management.

The central objective of conjoint measurement is to answer this question: what utility and as a result what willingness to pay does a customer associate with a given product? The respondents are not asked directly about price, but rather are confronted with alternative product-price profiles. In other words, they are asked about their preferences for combinations of different attribute levels, including different prices. The respondents only state their preferences for the combinations shown. From these all-encompassing preference statements, we can derive the effect not only of price but also of the product attributes which constitute the product-price combinations. Conjoint measurement is therefore not only well-suited for measuring the effects of price but also for quantifying the utility of non-price attributes.

Conjoint measurement provides answers to questions such as:

- How much is a certain improvement in quality, service, or design worth to a customer in terms of price?
- How much is a brand worth in terms of price, relative to other brands?
- How much is a customer willing to pay for special accessories or features or for better service?
- What effect does a price change have on the perceived utility and the preference?

Conjoint measurement is very important for price management. Every year, thousands of conjoint measurement studies are conducted around the world. The method has undergone steady advancement, not only because of its relevance but also thanks to continual improvements in computer-aided support. As a result, there are now numerous conjoint approaches [30, p. 705, 31, p. 2, 32].

Before we explore the most important uses, we would like to introduce the basic thinking behind classical conjoint measurement as well as an example of a typical approach.

To measure the effects of price using conjoint measurement, one proceeds as follows:

- Determine the attributes to include.
- Determine the levels for each attribute.
- Design the questionnaire and administer it.
- Calculate the preference function and part-worth utilities.
- Calculate the price-response function.

These steps cover the analysis of price effects, so that they can be translated into price recommendations, segmentation schemes, and positioning strategies. Choosing the attributes and setting their levels are of critical importance. This process should be done in collaboration with management, and in our experience, a workshop is the best format to facilitate the required discussion. Whenever possible, the judgments and opinions of management should be supplemented with customer interviews or focus groups. Setting the ranges for the levels is especially critical. The range should not be so narrow that it fails to cover the entire optimal interval. At the same time, including levels which are unrealistic or outside the normal intervals customers are accustomed to can skew the results.

Another problem is the number of levels per attribute. Several findings indicate that having different numbers of levels influences the overall results because more levels mean that a particular attribute gets weighted more heavily. Usually we recommend to use an identical or similar number of levels per attribute. In practice, however, this may not always make sense for prices. One often intentionally wants to test a greater number of price levels than levels of other attributes.

Once the attributes and their levels are set, we move to the third step: deciding on how to present the stimuli to the respondent. In the full-profile method, all attributes, including price, are shown in each profile. In other words, the respondent always sees a completely described product rather than a partial one. An alternative is to use the two-factor method with the help of a trade-off matrix. With this technique, the respondent need only to make trade-offs by weighing two attributes against each other. Under the Adaptive Conjoint Analysis (ACA) technique, the respondents compare a pair of profiles each comprising several attributes but not all. The full-profile method has the advantage that it closely resembles a real purchase decision. But it is also more complex for the respondent.

Conjoint measurements are easier to administrate and become more valid when the interviews are conducted using computer and video support. First, computer

Table 3.6 Attributes and levels for an automotive study

Attribute	Levels
• Brand	VW, Ford, Buick
• Price	$20,000, $22,000, $24,000
• Top speed	110, 120, 130 mph
• Gas mileage	42, 35, 28 mpg
Sample profile	
• Brand	Ford
• Price	$20,000
• Top speed	110 mph
• Gas mileage	42 mpg

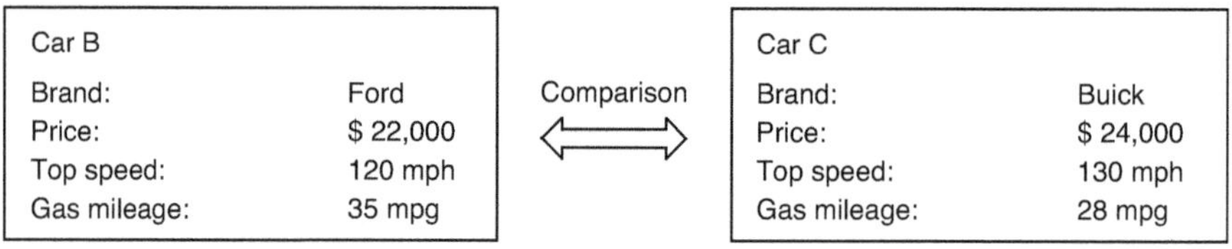

Car B		Comparison	Car C	
Brand:	Ford	⇐⇒	Brand:	Buick
Price:	$ 22,000		Price:	$ 24,000
Top speed:	120 mph		Top speed:	130 mph
Gas mileage:	35 mpg		Gas mileage:	28 mpg

Fig. 3.15 Paired comparison of two alternative cars (full-profile method)

support allows to handle a larger number of attributes and levels. Second, one can use several methods (also direct questioning) in parallel and build up the profiles step by step, such as with the Adaptive Conjoint Analysis programs from Sawtooth Software. The analysis of preferences and the calculation of part-worth utilities (step 4) are usually done on an individual respondent basis. With this approach, one avoids averaging out customer-specific differences and also receives input and indications for market segmentation and price differentiation. In step 5, the individual price-response functions are then aggregated to obtain the price-response function.

The following case demonstrates the conjoint measurement approach.

Case: Automotive Study

To resolve a price problem with conjoint, we helped an automobile manufacturer select the attributes and levels shown in Table 3.6. These were discussed and set in cooperation with the company's management.

Each alternative car profile is defined by four attributes, each of which will have one of three possible levels. This means one can construct 81 ($3 \times 3 \times 3 \times 3$) different "cars" in this study. We used the full-profile method in combination with paired comparisons. In each pair, the respondents see two "cars" and state which one they prefer. Figure 3.15 shows such a paired comparison.

Car C can reach a higher speed than Car B, but it is more expensive and has lower gas mileage. Car B also has a different brand than Car C. If the respondent chooses Car C, it means that the difference in brand and the higher maximum speed compensate for the higher price and the lower gas mileage. The paired comparison requires the respondent to weigh the advantages and disadvantages of each profile against the other. This corresponds to a typical purchase situation and is more realistic than asking a direct question about price. The responses to a series of similar paired comparisons reveal how important each individual attribute is for the respondent. Furthermore, we can determine how much utility the respondent derives from each level of each attribute.

One problem lies in the total number of paired comparisons which a respondent must make. With 81 potential "cars" in the study, 3,240 paired comparisons are possible. Using a fractional design, the number of required paired comparisons can be significantly reduced. In practice, between 10 and 20 paired comparisons are usually sufficient.

Once the data have been collected, the part-worth utilities can be calculated. These are the contributions which each individual level makes to the total utility. The software (e.g., Sawtooth Software) supports both the data collection and the analysis. The sample results in Fig. 3.16 are for one individual respondent.

The part-worth utilities show how the total utility of the car changes when one swaps one attribute level for another. The largest differences come from changing the level of the "price" attribute, the smallest when we change the level for the attribute "top speed." The influence on customer preferences and purchase decisions varies by attribute.

The part-worth utilities can also help determine the importance of each attribute. As a rule, the larger the range of part-worth utilities, the more important the attribute is. The importance w_j for the attribute j is determined by the difference between the largest and smallest part-worth utilities for the level. These values can be transformed into a relative importance $\bar{w}_j$ (in percent):

$$\text{Relative importance } \bar{w}_j = \frac{\text{Importance of an attribute } w_j}{\text{Sum of importances } \sum\limits_{j=1} w_j} \times 100\% \qquad (3.10)$$

Table 3.7 shows the absolute and relative importance for the attributes. Price represents the most important attribute for this respondent, followed by brand and gas mileage. The top speed is only in fourth place for this respondent. This respondent's weighting of price as a more important criterion than brand is rather typical for the less expensive compact and mid-sized car segment [33, p. 26].

The part-worth utilities can be used directly to express the value of additional attribute levels in terms of price units. In the case of the buyer in Fig. 3.17:

- The value of the VW brand exceeds that of the Ford brand $862.
- Increasing the top speed from 110 to 130 mph has a value of $215.
- Improving the gas mileage from 28 to 42 mpg is worth $554

Here we are using a linear preference model. In order to determine the total utility for a particular car model, one adds up the part-worth utilities listed in Fig. 3.16 for each respective attribute level. Table 3.8 shows this process for three cars.

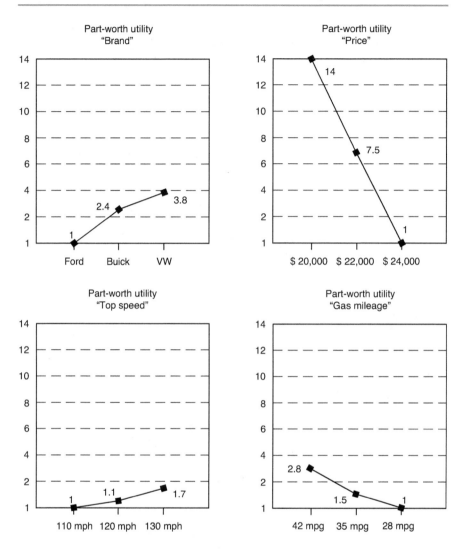

Fig. 3.16 Part-worth utilities for one respondent

Table 3.7 Calculating the importance of the attributes

Attribute	Importance w_j	Relative importance $\bar{w}_j$
Price	$14.0 - 1.0 = 13.0$	$13.0/18.3 \times 100\ \% = 71.0\%$
Brand	$3.8 - 1.0 = 2.8$	$2.8/18.3 \times 100\ \% = 15.3\%$
Gas mileage	$2.8 - 1.0 = 1.8$	$1.8/18.3 \times 100\ \% = 9.9\%$
Top speed	$1.7 - 1.0 = 0.7$	$0.7/18.3 \times 100\ \% = 3.8\%$
Total	18.3	100%

Market share
of car A

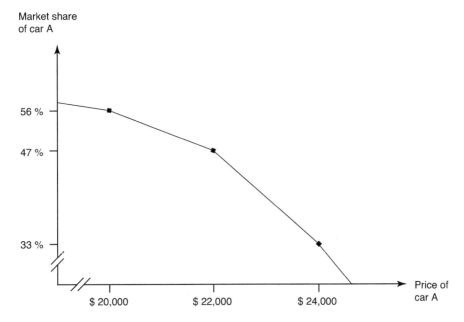

Fig. 3.17 Price-response function for car A

Table 3.8 Calculating the utility value for three cars—individual basis

Car A		Car B		Car C	
Level	Part-worth utility	Level	Part-worth utility	Level	Part-worth utility
VW	3.8	Ford	1.0	Buick	2.4
$20,000	14.0	$22,000	7.5	$24,000	1.0
110 mph	1.0	120 mph	1.1	130 mph	1.7
42 mpg	2.8	35 mpg	1.5	28 mpg	1.0
Utility	21.6	Utility	11.1	Utility	6.1

Car A has the highest total utility and, among these three alternatives, would be the one respondents prefer. Car C could achieve a higher total utility than Car B, if its price were $2000 lower. But there is no combination of technical changes which would help Car B or Car C ever have a greater total utility than Car A. This is due to the large difference in the utility contributed by the attribute "price" and its high importance to customers.

In the discussion below, we will consider only Cars A, B, and C for the determination of individual price-response functions. The purchase decision in this case is "yes-no."

Table 3.9 Market share calculations for Car A and one individual respondent

Price	$20,000	$22,000	$24,000
Part-worth utility of the attribute "price"	14	7.5	1
Sum of part-worth utilities without price (Car A)	7.6	7.6	7.6
Total utility at p_i	21.6	15.1	8.6
Total utility across all profiles	38.8	32.3	25.8
Market share of profile i	56%	47%	33%

From Utility to Sales Volume

In order to go from utility to sales volumes, there are two basic models. The deterministic model assumes that the product with the greatest total utility will be purchased. The stochastic model assumes that the utility values determine the purchase probabilities. We use the stochastic model in the following example. In order to generate a price-response function from the utilities, we use the attraction model. Purchase probabilities can be interpreted as market shares:

$$\text{Market share } m_i = \frac{\text{Utility of model } i}{\text{Sum of utilities of all models}} \qquad (3.11)$$

With this approach, we obtain the "purchase probabilities" for each respondent and for the product under consideration at three alternative prices. This process is shown for a selected respondent in Table 3.9 and displayed graphically in Fig. 3.17. When the price increases from $20,000 to $22,000, the market share declines from 56% to 47% (price elasticity of −1.6). If the price rises from $22,000 to $24,000, the market share drops to 33% and the absolute price elasticity increases sharply to −3.3. We arrive at an overall market share by aggregating the results across all respondents.

An approach to determining market shares which comes very close to reality is based on the multinomial logit model and accounts for the individual total utility as well as for the relation on the market to rival products. If Car A and Car B have similar utility values, the purchase probabilities change more sharply when one model gains additional utility than they do when one model is already strongly preferred.

Further Developments in Conjoint Measurement

We focus now on the approaches which have the highest relevance in the literature and in practice. These approaches differ in how they obtain the preference judgments and the choice of algorithms for the estimations [31, p. 2, 32, p. 45, 34, p. 610]. Fundamentally we differentiate between:

- Classic approaches (trade-off and profile methods)
- Hybrid approaches (ACA (Adaptive Conjoint Analysis) or ACBC (Adaptive Choice-based Conjoint))

- Discrete Choice Modeling (DCM), Choice-Based Conjoint (CBC), and Constant-Sum Conjoint (CSC)

The *classic approach* encounters validity problems when the number of attributes is large. To address these problems, researchers developed hybrid approaches to conjoint measurement.

Hybrid approaches combine compositional and decompositional methods. They use scoring models as well as conjoint measurement. Combining these two approaches allows one to apply comprehensive fractional conjoint designs across several people [30, p. 706, 34, p. 612]. With hybrid analyses, respondents are asked in an initial (compositional) phase to make isolated judgments on the importance of attributes and their levels. In the second (decompositional) phase, they evaluate selected combinations of attributes. These approaches alleviate the cognitive burden on the respondent. But the effort to collect data increases with these approaches. The most commonly used form of hybrid conjoint measurement is *ACA (Adaptive Conjoint Analysis)*.

ACA adapts the computer-supported interview to each individual on an ongoing basis. The respondent's answers are analyzed during the interview so that the subsequent questions focus on the area which is most important to the respondent. This reduces the number of required paired comparisons and shortens the interview, which in turn increases the respondents' engagement and the quality of individual answers.

An ACA interview typically comprises the following phases:

- Determine unacceptable attributes (optional)
- Rate preferences for the attribute levels
- Evaluate importance of the attributes
- Paired comparisons

In order to put meaningful decision alternatives in front of the respondent, it is important that they fall into the respondent's "accepted set." To assure this, in the first phase, each respondent should rule out attribute levels which are unacceptable. These levels are then excluded from the rest of the interview. Let's assume we are conducting an ACA on cars. If the respondent indicates in the first phase that he or she will not buy a Ford under any circumstances, then that level will be eliminated from the attribute "brand" from that point onward. This increases the relevance of the profiles later in the interview and reduces the number of paired comparisons required.

In the next phase, the individual respondent states his or her preferences for the levels of the nondirectional attributes. These are attributes which either have no a priori order (e.g., brand) or whose preferences do not necessarily increase as the level of the attribute increases (e.g., engine power). One cannot assume with certainty that all car buyers prefer a car with a more powerful engine. In contrast, for the directional attributes such as price, one can generally assume that the level of the

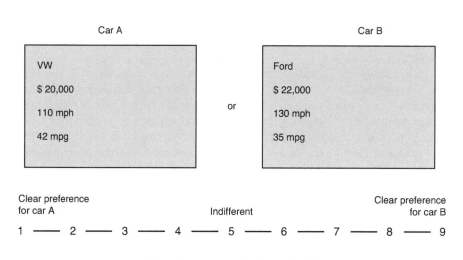

Fig. 3.18 Paired comparison with Adaptive Conjoint Analysis (ACA)

attribute correlates with preference, i.e., a lower price is generally preferable to a higher one (except sometimes for luxury goods).

In the third phase, the respondents are asked to rate the importance of individual attributes on a scale. For each attribute, the respondents will see the worst and the best level compared to each other and will be asked how important that difference is to them. Once these importance ratings are gathered, preliminary estimates of preferences and utility values are made. The ACA uses these values to determine what questions to pose in the next interview stage, which involves a series of paired comparisons and represents the core of the method. Figure 3.18 shows such a paired comparison. The respondent is asked to rate preferences for the two alternative cars on a scale from one to nine, where one represents a clear preference for the left-hand car and nine represents a clear preference for the right-hand one. If the respondent is indifferent, a five is indicated.

The paired comparisons are set up with the overall utilities for each "car" roughly similar, so that the respondent is close to being indifferent between the two options. As soon as the respondent indicates a preference, the ACA program uses that information to improve the estimates of the utility values and to select a new paired comparison. Because the estimated utilities are optimized from question to question, it becomes increasingly difficult for the respondent to express a preference for either alternative. Based on these utility values, in the next phase, one can estimate price-response functions using a market simulation model [34]. A detailed description of

"Which of the following products would you buy?
(Please assume that all other attributes are identical)"

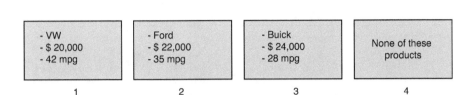

"Please mark the number corresponding to your choice"

Fig. 3.19 Purchase decision (choice-based conjoint)

the ACA process as well as its advantages and disadvantages can be found in Herrmann et al. [35].

An additional hybrid approach to conjoint analysis is Adaptive Choice-Based Conjoint (ACBC) offered by the software firm Sawtooth. In this approach, the respondents' preference rankings of attributes and levels lead to a bundle of products which the respondent would actually consider. One then conducts a conjoint measurement survey using this "consideration set" [36].

The next approach we will look at is *Discrete Choice Modeling (DCM)*. DCM is a category of conjoint models which ask for purchase decisions ("buy" or "not buy") instead of preferences. Choice-Based Conjoint (CBC) is the name of the software which Sawtooth developed for that purpose. *Constant-Sum Conjoint (CSC)* is a further development of CBC and belongs to the DCM category.

Figure 3.19 shows a typical line of questioning within a CBC interview. In contrast to traditional conjoint and ACA, the respondent must make a decision to purchase. The respondents are not forced to buy one of the alternatives; for each question they have the option to choose none of the alternatives shown.

In terms of the underlying assumptions, CBC is fundamentally different from the methods we have discussed so far [37]. Because the possibility to determine utility values at the individual level is limited, CBC lends itself best to markets with relatively homogenous preference structures. CBC is today one of the frequently used conjoint methods [38]. Its popularity is attributed among other things to its ability to generate valid measurements of willingness to pay [39]. A thorough discussion of the advantages and disadvantages of this approach can be found in DeSabro et al. [40].

Finally, we would like to call attention to another development of the CBC method. In recent years, the use of *Constant-Sum-Conjoint (CSC)* has established itself as state of the art in price research. In contrast to the discrete choice options "choose one" and "best-worst" of previous methods, the respondents in a CSC approach indicate their preferences by using points. The total number of points to distribute remains constant, e.g., 10 or 100. One could also use hierarchical Bayes

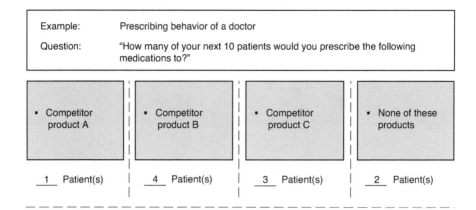

Fig. 3.20 Decision situation using Constant Sum Conjoint

models, which allow one to make utility estimates at the individual level [41, 42]. The associated software is HB-Sum from Sawtooth [43]. The task here is to allocate a fixed number of choice decisions across a set of products. The method recognizes the fact that a respondent may purchase two or more products with equal probability. For example, a doctor could use different medications for different patient types to treat a given illness. The method has the advantage that one can include existing products and new products. With the existing products—presumably known to the respondent already—one can dispense with the full-profile approach. All in all, this approach reflects the real decision situation rather well. The process has a high information efficiency and increases the validity relative to traditional conjoint measurement. Figure 3.20 shows a typical line of questioning. In this example, the doctor allocates a number of patients to each competing medication, based on how he would prescribe medication to them.

The performance capability of *Discrete Choice Modeling (DCM)* can be improved by combining it with other approaches. Albers et al. [44] show that using a combination of Choice-Based Conjoint Analysis with other approaches can simultaneously support product and communications decisions at the segment level. It also allows the derivation of willingness to pay for bundles. We refrain from generalizations, though, about the superiority of one conjoint analysis method over another. How appropriate a method is depends on the respective task at hand, the method of data collection, and in what context the data is collected [45, p. 116].

Technical progress has had a pronounced effect on conjoint measurement. Computer-based conjoint measurement surveys are the standard today. Due to the combination of powerful analytical techniques and modern information technology, it is possible to conduct a survey independent of the number of attributes and levels.

This means that complex products or decision situations can be analyzed using conjoint measurement. Srinivasan [46] has introduced the *Adaptive Self-Explication Method* (ASE Method), another powerful expansion of conjoint measurement. An alternative CBC technique is the *Restricted Click-Stream Analysis*, developed by Schlereth and Schulz [47]. It is comparable to other preference measurement methods in terms of validity. While CBC uses choice decisions, Schlereth and Schulz [47] address the information search during the purchase process. They argue that the relative time of attention a customer devotes to a product attribute correlates with the weight of its relative importance. Their empirical results show a comparable level of validity to established preference measurement methods.

The use of computers makes a more attractive graphical display of options possible through video and audio elements. It has been proven, for example, that a realistic visual representation of a product can replace the use of a prototype, without skewing the choice behavior [48]. In the future augmented reality will further improve the process. On the other hand, the availability of easy-to-use computer programs carries the risk that conjoint measurement will get used without an understanding of the method's complexity. With advanced and demanding techniques such as conjoint measurement, we must warn against a "paint by numbers" application. The more the data collection and the analysis are simplified, the greater the risk that the method will be applied without sufficient customization to the specific situation. This can lead to skewed results and incorrect interpretations. Here we recommend once again a multi-method approach. Whenever possible, one should cross-validate the conjoint results through other methods.

Conjoint measurement is seen by many practitioners as well as theoreticians as the best approach to measure customer preferences and price effects. While a variety of uses in practice have put the method's appropriateness for measuring demand preferences to the test, critics have referred to problems with validity, due in part to the hypothetical nature of the purchase situation [30, 49, p. 113, 50, p. 366]. High internal and external validities are therefore mutually exclusive. The internal validity expresses the extent to which the results of the study are intrinsically logical and can be interpreted unequivocally. The external validity relates to how well the results can be transferred to the real purchase situation.

Overview

Conjoint measurement does not ask customers directly about their price behavior. Instead, the price effects are derived indirectly from statements of preference or purchase intent. The respondents are requested to weigh value-to-customer against price. Conjoint measurement is extremely versatile, both for new and established products. The results are influenced by the study design. We therefore urge the utmost care and encourage advance, exploratory studies. Results should also be validated by other methods.

3.4.2   Observations

Price effects can also be measured through observations, which include experiments and market observations. With observations, the outcome of the research will not manifest itself through respondents' verbal explanations, but through their actual behavior.

3.4.2.1 Experiments

Price Experiments
In a price experiment, test buyers are exposed to alternative prices in a real or realistic purchase situation. We distinguish among field experiments, lab experiments, and a special form, direct marketing. As digitalization penetrates further into markets, it becomes increasingly easier to conduct price experiments [51].

Field experiments test the effects of pricing measures (price variation, price advertising, price display, forms of price differentiation) under real purchase conditions. The product under study is not removed or detached from its purchase environment. Only the independent variable (in this case, the price) is changed, while all other factors are held constant to the greatest extent possible. Normally the test subjects are not aware of the experiment.

We can distinguish between classic market testing approaches and store tests. The *classic test market* explores the effects of pricing measures in markets separated into regions. This form does not play a big role in practice, because of its high costs, the time required, and the inability to keep the test secret. Less costly methods such as store tests or simulated test markets have replaced it almost entirely. With a *store test*, the effects of pricing measures are examined in selected test stores. Usually for this kind of test, one chooses several test stores. These do not necessarily need to qualify as representative. Such tests can be expensive for manufacturers, because the retailers have to be paid for their participation.

A further refinement of the store test is the *mini test market*. The mini test market is a combination of store test and household panel. The capture of the data in the test stores happens with the help of scanners. The scanner allows purchases to be captured exactly, in real time, with precise allocation and at low cost. A benefit for price research is the extreme granularity of the data, as well as the ability to aggregate it in many ways. This leads to a wide range of measurement and segmentation possibilities.

At a product's point of purchase, one can collect data on price, time, location, and the buyer's basket. At the same time, one can collect data on alternative or substitute products the buyer did not select (and their prices), as well as the prices and sales volumes of other products. Altogether this dataset covers the competitive field in a comprehensive way and records all essential information for price research.

The *simulated test market* represents another alternative. A simulated test market takes place in virtual test studio modeled after a real market. The studio should be set up at a location (e.g., within a department store) which attracts a representative population and reflects the relevant retail structure. In the simulated test environment, test subjects participate in computer-aided price experiments. This form has time and cost advantages over the "real" test markets we described earlier. It allows a manufacturer to shield the product and price tests better from competitors, providing a greater level of secrecy than a classic test market.

Digitalization and e-commerce make price experiments easier to conduct. Online, computer-supported algorithms allow the creation of statistical models which collect, connect, and analyze data, with the ultimate goal of predicting customer behavior [52]. Prices can be changed for test purposes, and the volume effects measured without additional cost, because the data is transaction- and buyer-specific anyway. Any form of aggregation is possible. Amazon, for example, changes some prices several times a day in order to analyze the effects different prices have on volume [53]. As the share of e-commerce continues to grow, we expect a significant increase in field-based price experiments.

Test auctions offer yet another practical and meaningful form of price tests online. With the option to buy immediately (which corresponds to a fixed price for a product or service) one can test the effect of different prices. The following example illustrates the use of an online auction to optimize prices:

In this case, a dealer wants to sell 1000 Nikon Coolpix cameras on eBay, but does not know what price to charge. The dealer conducts the following price test:

- On the first day, the dealer offers 50 cameras at $400 apiece.
- On the second day, the dealer places 50 cameras on the platform at $350 each.
- On the third day, the dealer offers another 50 cameras at $300 each.

Figure 3.21 shows the resulting price-response function.

On the first day the dealer sold ten cameras. After cutting the price to $350 on the second day, the dealer sold 20 cameras. On the third day, after lowering the price to

Fig. 3.21 Online price test

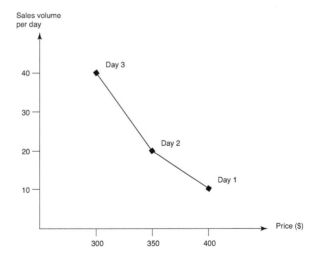

$300, the sales volume rose to 40 cameras. When one assumes no interdependence between the days, the result is a price-response function which offers the basis for price optimization.

In contrast to field experiments, *lab experiments* hold all variables constant to the greatest degree possible, except for price, so that one can analyze price's influence. One accepts that these scenarios are not fully reflective of reality. For the simulated purchase, the test persons receive an amount of money and are requested to shop with it. They see competing products in the simulation. Separate groups may see different price parameters (e.g., price level, price structure, presentation of the price) varied systematically in order to observe the effect on volume. Such tests are offered by firms such as Ipsos and GfK.

The newest form of lab experiment on price questions comes from the field of brain research. The so-called field of "neuro-pricing" investigates how the human brain reacts to price information (see Chap. 4). "The way we perceive prices is no different from the way we perceive other painful stimuli," says brain researcher Kai-Markus Müller [54]. Price perceptions trigger reactions in the brain which researchers can measure. Brain research can objectively capture processes which the consumer might not be aware of. In the next chapter, we will discuss this new field more deeply. The typical concerns for a lab experiment regarding validity and realism apply even more so to brain experiments. The test subjects must visit specialized labs and undergo a medical examination. How representative the samples and the measurement results are under these circumstances and how well they apply to the real world remain open questions.

> **Overview**
> The major advantage of lab experiments vs. field experiments lies in their lower costs, the ability to control external influences, less time commitment, and the secrecy. The primary problem with lab experiments is their limited external validity because the artificial purchase situations may not replicate the real purchase situation. The test subjects' awareness of their participation in such a test may lead them to exhibit behaviors they normally wouldn't.

Experimental Auctions

The significance of auctions has grown sharply as the Internet expanded [55, p. 625]. On auction platforms such as eBay or Alibaba, goods and services are sold to the highest bidder. Google earns billions of dollars by auctioning advertising space. Hal Varian, the chief economist of Google, claims that almost everything at Google is organized by auctions, even its initial public offering (IPO) [56, p. 85]. Auctions, however, are not only well-suited for setting prices; they also offer the opportunity to determine willingness to pay. A hallmark of the experimental auction is that the test subjects actually buy the products in the experiment.

The academic literature classifies auctions into four types: the English auction, the Dutch auction, the highest-price auction, and the Vickrey auction. Overviews of these auctions forms may be found in McAfee and McMillan [57, p. 702] as well as in Skiera and Spann [55, p. 628]. Skiera and Revenstorff [58] refer to the use of the Vickrey auction format as an instrument for the capture of willingness to pay. The Vickrey auction lends itself particularly well to determining price-response functions [58, 59]:

- In contrast to usual auctions, the Vickrey auction stands out due to two fundamental characteristics: first, the bidders cannot influence the purchase price directly via their bids. Second, the purchase price does not correspond to the highest bid, but instead is based on the offer of the second-highest bidder. The highest bidder gets the product but at a price equal to the second highest bid. The most prominent example of an auction platform which uses the Vickrey mechanism is eBay. The specific purchase price is based on the offer made by the second-highest bidder plus an amount equal to the minimum bidding increment in the auction.
- From a rational perspective, because of this bidding process, each individual bidder has the incentive to make bids at the level of their true willingness to pay [29, p. 38, 58, p. 226, 59, p. 20, 60, p. 22, 61, p. 3946]. Wolfstetter [61, p. 394] therefore characterizes the Vickrey auction as the only one which is incentive based.
- In addition to this compatibility, the Vickrey auction also has the advantage that all participants must make a bid.
- The participants' bids allow the derivation of price-response functions, optimal prices, and market shares.

An additional auction form is the so-called pay-per-bid auction. It is used both for auction processes with increasing as well as decreasing bids. Its special characteristic is that each bidding round has a countdown interval (e.g., 20 s) and the bidders are charged a fixed amount for each bid they make. As soon as a bid is made, the countdown starts again from the top. This gives competing bidders the chance to place their own higher (or lower) bid, for which they would also need to pay the fixed charge per bid. If a countdown interval ends without a fresh bid being placed, the winner of the auction has the option to purchase the object of the auction at a price corresponding to the most recent bid [62].

Overview
Experimental auctions represent new and innovative approaches to price research. Online auctions are relatively inexpensive and can replace or augment traditional approaches.

In addition to auctions, one can use lotteries to gather data on willingness to pay. This approach to measuring willingness to pay is suggested by Becker et al. [63] and works in two steps [50, p. 367]:

- In the first step, the test person is asked to reveal his or her willingness to pay in response to a direct price survey.
- In the second step, a price will be chosen per lottery. If this price is above the willingness to pay expressed by the test person, the test person is required to purchase the product at the price drawn in the lottery.

Similar to Vickrey auctions, lotteries are incentive-compatible. An empirical comparison between the Vickrey auction and the lottery demonstrated that both methods are reliable and valid in measuring individual willingness to pay [63, 64, p. 36].

3.4.2.2 Market Observations

Market Data
The market data used for price analysis typically has been collected at an earlier time for another purpose. In many markets, standardized data is available which can support price decisions. In addition to market research institutes such as IRI, Nielsen, or GfK, which collect data on volume, market share, and prices on a regular basis, retailers use scanner technology to gather data on prices and sales volumes. One can also obtain statistics from industry or trade associations and from government sources for price analyses.

The data are either in the form of time series or cross-sectional data. The latter can relate to different sales regions, countries, or market segments. An indispensable prerequisite for the use of market data to measure price effects is a sufficient level of variation in the independent variable price. In the event that the price was not changed over time or was not varied in the cross-sectional units, it is not possible to measure price effects. This situation is by no means an exception. The prices of competing firms often move in lockstep, so that the relative prices remain constant over time.

Normally one uses econometric regression methods to analyze market data. However, the predominance of this method in the literature does not correspond to its significance in practice. Customer surveys based on conjoint measurement, or the expert judgment technique, play a bigger role in practice. Price experiments are becoming increasingly popular, thanks to the Internet. Several problems with using historical data to determine price-response functions deserve consideration. If the price elasticity is low, one could observe large price differences, but these will have no significant influence on volume or market share. That means that despite a high level of variation in the independent variable, the dependent variable shows only slight variation. In contrast, if the price elasticity is high, the opposite effect tends to hold true. Relative prices hardly vary at all, because competitive prices adjust to price changes quickly. Telser [65] pointed to these weaknesses in using regression

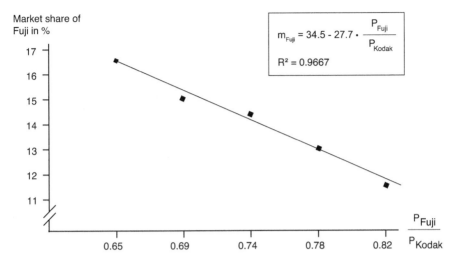

Fig. 3.22 Price-response function based on historical market data (Simon-Kucher & Partners)

to measure price effects. Our experience from more than four decades of pricing research and consulting underscores this concern.

A disadvantage of the falling back on market data is that the reaction of the customers does not provide any sound indication of the underlying cause of the reaction (e.g., price advertising, price variation, actions by a competitor). With respect to decision support, it is also disadvantageous that the data come from the past. Whether such historic price effects will apply to the future is always uncertain. Structural breaks in the market, such as the entry of a new competitor, make it necessary to re-examine price effects. In the wake of such structural shifts, the predictive validity of historical data is often low.

In Fig. 3.22 we illustrate the use of historical data to determine a price-response function. It concerns film for amateur use in the US market. Kodak was the market leader in the period in question, while Fuji was the attacker. The independent variable is the relative price p_{Fuji}/p_{Kodak} and the dependent variable is the market share of Fuji. Both the independent and the dependent variables show considerable variance. The linear price-response function $m_{Fuji} = 34.5 - 27.7 \times p_{Fuji}/p_{Kodak}$ explains 97% of the variance ($R^2 = 0.9667$). If we reduce the relative price from 0.78 to 0.74, which is 5.1%, the market share of Fuji increases by 8.6%. The price elasticity at this point is therefore $8.6/-5.1 = -1.69$.

When using regression analysis on the basis of market data, economic plausibility ("face validity") should be given the same weight as statistical criteria. There is no standard model which applies to all demand and competitive situations. In fact, it is absolutely necessary to examine carefully on a case-by-case basis which model, which variables, and which specifications are the right ones to choose.

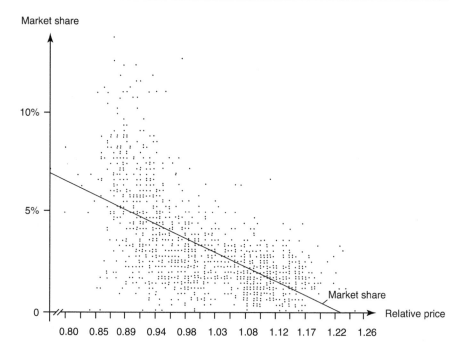

Fig. 3.23 Price-response function based on scanner data

Scanner data, which collect sales and prices directly at the cash register, are suitable for determining price-response functions. Figure 3.23 shows an example for a coffee brand whose sales and prices were collected in different store locations of a chain. The data interval is 1 week.

The availability of price and volume data depends on the industry sector. If no time-series data is available, one can perhaps use cross-sectional data instead. Time-series and cross-sectional data can also be combined in a pooled regression.

The price analyst must be creative in acquiring and interpreting data in order to get insights into the price effects. When using secondary data to determine price-volume relationships, one should keep the following recommendations in mind:

- Historical data should be prepared graphically and inspected visually; that step alone can lead to useful insights.
- The conditions which influenced the historical data must remain valid in the future. This assumption should be examined critically in the case of dynamic markets. Often there is—to use the econometric term—a structural break. That can render the results of an econometric analysis useless.
- With respect to price effects, one should test different hypotheses. Beyond price, one should consider as many other marketing instruments as possible.
- Economic plausibility is just as important as statistical accuracy.

Overview
In addition to establishing price-volume relationships, historical market data offers the possibility of gaining insights into the pricing behavior of competitors. Using market data, one can analyze the historical price actions and reactions of competitors in order to predict future behavior. Market data also help assessing competitors in terms of financial situation, strategy, future potential, and capacities.

Data from Online Auctions

With the advent of the Internet, new business models emerged online on the basis of *reverse pricing*. The purveyors included Priceline in the United States and companies such as ihrpreis.de in Germany. The price bids of the customers are binding and payment is generally made via credit card. As soon as a customer's bid is above the supplier's minimum price threshold (known only to the supplier), the customer receives the product and pays the amount he or she bid.

An example of such a price-response function is shown in Fig. 3.24. The product in question is a notebook. One sees that $250 is an important price threshold for this product. At prices below this level, the sales volume jumps. In comparison the price-response function is significantly flatter in the higher price ranges.

Figure 3.25 shows a second example of a price-response function derived from the Internet. This example involves the purchase of stock. Within a pre-defined price interval, the qualified buyer states the number of shares he or she would purchase at each price point. The offers are binding. One sees that the demand drops sharply in the range $170–$180. This form of price-response function is of the attraction type.

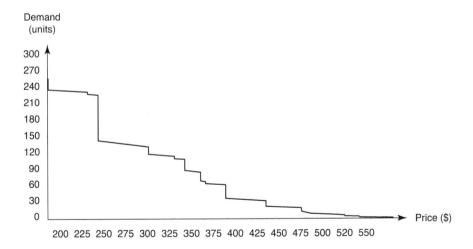

Fig. 3.24 Price-response function for a notebook (Simon-Kucher & Partners)

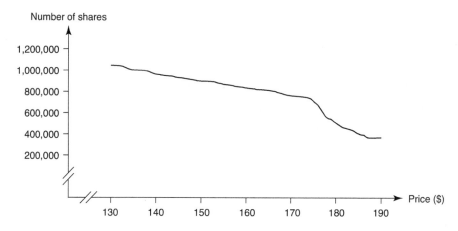

Fig. 3.25 Price-response function for a share of stock

On stock exchanges the demand curve is determined in a similar way. But in that case, the buyer names only his or her limit and not the desired amount at each different price. In aggregate, one sees a similar curve as the one shown in the figure.

Overview
Via the Internet one can determine true price-response functions with little effort. The data offer insights into the real willingness to pay of customers. In this manner, the Internet can contribute to the professionalization of price management.

3.4.3   Synopsis of Instruments

We have discussed numerous instruments for collecting relevant price information, which allows the calibration of price-response functions. Table 3.10 summarizes the strengths and weaknesses of these instruments. The analytical effort required should correspond to the relevance of the price decision to be made. The richness of the information collected is an important factor in choosing a method, but costs and time required also play a role.

3.4 Empirical Determination of the Price-Response Function 137

Table 3.10 Suitability of methods for determining price-response functions

Criterion	Method				
	Survey			Observation	
	Expert judgment	Direct customer survey	Indirect customer survey	Experiments	Market observations
Validity	Medium	Low/medium	High	Internal validity: high External validity: questionable	High
Reliability	Medium/high	Unclear	High	Medium/high	Low
Cost	Very low	Low/medium	Medium/high	High	Depends on availability and access
Methodological complexity	Low/medium	Low/medium	High	High	Medium
Usable for new products	Yes	For familiar products: good For true innovations: questionable	Questionable for true innovations	Yes	No
Usable for established products	Yes	Yes	Yes	Yes	Yes
Overall evaluation	Suitable	Limited suitability	Very suitable	Suitable	Limited suitability

Conclusion

In this chapter we looked at the role of economic analysis in price management. The quantification of price effects is an essential prerequisite for price optimization. We discussed what information is necessary in the context of price management and how to acquire that information. The goal of price management is to determine the optimal price. This requires the quantification of the price-response function and the price elasticity. We summarize this chapter:

- In order to understand the range of actions for pricing and to determine the optimal price, one must accurately analyze one's own enterprise, one's customers, and the competition.
- The pricing leeway is limited at the low end by marginal costs and at the upper end by value-to-customer as well as competitors' prices.
- Company information includes corporate goals and costs. Knowledge and a thorough understanding of the cost structure are essential for sound price decisions.
- Value-to-customer and willingness to pay are indispensable pieces of customer information for a price decision.
- The competition restricts a company's pricing leeway and influences the effects of one's own prices. Thus, the identification of the relevant competitors, the analysis of their prices, and the anticipation of their future price behavior are necessary.
- In order to make an optimal price decision, one must know the functional relationship between price and sales volume. The price-response function describes this relationship.
- The price elasticity is a measure of the influence of price on volume. It is the ratio of the percentage change in volume to the percentage change in the price which caused it. The price elasticity measures how strongly demand responds to a price change.
- To determine price-volume relationships, one has a toolbox of methods to choose from: expert judgment, direct and indirect customer surveys, experiments, and market observations. Each of these methods has advantages and disadvantages. In practice, expert judgment, indirect customer surveys, and the use of the Internet play important roles.
- Expert judgment is a simple and inexpensive method which is particularly suitable for new situations, such as the launch of a new product. It relies, however, on a company's internal knowledge.
- A powerful method for quantifying customer preferences and price effects is conjoint measurement. This method measures the total utility of a product and its constituent attributes from the customer's perspective. Customers

(continued)

are not asked directly about their price behavior. Instead, price effects are derived from statements on preferences.

- Conjoint measurement quantifies factors such as the value of brands, of technical features, or of services and expresses them in monetary units. This method is very versatile and provides the basis for determining a value-oriented price.
- Price experiments capture the effects of price on volume in real or simulated purchase situations. In addition to field and lab experiments, experimental auctions can be used to determine willingness to pay.
- Historical price and sales volume data can be employed to determine price-response functions. A prerequisite is that prices and sales volumes have sufficient variance. The data are only suitable for forward-looking price decisions when there have been no recent structural breaks in the market.
- The Internet offers new possibilities for collecting data for price management. True price-response functions can be determined online with little effort. One must be careful, though, in applying the findings to other purchase situations or channels.

This chapter has shown that a large number of determinants flow into price optimization. These factors reflect customers, competitors, and one's own business. They are consolidated into the price-response function, which allows the calculation of price elasticity. A price decision is only as good as the validity of the response measures on which it is based.

References

1. Marx, K. (1951). *Wages, Prices, and Profits* (p. 28). Moscow: Foreign Languages Publishing House.
2. Ramanujam, M. & Tacke, G. (2016). *Monetizing Innovation: How Smart Companies Design the Product Around the Price*. Hoboken, New Jersey: John Wiley & Sons.
3. Lockwood, T. (2009). *Design Thinking: Integrating Innovation, Customer Experience, and Brand Value*. New York: Allworth Press.
4. Freidank, C. C. (1994). Unterstützung des Target Costing durch die Prozesskostenrechnung. In K. Dellmann, & K. S. Franz (Eds.), *Neuere Entwicklungen im Kostenmanagement* (pp. 223–259). Bern: Paul Haupt.
5. Clifton, M. B., Townsend, W. P., Bird, H. M., & Albano, R. E. (2003). *Target Costing: Market Driven Product Design*. New York: CRC Press.
6. Herzberg, F. (1968). One more Time: How Do you Motivate Employees? *Harvard Business Review*, 46(1), 53–62.
7. Matzler, L., Hinterhuber, H. H., Bailom, F., & Sauerwein, E. (1996). How to Delight your Customers. *Journal of Product & Brand Management*, 5(2), 6–18.
8. Roland, D. (2017). The New Innovator's Dilemma: When Customers Won't Pay for Better. https://www.wsj.com/articles/when-new-and-improved-fails-insulin-maker-stumbles-when-customers-balk-1502809045. Accessed 14 February 2018.

9. Kotler, P., Armstrong, G., Wong, V., & Saunders, J. (2011). *Grundlagen des Marketing* (5. ed.). München: Pearson.
10. Fassnacht, M., & Köse, I. (2002). Marketingstrategien und Preisfindung für Unternehmensgründer. In H. Corsten (Ed.), *Dimensionen der Unternehmensgründung – Erfolgspotenziale der Selbstständigkeit* (pp. 159–199). Berlin: Erich Schmidt.
11. Gutenberg, E. (1984). *Der Absatz*. Grundlagen der Betriebswirtschaftslehre (Volume 2). Berlin: Springer.
12. Gossen, H. H. (1854). *Entwicklung der Gesetze des menschlichen Verkehrs und der daraus fließenden Regeln für menschliches Handeln*. Braunschweig: F. Vieweg.
13. Fog, B. (1960). *Industrial Pricing Policies*. Amsterdam: North Holland.
14. Kucher, E. (1985). *Scannerdaten und Preissensitivität bei Konsumgütern*. Wiesbaden: Gabler.
15. Gutenberg, E. (1965). *Zur Diskussion der polypolistischen Absatzkurve*. Jahrbücher für Nationalökonomie und Statistik (Volume 177, pp. 289–303).
16. Bijmolt, T., van Heerde, H. J., & Pieters, R. (2005). New Empirical Generalizations on the Determinants of Price Elasticity. *Journal of Marketing Research*, 42(2), 141–156.
17. Hanssens, D. (Ed.) (2015). *Empirical Generalizations about Marketing Impact*. Cambridge, MA: Marketing Science Institute.
18. Friedel, E. (2014). *Price Elasticity: Research on Magnitude and Determinants*. Frankfurt am Main: Peter Lang.
19. Anonymous. (2014). Auch ohne Maut: 19 Millionen Autofahrer zahlen drauf. http://www. focus.de/auto/ratgeber/kosten/adac-beitraege-2014-erhoeht-19-millionen-autofahrer-zahlen-bald-kraeftig-drauf-1_id_3518905.html. Accessed 04 June 2015.
20. Anonymous. (2015, 27 April). ADAC Gelber Engel, goldene Nase. *Wirtschaftswoche*, 18, p. 12.
21. Cohen, P., Hahn, R., Hall, J., Levitt, S. & Metcalfe, R. (2016). *Using Big Data to Estimate Consumer Surplus: The Case of Uber*, Working Paper: NBER.
22. Fong, N. M., Simester, D. I., & Anderson, E. T. (2010). *Private Label vs. National Brand Price Sensitivity: Evaluating Non-experimental Identification Strategies*. Working Paper: MIT.
23. Krishnamurthi, L., & Raj, S. P. (1991). An Empirical Analysis of the Relationship between Brand Loyalty and Consumer Price Elasticity. *Marketing Science*, 10(2), 172–183.
24. Olbrich, R., Battenfeld, D., & Grünblatt, M. (2005). Zum langfristigen Wirkungsverlauf von Preisaktionen. *Jahrbuch der Absatz- und Verbrauchsforschung*, 50(3), 266–287.
25. Koschate, N. (2002). *Kundenzufriedenheit und Preisverhalten: theoretische und empirisch experimentelle Analysen*. Wiesbaden: Gabler.
26. Gabor, A., Granger, C. W., & Sowter, A. S. (1971). Comments on "Psychophysics of Prices". *Journal of Marketing Research*, 8(2), 251–252.
27. Harrison, G. W., & Rutström, E. E. (2001). *Experimental Evidence of Hypothetical Bias in Value Elicitation Methods*. Columbia: The Darla Moore School of Business, University of South California. Working Paper B-00-05.
28. Stout, R. G. (1969). Developing Data to Estimate Price-Quantity Relationships. *Journal of Marketing*, 33(2), 34–36.
29. Völckner, F. (2006). Methoden zur Messung individueller Zahlungsbereitschaften: ein Überblick zum State of the Art. *Journal für Betriebswirtschaft*, 56(1), 33–60.
30. Hensel-Börner, S., & Sattler, H. (2000). Ein empirischer Validitätsvergleich zwischen der Customized Computerized Conjoint Analysis (CCC), der Adaptive Conjoint Analysis (ACA) und Self-Explicated-Verfahren. *Zeitschrift für Betriebswirtschaft*, 70(6), 705–727.
31. Hillig, T. (2006). *Verfahrensvarianten der Conjoint-Analyse zur Prognose von Kaufentscheidungen: Eine Monte-Carlo-Simulation*. Wiesbaden: Gabler.
32. Eggers, F., & Sattler, H. (2011). Preference Measurement with Conjoint Analysis. Overview of State-of-the-Art Approaches and Recent Developments. *GfK Marketing Intelligence Review*, 3 (1), 36–47.
33. DAT Group. (2014). Deutsche Automobil Treuhand Report 2014. http://www.dat.de/uploads/ DATReport_2014/pubData/source/804.pdf. Accessed 12 February 2015.

34. Backhaus, K., Erichson, B., Plinke, W., & Weber, R. (2011). *Multivariate Analysemethoden: Eine anwendungsorientierte Einführung* (13. ed.). Heidelberg: Springer.
35. Herrmann, A., Schmidt-Gallas, D., & Huber, F. (2001). Adaptive Conjoint Analysis: Understanding the Methodology and Assessing Reliability and Validity. In A. Gustafsson, A. Herrmann, & F. Huber (Eds.), *Conjoint Measurement: Methods and Applications* (2. ed., pp. 279–304). Berlin: Springer.
36. ACBC Technical Paper. (2014). *Sawtooth Software Technical Paper Series*.
37. Louvriere, J. J., & Woodworth, G. G. (1983). Design and Analysis of Simulated Choice or Allocation Experiments: An Approach Based on Aggregate Data. *Journal of Marketing Research*, 20(4), 350–367.
38. Hartmann, A., & Sattler, H. (2002). *Commercial Use of Conjoint Analysis in Germany, Austria and Switzerland*. Research Papers on Marketing and Retailing (6 ed.). Hamburg: University of Hamburg.
39. Huber, J. (1997). What We Have Learned from 20 Years of Conjoint Research: When to Use Self-Explicated, Graded Pairs, Full Profiles or Choice Experiments. *Sawtooth Software Research Paper Series*, 1–15.
40. DeSabro, W. S., Ramaswamy, V., & Cohen, S. H. (1995). Market Segmentation with Choice Based Conjoint Analysis. *Marketing Letters*, 6(2), 137–147.
41. Gensler, S. (2003). *Heterogenität in der Präferenzanalyse*. Wiesbaden: Springer.
42. Rossi, S. E., & Allenby, G. M. (2003). Bayesian Statistics and Marketing. *Marketing Science*, 22(3), 304–328.
43. Deal, K. (2002). Hierarchical Bayesian Applications Expand. *Marketing Research*, 14(2), 43–44.
44. Albers, S., Becker, J. U., Clement, M., Papies, D., & Schneider, H. (2007). Messung von Zahlungsbereitschaften und ihr Einsatz für die Preisbündelung. *Marketing – Zeitschrift für Forschung und Praxis*, 29(1), 7–22.
45. Weiber, R., & Rosendahl, T. (1997). Anwendungsprobleme der Conjoint-Analyse: Die Eignung conjointanalytischer Untersuchungsansätze zur Abbildung realer Entscheidungsprozesse. *Marketing – Zeitschrift für Forschung und Praxis*, 19(2), 107–118.
46. Srinivasan, V. (2006). Adaptive Self-Explication of Multi-Attribute Preferences. Monterey. Presented at the ART Forum, 12. June 2006.
47. Schlereth, C., & Schulz, F. (2014). Schnelle und einfache Messung von Bedeutungsgewichten mit der Restricted-Click-Stream Analyse: Ein Vergleich mit etablierten Präferenzmessmethoden. *Schmalenbachs Zeitschrift für betriebswirtschaftliche Forschung*, 66 (8), 630–657.
48. Jaeger, S. R., Hedderley, D., & MacFie, H. J. H. (2001). Methodological Issues in Conjoint Analysis: A Case Study. *European Journal of Marketing*, 35(11/12), 1217–1237.
49. Heidbrink, M. (2007). *Reliabilität und Validität von Verfahren der Präferenzmessung: Ein meta-analytischer Vergleich verschiedener Verfahren der Conjoint-Analyse*. Saarbrücken: VDM Verlag Dr. Müller.
50. Sattler, H., & Nitschke, T. (2003). Ein empirischer Vergleich von Instrumenten zur Erhebung von Zahlungsbereitschaften. *Schmalenbachs Zeitschrift für betriebswirtschaftliche Forschung*, 55(4), 364–381.
51. Müller, H. C. (2014, December 15). Digitalisierung der Betriebswirtschaft. *Handelsblatt*, 241, pp. 14–15.
52. Hoffmann, T., & Schölkopf, B. (2015, January 29). Vom Monopol auf Daten ist abzuraten. *Frankfurter Allgemeine Zeitung*, 24, p. 14.
53. Rueter, T. (2014). *The price is right – then it's not*. http://discover.360pi.com/acton/attachment/ 9666/f-01e2/1/-/-/-/-/IR_ThePriceIsRight_1408.pdf. Accessed 12 February 2015.
54. Müller, K.-M. (2012). *NeuroPricing*. Freiburg: Haufe-Lexware.
55. Skiera, B., & Spann, M. (2003). Auktionen. In H. Diller, & A. Herrmann (Eds.), *Handbuch Preispolitik: Strategien – Planung – Organisation – Umsetzung* (pp. 622–641). Wiesbaden: Gabler.

56. Bernau, P., & Budras, C. (2015). Google macht uns Angst, Herr Varian. *Vivanty*, pp. 84–89.
57. McAfee, R. P., & McMillan, J. (1987). Auctions and Bidding. *Journal of Economic Literature*, 25(2), 689–708.
58. Skiera, B., & Revenstorff, I. (1999). Auktionen als Instrument zur Erhebung von Zahlungsbereitschaften. *Schmalenbachs Zeitschrift für betriebswirtschaftliche Forschung*, 51 (3), 224–242.
59. Vickrey, W. (1961). Counterspeculation, Auctions and Competitive Sealed Tenders. *Journal of Finance*, 16(1), 8–37.
60. Wertenbroch, K., & Skiera, B. (2002). Measuring Consumers' Willingness to Pay at the Point of Purchase. *Journal of Marketing Research*, 39(2), 228–241.
61. Wolfstetter, E. (1996). Auctions: An Introduction. *Journal of Economic Surveys*, 10(4), 367–420.
62. Kim, J.-Y., Brünner, T., Skiera, B., & Natter, M. (2014). A Comparison of Different Pay-Per-Bid Auction Formats. *International Journal of Research in Marketing*, 31(4), 368–379.
63. Becker, G., DeGroot, M., & Marschak, J. (1964). Measuring Utility by a Single-Response Sequential Method. *Behavorial Science*, 8(9), 226–232.
64. Schreier, M., & Werfer, J. (2007). Auktionen versus Lotterien: Ein empirischer Vergleich zur Messung von Zahlungsbereitschaften. *Die Betriebswirtschaft*, 67(1), 22–40.
65. Telser, L. G. (1967). The Demand for Branded Goods as Estimated From Consumer Panel Data. *The Review of Economic Statistics*, 44(3), 300–324.

Analysis: The Psychology of Price

4

Abstract

The psychology of price is supplementary to the perspectives of classical economics and thus contributes to a more comprehensive understanding of the effects of price. Economics and marketing are not solely based on the rational assumptions of *homo oeconomicus*, which form the basis of classical theory. Price management and its processes should not be seen exclusively from the economic point of view. Perspectives from behavioral sciences should support them as well. This chapter provides an overview of price psychology and illustrates the variety of themes within the new research field "behavioral pricing."

4.1 Introduction

In Chap. 3 we dealt with the economics of price. Price serves as the independent (causal) variable, while sales volume serves as the dependent variable. The objective in the last chapter was to grasp the quantitative relationships between these variables. From a theoretical perspective, our basis for exploring this relationship was the so-called stimulus-response model (S-R Model). Quantitative classical economics does not concern itself deeply with the "why" in price response, i.e., what goes on between the stimulus ("price") and the response ("sales volume"). In other words, we were not trying to explain what is going on within the "organism" of the buyer. That is why we also refer to the S-R Model as a black box. Another important tenet of economic analysis is its assumption that the customer acts in a well-informed and mostly rational manner. The customer knows a product's price and is able to assess the product's value. The price-response function, therefore, has a negative slope except under rare circumstances.

The reality of price management, however, is more complex and fraught with uncertainty. In the so-called black box between the stimulus "price" and the response "sales volume" lies a critical and complex aspect: the behavior of the customer. This includes perceptions, emotions, risk tolerance, judgments, and post-purchase experiences. The *stimulus-organism-response model (S-O-R Model)* incorporates these intervening variables.

Every consumer knows that he or she does not always behave as the rational *homo oeconomicus*. It is therefore no surprise that the S-R model offers an incomplete picture of a customer's real price behavior. The perception of price depends on the context and the situation. Price knowledge and price recall influence the effect of prices. Likewise, trust in the supplier also drives a customer's behavior. These aspects lead to many questions and consequences for price management:

- How should one communicate prices?
- What are price anchors and what significance do they have?
- Should a supplier offer discounts and make special offers?
- How should one represent one's price relative to the competition's prices?
- Should a supplier use a one-dimensional or a multidimensional price structure?
- How does one configure a time-based price structure (e.g., 1 payment per year or 12 monthly payments)?
- What is the effect of adding product alternatives or price alternatives?
- How should one view flat rate prices?

The phenomena behind these questions in no way eliminate or suppress the importance of the price-response function. It will always exist. The function shows how many units of a product will be sold at a certain price. But in many cases, the sales volume does not only depend on the price itself, namely, the "objective price." It will also depend on how the customer perceives the price, what role the price plays for the customer (e.g., as an indicator of prestige or quality), and how and in what context the price is communicated. Price design and price communication can exert a strong influence on the price-response function. S-O-R models explain why a customer responds to a price in a particular way.

In this chapter we will explore two research traditions and their findings in depth. One is the older field of *price psychology*, and the other is the newer research field *behavioral economics* or *behavioral pricing*. Daniel Kahneman and Amos Tversky [1] founded behavioral economics when they published their "prospect theory" in 1979. Kahneman received the Nobel Prize in 2002, in part for this work. This branch of research, which strangely enough was not founded by economists, has already changed economic theory considerably. We expect it will continue to do so. For a more in-depth treatment of the core theories, we recommend Kahneman's [2] bestseller *Thinking, Fast and Slow*. The number of authors and publications on behavioral economics is exploding. In 2017, Richard Thaler, who also works in this field, received a Nobel Prize. Price plays a central role in this context, with surprising and often counterintuitive findings. It is not unusual to discover patterns of behavior which one could call "irrational" [3, 4]. Whether these behaviors are truly irrational or merely reflect the efforts of customers to simplify their decision-making, however, remains open to debate. Beyond these new insights, there are other psychological effects of price which have been known for a long time and which contradict the fundamental economic principle that "higher prices lead to lower volumes." We will explore these effects next, before we introduce the newer findings on behavioral pricing. The two areas have some overlap.

4.2 Traditional Psychology of Price

4.2.1 Prestige Effects of Price

Researchers have studied psychological price effects for over a century. The prestige effect emerged at the outset of that work. Back in 1899, Thorstein Veblen published his highly regarded book *The Theory of the Leisure Class* [5]. What one may generally refer to as the "snob effect" is also known as the Veblen effect. When this effect occurs, it leads to higher demand for a product even when prices increase, because consumers want to use that product to establish or reinforce a higher social status relative to others. Veblen [5, p. 36] expressed this as follows: "In order to gain and to hold the esteem of men, it is not sufficient merely to possess wealth or power. The wealth or power must be put in evidence, for esteem is awarded only on evidence." In line with the classification of needs we discussed in Chap. 2, this effect derives from a product's symbolic performance features. For "Veblen" goods, the primary effect of a higher price is not diminution of the net value, as classical theory would teach us to believe, but rather higher value due to the higher price. The higher price sends the signal that the consumer can afford more expensive products and therefore occupies a higher social rank than people who can only afford to buy less expensive products [6].

Such Veblen effects are in fact observed in practice. Delvaux, a Belgian manufacturer of exclusive handbags, put through a massive price increase in conjunction with a repositioning of its brand. As a result, its sales volume grew sharply. Consumers now viewed Delvaux as a relevant alternative to Louis Vuitton bags. When the sales volume of the famous whiskey brand Chivas Regal stagnated, its manufacturer opted for a repositioning. They developed a more modern, appealing label and raised the price by 20%. The product itself remained unchanged, but sales volume increased significantly [7]. The price of a backstitched Chanel bag has risen by 70% over the last 5 years, and the classic Louis Vuitton bag "Speedy" is now 32% more expensive than it was 7 years ago. Other luxury goods manufacturers have made similar increases in the last few years. Mulberry and Prada, however, have appeared to reach a point at which additional price increases will no longer have a positive effect on sales volumes. The revenue growth rates of these firms have declined. Chanel, in contrast, has not suffered this consequence despite its enormous price increases [8].

As these examples show, prestige effects can be very powerful for luxury goods. The price-response function has a positive slope, at least on some portions of the curve. Luxury goods suppliers need to know their price-response functions. Otherwise they are poking around in the dark. If one is uncertain, it makes sense to ease one's way gradually into the higher price range [9]. It is often wise, as in the case of Chivas Regal and Delvaux, to combine an upward price repositioning with a new design or improvements to packaging.

4.2.2 Giffen Paradox

Is it possible that sales volumes rise when the price goes up, even amid "normal" economic behavior? This apparent contradiction to the principles of economics does indeed exist. One speaks of a Giffen Paradox, named after the Scottish statistician Robert Giffen (1837–1910) [10]. This paradox applies when certain limitations on purchasing power or budgets take hold. Let us assume that a consumer on a limited budget eats only bread and meat. Now assume that the prices for both foods increase. The consumer may now need to eat more bread in order to meet his or her calorie requirements, because meat is no longer affordable, at least not in large quantities. The consumer, in other words, eats more bread even though the price has increased. There is, however, little empirical proof of the existence of the Giffen Paradox. Even Alfred Marshal, the person who made the Giffen Paradox known, said that "such cases are rare" [11, p. 132]. One of those rare empirical cases occurred in China. When the price of rice rose by 1%, consumption of rice rose by 0.24%. The price elasticity was positive and had a value of 0.24 [12]. Nonetheless, the Giffen Paradox has little relevance for pricing practices in highly developed countries.

At this point we feel obligated to issue a word of caution. Not all data which appear to link higher prices and higher sales volume mean that the price elasticity is truly positive. An example is the market for firewood. In 2005, a cubic meter of firewood cost $16. By 2012, the price had doubled to $32. Over the same period, consumption almost doubled as well. In a large forest range, sales volume was 10,000 m^3 in 2005 and 18,000 m^3 in 2012 [13, p. 13]. Is this a Giffen Paradox? In our opinion, it is not. We argue that the demand curve for firewood shifted upward between 2005 and 2012 and led to the sharp price increase. One must be careful not to confuse correlation with causation when interpreting price and volume data. One could interpret the price-volume change for firewood incorrectly and draw a price-response function with a positive slope. That would have resulted in a positive price elasticity of 0.8 (=80% volume increase ÷ 100% price increase). This (mis)inter-pretation may prompt one to raise prices further, in order to drive an additional volume increase. Most likely that would be a mistake.

4.2.3 The Price as a Quality Indicator

Within the models of the classical economics of price, one assumes that customers have complete information. They can assess the quality of a product independent of its price. The price then goes into the utility function as a negative. From the perspective of the purchase decision, its only effect is to reduce one's available budget. Thus, the price-response function has a negative slope. But this assumption of a quality assessment, independent of price, may collide with reality.

Price can serve as a quality indicator inducing a positive slope for parts of the price-response function. This phenomenon has been empirically proven on many occasions. Price has served as a quality indicator for products as diverse as furniture, carpets, shampoo, toothpaste, coffee, jams and jellies, and radios. Similar effects have been observed in the service sector (e.g., restaurants and hotels) [14–17]. Increases in sales volume in the wake of price increases have been reported for nasal sprays, nylon stockings, ink, and electrical goods. The sales volume for one electric razor increased by a factor of four after a significant price increase brought the razor closer to price parity with the market and quality leader Braun. The price gap to Braun was still large enough to serve as an incentive to buy, but not too large so that most customers would doubt the quality of the razor.

Price's ability to act as a quality indicator is by no means limited to consumer goods. It also applies to B2B. A software firm introduced a corporate cloud software package at an extremely low price of $19.90 per desk per month. Comparable competing products sold at more than $100 per month. After several months, the company's CEO realized that "small businesses are really excited about our prices. For the first time, they can afford this kind of software. But larger companies think our price point is so low that they have no faith in our product. Our extremely low price becomes a barrier to sales rather than an advantage." The solution lay in product and price differentiation. The company loaded up its product with additional features and then offered this new package to larger companies at a significantly higher monthly fee. The package was still rather inexpensive, but it now fits better into a more conventional price-value framework. This adaptation helped the firm rid itself of the negative image fostered by the initial low price.

The belief in a positive price-quality relationship may lead customers to feel that less expensive products actually "function" worse compared to more expensive ones. This perception can hold true even when there are in fact no physical differences in the products. In a test, people who consumed an energy drink which supposedly enhanced mental performance did significantly better at solving puzzles when the drink had a higher price. In another experiment, test patients who took a pain relief medication rated its efficacy to be significantly better when the medication had a higher price [18]. In medicine, such placebo effects are well known.

Price assumes the role of quality indicator whenever customers are not able to assess the quality of a product adequately. This happens when the customers lack the time or the ability or when a thorough assessment is too expensive. So they simplify their decision-making and use price as a proxy for quality. In reality, a customer often has no choice but to make a purchase decision on the basis of incomplete information. Customers try to reduce their perceived risks and the resulting cognitive dissonance by using other criteria or indicators to assess the quality. They fall back on indicators which are readily visible or accessible and which presumably correlate well with "objective" quality. In addition to price, customers may use indicators such as the country of origin (e.g., "Made in . . ."), brand name, manufacturer, retailer, or the sales person to determine quality. Price in particular has been frequently found to be a quality indicator [14, 17, 19]. Customers often presume strong links between price and quality and associate higher quality with more expensive products.

These heuristics, such as price-based quality judgments, can be rational from an economic perspective. The search for objective quality information has direct costs (e.g., test reports, Internet searches) as well as opportunity costs (e.g., lost time). The total cost for purchasing a product is the sum of the actual price and these search costs. When a customer assumes a positive correlation between price and quality and thus saves search costs, it can be a "cheaper" solution to buy a more expensive product. It is possible that the Internet has already changed this situation and will continue to do so. Easier access to information plays a role, but the availability of reviews from actual customers may be even more decisive [20–22]. They can serve as partial or complete substitutes for traditional quality indicators such as brand and price.

Why do customers use price as a quality indicator? There are several plausible reasons:

- Experience shows that high prices, in all likelihood, are a better guarantee of good quality than low prices. Such experiences manifest themselves in sayings such as "quality has its price," "you can't get something for nothing," or "you get what you pay for."
- The price is often one-dimensional and known at the time of purchase. Price allows a potential buyer to make immediate objective comparisons among products. For consumer goods, the price is often fixed and thus non-negotiable. Price plays less of a role as a quality indicator when prices are negotiable (e.g., for industrial goods or at an Oriental bazaar).
- Price is a signal of high credibility which the seller transmits (in contrast, say, to verbal claims in advertisements). For many customers, there is a close relationship between price and input costs. In other words, the cost-plus pricing approach predominates in the minds of customers as well, not just sellers.

Price-based quality judgments are most relevant for products with the following characteristics:

- Brands and manufacturer names do not play a major role.
- First-hand experience is either lacking or impossible to obtain, either because the product is new or is rarely purchased. For new products, price is an effective quality indicator only when it fits into frames of reference familiar to the customer. It does not apply to true innovations, whose value and perhaps prices often lie outside the buyer's familiar frames of reference.
- The customer's last purchase or usage was in the distant past.
- Customers normally do not share their experiences with each other about that particular product.
- The objective quality is hard to estimate either because of the technical complexity or because of the key importance of features such as durability and reliability. This is especially true for experience goods or credence goods.

- The customer perceives significant quality differences across products.
- The absolute price is not too high. Products which are expensive in absolute terms make the search for objective quality information more worthwhile and make it riskier to rely on price as a quality indicator. The greater the stakes, the less important a proxy indicator such as price becomes.

Furthermore, we can assume that the price becomes more powerful as a quality indicator as:

- Time pressure increases.
- Purchasing complexity increases.
- Price transparency decreases.
- Trust in whoever "offers" the price information increases.

Likewise, personal, customer-specific factors play an important role. Price's significance as a quality indication is greater:

- The lower a customer's self-confidence is
- The less frugal the customer is
- The greater the desire for a quick and easy purchase is
- The greater the desire to avoid cognitive dissonance is
- The greater the buyer's purchasing power is
- The less knowledgeable the buyer is about the product

The existence of price-based quality judgments has numerous implications for price management. They include price range, market segmentation, market entry strategy, and price communication.

4.2.4 Special Cases

Beyond the prestige effect, the Giffen Paradox, and quality indications, there are other special cases in which one may observe a positive relationship between price and sales volume. However, one should always be careful when interpreting such situations, as the firewood example showed. It is possible that one is not observing a price-response curve with a positive slope after all. Instead, one is observing a shift in the price-response curve which resulted from changes in the underlying demand or supply. An interesting case here is the BahnCard in Germany. For a renewable annual fee, this card entitles its owner to discounts on tickets for Germany's passenger rail system, owned by the German Railroad Corporation (Deutsche Bahn). A BahnCard50 gives the cardholder a 50% discount on all tickets. A BahnCard100 means that the cardholder receives a discount of 100% on a passenger train ticket. (Yes, they can ride anywhere, anytime, for free.)

The idea of a ticket which someone buys only once per year is not new. The Deutsche Bahn offered a personalized annual "network pass" for years, but few people were aware of it, and fewer than a thousand people per year actually bought one. Simon-Kucher suggested that the Deutsche Bahn incorporate this pass into the existing BahnCard system as the BahnCard100. This move caused sales to multiply, despite a price increase. Today the price of a BahnCard100 is €4270 in second class and €7225 in first class, significantly more than before. The number of BahnCard100 cardholders has risen to over 47,000.

When prestige, quality indication, or other similar price effects exist in a market, they have a significant impact on price positioning, tactical choices, and price communication. The optimal price never lies in the part of the price-response function with a positive slope, but always at a higher price. These circumstances also defuse price's ability to act as a competitive weapon; price cuts and special offers are neither advisable nor effective. If a seller wants to increase its market share through aggressive low prices in a market where prestige or similar effects matter, the action is doomed to fail. In the worst case, sales volume and market share may actually drop despite the lower prices. These effects also make market entry via aggressive pricing, or the so-called penetration pricing, more difficult. Attempts to win over customers with lower prices will not work. These two effects explain why discounts on no-name products or weak brands are often ineffective. Customers associate the reduced price with lower quality or low prestige. This happened to the Volkswagen Phaeton, which was a good automobile in terms of quality. But the Phaeton did not sell well in Germany, because it lacked sufficient prestige. The Volkswagen brand, while very strong in the medium segment, does not have the power to hold its own in the luxury or premium segments. As a result, even low prices compared to other luxury cars and favorable leasing rates did not have a noticeable effect on sales volume for the Phaeton. Weak brands hardly respond to price cuts.

What should sellers do when they are unable to use price as a competitive weapon? The best method may be to position the product in a price range which corresponds to the true quality the product delivers. This approach requires patience, as customers need to objectively understand and appreciate the product's quality and its price-value relationship.

4.3   Behavioral Pricing

Behavioral pricing can be viewed as a subcategory of behavioral economics. Almost all the insights of behavioral economics research come from experiments in which price generally plays a secondary role, not a primary one. In one of the standard works on the topic, *Thinking, Fast and Slow*, author and Nobel Prize winner Daniel Kahneman [2] uses the term "pricing" only twice. The word "price" does not appear at all in the index. Nonetheless, the findings from this field of research have enormous importance for price management. Enrico Trevisan [4] demonstrated this by applying behavioral economics insights to pricing in his book *The Irrational Consumer*. The word "price" is the most common keyword in the book, appearing over 60 times. The term "pricing" also appears around 20 times.

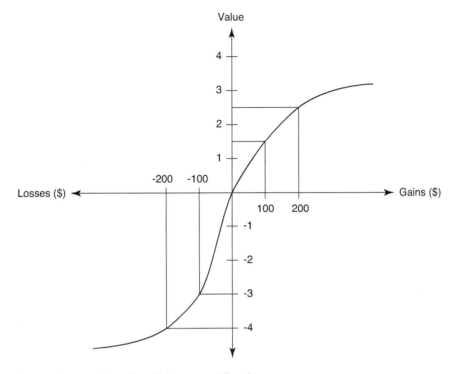

Fig. 4.1 Prospect theory from Kahneman and Tversky

4.3.1 Theoretical Basis

Behavioral pricing builds on theoretical models which we present briefly. Many price phenomena for which classical economics has no explanation can be understood and categorized with the help of these models.

4.3.1.1 Prospect Theory

The law of diminishing marginal utility was formulated in 1854 by Hermann Heinrich Gossen [23] and is one of the most widely known laws of economics. It says that the marginal utility of a product decreases with every unit a customer consumes. Gossen made no explicit distinction between gains and losses. The psychologists Kahneman and Tversky [1] modified Gossen's idea with their so-called prospect theory. They differentiate between the marginal values of gains and losses. The basic concept of prospect theory is shown in Fig. 4.1.

The positive branch of the value function in the upper right quadrant corresponds to Gossen's law. The perceived value of a gain is continuously increasing, but the difference in value of each additional unit gets smaller. The value of the first $100 gain is greater than the value from an additional gain of $100. The curve for losses is in the lower left quadrant. Perhaps the term "marginal harm" would be more appropriate than marginal value of losses. The marginal harm increases as the extent of the loss or harm increases. This is no surprise. It is what we would expect based on Gossen's law. The real breakthrough message from prospect theory is this: for any absolute gain or loss of identical size, the difference in value from the loss is greater than the corresponding positive value from the gain. That leads to surprising yet very realistic consequences. One is that it is not the absolute net value which matters. What matters are the gains and losses which make up that net value and their order.

The following real-life case illustrates this effect. Think about a lottery drawing which includes six numbers. Millions watch the lottery drawing live on television. The positive value increases immediately and dramatically for those who had five or six of the lottery numbers correct. Shortly thereafter, the lottery commission announced that it has nullified that evening's drawing because two balls failed to roll into the drum. This news certainly results in a very large negative value for the presumptive winners that evening, because they had just had a huge gain "taken away."[1] From the standpoint of classical economics, however, nothing has changed for these "winners." They did not have an extra $1 million before the drawing, and they do not have an extra $1 million after the drawing. But in reality, the net value for the "winners" will be negative—and presumably large. It probably takes days, if not weeks, for such people to overcome their disappointment from that experience.

Prospect theory has vast potential for pricing. Paying a price creates a negative value. One perceives the amount that one pays as a loss. The purchase and use of the product, in contrast, generate positive value. The asymmetry of positive and negative values results in some strange effects. One is known as the endowment effect, which an experiment conducted by Kahneman [24] illustrates. A number of students were divided into two groups. Students in one group received mugs bearing their university's logo. They were worth about $6 each. The students in the other group received nothing, but they could buy the mugs from the students in the first group. The average asking price for the mugs was $7.12. The students who could buy the mugs offered on average only $2.87, a highly significant difference. Because the students were split randomly into two groups, we should assume that each group would derive the same value from the mug and have the same price expectations. Classical economics cannot explain the large discrepancy between the two prices. But prospect theory can. The negative value of giving up something we already own is significantly greater than the positive value we get from a good that we first need to buy. We are all reluctant to part with what we have either purchased or received as a gift.

Prospect theory may also help explain price structures which would seem absurd at first glance. An established tactic for automotive sales in the United States is the so-called cash-back. One purchases a car for $30,000 and receives $2000 in cash-back. How does that make any sense? Prospect theory provides an answer. The payment of $30,000 generates a significant negative value, balanced out by the positive value of acquiring the new car. On top of that comes an additional positive

---

[1]This actually happened in the German national "Lotto" on April 3, 2013.

value in the form of $2000 in cash. Apparently this price structure leaves some car buyers with a perceived net value that is higher than if they had just paid $28,000 for the car straight up and received no cash-back. If the dealership accepts payment via check, transfer, or credit card, the positive value may even be greater than paying in cash, because those other forms of payment generate less negative value. The "cash-back," in contrast, comes in the form of physical money.

As in the case of cash-back, customers can integrate elements of the price and arrive at a holistic impression. Or they can segregate the price elements, make discrete judgments on each component, and then combine these to arrive at an overall assessment. If we work under the assumption that customers strive to maximize their value, then customers will try subconsciously to minimize perceived losses and maximize their gains.

The value function in the loss or negative area leads to the conclusion that multiple losses will feel less unpleasant when one sums them up into one loss, in line with the idea of diminishing negative marginal value. Multiple negative price effects, each subject to a separate judgment by the customer, will have in aggregate a greater negative value than one single negative judgment of the same magnitude. Bauer and Wübker [25] use bank account fees to illustrate this. Customers are more likely to accept an integrated fee of $36 per year than a fee of $3 per month, even though the total annual expenditure is identical. Salesforce, an international supplier of cloud computing solutions, takes advantage of this principle. The company publishes its prices on a per-month basis, but customers must commit to pay 1 year in advance with a notice period of likewise 1 year. Schulz et al. [26] studied the effects of prospect theory and mental accounting when someone pays monthly, which is common, say, for electricity bills. Under this billing method, consumers must either settle a balance at the end of the billing year or receive a rebate, based on the difference between their prepaid amount and actual monthly usage. The researchers found that receiving a refund lowers a customer's price awareness and increased the likelihood he or she will recommend the company. The likelihood that this customer will switch suppliers declines. This holds true as long as the rebate is not too high. It is advisable for companies who use this method to set their monthly rates high enough to reduce the chances that the customer will need to make a year-end payment or, conversely, increase the chances that the customer receives a refund.

One should avoid making snap generalizations of these insights. Should a fitness studio charge an annual fee or ask customers to pay in 12 monthly installments? Gourville and Soman [27] investigated this question. Using prospect theory, one would lean toward selecting the annual payment, because it only "hurts" the customer once and this minimizes the negative value. The fitness studio would also seem to prefer the onetime payment, because it receives more capital sooner and incurs lower transaction costs. But in the case of fitness studios, there is another effect in play. After making their payments, the customers want to "earn back" their money and visit the fitness studio on a more regular basis. The frequency of visits declines, however, the more distant the time of payment lies in the past. The monthly payment creates a fresh incentive each month for the customers to "earn back" their money. The usage intensity remains higher, and—more importantly—the renewal rate at year's end is significantly higher. In this case, one would thus recommend a system of monthly payments, in contradiction to prospect theory.

The evaluation of multiple gains is the opposite of how one evaluates multiple losses. Several discrete gains, taken together, will be perceived as better than one single gain of the same magnitude. The customers see higher total value from separate, discrete gains. As a result, segregation of the individual gains leads to higher value than integration. Several discounts across different goods will be viewed by the customer as better than one discount off the entire bundle, even when the total discounts in these scenarios are identical. Receiving 12 monthly bonuses of $100 each generates higher value than a onetime annual bonus payment of $1200.

4.3.1.2 Mental Accounting

Richard Thaler [28], the winner of the 2017 Nobel Prize in economics, introduced the theory of *mental accounting* which represents a broadening of prospect theory. According to this concept, the customer books "gains" and "losses" to separate mental accounts [29]. Each account has its own value curve for gains and losses. The accounts are defined by different categories, e.g., food, vacation, hobbies, car, or gifts. Such a categorization helps consumers plan their spending and maintain an overview of their budgets (e.g., "I will spend a maximum of $x on vacation"). Spending behavior and price sensitivity can vary from account to account [30–32].

A seller should know which account a consumer ascribes a particular product to and what the price sensitivity is in that category. Enormous differences exist here. One study looked at how consumers in different countries feel about the food and grocery category. According to a survey by GfK, price is the only criterion for half of all Germans when they do grocery shopping. Food accounts for 10% of Germans' household spending, compared to 15% in Italy and Spain and 13.4% in France. Americans, in contrast, spend just 6.9% of their household budget on food [33]. The mental account for cars and auto accessories paints a different picture. Germans spend considerably more for motor oil than they do for edible oils. The mental account labeled "car" appears to be very special for Germans. When buying a car, some customers will spend more than $2000 extra for a "comfort" seat for the driver. Yet they would spend "only" $800 for a new office chair. This difference supports the theory that people allocate products to different mental accounts, even when the products share some similarities.

A famous experiment reveals the unusual effects of mental accounting. Assume that a theater ticket costs $10. In the experiment there are two groups. One group is informed that they are standing in front of the theater and realize that they have lost their tickets. The other group is told that they still need to buy a ticket at the box office, but they had lost a $10 bill shortly before arriving at the theater. How many of the test subjects still decide to go the show, and why? In the first group, 54% decided to buy another ticket to replace the one they lost. In the second group, however, 88% decided to buy a ticket after losing $10 moments earlier. The ones who lost their tickets booked both the price for the lost ticket and the price of the replacement ticket to the account "going to the theater." The total "mental" price charged to that bucket rose to $20. That was too expensive for 46% of the test subjects. The ones who lost the $10 bill booked the loss to their "cash" account. Their total "mental" price for going to the theater remained at $10, and 88% of them chose to attend the show. Gains and losses are booked to different accounts. Loss aversion is particularly pronounced. One consequence of such aversion is that people usually realize losses from stock purchases too late [34].

A seller can attempt to influence the choice of account in order to get the customer to "book" the product in question in a more favorable category. If one lands in an account where only low prices matter (such as food and grocery in Germany), it will be difficult to charge or maintain high prices. In a study for Huf, the European market leader for upscale, modern timber-frame homes, we learned that prefabricated houses have an extremely inexpensive image in France. Consumers there place such houses in a low-price category with correspondingly high price sensitivity. Houses from Huf do not fit that category. Huf is not able and does not want to compete on price in that segment. We recommended that Huf positions itself as far away as possible from prefab houses and establish Huf houses as a stand-alone category. That is the equivalent of opening a new mental account. If a company succeeds in doing that, it opens up an entirely different set of pricing opportunities than would exist if one were stuck in an existing, price-sensitive account.

Overview
We summarize key points on prospect theory and mental accounting:

- The value functions for gains and losses are asymmetric, according to prospect theory. When a loss and gain are of equal magnitude, the negative value from the loss is larger than the positive value from the gain.
- It is important to know whether multiple gains or losses are integrated or judged separately.
- Paying prices below a reference price is viewed as a gain under prospect theory; paying prices in excess of a reference price is perceived as a loss.
- The mental accounting theory states that consumers allocate gains and losses to different mental accounts.

4.3.1.3 Other Theories
There is a range of other psychological theories which are relevant for price management, but they are less important than prospect theory. Therefore, we only describe them briefly:

The *Weber law*—as well as the *Weber-Fechner law*—belongs to the classical laws of psychophysics, a subdiscipline of experimental perceptual psychology. The central tenet of the Weber law is that the perception of differences between two stimuli depends on the initial stimulus. The greater the intensity of the initial stimulus, the larger the change or difference in stimuli must be in order to be perceived. An application to price would appear as follows: if a price cut on an $8 bottle of wine must be at least $2 for the customer to notice (perceive) it, then the price cut on a $12 bottle of wine must be at least $3 to effect the same perception of a price difference. In percent, the magnitude of the change in the second stimulus must correspond with the magnitude of the change of the first stimulus.

The Weber-Fechner law, in contrast, assumes a logarithmic transformation of the objective intensity of the stimulus into the strength of the subjective sensation. There are upper and lower bounds for sensitivity. Applied to price, this means that how one feels about a price difference still depends on the first or starting price. But for an identical price difference, the subjective perception grows underproportionally as the absolute price level increases. Thus, the higher the price is, the greater a discount or price cut a company must make to attract the customers' attention. In an experiment, respondents were ready to travel a longer distance when a store offered a $5 discount on a product whose normal price was $15. If the normal price was $120 and the discount was still $5, customers were no longer willing to travel a longer distance. This finding hints at irrationality, because the savings in each case is $5. The Weber-Fechner law offers a potential explanation [31]. Price changes and price differences are categorized in relative terms, not absolute ones.

The *Adaptation-Level Theory* from Helson [35] states that people form sensory judgments by comparing a perceived stimulus against an adaptation level based on previous experience. The price one perceives at a given moment is compared against an internal reference price, called an adaptation level. In other words, people compare current prices to how they have perceived prices in the past for the same product.

In contrast to the Adaptation-Level Theory, which is based on a reference point, the Range Theory uses a reference range for orientation. According to the *Range Theory* from Volkmann [36], individuals use their price recollections to form an upper and lower bound for their price expectations. The relative position within this price range determines how the current price is seen. Thus, a customer may decide not to make a purchase when a price is too low or a discount too high. An example of this is the US news magazine *Time*, which offered "preferred subscribers" a discount of 90%. The newsstand price for 52 issues was $305.49. The publisher offered subscribers a discount of $275.49, which resulted in a price of $30. Such a low price may cast doubt on the credibility of the entire price structure.

Assimilation-Contrast Theory makes assumptions similar to the Adaptation-Level Theory, in that individuals compare new stimuli with what they have encountered in the past [37]. A stimulus will be judged differently based on past experience. According to the Assimilation-Contrast Theory, new price stimuli which resemble a reference price drawn from past experience will be viewed as more similar than they truly are (assimilation effect), whereas new price stimuli which differ sharply from recollected reference prices will be perceived as larger outliers than they objectively are (contrast effect).

The consequences of these theories partially overlap with findings from behavioral pricing experiments. One example is the price anchor effect.

4.3.2 Behavioral Pricing Effects

Behavioral pricing includes a range of effects which appear at first glance to be irrational but which warrant consideration in price management.

4.3.2.1 Price Threshold Effect

A price threshold is a price point which triggers a pronounced change in sales volume whenever it is crossed. In general, these price thresholds are just below round numbers such as 5, 10, or 100. The most important reason commonly cited for these effects is that customers read the digits in a price from left to right and perceive them with decreasing intensity [38]. The first digit, therefore, has the greatest influence on the price perception. A price of 9.95 is perceived as "nine plus something." According to this hypothesis, customers underestimate prices which lie under round numbers. Implicit in this conclusion is the idea that customers will overestimate prices which lie just above round numbers [39].

The fact—or, rather, the belief—that such price threshold effects exist makes the use of these odd prices extraordinarily popular in practice. This practice is particularly common in retail [40, 41, p. 59, 42, p. 135]. Kucher [43, p. 35] looked at the frequency distribution for the end digit of 18,096 prices of consumer goods. None of the prices in the sample ended in zero. The end digit of nine accounted for 43.5% of all prices. Later studies have tended to confirm these findings. Levy et al. [44], whose study encompassed over 18,000 food and grocery products, reported that 69% of prices ended in nine. Thomas and Morwitz [45] have also found that prices which lie just below a round number (e.g.. $2.99) are perceived as being significantly less expensive than the round price (e.g., $3.00). Even though consumers may realize that the price difference is completely negligible, they still subconsciously fall under its influence.

When a price threshold effect exists, the price-response function shows a kink at the price threshold. Figure 4.2 illustrates this for a numerical example with a price threshold of $10. Left of the threshold, the price-response function is defined as $q = 150 - 10p$ with q as the sales volume and p as the price. Right of the threshold, the function is $q = 120 - 8p$. The function has a break at $p = 10$ after which the sales volume drops suddenly from 50 to 40 units.

Because consumers are used to odd prices, they often show increased price sensitivity when a price exceeds the price threshold. The comparison of price increases for two brands of sparkling wine, Mumm and Fürst Metternich, indicates the existence of a price threshold effect for the Mumm brand, as Table 4.1 shows [46–48].

In both cases, the price increase in percentage terms was similar (10% for Mumm and 9.7% for Fürst Metternich). The price increase for Mumm took the price across the threshold of €5. The sales volume decline was significantly larger than the decline from the price increase for Fürst Metternich. The price elasticity for Mumm was −3.64. The price elasticity for Fürst Metternich, whose price increase did not exceed a threshold, was significantly lower at −0.62.

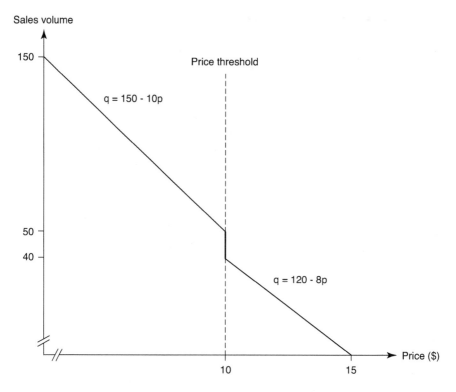

Fig. 4.2 Price-response function with price threshold effect

Table 4.1 Price increases and their effects for two brands of sparkling wine

	Mumm		Fürst Metternich	
	Before	After	Before	After
Price (€)	4.99	5.49	7.75	8.50
Volume (Index)	100	63.7	100	94
Price elasticity	−3.64		−0.62	

   Despite more and more reported cases, there is neither convincing scientific proof nor anything generally valid which proves the price threshold effect. Ginzberg [49] had already investigated the phenomenon back in 1936. Dean [50, p. 490] reported in 1951 on an experiment conducted by a mail-order company, which systematically varied prices around a price threshold: "The results are shockingly variable [...] sometimes moving a price from \$2.98 to \$3.00 greatly increased sales, and sometimes it lowered them. There was no clear evidence of concentration of sales response at any figure." Kucher was also unable to establish any systematic effect from exceeding a price threshold [43, p. 40]. These ambiguous findings favor a hypothesis put forward by Gabor and Granger [51] that the belief in price threshold effects was born out of prevailing marketplace practices. In a similar vein, Kaas and Hay [52, p. 345] see the price threshold effect as "the result of a self-fulfilling prophecy." Everyone believes that everyone else is doing it, and ultimately consumers behave in line with the hypothesis. That would certainly correspond to what the Adaptation-Level Theory suggests. Price thresholds would thus be more of a tactical than a strategic issue.

Price threshold effects create problems when there are inflationary tendencies because they can hinder a company's efforts to pass on cost increases. The situation is particularly volatile when some competitors are forced to breach a price threshold due to their cost situation, while others can maintain prices below the threshold. In this case it makes sense to exceed the threshold with a significant price increase, not a slight one. If there is indeed a strong price threshold effect, it would at least be offset partially by the higher unit contribution margin. Another tactic, albeit a problematic one, is to reduce a package size in order to keep the price below the threshold. The idea that foregone potential may lie in a price threshold is something which Diller and Brielmaier [53] calculated. They show that sticking with a policy of "pricing on the 9's" can lead to considerable lost profits when the price threshold effect is not valid. Gedenk and Sattler [54] also argue that misinterpretation of price thresholds can lead to considerable negative consequences. When retailers achieve a return on sales of 1%, increasing prices from \$0.99 to \$1.00, assuming no change in sales volume, would double their profit. Even if the sales volume dropped significantly (say, by 10%), the profit effect would still be positive. Based on our experience, it makes little sense to have prices which end in 0.95, 4.90, or 9.50. As long as one remains below the price threshold, one should fully exhaust the potential, i.e., charge prices ending in 0.99, 4.99, or 9.99. These slight price differences are liable to have hardly any negative effect on sales volume, but they can yield significant profit improvements when unit contribution margin is low.

Some hypotheses refer to the influence of the last digit in price perception. We can distinguish between a price image effect and a quality image effect. According to one study, the end digit of nine signals a particularly favorable offer (price image effect), but it can also serve as an indicator of lower quality (quality image effect). The end digit 0, on the other hand, is more likely to be seen as a "normal price" which triggers neither a price nor a quality image effect [55].

4.3.2.2 Price Anchor Effects

If customers feel uncertain about their price judgment, they search for a reference point or a so-called anchor. This leads to interesting effects. Different indicators can serve as price anchor, and there is not always a conscious process at work. Price anchors are often used subconsciously [56].

An old story illustrates such an anchor effect [57]. The brothers Sid and Harry ran a clothing store in New York in the 1930s. Sid was the salesman, Harry the tailor. Sid would play dumb if he noticed that a customer liked a suit. If the customer asked about the price, Sid would call out to Harry back in the tailor shop: "Harry, how much does this suit cost?" "That nice suit? \$42", Harry would shout. Sid then acted as if he didn't understand: "How much?" "\$42!", Harry repeated. Sid would then turn to the customer and say that the suit's price is \$22. The customer did not hesitate, immediately putting $22 on the counter and leaving with the suit. The brothers' price anchor had worked as planned.

Price anchors even work effectively on businesspeople, not only consumers. Mussweiler et al. [58] conducted an experiment which required participants to estimate the price of a used car. Apparently for no reason, someone stood next to the car and made an unprompted statement about its price: "This car is worth x euros." In one study involving 60 automotive experts, a car's value was estimated at €3563, when the neutral and seemingly random person next to the car gave a price anchor of €3800. Yet the estimated value was €2520 when the prompt for the car's price was €2800. The off-the-cuff remarks of some random person were powerful enough to change the perception of car experts by €1043. Based on a price at the midpoint of €3300, this is a change of 32%. Many other studies attest to similar anchor effects. Mussweiler et al. [58, p. 1143] observe that "the findings indicate that anchoring is an exceptionally robust phenomenon that is difficult to avoid."

Under price anchor effects, it can be worthwhile to include a product in one's portfolio even if no one ever buys it. The following story illustrates such a case. A customer enters a store to buy a piece of luggage. The saleswoman asks him how much he is planning to spend. "I was thinking $200," the customer responds. "That would get you a good suitcase," the saleswoman says. "But before we narrow down the selection, may I show you something nice?" she asks. She adds that her goal is only to inform him about their product range, and not to pressure him into buying an expensive suitcase. The saleswoman then shows the customer a suitcase for $500, a top model in terms of quality, design, and brand. Then she points out the suitcases in the price category the customer mentioned but steers his attention toward pieces which cost $250–$300, slightly more than the $200 he said he had in mind. How will the customer react? There is a high probability that the anchor effect from the top-of-the-line $500 suitcase will prompt him to buy one for $250 or $300 and not for $200 as he originally planned. Even when nobody ever buys the expensive suitcase for $500, it still makes sense for the store to have it in its assortment. The price of $500 sets an anchor which changes the perception of prices in the $200–$300 range and shifts the customer's willingness to pay upward.

4.3.2.3 The Magic of the Middle

Another interesting effect is the tendency of customers to pick a middle option. How a price is positioned relative to other prices can have a strong influence on customer behavior. Even a price of $10 can spur entirely different customer reactions, depending on whether the price is the highest, the lowest, or the middle price in the product category. Let us assume a customer needs to buy a padlock. The customer cannot recall the last time he had purchased one and has no idea how much they currently cost. The local home improvement store has a range of appropriate padlocks priced between $4 and $12. How does the customer react? His security requirements do not justify buying the expensive lock, yet he doubts the quality of the least expensive ones, so he chooses a lock from the middle price range for $8.

If customers do not know how much a product costs and have no clear special needs (e.g., high quality or the lowest price), they will typically gravitate toward a price in the middle. If the price range for the padlocks at the home improvement store would have been $4–$16 instead of $4–$12, the customer would have likely purchased a lock for $10. That would have provided the store 25% more revenue and maybe a higher contribution margin. One observes the same behaviors in a restaurant when customers select a wine. The guests review the wine menu and most will end up choosing a bottle from the medium price range. The most expensive and least expensive wines are rarely purchased. The middle tendency means that a supplier can use the price range to guide the purchase of a particular product. The less a customer knows about a product's features and prices, the stronger this effect is. This behavior can to some degree be rational, given the limited information the customer has. Choosing a product from the medium price range reduces the risk that the customer gets a poor quality product and likewise reduces the risk of overspending. At the same time, the customer avoids excessive search costs.

4.3.2.4 Assortment Effect

This form of customer behavior opens up opportunities in terms of assortment planning and the associated price management. Let us assume that a restaurant offers meals in the range of $10–$20, and 20% of the demand goes to the meals priced at $18. If the restaurant adds a meal at $25, the share of the $18 meal is likely to increase. Analogously, if the restaurant adds a meal which is less expensive than the previously least expensive meal, sales for the latter $10 option will likely increase, even though few customers ever bought it in the past [59].

A very astounding result of behavioral pricing research is shown in Fig. 4.3. This experiment for the business magazine *The Economist* included two tests.

In offer A only two alternatives were offered: an online subscription at $59 per year and a combined subscription (print and online) at $125 per year. Some 68% of respondents chose the less expensive online subscription, while 32% chose the more expensive combination. Offer B introduced a third alternative, a print-only subscription for $125, the same price as the combined print-online subscription. In this version, 84% of respondents chose the combination at $125. No one chose the print-only option. This result defies rationality under classical economics. Solely by introducing an alternative nobody wanted, the share of respondents choosing the

Offer A		
Online	$59	68%
Print + Online	$125	32%

Offer B		
Online	$59	16%
Print	$125	0%
Print + Online	$125	84%

Fig. 4.3 Sales volume effect of two and three alternatives [3]

combined offer rose by 52 percentage points, from 32% to 84%. Let us assume that both offer A and offer B attract 10,000 new subscribers. The additional revenue from offer A is $801,200, while the revenue from offer B totals $1.14 million or 42.8% more. The average price per new subscriber was $80.12 in offer A and $114.40 under offer B.

How does one explain this phenomenon? One possible explanation is the "magic of zero." By setting the print-only and the combined offers at the same price, the customer gets additional value in the latter offer for a price of zero. Many customers find this irresistible and select the value-added offer, in this case the combined subscription. Thaler [28] calls this the "deal effect." The anchor argument can also play a role. Because two of the three offers in offer B are at $125, the price anchor shifts higher.

The phenomenon detected by Ariely [3], that the introduction of an additional alternative exerts a strong influence on product choice, is something which Simon-Kucher & Partners frequently observes in consulting projects. Figure 4.4 shows the results of a study with two offers. In offer A, respondents saw two alternatives: a checking account for €1 per month and a checking account with credit card for €2.50 per month. Some 59% chose the combination, while 41% chose the stand-alone checking account option [60].

In offer B the credit card was introduced as a third alternative, at the same price as the combination offer. The design corresponds to the one from Ariely [3], and the results also resemble the ones from his experiment. Only 2% chose the stand-alone credit card, but the share of respondents choosing the combination jumped to 81% from 59%. The average revenue per customer rose from €1.89 to €2.42, an increase of 28%. That additional revenue came without a price increase, merely through a portfolio change.

As these examples show, the addition of a product alternative can have dramatic effects. The test shown in Table 4.2 illustrates an expanded assortment effect. The test groups were shown a different number of bank accounts at prices of €0, €2, €4, €8, and €10. The alternatives with higher prices also had a high level of performance (e.g., more or better features) [61].

When offered only two alternatives at prices €0 and €1, 66% of the respondents chose the account with a price of €0. The average monthly price achieved thus came to €0.33. When one adds a third alternative priced at €2, 56% of the respondents

Offer A		
Checking account	€1.00	41%
Checking + Credit card	€2.50	59%

Offer B		
Checking account	€1.00	17%
Credit card	€2.50	2%
Checking + Credit card	€2.50	81%

Fig. 4.4 Banking products with two and three alternatives

Table 4.2 Assortment effects for alternative bank accounts

| Number of alternative offers | Price per month (in €) | Most frequently chosen alternative | | Average price achieved (in €) |
		Price in €	Share in percent	
2	0, 1	0	66	0.33
3	0, 1, 2	1	56	1.20
4	0, 1, 2, 4	2	54	2.18
5	0, 1, 2, 4, 8	4	44	3.96
6	0, 1, 2, 4, 8, 10	8	40	5.88

preferred the account for €1 and the average price rose to €1.20. Each additional alternative shifted the most frequently chosen offer to the one with the second highest price. As a result, the average price with six alternatives rose to €5.88. Note that less expensive offers always remained available. In each step, only a more expensive alternative was added. The effect of the additional alternative was thus stronger than the "magic of zero," although the free offer was chosen by 66% of the respondents when only two alternatives were offered. An increasing number of respondents opted for higher-priced offers. One explanation for this finding is that the value gain from the greater performance more than offsets the value loss from the higher price of the additional alternative. But that conclusion is inconsistent with the stated preferences. If that hypothesis were true, then the majority of respondents would have chosen the offer for €1 (among two alternatives) or would have selected the highest-priced offer in the subsequent steps as alternatives were added. In reality the greater number of alternatives shifted the willingness to pay upwards.

One could be tempted to say that a company should offer the greatest possible number of alternatives. We would like to warn against that. Overextending the assortment reduces the willingness of customers to deal with the greater complexity. Empirical studies have shown that having too many alternatives can make the purchase decision so difficult that the customer refuses to buy at all [62, 63].

The following project example comes from the telecommunications sector. In the first test, respondents could choose between two plans with monthly prices of $25 and $60. Some 78% of the respondents chose the less expensive plan, while 22% selected the more expensive one. The average revenue per user (ARPU) from this test came to $32.80. This revenue includes all additional fees, even those for incoming calls from other networks. In the second test, the respondents could choose among three plans priced at $25, $50, and $60. The highest and lowest prices remained the same; the only difference was the $50 plan inserted in between them. The results confirm the effects we have seen before. In the second test, only 44% of respondents chose the least expensive plan, compared with 78% in the first test. Almost as many (42%) went for the new $50 plan, and the remaining 14% chose the most expensive plan. The ARPU, including all additional fees, increased to $40.50, or 23% more than in the first test. This is an enormous amount of additional revenue.

What are the possible explanations for selecting the middle option in this case? Here are four hypotheses:

- *Uncertainty:* Customers don't have a good estimate of their monthly usage, so they fall back on the "magic of the middle" and think that they will not be too far off with the middle option.
- *Quality expectations:* The customer thinks: "If the basic fee is so low, the service probably isn't good enough."
- *Peace of mind/risk avoidance:* "If I end up making a lot of calls, it can get really expensive with the low base fee and high variable charges."
- *Status:* "I can afford it."

In reality, these motivations do not manifest themselves in their pure forms. Rather, they interact. All of these empirical cases clearly demonstrate that psychological effects are extremely important and relevant for price setting and assortment planning. Small changes in the assortment or in the price structure can have a dramatic impact on revenue and profit, without any increases in costs.

4.3.2.5 Additional Effects

In addition to the phenomena we have described so far, there are several other effects which are less important for price management. They include the possession effect, the separation effect, and the self-control effect. Trevisan [4] offers thorough treatments of each of these effects in his book.

Other phenomena which affect pricing include the price figure effect and the price shading effects. Price figure effects occur when customers perceive the ordering of the price digits in a certain way. One simple example is decreasing digits (e.g., $4.32) or increasing digits (e.g., $2.34). Another variant is to use identical digits (e.g., $4.44). Stiving and Winer [55] found in a study that customers do not perceive prices as whole, singular things, but instead have a perception for each individual digit. We can find no general validity for the price figure effect, except for the proven dominance of the "left-to-right" comparison. Digits closer to the left tend to have a greater influence on price perception than digits closer to the right. This would speak for having an increasing sequence of digits from left to right. One should be careful with such a recommendation, however, because research findings on this topic have been very mixed and do not allow for any definitive conclusions. Nonetheless, one sees the prominent use of price figures in practice. Two European electronics retail chains, Media Markt and Saturn, often use prices such as $444 or $555. These two chains must be assuming that the price figure effect is influencing price perception to their advantage.

Price shading effects reflect the translation or generalization of learned relationships [64, p. 131] which influence the way the customer interprets how the price is presented. These interpretations "rub off" on their perception of price. The visual presentation and the communication of prices play an important role in this regard. One can strongly influence price perception by using phrases such as "lowest price," "rock bottom price," "crazy low price," or "unbeatably low price." The number and selection of advertised prices, as well as their color, font, and font size, all affect price perception [65, p. 130, 66, p. 88]. It appears that the magazine *Scientific American* is trying to take advantage of this effect. They not only label their subscriptions as offering "maximum savings" but also note that prices will be higher in the next offer. This form of communication places additional pressure on the customer to use their "last chance" at the current offer. It is doubtful, though, that such a threat leads to the hoped-for increase in sales. Müller-Hagedorn et al. [67] found that a judgment about how low or favorable prices are depends on the number of advertised products as well as the expenditure per shopping trip. Flyers with many low-priced products had a very strong effect on the perception of a store as inexpensive or affordable. More and more supermarkets are inducing customers with weekend or limited-time discounts. "With very large discounts on individual products, the discount chains are trying to attract customers who then complete their entire week's shopping in the store" [68]. In these cases, the retailers are hoping that the deep discounts on a few individual products rub off on the customers' perception of the store as a whole. Inman et al. [69] were able to show that conditions which signal scarcity can drive sales volumes sharply higher. These may include time limits ("this week only" or "today only") or volume limits ("maximum two per customer"). The restrictions suggest to the customer that the price is favorable and the supply scarce.

The 2012 Olympic Games in London were a spectacular success. These Games also saw the application of a number of innovative pricing schemes [70]. The price digits themselves were meant to send signals on their own, without further commentary. The lowest (standard) price was £20.12 and the most expensive ticket was £2012. The number 2012 was reflected time and again in the price digits. One knew at one glance what these prices were for: Olympia London 2012. For children and young adults, the motto "pay your age" applied, which means one paid as much (or as little) as one's age. A 6-year-old paid £6 for a ticket, and a 16-year-old would pay £16. This price structure had a very positive resonance. The media reported on it thousands of times. Even the queen and the prime minister openly praised the pay-your-age prices. These prices were not only communicated effectively but were perceived as very fair. Seniors could also buy reasonably priced tickets.

Otherwise, there were no discounts available. The management of the London Olympics stuck firmly to this policy, even when certain events did not sell out. This sent the clear signal that the tickets and the events were worth their price. There were also no ticket bundles, a common practice in sports under which attractive and less attractive events are combined into a single package. Local public transportation, however, was bundled together with the tickets. The organization relied very heavily on the Internet both for communications and sales. Approximately 99% of tickets were sold online. The goal prior to the Olympic Games was ticket revenues of £376 million. The ingenious price structure and communication campaign ultimately generated ticket revenues of £660 million. That was 75% more than planned and more ticket revenue than from the preceding three Olympic Games (Beijing, Athens, and Sydney) combined. This case demonstrates the kind of revenue and profit potential that lies in psychologically savvy price management.

Tax-free days or weekends are another popular tactic which retailers use. By not charging sales tax (i.e., paying the sales tax on behalf of the customer), the customers often feel they are receiving a discount equivalent to the amount of sales tax. This is an error. If the sales tax is 20%, the customer does not receive a discount of 20% on their purchase, but rather an effective discount of 16.6%. The price with tax on a $100 purchase would have been $120. Removing the $20 tax means the effective discount is $20 \div 120 = 16.7\%$.

4.3.3   Neuro-Pricing

The latest direction in research builds on behavioral pricing and expands it into the measurement of physical reactions to price stimuli. Brain research explores neural processes which take place subconsciously. "How we perceive prices is no different from how we perceive other stimuli," [65] says a brain researcher. Price perceptions trigger reactions in the brain which can be measured with a high level of precision. The most widely known process for this is MRI, but researchers also use positron emission tomography, magnetoencephalography, and electroencephalography (commonly known as EEG) [71].

Advertising stimuli and product stimuli are at the forefront of this field of research, but certain results refer to price-related stimuli. Elger [72] reports that "a discount sign massively suppresses the usual strategies of weighing the pros and cons of making a purchase." The mere presence of a discount sign unleashes a reaction in the brain which lessens one's ability to make rational judgments. One finding is that price information activates the brain's pain center and is processed there. It is actually no surprise that customers associate prices with unpleasant feelings.

Neuro-pricing can provide valuable information to supplement classical methods. It can objectively measure processes which the customers are not aware of but which influence their purchase decision. It accomplishes this without relying on verbal responses from the test subjects. The goal of neuro-pricing research is to understand such processes better and to influence them from the seller's perspective. It is evident that this is an ethically sensitive area.

The external validity of the research results is questionable. It begins with the sampling. While the sample selection follows the same principles as classical market research, there are some crucial differences. First, the research subjects need to go to a special lab. Many potential candidates are unwilling to subject themselves to physiological brain research for marketing purposes. The measurement situation is also far removed from a typical purchase situation. Given all these circumstances, one can doubt the extent to which the measurement results can be extrapolated to reality.

Until now, relatively few results have come to light from which one can derive practical price recommendations. One author cites a study he conducted on Starbucks coffee, which led him to the following conclusion: "The willingness to pay for a cup of coffee at Starbucks is apparently much higher than the company itself believes. Starbucks is letting millions in profits slip through its fingers because it is not taking consumers' willingness to pay into account" [65]. Anyone with halfway decent knowledge of the coffee market knows that prices at Starbucks are already very high. Thus, one should take these statements with great caution.

Brain research does, however, deliver some interesting insights into the design of prices. The usual notation for price, say $16.70, activates the brain's pain centers particularly strongly. The activation is less pronounced when one leaves out the currency symbol and simply writes "16.70." The brain does not immediately interpret such a number as a price. The activation is weaker still when one uses whole numbers, i.e., rounds the price up to 17 in this case. One finds this form of price communication in some restaurants. When the price is expressed in words, such as "seventeen," the perceived pain is the lowest of all forms. It remains to be seen whether menus and price lists will start to appear in this form. The use of currency symbols in advertising should be avoided, unless self-image and prestige matter to the customer and are conveyed by the price. There are also findings related to the effects of colors (e.g., red price tags signal a discount or special offer) and cash payments, which activate the pain centers more than card payments.

The use of brain research for marketing and pricing is still in a very early stage. Many of the findings in this field are preliminary. But there can be no doubt that this technology will bring new insights. It is too early to speculate, though, what effects it will have on price management.

4.3.4 Overall Assessment

Behavioral and neural economics have already changed classical economics and will continue to do so. The results of the behavioral research we have presented are fascinating. The new approaches can explain many phenomena for which classical economics has no answer. However, we still advise caution. We are convinced that the fundamental laws of economics will continue to govern most transactions. A higher price may under certain circumstances lead to higher sales volume. But that is the exception to the rule. Another problem lies in generalizing the results. When is it better to have a customer pay once per year, and when is it better to have quarterly payments or monthly payments? There is neither a general answer to that question nor a clear and unambiguous way to frame up the problem. Philip Mirowski, an economic historian and philosopher, is right in his criticism that behavioral economics may be "undermining the foundation of rational activity, but putting nothing up in its place" [73]. Behavioral economics does not yet offer a complete, unified theory.

Some of the test results of behavioral economics must be challenged critically. Most of the findings derive from lab situations whose applicability to real-life situations is dubious. Some stimuli are presented in such a way that they can guide behavior in a certain direction. These concerns apply to an ever greater degree to brain research. Beck [74] came to this conclusion: "The theoretical and empirical evidence against behavioral economics means we should be cautious and not completely throw out the idea of the 'rational man.'" People are not as rational as classical economics sees them, nor are they as irrational as some behavioral economists presume. In price management, one may be best advised to consider both research traditions but do so with care. Moreover, the combination of both research streams, i.e., linking experimental approaches with econometric modeling and real-life data, shows a lot of research potential with high relevance for corporate price management [75].

Conclusion
When analyzing price effects, one should not only consider economic aspects but also insights from behavioral science. The psychology of price supplements the classical economic view and thus makes an essential contribution to a more comprehensive understanding of price effects. The behavioral field has seen breakthroughs in recent years which lie closer to reality than the assumptions which underpin classical economic models. Both viewpoints should therefore be considered in price design and price communication in order to achieve optimal results. We stress the following points:

- The stimulus-organism-response (S-O-R) model expands the economic black box model and contributes to a better understanding of the effects of price.
- Numerous price phenomena which appear to be counterintuitive or even irrational from a purely economic perspective can be explained with the help of behavioral science and offer guidance for effective pricing measures.
- The price is not only a feature with negative value. It can also confer prestige or serve as a quality indicator, which means that some portions of the price-response function can have an upward slope. The price elasticity is positive in these cases.
- Prospect theory assumes that the utilities of gains and losses are asymmetrical. Due to loss aversion, the loss value is greater than the gain value in absolute terms. This asymmetry has consequences for design and communication of prices and price structures.
- Mental accounting assumes that consumers sort products into categories and react differently to prices depending on the category.
- Customers often use rubrics or tactics to simplify their pricing decisions when they have limited capacity to collect or review information or have low interest (low involvement) in the product. From these behaviors emerge many phenomena such as the magic of the middle, price threshold effects, price anchor effects, and assortment effects which all have major implications for price management.
- Modern brain research on prices and their effects is still in a very early stage. This field has revealed that prices activate the brain's pain center and

(continued)

that the presentation of a price can have considerable influence on a purchase decision.

This chapter has shed light on the variety of research in the field of behavioral pricing. These new insights have already had a strong influence on economics. We expect more breakthroughs to emerge (e.g., from brain research). Customer behavior cannot be explained solely by the rationality hypotheses of *homo oeconomicus*, which form the basis of classical theory. Many insights from behavioral science are surprising and appear to be irrational at first glance. But in reality, they come closer to representing customer behavior than classical economic models do. This has many specific and concrete consequences for price management. Nonetheless, we urge caution. Many findings were derived under conditions which are quite different from typical purchase situations. The extent to which the findings may be generalized is not well known. We do, however, expect additional important insights from this area of research. Price management should take behavioral science into account and not rely solely on the tenets of classical economics.

References

1. Kahneman, D., & Tversky, A. (1979). Prospect Theory: An Analysis of Decision under Risk. *Econometrica*, 47(2), 263–291.
2. Kahneman, D. (2012). *Thinking, Fast and Slow*. Farrar, Straus and Giroux: New York.
3. Ariely, D. (2010). *Predictably Irrational: The Hidden Forces that Shape our Decisions*. New York: Harper Perennial.
4. Trevisan, E. (2013). *The Irrational Consumer: Applying Behavioural Economics to Your Business Strategy*. Farnham: Gower.
5. Veblen, T. (1899). *Theory of the Leisure Class*. New York: Macmillan.
6. Fassnacht, M., & Dahm, J. M. (2018). The Veblen Effect and (In)Conspicuous Consumption A State of the Art Article. *Luxury Research Journal*, 1(4), 343–371.
7. Rohwetter, M. (2012). Das will ich haben!. http://www.zeit.de/2012/18/Verkaeufer. Accessed 17 March 2015.
8. Milligan, L. (2014). Would You Pay 70 Per Cent More for Chanel? http://www.vogue.co.uk/news/2014/03/05/price-increases-for-luxury-items%2D%2D-chanel-louis-vuitton-bags. Accessed 2 April 2015.
9. Fassnacht, M., Kluge, P.N., Mohr, H. (2013). Pricing Luxury Brands: Specificities, Conceptualization, and Performance Impact. *Marketing ZFP – Journal of Research and Management*. 35 (2), 104–117.
10. Krelle, W. (1976). *Preistheorie*. Tübingen: J.C.B. Mohr.
11. Marshall, A. (1920). *Principles of Economics: An Introductory Volume*. London: Macmillan.
12. Tigges, K. (2007). Chinesen sind paradox: Wirtschaftstheorie. http://www.faz.net/aktuell/wirtschaft/wirtschaftstheorie-chinesen-sind-paradox-1461300.html. Accessed 17 March 2015.
13. Grossarth, J. (2013). Tannen zapfen: Das Brennholz wird knapp. http://www.faz.net/das-brennholz-wird-knapp-tannen-zapfen-12047380.html. Accessed 17 March 2015.

14. Völckner, F. (2006). Determinanten der Informationsfunktion des Preises: Eine empirische Analyse. *Zeitschrift für Betriebswirtschaft*, 76(5), 473–497.
15. Anonymous (2013). Was ist Preis-Wert? http://www.gfk-compact.com/index.php?article_id=236&clang=0. Accessed 17 March 2015.
16. Teas, R. K., & Agarwal, S. (2000). The Effects of Extrinsic Product Cues on Consumers' Perceptions of Quality, Sacrifice, and Value. *Journal of the Academy of Marketing Science*, 28 (2), 278–290.
17. Brucks, M., Zeithaml, V. A., Naylor, G. (2000). Price and Brand Name As Indicators of Quality Dimensions for Consumer Durables. *Journal of the Academy of Marketing Science*, 28(3), 359–374.
18. Shiv, B., Carmon, Z., Ariely, D. (2005). Placebo Effects of Marketing Actions: Consumers May Get What They Pay For. *Journal of Marketing Research*, 42(4), 383–393.
19. Grewal, D., Nordfält, J., Roggeveen, A., Olbrich, R., Jansen, C. H. (2014). Price-Quality Relationship in Pricing Strategies for Private Labels. *Journal of Product & Brand Management*, 23(6), 429–438.
20. Hu, M., & Liu, B. (2004, August). Mining and Summarizing Customer Reviews. *Proceedings of the tenth ACM SIGKDD international conference on Knowledge discovery and data mining* (pp. 168–177). ACM.
21. Yang, Z., & Fang, X. (2004). Online Service Quality Dimensions and their Relationships with Satisfaction. *International Journal of Service Industry Management*, 15(3), 302–326.
22. Cheung, C. M., & Thadani, D. R. (2012). The Impact of Electronic Word-of-Mouth Communication: A Literature Analysis and Integrative Model. *Decision Support Systems*, 54(1), 461–470.
23. Gossen, H. H. (1854). *Entwickelung der Gesetze des menschlichen Verkehrs und der daraus fließenden Regeln für menschliches Handeln*. Braunschweig: F. Vieweg.
24. Kahneman, D., Knetsch, J. L., Thaler, R. (1990). Experimental Tests of the Endowment Effect and the Coase Theorem. *Journal of Political Economy*, 98(6), 1325–1348.
25. Bauer, C., & Wübker, G. (2015). *Power Pricing für Banken: Wege aus der Ertragskrise*. Frankfurt am Main: Campus.
26. Schulz, F., Schlereth, C., Mazar, N., Skiera, B. (2015). Payment Systems: Paying Too Much Today and Being Satisfied Tomorrow. *International Journal of Research in Marketing*, 32(3), 238–250.
27. Gourville, J. T., & Soman, D. (1998). Payment Depreciation: the Behavioral Effects of Temporally Separating Payments From Consumption. *Journal of Consumer Research*, 25(2), 160–174.
28. Thaler, R. (1980). Toward a Positive Theory of Consumer Choice. *Journal of Economic Behavior & Organization*, 1(1), 39–60.
29. Thaler, R. (1985). Mental Accounting and Consumer Choice. *Marketing Science*, 4(3), 199–214.
30. Thaler, R. H., & Sunstein, C. R. (2009). *Improving Decisions about Health, Wealth and Happiness*. London: Penguin.
31. Thaler, R. H. (1999). Mental Accounting Matters. *Journal of Behavioral Decision Making*, 12 (3), 183–206.
32. Thaler, R. H. (1994). *Quasi Rational Economics*. New York: Russell Sage Foundation.
33. Strobel y Serra, J. (2012). Schluss mit der Geschmacklosigkeit!: Die Ernährung der Deutschen. http://www.faz.net/aktuell/feuilleton/die-ernaehrung-der-deutschen-schluss-mit-der-geschmacklosigkeit-11680616.html. Accessed 17 March 2015.
34. Tversky, A., & Kahneman, D. (1981). The Framing of Decisions and the Psychology of Choice. *Science*, 211(4481), 453–458.
35. Helson, H. (1964). Current Trends and Issues in Adaptation-Level Theory. *American Psychologist*, 19(1), 26–38.

36. Volkmann, J. (1951). Scales of Judgment and their Implications for Social Psychology. In J. H. Rohrer, & M. Sherif (Eds.), *Social Psychology at the Crossroads. The University of Oklahoma Lectures in Social Psychology* (p. 273–298). Oxford: Harper.

37. Sherif, M., & Hovland, C. I. (1961). *Social Judgment: Assimilation and Contrast Effects in Communication and Attitude Change. Yale Studies in Attitude and Communication.* New Haven: Yale University Press.

38. Baumgartner, B., & Steiner, W. J. (2007). Are Consumers Heterogeneous in their Preferences for Odd and Even Prices? Findings from a Choice-Based Conjoint Study. *International Journal of Research in Marketing,* 24(4), 312–323.

39. Gedenk, K., & Sattler, H. (1999). The Impact of Price Thresholds on Profit Contribution – Should Retailers set 9-ending Prices? *Journal of Retailing,* 75(1), 33–57.

40. Pauwels, K., Srinivasan, S., Franses, P. H. (2007). When Do Price Thresholds Matter in Retail Categories? *Marketing Science,* 26(1), 83–100.

41. Bösener, K. (2015). *Kundenzufriedenheit, Kundenbegeisterung und Kundenpreisverhalten. Fokus Dienstleistungsmarketing.* Wiesbaden: Gabler.

42. Schröder, H. (2012). *Handelsmarketing: Strategien und Instrumente für den stationären Einzelhandel und für Online-Shops mit Praxisbeispielen* (2nd ed.). Wiesbaden: Gabler.

43. Kucher, E. (1985). *Scannerdaten und Preissensitivität bei Konsumgütern.* Wiesbaden: Gabler.

44. Levy, D., Lee, D., Chen, H., Kauffman, R. J., Bergen, M. (2011). Price Points and Price Rigidity. *Review of Economics and Statistics,* 93(4), 1417–1431.

45. Thomas, M., & Morwitz, V. (2005). Penny Wise and Pound Foolish: The Left-Digit Effect in Price Cognition. *Journal of Consumer Research,* 32(1), 54–64.

46. Anonymous (2005). Rotkäppchen-Mumm steigert Absatz. http://www.lebensmittelzeitung.net. Accessed 17 December 2014.

47. Anonymous (2006, April 26). Rotkäppchen will nach Rekordjahr Preise erhöhen Jeder dritte Sekt stammt aus dem ostdeutschen Konzern / Neuer Rosé / Mumm verliert weiter: Unternehmen. *Frankfurter Allgemeine Zeitung,* p. 23.

48. Anonymous (2007). Sekt löst Turbulenzen aus. http://www.lebensmittelzeitung.net. Accessed 17 March 2015.

49. Ginzberg, E. (1936). Customary Prices. *The American Economic Review,* 26(2), 296–310.

50. Dean, J. (1951). *Managerial Economics.* New Jersey: Prentice Hall.

51. Gabor, A., & Granger, C. W. J. (1964). Price Sensitivity of the Consumer. *Journal of Advertising Research,* 4(4), 40–44.

52. Kaas, K. P., & Hay, C. (1984). Preisschwellen bei Konsumgütern: Eine theoretische und empirische Analyse. *Schmalenbachs Zeitschrift für betriebswirtschaftliche Forschung,* 36(5), 333–346.

53. Diller, H., & Brielmaier, A. (1996). Die Wirkung gebrochener und runder Preise: Ergebnisse eines Feldexperiments im Drogeriewarensektor. *Schmalenbachs Zeitschrift für betriebswirtschaftliche Forschung,* 48(7/8), 695–710.

54. Gedenk, K., & Sattler, H. (1999). Preisschwellen und Deckungsbeitrag: Verschenkt der Handel große Potentiale? *Schmalenbachs Zeitschrift für betriebswirtschaftliche Forschung,* 51(1), 33–59.

55. Stiving, M., & Winer, R. S. (1997). An Empirical Analysis of Price Endings with Scanner Data. *Journal of Consumer Research,* 24(1), 57–67.

56. Jung M. H., Perfecto H., Leif D. N. (2016) Anchoring in Payment: Evaluating a Judgmental Heuristic in Field Experimental Settings. *Journal of Marketing Research,* 53(3), 354–368.

57. Cialdini, R. B. (2008). *Influence: Science and Practice* (5th ed.) Boston: Allyn and Bacon.

58. Mussweiler, T., Strack, F., Pfeiffer, T. (2000). Overcoming the Inevitable Anchoring Effect: Considering the Opposite Compensates for Selective Accessibility. *Personality and Social Psychology Bulletin,* 26(9), 1142–1150.

59. Huber, J., & Puto, C. (1983). Market Boundaries and Product Choice: Illustrating Attraction and Substitution Effects. *Journal of Consumer Research,* 10(1), 31–44.

60. Trevisan, E. (2014). *The Impact of Behavioral Pricing*. Bonn: Simon-Kucher & Partners. August.
61. Trevisan, E., Di Donato, M., Brusco, R. (2013). Zero-Pricing. *The Journal of Professional Pricing*, 22(4), 10–16.
62. Polman, E. (2012). Effects of Self-Other Decision Making on Regulatory Focus and Choice Overload. *Journal of Personality and Social Psychology*, 102(5), 980–993.
63. Iyengar, S. S., & Lepper, M. R. (2000). When Choice is Demotivating: Can One Desire too much of a Good Thing? *Journal of Personality and Social Psychology*, 79(6), 995–1006.
64. Diller, H. (2008). *Preispolitik* (4th ed.) Stuttgart: Kohlhammer.
65. Müller, K.-M. (2012). *NeuroPricing: Wie Kunden über Preise denken*. Freiburg im Breisgau: Haufe.
66. Pechtl, H. (2014). *Preispolitik: Behavioral Pricing und Preissysteme* (2nd ed.) Konstanz: UVK/Lucius.
67. Müller-Hagedorn, L., Schuckel, M., Helnerus, K. (2005). *Zur Gestaltung von Einzelhandelswerbung. Die Auswirkungen von Art und Anzahl der Artikel sowie der Abbildungsgröße*. Working paper, Vol. 14. Cologne: University of Cologne.
68. Schnitzler, J. (2015). "Framstag" und "Supersamstag". http://www.wdr2.de/service/ quintessenz/lockangebote-100.html. Accessed 17 March 2015.
69. Inman, J. J., Peter, A. C., Raghubir, P. (1997). Framing the Deal: The Role of Restrictions in Accentuating Deal Value. *Journal of Consumer Research*, 24(1), 68–79.
70. Williamson, P. (2012). *Pricing for the London Olympics 2012*. Bonn: Simon-Kucher & Partners World Meeting. December.
71. Kenning, P., Plassmann, H., Ahlert, D. (2007). Applications of Functional Magnetic Resonance Imaging for Market Research. *Qualitative Market Research: An International Journal*, 10(2), 135–152.
72. Elger, C. E. (2008). Freiheitsgrade: Werbung, Manipulation und Freiheit aus Sicht der Hirnforschung. *Forschung & Lehre* (3), 154–155.
73. Anonymous (2013, February 16). Die Ökonomen haben ihre Erzählung widerrufen. *Frankfurter Allgemeine Zeitung*, p. 40.
74. Beck, H. (2013, February 11). Der Mensch ist kein kognitiver Versager. *Frankfurter Allgemeine Zeitung*, p. 18.
75. Koschate-Fischer, N., Wüllner, K. (2017). New Developments in Behavioral Pricing Research. *Journal of Business Economics*, 82(6), 809–875.

Decision: One-Dimensional Prices

5

Abstract

This chapter deals with decision-making for one-dimensional prices. In other words, it involves setting a price for one product in one period. Rigid processes such as cost-plus or competition-oriented pricing, which consider only one factor, are in widespread use in practice, but they are not up to the challenges and complexities of price setting. Comprehensive processes take all relevant factors, such as goals, volume effects, costs, and competitive behavior, into account in the price decision. With their help, one can derive general rules for optimal prices. The price in this case is an elasticity-dependent markup on marginal costs. In the case of an oligopoly, the complexity is greater because one must take competitive reaction into account. Signaling can be used to influence such reactions.

5.1 Introduction

We will discuss price decisions in three separate chapters. This chapter is about the optimization of one-dimensional prices, where we examine pricing for one product and for one period. The price in this case consists of only one parameter or one dimension. In Chap. 6, we will explore optimization across multiple products and prices. In that chapter we use the term "price differentiation" to describe situations when a company has different prices for the same product or for variants of the product. We will also look at prices for multiple products whose sales or costs are interrelated. Topics include price bundling and pricing for product lines. Finally, in Chap. 7, we will examine long-term price optimization, which requires price setting across multiple periods. Table 5.1 explains the different types of price decisions.

Obviously decisions for multidimensional prices are more complex and difficult than those for one-dimensional prices. At the same time, the profit potential from multidimensional price structures is higher, which makes the extra effort

© Springer Nature Switzerland AG 2019
H. Simon, M. Fassnacht, *Price Management*,
https://doi.org/10.1007/978-3-319-99456-7_5

Table 5.1 Categorization of price decisions

	Number of products		Number of prices	
Price decision	1	>1	1	>1
One-dimensional prices (Chap. 5)	x	–	x	–
Price differentiation (Chap. 6)	x	–	–	x
Pricing for multiple products (Chap. 6)	–	x	–	x
Price decisions over time (Chap. 7)	x	–	–	x

worthwhile. A market's profit opportunities are more effectively exploited through multidimensional prices than through one-dimensional prices.

5.2   Categorization of One-Dimensional Pricing Processes

We use the categorization of one-dimensional pricing processes suggested by Wiltinger [1, pp. 100–108]. The main criterion for this categorization is the information each process relies on and how that information is used. The three categories are rigid processes which rely only on one aspect, flexible-intuitive processes, and comprehensive processes.

The rigid pricing processes use a single source of information, such as one's own costs or the competitors' prices, in one step. When decision-makers process several types of information and do so in multiple steps, Wiltinger [1, p. 102] refers to this as a flexible-intuitive pricing process. In the first step, one comes up with an initial idea for the price based on primary information. In subsequent steps, the decision-makers bring in additional information and make intuitive revisions to the preliminary price. Primary information corresponds to the nature of the process itself, i.e., costs in the case of the cost-plus process or competitors' prices if competition-oriented pricing is applied. Secondary information supplements the primary information and is used in both the flexible-intuitive and the comprehensive processes. This information could include actual prices from previous periods or information about maximum prices. Comprehensive pricing processes are characterized by information processing in parallel. One incorporates market, cost, and goal information into the price decision. Several price alternatives are developed, evaluated, and compared. The comprehensive processes can include profit calculations, decision trees, and decision-support systems, as well as marginal analyses.

Categorization of pricing processes based on the information they rely on has three advantages. First, it addresses the data collection in the analysis phase. Second, taking different types of information into account in the context of flexible-intuitive or comprehensive processes resembles how companies actually make price decisions. Third, this criterion (information collection and usage) creates awareness of the complexity of price decisions.

5.3   Rigid Pricing Processes

We consider cost-plus pricing and competition-oriented pricing to be rigid pricing processes.

5.3.1   Cost-Plus Pricing

Cost-plus pricing means that the price p is determined by a percentage markup on unit costs:

$$p = (1 + \text{markup}) \times \text{unit costs} \tag{5.1}$$

The markup basis could be either total unit costs (full-cost calculation) or variable unit costs (partial cost calculation). The markup percentage is based on what is common in the industry, habits of the particular firm, or rules of thumb.

Under cost-plus pricing, each change in costs leads to a proportional change in price. Changes in other parameters, such as shifts in demand, are ignored. One example is the discount retailer ALDI, which lowers its prices when commodity prices fall. Around 75% of companies practice cost-oriented pricing [2, p. 22, 3, p. 137, 4, p. 14]. Cost-plus pricing has serious disadvantages. Especially problematic is the use of a full-cost calculation as the basis for the markup. If sales volumes decline, the fully loaded unit cost rises, as does the price. That normally leads to further sales volume declines, which in turn result in even higher prices. The opposite applies when demand increases, namely, full unit costs, and prices go down. In short, pricing on the basis of fully loaded costs ignores the influence of price on demand. Companies using this approach run the risk of pricing themselves out of the market when demand weakens or missing out on significant profit opportunities when demand increases.

Another problem with full-cost pricing arises when a company manufactures several different kinds of products. It is rare to have a situation when one can cleanly allocate shared costs to the product responsible for them. Traditional cost-allocation methods such as fixed percentages, units of service, step-down method, and activity-based costing all endeavor to allocate shared costs as closely as possible to the products which generated the costs [5, pp. 107–124]. Yet there is enough room for subjectivity in such measurements that the allocation of shared costs and resulting markup levels on unit costs can only be considered "acceptable." In the United States, they must be "logical and reasonable," but they are never truly objective or 100% accurate [6, p. 677].

Nonetheless, cost-plus pricing is a popular method in practice thanks to its ease of use. Under specific conditions it is also theoretically acceptable as a pricing method. From a strategic standpoint, unit costs define the lower limit for prices. The unit costs on a fully loaded basis form the long-term lower limit for prices. In the short term, the price should at least cover variable unit costs. We summarize the advantages and disadvantages of cost-plus pricing.

Advantages:

- The process is simple and easy to use.
- The prices are based on "hard" cost data. Cost-plus appears to reduce the uncertainty around pricing better than a market-oriented process does.
- Companies with large assortments are compelled to use simple, schematic processes to set prices.
- From a competitive standpoint, cost-plus pricing can lead to optimal prices when competitors have similar cost structures and use the same markups. Under such circumstances, cost-plus pricing actually corresponds to a form of tacit coordination among competitors.

Disadvantages:

- The method does not explicitly take the demand side into account.
- Customers' willingness to pay does not derive from the cost of a product, but rather from its performance and the resulting value-to-customer.
- The use of cost-plus pricing on a fully loaded cost basis takes fixed costs into account, which is a logical fallacy. Fixed costs should not influence the optimal price.

5.3.2 Competition-Oriented Pricing

Competition-oriented pricing means that competitors' prices form the basis for a company's price setting. Rigid competition-oriented pricing uses no other information except competitors' prices in the price decision. One commonly finds this form of pricing in markets for homogenous products such as oil, gas, or electricity. One also observes this process frequently in retail. One CEO of a large retail chain told us that his company follows ALDI's lead on prices for several hundred products.

One variant is flexible-intuitive competition-oriented pricing. This method lets additional information beyond competitors' prices flow into the price decisions, such as how competitors might respond to one's own price actions. One could, for example, use the price of the largest competitor (ostensibly the market's price leader) as a basis and then adjust one's own price by a certain percentage based on advice from the sales team.

Competition-oriented pricing has two forms, the adjustment strategy and the niche strategy.

5.3.2.1 Adjustment Strategy
The adjustment strategy calls for price setting using an "orientation price" as a basis. The orientation price is usually the one set by the price leader or market leader. This strategy is also known as "price follower" strategy. Companies have adopted this

strategy in many markets, including air travel, petroleum products, and telecommunications.

The prerequisites for an adjustment strategy are similar cost structures among the market leader and the followers and a certain level of trust in the price leader. Beyond that, the strategy also assumes that the market leader's price policies are not consciously aimed at weakening the price followers.

The results of the adjustment strategy are similar to those from cost-plus pricing based on customary industry markups. Pricing policies are tacitly coordinated and competitive mechanisms are suppressed. The adjustment strategy represents a widely used rule of thumb and allows the price leader to reliably anticipate how competitors (followers) will respond to its price changes. In this manner, the adjustment strategy can lead to optimal results for all competitors.

5.3.2.2 Niche Strategy

In contrast to the adjustment strategy, the niche strategy is defined by conscious differentiation from competitors' prices. The price is set at a spot in the market not yet occupied by any other price. Such a price position can lie within an uncovered range between other prices or lie at the upper or lower end of the prevailing price range. The more fragmented a market is in terms of the purchasing power and the preferences of customers, the more fundamentally sound the niche strategy is. It may also be less likely to warrant competitive reactions. One possibility is that the distance between the niche price and the existing prices stimulates latent demand in a viable market segment which previously did not buy the product. Bargain airlines exemplify this. If most of the customers responding to the niche price represent this latent demand, the effect on sales of established competitors will be barely noticeable. This means they are unlikely to respond. The niche strategy can also be used to avoid undesirable competitive reactions. In the spirit of a "blue ocean strategy," one consciously sidesteps the competition [7].

The market for household cleaning products offers an interesting illustration. Three of the five most important brands lie price-wise in a very narrow range. The fifth brand has a noticeably lower niche price, the fourth a noticeably higher one. Table 5.2 shows that the price elasticities in the upper and lower niches are significantly lower than in the more crowded segment. Apparently, the niche brands can extricate themselves from price competition to some extent. Their price actions have small effects on the sales volumes of the brands in the medium segment.

Table 5.2 Price elasticities in different price ranges

Product	Deviation from median price (%)	Price elasticity (absolute value)
Brand 4	7	1.34
Brand 1	+0.6	6.28
Brand 2	0	3.58
Brand 3	−2.7	5.61
Brand 5	−8.9	1.73

One should be wary of two problems arising from competition-oriented price decisions. First, information of competitive prices in many markets is unreliable. Second, the performance levels of companies and their products are often not directly comparable.

5.4   Comprehensive Pricing Process

Comprehensive pricing processes take both market and cost information into account. These processes include contribution margin calculations, decision trees, decision-support systems, and marginal analyses. They compare and evaluate several alternative prices [1, p. 104]. While contribution margin calculations and decision-tree processes consider only a few price points, decision-support systems can incorporate a larger number of price points. Marginal analyses consolidate a seemingly endless number of price points into the form of a function and allow for very granular evaluation of potential price points.

One-sided, rigid, and flexible-intuitive processes share one major limitation: they do not make any assumptions about interrelationships between price and its determining factors [1, p. 105]. In a one-sided, rigid pricing process, the price is a function of costs or competitors' prices, i.e., the costs or the competition determines the price. In comprehensive processes, all of the factors which influence and have an effect on price are themselves a function of price. This means that the costs, demand, and competitors' prices—as shown in Fig. 1.7—must be considered as dependent on price. From a logical standpoint, this is the only correct decision process. Every variable which depends on a decision must be considered when making that decision.

5.4.1   Break-Even Analysis

Break-even analysis incorporates information on costs and sales volume and includes the evaluation of several price alternatives. Conceptually, it calls for strict separation between fixed and variable cost components [8, 9, p. 76]. The fixed costs are treated as a block. Because they are by definition independent of any decision for a particular planning period, the fixed costs should not influence a pending price decision. The focus here is on the profit contribution margin. The break-even volume or the maximum total contribution margin can serve as criteria for the price decision.

The break-even analysis follows these steps:

1. Selection of a potential price.
2. Calculation of the unit contribution margin by subtracting the variable unit costs k from price p. The break-even analysis assumes a linear cost function, so that variable unit costs and marginal costs are both constant and identical. The unit contribution margin is:

$$d = p - k \tag{5.2}$$

3. Calculation of the break-even volume q_{BE} by dividing the fixed costs C_{fix} by the unit contribution margin d:

$$q_{BE} = \frac{C_{fix}}{d} \tag{5.3}$$

This volume will cover the fixed costs exactly, and the profit is zero. The break-even volume is therefore also referred to as the profit threshold.

4. Assessment of whether the break-even volume will be exceeded or not at the selected price. If the expected sales volume exceeds the break-even volume, it means the product will earn a profit; if the anticipated volume is less than the break-even volume, the product will lose money.

Implicit in the fourth step is the existence and application of a price-response function, as one must determine what sales volume would result at a certain price.

If one has completed steps one to four for only one price, then the result can only be used for a "yes-no" decision on whether to offer the product at that price. In order to use the break-even analysis for a price decision, one should complete steps one to four for several alternative prices. In step four, one must assess which price has the highest probability of achieving or exceeding the break-even volume.

Table 5.3 explains this approach using a simple example with variable unit costs of $5 and fixed costs of $100,000. The table shows the break-even volumes for five alternative prices.

Figure 5.1 shows this relationship graphically. The break-even volume declines exponentially as the price increases. One should not conclude on this basis, however, that lower break-even volumes are easier to achieve. They are associated with higher prices, which will typically reduce volumes.

Table 5.3 Break-even volumes for alternative prices

Price p ($)	Unit contribution margin d ($)	Break-even volume q_{BE} (units)
6	1	100,000
7	2	50,000
8	3	33,333
9	4	25,000
10	5	20,000

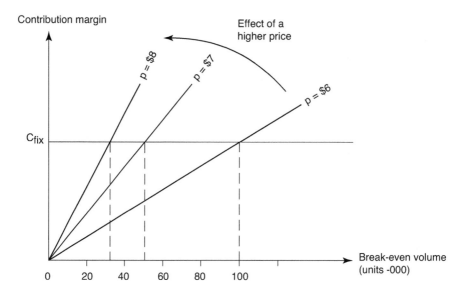

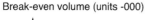

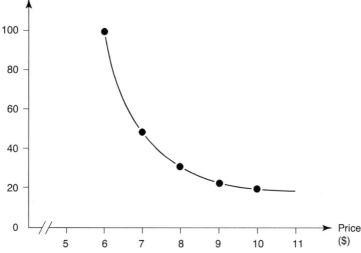

Fig. 5.1 The relationship between break-even volumes and price

It is incumbent upon management to determine which combination of price and break-even volume appears to be the best. The use of break-even analysis as support for a price decision only makes sense when the probabilities of achieving the alternative break-even volumes show significant differences. Often the probabilities of achieving or exceeding the different break-even volumes (at the different prices) are similar. In other words, the break-even criterion does not differentiate

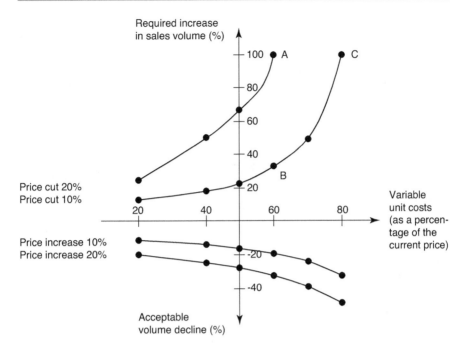

Fig. 5.2 Curves for the same level of profits

sufficiently. Break-even volumes are an incomplete criterion, because they do not take into account what happens beyond the break-even point. Nonetheless, break-even analysis represents a practical instrument for "yes-no" decisions such as whether to launch, keep, or eliminate a product. It is less well suited for price decisions.

The same procedure can be used to decide on price changes. Figure 5.2 shows a simple example for a price cut or price increase. We look at the price change and the required change in sales volume. The horizontal axis shows the variable unit costs as a percentage of the current price. The vertical axis shows the required increase in sales volume (up) and the acceptable volume decline (down) to achieve the same profit. We consider price changes of 10% and 20%.

Let us look first at the price decline curves in the upper part of the figure. The curve for price cuts of 20% shows that when variable unit costs have a share of 60% of the current price, the required volume increase to maintain constant profit is 100% (point A). If the price cut is only 10%, then the required volume increase is 33% (point B). This numerical case clarifies how sensitive profit is to price changes, when the variable unit costs are relatively high. The higher the variable unit costs, the steeper the curve is. If variable unit costs amount to 80% of the current price, a volume increase of 100% is necessary to offset a price decrease of 10% in order to maintain profit (point C).

In contrast, the curves for price increases of 10% and 20% in the lower portion of Fig. 5.2 are much flatter and lie closer together. This proves that the tolerable declines in sales volume react less sensitively to the percentage share of variable unit costs. Figures of this kind offer useful decision support when assessing price changes. They show clearly what changes in sales volumes are necessary to keep profit constant.

Contribution Margin Maximization
A focus on the total expected contribution margin at a specific price is better for price setting than an orientation solely on the break-even volume. Because the fixed costs are constant, the price which yields the highest contribution margin is also the one which maximizes profit. Contribution margin maximization is identical to profit maximization. A prerequisite for calculating contribution margins is that one specifies price alternatives and can estimate the sales volumes at those prices. In other words, one explicitly takes the effect of price on volume into account. This approach is shown in Fig. 5.3.

Contribution margin maximization represents a logically sound method for price optimization. One advantage is its simplicity. It requires no functions or sophisticated mathematical optimization methods. One must only calculate contribution margins for a small number of alternative prices and compare them. This process is therefore very relevant in practice. It is clearly superior to cost-plus decision-making.

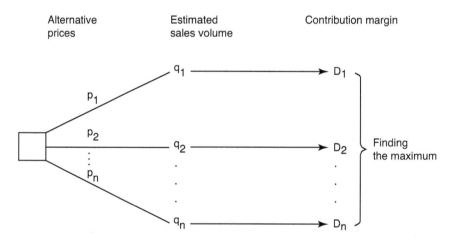

Fig. 5.3 Contribution margin maximization

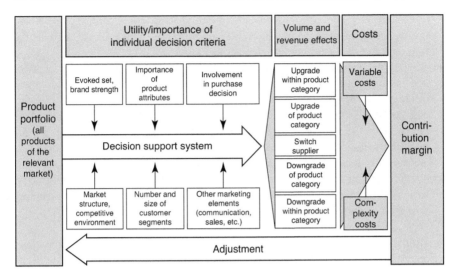

Fig. 5.4 Structure of a decision-support system

5.4.2 Decision-Support Systems

The methods we have shown so far are not always adequate to deal with the complexity of real-life price decisions. The use of comprehensive decision-support systems can be more appropriate.

Decision-support systems integrate information about customer preferences and needs, the buying decision, the market structure and trends (for competitive products as well as one's own), as well as other marketing instruments (communication, sales, and distribution). This information, as shown in Fig. 5.4, is consolidated into a decision-support system and allows one to forecast sales volumes at different prices. One can consider a vast number of price effects: customers' switching among different suppliers, switching between product categories of the same supplier, and switching within a product category. If one includes costs in the system, one can make profit calculations.

In order to express a real buying decision in a decision-support system, one should consider the following influence factors:

- First, one must precisely define the relevant market. Does the market for automobiles, for example, include only premium class vehicles or mass market ones as well? Do future product decisions affect only private customers/ consumers, or will they also have an influence on the buying decisions of business customers? The definition of the relevant market determines which products (competitors and one's own) should be incorporated into the system.

- The core elements of a decision-support system are customer needs and preferences as well as the purchase decision processes. One collects the information on these two aspects through customer surveys.
- Buying decision processes differ by product and situation. The process for low-involvement products is different from the one for high-involvement products [10, p. 41].
- The last step in the development of a decision-support system is the calibration. One adjusts the market share forecast, derived from the collected data and the underlying algorithms, to reflect reality as closely as possible. These adjustments are made by hand. The resulting market shares form a base scenario, which one uses for subsequent simulations. This process resembles one used in meteorology, which calibrates complex weather forecasting models using historical data, before forecasting future weather [11].

Ultimately, one wants to emulate an individual customer's decision context and price-response as realistically as possible. That requires a deep understanding of the relevant features at the individual customer level. How detailed the statements and outputs of a decision-support system should be depends on the questions management would like to have answered.

Case Study: Decision-Support System for an Innovation
Companies face a high level of uncertainty regarding the optimal price when they launch a new product. This is most critical for innovations, which create new markets. Mistakes made in the initial positioning are hard to correct. The use of a decision-support system is helpful in these situations in order to quantify the effects of different price levels on sales and profit. Figure 5.5 shows the use of such a system for a very innovative professional system for ironing shirts. The left-hand side of Fig. 5.5 shows a picture of the ironing system as well as the product specs and price of a basic configuration. The right-hand side depicts the price-response curves for three product variants, derived from a decision-support system. If one includes the costs of the different variants, one can calculate the associated profits. One can make fundamental price decisions on this basis, taking strategic goals (volume targets, profit targets) into account. Critical success factors of a decision-support system are the precise determination of the value-to-customer for individual product attributes and prices, as well as the quantification of the market potential.

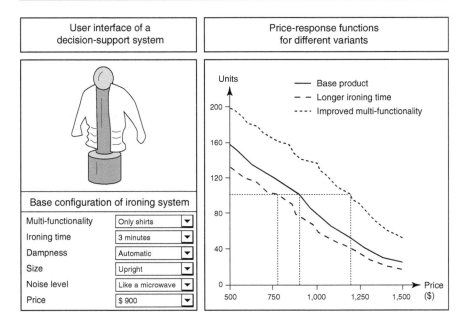

Fig. 5.5 User interface and price-response functions of a decision-support system for an ironing system

---

Overview

We summarize the use of decision-support systems:

- Decision-support systems are very well suited to support complex price decisions.
- Two things are particularly important: (1) the adaptation and calibration of the model to the specific situation and (2) deep methodological expertise. Standardized models applied without a thorough understanding of neither the methodology nor the system's interrelationships significantly increase the risk of mistakes.
- To achieve valid and reliable results, we recommend the integration of multiple information sources and multiple analytical methods.

5.4.3 Mathematical Price Optimization

The most elegant and precise form of price optimization is the mathematical price optimization. It determines the profit-maximizing price by expressing price-volume relationships as mathematical functions. It examines all prices within specific intervals, rather than a small number of selected price points. The optimal price is not determined through the comparison of discrete values, but through examination of the entire profit curve. In this way, one can derive simple optimality rules for specific price-response and cost functions.

5.4.3.1 Monopoly Case

First, we look at the case of a monopolist. We do not need to take any competitive prices into account. The profit function is:

$$\pi = R - C = p \times q(p) - C[q(p)] \tag{5.4}$$

with R = revenue, C = costs, p = price, q = quantity, and $q(p)$ as the price-response function. In order to maximize profit, we differentiate the profit function and get:

$$\frac{\partial \pi}{\partial p} = \underbrace{q(p) + p\frac{\partial q}{\partial p}}_{\text{marginal revenue}} - \underbrace{\frac{\partial C}{\partial q}\frac{\partial q}{\partial p}}_{\text{marginal costs}} = 0 \tag{5.5}$$

At the optimal price p^*, this derivative equals zero. This is the case when marginal revenue and marginal costs (as a function of price) are equal. The condition "marginal revenue = marginal cost" dictates that the changes in revenue and cost are in balance. If the price is lower than the optimal price, the costs will increase faster than the revenue. Conversely, if the price is higher than the optimal price, the revenue falls faster than the costs. In either case, profit is lower than at the optimal price p^*.

One can explain the effects of a deviation of the price from its optimum on the basis of the unit contribution margin and the volume, which move in opposite directions as the price changes.

- *Price increases from the optimum*: Relative to the optimal price, a price increase results in a higher unit contribution margin. The percentage increase in the unit contribution margin is less, however, than the percentage decline in sales volume. This has a net negative effect on profit.
- *Price decreases from the optimum*: A price decrease from the optimal price results in higher sales volumes, but the percentage increase in volume is less than the percentage decline in unit contribution margin. This likewise has a net negative effect on profit.

Condition (5.5) also recognizes that only the marginal costs influence the optimal price. The optimal price does not depend on fixed costs. When we take the derivative of the profit function, fixed costs disappear from the equation because they are a constant. Every pricing method which attempts to set an optimal price as a function of fixed costs is logically incorrect.

We can use price elasticities to derive a simple formula for the optimal price p^* (from (5.5)), the so-called Amoroso-Robinson relation[1]:

$$p^* = \frac{\varepsilon}{1 + \varepsilon} C'$$ (5.6)

with $\varepsilon = \frac{\partial q}{\partial p} \frac{p^*}{q}$ as the price elasticity and $C' = \frac{\partial C}{\partial q}$ as marginal costs (as a function of volume).

The optimal price is thus an elasticity-based markup on marginal costs. What is shown in (5.6), however, does not solve for the optimal price p^*; rather it is simply a reformulation of the necessary condition "marginal revenue = marginal cost." The price elasticity and the marginal cost C' can themselves be a function of price. The higher the price elasticity is (in absolute terms), i.e., the more sensitive demand is to price changes, the lower the optimal price will be. The optimal price always lies in a range for which the price elasticity (in absolute terms) is greater than 1. Because the price elasticity at the revenue-maximizing price is equal to -1, the profit-maximizing price is always higher than the revenue-maximizing price. A price increase will increase profit when the price elasticity is less than 1 in absolute terms. For example, if a price increase of 10% results in a volume decline of 5%, the price elasticity is -0.5, and it makes sense to raise prices.

5.4.3.2 Price Optimization for a Multiplicative Price-Response Function

As we know from Chap. 3, the multiplicative price-response function has a constant price elasticity. If the marginal costs are also constant, i.e., the cost function is linear, then one can use formula (5.6) directly as a rule for price decisions. If the price elasticity has a value of -2, for example, the optimal markup factor is 2. One adds 100% to the marginal costs. If the price elasticity is -3, the markup factor is 1.5, which means a markup of 50% on marginal costs. If the price elasticity is -5, the markup is only 25%. The closer the price elasticity gets to one, the more the markup factor rises. At a price elasticity of -1.2, the markup is 500%.

5.4.3.3 Price Optimization for a Linear Price-Response Function

For a linear price-response function and a linear cost function, the formula for the optimal price is[2]:

$$p^* = \frac{1}{2}\left(\frac{a}{b} + k\right)$$ (5.7)

The quotient a/b is the maximum price, i.e., the price at which the sales volume would be zero.

---

[1]One multiplies (5.5) with $\frac{p}{q}$, expresses the price elasticity as ε according to (3.3), and solves for p^*.

[2]For the derivation, see the Background Information at the end of the chapter.

The optimal price p^* lies exactly at the midpoint between the variable unit costs k and this maximum price. In order to determine the optimal price in the linear case, one therefore only needs to know the variable unit costs and the maximum price.

From Eq. (5.7) it follows that a cost increase should result in a price increase of only half that amount. In the same vein, only half of a cost decrease would be passed on to customers. In reality one actually observes that firms do not fully pass on cost changes in their prices. When milk prices rose by ten cents, for example, ALDI only passed seven cents of the increase on to consumers [12]. Cost savings, in contrast, are usually passed on directly to consumers, according to the homepage of ALDI Süd, one of the company's two operating units [13]. (ALDI Nord, the other unit, operates the Trader Joe's chain in the United States.)

In another case, a building cleaning services firm passes on only 80% of its labor cost increase to its customers [14]. After a decline in oil prices, Ryanair CEO Michael O'Leary [15] said the company would pass on almost all, but not all, of the savings to its customers. One can interpret "almost all" as meaning that only part of the savings will be reflected in lower ticket prices—probably a wise move.

We will now demonstrate price optimization for linear price-response and cost functions for a fashion brand. The fixed costs are $2.95 million. The variable unit costs are $60. The price-response function is:

$$q = 300,000 - 2,000p \tag{5.8}$$

so that the maximum price $p^{\mathrm{max}} = 300,000/2000 = \$150$. The optimal price is therefore:

$$p^* = \frac{1}{2}(150 + 60) = \$105 \tag{5.9}$$

Figure 5.6 displays this optimization graphically. The price of $105 lies exactly between the variable unit cost of $60 and the maximum price of $150. The total contribution margin, which is the product of the unit contribution margin and the sales volume, appears graphically as a rectangle. The profit curve describes the size of the rectangle. The area of the rectangle (and thus the total contribution margin) reaches its maximum when the price lies at the midpoint between the variable unit costs and the maximum price. The sales volume at this price is 90,000 units. The maximum profit is $1.1 million. The more the company deviates from the profit-maximizing price, the more strongly the profit declines. The profit curve is symmetrical, which means that upward price deviations from the optimal price have the same effect on profit as downward price deviations of the same magnitude.

5.4.3.4 Price Optimization for a Gutenberg Function

The Gutenberg price-response function (see Fig. 3.6) leads to more complex profit curves. These can have either a global maximum or two local maxima. At each of these points, the general condition "marginal revenue = marginal costs" is fulfilled.

Sales volume (units -000.000)
Profit ($ mill.)

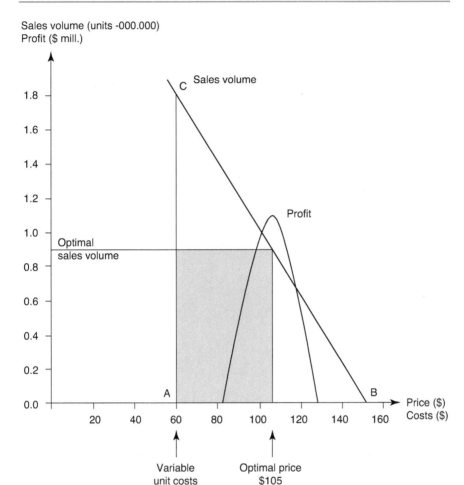

Fig. 5.6 Determining the optimal price (linear price-response and cost function)

Thus, it is not enough to know only one price at which this condition holds. One must be sure to find the global profit maximum.

The different cases are best illustrated using numerical examples. We assume the following Gutenberg price-response function:

$$q = a - c_1 \sinh[c_2(p - \bar{p})] \tag{5.10}$$

The variable $\bar{p}$ represents either the competitive price (when one is looking at the price difference to competitors) or the previous price (when one is looking at the effect of a price change). In each example, we set $a = 10$ and $\bar{p} = 2$. We assume a linear cost function with variable unit costs of k. There are three possible cases, as shown in Table 5.4:

Table 5.4 Parameter
values for the three cases of
Gutenberg function

Parameter	Case 1	Case 2	Case 3
c_1	3	0.2	0.4
c_2	1	5	4
k	1.20	0.65	0.25

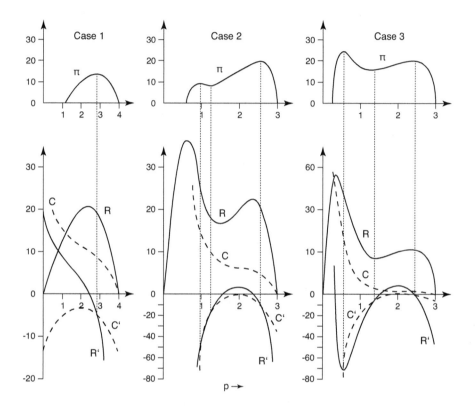

Fig. 5.7 The three cases of Gutenberg function

- Case 1: There is only one profit maximum.
- Case 2: There are two profit maxima, and the profit is highest at the higher price.
- Case 3: There are two profit maxima, and the profit is highest at the lower price.

Figure 5.7 illustrates these three cases.

The upper part of the figure shows the profit functions, from which one can readily recognize the profit maxima and the optimal prices. The lower part explains how these curves were derived. For this purpose, the solid-line curves show revenue R and marginal revenue R'. The dashed-line curves indicate costs C and marginal costs C'. The thin vertical lines mark the respective positions of the maxima and

Table 5.5 Optimal vales for the three cases of the Gutenberg function

Result	Case 1	Case 2	Case 3
Optimal price p^*	2.87	2.46	0.54
Profit maximum	11.77	16.31	22.84
Local optimal price	–	0.96	2.40
Local profit maximum	–	8.72	19.46

minima of the profit function, which always coincide where marginal revenue equals marginal cost, i.e., where the curves intersect.

Case 1: One Profit Maximum
If the Gutenberg function is only slightly kinked, then there is only one profit maximum. Price cuts do not attract enough demand and thus reduce the profit. The optimal price lies at the upper end of the monopolistic part of the Gutenberg function.

Case 2: Two Profit Maxima; the Higher Price Is Optimal
The Gutenberg function has a stronger kink in this case, so that there is a second profit maximum at a low price. But the kink is not pronounced enough, which means that the larger sales volume at the lower price point cannot compensate for the decline in the unit contribution margin. The upper price yields the higher profit. The optimal price once again lies in the upper end of the monopolistic part of the function. This indicates a premium positioning.

Case 3: Two Profit Maxima; the Lower Price Is Optimal
This applies when the Gutenberg function has a pronounced kink. Sales volume responds much more strongly to large price deviations or cuts than to small price deviations or cuts. The more the price elasticity increases with the extent of the price cut, the greater the chances that case 3 occurs and that the global profit maximum is achieved at a low price. A low-price positioning is optimal in such a case.

Table 5.5 provides an overview of the optimal values for the three cases of the Gutenberg function.

The cost function has implications for the price positioning. Marginal costs which are constant and low or decline with volume favor a low-price positioning, while constant and high or progressively increasing marginal costs make a premium price positioning more advantageous.

If we summarize the aspects of cost and price effects (the latter categorized into "weakly kinked" and "strongly kinked" price-response functions), we can derive the qualitative recommendations shown in Table 5.6.

Table 5.6 Qualitative recommendations for different constellations of Gutenberg functions and marginal costs

Marginal costs	Price-response function	
	Weakly kinked	Strongly kinked
Constant high or progressively increasing	Premium price definitely optimal	Premium price tends to be optimal
Constant low or progressively decreasing	Premium price tends to be optimal	Low price is definitely optimal

Overview

To sum up, we state the following regarding price positioning with a Gutenberg price-response function. Two local profit maxima could exist. The first lies at a premium price; the second, if it exists, is at a noticeably lower price. A prerequisite for the lower-priced profit maximum is a strong kink in the price-response function as well as low marginal costs. Due to the potential existence of two profit maxima, the measurement and analysis of the price-response function must include a wide price interval. Finding only one price where marginal revenue and marginal costs are equal does not guarantee maximum profit. One has to investigate which of the two profit maxima is the global maximum.

5.4.4   Price Optimization in Oligopoly

In the case of an oligopoly, a company must take the reactions of competitors into account. This makes the price decision significantly more complicated. In general, there is no definitive optimal price in an oligopoly. The price depends instead on assumptions about the behavior of competitors. The challenge is to set the price in a way that it is optimal after competitors respond. In order to do this with precision, one must consider the reaction functions of the competitors and not just the price-response function of the customers:

$$p_i = r_i(p_1, \ldots, p_{i-1}, p_{i+1}, \ldots p_n), \quad i = 1, \ldots, n \tag{5.11}$$

The reaction function r_i describes how the oligopolist i will react to price measures taken by competitor j. Theoretically, one can justify differences across individual reaction functions, because competitors may indeed react differently. Determining such detailed functions empirically, however, is not practical. Similar to the estimation of the price-response function, it makes sense to use an aggregated form of the reaction function. The average price of the competitors then serves as the explanatory variable from the perspective of the oligopolist j, giving us the formula:

$$\bar{p}_j = r(p_j) \tag{5.12}$$

Thus, one needs to determine only one reaction function, but this also means that any differentiated reaction by competitors will not be captured. A compromise between (5.11) and (5.12) could be to group together brands which show similar reactions (e.g., store brands vs. manufacturer brands or branded goods vs. no-name goods). As a rule, one normally opts for the simpler form. We use a simplified version for the following line of thought.

By inserting the reaction function (5.12) into the price-response function (without a product index):

$$q = f(p, \bar{p}) \qquad (5.13)$$

we get:

$$q = f[p, \bar{p}(p)] \qquad (5.14)$$

The sales volume q depends here on one's own price p and on the competitors' price $\bar{p}$, which in turn depends on one's own price. In order to determine the optimal price, we differentiate the profit function with respect to p and set the derivative equal to zero:

$$\frac{\partial \pi}{\partial p} = \underbrace{q + p^* \frac{\partial q}{\partial p}}_{\text{marginal revenue}} - \underbrace{C' \frac{\partial q}{\partial p}}_{\text{marginal costs}} = 0 \qquad (5.15)$$

with $C' = \frac{\partial C}{\partial q}$ as marginal cost based on volume. The fundamental principle "marginal revenue $=$ marginal costs" remains unchanged in an oligopoly. After additional steps we get the following formula for the optimal price[2]:

$$p^* = \frac{\varepsilon + \sigma \varepsilon_k}{1 + \varepsilon + \sigma \varepsilon_k} C' \qquad (5.16)$$

with $\varepsilon = \frac{\partial q}{\partial p} \times \frac{p}{q}$ direct price elasticity, $\varepsilon_k = \frac{\partial q}{\partial \bar{p}} \times \frac{\bar{p}}{q}$ cross-price elasticity for the product in question vs. the competitors' price, and $\sigma = \frac{\partial \bar{p}}{\partial p} \times p\bar{p}$ reaction elasticity of the competitors' price vs. the price of the product in question.

The *reaction elasticity* indicates the percentage change in the competitors' price when one's own price changes by 1%.

The optimality condition structurally resembles the Amoroso-Robinson relation (5.6). But in an oligopoly, the markup to marginal costs is determined not only by the direct price elasticity, but rather by an "adjusted" elasticity which incorporates competitive reaction ($\varepsilon + \sigma \varepsilon_k$). The expression ($\varepsilon + \sigma \varepsilon_k$) can be interpreted as "price elasticity after competitive reaction."

To determine the markup, one must not only know the direct price elasticity but also the cross-price elasticity and the reaction elasticity. We note here once again that

(5.16) does not solve for p^* because all expressions on the right-hand side of the equation can depend on p^*.

The cross-price elasticity between competing products is positive. The reaction elasticity will normally be either zero or positive, i.e., the competition either does not respond at all or moves its prices in the same direction as the initiator's change. In the latter case, the optimal price, taking competitive reaction into account, is equal to or higher than the price when one does not take the reaction into account and makes decisions on the basis of the "monopolistic" Amoroso-Robinson relation (5.6). If the reaction elasticity is zero, formula (5.16) corresponds to the Amoroso-Robinson relation.

In the case of multiplicative price-response and reaction functions, formula (5.16) can be used directly as a rule for price decisions. Let us assume these values: price elasticity $= -2$, cross-price elasticity $= 0.5$, and reaction elasticity $= 1$. Then the equation yields a markup factor of 3, assuming constant marginal costs (i.e., a linear cost function). That means that marginal cost should be marked up by 200%. If the cross-price elasticity is 0.6, the percentage markup increases to 250%. If the reaction elasticity is 0.5, keeping all the other original parameters the same, the markup percentage is only 133%. A lower reaction elasticity reduces the optimal markup.

Overview

We summarize the key points for price optimization, taking competitive reaction into account:

- The conditions for an optimal price in an oligopoly can be expressed in a form similar to the Amoroso-Robinson relation.
- The optimal price is equal to the marginal costs multiplied by a markup factor which depends on the direct price elasticity, the cross-price elasticity, and the reaction elasticity.

5.4.4.1 Linear Price-Response Function, Linear Reaction Function

Now we will consider the case of linear price-response and reaction functions. In general, we assume that the cost function is also linear.

If we incorporate the linear reaction function:

$$\bar{p} = \alpha + \beta p \qquad (5.17)$$

into the linear price-response function $q = a - bp + c\bar{p}$, we get a price-response function with competitive reaction:

$$q = (a + c\alpha) - (b - c\beta)p. \qquad (5.18)$$

One can apply the monopolistic decision-making rule in formula (5.7) to this "reaction-adjusted" function, in order to get the optimal price:

$$p^* = \frac{1}{2}\left(\frac{a + c\alpha}{b - c\beta} + k\right). \tag{5.19}$$

The ratio in parentheses corresponds to the reaction-adjusted maximum price. The optimal price lies exactly at the midpoint between this maximum price and the variable unit costs k. The optimal price is dependent on all the parameters in the price-response and reaction functions.

As with the case of constant elasticities, the optimal price in (5.19) rises with the competitive reaction parameter β. The stronger the competition reacts to one's own price changes, the higher the optimal price will be.

5.4.4.2 Case Study

We shed light on reaction behavior by investigating a case study from the market for household cleaning products. Figure 5.8 shows the actual price trends for the four most important brands.

The time period observed is 2 years and 4 months. As a visual inspection reveals, the prices for the brands A, B, C, and D have followed a similar development. It appears that a reaction interdependence exists. The linear reaction function (5.17) does a good job of explaining the development of market-share-weighted

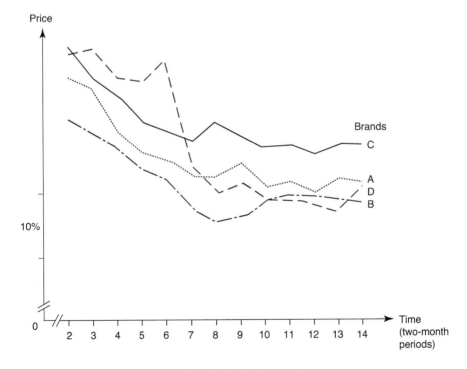

Fig. 5.8 Price trends in a market for households cleaning products

Table 5.7 Linear reaction
function for four household
cleaners

Variable				
Dependent	Independent	α	β	R^2
$\bar{p}_A$	p_A	0.131	0.927	0.9462
$\bar{p}_B$	p_B	−0.306	1.284	0.8882
$\bar{p}_C$	p_C	−0.184	1.037	0.8464
$\bar{p}_D$	p_D	0.876	0.436	0.7180

competitors' prices. The coefficients of determination R^2 are all high, and all coefficients are statistically significant at the 10% level. Table 5.7 shows the results.

For a demonstration of price determination, we choose the brand D, whose reaction coefficient β has a value of 0.436. The linear price-response function we use here is a version in which the price difference (and not the absolute price) serves as the independent variable. As price-response function for D, we obtain:

$$q_D = 3,373 - 8,624(p_D - \bar{p}_D) \qquad (5.20)$$

The "reaction-adjusted" maximum price for D is $2.25 per kilogram, i.e., the "reaction-adjusted" price-response function intersects with the price axis at $2.25. The marginal costs are $0.85. For the optimal price, taking competitive reaction into account, we use formula (5.19) and get:

$$p^* = \frac{1}{2}(2.25 + 0.85) = 1.55. \qquad (5.21)$$

If the competition responds according to the estimated function, they would also set their price (on average) at $0.876 + 0.436 \times 1.55 = 1.55$, i.e., at the same level.

Under this price constellation, brand D will have a sales volume of 3373 tons and would earn a contribution margin of $2.361 million. The direct price elasticity and the cross-price elasticity are equal in absolute terms $|\varepsilon| = \varepsilon_k = 3.96$. The reaction elasticity σ is 0.436, as: $\bar{p}_D = p_D$.

It is interesting to compare this optimal price with the one derived without taking competitive reaction into account. To demonstrate this, we assume a competitive price of $1.55 and consider this price as a given. The optimal price without competitive reaction works out to:

$$p^* = \frac{1}{2}(1.94 + 0.85) = 1.40. \qquad (5.22)$$

If the competition really does not react, at that price, brand D achieves a sales volume of 4667 tons and a contribution margin of $2.567 million. That is more than the $2.361 million in the situation above. In reality, i.e., if the measured reaction function is valid, the competition will react and set its price at $p_D = 0.876 + 0.436 \times 1.40 = \$1.49$. At this price, brand D sells only 4149 tones (instead of the erroneously expected 4667). The contribution margin falls to $2.282 million, which is smaller than the optimal value when taking competitive reaction into account ($2.361 million).

5.4.4.3 Price Optimization with Subjective Estimations of Competitive Reaction

Subjective estimation by managers can serve as an alternative to the econometric calibration of reaction functions using historical price data. Based on such estimates, we can derive reaction-adjusted price-response functions. Figure 5.9 illustrates this approach. The managers were asked to predict the expected competitive reaction to

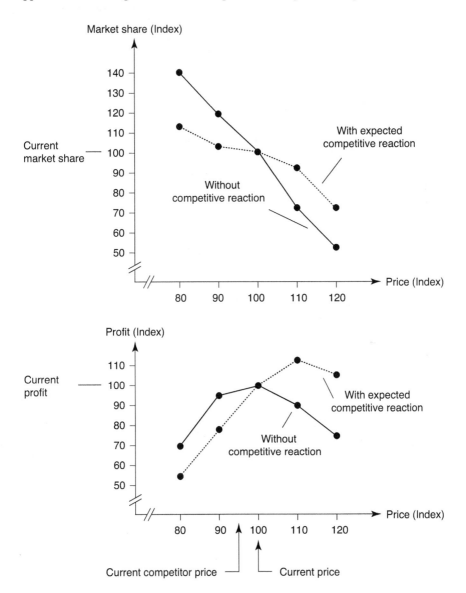

Fig. 5.9 Price-response functions and profit curves based on subjective estimation (with and without competitive reaction)

five alternative prices, and the resulting market shares were determined based on their reaction assumptions. In the case of a price cut, the managers expected a competitive reaction, as they did for a price increase of 10%. In contrast, the managers anticipated that competitors would not follow a price increase of 20%. With this reaction, a price increase to $p = 110$ is optimal.

The method of subjective estimation is easy to apply and more flexible than reaction functions derived from market data. All aspects which can influence reaction behavior can be considered. On the other hand, these approximations do not always solve the problem of competitive reaction. Managers are often more uncertain about competitive reactions than about estimating price-response functions.

5.4.5   Reaction Hypotheses in an Oligopoly

The assumption of a fixed (e.g., linear or multiplicative) reaction function means that the competition will respond to every price move in the manner prescribed by the function. Oligopoly theories based on such rigid reaction patterns are called heuristic. More sophisticated oligopoly theories do not mandate a specific reaction, but instead deduce the reaction from the optimization context. The primary impulses behind those theories are ideas derived from game theory. Game theory provides managers with a general framework for strategic thinking, even though it offers few firm rules for price decisions.

In order to anticipate competitors' reactions, one must put oneself in their situation—inside their heads, so to speak—and ask what reactions would be optimal for them. It is obvious that prerequisites for answering such questions include knowledge of the competitors' goals, costs, financial situation, etc. The answers to many of these questions will rely on speculation.

The situation is made even more complicated because the competitors' thought processes will include their speculation about *our* response to *their* response. In fact, it can play an important role in their decision. We therefore not only need to infer what the competition thinks about its own situation but ours as well. For now, we will consider the first of these steps: how will our pricing moves affect the competition? We assume that the competition is interested in profit maximization, just as we are. A competitor will therefore only react when its reaction will yield a higher profit than the do-nothing option.

In order to make the oligopolistic relationships easy to understand and to come up with solutions, we will use a linear price-response function. The oligopoly we are looking at is symmetrical and consists of oligopolists A and B (a so-called duopoly). The price-response function of oligopolist i is:

$$q_i = a - bp_i + cp_j; \quad i,j = \mathrm{A}, \mathrm{B} \tag{5.23}$$

Table 5.8 Results with and without reaction

		Duopolist A	Duopolist B
Starting situation	Price in $	20	20
	Volume in units	500	500
	Profit in $	6500	6500
Without reaction of competitor B	Price in $	17.50	20.00
	Volume in units	625 (+125)	437.5 (−62.5)
	Profit in $	6812.50 (+312.50)	5562.50 (−937.50)
With reaction of competitor B	Price in $	17.50	17.50
	Volume in units	562.50 (+62.50)	562.50 (+62.50)
	Profit in $	6031.00 (−369.00)	6031.00 (−369.00)

with the parameters $a = 1000$, $b = 50$, $c = 25$. The cost function is likewise linear with $C_{fix} = \$1000$ and $k = \$5$.

In Table 5.8 we show three situations. In the starting situation, both competitors have the same price $p_{A0} = p_{B0} = 20$. They each sell 500 units and achieve a profit of \$500.

Duopolist A now undertakes an examination of its pricing. We consider two alternative cases. In the first, A assumes that B will not react. In the second, A assumes that B will react.

5.4.5.1 Cournot Hypothesis

Case 1: A assumes that B will not react and maintain its current price of $p_{B0} = 20$. This reflects the so-called Cournot hypothesis, the oldest of the heuristic oligopoly hypotheses. A's price-response function is then:

$$q_A = (a + cp_{B0}) - bp_A = (1,000 + 25 \times 20) - 50p_A \qquad (5.24)$$

Under this assumption, the optimal price can be calculated as in a monopoly situation according to formula (5.7). This results in:

$$p_A^* = \frac{1}{2}\left(\frac{a + cp_{B0}}{b} + k\right) = \frac{1}{2}\left(\frac{1,500}{50} + 5\right) = 17.50 \qquad (5.25)$$

This price is referred to as the Cournot price. If B in fact does not respond, A achieves a volume of 625 units and earns a profit of \$6812.50, which is greater than the profit of \$6500 in the starting situation. What happens to the profit of B? If B does nothing, it loses customers to A. B's volume declines from 500 to 437.50 units, and as a result its profit drops to \$5562.50. Table 5.8 shows these results. Assuming that duopolist B is not "stupid" or uninformed, it will not accept this deterioration of its profit situation. B most likely will respond. If B likewise cuts its price to $17.50, the price-response function for A is:

$$q_A = a - (b - c)p_A = 1,000 - 25p_A \qquad (5.26)$$

Due to the reaction of B, A's sales volume does not increase to 625, as A had originally and now incorrectly anticipated. It rises only to 562.50 units, which yields a profit of only $6031. This is lower than the starting profit of $6500. B's profit also falls to $6031, but that is still better than B's "do-nothing" profit of only $5562. Table 5.8 shows these results. Thus, there is a high probability that B will respond to A's price cut with one of its own. If A expects this to happen, it would forgo the price cut and leave the price unchanged at $20, because a price cut combined with a reaction from B would leave A worse off.

5.4.5.2 Chamberlin Hypothesis

Case 2: In A's review of its pricing policies, A now assumes that B will respond in full to its price change, i.e., that the price-response function shown in (5.26) applies. If A optimizes under this assumption, its optimal price would be:

$$p_A^* = \frac{1}{2}\left(\frac{a}{b-c} + k\right) = \frac{1}{2}\left(\frac{1,000}{25} + 5\right) = 22.50 \qquad (5.27)$$

This price is the so-called Chamberlin price. At this price, A would sell 437.50 units and earn a profit of $6656, which is higher than the initial profit of $6500.

What are the consequences for B? If B reacts in the manner which A anticipates and matches the price increase to $22.50, B would also achieve a profit of $6656, an improvement over its starting situation. But B does even better if it does not react. In that case, its sales volume would increase to 562.50 units thanks to the inflow of switching customers. B's profit would increase to $7438. Assuming the duopolist B does not think further, it would not react to A's price increase. The "do-nothing" response from B, however, would mean that A's price increased to $22.50 would reduce A's profit to $5562.50. If A therefore feels that B will not react, A will act swiftly to rescind its decision to raise its price and keep the price at the old level.

5.4.5.3 Game Theory Interpretation

The line of thinking shown above ascribes intelligent behavior to the duopolist B rather than adherence to a rigid response. But the thought process of B, or at least A's understanding of it, ended at least one step too early.

The line of thinking was as follows:

- B does not react to A's price increase, because the "do-nothing" response leaves B better off.
- A knows that and decides not to raise its price. Both companies remain stuck in the starting situation. If B thinks further ahead, it would realize that its "do-

Table 5.9 The oligopoly situation as prisoner's dilemma

Options	B doesn't raise ($p_B = \$20$)	B raises ($p_B = \$22.50$)
A doesn't raise ($p_A = \$20$)	Field 1 $\pi_A = \$6500$ $\pi_B = \$6500$	Field 2 $\pi_A = \$7438$ $\pi_B = \$5563$
A raises ($p_A = \$22.50$)	Field 3 $\pi_A = \$5563$ $\pi_B = \$7438$	Field 4 $\pi_A = \$6656$ $\pi_B = \$6656$

nothing" response to A's price increase would have left it better off than a reaction would have but prevented A from implementing a price increase. That standstill hardens the positions on both sides and leaves B's profit at $G_B = 6500$, which is less than its profit of $G_B = 6656$ had it followed A's increase.

The situation captured in Table 5.9 is known in game theory as the prisoner's dilemma. The option "don't raise" corresponds to a "betrayal" of the other prisoner. The option "raise price" is the equivalent of the "remain silent" option.

The success of an oligopolist depends on its reactions to its competitors. Price changes by competitors can have an immediate and noticeable effect on one's own profit. Price changes in an oligopoly are burdened with greater uncertainty due to the potential competitive reactions. The simplest way to reduce this uncertainty would be an arrangement or a contractual agreement among the oligopolists. But such price cartels are not only forbidden under antitrust and competition laws, they are also punished with increasing severity.

The pricing situation takes on the character of a dilemma in particular when the price increase would be binding for a longer time period (because of organizational, contractual, or other reasons). If A increases its price, but B does not follow, then A has a worsened profit position (Field 3, $p_A = \$22.50$; $p_B = \$20$). This option is attractive for B, because it does well in Field 3. A price increase is thus risky for the company which takes the initiative; it is referred to as playing the "martyr role." The martyr also runs the risk of needing to rescind the price increase, which could damage its image. If A does not trust B, A will choose a strategy which in the worst case earns it the maximum profit (a max-min strategy). In other words, it would leave the price unchanged at $p_A = \$20$. A's profit of $\$6500$ at that level is the least endangered.

But when A can assume, on the basis of prior experience, that B will follow its price increase, then A would raise its price. If B does indeed follow, according to the Chamberlin hypothesis, the profits of both duopolists increase compared to the starting situation and represent a collective maximum. This situation can also be achieved via cost-plus calculations at customary industry markups, through the strategy of price adjustments or through price leadership. Such rules of thumb can lead to optimal results in an oligopoly.

Stigler [16] considers price leadership the best solution to the oligopoly problem. Much speaks in favor of this strategy. It leads to satisfactory results for all competitors, at least when they have similar cost and sales volume positions. But it also has its limitations. Price leadership and similar behaviors demand a considerable amount of strategic intelligence and mutual trust among competitors. It also requires a certain similarity across costs, goals, and demand structure. Such conditions are most likely to occur in established and mature markets with a stable number of competitors who "know each other well." But even under such circumstances, one still runs into "dumb" industries or companies who wage price wars.

Such aligned conduct rarely occurs in dynamic markets. New competitors, especially ones entering from other countries or other industries (diversification), are likely to dismiss established price setting rules and force their way into the market using aggressive prices. When different cost positions exist or are achievable (e.g., through experience-curve or network effects), then an equilibrium with respect to prices is just as unlikely. The new and growing market for inter-city and long-distance bus lines in Europe, and the re-emergence of the market in some regions of the United States, has been characterized by price wars from the start. These have been so severe that some competitors did not even survive for more than a year [17]. In these early phases of a market, two goals dominate competitors' thinking. First, they want to use low prices to lure customers onto the bus and away from driving or taking the train. Second, they want to force financially weaker competitors out of the market in order to gain market share [18]. Within 3 years, Flixbus reached both goals. It has more than 90% of the German market, and only three competitors are left [19]. After such mergers or acquisitions, prices typically start to shift upwards. That happened in this market, with prices rising by 15% on average in the span of one quarter [20].

The market for cloud services found itself in the same situation, with a price war raging between Amazon and Google [21]. The financial strength of competitors is decisive for success or failure, especially in early market stages. Stronger companies can withstand losses or forgo profits for longer periods while expanding their capacity and their market shares.

Overview
We summarize the key aspects of price optimization in an oligopoly:

- In an oligopoly there is no definitive optimal price. The optimal price instead depends on competitive reactions. Therefore, competitive reactions must be included in setting prices.
- Oligopolies can succeed in achieving or at least approximating a collective monopoly price if the following conditions hold: competitors have similar cost and market positions, pursue similar goals, have sufficient strategic intelligence, and possess a certain level of trust in each other.
- Oligopolies are better off abstaining from significant price changes if these conditions do not apply or one or more of them decide for whatever reason

(continued)

not to move their prices toward that collective monopoly price. One may increase prices, however, to compensate for higher costs which affect all oligopolists. Price cuts may likewise confer no sustained advantage on the initiator, because competitors are likely to respond in kind and provoke a price war.

5.4.5.4 Signaling

Signaling refers to public indications, or signals, which the oligopolist sends to the market in the run-up to planned price adjustments. These signals may be transmitted via press, radio, television, the Internet, or other communications channels. Porter [22, p. 75] defines a market signal as "any action by a competitor which provides a direct or indirect indication of its intentions, motives, goals, or internal situation." The signals can come in the form of actions or statements [23, p. 28]. Statements are viewed as less credible than actions, as some companies will bluff in an attempt to mislead competitors. To signal effectively, a company's actions must be consistent with its statements and vice versa [24, p. 113].

The concept of signaling is based on the idea that an action of a company will draw a reaction, as long as that company is in a competitive situation, i.e., the cross-price elasticity is not zero [25, p. 8]. The concept begs the question about the goals which competing companies are pursuing when they make price cuts or price increases. The interpretation of these goals can prompt a signal which can likewise be met with a reaction.

Signaling can help a company:

- Discourage or prevent a potential competitor from entering a market.
- Justify price changes, especially price cuts. For example, if a company has a product at the end of its life cycle, it may want to discount that product to clear inventory. Communicating this intent and a limited time period may prevent competitors from misinterpreting the price cut as aggressive and from making similar price cuts.
- Motivate competitors to follow a particular behavior. This can be important for price increases. In these cases, companies often communicate the rationale behind the increase so that not only competitors but also customers (retailers, resellers, consumers) become aware of and ideally accept the necessity of the price increase.

The interpretation of market signals is vitally important. A price cut by one competitor may represent an attempt to gain market share or a desire to reduce inventories [26, p. 755]. The former may be perceived as a much more aggressive action [27, p. 225]. This situation explains why the same price move may prompt different reactions. A precise examination of the characteristics of the signals offers valuable clues into its intent. Heil and Bungert [28, p. 93] have classified the characteristics of signals as follows:

- The signal's effect describes the assessment of the reacting company on the extent to which the announced or implemented price changes of a competitor will affect one's own profit or market share.
- The signal's aggressiveness is determined by the amount of the price cut and the associated threat it poses to competitors.
- A signal is considered clear when it allows little room for interpretation. Clear signals often lead to immediate reactions. Unclear signals allow wider latitude for (mis)interpretation.
- Signal consistency refers to the alignment of signals the same company sends in other markets or market segments.
- The extent to which a signal is binding is a function of how reversible it is.
- The credibility of the sender affects the likelihood that the announced plan will actually be implemented. It is a decisive factor in signaling.

The market for automotive insurance in Germany offers an example for successful signaling. For years, the market had endured price wars instigated by one of the market leaders. In October 2011, the German business press reported that "Germany's largest insurance group, Allianz, is going to raise prices drastically, effective January 1, 2012" [29]. All other insurance companies publicly announced that they would raise their prices as well. In the course of 2012, prices rose by 7% on average. Then the chairman of HUK-Coburg, Allianz's biggest rival, announced that "in 2013, prices should rise again" [30]. Prices did indeed rise by around 6% in 2013. Price leadership only emerges when a company takes on that role and its competitors recognize it as the price leader.

Companies also use signaling to announce a retaliation, in an effort to discourage their competitors from taking a course of action such as a price cut. Im Tak-Uk, the chief operating officer of Korean car manufacturer Hyundai, claimed publicly that if ". . . Japanese car makers become aggressive in raising incentives and the red light comes on in achieving our sales target, we will consider raising incentives for buyers" [31, p. 24]. "Incentives" are higher discounts or, in other words, price cuts. The statement could hardly be any clearer.

Such statements must be carefully formulated, however, to avoid the risk of violating antitrust or competition law. Not only are direct incitements of competitors to cooperative behavior forbidden, but a "message in a bottle" approach or a letter directed at customers to inform them of a price increase may be viewed critically if the underlying intent is perceived to be an attempt to inform competitors, not customers. A company must adopt clear rules regarding corporate communication in order to stay clear of antitrust concerns.

Overview

We identify these key points regarding signaling:

- Price changes in an oligopoly require careful preparation. Signaling serves as a means to communicate one's intent to the market in advance and, as a result, to prompt a desired reaction from other oligopolist.
- Signaling can inform all market participants about a planned action. Competitors have an option to send a signal themselves and/or to adjust their behavior. The signals also inform customers. This can improve the acceptance of a price increase or intensify the effects of a price decrease.
- Signaling can increase the chances that an advantageous result for all oligopolies emerges.

Conclusion

In this chapter we introduced methods, decision rules, and guidelines for one-dimensional prices. We summarize the processes and the determination of an optimal price as follows:

- Rigid processes consider either only costs (cost-plus pricing) or competitors' prices (competition-based pricing).
- The comprehensive processes, which include break-even calculations, decision-support systems, as well marginal analysis, capture the interrelationships between price and its determinants. They consider market, costs, and goal information simultaneously.
- Break-even analysis is best suited for "yes-no" decisions and provides help for decisions on price increases and decreases.
- Decision-support systems use simulations of the market. They consolidate information on customer preferences and needs, the purchase decision process, market structure, and trends. This forms the basis for robust decisions.
- Marginal analysis transforms price-volume relationships systematically into mathematical functions. This allows the determination of the optimal price from all potential prices, not just among a few discrete price points. These models also provide general rules for the optimal price.
- The optimal price is determined by the so-called Amoroso-Robinson relation and results from an elasticity-dependent markup on marginal costs. Fixed costs have no influence on the optimal price.

(continued)

- Because multiplicative price-response functions have a constant price elasticity, the Amoroso-Robinson relation can be used directly as a decision rule.
- If the price-response function and cost function are linear, the optimal price lies at the midpoint between maximum price and marginal cost. Only half of the changes in marginal cost are passed along to customers.
- When the price-response function has a Gutenberg form, there can be two profit maxima, one at a high and one at a very low price. In such cases one must consider a wide price interval.
- For price optimization in a monopoly, one must take only the response of customers into account.
- For price optimization in an oligopoly, one must also anticipate the reactions of competitors.
- Signaling is a means to influence the reactions of competitors.
- Proper price optimization always requires the incorporation of goals, the price-response function, and costs. In a competitive market, one must also include competitors' prices. If there is an interdependence of reactions among competitors, such as in an oligopoly, one must take competitors' reactions into account.

5.5 Background Information

To derive (5.7): If the price-response function is linear, i.e., $q = a - bp$, and the cost function also has a linear form $C = C_{fix} + kq = C_{fix} + k(a - bp)$ with k as variable unit costs, the profit function is defined as $\pi = (a - bp)p - C_{fix} - k(a - bp)$. If one solves for p under the "marginal revenue = marginal cost" condition, one gets this formula for the optimal price:

$$p^* = \frac{1}{2}\left(\frac{a}{b} + k\right)$$

The derivation of (5.14) $\frac{\partial q}{\partial p}$ differs from its monopolistic counterpart through an additional addend which incorporates competitive reaction:

$$\frac{\partial q}{\partial p} = \frac{\partial q}{\partial p} + \frac{\partial q}{\partial \bar{p}} \frac{\partial \bar{p}}{\partial p} \tag{5.28}$$

If we insert (5.28) into (5.15), we get:

$$q + (p^* - C')\left(\frac{\partial q}{\partial p} + \frac{\partial q}{\partial \bar{p}}\frac{\partial \bar{p}}{\partial p}\right) = 0. \tag{5.29}$$

The multiplication by $\frac{p}{q}$ as well as the expansion of the last fraction with $\frac{\bar{p}}{p}$ lead to:

$$p + (p^* - C')\left(\frac{\partial q}{\partial p}\frac{p}{q} + \frac{\partial \bar{p}}{\partial p}\frac{p}{\bar{p}}\frac{\partial q}{\partial \bar{p}}\frac{\bar{p}}{q}\right) = 0. \tag{5.30}$$

If one inserts into (5.30) the elasticity expressions below, it yields:

$$p^* + (p^* - C')(\varepsilon + \sigma\varepsilon_k) = 0, \tag{5.31}$$

with $\varepsilon = \frac{\partial q}{\partial p} \times \frac{p}{q}$ direct price elasticity, $\varepsilon_k = \frac{\partial q}{\partial \bar{p}} \times \frac{\bar{p}}{q}$ cross-price elasticity of the product in question vs. the competitor's price, and $\sigma = \frac{\partial \bar{p}}{\partial p} \times p\bar{p}$ reaction elasticity of the competitor's price vs. the price of the product in question.
One brings p^* to the left side and gets (5.16).

References

1. Wiltinger, K. (1998). *Preismanagement in der unternehmerischen Praxis. Probleme der organisatorischen Implementierung*. Wiesbaden: Gabler.
2. Graumann, J. (1994). *Die Preispolitik in deutschen Unternehmen. Ein Untersuchungsbericht über Preisstrategien, Kalkulationsmethoden, Konditionensysteme und ihre betriebswirtschaftlichen Auswirkungen*. München: Norbert Müller.
3. Wied-Nebbeling, S. (1985). *Das Preisverhalten in der Industrie. Ergebnisse einer erneuten Befragung*. Tübingen: J. C. B. Mohr (Paul Siebeck).
4. Fabiani, S., Druant, M., Hernando, I., Kwapil, C., Landau, B., Loupias, C., Martins, F., Mathä, T. Y., Sabbatini, R., Stahl, H. & Stokman, A.C.J. (2005). *The Pricing Behaviour of Firms in the Euro Area. New Survey Evidence*. Working Paper, No. 535. European Central Bank.
5. Götze, U. (2010). *Kostenrechnung und Kostenmanagement* (5th ed.). Berlin: Springer.
6. Plinke, W. (2000). Grundzüge der Kosten- und Leistungsrechnung. In M. Kleinaltenkamp, & W. Plinke (Eds.), *Technischer Vertrieb. Grundlagen des Business-to-Business Marketing* (2nd ed., pp. 615–690). Berlin: Springer.
7. Kim, W. C., & Mauborgne, R. (2005). *Blue Ocean Strategy. How to Create Uncontested Market Space and Make the Competition Irrelevant*. Boston/Massachusetts: Harvard Business School Press.
8. Kilger, W., Pampel, J. R., & Vikas, K. (2012). *Flexible Plankostenrechnung und Deckungsbeitragsrechnung* (13th ed.). Wiesbaden: Gabler.
9. Dahmen, A. (2014). *Kostenrechnung* (3rd ed.). Frankfurt am Main: Vahlen.
10. Rumler, A. (2002). *Marketing für mittelständische Unternehmen*. Berlin: Teia.
11. Hoffman, R. N. (2004). Controlling Hurricanes – Can Hurricanes or Other Tropical Storms be Moderated or Deflected? *Scientific American, 291*(4), 68–75.
12. Anonymous. (2008, June 12). Preiserhöhung passé. *General-Anzeiger Bonn*, p. 20.
13. Anonymous. (2015). ALDI SÜD oder: die Konzentration auf das Wesentliche. https://unternehmen.aldi-sued.de/de/ueber-aldi-sued/philosophie/. Accessed 19 February 2015.
14. Berg, W. (2015). Preiserhöhung. *Postwurfsendung der Gebäudereinigung Berg GmbH*. January 2015.
15. Anonymous. (2015, February 09) Die Luft wird dünner. *General-Anzeiger Bonn*, p. 7.

16. Stigler, G. J. (1947). The Kinky Oligopoly Demand Curve and Rigid Prices. *Journal of Political Economy, 55*(5), pp. 432–449.
17. Anonymous. (2014, December 31) Fernbusse werden langsam profitabel. *Frankfurter Allgemeine Zeitung,* p. 18.
18. Anonymous. (2015, September 19). Fernbusbranche rechnet mit teureren Tickets. *General-Anzeiger Bonn,* p. 12.
19. Anonymous. (2015, September 21). Jeder zweite Fernbuspassagier ist berufstätig. *Frankfurter Allgemeine Zeitung,* p. 22.
20. Anonymous. (2015, April 27). Institut: Fernbusse werden teurer. *General-Anzeiger Bonn,* p. 7.
21. Hook, L. (2015). Amazon to Bring Cloud Services Out of Shadows. *Financial Times.* 14 April, p. 13.
22. Porter, M. E. (2004). *Competitive Strategy. Techniques for Analyzing Industries and Competitors.* New York: The Free Press.
23. Gelbrich, K., Wünschmann, S., & Müller, S. (2008). *Erfolgsfaktoren des Marketing.* Dresden: Vahlen.
24. Simon, H. (2009). *33 Sofortmaßnahmen gegen die Krise. Wege für Ihr Unternehmen.* Frankfurt am Main: Campus.
25. Heil, O. P. & Schunk, H. (2003). Wettbewerber-Interaktion. Wettbewerber-Reputation und Preiskriege. *Marketing- und Management-Transfer. Institutszeitschrift der Professur Zentes. Universität des Saarlands* 24, pp. 8–16.
26. Kotler, A., Armstrong, G., Wong, V., & Saunders, J. (2011). *Grundlagen des Marketing* (5th ed.). München: Pearson.
27. Schunk, H., Fürst, R., & Heil, O. P. (2003). Marktstrategischer Einsatz von Signaling in der Hersteller-Handels-Dyade. In D. Ahlert, R. Olbrich, & H. Schröder (Eds.), *Jahrbuch Vertriebs- und Handelsmanagement* (pp. 221–233). Frankfurt am Main: Deutscher Fachverlag.
28. Heil, O. P., & Bungert, M. D. (2005). Competitive Market Signaling. A Behavioural Approach to Manage Competitive Interaction. *Marketing – Journal of Research and Management, 1*(2), pp. 91–99.
29. Anonymous. (2011, October 26). Allianz erhöht Autotarife. Versicherungskonzern nimmt Kundenschwund in Kauf. *Financial Times Deutschland,* p. 1.
30. Anonymous. (2013, March 20). Kfz-Versicherung 2013. Aktuelle Entwicklungen in einem dynamischen Markt. 9. MCC-Kongress. http://www.my-experten.de/upload/exp13pdf00010136.pdf. Accessed 20 January 2015.
31. Hyundai Seeks Solution on the High End. (2013) *The Wall Street Journal Europe.* 19 February, p. 24.

Decision: Multidimensional Prices

6

Abstract

One-dimensional pricing, discussed in the preceding chapter, is rather the exception than the rule in economic reality. Companies typically charge different prices for the same product depending on target group, region, time, or purchase volume. This kind of price differentiation requires the setting of multiple prices or price parameters. Almost all companies offer several products, and their sales are often interdependent. Price management needs to take these inter dependencies into account, because they can have strong effects on a product line's profit. Offering several products in one package, normally at a reduced price, is referred to as price bundling. This method is effective for finer market segmentation and for better exploiting willingness to pay. The optimization of multidimensional prices requires a deeper understanding of interactions and dependencies, and more detailed information, than one-dimensional pricing. This chapter provides the reader with the necessary knowledge.

6.1 Introduction

In Chap. 5, we looked at the determination of an optimal, one-dimensional price. In this chapter we deal with multidimensional prices, which means we need to examine and optimize multiple prices at the same time. This can involve several prices or price parameters for one product, which is the case with price differentiation. It can also involve several prices for several products, such as the pricing for a product line or price bundling.

Multidimensional pricing is highly complex. Instead of one price decision, a company must make several. An automotive original equipment manufacturer, for example, offers a range of model variants whose prices and sales volumes are interdependent. Discount systems require the setting of many parameters such as discount levels as well as volume or revenue thresholds. Multidimensional price

© Springer Nature Switzerland AG 2019
H. Simon, M. Fassnacht, *Price Management*,
https://doi.org/10.1007/978-3-319-99456-7_6

structures, such as those for software or banking services, may have several hundred price parameters.

Section 6.2 discusses the fundamental concept of price differentiation (price discrimination). Section 6.3 then analyzes price decisions across multiple products.

6.2   Price Differentiation

Customers are confronted with differentiated prices for almost all products and services. Coca-Cola provides a distinct example of this. Figure 6.1 shows the price for a cold 20-ounce bottle of Coca-Cola ranging from $1.25 to $3.49, depending on where the customer buys it. The most expensive cola thus costs roughly 2.8 times as much as the least expensive, which is a remarkable difference for an identical product sold ubiquitously within one city. The fact that customers regularly pay each of these prices shows that customers have different willingness to pay.

Coca-Cola demonstrates an example of price differentiation generally accepted by customers, not least because the customers themselves choose where to buy and thus what price to pay. We refer to such cases as price differentiation by self-selection.

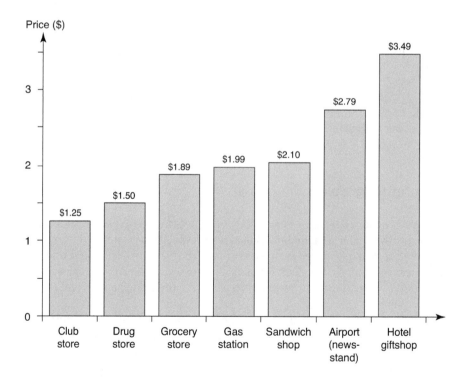

Fig. 6.1 Prices for a cold 20-ounce bottle of Coca-Cola in a major US city (excluding taxes and deposits)

The following test shows that the willingness to pay for the same product can be very different depending on the situation. Let us say a person is relaxing at the beach. A friend offers to bring back a drink and asks what is the most that the person is willing to spend. Then he reveals an additional piece of information. In Test A, the friend says: "I'm going to buy the drink at the food stand," and in Test B he says, "I'm buying the drink at that nice hotel by the beach." The test people in Group A named a maximum price of $1.50, while those in Group B said $2.65 [1, p. 150]. Price differentiation is a sensitive topic. In Japan, Coca-Cola tried to differentiate prices according to temperature [2]. When it is hot outside, a soft drink provides higher value. Therefore, it seems logical to charge a higher price on hot days. The technology is simple: one needs only to install thermometers in vending machines and automatically adjust the price based on the temperature. News of the plans leaked, though, and touched off protests. Consumers considered that kind of differentiation to be unfair. Coca-Cola therefore scrapped the project. Then in Spain, the marketing agency Momentum tried the opposite tactic. The cola price dropped when the temperature rose. But that was considered to be more of a gag than a serious move [3].

The world teems with examples of price differentiation. As with Coca-Cola, the prices for millions of goods vary by distribution channel. Massive amounts of fast-moving consumer goods and fashion items are sold under discount programs, some of which call for prices up to 75% below the normal price. Hotels differentiate their prices according to demand; when there is a trade fair in town, prices can be a multiple of normal prices. The air travel industry believes in the idea that it should sell every seat at a different price if possible. Charges for electricity and telecommunications vary by time of day or day of week. Restaurants offer lunch menus at reduced prices; in the evening the same menu items can cost significantly more. Lower prices for advance purchases and discounts for early bookings are very common. Prices for rental cars are differentiated by availability and a thousand other criteria. Insurance companies, hotel chains, telecom companies, and tour operators all offer special discounts to members of associations such as the American Automobile Association (AAA) and similar organizations. AAA members receive discounts of 10% at many hotels and a variety of other places such as factory outlet malls. Cinemas, theaters, and some sports teams offer lower prices to students and seniors. One can get a bulk or volume discount for almost anything. And many prices show stark differences for the same product internationally. In one sentence: price differentiation is a ubiquitous phenomenon. Companies that do not practice price differentiation are sacrificing a substantial amount of profit.

6.2.1 Market Segmentation as the Foundation for Price Differentiation

A market typically comprises customers with different willingness to pay, incomes, preferences, and purchasing habits. A company can treat these different customers individually or in aggregate. But in most cases, completely individualized price management is neither feasible nor economically sensible. The practical implementation fails because individual price elasticities are not exactly known and because price setting at the individual level is organizationally difficult. From an economic standpoint, total disaggregation makes no sense in most cases because subgroups or segments of customers share similar behaviors, making the cost of serving each individual customer prohibitive relative to the increased revenue at stake.

The role of a price-based market segmentation is therefore to allocate customers to segments based on certain criteria. The customers in a segment should be as homogenous as possible, while the segments themselves should be as heterogeneous as possible. Price differentiation addresses these different customer segments with different prices, taking advantage of the heterogeneity in willingness to pay across segments. The price-driven market segmentation involves two tasks: identifying the segments and addressing them.

Identification of Market Segments
Identifying market segments first requires the establishment of criteria and the definition of segments based on these criteria. The next step is to operationalize the segments, so that they can be addressed with segment-specific marketing actions. The segmentation criteria fall into two basic groups: demographic (characteristics of the buyers) and behavioral (characteristics of how they act) criteria (Fig. 6.2).

The segmentation criteria should fulfill the following requirements:

- Behavioral relevance: The segmentation criteria should have a strong link to aspects of the customer's buying and consumption behavior.
- Observable and measurable: The company should select criteria which are readily observable and consistently measurable.
- Stable over time: The distribution of customers across the segments should remain relatively stable over time, reflecting consistent behavior.
- Reachable: The company should have marketing instruments at its disposal to address and serve the segments.

Buyer characteristics	Behavioral characteristics
1. Demographic Region, sex, age, household size, ...	1. Purchase behavior Buyer vs. non-buyer, frequent vs. occasional user, ...
2. Socioeconomic Income, purchasing power, education, career, ...	2. Price-related behavior Price elasticity, willingness to pay, price sensitivity, price attitude, price knowledge, discount behavior, ...
3. Psychographic Personality, lifestyle, ...	3. Behavior vis-a-vis other marketing instruments

Fig. 6.2 Market segmentation criteria

The dilemma often is that only the behavioral characteristics are directly relevant for cultivating a specific segment. Yet these criteria are hard to observe in most cases and the segments built from them hard to reach. In contrast, it is easier to observe buyers' demographic traits and characteristics and target the segments based on those criteria, even though their behavioral relevance is often unclear or dubious. One possibility to resolve this problem is to take a multistep approach:

1. The segments will first be defined on the basis of behavioral characteristics.
2. The relationship between behavioral and general buyer characteristics is then determined.
3. The segments to target will then be redefined on the basis of general buyer characteristics that have a strong correlation with the behavioral characteristics.

Steps 1 and 2 may be done in succession (e.g., with the help of multiple regression analyses) or simultaneously (e.g., with cluster analysis).

Figure 6.3 shows how a market segmentation based on price elasticities might look: This is a household appliance brand for which price elasticities were determined in ten European regions. The measured elasticities have absolute values between 1.4 and 2.8, which is a rather wide range. The most important reason for these differences is the high divergence of brand value across individual regions. A uniform price makes no sense, because the company would be sacrificing a considerable amount of profit. Having ten different prices, however, did not seem feasible to the company's management in this case. They agreed therefore on three segments:

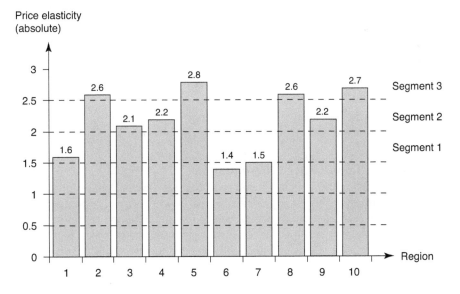

Fig. 6.3 Regional segmentation based on price elasticity (Simon-Kucher & Partners)

- Segment 1: relatively low price elasticity in a range from 1.4 to 1.9 (regions 1, 6, 7)
- Segment 2: medium price elasticity in a range from 2.0 to 2.5 (regions 3, 4, 9)
- Segment 3: high price elasticity, greater than 2.5 (regions 2, 5, 8, 10)

The company then aimed to have optimal prices in these three segments based on the respective elasticities.

There are two basic, conceivable approaches to a price-based market segmentation:

1. The segments will be developed based on criteria which one expects ex ante to lead to certain price reactions; price elasticities will then be calculated for these segments.
2. The price elasticities of individual customers will be measured first, and then the customers with similar price elasticities will be aggregated into segments.

The second task involves determining and implementing segment-specific strategies. Price differentiation addresses these tasks in parallel, namely, the determination of the optimal price for each segment and its implementation. In this regard, an effective demarcation of each market segment, known as fencing, plays a central role. Fencing is designed to prevent customers with higher willingness to pay from buying at lower prices.

E-commerce and Big Data provide an increasingly profound basis for market segmentation. Actual purchasing behavior is automatically recorded, and addressability improves radically. In the extreme, individualization of prices will become technically possible.

Price-based market segmentation is not a method per se. It is a complex exercise which can be handled with different methods. These methods range from pure intuition to multivariate analyses such as cluster analysis.

6.2.2   Theoretical Basis of Price Differentiation

The goal of price differentiation is to exploit customers' different willingness to pay, in order to earn more profit than a uniform price would yield.

6.2.2.1 Definition of Price Differentiation

Price differentiation occurs when a company charges different prices for products which are identical or very similar in terms of space/location, time, performance, and quantity. Product variants are explicitly included in this definition because there are close substitutive relationships between them from a demand perspective [4, p. 25].

The following prerequisites must be present for price differentiation [5, pp. 14–16]:

- The customers have different willingness to pay and, thus, different price elasticities.
- It is possible to group the different customers into at least two segments, which are distinct from one another.
- The company possesses a certain monopolistic leeway, which is typical in imperfect markets, to extract consumer surplus or rents. The price elasticity therefore cannot be infinite.

The first two prerequisites are generally met in practice. Companies must undertake appropriate measures, though, for the third to take effect. The third condition may require controls. Companies can establish a monopolistic space more easily when customers perceive their products or services to have a unique selling proposition.

6.2.2.2 Goals of Price Differentiation

In addition to increased profit through the extraction of consumer surplus, companies can pursue other goals through price differentiation. The strategic triangle in Fig. 6.4 illustrates this.

A cost reduction for the customer is achievable, for example, through a volume discount. If a customer is offered such a discount, that customer can be induced to buy a higher quantity (variable-quantity case). At the same time, transaction costs are lowered. This means that higher volumes are achieved not because more customers buy but because the same customers buy more. Customer-related goals of price differentiation focus on higher customer retention and customer satisfaction, which

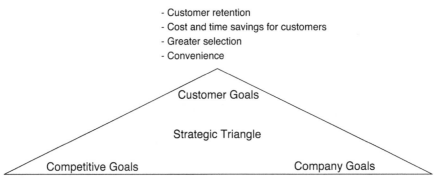

Fig. 6.4 Goals of price differentiation

can be achieved through loyalty discounts or two-dimensional price schemes such as offered by Amazon Prime.

Price differentiation also allows a company to pursue competitive goals. One reactive approach is to adjust one's price structure based on that of the competitors. One observes this when customers intensively compare prices and price structures. Proactive competitive goals include building up switching barriers for customers (e.g., through bonus programs) or erecting barriers to entry for competitors. Differentiated prices result as well when companies strive to avoid the competition and claim niches in the price spectrum.

6.2.2.3 Tasks to Achieve Price Differentiation

Segment-specific price differentiation comprises two tasks: first, determination of the optimal price for each segment. Second, implementation of the price differentiation in such a way that the intended goals are achieved and arbitrage is prevented. We distinguish among three cases:

Case 1: Completely Isolated Market Segments
The segments may be addressed separately, and arbitrage between them does not occur. The sales volume in segment i depends only on price p_i^*. The cross-price elasticity between the segments, therefore, is zero. For the optimization, it does not matter whether the separation of the segments is "natural" or "arbitrary." What matters is whether the separation is actually effective.

Under these conditions, price differentiation is simple. The optimal price in each market segment is determined through the segment-specific Amoroso-Robinson relation:

$$p_i^* = \frac{\varepsilon_i}{1 + \varepsilon_i} C_i' \tag{6.1}$$

where ε_i is the segment-specific price elasticity and C_i' represents the segment-specific marginal costs. In other words, each segment must meet the "marginal revenue = marginal cost" condition. Thus, if marginal costs (regarding price) in two segments are equal, the marginal revenue (but not the prices!) must also be equal in the optimal case.

Case 2: Partially Separated Market Segments
If there is no separation or isolation of the segments as in Case 1, the segment-specific price-response function has the following form:

$$q_i = f(p_1, \ldots, p_i, \ldots, p_n) \tag{6.2}$$

The cross-price elasticity between the two segments is positive, just as it would be for competitive products. This means that a price increase in one segment leads to a partial shift of customers to the segment with the lower price.[1] The optimal, segment-specific prices are determined via the partial derivative of the profit function and solving the resulting system of equations. Several steps yield the optimality condition:

$$p_i^* = \frac{\varepsilon_i}{1 + \varepsilon_i} C_i' - \sum_{\substack{j=1 \\ j \neq i}}^{n} \left(p_j - C_j' \right) \frac{\varepsilon_{ij}}{(1 + \varepsilon_i)} \frac{q_j}{q_i} \tag{6.3}$$

with ε_i as the direct price elasticity and ε_{ij} as the cross-price elasticity of segment j relative to price p_i. Equation (6.3) corresponds structurally to the so-called Niehans formula (6.8) for the price optimization of multiproduct companies. In the first addend, one sees the Amoroso-Robinson relation. The summation term considers the influence of the price p_i on the demand in the other segments. In this expression, only $(1 + \varepsilon_i)$ is negative, so that in total the summation term will be negative. Together with the negative sign in front of the summation term, this results in an optimal price that is higher than the optimal price for completely separated or isolated market segments.

The difference between the optimal prices in the different market segments is larger[2]:

- The larger the cross-price elasticities ε_{ij} are.
- The larger the unit contribution margins in the other segments are.
- The larger segment j is volume-wise compared to segment i.

Case 3: Classic Model of Price Differentiation
In this case we assume that there is only one price-response function on the basis of which one can determine optimal prices and segments simultaneously (although the segments will not be optimally partitioned).

Classic price differentiation is best illustrated using a linear price-response function.[3] The profit increase from the use of price differentiation is a result of the extraction of consumer surplus. Figure 6.5 compares uniform pricing and classic price differentiation. We assume a monopoly situation, constant marginal costs, no costs for price differentiation, and a linear price-response function.

---

[1] The shift by customers only takes place when the price difference is greater than the arbitrage costs. A situation with positive arbitrage costs and a small number of segments resembles an incomplete oligopoly. This situation is different from the competitive case, however, because the supplier determines all the segment-specific prices. Competitive reaction is not an issue. This situation thus corresponds to the collective profit maximization in an oligopoly.

[2] These statements apply ceteris paribus, i.e., when only the respective variable changes.

[3] Prerequisite for the applicability of price differentiation on this basis is that the aggregated linear price-response function results from an equal distribution of the willingness to pay of each individual. If this linearity instead results from the fact that each individual price-response function is already linear, i.e., that each individual customer buys more at a lower price ("variable-quantity case"), then price differentiation does not work. The use of price differentiation therefore presumes knowledge of the individual responses to different prices.

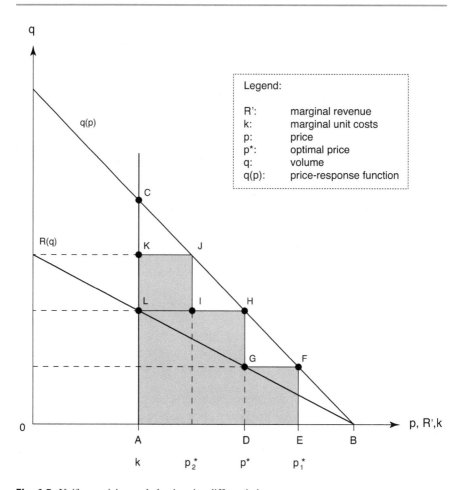

Fig. 6.5 Uniform pricing and classic price differentiation

The total profit potential corresponds to the area of the triangle A-B-C. The profit-maximizing uniform price p^* lies according to formula (5.7) at the midpoint between the maximum price B and the variable unit cost k. At the uniform price p^*, a company earns a profit defined by the rectangle A-D-H-L. The profit from the uniform price is thus represented by a rectangle which lies within the "profit potential triangle" A-B-C. The area of the triangle D-B-H corresponds to the consumer surplus, i.e., the unextracted willingness to pay.

If one uses price differentiation with three prices p_1^*, p^* and p_2^*, one increases profit by the amounts defined by the rectangles D-E-F-G and L-I-J-K. The consumer surplus in this case declines to the amounts defined by the triangles I-H-J, G-F-H, and E-B-F. This makes it clear that the higher profit from price differentiation results from the reduction of consumer surplus. One can thus express the task of classic price differentiation by saying that one must move from "rectangle to triangle."

From the figure it is also easy to see that when we have a linear price-response function and cost function as well as completely individual, perfect price differentiation, the total profit is twice as large as with a uniform price.[4] The combined surface of the two triangles D-B-H and L-H-C is the same as that of the rectangle A-D-H-L.

6.2.3 Implementation of Price Differentiation

The issue of how to separate or "fence" the market segments is not solved by finding the optimal prices. It is crucial that a company succeeds in getting the customers in the individual segments to accept the prices and not undermine them. The resulting problems depend on both the form of the price differentiation and its conditions. To explore and understand the problems, we will first break down the types of price differentiation according to Pigou's taxonomy. Then we will deal with the individual implementation forms of price differentiation.

Pigou distinguishes between first-, second-, and third-degree price differentiation depending on the extent to which the differentiation extracts consumer surplus [6, p. 279].

Under *first-degree price differentiation*, the seller charges the exact maximum price for each individual. The entire consumer surplus is thus extracted, which is why one also refers to this case as perfect price differentiation.

If a seller is able to divide the customers in segments with different maximum prices, and then set prices which target each segment, then one refers to this as *second-degree price differentiation*.

Customers are still free to self-select, meaning they are not bound to any segment. Because the seller has no control costs, implementation is relatively unproblematic. The challenge with second-degree price differentiation is deciding on products with sensible price-value relationships which optimally address their respective market segment.

Under *third-degree price differentiation*, the segments are identified on the basis of observable and addressable criteria. The optimal price for each segment will then be determined on this basis. Switching between segments under third-degree price differentiation is either not possible or possible only at a cost, because access to each segment is linked to meeting the respective segmentation criteria.

Figure 6.6 shows the connection between the three types of price differentiation according to Pigou and the most common forms of implementation. One should

---

[4]The general derivation of these relationships is as follows: out of the aggregated price-response function $q = a - bp = b(p^{max} - p)$ results the function for the segment i as $q_i = b(p_{i-1} - p_i)$ with $i = 1,\ldots,n$, where p_{i-1} is the next-highest price to p_i and $p_0 = p^{max} = a/b$. As one can see, p_{i-1} becomes the maximum price for segment i. All customers, whose willingness to pay is greater than p_{i-1}, belong to segment $i-1$. For a given number of segments n, we insert the formula $q_i = b$ $(p_{i-1} - p_i)$ with $i = 1,\ldots,n$ into the profit equation and differentiate the equation with respect to the individual prices. Assuming that marginal costs are equal for all segments, one can explicitly define the segment-specific optimal prices p_i^* $(i = 1,\ldots,n)$.

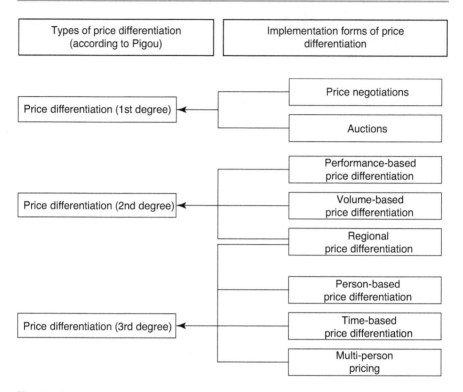

Fig. 6.6 Types of price differentiation and their implementation forms

notice that regional price differentiation can be categorized as second-degree or third-degree price differentiation. Depending on the distance, customers could react to regional price differences by going out of their way to buy the product at a lower price. This happens, for example, when gasoline, cigarettes, alcohol, or other products are significantly less expensive in one state or country than in a neighboring one. When such a journey is not possible, then third-degree price differentiation applies. This can happen, for example, when a purchase requires an address in a given region, state, or country.

6.2.3.1 Individual Price Differentiation (First Degree)

Individual price differentiation means that each customer pays one price, ideally the price which corresponds precisely to his or her willingness to pay, the so-called maximum price. In this manner, some universities in the United States charge tuition based on the income situation of the individual student [7, p. 228]. Fencing measures are not necessary for first-degree price differentiation, because arbitrage is not possible.

But individual price differentiation is rarely used; it requires that the seller knows the willingness to pay of each individual customer. The actual willingness to pay is difficult to ascertain. A company collecting such information and setting individualized prices incurs costs which may be higher than the additional revenue the company would get if it extracted the entire consumer surplus.

The Internet has led to increased usage of individual price differentiation [8]. The greater ease of evaluating customer data on the Internet cannot only be used to offer each customer individually customized products but also to charge individualized prices. Auctions also play a big role on the Internet. They can be very effective for extracting the willingness to pay.

Examples which at least approximate first-degree price differentiation occur in negotiations and in auctions.

- *Price negotiations:* In many industries, the final transaction price is not set by the seller, but rather the result of a negotiation. In B2B, this is the predominant form for setting prices. In an individual price negotiation, the result depends essentially on the negotiating positions and strengths of each party, which means one can interpret this as individual price differentiation.
- *Auctions:* Auctions result in individual prices when the product or service is auctioned multiple times. This can lead to different prices which reflect the individual willingness to pay of the winning bidders. In Chap. 3 we described auctions as an instrument to collect information on individual willingness to pay.

6.2.3.2 Price Differentiation Through Self-Selection (Second Degree)
Under second-degree price differentiation, buyers allocate themselves to a price segment. In this context, the two basic forms of implementation are performance-based and volume-based price differentiation.

Performance-Based Price Differentiation
Performance-based price differentiation exists when a company sells versions of a product which differ in terms of performance and price but are otherwise identical across the dimensions location, time, and volume. Under this form of price differen-tiation, a company may also differentiate other marketing instruments besides price.

Examples for product-specific differentiation include credit cards (standard, gold, platinum), airline tickets (economy, premium economy, business, first class), or train tickets (first class, second class).

Table 6.1 shows performance-based price differentiation for video-on-demand offers. Netflix offers three subscription levels with different film quality and different performance attributes.

A prerequisite for successful performance-based price differentiation is that the differences in value are both meaningful to and actually perceived by the customers.

For example, the difference between business class and economy class on intra-European Lufthansa flights is rather slight. The main thing separating the two classes is a curtain. The differences in service are limited. As a result, business class on some flights has many open seats, while the economy section is full. On long-distance flights, Lufthansa and many other airlines such as United Airlines have

Table 6.1 Performance-based price differentiation: Netflix video-on-demand [9]

	Base package (SD)	Standard package (HD)	Premium package (Ultra-HD)
Price (monthly)	$7.99	$10.99	$13.99
Performance attributes	• No HD quality • Watch films and TV series only on one device	• HD quality • Watch films and TV series simultaneously on up to two devices	• HD quality • Ultra-HD quality (when available) • Watch films and TV series simultaneously on up to four devices

Table 6.2 Performance-based price differentiation: *Financial Times* [10]

	Newspaper + online	Premium online	Standard online
Price (per week)	$11.77	$9.75	$6.45
Financial Times (FT) blogs	x	x	x
Unlimited access to articles	x	x	x
E-paper access	x	x	–
Daily home or office delivery	x	–	–

introduced a new intermediate class of service called premium economy. The major advantages passengers enjoy in this cabin are more legroom and a larger video screen, as well as a welcome drink. This class could be attractive for business travelers who cannot travel in the significantly more expensive business class due to internal restrictions at their company. United Airlines and American Airlines have also introduced "basic economy" fares, which offer even less service. Passengers cannot choose their seat (the airline assigns it at check-in), cannot use the overhead bins, and must board the plane in the last group.

The *Financial Times* offers subscriptions which have different performance levels (Table 6.2).

In contrast to the prices for plane tickets, price differentiation for opera tickets and theater tickets is based on the seat's location and distance relative to stage. The drivers of value in this case are the sight lines to the stage, the acoustics, or the prestige of sitting closer to the stage. Patrons accept such price differences.

An example of performance-based differentiation in B2B is the construction of lighting modules for office buildings and shopping centers. The modules have a variety of functions, but at first only a basic selection will be activated at a set price. If the customer wants additional lighting options, these can be activated for an additional price.

Performance-based price differentiation is often accompanied by sales channel differentiation. The Coca-Cola example shown in Fig. 6.1 reflects price differentiation by sales channel. Another example of sales channel differentiation is the factory outlet center, where consumers can buy branded products at much lower prices than in specialty retail stores. However, there is often product differentiation as well, in that the outlets sell merchandise from the previous season or sell products manufactured to lower-quality specifications. A new form of price differentiation in conjunction with sales channel differentiation is online shopping. Whoever buys with a tablet or smartphone may be paying a surcharge because online shops use tracking systems which show what device a customer is using to go online. Home Depot, for example, shows different results for the same online search depending on what operating system the customer is using. On average, users of Android phones were shown 6% higher prices [11].

Volume-Based Price Differentiation

The starting point for volume-based price differentiation is Gossen's first law, which states that the marginal utility of a product decreases as volume increases [12]. Each additional unit of a product gives the user a smaller amount of incremental utility. The first glass of beer at an inn provides a thirsty hiker a greater level of utility than the second, third, or fifth glass. Because this involves a change in utility relative to a variation in the volume consumed, volume-based price differentiation applies primarily to the "variable-quantity case." The customer compares price and utility for the product, unit by unit, and buys the nth unit only when its utility is greater than the price. Volume-based price differentiation therefore does not involve any discrimination by the seller. By choosing their own volume levels, however, each customer pays a different average price. This type of pricing is also known as *nonlinear*, because the unit price to pay declines with increasing volume and is therefore in a nonlinear relationship to the volume purchased [13, p. 25]. We find an example for nonlinear pricing at a parking garage in Houston. The customer pays a rate of $4.50 per hour to park. The maximum charge for the entire time the garage is open (6 a.m.– 10 p.m.) is $18 which corresponds to $1.13 per hour if the full 16 h are used [14].

Volume-based price differentiation is useful for homogeneous and heterogeneous groups of customers. Each case is described below. We assume that marginal costs are zero.

- *Homogeneity of customers:* If all customers have the same maximum price for the first, second, third, etc., unit of a product, then it is sufficient to consider just one customer. This situation is shown structurally in Fig. 6.7. The entire profit potential to extract is the area of the triangle 0-A-B. With uniform pricing, only half of this potential will be exploited, as already shown. This consideration is analogous to classical price differentiation with the difference that there, one applies price differentiation across the different customers, whereas here one sees price differentiation according to purchase volume. In comparison to uniform price setting, volume-based price differentiation is more advantageous when the customers are homogeneous. The right side of the figure shows that it fully extracts the potential in the profit triangle.
- *Heterogeneity of customers:* In reality, customers are never completely homogeneous. In order to discuss volume-based price differentiation for heterogeneous customers, we refer to the example in Table 6.3. The company in question operates movie theaters. The three customer segments A, B, and C have different

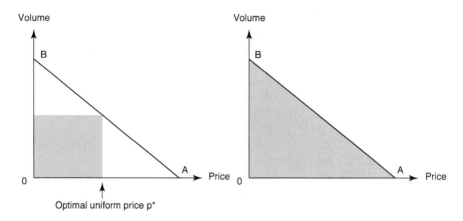

Fig. 6.7 Uniform pricing vs. nonlinear pricing with homogeneous customers

Table 6.3 Volume-based price differentiation with three heterogeneous consumer segments A, B, and C

Trip	Maximum price ($) A	B	C	Optimal nonlinear price structure ($)	Volume (in 1000)	Profit $ (in 1000)
1	9.00	10.00	12.00	9.00	3	27.00
2	6.00	7.50	10.00	6.00	3	18.00
3	3.50	5.50	8.00	5.50	2	11.00
4	2.00	4.00	6.00	4.00	2	8.00
5	1.10	1.50	3.50	3.50	1	3.50
Total					11	67.50
Optimal uniform price				5.50	9	49.50

maximum prices for the first, second, third, etc., movie in a month. The optimal uniform price is $p^* = \$5.50$. At this price, Segment A's customers would go to the movies 2000 times, B's would go 3000, and C's would go 4000 times. That works out to 9000 visits in a month and a profit of \$49,500.

Finding the optimal nonlinear price differentiation takes several steps. The first step is to determine the profit-maximizing price for the first visit. This price is $p_1^* = \$9$; customers from all three segments attend, and the profit is \$27,000. If the price were $p_1 = \$10$, only customers from Segments B and C would attend, and the profit would fall to \$20,000. If the cinema charged $p_1 = \$12$ for that first visit, only segment C would visit and profits would be just \$12,000.

If we conduct this step for all subsequent trips to the movie theater, we get the nonlinear price structure shown in Table 6.3. The optimal prices vary between \$9 for the first visit and \$3.50 for the fifth visit. The total profit of \$67,500 is much higher than the profit from uniform pricing, which would be \$49,500.

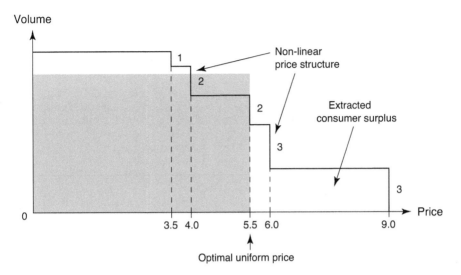

Fig. 6.8 Uniform pricing vs. volume-based price differentiation with heterogeneous customers

Figure 6.8 illustrates the profit effects of this case of volume-based price differentiation with heterogeneous customer segments. The shaded area corresponds to the profit from uniform pricing, while the area below the stepped curve represents the profit from nonlinear pricing. It extracts consumer surplus and at the same time activates demand below the optimal uniform price. In a volume-based price differentiation structure, the price can fall as low as the level of marginal costs as volume increases. Compared to uniform pricing, this allows a better capture of profit potential, both above and below the optimal uniform price.

Volume-based price differentiation can take on several forms (Table 6.4). We will elaborate briefly on the most important and most common ones.

The *two-part tariff* comprises a fixed, one-time fee for a given time period and an additional price per unit. A typical example is the classic price model for a phone plan, which has a monthly base price and a price per minute. The typical price model for electricity has the same structure. The price for each additional unit in a two-part tariff is constant, but the average overall unit price the customer pays declines as volume increases. This happens because the base price is distributed across more units.

The *block tariff* is a combination of a two-part tariff and a uniform price. Generally speaking, a number of two-part tariffs ($=n$) are combined in such a way that n volume intervals result. Figure 6.9 shows an example of a block tariff for an energy utility. It comprises a fixed price as well as a price for the unit of consumption. The higher the fixed price is, the lower the variable price. The break-even point, at which the transition from the low consumption tariff to a base price tariff is advantageous, is at 114.61 kWh.

Volume discounts grant higher discount rates for larger volumes, so that the average price declines as volume increases. Here we distinguish between total

Table 6.4 Forms of volume-based price differentiation (nonlinear pricing)

Form	Definition	Notation
Two-part tariff	$p(q) = f + p \times q$	$p(q)$: price to pay f: fixed base price
Block tariff	$p(q) = \begin{cases} p_1 \times q, & \text{for } q < q_b \\ f + p_2 \times q, & \text{for } q \geq q_b \end{cases}$	p: price q: volume q_b: volume break (beyond which a different price applies)
Total volume discount	$p(q) = \begin{cases} p_1 \times q, & \text{for } q < q_b \\ p_2 \times q, & \text{for } q \geq q_b \end{cases}$	
Incremental volume discount	$p(q) = \begin{cases} p_1 \times q, & \text{for } q < q_b \\ (p_1 - p_2) \times q + p_2 \times q & \text{for } q \geq q_b \end{cases}$	
Price point	Prices are explicitly specified for different volumes	
Continuous price structure	A continuous differentiable function which shares characteristics with the other types of nonlinear pricing	

volume discounts and incremental discounts. If the discount rate is applied across the entire volume purchased, one speaks of a total volume or full volume discount. The fact that a discount rate beyond a particular volume threshold would apply to the entire volume gives rise to volume ranges which are inefficient for the customer. In such cases it makes sense to buy the volume at the next-largest volume threshold (at which point the discount rate increases, i.e., the price for the entire volume drops further). Figure 6.10 provides an example of this structure. The customer would probably purchase 250 units instead of the 241 he or she actually needs, because the discount rate at 250 units or beyond would apply to the entire volume.

If the discount rate applies only to the volume within a certain interval, one speaks of an *incremental discount*. In the *price point* system, it means that specific prices are set for discrete purchase volumes. This implies that a customer can only buy specified amounts. An example is a photographer who offers passport photos only in fixed volumes, i.e., 3, 6, and 12. Three photos cost $18 (or $6 apiece), while 6 photos cost $27 (or $4.50 apiece), and 12 photos cost $48 (or $4 apiece).

In a *continuous price structure,* the volume-dependent price degression is described by a mathematical formula. It has little relevance in practice; we include it for the sake of completeness.

6.2.3.3 Price Differentiation Based on Customer Criteria (Third Degree)

For third-degree price differentiation, we distinguish among four implementation forms: personal or person-based, time-based, regional, and multi-person. The common denominator in all forms is that the customer does not self-select his or her segment but instead is allocated by the seller to a segment based on specified characteristics. These characteristics should have a connection to customers' willingness to pay.

Tariff	Energy price		Legend:	
	Base price	Unit price	p(q):	Total price dependent on volume
Low-consumption tariff	$0.00/month	ct31.99/kWh		
Fixed price tariff	$12.08/month	ct21.45/kWh	kWh:	Kilowatt hour

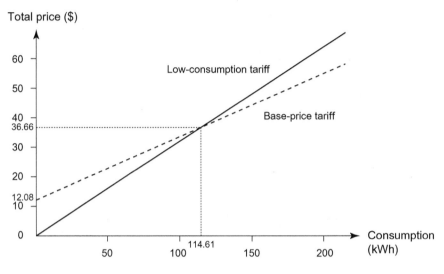

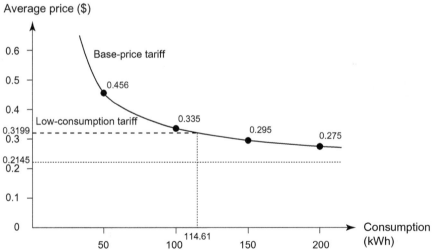

Fig. 6.9 Example of a block tariff

Volume	Discount
> 10 units	9%
> 20 units	12%
> 50 units	15%
> 100 units	17%
> 250 units	20%
> 500 units	23%

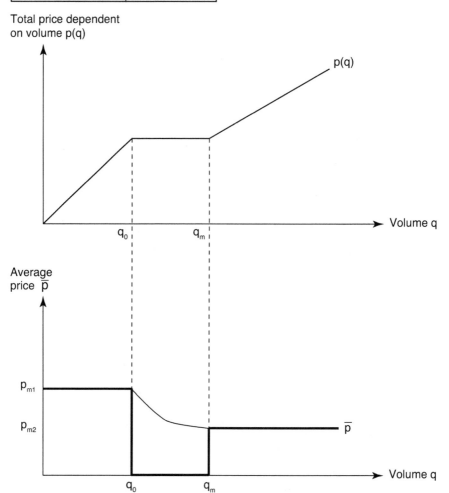

Fig. 6.10 Example of a total-volume discount

Person-Based Differentiation

Person-based price differentiation depends on a segmentation according to the characteristics of the buyers. These could be sociodemographic such as age (prices for children or seniors), school status (college student, high school student), or work or group affiliations (associations, parties). Implementation of this form of price differentiation is easy and straightforward for services. But attempts to capture such segment-based willingness to pay might not work for products where it is hard to trace purchase or usage. There are also additional costs associated with checking the effectiveness of a segmentation according to observable buyer characteristics.

The buyer characteristics should reflect the buying behavior of the customers. Examples of price differentiation according to purchase behavior are in-package coupons, loyalty rebates, or simply the amount purchased. Drugstore chains like Müller, CVS, and Walgreens print discounts on the customer's receipt, which the customer can redeem on the next purchase. This method can have a strong effect on customer retention. It also leads to a form of self-selection, as the customers decide whether to apply the discount to their next purchase. Other examples of person-based price differentiation include:

- In museums, the education status of the customers is a criterion for price differentiation. At the Museum of Modern Art in New York City, students pay $14, while adults pay $25.
- Age is frequently used as criterion for price differentiation. At Walt Disney World, children aged 0–3 years are admitted to the Magic Kingdom free, while children aged 4–9 pay $101 on a "value" day and visitors aged 10 and older pay $107. At the Europa-Park, children aged 4–11 and seniors (60 and older) pay €37 for admission, while adults in age range 12–60 pay €42.50. Best Western Hotels & Resorts offer a discount of at least 10% for people aged 55 and up. Numerous transportation providers likewise offer discounted tickets to seniors.
- The ADAC, the German counterpart to AAA in the United States, differentiates between new and experienced drivers. A driver who has had a license for a year or less pays no fees, while drivers who are not beginners must pay €49 per year. AAA offers free membership to teenage drivers with a learner's permit as long as someone else in the family is a member.
- Age-dependent premiums are also common for automobile insurance.[5] Drivers in the age group 50–59 pay the lowest premiums at $480 on average. Drivers aged 24 and under pay $1948 on average per year, or 306% more. For drivers aged 60 and up, the same insurance they had before turning 60 now costs around 10% more on average, or $529. These prices are not, however, proportional to the accident risk. Drivers aged 50–59 have 285 accidents per 100 million miles driven. For drivers aged 60 and older, the accident rate increases by 692% to 2257 per 100 million miles driven. The premium difference of 10% is far less than the increased accident rate and therefore the increased cost to the insurer. The picture is similar for drivers up to age 24. They are responsible for 4085 accidents

---

[5]The described data comes from a comparison site and does not refer to a specific company.

per 100 million miles driven, or 1333% more than the drivers aged 50–59. Yet they pay only 306% more [15].

- Some health insurers distinguish between smokers and non-smokers. Insurers plan to use health-related apps to gather health and fitness data and grant discounts for healthier living. Similarly, automotive insurance companies are installing black boxes in cars to monitor a drivers' behavior and adjust premiums up or down accordingly.
- Associations and clubs offer different prices to members and nonmembers. The American Marketing Association charges members $550 for a ticket to their annual conference, while nonmembers must pay $765.
- Swiss transportation companies offer young people the "Swiss Travel Pass" at a reduced rate of around 17% [16].

Time-Based Price Differentiation

Time-based price differentiation means that a seller charges different prices over the course of various time periods for a product which is otherwise identical in terms of location, performance, and volume in each period. In a similar vein, one also refers to this as "dynamic pricing" when certain conditions apply.

Examples of time-based price differentiation include time of day (telephone, electricity), weekdays (admissions, transportation tickets), or season (air travel, tourism). Selected examples are shown in Table 6.5. A fitness studio, for example, may charge different prices depending on time of the day. Mornings and evenings are less expensive than during the day ($31.90/$29.90 vs. $49 per month). Movie theaters and spas tend to vary prices by day of week.

Additional examples of time-based price differentiation include:

- Lufthansa offers a weekend price for direct flights within Germany. In contrast, Ryanair flights on Tuesdays and Wednesdays are particularly inexpensive.

Table 6.5 Examples of time-based price differentiation [17–20]

Fitness studio		Parking (airport)		Movie theater		Wellness hotel (single room)	
Time	Price	Time	Price	Time	Price	Time	Price
No restrictions	$39.90 per month	Daily price (Mo–Sa)	$29	Mo/Tu/We	$7.00	Fr/Sa/ Holidays	$220
		Sunday/ Holidays	$3	Th–Su (before 5 p.m.)	$8.00	Su–Th	$149
10.00 a.m.– noon	$31.90 per month	–		Th (after 5 p. m.)	$9.00		
7:30–9:30 p. m.	$29.90 per month	–		Fr–Su and holidays (after 5 p.m.)	$10.00		

Table 6.6 Price differentiation of hotels in Frankfurt am Main (standard room, with or without breakfast) [22–27]

	Single room Monday–Friday	Single room Weekend	Single room Trade fair
Le Méridien Parkhotel Frankfurt	219.00 incl.	139.00 incl.	369.00 incl.
Mercure Hotel & Residenz Frankfurt	79.00 excl.	79.00 excl.	199.00 excl.
Maritim Hotel	122.55 excl.	84.55 incl.	437.00 excl.
Marriott Hotel, Frankfurter Messe	189.00 incl.	129.00 excl.	479.00 excl.
Sheraton Hotel & Towers	224.00 incl.	185.00 incl.	274.00 incl.
Steigenberger Frankfurter Hof	249.00 excl.	199.00 excl.	649.00 excl.

All prices are in Euros

- A bakery chain has a "happy hour" offer: in the last hour before the store closes, customers receive a 30% discount on bread purchases.
- Hotel room prices show very wide variation, depending on whether there is a trade fair or other major event in town. Table 6.6 illustrates this for selected hotels in Frankfurt am Main, Germany. Major cities in the United States show similar schemes, with prices in Chicago increasing by as much as three times standard rates during a trade fair.
- Vacation homes' prices vary depending on the season. In summer, the demand for vacation houses is higher. As a result, prices increase. It may happen that in peak season one has to pay more than three times higher prices than in the off-season.
- Due to greater demand, products sold online are sometimes more expensive during the evening [21].

Amazon is proof of just how strongly digitalization has inspired price differentiation. The online retailer changes prices more than 2.5 million times per day. Best Buy and Walmart, whose focus remains on the classic brick-and-mortar market, change prices around 50,000 times per month. Their activity is less than 0.1% of Amazon's in this regard.

Time-based price differentiation is also used to manage capacity. Prices are increased whenever demand for a product or service spikes, in order to maintain a stable level of capacity utilization. A case in point of dynamic price differentiation is the "surge pricing" of the ride-sharing service Uber. The greater the demand is at certain times, the higher the prices are. During a snowstorm in New York City, Uber temporarily raised prices drastically, with prices ranging between two and four times normal prices [28]. A special application of dynamic pricing would be to solve one of the costliest problems of modern societies: traffic congestion on roads. This is one of the most promising areas for dynamic pricing, but so far it has rarely been used as a means to alleviate congestion. Note that we are not talking here about fixed tolls. Currently we find congestion pricing in the United States (e.g., on some highways in Minneapolis, Washington, DC, San Diego, Denver, and Orange County, CA). In the latter area, the price varies between $1.15 and $9.25 per trip and is posted prior to highway entry. Thus, motorists can choose between priced and non-priced lanes.

Singapore is the pioneer in this field. Cars are charged an additional fee ("central area pricing") when they enter the central business district. The use of private cars decreased by 73%, while carpooling increased by 30%. Congestion pricing was later extended to three major freeways. Average speed on one freeway increased from 31 to 67 km/h. It seems that everybody who visits Singapore is astonished how much better the traffic flows than in other large cities. The difference is all due to pricing [29].

Time-based price differentiation is also popular among restaurants. A common form is to offer a "happy hour" during which prices are reduced for a few hours, usually in the late afternoon or early evening. Whether that makes sense, however, depends on the price elasticity. It may happen that the reduced prices do not attract enough additional customers. Some restaurants lower their prices on slower week-days with weak demand, but this raises the same concern. In contrast, higher prices in periods of strong demand are a relatively safe bet. Amid excess demand, the higher prices allow the restaurant to better manage capacity; they do not need to turn away customers because they do not have enough room for them. The downside risk is that core customers may be offended by the higher prices during these peak periods. Customers who have less demand for a service at a given time see lower prices. Peak-load pricing and revenue management tackle such problems and will be discussed in detail in the chapter on implementation (see Chap. 9).

If there is no possibility for arbitrage, time-based price differentiations by time of day, day of week, or season are effective means to increase profits. The approach requires little or no additional costs for control.

Multi-Person Pricing
Multi-person pricing involves the sale of products or services to groups of people. Companies which use multi-person pricing include:

- Travel agents: some allow partners or children to travel on vacation at reduced prices or for free.
- Airlines: some, under certain conditions, offer the opportunity for spouses or another companion to fly at half price or for free.
- Public transportation: children ride for free when accompanied by their parents.
- Restaurants: the main course for a second person is half price or free.
- Music streaming: Apple Music and Spotify offer special family rates, so that it is not necessary for each individual family member to have a separate subscription. Apple's family package costs $14.99 for up to six users, while at Spotify each additional member pays $5 [30, 31].

We identify three forms of multi-person pricing [32, p. 19f].

- Under variable-quantity multi-person pricing, each individual customer fulfills his or her own demand, such as in a combined order from a catalog or online retailer.

- Under fixed-quantity multi-person pricing, each customer orders an identical amount of the product or service. This form of multi-person pricing includes, for example, tickets for a museum at a reduced group rate.
- The third form is single-product multi-person pricing, when a group jointly purchases one product, i.e., a group ticket on the railroad or a software package which allows multiple users.

The profit increase from multi-person pricing derives from two effects. First, it better extracts the consumer surplus of heterogeneous customers, and second, it can transfer the consumer surplus from one customer to another.

These effects are shown in Fig. 6.11, where for simplicity's sake we assume that fixed costs and marginal costs are zero. A business traveler's spouse is considering accompanying the traveler on a trip. The traveler's maximum willingness to pay is $1000. The spouse's willingness to pay is $750. If the uniform one-person price for the flight is $1000, only the traveler would go on the trip. The profit would be $1000. If the airline offered a uniform price of $750, then both would fly. The profit rises to $1500 (2 × $750), making $750 the optimal uniform price. Using multi-person bundling, however, the airline sets the total price for the couple at $1750 ($1000 + $750). This is a profit increase of 16.7% relative to the optimal uniform price. Multi-person pricing takes advantage of the maximum willingness to pay of each individual in order to achieve higher profits.

We observe the transfer of one customer's surplus to another customer if we repeat this example with slightly modified figures. If the maximum willingness to pay of the business traveler is only $900 and the spouse's is $850, then the traveler would not even go alone if the price for a single traveler were $1000. Both would travel together, however, if the total price for two were $1750, because this combined price corresponds to the combined willingness to pay.

Regional Price Differentiation
We speak of regional price differentiation when a seller charges different prices for the same product depending on the region, i.e., where the customer is located or is buying. Table 6.7 shows car rental prices for different regions of the United States.

Regional price differentiation is applied in many markets. Examples include fuel, food, groceries, and many kinds of services. The rationales behind the price differentiation can include differences in purchasing power, buying behavior, costs, competition, and sales channels. The approach calls for the determination of an optimal price for the respective region based on the regional price elasticity and costs. To enable effective fencing, the boundaries of a region play a critical role. The problem is structurally similar to international price differentiation (Sect. 8.2.1).

6.2.3.4 Combination of Several Forms of Price Differentiation
So far, we have looked at the various implementation forms of price differentiation in their pure form, i.e., in isolation. But in practice, companies often combine several forms. These combinations serve to address customer segments even more precisely. Fassnacht [4, pp. 95–98] found that in the service sectors he investigated, 47.5% of

Fig. 6.11 Uniform pricing vs. multi-person pricing

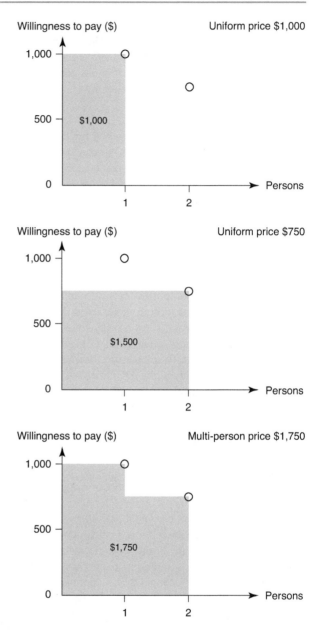

companies used two forms of price differentiation simultaneously, while 10% used three forms, and 0.7% used four forms. The most common combinations were time-based and performance-based (28.8%), time- and volume-based (25.8%), and person-based price differentiation in conjunction with price bundling (12.1%).

Table 6.7 Car rental prices in the United States (intermediate class, 1 week) [33]

City	Price per week ($)	Deviation from average (in %)
New York	345	+12.8
Chicago	370	+21.0
Los Angeles	245	−20.0
Detroit	360	+17.7
Miami	210	−31.4

Table 6.8 Multidimensional price differentiation at the American Marketing Association [34]

| Type | American Marketing Association | | |
	United States	Canada	International
Professional			
1 year	$240[a] + chapter dues	$195 + chapter dues	$195
2 years	$460[a] + chapter dues	–	–
3 years	$640[a] + chapter dues	–	–
Academic	$240[a] + chapter dues	$195 + chapter dues	$195
Young professionals	$120 + chapter dues	$120 + chapter dues	$105
Doctoral	$120 + chapter dues (optional)	$120 + chapter dues (optional)	$105
Student	$50 + chapter dues (optional)	$50 + chapter dues (optional)	$50
Group (offline application)			
4–9 members	$255 per member[b]	$255 per member[b]	–
10+ members	$230 per member[b]	$230 per member[b]	–

[a]Plus $30 application fee for new members
[b]Chapter dues included

One example for a multidimensional combination—an offering from the American Marketing Association—is shown in Table 6.8.

We observe the following implementation forms of price differentiation in this example:

- *Region-based price differentiation:* When one compares the different countries, one notices that the "International" fee is lower than the one for the United States and Canada. Moreover, the chapter dues vary significantly, from a high of $70 (e.g., for Chicago and Los Angeles) to a low of $24 lowest (e.g., for Tulsa).
- *Person-based price differentiation:* United States, Canadian, and international members pay different dues depending on their employment or qualifications (professional, academic, etc.).
- *Multi-person-based price differentiation:* Groups with four to nine members pay $255 per member, but the chapter dues are also included. Thus, the multi-person discount depends on the chapter dues. Groups with 10+ members pay $230 per

Table 6.9 Multidimensional price differentiation: Flinkster car sharing [35]

	Small car	Mid-sized car
Price per hour		
• 8:00–22:00 h	€5.00	€7.00
• 22:00–8:00 h	€1.50	€1.90
Daily price (first day)	€50.00	€70.00
Daily price (second day)	€29.00	€49.00
Consumption flat rate (electricity or gas) per kilometer	€0.18	€0.20
Registration costs (one-time)		
• Without BahnCard	€50.00	€50.00
• With BahnCard	Free	Free

Table 6.10 Multidimensional price differentiation: *The Economist* [36]

Weekly issue	Annual subscription (12 months)	Annual subscription, student (12 months)
Print or Digital	$152	$115
Print and Digital	$190	$142

member. For 10+ members this results in a discount of 26% for Chicago and Los Angeles and of 13% for Tulsa.

- *Volume-based price differentiation:* Members pay less for a 2- or 3-year membership than for a 1-year membership. They receive a discount of 11% for a 3-year membership relative to the annual dues. Thus, the prices decline with the duration of membership.

The example in Table 6.9 shows another combination of several forms of price differentiation:

- *Time-based* price differentiation: the hourly price varies depending on whether the car is rented during the day or overnight.
- *Person-based* price differentiation: Customers pay different registration costs depending on whether they have a BahnCard.
- *Performance-based* price differentiation (first case): The price per hour varies depending on the size of the car rented.
- *Performance-based* price differentiation (second case): The price per kilometer also varies depending on the size of the car rented.
- *Volume-based* price differentiation: The price for the second day is lower than the price for the first day.

The example of *The Economist* in Table 6.10 likewise shows a combination of multiple forms of price differentiation:

- *Person-based* price differentiation: students receive a discount of around 25%.
- *Performance-based* price differentiation: the price of the magazine depends on the form(s) the reader chooses, i.e., print or digital.

The advantage of such combinations of price differentiation is that customers can choose among different performance parameters and pay different prices, so that consumer surpluses are effectively extracted. When a company offers such a combination of price differentiation forms, however, it should be aware that the customers can perceive the complexity to be very high. The company must evaluate case by case whether this complexity is desirable from the perspective of price transparency. High complexity makes it hard for the customer to compare prices, but it can also lead to the intended incentive effects not taking hold or to outright customer resistance. At the same time, the use of multiple forms of price differentiation creates additional costs. These can be split into internal and external costs. The internal costs include market research activities and additional organizational efforts. The external costs from price differentiation stem from the potential customer frustration. The customers may perceive the differentiation as a nontransparent price structure which is hard to understand. This can lead to frustration, to more customer service inquiries, or ultimately to customers' switching suppliers. The maxim therefore is that a seller should *optimize* not *maximize* the number of price differentiation forms.

The costs of price differentiation may in fact outpace the increased utility of implementation forms. At the same time, the value for the seller, i.e., the profit increase, rises underproportionally. These countervailing effects lead to an optimal number of implementation forms. Figure 6.12 shows this relationship schematically.

Even in industries with complex price structures, we occasionally find companies which use a *simple price structure*. The increase in complexity caused by some sellers opens up "niches of simplicity" for competitors. One example of such simplification is the concept of a single price for unlimited use of a good, a so-called flat rate. This concept results in a fundamental simplification for the customer, who can, for example, make phone calls or send text messages of any length at any time, 24 hours a day, 7 days a week for one fixed price. Flat rates have entered more and more areas of day-to-day life [37]. Examples include the BahnCard 100 of the German Railway, which allows unlimited train travel. For a flat annual fee, Amazon's Prime program offers free 2-day delivery throughout the United States on any eligible product, as well as an e-book flat rate under the name "Kindle Unlimited," an extensive video-on-demand program, and a streaming service called "Prime Music." The annual price for Amazon Prime is $99 in the United States and €69 in the European Union. Different transit companies in Switzerland offer a combined flat rate called the "Swiss Travel Pass," which allows the pass holder unlimited use of rail, bus, and boat service for a period of either 3, 4, 8, or 15 days [16].

Service contracts for automobiles at fixed monthly rates also fit this pattern. This development indicates that customers seem to appreciate the reduction in complexity. Fritz et al. [38] found that transparency and cost controls—and not only the

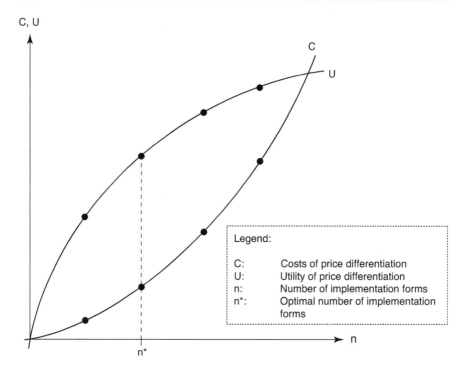

Fig. 6.12 Costs and utility of price differentiation

simplification of the purchase decision—play a role when complicated price comparisons are no longer necessary. Companies who use simple forms of pricing have a cost advantage because they do not incur the implementation costs of complex, differentiated price structures.

6.3   Price Decisions Across Products

6.3.1   Price Decisions for Product Lines

It is rare that a company offers only one product or one service; most firms offer multiple products and/or services. Whether this multiproduct nature has consequences for price management depends on the extent of volume and cost interdependencies between the individual products. Unless the products are in completely separate markets or market segments, it is likely that such interdependencies exist.

6.3.1.1 Theoretical Basis
When interdependencies exist between products of a product line, the profit-maximizing price should not be determined for each product in isolation. The

maximization of the firm's profit requires that one takes the interdependencies into account. We distinguish among four different interrelationships between products.

Substitutive Relationships

Products which satisfy the same or similar needs are considered to have a competitive or substitutive relationship with each other. The customers typically choose to buy one product out of several alternatives or they buy less of one product when they buy more of another. Thus, the cross-price elasticity between substitute products is positive. When the price of one product rises, demand for it will tend to be less, and the demand for its substitutes will increase. Examples of products which are considered complete substitutes are cars or vacation packages. One also sees a gradual substitution between different types of wine or between rail trips and airline trips.

Normally a company which has substitutive products within its product line will endeavor to keep cannibalization between its own products at a low level. Price management is an important instrument to achieve this objective.

Complementary Relationships

Products have a complementary relationship to each other when they provide value in combination. If customers buy more of one product, they also buy more of the other. The cross-price elasticity between complementary products is negative, i.e., a price increase in one product reduces not only the sales volume of that product but that of its complement as well. The extent of the complementary relationship can be fixed (limitational) or variable. Examples of fixed relationships are cars and air conditioning systems or houses and heating units. Variable relationships in complementary products include coffee and sugar or wine and cheese.

Dynamic Relationships

Time often plays a role in the interrelationships across products. The purchase of a primary product is often followed over time by the purchase of other related products or services. For products subject to extensive wear and tear such as diesel engines, machine tools, or jet engines, the expenditures on such follow-on products and services can be a multiple of the purchase price of the primary product. Other examples for dynamic relationships across products include copiers and cartridges or blood sugar test devices and test strips.

In some cases, it can be optimal to sell the primary product at prices below costs. The overall result can still be optimal, as long as the follow-on products are sold at prices with high margins. This differentiated pricing policy is based on the fact that the price elasticities for the primary and the follow-on products are sharply different.

From a dynamic perspective, the borders between substitutive and complementary can blur. Two products which from a static point of view could be considered substitutes can be complementary over time. That can result, for example, from a need for variety, as many customers opt for a suite of brands or variants over time instead of buying just one brand or one variant all the time. Soft drinks, yogurt, and ice cream fit that description.

Information Transfer

In addition to usage-based relationships between a company's products, there are more general information transfers. A positive or negative experience with one product can get transferred to other products of the same manufacturer, and that transferred experience can have a correspondingly positive or negative impact on willingness to pay for those other products. Simon [39, pp. 32–43] has analyzed such goodwill transfers extensively. They are widespread. Their significance for price management depends on the intensity of the information transfer. It can make sense to offer certain introductory, entry-level, or basic products at favorably low or even negative prices, in order to provide the customer with a positive experience and create goodwill which carries over to the company's other products.

6.3.1.2 Price Optimization for Product Lines

We consider a monopolistic case and assume a cross-product price-response function for multiple products of the following general form:

$$q_i = f\left(p_1, \ldots, p_i, \ldots, p_n\right) \tag{6.4}$$

where q_i is the sales volume of product i. The variables $p_1, \ldots, p_n$ represent the prices of the n products in the product line. Because we are looking at a static case, we can leave out a time index.

For function (6.4), the direct price elasticities are:

$$\varepsilon_i = \frac{\partial q_i}{\partial p_i} \times \frac{p_i}{q_i} \tag{6.5}$$

and the cross-price elasticities are:

$$\varepsilon_{ij} = \frac{\partial q_i}{\partial p_j} \times \frac{p_j}{q_i} \tag{6.6}$$

The cross-price elasticity ε_{ij} indicates the percentage change in the sales of product i, when the price of product j varies by 1%.

The objective function is the maximization of the product line's total profit:

$$\text{Max}\,\pi = \sum_{i=1}^{n} [p_i q_i - C_i(q_i)] \tag{6.7}$$

$C_i(q_i)$ represents as usual the cost function of product i; we assume no cost interdependence. After taking the partial derivative of the profit function for all prices, and after some reformulations, we get the condition for the optimal price of product j[6]:

---

[6]For the derivation, see the Background Information at the end of the chapter.

$$p_j^* = \frac{\varepsilon_j}{1+\varepsilon_j}C_j' - \sum_{\substack{i=1 \\ i \neq j}}^{n}\left(p_i - C_i'\right)\frac{\varepsilon_{ij}}{\left(1+\varepsilon_j\right)}\frac{q_i}{q_j} \qquad (6.8)$$

This is the so-called Niehans formula [40]. In the first addend of (6.8), we recognize the familiar Amoroso-Robinson relation (5.6), which determines the isolated optimal price, i.e., the price without considering interdependencies with other products. A cross-product optimal price is the sum of the isolated optimal price and a correction term which captures the value of the interrelationships across the product line. That correction term includes elasticities, sales volumes, and unit contribution margins. If one considers (6.8) for all n products simultaneously, each price depends on all the elasticities and all the marginal costs of the entire product line. It is not possible to provide a general statement about the effects of cross-product interrelationships on the optimal price, because all prices are dependent on each other. In order to arrive at interpretable conclusions, we have to make ceteris paribus assumptions. We need to assume that only one variable at a time changes on the right-hand side of (6.8). In addition to the necessary condition (6.8), the sufficient conditions have to be determined. These are met when the direct price effect coefficients for all products are larger than the indirect coefficients [41, pp. 38–55, 42, pp. 71–80].

When the product line comprises only *substitutive products*, all cross-price elasticities ε_{ij} are positive. In this case, and if $\varepsilon_j < -1$, the summation term in (6.8) is negative. It follows that the cross-product optimal price p_i^* ceteris paribus is higher than the isolated optimal price as given by the Amoroso-Robinson relation. Relative to the isolated optimal price, the cross-product optimal price p_j^* is higher:

- The greater the number of products is
- The higher the cross-price elasticities ε_{ij} are
- The larger the unit contribution margins of the other products are
- The closer the direct price elasticity ε_j is to -1
- The greater the ratio of the sales volumes of i and j is

If the relationships are purely substitutive, product-line pricing leads to higher prices than the pricing of individual products in isolation.

When the relationships are *exclusively complementary*, all cross-price elasticities ε_{ij} are negative, so if $\varepsilon_j < -1$, the summation term in (6.8) is positive. It will thus be subtracted from the Amoroso-Robinson term. It follows, then, that the cross-product optimal price p_j^* is lower:

- The more products the product line includes
- The larger the cross-price elasticities ε_{ij} are (in absolute terms)
- The larger the unit contribution margins for the other products are
- The closer the direct price elasticity ε_j is to -1
- The greater the ratio of the sales volumes of i and j is

Table 6.11 Parameters for an example of a substitutive relationship	Product i	a_i	b_i	b_{ij}	C_i'
	1	1000	50	25	5
	2	1000	50	10	5

A typical case of product-line pricing for complementary products are special offers or discounts of retailers. A retailer is willing to accept a low or even negative unit contribution margin for the product on special offer in the hope of luring customers who will also buy higher priced, more profitable products. From formula (6.8) one can see that the optimal price can be below the marginal costs of the relevant product and could even be negative (see Chap. 14). From a business standpoint, there is no justification for forbidding a multiproduct firm with interrelated products to sell some products below marginal costs.

Condition (6.8) also explains why the optimal price for the same product can differ from company to company, even when the costs are the same. That explains why gas stations at supermarkets sell gas at lower prices than stand-alone gas stations.

When there are both *substitutive and complementary* relationships within a product line, we cannot determine the sign of the summation term in (6.8) unequivocally. In such cases, the magnitude of the substitutive and complementary effects will determine whether the optimal cross-product price is higher or lower than the isolated optimal price. We illustrate the above insights with one example each for substitutive and complementary relationships.

Example with Substitutive Relationships

We assume linear price-response and cost functions with the parameters shown in Table 6.11. Except for the cross-price effect parameter b_{ij}, the parameters for both products are identical. To determine the cross-product optimal prices, we use (6.8) and get $p_1^* = \$18.16$ and $p_2^* = \$17.61$. The sufficient conditions for a global maximum profit are fulfilled, because all direct price effect parameters are greater than the indirect ones.

The result is explained in Fig. 6.13. It shows the profit situation for different combinations of p_1 and p_2 using iso-profit curves. The curves representing equal profit for each individual product (π_1 and π_2) are dashed, while the total profit π is represented by the solid line. The arrows show the direction of rising profit. An increase of price p_1 will, ceteris paribus, increase the revenue and the profit for product 2—assuming no change in its price and a positive unit contribution margin—as more demand flows to it. The interest of the company is not the profit of the individual product, but rather the total profit π. In Fig. 6.13 the point of maximum total profit is marked with a star. The cross-product optimal prices are $p_1^* = \$18.16$ and $p_2^* = \$17.61$.

For comparison we calculate the isolated optimal prices. We get $p_1^* = \$16.03$ and $p_2^* = \$14.10$. In Fig. 6.13 this price combination is indicated by the large dot. The results for cross-product and isolated optimal pricing are shown side by side in Table 6.12.

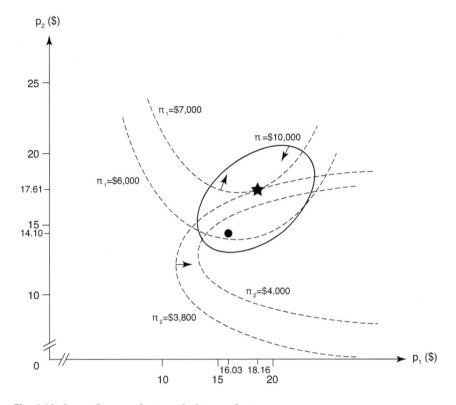

Fig. 6.13 Iso-profit curves for two substitute products

Table 6.12 Optimal values for an example of products with a substitutive relationship

Optimal value	Cross-product		Isolated	
	Product 1	Product 2	Product 1	Product 2
Price p_j^*	$18.16	$17.61	$16.03	$14.10
Volume q_j	532	301	551	455
Revenue R_i	$9663	$5305	$8835	$6418
Profit π_j	$7003	$3798	$6078	$4143
Total profit π	$10,801		$10,221	
Price elasticity ε_j	−1.71	−2.92	−1.50	−1.50
Cross-price elasticity ε_{ij}	0.83	0.60	0.64	0.35

The cross-product optimal prices for product 1 and product 2 are 13.3% and 24.9% above the respective isolated optimal prices. The difference is greater for product 2, because the negative impact of a lower price p_1 on the sales volume of product 1 is much stronger than the similar effect for product 2. This is explained by the higher cross-price effect coefficients (25 vs. 10).

The total profit with cross-product price optimization is $580 or 5.7% higher than the isolated optimum. The profit situation for the individual products is vastly different, however. Product 2, logically, shows a higher profit in isolation, with a difference of $345. For product 1, the opposite is true; its isolated profit is $925 lower than its profit in the combined, cross-product view. Interestingly, the total revenue follows the opposite trend. In the cross-product optimization, the total revenue is $285 or 1.9% lower. In our case, the company knowingly forgoes the opportunity to exploit the full revenue of product 2, in order to achieve higher revenue and profit from the more profitable product 1.

Example with Complementary Relationship

We maintain the parameter values for the two products shown in Table 6.11. The sign of the cross-effect parameter b_{ij} is negative, however, for complementary products.

The situation for complementary products is shown in Fig. 6.14. The iso-profit curve for products 1 and 2 are dashed, and the solid ellipse symbolizes the total profit π. The star marks the price combination which maximizes the total profit. The dot shows the price combination which results in the greatest total profit for the individual products in isolation. The arrows show the direction of increasing profit.

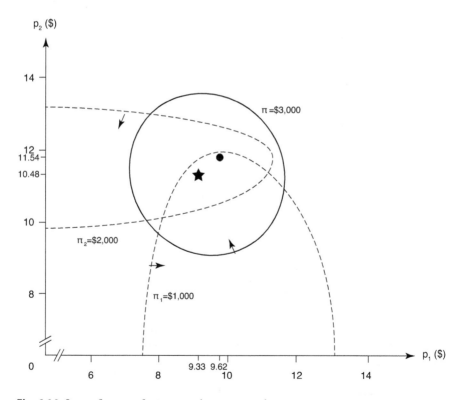

Fig. 6.14 Iso-profit curves for two complementary products

Table 6.13 Optimal values for an example of products with a complementary relationship

Optimal value	Cross-product		Isolated	
	Product 1	Product 2	Product 1	Product 2
Price p_j^*	$9.33	$10.48	$9.62	$11.54
Volume q_j	271	382	231	327
Revenue R_i	$2532	$4010	$2219	$3772
Profit π_j	$1175	$2098	$1065	$2138
Total profit π	$3273		$3203	
Price elasticity ε_j	−1.72	−1.37	−2.10	−1.80
Cross-price elasticity ε_{ij}	−0.97	−0.24	−1.30	−0.29

The iso-profit curve system is rotated in comparison to the one for substitute products. A price increase in product 1 reduces the profit of product 2, because its volume q_2 declines.

Table 6.13 shows the results. For a cross-product optimization the prices are lower, but the total profit is higher than in the isolated case. The company sacrifices $40 in profit from product 2 in order to generate an additional $110 in profit from product 1. In this case, the revenue with cross-product optimization is $554 higher

Implementation of Price Decisions for Product Lines

Price optimization across products is more complicated than isolated optimization. There are two problems associated with this. First, price optimization across products only makes sense when the respective cross-price effect coefficients can be measured with validity. Second, having a centralized competence for price decisions for all relevant products is a prerequisite.

To measure the cross-price coefficients, a company essentially must draw on all of the data sources and analytical methods described in Chap. 2. For larger numbers of products ($n > 3$), however, there are additional difficulties. The primary problem with econometric estimates is the multicollinearity of the various prices. The more appropriate approach would be expert estimates and/or conjoint measurement. The best approaches are decision-support models which allow detailed simulations of the substitutive or complementary relationships. Simon-Kucher & Partners has conducted thousands of such simulations for the automotive, pharmaceutical, banking, and other markets with good results [43].

Optimization across products can cause conflicts in a decentralized organization, because it involves the sacrifice of profit on one or several products in order to earn higher profits on other products. If the products belong to different profit centers, the "sacrificing" profit center has no interest in profit optimization across products. This is equally true for substitutive and complementary relationships.

The significance of these conflicts in practice is potentially large, as the following relationships illustrate:

- First purchase vs. parts and service
- Machine vs. consumables
- Business customers vs. private customers at a bank
- Passenger cars vs. commercial vehicles

If possible, the cross-product relationships should be considered in the setup of the organization. Another way to manage potential conflicts is to give the "sacrificing" profit center credit for its contribution to the profit of the other division or profit center. Although this credit is correct in theory, it can provoke resistance from the division required to grant the credit. The more reliably the relationships can be measured, the greater the likelihood that such a system will find acceptance.

6.3.2   Price Bundling

Bundling includes offering two or more products or services at one combined price. "Price bundling happens when a supplier combines several heterogeneous products into one package or bundle and then charges one total (bundle) price" [44, p. 12].
We find examples for price bundling in many sectors:

- Fast-food restaurants offer food and drinks at a fixed price.
- Cable and telecom providers offer packages which combine fixed-line telephony, mobile telephony, the Internet, and cable television.
- Internet or mobile contracts include access to streaming services such as Netflix or Spotify.
- Washing machine and dishwasher manufacturers offer packages which also include soaps or detergents.
- Software packages contain multiple applications.

Companies use price bundling to pursue different goals:

- Higher profits through price differentiation: Under price bundling, customers do pay the same bundle price, but because they will have differences in their willingness to pay for the bundle components, there is an implicit price differentiation.
- Price segmentation: When customers have the opportunity to choose between a bundled offer and the unbundled components, the existence of the bundle results in a different segmentation of the customers.
- Lowering price elasticity: The reduction of price elasticity can occur when the bundle combines a product with high elasticity with a product whose elasticity is low.
- Disguising individual prices: If only the price for the bundle is shown, the customers cannot easily infer what the price of an individual product in the bundle would be.

- Hiding a price increase: Price bundling is an appropriate instrument for cleverly communicating a price increase without customers' feeling they are being treated unfairly.
- Taking advantage of psychological price assessment processes: In the spirit of prospect theory (see Chap. 4), paying one total price for the bundle instead of paying separate prices for each individual component can lower the negative utility associated with paying multiple prices.

6.3.2.1 The Theory of Price Bundling

Price bundling appears in many forms. These are shown in Fig. 6.15. Most price bundling cases involve a "yes-no" decision, i.e., the customer either buys the bundle or not. The "variable-quantity" case occurs with tied sales and sales bonuses.

Older explanations of the optimality of price bundling referred to cost savings in production, transactions, and information as well as the complementarity among the bundle components [45–47]. It is obvious that cost savings can make bundling advantageous. Complementarity enhances the advantages of price bundling, but it is not a prerequisite. The bundling of noncomplementary products can also make sense.

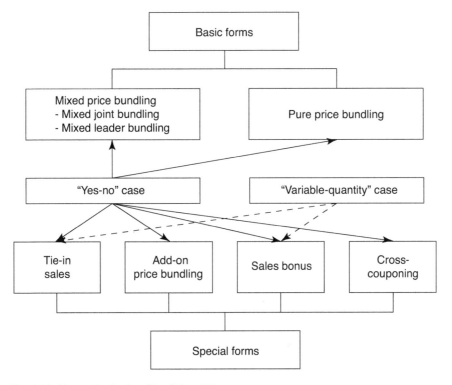

Fig. 6.15 Forms of price bundling [44, p. 35]

Table 6.14 Maximum
prices for individual
products and the price
bundle

Customer	Maximum prices (in $)		
	A	B	A + B
1	6.00	1.00	7.00
2	1.80	5.00	6.80
3	5.00	4.00	9.00
4	3.00	2.50	5.50
5	2.40	1.80	4.20

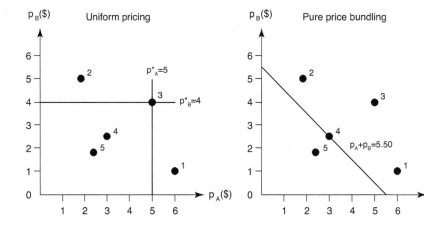

Fig. 6.16 Uniform pricing vs. price bundling

Adams and Yellen [48] have shown that price bundling allows a company to better extract the consumer surplus of heterogeneous customers than by selling to them at separate prices. Price bundling thus has similarity to nonlinear pricing. Oren et al. [49] apply the concept of nonlinear pricing across multiple products, with the following important differences:

- Price bundling only makes sense when the customers are heterogeneous, while nonlinear pricing is advantageous when customers are homogeneous or heterogeneous.
- Price bundling is primarily relevant for the "yes-no" case, less so for the "variable-quantity" case, while nonlinear pricing is only relevant for the latter case.

In order to explain these implications, we look at the example in Table 6.14. The table shows the maximum prices for products A and B for five customers. The maximum prices correspond to the value the respective customer derives from these products. The maximum price for the product bundle A + B equals the sum of the maximum prices for both products.

The positions of the maximum prices for products A and B for all customers are plotted on the left-hand side of Fig. 6.16. We assume that the variable unit costs are zero. That assumption neither limits nor alters the general validity of the underlying principle. The optimal individual prices are $p_A^* = \$5$ and $p_B^* = \$4$. Under this price constellation, the individual customers behave as follows: 1 buys only product A, 2 buys only product B, 3 buys A and B, and customers 4 and 5 buy neither product. Two units each of A and B are sold, and the total profit is $\$5 \times 2 + \$4 \times 2 = \$18$. The profits are $\pi_A = \$10$, $\pi_B = \$8$ and reach their respective maxima.

6.3.2.2 Forms of Price Bundling

Pure Bundling
With pure bundling the components of the bundle are sold exclusively as a package at one total price. It is not possible to purchase the individual components of the bundle. The customer can only decide whether or not to buy the bundle.

What happens when a firm offers products A and B in Table 6.14 as a price bundle? The optimal bundle price is $5.50. This situation is shown on the right-hand side of Fig. 6.16. Along the negatively sloped, 45-degree line, $p_A + p_B = \$5.50$. Pure bundling has the effect of turning the previous market structure (four customer segments, clearly visible on the left-hand side of the figure) into just two segments: buyers and non-buyers of the bundle. The buyers include customers 1, 2, 3, and 4, while customer 5 does not buy. Price bundling reduces the heterogeneity among customers [5, 50]. The firm generates a profit of $\$5.50 \times 4 = \$22$, which is 22% higher than the maximum profit in the unbundled situation. This is all the more surprising when you consider that the bundle price of $5.50 is considerably less than $9, the sum of the two isolated optimal prices for A and B. In order to win over customer 5 as well, the bundle price would need to be lowered to $4.20, which would reduce total profit to $5 \times \$4.20 = \$21$. This is still a higher profit than the optimum in the unbundled situation.

The reason for the profit improvement from $18 to $22 is that bundling does a better job of extracting consumer surplus. Pure bundling essentially means that the firm creates a new product. The bundle price is set in such a way that the consumer surplus from one product is transferred to the new combined product. In our example, customer 1 retains a consumer surplus of $\$6 - \$5 = \$1$ on product A in the unbundled situation, but the willingness to pay for product B is $3 too low. When the firm opts for pure bundling, its price represents a reduction in the sum of customer 1's two maximum prices for product A and B. At $5.50, the price is low enough that customer 1 is incentivized to buy the bundle. The situation for customer 2 is the opposite. There is a consumer surplus of $1 on product B, but the willingness to pay for product A is $3.2 too low. The reduction of the bundled price relative to the sum of the two individual maximum prices for A and B is exactly enough to induce customer 4 to buy the bundle. It is possible that even though the bundling increases overall profit, the firm earns less profit from an individual customer through bundling than it would earn by selling the products separately. That is the case for customer 3, who would buy both products for a total of $9 at their isolated optimal prices. Under pure bundling, customer 3 pays only $5.50, which reduces profit by $3.50 for that particular customer.

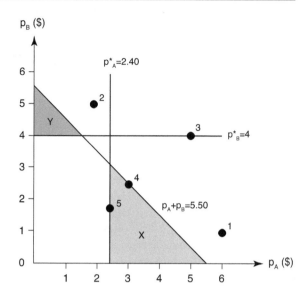

Fig. 6.17 Mixed price bundling

Mixed Bundling

With mixed bundling, customers can buy the bundle at a fixed price or can buy any of the bundle components separately at their individual prices. This is also referred to as optional bundling. In most cases, the bundle price in mixed bundling is less than the sum of the individual prices [51].[7]

The example from Table 6.14 helps illuminate the advantages of mixed bundling. In addition to the bundle at a price of $5.50, we offer product A separately at a price of $2.40 and product B separately at $4 ($p_B$ must be higher than $3.10, so that the sum of the individual prices is not less than the bundle price). The mixed bundling is shown in Fig. 6.17.

In this new constellation, customer 5 now purchases product A (but only product A), so that the profit rises to $24.40 from $22. Generally speaking, the customers in triangle X become buyers of product A and the customers in triangle Y buyers of product B. This is above and beyond the customers who buy the bundle. Mixed bundling leads to an even finer market segmentation and extraction of consumer surplus.

Schmalensee [50, p. 227] summarizes his views on the topic of price bundling as follows: "The advantage of pure bundling is the ability to reduce effective buyer heterogeneity, while the advantage of unbundled sales is the ability to collect a high price for each good from some buyers who care little for the other good. Mixed bundling can make use of both these advantages by selling the bundle to a group of

---

[7]This must not always be the case. For collections, the price for a complete collection may be greater than the sum of the individual pieces.

buyers with accordingly reduced effective heterogeneity, while charging high mark ups to those on the fringes of the taste distribution who are mainly interested in only one of the two goods."

Special Forms of Price Bundling
Special forms of price bundling include:

- *Tie-in sales*: These are defined by a primary product (tying good) for which the customer must buy one or more homogeneous supplemental products (tied goods). The tying good is normally a durable product, while the tied goods are consumables. Examples include printers and cartridges or razors and blades.
- *Add-on price bundling:* Customers may purchase the secondary product (add-on product) only if they have already purchased the primary product. The difference to tie-in sales is that the customer can still use the primary product without purchasing any of the add-on products. Computer games for which a customer has the option to buy expansions but can still play the basic game on its own are an example.
- *Sales bonus*: Customers receive either a fixed amount of money or a percentage of their total expenditures as a credit or payout after a certain period of time. The distinguishing characteristic of this form is that it does not necessarily depend on what the customer buys in that time period, i.e., what comprises the individual bundle. Only the total expenditure matters. This form of bundling is often offered in conjunction with customer loyalty programs.
- *Cross-couponing*: This means that customers receive a coupon on product B after they purchase product A. This is an implicit form of price bundling.

Unbundling
Unbundling describes the separate sales of products or services which used to be offered as a bundle. The following conditions may make unbundling a favorable option:

- Higher profit margins from unbundling: This can happen when the individual products have a low price elasticity. This situation happens when the bundled price becomes very high as the bundling "system" evolves.
- Developing a market: A firm can sometimes tap into latent demand or new market segments by unbundling a product.
- Increasing standardization and compatibility: The more the bundle components become standardized and compatible, the riskier pure bundling becomes, as customers have the option to cobble together the same solution with components from multiple sellers. This creates a tension between fencing oneself off against competitors (via pure bundling) and expanding the market. As the life cycle of a product progresses and the market matures, the balance tips in favor of unbundling.

- Shifting the share of added value: In many industries there is a trend toward charging separately for services which used to be included in the purchase price of a product.

An interesting case is the television function in the BMW 7 series. The first generation of the navigation system in the 7 series included television at no extra charge. Subsequent generations offered television but for a separate charge. This separate price for the fifth generation is €1250 [52].

In the age of e-book readers, the unbundling of a book into its constituent chapters is becoming more common. Harvard Business School Publishing sells individual chapters of books as well as articles from the *Harvard Business Review* (HBR) for $8.95 each. Other publishers have adopted this à la carte model. Such offers are attractive to readers who may have interest only in certain topics or aspects of a book. An annual subscription to HBR costs $99. Someone who reads fewer than 11 articles in a year would be better off purchasing them individually. Someone who reads only five articles pays 50% less under the à la carte model. The unbundling carries certain risks for sellers, who should carefully consider the potential consequences before introducing it.

A revolutionary form of unbundling was introduced with iTunes, which made it possible to purchase an individual track without buying the entire album. Its spectacular success is due in part to the innovative price model. But that is no guarantee of future success. Music streaming services such as Spotify, Amazon, Deezer, or Tidal are offering flat rate models which allow customers to listen to as much music as they wish, online and offline, for monthly subscription fee [53, 54]. Similarly, Amazon provides unlimited access to Amazon Music for Prime subscribers.

Another controversial example of unbundling was the separation of checked baggage from the airline ticket. Started by Ryanair, many airlines now have a surcharge for checked baggage. The Sanifair concept at highway rest areas is another case of unbundling. Traditionally the use of a bathroom was free of charge along interstate highways (the Autobahn) in Germany. Starting in 2003, the use of the toilet cost 50 cents for everyone except children under a certain height limit. That was a family-friendly form of price differentiation. The disabled could also use the bathrooms free of charge. In exchange for the 50 cents, the customers received a coupon which they could redeem at one of the businesses at the rest area. This price model achieved a differentiation between those who only wanted to use the bathroom (and had to pay 50 cents) and those who wanted to buy other products as well and received a 50-cent coupon, i.e., free use of the bathroom. In 2010, the price to enter the bathroom was raised to 70 cents, but the value of the coupon remained at 50 cents.

Price Presentation

The implementation of price bundling happens in two steps. First, a firm determines the form of the price bundling. Then the firm sets the price level using one of three approaches:

1. Additive price bundling: The bundle price corresponds exactly to the sum of the prices for the individual products. We observe the use of additive price bundling on Amazon for books, kitchen, and household products.
2. Super-additive price bundling: The bundled price is higher than the sum of the individual prices. This form is rather rare. One example of its use is for complete collections of stamps, for which the seller can demand a premium for a complete set.
3. Sub-additive price bundling: The bundled price includes a discount, i.e., it is lower than the sum of the individual prices. This is the typical approach.

An important aspect of sub-additive price bundling is the way the price reduction is expressed. There are three options for presenting the price and/or discount:

- Joint-bundle pricing: a bundled price which includes a discount is shown together with the prices for the individual items (e.g., menus in a restaurant).
- Leader-bundle pricing: the customer receives the primary product at the regular price, but receives the additional bundle products at a steep discount or even for free. Clothing retailers such as Tie Rack or Jos. A. Bank use this approach to sell the first item at full price and additional items at half price or less.
- Composite-bundle pricing: All products in the bundle receive a discount. One example is an online service for wine, which offers a discount of $15 off the sum of the individual prices when the customer orders a package of six kinds of wine.

The combined offer of several products in the form of a bundle at one total price is an effective way to extract profit potential. Bundling reduces the heterogeneity of demand. It can be applied in pure or mixed form. Companies must consider on a case-by-case basis which form is superior or whether unbundling delivers better results. It is not possible to offer a general rule because bundling decisions hinge on the distribution of customers' willingness to pay.

Conclusion
In this chapter we demonstrated the optimization of multidimensional prices and the effects on profit. We summarize the chapter as follows:

- Compared to one-dimensional pricing, multidimensional pricing can generate significantly higher profits. The reason is that the profit potential, from a geometrical standpoint, resembles the area of a triangle. A one-dimensional or uniform price can only carve out a rectangle, whose area is necessarily smaller than the total area of the triangle.
- The optimization of multidimensional prices requires a deeper understanding and more differentiated information than one-dimensional pricing.

(continued)

- Price differentiation is worth considering whenever customers differ in their willingness to pay or other aspects relevant for pricing. Price differentiation can be based on time, region, product, volume, or other buyer characteristics. It is possible to combine several forms.
- The multidimensionality can derive from different price parameters. One can implement a volume-based price differentiation through a direct volume discount, through the combination of fixed and variable price components, in the form of two- or multipart tariffs, or through discrete price points. In all cases it is critical to maintain effective fencing, i.e., to prevent a customer with a higher willingness to pay from buying at a lower price. This is the only way to come as close as possible to extracting the profit potential from the profit triangle. Ineffective fencing poses a significant risk.
- Multi-person pricing involves transferring residual or unextracted willingness to pay from one customer to another customer.
- Companies who offer more than one product should consider the interdependencies between costs and products when they optimize prices. The prices for interdependent products should be optimized simultaneously. One should take into account the effects that the price of one product has on the profits of other products and thus on the total profit of the firm.
- For substitutive products, the general rule is that the difference between the cross-product optimal price of a product and its optimal price in isolation depends on the number of substitute products, the cross-price elasticities between these products, and the unit contribution margin of those products. The greater those factors are, the greater the difference is between the cross-product optimal prices and the isolated optimal prices.
- For complementary products, the opposite applies. The greater those factors are, the *lower* the cross-product optimal price of a product is relative to its isolated optimal price. In this case, the optimal price of a product can be below marginal costs or even negative.
- In price bundling, products are offered as a package rather than sold individually. Typically, the bundle price is lower than the sum of the individual prices. Price bundling can be employed in pure form (the customer can buy only the bundle) or in mixed form (the customer may buy the bundle or may buy the component products separately). The advantages of price bundling derive from the transfer of unextracted willingness to pay from one product to another. That is synonymous with saying that the customer heterogeneity is reduced so that the price differentiation becomes more effective. Price bundling can lead to significant profit improvements.

(continued)

- Price differentiation brings an increase in complexity and cost. One should therefore weigh the costs and benefits of pursuing it. What makes sense is not maximum price differentiation, but rather an optimal balance between the marginal gains and the marginal costs of differentiation. One should keep in mind organizational and legal aspects.

Although we cannot make generally valid statements about the advantages of price differentiation, we can say that price differentiation almost always makes sense. Prerequisites to its proper use, however, include gaining a thorough understanding of its various forms, generating the necessary data and information, and implementing effectively. If a company does not succeed in separating customer segments with different willingness to pay, price differentiation can actually destroy profits. When used properly, it can lead to considerable profit increases.

6.4   Background Information

In order to decide on the optimal prices $p_i^*, \ldots, p_n^*$, we determine the partial derivatives of the profit function across all prices. This leads to:

$$\frac{\partial \pi}{\partial p_j} = q_j + \left(p_j - C_j'\right)\frac{\partial q_j}{\partial p_j} + \sum_{\substack{i=1 \\ i \neq j}}^{n} \left(p_i - C_i'\right)\frac{\partial q_i}{\partial p_j} = 0 \qquad (6.9)$$

with C_i' as marginal costs of product i, $i = 1,\ldots,n$. For the overall optimization for the product line, we need to set the derivative for all n products equal to zero (necessary condition). A simple reformulation (dividing by q_j, multiplying by p_j, inserting the elasticity according to (6.7) and (6.8)) yields the optimality condition.

References

1. Poundstone, W. (2010). *Priceless: The Myth of Fair Value (And How to Take Advantage of It)*. New York: Hill and Wang.
2. Hays, C. L. (1999, October 28). Variable Price Coke Machine Being Tested. *The New York Times*, p. C1.
3. Morozov, E. (2013, April 10). Ihr wollt immer nur Effizienz und merkt nicht, dass dadurch die Gesellschaft kaputtgeht. *Frankfurter Allgemeine Zeitung*, p. 27.
4. Fassnacht, M. (1996). *Preisdifferenzierung bei Dienstleistungen: Implementationsformen und Determinanten*. Wiesbaden: Gabler.
5. Philips, L. (1983). *The Economics of Price Discrimination*. Cambridge: Cambridge University Press.

6. Pigou, A. C. (1932). *The Economics of Welfare* (ed. 4). London: Macmillan.
7. Pechtl, H. (2014). *Preispolitik: Behavioral Pricing und Preissysteme* (ed. 2). Wirtschaftswissenschaften. Konstanz: UVK/Lucius.
8. von Thenen, S. (2014). E-Commerce in privaten Haushalten 2013. *Wirtschaft und Statistik* 8, 450–454.
9. Netflix International (2018). https://www.netflix.com/. Accessed 27 February 2018.
10. Financial Times (2016). https://sub.ft.com/spa2_5/?countryCode=USA. Accessed 15 December 2016.
11. Hannak, A., Soeller, G., Lazer, D., Mislove, A. & Wilson, C. (2014): Measuring Price Discrimination and Steering on E-Commerce Web Sites, in: *IMC '14 Proceedings of the 2014 Conference on Internet Measurement Conference*, pp. 305–318.
12. Gossen, H. H. (1854). *Entwicklung der Gesetze des menschlichen Verkehrs, und der daraus fließenden Regeln für menschliches Handeln.* Braunschweig: Vieweg.
13. Tacke, G. (1989). *Nichtlineare Preisbildung: Höhere Gewinne durch Differenzierung.* Wiesbaden: Gabler.
14. BestParking.com (2016). http://www.bestparking.com/houston-parking. Accessed 15 December 2016.
15. Tefft, B. C. (2012). Motor Vehicle Crashes, Injuries, and Deaths in Relation to Driver Age: United States, 1995–2010. AAA Foundation for Traffic Safety. November 2012.
16. Swiss Travel System (2015). http://www.swisstravelsystem.com/de/tickets/swiss-travel-pass.html. Accessed 18 November 2015.
17. Fitness-Center Scheel (2015). http://www.fitness-center-scheel.de/fitness-center/preise-beitraege. Accessed 18 December 2016.
18. Flughafen Köln/Bonn (2015). http://www.koeln-bonn-airport.de/parken-anreise/parken.html. Accessed 18 December 2016.
19. Cinedom Kinobetriebe (2015). http://cinedom.de/kino/tree/node1006/city78. Accessed 18 December 2016.
20. Wald & Schlosshotel Friedrichsruhe (2015). http://schlosshotel-friedrichsruhe.de/. Accessed 18 December 2016.
21. Wienand, K. (2015). BILD lüftet das Geheimnis der Achterbahn-Preise. BILDplus. http://www.bild.de/bild-plus/geld/wirtschaft/online-shopping/wann-man-billig-einkaufen-kann-40108716.bild.html. Accessed 18 March 2015.
22. Iona Hotels (Deutschland) (2015). http://www.lemeridienparkhotelfrankfurt.com/de/. Accessed 18 March 2015.
23. Accor (2015). http://www.mercure.com/de/hotel-1204-mercure-hotel-residenz-frankfurt-messe/room.shtml. Accessed 18 March 2015.
24. Maritim (2015). http://www.maritim.de/de/hotels/deutschland/hotel-frankfurt/uebersicht#hotel_content. Accessed 18 March 2015.
25. Marriott International (2015). http://www.marriott.de/hotels/travel/fradt-frankfurt-marriott-hotel/. Accessed 18 March 2015.
26. LE-BE Hotel (2015). http://www.sheratonfrankfurtairport.com/de/club-lounge. Accessed 18 March 2015.
27. Steigenberger Hotels (2015). http://de.steigenberger.com/Frankfurt/Steigenberger-Frankfurter-Hof. Accessed 18 March 2015.
28. Hecking, M. (2014). Wenn der Algorithmus die Macht übernimmt. Manager magazin. http://www.manager-magazin.de/unternehmen/handel/uber-mytaxi-co-wenn-der-computer-den-preis-macht-a-946122.html. Accessed 13 June 2015.
29. Cramton, P., Geddes, R. R., & Ockenfels, A. (2018). *Markets for Road Use – Eliminating Congestion through Scheduling, Routing, and Real-Time Road Pricing.* Working Paper. Cologne: University of Cologne.
30. Apple (2016). https://support.apple.com/en-us/HT204939. Accessed 19 December 2016.
31. Spotify (2016). https://www.spotify.com/us/family/. Accessed 19 December 2016.

32. Wilger, G. (2004). *Mehrpersonen-Preisdifferenzierung: Ansätze zur optimalen Preisgestaltung für Gruppen*. Wiesbaden: Deutscher Universitätsverlag.
33. Hertz Autovermietung (2015). www.hertz.de. Accessed 18 December 2016.
34. American Marketing Association (2017). Membership Pricing. https://www.ama.org/member ship/Pages/Dues.aspx. Accessed 27 March 2018.
35. DB Rent (2015). https://www.flinkster.de/index.php?id=416&. Accessed 18 March 2015.
36. The Economist (2016). https://subscription.economist.com. Accessed 19 December 2016.
37. Berke, J., Bergermann, M., Klesse, H.-J., Kiani-Kress, R., Kroker, M., & Seiwert, M. (2007). Die Welt ist flat. *Wirtschaftswoche*, 52, 88–94.
38. Fritz, M., Schlereth, C., & Figge, S. (2011). Empirical Evaluation of Fair Use Flat Rate Strategies for Mobile Internet. *Business & Information Systems Engineering*, 3(5), 269–277.
39. Simon, H. (1985). *Goodwill und Marketingstrategie*. Wiesbaden: Gabler.
40. Niehans, J. (1956). Preistheoretischer Leitfaden für Verkehrswissenschaftler. *Schweizerisches Archiv für Verkehrswissenschaft und Verkehrspolitik*, 11(4), 293–320.
41. Krelle, W. (1976). *Preistheorie* (ed. 2). Tübingen: J.C.B. Mohr.
42. Selten, R. (1970). *Preispolitik der Mehrproduktunternehmung in der statischen Theorie. Ökonometrie und Unternehmensforschung*. Berlin: Springer.
43. Simon, H. (2012). How Price Consulting is Coming of Age. In G. E. Smith (Hrsg.), *Advances in Business Marketing and Purchasing. Visionary Pricing. Reflections and Advances in Honor of Dan Nimer* (pp. 61–79). Emerald: Bingley.
44. Wübker, G. (1998). *Preisbündelung: Formen, Theorie, Messung und Umsetzung*. Wiesbaden: Gabler.
45. Coase, R. H. (1960). The Problem of Social Cost. *The Journal of Law & Economics*, 3(1), 1–44.
46. Demsetz, H. (1968). The Cost of Transacting. *The Quarterly Journal of Economics*, 82(1), 33–53.
47. Burstein, M. L. (1960). The Economics of Tie-In Sales. *The Review of Economics and Statistics*, 42(1), 68–73.
48. Adams, W. J., & Yellen, J. L. (1976). Commodity Bundling and the Burden of Monopoly. *The Quarterly Journal of Economics*, 90(3), 475–498.
49. Oren, S., Smith, S., & Wilson, R. (1984). Pricing a Product Line. *The Journal of Business*, 57 (1), 73–100.
50. Schmalensee, R. (1984). Gaussian Demand and Commodity Bundling. *The Journal of Business*, 57(1), 211–230.
51. Prasad, A., Venkatesh, R., & Mahajan, V. (2015). Product Bundling or Reserved Product Pricing? Price Discrimination with Myopic and Strategic Consumers. *International Journal of Research in Marketing*, 32(1), 1–8.
52. Bayerische Motoren Werke (BMW) (2015). http://www.bmw.de/de/neufahrzeuge/7er/limou sine/2012/start.html. Accessed 05 November 2015.
53. Garraham, M., & Bradshaw, T. (2015, April 04). Jay Z Relaunches Tidal as a Friend of Artists. *Financial Times*, p. 10.
54. Gropp, M. (2015, April 01). Eine musikalische Unabhängigkeitserklärung: Popstars wie Madonna, Rihanna und Jay-Z fordern digitale Musikdienste mit einem eigenen Angebot heraus. *Frankfurter Allgemeine Zeitung*, p. 15.

Decision: Long-Term Price Optimization

7

Abstract

Any company's goal should be long-term—and not short-term—profit maximization. This goal is synonymous with the maximization of shareholder value. Up until now, we have not examined relationships across time periods. For long-term price optimization, it is necessary to take into account that the determinants of the optimal price can be dynamic—the goals, the price-response function, and the cost function. Competitive conditions also typically change over the life cycle of a product or market. In this chapter, we focus on how the effects of price changes, carryover effects, and the experience curve influence the optimal development of price. For the introductory phase of a product, we will examine two standard strategies—skimming and penetration strategy. We will then use several cases to demonstrate the differences between short-term and long-term optimal prices. The chapter will conclude with a qualitative perspective on price management and relationship marketing.

7.1 Determinants of Long-Term Optimal Prices

In Chap. 5 we looked at *one-dimensional* prices. Price optimization was centered on one product, one price, and one period. In Chap. 6 we expanded this view to include *multidimensional* price decisions, i.e., multiple prices for one product or multiple prices for multiple products. In both chapters, we assumed that the analyses cover only one time period, the so-called static analysis. When we spoke of time-based differentiation, we did not include relationships between periods. In other words, we opted for a *comparative-static* view. In this chapter, we will explicitly consider several periods, implying that the current price influences future sales volumes and profits. Such effects must be taken into account when a firm sets its current price. We will restrict ourselves, however, to one product [1]. The goal of the *multi-period* perspective is to set optimal prices over the longer term.

© Springer Nature Switzerland AG 2019
H. Simon, M. Fassnacht, *Price Management*,
https://doi.org/10.1007/978-3-319-99456-7_7

7.1.1 Long-Term Objective Function

The dynamic perspective affects all determinants of a price decision:

- The objective function (i.e., what we are trying to maximize)
- The price-response function
- The cost function

In reality, companies in most cases do not maximize short-term profit for one period but instead strive to secure and maximize profit over the longer term. That is what shareholder value is about, as described in Chap. 2. Incorporating multiple periods into planning means that cash flows occur at different points in time. These time differences are eliminated in the *long-term objective function* by discounting back to the time of the decision $t = 0$. The objective function for long-term profit maximization is the following:

$$\pi_L = \sum_{t=1}^{T} (p_t q_t - C_t)(1 + i)^{-t} \tag{7.1}$$

where π_L is the sum of discounted profits (the index L stands for long term), p_t is the price in the respective period $t = (1, \ldots, T)$, q_t is the sales volume in period t, C_t are the costs in period t, and i is the interest rate by which we discount.

If effects exist across periods, all prices p_t, $t = (1, \ldots, T)$ must be incorporated concurrently into the decision in order to maximize long-term profit. The main challenge with *long-term price optimization* lies in the consideration of higher short-term vs. higher long-term profits. A higher interest rate i leads to a steeper discounting of later cash flows, which means they contribute less to overall long-term profit. The higher the discount rate is, the greater the similarity will be between the long-term optimal price and its static counterpart. In practice, however, a company only sets and implements a binding price for period 1. Thus, a company generally settles for optimizing the price for period 1 and takes the future effects in quantitative form or at minimum in qualitative form into account.

7.1.2 Long-Term Price-Response Function

The long-term perspective leads to an expansion of the *price-response function*:

- The market and competitive conditions of a product change over time and often follow a pattern which is referred to as the product life cycle.
- The current price affects future sales volumes and future prices.

These conditions are fundamental determinants for long-term price optimization.

7.1.2.1 Product Life Cycle

The *life cycle* of a product or a brand is represented by a time series of sales. The life cycle concept is the most popular approach to describe and explain how sales develop over time. One commonly divides the product life cycle into the four phases: introduction, growth, maturity, and decline. A unified theoretical foundation for the concept does not exist. The typical S-shape of a life cycle curve is usually explained by results from diffusion research. One refers in particular to a hypothesis from Rogers [2], according to which the distribution of time intervals which elapse between the launch of a product and its adoption by individual consumers approximates a normal distribution. Those who adopt a new product quickly and those who take a very long time to adopt the new product are in the minority relative to the share of the general population which adopts the product in a medium amount of time.

The easy-to-understand life cycle concept has had a strong influence on marketing thinking. One should, however, avoid general assumptions about the shape of the life cycle curve. The life cycle of a product does not evolve according to some general law but rather from a constellation of *causal factors* which are specific to each product. These factors include the degree of innovation, how much learning the customers and distributors need to familiarize themselves with the product, and the competitive dynamics. Prices can have a strong influence on the rate of diffusion.

The life cycle concept is less useful for the later phases. The assumption that all products follow a natural life cycle which will automatically end with their decline is both misleading and dangerous. There are many products, and especially brands, which continue to enjoy uninterrupted demand and popularity despite their very advanced age. American brands like Ford and Coca-Cola as well as German brands such as Aspirin, Nivea, and Mercedes-Benz are all more than 100 years old, and none of them shows signs of age. Of course, the products and designs behind these brands have been adjusted to reflect new technologies and prevailing tastes. However, one cannot assume an automatic decline of a product or brand simply because it has been on the market for a certain amount of time. One must analyze and understand on a case-by-case basis the potential causal factors which may lead to such a decline.

Dynamics of Price Elasticity

In the context of price management, one of the most interesting questions is how *price elasticity* evolves over the course of the life cycle. One finds the first explicit comments on this topic in the work of Mickwitz [3], who postulated that the (absolute) price elasticity is low at the beginning, rises over the first three phases (introduction, growth, and maturity), and then drops again during the decline phase. Many other authors have adopted this hypothesis. Diffusion research appears to confirm this—the so-called early adopters, who are the first buyers and users of a new product, tend to have higher incomes and are less price sensitive than subsequent adopters [4, 5]. Simon [6], however, found the opposite pattern using empirical measurements. The (absolute) price elasticity was relatively high in the introductory phase, fell during the growth and maturity phases, and then rose once again in the decline phase. Friedel [7] confirmed these findings.

It is not possible to make generally valid statements on the development of price elasticity over the life cycle.[1] However, distinguishing between *true innovations* and *me-too products* seems to make sense. With some claim to general validity, we can state the following: the price elasticity may be relatively low at the beginning of the life cycle for true innovations and then will rise over time, especially as the number of competitors and the competitive intensity rise and the degree of product standardization increases. Me-too products face competition from the outset, so the price elasticity is therefore relatively high in the introduction phase. The elasticity then decreases over the course of the growth phase as customer awareness and trust increase. It reaches its minimum during the maturity phase and then rises again in the decline phase.

7.1.2.2 Competitive Dynamics

The changes in the competitive situation which occur over the course of the life cycle are very important for long-term oriented price management. Some authors ascribe *typical competitive situations* to the life cycle phases. According to these, the number of competitors and the competitive intensity rise in the first life cycle phases, reach their maximum in the maturity phase, and then decrease again in the decline phase. This development can be accompanied by a sharp increase or a decrease in the competitive intensity. As a result, the importance of price as a competitive instrument varies in these phases.

From a price management perspective, it makes more sense to look at the ratio between demand and capacity than solely at the number of competitors. It is likely that price will be used more aggressively when *overcapacity* builds up over the life cycle. In theory, overcapacity can occur in any phase of the life cycle. However, it is most typical at the entry into the maturity phase, especially when companies have overestimated growth. It is also common at the entry into the decline phase, when companies have not anticipated the decline. The probability of the aggressive use of price and price wars rises significantly in these phases. However, sometimes price wars break out even in the introduction phase because the objectives are to acquire market share and establish a position of market leadership. An example is scheduled long-distance buses, which were first permitted in Germany in 2013. This sector experienced a price war from the very start, causing most players to exit the market within the first 2 years.

7.1.2.3 Price Effects Across Periods

The current price p_t can have effects which extend beyond the current time period. These effects come in many forms and have different causes. First, the price in period t serves as an anchor for future prices. As we know from price psychology, such anchor effects can be significant. In this sense, there are only two types of price

---

[1]See Background Information at the end of this chapter.

decisions: the decision on the *introductory price* of a new product and the decision on whether to maintain or change the *existing price*. Only once, namely, at the launch of a new product, does a company have an opportunity to set a price with a clean slate. Every price after that reflects a decision to change or maintain the prevailing price.

In the static analysis, there is no independent effect due to a price change. The price effect and the price elasticity depend solely on the absolute price in the period under consideration. This assumption is not realistic in many cases. A price of $10 is likely to have a different effect depending on whether the product had a price of $15, $10, or $5 in the preceding period. The first case represents a price decrease of 33%, the second case represents a steady price, and in the third case, the customer is confronted with a price increase of 100%.

These scenarios give rise to the following questions:

- What kind of effects does a price change have?
  - Symmetrical or asymmetrical, i.e., do price cuts have the same effect as price increases, or different ones?
  - Proportional or disproportional?
- How does the return to equilibrium take place after a price change?
  - Immediately or gradually?
  - Relative to the new equilibrium, is there a short-term overreaction or underreaction in terms of sales volume?

In many cases, we have observed asymmetrical price effects. Nonetheless, one cannot generalize whether price decreases or price increases have a more pronounced effect [7]. That depends on competitive reaction, among other things. *Prospect theory* (see Chap. 4) assumes such an asymmetry, because people perceive a greater effect from a loss than from a gain of equal magnitude. This would mean that if the perceived loss from a price increase were equal to the perceived gain from a price decrease, the price elasticity of the price increase would be greater than that of the decrease [8].

Regarding proportionality of the effects of price changes, one can generally assume that minimal price changes have underproportional effects and large price changes have disproportionately large effects. This assumption is in line with the *Gutenberg Hypothesis* (see Chap. 3). Expert surveys confirm this form in most cases.

Another kind of price-change effect is referred to as *expectation or speculation effects*. These effects arise when customers develop certain expectations of future prices based on previous price changes. These can lead to seemingly paradoxical consumer reactions. A price decrease, for example, may result in lower demand. This happens when customers anticipate further price decreases and therefore postpone their purchases. The opposite effect occurs with price increases, which may lead to higher demand if customers fear that further price increases are coming. As a result, they actually buy more of the product in the short term, despite the current higher price. A price increase for heating oil is often seen as a harbinger of additional increases. To protect themselves against those anticipated additional increases,

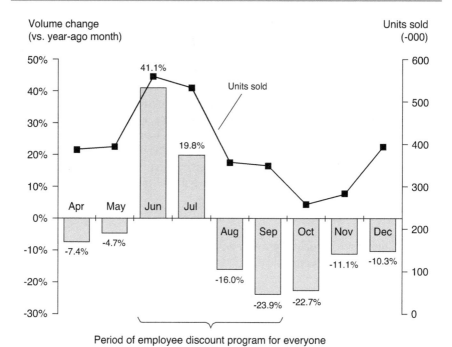

Fig. 7.1 GM employee discount promotion—pull-forward effect

customers stock up on oil even though its price has just gone up. The opposite effect is typical for electronics. Price decreases lend support to the expectation that prices will fall even more. Customers wait instead of buying.

If instead the customers have the expectation that the price increases or price cuts are only temporary, the opposite purchase behaviors occur. Price increases will damp demand, because one expects lower prices to follow. After price cuts, demand is pulled forward, in order to seize the opportunity to buy at lower prices. The latter effect is especially true for discounted special offers, or what are commonly referred to as "limited time offers." The temporary price reduction often does not lead to an increase in overall sales. Rather, customers buy more during the period of the limited time offer and then buy less in subsequent periods. For consumer goods, this is sometimes referred to as "pantry filling." For durable goods, it means that customers pull their purchases forward.

A case study of General Motors (GM) illustrates this pull-forward effect. Because business was very poor in the spring of 2005, GM decided to give the entire market access to the discount rates it normally only offered to its employees. This action began on June 1, 2005, and ran until the end of September. Figure 7.1 shows the results.

The unusual action took off like a rocket. Sales volume rose by 41.1% year-on-year in June and then increased by 19.8% year-on-year in July. However, the euphoria quickly subsided. It turned out that the additional purchases in the summer months were "borrowed" from the future. Even though the action ran through September, sales started to show a massive decline in August. The growth rates for GM were negative for the remainder of 2005. The solid curve shows how dramatically sales volumes declined from August onward. After selling almost 600,000 vehicles in June, GM sold fewer than 300,000 vehicles in October. GM had given an average discount of $3623 per vehicle and posted a loss of $10.5 billion. Its market capitalization sank from $20.9 billion in August to $12.5 billion in December.

The question of how sales volume adjusts after a price change also warrants attention. In order to discuss this, we assume that sales volume has an *equilibrium level* for the old price as well as for the new price. In Fig. 7.2, we show three adjustment forms each for price increases and price decreases. In Case A, the adjustment is immediate. Demand responds right away to the price change. Short- and long-term price elasticities are identical. In Case B, sales volume approaches its new equilibrium gradually. This is called a *partial-adjustment model*. The short-term price elasticity is lower than the long-term one. Case C in contrast shows a price change response which is very strong in the short term but ebbs over time. The short-term price elasticity is higher (in absolute terms) than the long-term one. In an empirical analysis of scanner data for consumer goods, Kucher [9] confirmed that the adjustment form shown in Case C is predominant.

Under dynamic conditions, sales volume is not only influenced by the current price level but also by the price of the previous period. Price cuts can stimulate sales volume. The effect can be proportional or underproportional, as well as symmetric or asymmetric. When expectation effects are present, price changes will be interpreted as indicators for additional price changes in a certain direction. Demand then responds in line with the respective expectation.

7.1.2.4 Carryover Effects

We describe *carryover* as the effect which sales volume in period t has on sales volume in subsequent periods. Such effects can have many causes, the most important one being *repurchase behavior*. If a customer is satisfied with a product purchased once, there is a high probability that he or she will buy that product again. The customers' spreading the word about the experience (word of mouth) or their social interaction can also mean that current sales volume has an effect on future volume. Common to all of these causes is that they are not directly related to the price but rather to the features of the product, the individual decision processes, and social interactions. These relationships can be very important for long-term oriented price optimization, because the price in period t continues to affect sales in future periods through the carryover effect.

The simplest form of a carryover effect, within the context of a linear price-response function, is modeled as follows:

$$q_t = a + \lambda q_{t-1} - bp_t. \tag{7.2}$$

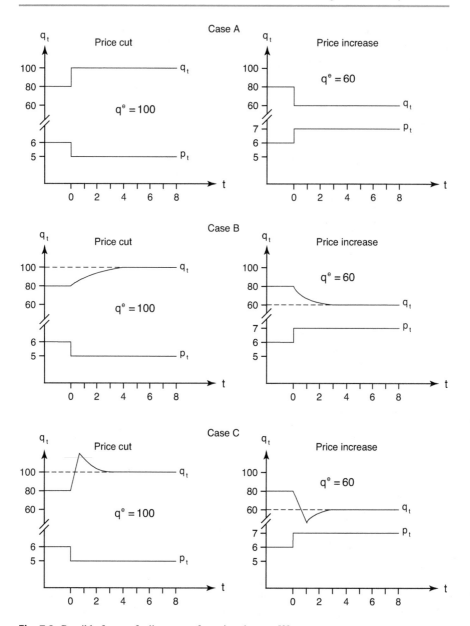

Fig. 7.2 Possible forms of adjustment after price changes [9]

We refer to the parameter λ as the *carryover coefficient*.[2] The parameter λ has been empirically estimated in numerous studies and almost always makes a

---

[2]The literature contains many similar descriptions such as "brand loyalty parameter," "new buyer holdover," or "repeat purchase parameter."

Table 7.1 Empirically measured carryover coefficients for consumer goods

Product category	Econometrically estimated		Calculated from panel data	
	n	λ	n	λ
Cosmetics	9	0.6344	–	–
Pharmaceuticals	25	0.6272	–	–
Beverages	22	0.6080	–	–
Cigarettes	46	0.5680	–	–
Gasoline	14	0.5630	–	–
Coffee	16	0.5044	12	0.5294
Orange juice	7	0.4940	12	0.3839
Margarine	25	0.4603	12	0.5139
Laundry detergent	29	0.3832	12	0.4195
Flour (branded)	–	–	9	0.4885
Paper towels	–	–	6	0.4811
Ketchup	–	–	8	0.3948
Toothpaste	–	–	12	0.3749
Shampoo	–	–	12	0.3084

significant contribution to explaining how sales volumes developed. One should be careful, however, when drawing conclusions about the causality relevant for long-term price optimization. λ can also capture underlying market trends which are not based on a causal relationship between the sales volumes q_t and q_{t-1}.[3]

Function (7.2) can apply to consumer goods and to durable goods. However, one must observe the time differentials between the purchase and the repurchase. The carryover coefficient is especially high for consumer goods which are bought habitually or to which the consumer has a strong emotional attachment. Such products include cigarettes, pharmaceuticals, or cosmetics. Table 7.1 shows a sample of empirically measured carryover coefficients, where n indicates the number of products investigated.

Because of customer loyalty, one also expects a high carryover coefficient for services such as telecommunications, utilities, health care, and tax advisory services. For durable goods such as cars or household appliances, there are large time intervals between replacement purchases. However, the relationship expressed in the formula still applies. Over 90% of first-time buyers of the brand Miele, a market leader in premium washing machines, purchase another Miele product as a replacement. Table 7.2 shows selected carryover coefficients for compact cars.

The magnitude of the carryover effect is closely related to the concept of *customer value* or *customer lifetime value*, which we explore in detail later. Carryover effects can play an important role for consumer goods and durable goods. They result from repeat purchases and brand loyalty. The magnitude of the carryover coefficient

---

[3]See Background Information at the end of the chapter.

Table 7.2 Carryover
coefficients for
compact cars

Brand	Carryover λ
VW Golf	0.615
Opel Kadett	0.460
Fiat 128	0.503
Ford Escort	0.656
Peugeot 204	0.357

serves as a measure of this effect. Empirical values for this coefficient are typically in the range between 0.3 and 0.6 and vary by product group and brand. Carryover effects have an influence on the long-term optimal price.

7.1.3   Long-Term Cost Function

In the long term, one cannot assume constant unit and marginal costs. Two factors lead to changes in costs over the course of the life cycle. First, a company can use more efficient processes as sales volumes (and production volumes) increase and thus achieve *economies of scale*. However, these are essentially a static phenomenon. The fundamental difference between static economies of scale and dynamic cost relationships is that the former arise solely from bringing more capacity on line and happen without delay due to the time necessary to build and ramp up the additional capacity. The latter, in contrast, result from a time-consuming learning process. The production and marketing activities themselves represent learning processes which lead to the accumulation of know-how and experience. A customary measure for this experience is the total amount produced of the respective product, or the *cumulative volume*.

Experience Curve

The relationship between the *cumulative volume* and the *unit costs* is called the experience curve. It is assumed that unit costs decline exponentially with the cumulative volume. In management, the *experience curve* is widely used to support strategic planning. It has also been the subject of a long tradition of scientific studies. The first systematic investigation dates back to 1936 when Wright [10, pp. 122–128] analyzed the relationship between the number of hours required to manufacture an aircraft and the cumulative number of aircraft produced. Numerous studies during World War II likewise observed this relationship. The work from Henderson [11–13] helped the concept to achieve its breakthrough to the management level and into strategic planning. The experience curve played a standout role in the electronics industry. Companies such as Texas Instruments, National Semiconductor, and Intel based their strategies on this relationship with unwavering consistency. Figure 7.3 shows a contemporary example. It shows the costs associated with DNA sequencing tracked and analyzed by the National Human Genome Research Institute (NHGRI) from 2001 until 2015. This information serves as an important benchmark for assessing improvements in DNA sequencing technologies and for establishing the

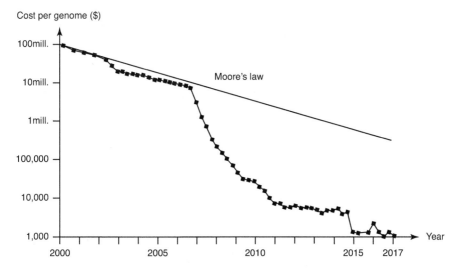

Fig. 7.3 Experience curve of cost per genome in DNA sequencing [14]

DNA sequencing capacity of the NHGRI Genome Sequencing Program (GSP). One observes a rapid cost decline from 2008 onward, due to the improvements in DNA sequencing technologies and data production pipelines [14].

Nowadays, the experience curve is perceived with a certain skepticism. Some firms went to extremes in using the concept to develop their pricing strategies and then ran into difficulties when they overestimated the extent of the competitive advantage the experience curve would enable them to achieve. It appears that experience spreads to competitors faster than formerly believed.

The relationship between the unit costs k_t (adjusted for inflation) and the cumulative production volume Q_t, as postulated by the experience curve, can be formally expressed as:

$$k_t = k_0'(Q_t/Q_0)^\chi, \tag{7.3}$$

where k_0' is the initial unit costs for $Q_t = Q_0$, Q_0 is the initial volume (or the amount manufactured up to $t = 0$, e.g., pilot production), and χ is a parameter, $\chi < 0$.

The parameter χ is the elasticity of unit costs relative to the cumulative volume. It expresses by how many percent unit costs decline when the cumulative volume rises by 1%. The model in (7.3) has a constant elasticity, i.e., the percentage decline in k_t based on a change of cumulative volume Q_t is a constant. The absolute cost degression will, however, become smaller with increasing cumulative volume. Because Q_0 is a constant, we can simplify (7.3) to:

$$k_t = k_0 Q_t^\chi, \quad \text{with } k_0 = k_0'/Q_0^\chi. \tag{7.4}$$

After taking the logarithm, we get a linear function:

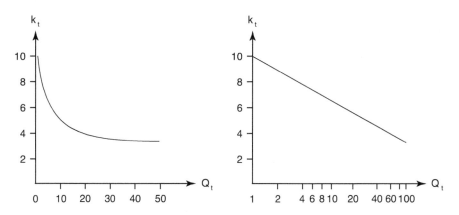

Fig. 7.4 Experience curve in exponential and logarithmic form

$$\ln k_t = \ln k_0 + \chi \ln Q_t. \tag{7.5}$$

Figure 7.4 shows the exponential and logarithmic versions of the experience curve. In the typical version, the experience curve concept is verbally formulated in such a way that the real unit costs drop by a certain percentage rate for every doubling of the cumulative volume. This is referred to as the *learning rate*.[4] In Fig. 7.4 we assume a learning rate of $\alpha = 20\%$ and starting costs k_0 of 10.

Despite the critical views of some observers, the experience curve continues to play a major role in practice. This applies mostly to forecasts of costs and prices. The experience curve has a certain similarity to Moore's Law. This law, which celebrated its 50th anniversary in 2015, says that the costs per transistor drop by half every 18–24 months. Moore's Law has maintained its validity over five decades, and it is expected to remain valid for several more years.

Figures 7.5 and 7.6 illustrate two cases of enormous cost degressions [15]. Figure 7.5 shows the cost per transistor cycle in dollars. The dimension of the vertical axis is logarithmic.

The horizontal axis shows time, in accordance with Moore's Law, rather than cumulative volume. However, the volume grew exponentially as well, similar to the rate at which the costs declined. Figure 7.6 shows several successive product generations for two types of batteries. We see that the cost degression effects kick up with each new generation. One can assume the validity of the experience curve in almost all sectors characterized by a high level of technological progress.

Such experience curves are useful for making long-term price forecasts. Besides the price forecast, there is another important question for long-term price optimization: should a company use price aggressively in order to drive volumes up and, thus, costs down, or should the company wait until costs have fallen and then reduce

---

[4]See Background Information at the end of the chapter.

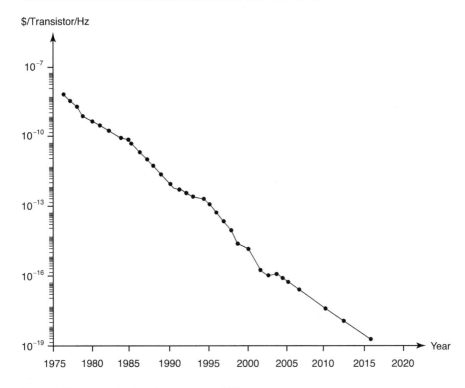

Fig. 7.5 Cost dynamics for microprocessors [15]

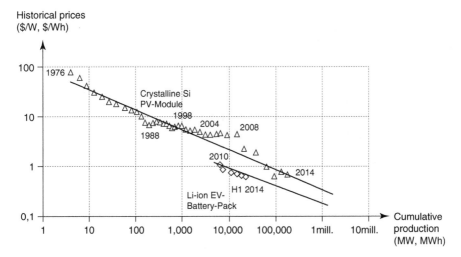

Fig. 7.6 Cost dynamics for batteries [16]

prices? The original viewpoint put forth by Henderson [12] called for proactive price cuts in order to achieve the highest possible relative market share. The relative market share, defined as the ratio of one's own market share to that of the strongest competitor, serves as a measure of the *competitive gap* relative to the cumulative volume (experience) and therefore the costs. An aggressive price policy to grow market share comes into question in the early phases of the life cycle. In these phases, the growth rates are high and the cumulative volumes low, so that a doubling of the cumulative volume and its associated cost decreases are achievable in a short amount of time. Even when the price at the outset is near to or less than unit costs, a swift decrease in costs can lead to positive margins over the longer term.

This kind of pricing is very important for online businesses. However, the main reason here is not costs but rather the ability to rapidly establish a dominant market position. Many digital markets tend toward natural monopolies because of network effects, which suggest the importance of seizing market leadership and establishing oneself as a quasi-monopolist.

Overview

In summary, the experience curve represents the most relevant operationalization of dynamic cost effects. According to the concept, the inflation-adjusted unit costs fall by a certain percentage (the "learning rate") every time the cumulative volume doubles. These effects must be taken into account in long-term price optimization and in price forecasting.

7.2   Long-Term Price Optimization

Having looked at the determining factors, we will now examine how these relationships affect long-term optimal prices. Figure 7.7 shows the complex web of interrelationships to consider.

We encounter a much greater complexity than for one-dimensional price decisions. We will only consider the case without competitive reaction; otherwise, the complexity would be even greater. This complexity results from the fact that the current price p_t can have various effects on future sales volumes, revenues, costs, and profits. It is imperative to consider these effects when optimizing p_t. To be precise, one needs to optimize all prices—for the current and future periods—simultaneously. However, as we indicated previously, only the price p_t is binding and implemented immediately. All future prices are tentative and can be corrected later if there are deviations in expected or actual developments. In practice, the *simultaneous optimization* of all future prices plays no role. We restrict ourselves therefore to the long-term optimal price for period t. We are particularly interested in the extent to which that price deviates from the short-term optimal price, which considers only the current period. Under what circumstances is it higher, and under what circumstances is it lower? First we look at *qualitative rules of thumb* for long-term

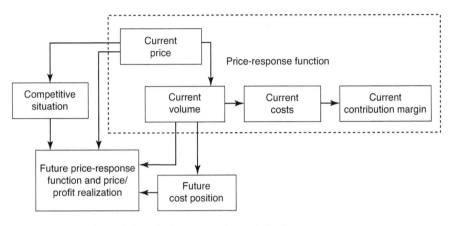

Fig. 7.7 Systems interrelations for long-term price optimization

price optimization. Then we will examine the effects that the determinants of the dynamic price-response and cost functions have on the long-term optimal price.

7.2.1 Rules of Thumb for Long-Term Price Decisions

Various rules of thumb have been suggested for pricing over the product life cycle. They consider the determinants of long-term price optimization only in a qualitative way but nonetheless contain useful, practical recommendations.

7.2.1.1 Price Decisions in the Launch and Growth Phase

For long-term oriented pricing for new products in the launch and growth phases, there are two basic recommendations: *skimming strategy* and *penetration strategy*. They are shown in idealized form in Fig. 7.8.

Skimming Strategy

Under a *skimming strategy*, the price of the new product will be set at a comparatively high level. That price will usually not be maintained over time but lowered in successive steps. What exactly the term "high" launch price means remains open in the qualitative discussion. In the interest of precision and consistency, we will refer to a skimming price as one which is noticeably above the short-term, profit-maximizing price for the launch period.

The launch of the original Apple iPhone offers a clear example of a skimming strategy. Figure 7.9 shows the development of prices for the version with 8 GB of memory.

The launch price of $599 was very high. A mere 3 months later, Apple cut the price massively to $399. What could have been the reasons for the high introductory price? The price of $599 signaled the highest technical competence and quality as well as prestige. Despite the high price, there were long lines of customers waiting

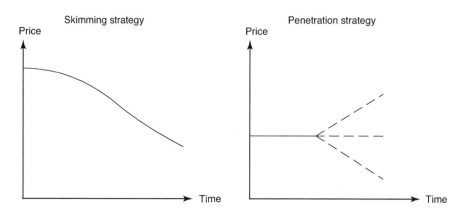

Fig. 7.8 Skimming and penetration strategy

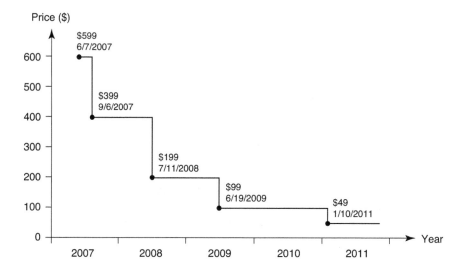

Fig. 7.9 Skimming strategy of the iPhone with 8 GB of memory

outside Apple stores when the iPhone was launched. The massive price cut to $399
led to a strong boost in demand, and we assume that this boost was stronger (after a
$200 price cut) than demand would have been if the original launch price were $399.
In other words, there was a significant price-change effect. In the spirit of prospect
theory, the price cut itself represents an additional utility gain. The flipside, however,
is that the discount touched off outrage and protests among the early adopters who
had paid $599 for the product. Apple responded with a $100 coupon for these initial
buyers.

In the ensuing years, Apple slashed the price further. Apple's clear-cut skimming
strategy, designed to exploit the differences in willingness to pay over time, was not
entirely driven by demand. Costs also fell sharply thanks to technological

advancements and the "explosion" in sales volumes. Apple sold 169 million iPhones in its 2013/2014 fiscal year. This generated revenue of $101.9 billion, which represented around 55% of Apple's total revenue [17]. Dividing revenue by unit sales yields an average price of $603 per iPhone. Interesting, in contrast, are the reported figures on cost. According to IHS Technology, manufacturing costs in 2014 ranged from $200 for the iPhone 6 to $216 for the iPhone 6 Plus [18]. With the ensuing generations of the iPhone, the success continued. In the first 10 years, 1.2 billion iPhones had been sold generating a cumulative revenue of $768 billion and a total profit beyond $100 billion. The market capitalization of Apple was $898 billion in late 2017, making it the most valuable company in the world. The average price of all iPhones sold is $640, about double the price of all other smartphones. With this outstanding price position the iPhone has been grabbing roughly 80% of total profits in the global smartphone market [19]. The price strategy made a fundamental contribution to this success.

Penetration Strategy

The *penetration strategy* calls for a conspicuously low price when the product is introduced. The penetration price should be noticeably below the short-term profit-maximizing price for the launch period. There is no general rule, however, for what should happen to the price over time after the launch.

Toyota followed a classic penetration strategy when it launched its new premium brand Lexus in the United States. Lexus was a new, unknown brand name, and the associated advertisements made no connection between Lexus and Toyota. Nonetheless, it was widely known that Lexus was made by Toyota, which sold over one million cars annually in the United States. Toyota achieved top sales from its Corolla and Camry models, which enjoyed outstanding reputations for reliability and high residual values. That was hardly a basis, however, to believe in Toyota's ability to introduce a model with a premium price position. Lexus entered the market with a price of $35,000 and sold 16,000 vehicles in the first year.

The price then rose by a total of 48% over the next 6 years. In the second year, sales volume jumped to 63,000 units. The early buyers of the Lexus LS400 spread positive word of mouth for the product. *Consumer Reports* described the LS400 enthusiastically in its annual issue: "[The LS400] combines advanced technology with almost every conceivable form of comfort, safety, and accessories, which make this the most highly-rated car we have ever tested." The LS400 became the standard for a favorable price-value ratio in its segment and consistently appeared at the top of customer satisfaction rankings. The original uncertainty about whether Toyota could build a true premium car had vanished. Toyota continually raised the prices for the Lexus models. The low introductory price helped facilitate the Lexus's market entry and helped attract attention and start building an enviable reputation. This is a classic example of a penetration strategy. The price of $35,000 at launch was certainly too low to maximize Toyota's short-term profits, but it created the foundation for the brand's long-term success. In contrast to its success in the United States, the Lexus never established itself in Germany. One reason for that could be the fact that premium and luxury car prices in Germany serve more strongly as indicators of

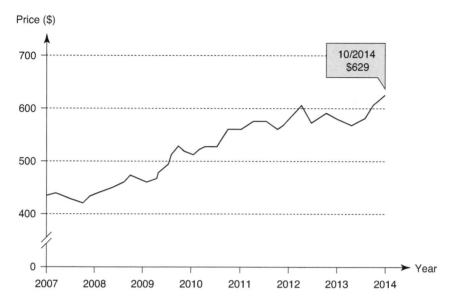

Fig. 7.10   Penetration strategy at Intel [20]

quality and status than they do in the United States. Under such circumstances, a penetration strategy will not work.

The chip manufacturer Intel offers another example of a successful penetration strategy. Intel introduced the x86 chip for server systems in 2007 at $429 per chip. The low price helped Intel achieve market leadership in this segment. Through 2014 Intel had raised the price of the x86 chip in several steps to $629. The ability to implement such price increases is a testament to considerable pricing power. In other markets, however, even Intel's prices have fallen. Chips for notebooks, for example, declined massively by 33%. Figure 7.10 shows Intel's penetration strategy in the US market for server chips.

Both strategic options touch a wide range of other aspects which are listed in Table 7.3.

The arguments for either strategy are self-explanatory and require no further elaboration. Because the two strategies are diametrically opposed, an argument in favor of one is an argument against the other. In essence, the decision boils down to how the company views the strategic alternatives in light of the classic problem: weighing short-term relatively certain profits against long-term relatively uncertain profit opportunities. The skimming strategy yields higher profits early on. The penetration strategy is expected to bring in higher profits over the long term. The preference for one strategy over the other also depends on the financial strength of the company. A company which needs liquidity in the short term will opt for a skimming strategy because that strategy places more emphasis on short-term profits and cash flows. It is advisable when either no long-term effects exist or long-term returns cannot be estimated at the moment, either because they are too uncertain or

Table 7.3 Arguments for skimming and penetration strategy

Skimming strategy	Penetration strategy
• Realize higher short-term profits, which are not affected by discounting • For true innovations: profit realization during the period of monopolistic market position; reduction of long-term competitive risk; and rapid amortization of R&D expenditure • Profit realization in the early stages of the life cycle; reduction of the risk of obsolescence • Creation of leeway to cut prices later and take advantage of potential positive price-change effects • Gradual extraction of willingness to pay (consumer surplus) when possible (time-based price differentiation) • Avoidance of the need for price increases (being on the safe side) • Positive price and quality indication via the high pricew • Avoidance of having to build up high capacity, and thus lower demands on financial resources	• High total contribution margin through rapid sales volume growth, despite low unit contribution margin • Establishment of a long-term and superior market position (higher prices and/or higher sales volumes in the future) due to positive intrapersonal carryover effects (consumer goods) or interpersonal carryover effects (durable goods) • Rapid acquisition of market leadership and the establishment of a monopoly position • Taking advantage of static economies of scale; short-term cost reductions • Rapid increase in cumulative volume, and thus a quick move down the experience curve; establishment of a cost advantage which competitors will have difficulty matching • Reduction of the risk of failure because the low launch price is associated with lower probability of a flop • Ward off potential competitors from entering the market

because the discount rate is very high. The penetration strategy, in contrast, is justified by a more long-term perspective and presumes far-sighted planning. It may require a readiness to accept losses in the short term, greater financial strength, and a higher appetite for risk.

In the e-commerce and software sectors, there are examples of penetration strategies at the company level which have been in place for years. Amazon was founded in 1994, and through 2015, it had shown a profit in only one financial year [21]. But in late 2017, Amazon enjoyed a market capitalization of $571 billion. That market capitalization is double Walmart's market capitalization ($288 billion), even though Walmart's revenue is more than three times greater than Amazon's. The firm Salesforce has seen a similar development since its founding in 1999. The software firm has never recorded a profit for a full year. However, its market capitalization was $77 billion in late 2017. Both firms pursue a pronounced, company-wide, and enduring penetration strategy which has occasionally included pricing below cost. The goal is to build up the largest possible base of customers and revenue in the hope that this base will eventually yield high profits and shareholder value. The stock exchanges have apparently signaled their support for this strategy.

A study of the digital camera market conducted by Spann et al. [22] revealed that most firms pursue neither a conscious skimming nor a penetration strategy. Instead, they orient their launch prices on the price level of competitors. In our experience, this also applies to discount policies. Even innovations are sold at high discounts early in the product life cycle. Under the classification scheme we introduced in Chap. 5, the camera manufacturers are practicing competition-oriented pricing. That indicates relatively slight product differentiation as well as short-term oriented price management in this intensely competitive market.

7.2.1.2 Price Decisions in Later Phases

With the beginning of the maturity phase, and sometimes during the growth phase— the boundary between the phases is fuzzy anyway—additional competitors will enter the market. A second aspect is that upon market maturity, competition turns into a zero-sum game. In other words, growth is only possible at the expense of competition, in that one competitor takes away market share from others. This shift can strongly impact price management.

In anticipation of market entry by competitors, companies have the options shown in Fig. 7.11 available. A *proactive price cut* means that the pioneer cuts prices before the competitor actually enters the market. The proactive price cut represents a compromise between short- and long-term profit maximization. In the short term, the company sacrifices some profit but defends its long-term market position more effectively. This strategy also avoids frustrating existing customers when the company has to cut prices under acute pressure from newly entered competitors. Despite these potential advantages, proactive price cuts tend to be an exception in practice. Few companies reduce their prices as long as there is no competition. Another argument is that the reduced price will deter competitors from entering the market and is called *entry-limit pricing*. However, in reality, this method hardly ever deters competitors if the market is attractive.

For these reasons, pioneers lean toward choosing the second option. This option calls for a price reduction after competitive entry, or what we refer to as a *reactive price cut*. The established competitor cuts the price only after the competitor has entered the market and when market share is actually at risk. The German grocery trade offers an example. When ADLI adds a new branded product to its assortment, either at or slightly below the competitors' price level, LIDL responds with a significant cut in its everyday price. ALDI follows that price cut and in some cases

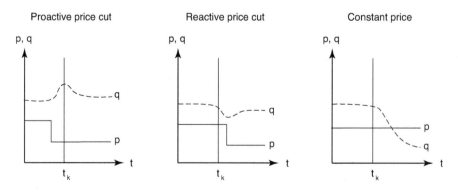

Fig. 7.11 Alternative strategic options for market entry of competition

other discounters enter the fray, until the price settles at a level well below the previous price level. In 2015, ADLI sold the Red Bull 250 mL can for €0.95. The supermarket chains EDEKA and REWE cut their prices to the same level, so that one could buy the 250 mL can at those stores for as low as €0.95 [23].

Gillette, the shaving specialist, took a different approach. When the French company BIC indicated it planned to enter the market for disposable razors, Gillette reduced its prices proactively. Several months prior to BIC's actual market entry, Gillette introduced a new model which was 31% less expensive than the previous product. Gillette thus defended its market position and fended off the attack from BIC. Apparently, the company had learned its lesson after previous attacks from BIC in the markets for ballpoint pens and lighters. In those markets, Gillette had cut its prices only after BIC had already claimed considerable market share. Gillette lost its market leadership in both these markets.

Under the "constant prices" option, the market leader maintains its (high) price even after a competitor enters and consciously accepts some loss in market share. This strategy can be both sensible and profitable if the market-leading company plans to withdraw from the market or introduce a successor product. Older products can still generate a stream of profits for a long time if the company possesses a base of very loyal customers.

The entry of a competitive product in the decline phase presents a new situation which demands increased vigilance regarding pricing. If we limit ourselves solely to the product which is approaching the end of its life cycle, then it is generally optimal to reduce the price if and when the price elasticity increases (in absolute terms). This measure cannot hinder the decline completely but can mitigate it compared to the case when prices stay constant. Pricing measures can do little or nothing, however, to halt or slow the decline of products which are obsolete or otherwise no longer competitive.

The alternative to cutting prices is the *harvesting strategy*, under which the company maintains a high price in the decline phase. This strategy can make sense—the company accepts a decline in sales volume but continues to achieve high margins. Keeping prices high is also indicated if the company is planning to introduce a new product to succeed the old one. One can then avoid having to raise the price of the new product significantly relative to the old product's price. Furthermore, the comparatively high price for the older product can accelerate cannibalization and thus the older product's demise. One does not actively withdraw it from the market, which may risk upsetting existing customers. Instead, they switch on their own volition to the new product because of the older product's high price.

7.2.2   Quantitative Optimization of Long-Term Prices

In this section, we will address the interdependence between the long-term optimal price and its determinants and the differences to the short-term optimal price. We begin by looking at just one determinant, either the dynamic price-response function or the dynamic cost function, in order to see the respective effects in isolation.

7.2.2.1 Long-Term Optimal Price with a Dynamic Price-Response Function

We maximize the long-term profit according to the objective function (7.1). We use the dynamic price-response function $q_t = f(p_t, \ldots, p_{t-T})$. After some reformulations, we get the condition for the long-term optimal price [24]:

$$p_t^* = \frac{\varepsilon_t}{1 + \varepsilon_t} C_t' - \frac{\varepsilon_t}{1 + \varepsilon_t} m_t = \frac{\varepsilon_t}{1 + \varepsilon_t} \left(C_t' - m_t \right) \tag{7.6}$$

where p_t^* is the long-term optimal price, ε_t is the short-term price elasticity, and

$$m_t = \sum_{\tau=1}^{T} \frac{\varepsilon_{t+\tau,t}}{\varepsilon_t} \left(p_{t+\tau} - C_{t+\tau}' \right) \times \frac{q_{t+\tau}}{q_t} (1 + i)^{-\tau} \tag{7.7}$$

and

$$\varepsilon_{t+\tau,t} = \frac{\partial q_{t+\tau}}{\partial p_t} \frac{p_t}{q_{t+\tau}}. \tag{7.8}$$

$\varepsilon_{t+\tau,t}$ is the dynamic price elasticity and captures the effect of price measures taken in period t on the sales volume in period $t + \tau$. In line with the usual notation, q_t denotes the sales volume, p_t the price, C_t' the marginal cost, and i the discount rate.

The condition (7.6) in this form is well suited for an intuitively appealing interpretation. The condition for the long-term optimal price differs from its short-term counterpart, the *Amoroso-Robinson relation* (5.6), by the additional term m_t. This term corresponds to the discounted cash value of future contribution margins which result from a price change in period t. These effects, which take hold in later periods, are attributable to price measures taken in t and therefore act (depending on the sign) like a reduction or an increase in marginal costs in an amount equal to their cash value. A deviation of the long-term optimal price from the short-term optimal price means that the company forgoes short-term profits in exchange for higher long-term profits.

The long-term optimal price is lower than the short-term optimal price when the correction term m_t is positive. This is the case when all the dynamic price elasticities are negative, i.e., a lower price today leads to higher sales volumes in the future. It is obvious that this is true for positive carryover effects. On the other hand, the long-term optimal price is higher than its short-term counterpart when all the dynamic price elasticities are positive. That is synonymous with saying that a lower price at the present time will reduce sales volumes in the future. This occurs when the additional sales in the current period are "borrowed" from future sales (pull-forward effect). The presence of a price-change effect can also lead to a negative m_t and therefore to a higher long-term optimal price.

When the signs of the dynamic price elasticities are uniform, we can draw the following ceteris paribus conclusions: the deviation of the long-term optimal price from the short-term optimal price is more pronounced:

- The larger the ratio $\varepsilon_{t+\tau,1}/\varepsilon_t$ of the dynamic and short-term elasticities is (in absolute terms).
- The greater the future contribution margins are.
- The lower the discount rate i is.
- The longer the planning horizon T is.
- The larger the ratio $q_{t+\tau}/q_t$ is. Because this ratio is larger in the upward, growth part of the life cycle curve than in the later phases (ceteris paribus), the deviation between the prices will be greater at the beginning of the life cycle than in the later phases.

The common denominator in these statements is that the relevant deviation increases the greater the future profit effects from current price measures are. The larger m_t is in absolute terms, the more the marginal costs will be changed through the dynamic correction.

The short-term profit sacrifice associated with the long-term price optimization can be interpreted as a *marketing investment* which yields a long-term profit.

Long-Term Optimal Price with Carryover

If there is a carryover effect according to formula (7.2), we can express the correction term m_t very simply. Here we assume that the future unit contribution margins $p - C'$ are constant:

$$m_t = \left[\frac{1}{1 - \lambda/(1+i)} - 1 \right] (p - C'). \tag{7.9}$$

Let us illustrate this through a numerical example with a carryover coefficient of $\lambda = 0.45$. As we know from Table 7.1, this magnitude is typical for consumer goods. The time period is 2 months, and the discount rate i is 2% (which corresponds to 12.6% per year). The other parameters of the linear dynamic price-response function according to (7.2) are $a = 100$, $b = 10$, $C' = 5$, and $q_0 = 40$.

The optimal prices, sales volumes, and profits for long- and short-term optimization are summarized in Table 7.4. The long-term optimal price in period 1 is 9% lower than the short-term optimal price. For period 2 the opposite is true, although the price difference is smaller. The company follows a penetration strategy with the long-term optimization, so that in period 1 the sales volume is higher, but the profit is lower. In the second period, the stronger starting situation (thanks to the carryover effect) is used to achieve a higher profit. The profit sacrifice in period 1 is $5.78. This

Table 7.4 Results of long-term and short-term optimization

Optimization	t	p_t ($)	q_t	Profit ($)	Capital value ($)
Long-term	1	7.64	41.6	109.82	225.57
	2	8.44	34.3	118.06	
Short-term	1	8.40	34.0	115.60	220.11
	2	8.27	32.6	106.60	

"marketing investment" leads to a total profit of $227.88, which is $5.68 higher than with short-term optimization. This difference will be greater, the stronger the carryover effect is.

Long-Term Optimal Price with Price-Change Effects

Now we look at a symmetrical price-change effect, i.e., a price increase or price decrease of equal magnitude has the same effect on sales volume. This kind of effect leads to the long-term optimal price being lower than the short-term optimal price. Through the higher initial price, a company creates leeway for future price cuts, whose implementation stimulates sales volume due to the price-change effect. At the beginning of the life cycle, price-change effects favor a skimming strategy followed by subsequent price cuts.

Price-change effects which are asymmetrical—which means that price cuts have a stronger effect on sales volume than price increases—give rise to a long-term optimal price strategy referred to as *pulsation*. The optimal price "pulses" between an upper and lower bound. Figure 7.12 shows such a *pulsation strategy*, with the following dynamic price-response function (+ stands for price increase, − for price cut):

$$q_t = a_t - c_1(p_t - p_{t-1})^+ - c_2(p_t - p_{t-1})^-.$$

An empirical example for a consumer durable illustrates this strategy. Because advertising played an important role in this case, we included a logarithmic advertising variable $\ln A_t$ and estimated the following function:

$$q_t = 2866 + 1249.5\ln A_t - 39.57(p_t - p_{t-1})^+ - 40.48(p_t - p_{t-1})^-. \qquad (7.10)$$

All of the parameters were significant at the 5% level. Price increases and price cuts have asymmetrical effects.

With marginal costs of $C' = \$180$ and a discount rate of 0%, the lower optimal price is $233.40, and the upper optimal price is $269.48. The average profit per period using the pulsation strategy is $176.15. The optimal uniform price would be

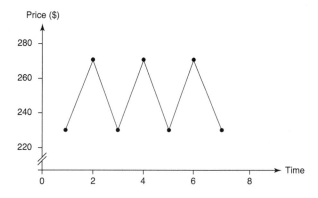

Fig. 7.12 Pulsing price strategy with asymmetrical price change

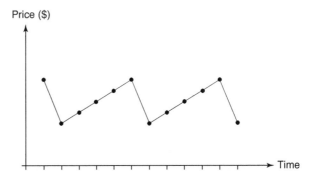

Fig. 7.13 Pulsation effect with overproportional price change strategy

$242.26 and would generate a profit of $153.39. The profit using price pulsation is 14.8% higher. The so-called "Hi-Lo" discount strategy follows such a *pulsation pattern* [25]. High and low prices alternate in a more or less regular rhythm. Asymmetrical price-change effects offer a logical explanation for this pricing scheme.

For *disproportional price-change effects*, as implied by the Gutenberg model, the price-change effect is slight (underproportional) if the price changes are small and significantly more pronounced (overproportional) for larger price changes. This response pattern makes it advantageous to execute repeated, massive price cuts and then raise the price again in small steps. This asymmetrical pulsation is shown graphically in Fig. 7.13.

In reality, one can indeed observe that upward price adjustments take place in several steps. In our consulting practice, we sometimes advise clients to use that tactic. Regarding a price increase for a fast-moving consumer good on the heels of a tax increase, the motto was: "two moderate price increases, in our experience, will have a less negative effect on the market share than a massive price increase in one step" [26].

In a conjoint measurement analysis for an industrial respirator, it turned out that the product offered superior value which would allow the manufacturer to raise prices by 25%. Instead of using that leeway in one large step, the company made three price increases of 7% each, with virtually no loss of sales volume or customers.

One should be careful, however, when making massive price cuts, because of the risk that one may not be able to return prices back to their old levels. Competition laws in some countries forbid the practice of raising prices with the intent of making substantial cuts later as part of a discount or promotion campaign. It can be misleading to attract customers with a large price cut when the higher price (against which the discount is measured) was only available for an unreasonably short time. Because such cases hinge on what the previous price levels were and how long they were in effect, the burden of proof lies with the seller.

Overview
Under price-change effects (i.e., price cuts provide an additional stimulus to sales volume), the long-term optimal price lies above the short-term optimal price. A skimming strategy followed by later price decreases is called for in this scenario. Setting a high initial price creates *price decrease potential* which can be used to drive higher sales volume in later periods. If price-change effects are asymmetrical, meaning that price decreases have a stronger effect than price increases, pulsation pricing is optimal. If price-change effects are disproportional, recommendations are asymmetrical. Price increases should be implemented in smaller steps, while price cuts should be made in larger steps. If expectation effects exist, optimal price paths can be different, depending on the direction of the price expectations.

7.2.2.2 Long-Term Optimal Price with Dynamic Cost Functions

In this section, we assume the existence of a dynamic cost function. This means that costs depend on previous sales volumes (and thus previous prices) and that the current prices have an influence on the current sales volumes and thus the future costs. On the sales side, we assume no dynamic interrelationships.

We plug the dynamic cost function $k_{t+\tau} = k(p_t, \ldots, p_{t+\tau-1})$ into the objective function (7.1) for long-term profit and differentiate with respect to p_t. The unit costs k_t within period t are constant. After several simplifications, we can write the condition for the long-term optimal price as follows [24][5]:

$$p_t^* = \frac{\varepsilon_t}{1 + \varepsilon_t}(k_t - z_t) \qquad (7.11)$$

where

$$z_t = -\sum_{\tau=1}^{T} \frac{\chi_{t+\tau,t}}{\varepsilon_t} \times k_{t+\tau} \times \frac{q_{t+\tau}}{q_t}(1+i)^{-\tau} \quad \text{and} \quad \chi_{t+\tau,t} = \frac{\partial k_{t+\tau}}{\partial p_t} \times \frac{p_t}{k_{t+\tau}}. \qquad (7.12)$$

If the unit cost elasticity $\chi_{t+\tau,t}$ is positive (this is the normal case), the long-term optimal price will be below the short-term optimal price. The discrepancy between the two prices will be larger:

- The larger the unit cost elasticity $\chi_{t+\tau,t}$ is.
- The larger the unit costs $k_{t+\tau}$ are.
- The greater the ratio $q_{t+\tau}/q_t$ is. This ratio can be particularly high at the beginning of the life cycle, so that "investments" in experience pay off especially well in this phase.

---

[5]Derivation: see Background Information at the end of the chapter.

- The lower the discount rate i is.

Our earlier interpretation of the dynamic price optimization as "investment" applies analogously here. The short-term profit sacrifice is worthwhile, because a more favorable cost position can be achieved over the long term, which in turn leads to higher long-term profits.

To sum up, we conclude the following regarding cost dynamics: if a price cut in the current period and the increase in sales volume which results lead to lower unit costs in subsequent periods, then the long-term optimal price is lower than the short-term optimal price. Going below the short-term optimal price means that a short-term profit sacrifice is accepted in favor of higher profit in the long term.

Considering the dynamics can lead to a situation where the long-term optimal price lies below the current unit costs (both total and marginal). Under dynamic conditions, one cannot generally determine a fixed lower bound for price. Carryover and experience curve effects can contribute to a significant reduction in the long-term optimal price. The long-term optimal price is more likely to be below marginal costs:

- The smaller the difference is between the short-term optimal price and the short-term lower price limit, i.e., the marginal cost.
- The higher the carryover coefficient is.
- The greater the learning rate of the experience curve is.

Below-cost prices have empirical relevance above all for new products because the carryover effect and the learning rate tend to be high for new products. If marginal costs are zero or close to zero, which is true for many digital products, the long-term optimal price can even be negative (see Chap. 14).

7.2.2.3 Synopsis on Long-Term Price Optimization

In the previous sections, we showed how dynamic relationships on the demand and on the cost side influence the long-term optimal price. The optimality conditions were formulated in such a way that the long-term optimal price is expressed in comparison to the short-term optimal price. This approach makes it easier to understand the long-term price optimization and allows clear conclusions on the direction of the effects from the dynamics. In practice, a step-by-step approach is recommended to determine the long-term optimal price, under which one first determines the short-term optimal price and then determines the sign and the magnitude of the dynamic deviation from that price. The recommendations based on the respective, isolated dynamic effects are summarized in Table 7.5.

Each of the effects listed above was examined in isolation, and thus the conclusions in Table 7.5 apply only for the respective isolated effects. In reality, these effects can occur simultaneously and either reinforce or offset each other. Thus, if there is a positive carryover effect and a concurrent experience curve effect, the long-term optimal price falls sharply. Those two effects together favor a penetration strategy. At the same time, simultaneous carryover and price-change effects do not allow any clear guidance, because these are offsetting effects.

Table 7.5 Dynamic effects and their impact on the long-term optimal price

Type of dynamic effect	Long-term optimal price (relative to short-term optimal price)
Positive carryover	Lower
Negative carryover	Higher
Partially positive, partially negative carryover	Undetermined
Price-change effect	Higher
Asymmetrical price-change effect with strong volume effect from a price cut	Pulsation
Overproportional price-change effect	Massive price cut in one step, small price increases, and step-by-step
Expectation and speculation effects with expectation of a price cut (and vice versa)	Undetermined
Experience curve	Lower

The possibility of opposing dynamic price and costs effects has an important implication for long-term price optimization. It is not possible to offer general guidance about the level and the development of the long-term optimal price. Which dynamic effects will take hold—as well as how strong they are relative to each other and over what time intervals they unfold—will depend on the product and market situation.

7.3   Long-Term Price Decisions and Relationship Marketing

In the recent past, marketing has focused intensively on the *customer relationship*. Therefore, one also talks about *relationship marketing*. While transaction marketing asks the question "how do I sell a product?", relationship marketing asks "how do I acquire and keep a customer?". Relationship marketing comes to the forefront when customers can be identified and the data on their transactions can be captured and stored. The rise of relationship marketing is in part attributable to both the improvement and the spread of information technology (customer cards, customer relationship management (CRM), internet, etc.). Granted, customers have traditionally been known and their transactions documented in many sectors, such as banking, insurance, book clubs, newspaper and magazine publishing, energy utilities, telecommunications, mail order, and B2B. But the penetration of customer cards, for example, has enabled more and more companies to systematically document and influence customer transactions and customer relationships. These include airlines, passenger railroads, brick-and-mortar retail, hotels, and many other service providers. Internet and e-commerce have made an enormous contribution to a deeper understanding of the relationships between customers and suppliers.

Relationship marketing is not specifically focused on price nor is it limited to price. It covers the entire marketing mix. Nonetheless, it offers many touch points for pricing. Large online sellers such as Amazon vary some of their prices over the course of a day: a television, for example, might cost $100 less in the morning than it does in the afternoon. The underlying dynamics analyze the number of customers and their preferences at given points in time. This approach has now spread to brick-and-mortar retailers, who install electronic price tags on their store shelves and, thus, can change prices more frequently. Individualized prices, which tailor the prices to each customer based on different characteristics, are a hot topic in e-commerce. So far, however, online sellers such as Amazon have focused more on individualized discounts by customer [27].

Relationship marketing involves maximizing the long-term profit generated by a customer. The long-term objective function (7.1) can also be applied to an individual customer or customer group. The so-called *customer value*[6] is the net present value of the contribution margins that a specific customer will provide the company. Effects such as carryover result from customer loyalty. A cost dynamic may also exist because an entrenched customer relationship lowers transaction costs. When a company has had a reliable relationship with a customer over many years, it can dispense with credit checks or accept and honor oral agreements. An example is Amazon's relationship marketing. In order to achieve a closer customer relationship, Amazon introduced the "Fire-TV stick" which makes it possible for customers to watch online videos in HD quality on their television screens, preferably videos offered through the Amazon Prime streaming service. In order to make that offer even more attractive, Amazon offered the stick in Germany for only €7 in combination with an annual subscription, instead of the usual €39 [28].

The topic of customer value is gaining more attention and greater importance in financial reporting. The value of a customer base (one speaks of customer equity, customer lifetime value [29], or customer capital [30, 31]) can make a significant contribution to the overall value of a company. What matters is not the number of customers or their loyalty over time but rather the cash flow per period and per customer, which in turn depends on the price. This dependence has several causes. On the one hand, the price directly influences the average revenue per customer (one sometimes refers to this as ARPU = average revenue per user). On the other hand, the customer loyalty and the duration of the relationship depend on the form of the price and the price incentives. In 2014, the telecommunications company O_2 credited its UK customers with an allotment of free minutes, SMS, and data volume, scaled according to the length of time that customer had been on a particular plan. For example, a customer that had spent more than 3 months on the "3G Pay & Go Go

---

[6]One must distinguish between customer value and value-to-customer, even though they are often used synonymously in practice. Value-to-customer describes the benefit that a business provides to a customer (see Chap. 3).

Go" plan would receive 150 min, 1000 SMS, and 500 MB of data volume instead of the usual 75 min, 500 SMS, and 250 MB in data volume, at the same price of £10. The customer value represents the decisive criterion for the investment in the acquisition of new customers, the retention of existing customers, or the reacquisition of lost customers. The corresponding investments can come in the form of expenditures (promotions, giveaways, etc.) or in the form of discounts.

7.3.1   Long-Term Price Decisions and Customer Acquisition

The price plays a decisive role in new customer acquisition. Many price offers in various industries are directed at the acquisition of new customers:

- Telecommunications and cable companies are making special offers to attract switchers or new customers. Long-term customers often need to threaten to switch in order to receive similar offers [32].
- Computer or software firms provide their devices or their products to schools and other educational institutions either at very low prices or even free of charge in order to get the students accustomed to their systems and acquire them as customers in the future.
- In the pharmaceutical industry, it is customary for doctors to receive free samples of a new medication. The doctors learn about the new medication, and if their experience is positive, they may prescribe it regularly.
- A very widespread tactic is rent-free periods for new tenants. Such offers are attractive for new tenants because they are already burdened with costs for moving and refurbishing. The landlord, meanwhile, avoids needing to reduce the regular (nominal) rent, which may help determine the value of the building if he or she wants to sell it.
- It is common for software-as-a-service (SaaS) to include low introductory prices or free usage for a limited period for new customers. The firm Scopevisio offers a free 30-day test version.
- Some companies such as Amazon (e.g., Amazon Vine) have programs which go even further and pay potential customers to test new products.
- Customers are sometimes paid to become customers. Commerzbank pays each new customer €50. During its introduction phase, PayPal paid new customers $10. The Chinese bike rental service Mobike pays its customers for using its bikes. This practice can be interpreted as a negative price, because the customer not only does not pay anything but actually receives money from the seller [33] (see Chap. 14).

Each of these cases involves a "marketing investment" in form of price reductions. The optimal level of investment depends on the respective customer value. This is ceteris paribus (i.e., for the same expenditure or cost per period) higher for younger customers than for older ones. Volkswagen's tactic to offer a special discount to people who have just earned their driver licenses makes sense under this aspect. In the same manner, it is attractive for health insurers to use low premiums to acquire young customers because they cause much lower costs than older ones and many remain loyal to the insurer for a long time. Under these mechanisms, the long-term optimal price is always lower than the short-term optimal price.

Price communication plays an important role in the acquisition phase. Noncustomers will be less well informed about a supplier's prices than existing customers. New customers do not perceive price differences the same way that old, loyal customers do. Thus it is important for a company to explain the reasons behind price differences, but at the same time, it is advantageous to make the transactions for new and existing customers different. New customers will only buy when they perceive a price advantage. Clever price communication can also trigger the first contact between customer and company. That can include frequent repetition of the price, such as the Dollar Shave Club, which has the price-per-day for a shave in the name of the company. Innovative or even humorous price setting can generate interest. One eyewear chain, for example, offers discounts based on the age of the customer. The London Olympics applied the same approach for children.

7.3.2   Long-Term Price Decisions and Customer Retention

Customer loyalty stands out as a factor of long-term profitability. Studies frequently claim that companies earn above-average profits from loyal long-term customers [34]. It is supposed to be significantly less expensive to keep a customer than to acquire a new one. The price is an important instrument for customer retention. A number of studies point out why customers switch suppliers, and the following cross-industry finding from Simon-Kucher & Partners may be viewed as rather representative: 52% of customer cited service- or behavior-related issues as the primary reason for switching, while 29% cited price and 18% identified poor product quality as their primary reason for switching. Price plays a central role in customer retention, in part because it is easier and faster to change than service, employee behavior, or product quality. However, this does not imply that a company has leeway to lower prices sufficiently to retain potential switchers, nor does it imply that offering such discounts is wise. One should be very careful with such moves in order to avoid a detrimental impact on contribution margin and profit. Generally speaking, it seems that existing customers, especially the so-called "strategic" customers, are often granted excessive discounts. Therefore, we adamantly warn against making premature or unnecessary concessions to existing customers. One can sacrifice some customer satisfaction for the sake of profit. The goal of a business is not to maximize customer satisfaction but to maximize long-term profit. The customer should be satisfied with a company's performance, but a certain level of dissatisfaction with the price is tolerable and often unavoidable [35].

Customer retention or loyalty programs are very popular nowadays. Customer loyalty has a positive connotation, so that almost every company feels obligated to

foster it. Most customer loyalty programs have some kind of special price component. Potential indirect measures within customer loyalty pricing include volume-
based discounts as well as time- and loyalty-dependent prices [36]. A typical
example for *retention-oriented pricing* is frequent flier programs which offer points
which can be redeemed for future travel.

Pricing policies aimed at increasing customer loyalty focus on concessions which
the seller makes depending on the duration or the intensity (in terms of revenue,
purchase frequency, etc.) of the customer relationship. The *loyal repeat customer*,
who buys a lot and buys often, has a better standing in the eyes of the seller than the
ad hoc or *casual customer*.

- The length of a relationship with an auto insurer as well as accident frequency can
  lower or raise a customer's premium. The differences can become quite large
  over time.
- The granting of discounts over time is facilitated when there is a contractual
  relationship between the customer and the company. Under such contracts, sellers
  often receive regular payments from customers, so that the "investment" in a
  discount can be amortized by the revenue stream from the customer. Examples
  include magazine subscriptions, which are generally lower priced the longer the
  commitment is. The magazine *Time* offered a "preferred customer" rate in the
  form of a 2-year subscription at 86% off the newsstand price. If a customer opted
  for immediate payment, the subscription would additionally be extended for
  6 months free of charge [37].
- A regional utility offered a bonus system to its contract customers. The longer the
  customer's contract, the higher the bonus, which would be applied to the annual
  base fee. The bonus was 5% for 1 year, 10% for 2 years, and 15% for 3 years and
  beyond.
- In retail, a common system is to pay out revenue bonuses in the form of coupons
  for future purchases rather than as cash. The office supply chain Staples, the
  sporting goods retailer Dick's, and clothing stores such as Gap use such schemes.
- An all-time classic example is the discount stamp, such as the S&H Green Stamps
  which were popular in the United States for decades. The buyers receive a certain
  number of discount stamps depending on the value of their purchases and then
  paste these stamps in a booklet. Customers can redeem completed books for a
  certain amount, traditionally around 3% of the purchase value. Contemporary
  versions of such programs in the age of smartphone apps include the bonus stars
  from Starbucks. After customers have accumulated a certain number of stars (the
  equivalent of a full book of stamps back in the old days), the customers can
  redeem those stars for any eligible product of their choice. In this case, the
  discount is variable rather than fixed because it depends on which product the
  customer chooses when the stars are redeemed.
- Even more effective, but less common, are systems which call for customers to
  make an upfront payment which entitles them to discounts on subsequent
  purchases within a specified timeframe. One of the most successful and best-
  known examples is the Amazon Prime program, which is similar in structure to

the BahnCard of the German Railway Corporation (see Chap. 4). Amazon Prime customers receive guaranteed delivery within 2 days. The program also includes free e-books, discounts on e-books and videos, and access to video and music streaming content. In the European Union, the price for Amazon Prime is €69 per year, while the price in the United States is $99. The worldwide enrollment in the Prime program is estimated in 2017 at 65 million customers, who generate $65 billion in revenue. Amazon Prime members spend over $1000 a year on Amazon, or 4.6 times more than non-Prime customers. Customers in the United States who purchased Prime tripled their spending with Amazon to $1500 per year. Amazon supposedly earns no money from Prime's membership fees, however, because the costs per Prime customer exceed the fees. Amazon sees the program as an investment in customer loyalty. "If they can make customers more loyal, they can make more profit, even if they have to subsidize Prime," said one former Amazon manager [38]. Such systems create a stronger bonding effect than loyalty bonuses which are "given away" because the customers want to earn back the upfront money they paid. For this reason, these systems have significant potential for other industries.

Companies are limited only by their own imaginations when it comes to price-related customer retention or loyalty systems. One should, however, carefully weigh the costs and the effects of such programs. How strong is the loyalty effect in reality? Can it be measured and verified? And do the systems pay off when one compares the discounts versus the margins which the company sacrifices? An additional problem is that most customer loyalty programs, especially those which are purely discount-based, are easy for competitors to replicate. Many customer loyalty programs offer nothing more than price cuts in the form of discounts. When every competitor can simply duplicate that method, the only thing one has accomplished is the start of a downward price spiral. In the end, there is no net gain in customer loyalty, but prices end up at a lower level. One should therefore proceed carefully when thinking about using price as a means to drive customer loyalty.

7.3.3 Long-Term Price Decisions and Winning Back Customers

The issue of price and *winning back customers* is a difficult one. Our experience and the literature show that *programs to win back customers* can certainly be effective. We have determined in several industries that between 10% and 30% of lost customers can be won back. Price can play a decisive role in this. Often a company makes the lost customer a less expensive offer, but one must once again keep an eye on the effects on profit. The goal is not to win back the customer per se but rather to improve the company's profit situation. If the conditions offered to the customer do not result in a sufficient margin or even cause a negative margin, then the offer does not serve the profit goal. It would make more sense to try win the customer back through better service or quality, so that one can avoid making price concessions which hurt margins. If the conditions offered to win back the customer apply only for a limited time, then the move can in fact fit within a long-term price strategy. In that context, the situation resembles a new customer acquisition, which means a temporary investment made in the hope of acquiring (or, in this case, reacquiring) a profitable customer.

Conclusion

Incorporating multiple time periods makes price decisions much more complex. But in many industries, the effects across periods are so strong that neglecting them can be detrimental to long-term profit. We summarize this chapter in the following points:

- Long-term price optimization touches every determinant of a price decision, namely, the objective function, the price-response relationship, and the costs.
- The goal is not to maximize short-term profit (one period) but rather to maximize profit over several periods. This requires the discounting of cash flows from future periods.
- The dynamic price-response function captures the circumstances of the product life cycle and effects across periods.
- The product life cycle follows no fixed laws but rather indicates that market and competitive conditions—and thus the optimal price level—are subject to change over time.
- One observes patterns of price elasticity and competitive dynamics which have implications for long-term price optimization.
- Price-response relationships across periods can be categorized into carry-over effects, price-change effects, and expectation and speculation effects.
- Cost dynamics, especially in the form of the experience curve, play an important role for long-term price optimization. The experience curve should be interpreted and used with caution.
- Skimming and penetration strategies provide guidance for long-term oriented price decisions. The skimming strategy calls for a product launch at a comparatively high price, followed by price decreases. The penetration strategy begins with a low price, but the subsequent price trajectory follows no general pattern.
- Competitive entry, especially when it occurs in the growth phase or early in the maturity phase, can be met with proactive or reactive price cuts. The proactive price cut is aimed at defending the pioneer's market leadership but includes the risk of a short-term profit sacrifice. The reactive price cut risks that customers get upset when the price is cut in the face of new competitive pressure. Reactive price cuts can trigger a downward price spiral. The third alternative is to maintain the high price, but that requires accepting some decline in market share.

(continued)

- In the maturity phase, the focus should shift to a resolute profit orientation because the lack of market growth leads to a zero-sum game. One should avoid aggressive prices and price wars and strive instead for a more peaceful form of price competition.
- In the decline phase, a company may consider price cuts in order to offset the drop in demand. But often it makes more sense to keep prices high and pursue a harvesting strategy.
- Quantitative analysis allows the determination of the exact conditions under which the long-term optimal price is higher or lower than the short-term optimal price.
- Along those lines, the long-term optimal price is lower than its short-term counterpart when:
  - Positive carryover effects exist.
  - The experience curve applies.
- In contrast, the long-term optimal price is higher when:
  - Negative carryover effects exist.
  - Price-change effects exist.
  - Expectation and speculation effects occur (in some cases).
- Asymmetrical or disproportional price-change effects can favor price pulsation strategies.
- Overproportional price changes indicate that a company should make price cuts in one large step and price increases in several small steps.
- In the context of relationship marketing, one should take long-term price optimization into account. Pricing plays an important role in all three phases of relationship marketing: customer acquisition, customer retention, and winning back customers.
- The influence of price on customer value and therefore on enterprise value is important for financial reporting. Price has an effect on cash flow as well as direct and indirect effects on the number of customers and on customer loyalty and therefore plays a major role in the determination of enterprise value.

Our discussion in this chapter demonstrates that long-term price optimization requires a high degree of understanding as well as very detailed information. Our primary objective was to illustrate the interactions intuitively. We hope that the reader has gained insights which will be helpful for better long-term oriented price management.

7.4   Background Information

1. Looking at the individual components of price elasticity helps to understand how the elasticity might develop over time:

$$\varepsilon_t = \frac{\partial q_t}{\partial p_t} \times \frac{p_t}{q_t}.$$

These are the absolute price effect $\partial q_t/\partial p_t$, the sales volume q_t, and the price p_t.

   If we assume a typical life cycle with an uptrend and a downtrend, the volume q_t will grow up to its maximum level in the maturity phase. Assuming an unchanged price effect and the same price (ceteris paribus) ε_t will decline in the upward trend of the life cycle. The opposite applies to the downward trend. This increase in volume will often be accompanied by a decline in prices. The decline in the elasticity will be intensified in that case. In order to have a price elasticity which gets larger (in absolute terms) in the uptrend of the life cycle, as postulated by Mickwitz [3], the following conditions must be fulfilled:

   - At a constant price, the price effect must increase more sharply than the sales volume. When one recalls realistic magnitudes for the growth of q_t (the sales volume can often increase 10-, 20-, or even 100-fold), the problem with this assumption becomes evident.
   - If the price is declining, the price effect needs to increase even faster than the ratio (p_t/q_t) declines. Such a development is even more unlikely, especially in markets with strong experience curve effects. Within a few years, the prices for calculators, quartz watches, mobile phones, or digital cameras have fallen to a mere a fraction of their initial level.

   One should always keep in mind that the price elasticity is a relative measure. If there is a price cut of 10% in the introductory phase and the sales volume rises from 10 units to 14 units (i.e., 4 additional units), then $\varepsilon_t = -4$. If the sales volume has risen later to 1000 units, then the same price decrease must increase sales by 400 units so that an elasticity $\varepsilon_t = -4$ results. Such a development is unlikely, at least without a significant change in the market structure.

2. In Eq. (7.2), the carryover coefficient is assumed to be constant. However, if one accepts the product life cycle, then the ability of a product to retain existing customers or attract new customers will diminish over time. This is to be expected at least at the onset of the maturity and the decline phases. The carryover coefficient would therefore decline over time. If we assume an exponential decline at a rate of $(1 - r)$, this results in the following modification to (7.2)

$$q_t = a + \lambda r^t q_{t-1} - b p_t.$$

Such a carryover model which varies over time remains simple and usable from a measurement standpoint. This model can capture very different forms of the life cycle [6].

3. The link between the learning rate α and the elasticity χ becomes clear when one inserts $Q_t = 2Q_0$ and $k_t = (1 - \alpha)k_0$ in (7.3).

One gets (for $Q_0 = 1$):

$$(1 - \alpha)k_0 = k_0 2^\chi,$$

which after taking the logarithm and after solving results in:

$$\text{Cost elasticity } \chi = \ln (1 - \alpha)/\ln 2$$

or:

$$\text{Learning rate } \alpha = 1 - 2^\chi.$$

The difference $(1 - \alpha)$ is referred to as the *slope* of the experience curve.

4. Derivation of the long-term optimality condition with a dynamic cost function: If we differentiate the long-term profit function with respect to p_t we get:

$$\frac{\partial \pi_L}{\partial p_t} = q_t + (p_t - k_t)\frac{\partial q_t}{\partial p_t} - \sum_{\tau=1}^{T} \frac{\partial k_{t+\tau}}{\partial p_t} q_{t+\tau}(1 + i)^{-\tau} = 0.$$

Multiplying by p_t/q_t and inserting ε_t for the price elasticity results in:

$$p_t + (p_t - k_t)\varepsilon_t - \sum_{\tau=1}^{T} \frac{\partial k_{t+\tau}}{\partial p_t} \times \frac{p_t q_{t+\tau}}{q_t}(1 + i)^{-\tau} = 0.$$

One expands the addends with $k_{t+\tau}/k_{t+\tau}$ and plugs in

$$\chi_{t+\tau,t} = \frac{\partial k_{t+\tau}}{\partial p_t} \times \frac{p_t}{k_{t+\tau}}$$

as the elasticity of the unit costs in $t + \tau$ with respect to the price in t. Solving for p_t leads to:

$$p_t^* = \frac{\varepsilon_t}{1+\varepsilon_t} k_t + \frac{1}{1+\varepsilon_t} \sum_{\tau=1}^{T} \chi_{t+\tau,t} \times k_{t+\tau} \times \frac{q_{t+\tau}}{q_t} (1+i)^{-\tau}.$$

This can be written as:

$$p_t^* = \frac{\varepsilon_t}{1+\varepsilon_t} (k_t - z_t)$$

where

$$z_t = -\sum_{\tau=1}^{T} \frac{\chi_{t+\tau,t}}{\varepsilon_t} \times k_{t+\tau} \times \frac{q_{t+\tau}}{q_t} (1+i)^{-\tau}.$$

References

1. Simon, H. (1985). *Goodwill und Marketingstrategie*. Wiesbaden: Gabler.
2. Rogers, E. M. (1962). *Diffusion of Innovations*. New York: The Free Press.
3. Mickwitz, G. (1959). *Marketing and Competition*. Helsingfors: Centraltryckeriet.
4. Robertson, T. (1960). The Process of Innovation and the Diffusion of Innovation. *Journal of Marketing*, 31(1), 14–19.
5. Rogers, E. M. (1983). *Diffusion of Innovations*. New York: The Free Press.
6. Simon, H. (1979). Dynamische Erklärungen des Nachfragerverhaltens aus Carryover-Effekt und Responsefunktion. In H. Meffert, H. Steffenhagen, & H. Freter (Eds.), *Konsumentenverhalten und Information* (pp. 415–444). Wiesbaden: Gabler.
7. Friedel, E. (2014). *Price Elasticity: Research on Magnitude and Determinants*. Frankfurt am Main: Peter Lang.
8. Thaler, R. H. (1985). Mental Accounting and Consumer Choice. *Marketing Science*, 3(4), 199–214.
9. Kucher, E. (1985). *Scannerdaten und Preissensitivität bei Konsumgütern*. Wiesbaden: Gabler.
10. Wright, J. (1936). Factors Affecting the Cost of Airplanes. *Journal of Aeronautical Sciences*, 4 (3), 122–128.
11. Henderson, B. (1968). *Perspectives on Experience*. Boston: The Boston Consulting Group.
12. Henderson, B. (1984). *Die Erfahrungskurve in der Unternehmensstrategie*. Frankfurt am Main: Campus.
13. Henderson, B. (1984). The Application and Misapplication of the Experience Curve. *Journal of Business Strategy*, 4(3), 3–9.
14. National Human Genome Research Institute (2016). The Cost of Sequencing a Human Genome. https://genome.gov/sequencingcosts/. Accessed 19 December 2016.
15. Kurzweil, R. (2005). *The Singularity Is Near*. New York: Penguin.
16. Korstenhorst, J. (2015). *The Accelerating Energy Revolution*. Rotterdam: Cleantech Summit.
17. Apple Annual Report 2014 (2015). http://investor.apple.com/secfiling.cfm?filingid=1193125-14-383437. Accessed 14 February 2018.

18. Kirst, V. (2014). Ein iPhone 6 kostet 156 Euro in der Produktion. http://www.welt.de/wirtschaft/webwelt/article132573424/Ein-iPhone-6-kostet-156-Euro-in-der-Produktion.html. Accessed 22 February 2015.

19. Anonymous. (2017). Die Welt des iPhone. *Absatzwirtschaft*, 12/2017, 26–27 and own calculations.

20. Clark, D. (2014, May 14). Intel's Sway Boosts Prices for Server Chips. *The Wall Street Journal*, p. 10.

21. Clark, M., & Young, A. (2013). Amazon: Nearly 20 Years In Business And It Still Doesn't Make Money, But Investors Don't Seem To Care. http://www.ibtimes.com/amazon-nearly-20-years-business-it-still-doesnt-make-money-investors-dont-seem-care-1513368. Accessed 30 November 2015.

22. Spann, M., Fischer, M., & Tellis, G. J. (2015). Skimming or Penetration? Strategic Dynamic Pricing for New Products. *Marketing Science*, 34(2), 235–249.

23. Reichmann, E. (2015). ALDI und LIDL liefern sich erbitterten Preiskampf. http://www.stern.de/wirtschaft/news/preiskampf%2D%2Ddiscounter-aldi-und-lidl-werden-noch-guenstiger-6346226.html. Accessed 3 September 2015.

24. Simon, H. (1992). *Preismanagement: Analyse – Strategie – Umsetzung*. Wiesbaden: Gabler.

25. Fassnacht, M., & El Husseini, S. (2013). EDLP vs. Hi-Lo Pricing Strategies in Retailing – A State of the Art Article. *Journal of Business Economics*, 83(3), 259–289.

26. Anonymous. (1991, June 14). Zigaretten werden in zwei Schritten teurer. *Frankfurter Allgemeine Zeitung*, p. 21.

27. Gassmann, M., & Reimann, E. (2015). Wann Sie im Internet am billigsten einkaufen. http://www.welt.de/wirtschaft/article138271393/Wann-Sie-im-Internet-am-billigsten-einkaufen.html. Accessed 6 June 2015.

28. Anonymous. (2015, March 25). Amazon bindet jetzt auch die Fernsehkunden an sich. *Frankfurter Allgemeine Zeitung*, p. 21.

29. Berger, P., & Nasr, L. (1998). Customer Lifetime Value: Marketing Models and Applications. *Journal of Interactive Marketing*, 12(1), 18–30.

30. Reinartz, W., & Kumar, V. (2000). On the Profitability of Long-Life Customers in a Noncontractual Setting: An Empirical Investigation and Implications for Marketing. *Journal of Marketing*, 64(4), 17–35.

31. Rust, R., Lemon, K., & Zeithaml, V. A. (2004). Return on Marketing: Using Customer Equity to Focus Marketing Strategy. *Journal of Marketing*, 68(1), 109–127.

32. Budras, C. (2015). Kunden, wacht auf!. http://www.faz.net/aktuell/finanzen/meine-finanzen/geld-ausgeben/rabatte-kunden-wacht-auf-13442417.html. Accessed 23 February 2015.

33. Kuhr, D. (2013). Amazons zweifelhafte Sternchen. http://www.sueddeutsche.de/geld/exklusive-kundenbewertungen-amazons-zweifelhafte-sternchen-1.1791159. Accessed 28 February 2015.

34. Wieseke, J., Alavi, S., & Habel, J. (2014). Willing to Pay More, Eager to Pay Less: The Role of Customer Loyalty in Price Negotiations. *Journal of Marketing*, 78(6), 17–37.

35. Simon, H., Bilstein, F., & Luby, F. (2006). *Manage for Profit, not for Market Share*. Boston: Harvard Business School Publishing.

36. Simon, H., & Dahlhoff, D. (1998). Target Pricing und Target Costing mit Conjoint Measurement. *Controlling*, 10(2), 92–96.

37. Anonymous. (2015). Abonenntenangebot. *Time*.

38. Woo, S. (2011). Amazon "Primes" Pump for Loyalty. http://www.wsj.com/articles/SB10001424052970203503204577036102353359784. Accessed 28 February 2015.

Price Management and Institutional Context

8

Abstract

In the previous chapters, we have looked at price decisions without taking the institutional or economic context into account. For example, we have proceeded as if there were no inflation or deflation. The reality is that such phenomena exist, and the question is whether and to what extent they influence the optimal price. Internationalization also poses special challenges to price management. The market environment typically differs from country to country due to trade practices and consumer preferences. Domestic markets can be partially protected by tariffs, trade barriers, and different currencies. This chapter deals with the effects which inflation and deflation, foreign exchange, and internationalization have on price.

8.1 Price and Inflation

We have observed inflationary tendencies in many countries, at least since the gold standard was abandoned in 1971. Central banks generally aim for an annual inflation rate of around 2%. Figure 8.1 shows the development of consumer prices in the United States between 1991 and 2015. In this period, the consumer price index rose from 100 to 157 [1]. That corresponds to an average annual inflation of 1.9%. This results, as the curve shows, in a decline of the value of the dollar of 36.3%. In other words, $100 in 1991 only had the purchasing power of $63.69 in 2015. An annual inflation rate of 1.9% may not seem very high, but since 1991, the cumulative effect of inflation has led to a massive devaluation of the dollar by more than a third.

The trend shown in Fig. 8.1 for the United States is typical for most highly developed nations. One exception is Japan, where prices have increased only minimally since the beginning of the 1990s. It is doubtful that the trend toward lower inflation rates, or even deflation, in Western nations in 2014–2017 will last.

© Springer Nature Switzerland AG 2019
H. Simon, M. Fassnacht, *Price Management*,
https://doi.org/10.1007/978-3-319-99456-7_8

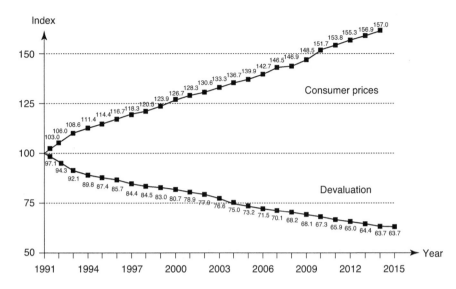

Fig. 8.1 Consumer price index (CPI) for the United States

The massive expansion of the money supply by central banks in Europe, the United States, and Japan in the aftermath of the great recession in 2009 may lead again to higher inflation rates in the medium term. The topic of inflation will remain relevant for price management.

8.1.1 Varying Inflation Rates and Net Market Position

Looking at inflation rates for an overall economy hides the fact that inflation affects individual industries and companies in very different ways. Between 2000 and 2010, the telecommunications sector in Germany achieved a nominal increase in revenue of 5% (over the entire period, not annually). Adjusted for inflation, however, the sector experienced a decline of 10% in real terms, thanks to sharp decreases in telecommunication prices. This came despite numerous innovations and significantly better performance. The industry was not even able to increase prices at the rate of inflation. In contrast, the German automobile industry showed a nominal growth of 30% and real growth of 11% over the same period. Based on its improved performance, the industry was able to raise its prices by more than the rate of inflation [2]. In the Global Pricing Study conducted by Simon-Kucher & Partners [3], for which 3904 managers around the world were surveyed, roughly one third of the respondents said they had raised prices below the rate of inflation, one third at the rate, and one third above the rate. That means that individual companies and industries are affected very differently by inflation. Some gain advantages from inflationary tendencies, while others must accept price declines in real terms.

Inflation has effects on selling prices as well as on procurement prices, i.e., costs. How the difference between selling costs and procurement costs develops over time is decisive for the profit situation. This difference, which one refers to as the "net position," "is an indicator of the extent to which a company can pass on the price increases it faces and the extent to which it must absorb them" [4, p. 442]. We assume for the following analysis that the company must accept the trend in procurement prices. How the net position evolves will then obviously dep22end on any change of the price-response function.

8.1.2 Inflation-Neutral Trend

We assume linear cost and price-response functions. The procurement and the consumption of the inputs take place within the same period. We assume that the variable unit costs increase from k_0 in period 0 to $k_1 = (1 + r)k_0$ in period 1 and that the price-response function in period 0 is:

$$q_0 = a - bp_0. \tag{8.1}$$

It changes in period 1 to:

$$q_1 = a - \frac{b}{1 + w}p_1, \tag{8.2}$$

where w is the rate of change of the maximum price, because $p_1^{\max} = (1 + w)p_0^{\max}$.

We characterize the change of the price-response function as *inflation-neutral* if w is equal to the rate of the cost increase r. The equation $p_1' = (1 + r)p_0$ then applies to all prices. After we plug that into (8.1) we get:

$$q_1' = a - b\frac{1 + r}{1 + w}p_0' = a - bp_0' = q_0. \tag{8.3}$$

In other words, if the maximum price increases at the same rate that costs do, the sales volume does not change.

If $w = r$ the optimal price p_1^* also rises at that rate, as does the nominal profit π_1. The "real" or inflation-adjusted profit $\pi_1^{\text{real}} = \pi_1 \div (1 + r)$ remains unchanged.

8.1.3 Non-Inflation-Neutral Trend

The trend in costs and volume is not inflation-neutral if the price increase rate w deviates from the cost increase rate r. If $r > w$, i.e., the variable unit costs rise at a faster rate than the maximum price, it follows that:

Table 8.1 Effects of different rates of increase for costs and maximum price on optimal prices and profits (*top figure* optimal price, *middle figure* nominal profit, *bottom figure* real profit)

		Cost increase r (%)			
		0	10	15	20
Maximum price increase w (%)	0	$p_1 = \$7.00$ $\pi_1 = \$90.00$ $\pi_1^{real} = \$90.00$	$\$7.20$ $\$78.40$ $\$71.30$	$\$7.30$ $\$72.90$ $\$63.39$	$\$7.40$ $\$67.60$ $\$56.50$
	10	$\$7.50$ $\$111.40$ $\$111.40$	$\$7.70$ $\$99.00$ $\$90.00$	$\$7.80$ $\$93.09$ $\$80.95$	$\$7.90$ $\$87.36$ $\$72.80$
	15	$\$7.75$ $\$122.28$ $\$122.28$	$\$7.95$ $\$109.58$ $\$99.62$	$\$8.05$ $\$103.50$ $\$90.00$	$\$8.15$ $\$97.58$ $\$81.32$
	20	$\$8.00$ $\$133.30$ $\$133.30$	$\$8.20$ $\$120.33$ $\$109.30$	$\$8.30$ $\$114.08$ $\$99.20$	$\$8.40$ $\$108.00$ $\$90.00$

- The optimal price increases percentage-wise less than the costs.
- The rate of increase in the nominal profit can be weaker, stronger, or identical to that of costs.
- The real, i.e., inflation adjusted, profit declines.

When $r < w$ the opposite conclusions apply. In that situation, the company may harvest unexpected profits (e.g., in the chemical industry or aviation, when the oil price declines). But this situation is mostly temporary.

We illustrate this relationship with a numerical example, where $k_0 = 4$, $a = 100$ and $b = 10$. The optimal prices as well as the nominal and real profits are shown in Table 8.1.

We call particular attention to the cases where $w = 10\%$, $r = 15\%$ as well as where $w = 15\%$, $r = 20\%$. In these cases, the nominal profit increases, but the real profit declines.

The example shows that passing on cost increases to customers in a schematic manner is dangerous.

The most important insights from the discussion are:

- When passing on cost increases in the form of higher prices, one must be aware of whether and how the price-response function shifts over time.
- The optimal price increase will correspond to the rate of the cost increase only when the maximum price also grows at the same rate. In that case, the real profit remains the same. In all other cases, the optimal price grows at a different rate than the costs.

8.1.4 Tactical Considerations on Price and Inflation

We have observed in various studies that a high inflation rate leads to a higher price elasticity. A pure orientation on the cost side can therefore lead to dangerous missteps. For countries with extremely high inflation rates, such as Brazil, this process gets turned on its head. In one study, we found a price elasticity of close to zero. The explanation for this surprising finding lies in the reference or anchor prices. When the inflation rate is extremely high, buyers lose this reference basis. Such findings underscore the importance of being vigilant on the sales side. Measuring changes in the price-response function, however, poses significant problems. One could consider making rolling adjustments to the parameters by examining the price-response function against the latest data at regular intervals.

There is another aspect of price management in an inflationary environment which warrants attention. When all suppliers in a market are affected by the same cost increase, the probability is high that all will follow if one supplier raises prices. Under such circumstances, it can be optimal to pass through the cost increase in full. That applies when the total sales volume in the market is price inelastic and market shares depend on price.

Adjustable price clauses in B2B markets can automate the required price changes to some degree and thus lessen the resistance of customers. But one should be careful here as well. Shapiro [5] reports on a manufacturer who linked product prices to the price of copper, because its products contained a large amount of the metal. But because the other costs and the willingness to pay developed differently from the copper price, prices became more and more inadequate over time.

One should keep the following tactical recommendations in mind when adjusting prices vis-à-vis inflation:

- Set clear objectives for price increases: this should happen top-down.
- Break the price objectives down by customer segments, product segments, and channels.
- Pursue the price increase objectives by implementing concrete measures: raise list prices, change the discount system, change payment terms, introduce surcharges, etc.
- Prepare the pricing measures with proper communication:
  - Develop high-level communication/announcements by the CEO, e.g., through interviews.
  - Communicate internally to sales.
  - Prepare convincing arguments for customers.
  - Review contracts.
  - Use adjustable price clauses or indexing.
- Implement the price increase measures:
  - Plan all the details, e.g., sequencing, target customers.
  - Closely monitor the implementation; adjust measures if necessary.

- Watch the competition carefully.
- Perhaps offer the sales team an incentive based on price increase realization.
• Monitor precisely: compare the implemented price increase vs. original objectives in as close to real-time as possible.

The greatest risk posed by inflationary developments is to implement the necessary price increases either too late or not at all. It is hard to catch up after missing these opportunities.

The opposite applies when an economy experiences deflation. One should avoid premature price cuts and try to stem the decline in prices. Avoiding a downward price spiral and refraining from price wars become high priorities in a deflationary environment [6]. The deflation in Japan, which has now lasted for over two decades, may explain why 84% of Japanese companies are involved in price wars. That percentage is well above the average in other countries, which is "only" 46% [3]. The deflationary price trend could also be behind the fact that Japanese firms have the lowest return on sales among all OECD nations [7, p. 33].

8.2   International Price Management

The international exchange of goods and services is growing at much faster rates than the gross domestic product of most countries. With the world's increasing economic integration, it is inevitable that the role of international price management changes. There are two countervailing trends related to this. First, the importance of international price management increases for a company when its share of foreign sales goes up. On the other hand, it is becoming more difficult to implement and maintain price differentials across countries. This is the case because modern transportation and information technology, combined with political developments, have made previously distinct and separate national markets more similar and lowered the barriers between them.

This is particularly true in the European single market, whose establishment was expected to lead to a strong convergence of prices. But even today this expectation remains only partially fulfilled. "The differential in inflation rates between the euro area and Germany, which had leveled off in the interim, has now grown slightly larger," according to a report from Germany's Bundesbank [8, p. 21].

8.2.1   Problems and Practices

One challenge in international price management lies in the enormous price differences which sometimes exist across countries. Below we illustrate international price differentiation for selected industries.

Table 8.2 Price differences for the Apple iPhone 7 with 32 GB [9]

Country	Price in $ (without VAT)	Deviation from average (in %)
USA	649.00	−11.4
Japan	631.87	−13.78
Germany	807.01	+10.12
UK	758.62	+3.52
France	817.68	+11.58

Table 8.3 Price difference for a women's leather shoe [10]

Country	Price in US$	Deviation from average (in %)
UK	152.00	−17.58
USA	189.00	+2.48
Japan	257.60	+39.67
Russia	192.85	+4.57
European Union	178.25	−3.35
Spain	128.20	−30.49

Smartphones exhibit large price differences across countries, as we show in Table 8.2 for the Apple iPhone.

The global brand Zara also implements significant price differences around the world. Table 8.3 shows the prices for a women's basic leather shoe.

The fashion firm Brax differentiates its prices across European countries. While a pair of cotton pants costs €99.95 in Germany, the same pants have a price of €120.50 in Denmark and €174.47 in Switzerland. Those are differences of 21 and 74%, respectively.

The international price differentiation is a special form of regional price differentiation. What distinguishes it are special characteristics such as different currencies, parallel imports, and customs or other forms of government intervention. High arbitrage costs can exist when one crosses an international border, compared with covering a similar distance within a country. As long as such barriers exist, Boston will be further away from Montreal than from Philadelphia, economically speaking, even though the distance in miles is roughly the same, and the Internet makes it easy to compare prices across countries. High international price differences are common in food and grocery. A bottle of French red wine sells for €1.99 in Germany, while the same bottle costs CHF 6.99 in Switzerland and £4.50 in Great Britain, which corresponds to a price difference of more than 160% [11]. Another example of international price differentiation are handbags from luxury brand Chanel in Europe and China. While Chanel's classic bag in Europe has a price of €3350, the price for the same bag stood at €5444 in China, or 63% more. Chanel plans to change its price strategy, however, and reduce this gap by raising the European price and lowering the price in China [12].

One can observe considerable international price differences even for the exact same level of performance. One example is air travel, as the price for a flight can depend on where it is booked. The price for a flight from Paris to Frankfurt on the German site of the travel agency Opodo costs €202, but €247 on the Irish page. According to one expert, such price differences can regularly be as large as 20%. The price search engine Kayak.com has internationalized its searches for that reason. In other words, it searches across several countries for the price of the same flight [13]. A new EU regulation illustrates just how much the Internet can sharply limit opportunities for price differentiation. The regulation prohibits "geo-blocking" for subscribers of video services such as Netflix. This means that customers have cross-border access to content they have paid for in their home country [14].

The reasons behind international price differentiation are manifold:

- Purchase behavior and preferences
- Competitive structure and behavior
- Costs
- Currency fluctuations
- Delivery and payment conditions
- International brand positioning
- Parallel imports
- Taxes, customs, quotas, and other government measures

The international pricing practice is dominated by cost-plus thinking to a greater extent than the domestic pricing practice [15]. In many books on international marketing, one will find pricing recommendations of a cost-plus nature [16, 17, p. 258]. Academics and practitioners debate which cost basis should be used for international business: marginal or fully loaded costs [18]. An older viewpoint considers the export business as incremental or additional to the core domestic business, so that one can use marginal costs as the calculation basis. Under this view, the core domestic business should cover fixed and variable costs, while the foreign business only needs to generate contribution margins. As long as foreign revenue constitutes a small part of total revenue, one may accept that approach. If a company sets its prices using this method, the foreign prices tend to be lower than the domestic prices. In each specific case, however, this will depend on the additional costs of the exports.

But if a significant portion of the revenue comes from abroad, which is the case today for many companies, the custom is to use a fully loaded cost calculation. Under this method, the calculation of prices for foreign sales incorporates not only the fixed costs but also the additional costs for shipping, insurance, packaging, distribution, etc. This results in foreign prices which are typically higher than domestic prices. One refers to the phenomenon of higher foreign prices as "international price escalation" [18, 19]. In practice, one observes foreign prices which are higher or lower than the corresponding domestic prices, depending on the product and the countries of origin and sale.

One explanation for the preference for cost-plus thinking relates to the higher perceived uncertainty when conducting business abroad, leading companies to fall back even more strongly on the apparently safer cost-plus calculation. Of course this method is just as inadequate for foreign business as it is for the domestic business. Cost-plus pricing in an international context takes neither the country-specifics on the demand side nor the competitive aspects into account.

What also stands out are the efforts to invoice the export business in one's own currency to the greatest extent possible. Many companies interpret this as an indicator of their market and competitive strength. The major advantage for the supplier of invoicing in its own currency is that it shifts the exchange rate risk to the customers. The flipside is that the price may be anything but optimal once it has been converted into the customer's currency. It is an illusion that invoicing in one's own currency can eliminate exchange rate problems.

A local market is characterized by its idiosyncratic customer behavior and its competitive structure. This can result in different optimal prices, i.e., regional price differentiation, as we showed in Chap. 6. At the international level, it is obvious that one needs to pay attention to purchasing power and preferences of customers as well as the size, number, and behavior of competitors. Each country should be analyzed along these lines, and one can devise an appropriate price strategy on this basis. The coordination of international prices begins only after this stage is completed. One problem can be the availability of valid market data (especially in emerging markets). The situation has improved in recent years, however, because of the spread of global consulting and market research firms.

Countries often have different inflation rates, which will influence the respective prices. With a free market mechanism, these differences in inflation are reflected in exchange rate changes. Such changes are an important factor for international price management. Within the euro zone, however, this problem no longer exists, since there is only one currency, the euro.

A change in exchange rates can have very strong effects on price management. When the Swiss National Bank let the Swiss franc float starting on January 15, 2015, the currency rose abruptly by 20%. Products on the German side of the Rhine, which marks the border, were suddenly much less expensive in terms of Swiss francs. Products offered in Switzerland to German customers (who think and calculate in euros) became more expensive. Supermarket prices in Switzerland are up to 39% higher than in Germany. This large price difference has made imports into Switzerland less expensive, from which the Swiss retailers can benefit [20]. The price advantage of Swiss customers who shop in Germany is amplified by the reimbursement of value-added tax. In this period, a German supermarket on the border was issuing 2000 receipts per day which Swiss shoppers submitted to get their value-added tax back. As a result there was a run on German shops. But it is not only the Swiss who feel the effects of the price difference between Germany and Switzerland. A price spread developed within Germany itself, with prices for the exact same product higher near the Swiss border than in other parts of Germany: the price of a package of oatmeal was €1.49 in the town of Lörrach, near the Swiss border, but the same product was offered for 69 cents in the city of Mannheim

[21]. The local transportation authority in Basel deployed more light-rail trains on the stretch to Weil am Rhein, while Swiss retailers resorted to massive discounts in order to avoid losing even more customers [22]. This case shows an important consequence of exchange rate effects. These do not only affect exporters but suppliers on both sides of the exchange rate "border." The rise in value of the Swiss franc did more than make business difficult for Swiss exporters and easier for companies who import goods from the euro zone into Switzerland. Suppliers who sell exclusively in Switzerland (e.g., retailers in the border areas) and suppliers who sell only in Germany (likewise retailers in the border area) feel the effects, either positive or negative. The effects are also not limited to retail. They apply to any company which is in competition with companies from the other currency area.

In the next section, we will analyze how currency fluctuations, parallel imports, and government intervention affect international price management.

8.2.2   Price and Exchange Rates

To take a closer look at the exchange rate aspect, let us consider a European firm which wants to maximize its profit in euros. It exports into the United States, where the selling price for its product is denominated in dollars. For simplicity's sake, we will ignore taxes, customs duties, additional export costs, etc. We also assume a complete separation of the European and the American markets, i.e., no interdependencies such as parallel imports exist. Finally, we assume linear price-response and cost functions.

Because the US price is in dollars, the price-response function in the United States is:

$$q = a - bp_\$ \tag{8.4}$$

with q = volume in the United States, $p_\$$ = price in dollars, and a, b = parameters.

All costs, however, are incurred in euros, so that the cost function is as follows:

$$C_{\text{Euro}} = C_{\text{fix}} + kq \tag{8.5}$$

with C_{fix} as fixed costs and k as variable unit cost in euros.

This results in the following profit function in euros:

$$\pi_{\text{Euro}} = (a - bp_\$)(wp_\$ - k) - C_{\text{fix}} \tag{8.6}$$

with w = exchange rate ($\$/€$).

After taking the derivative and reformulating, we get the formula for the optimal US price:

$$p_{\$}^{*} = \frac{1}{2}\left(\frac{a}{b} + w \times k\right).\tag{8.7}$$

In contrast to the usual formula for the optimal price, the variable unit costs (measured in euros) are multiplied by the exchange rate w to transform them into dollars. The fraction $a \div b$ expresses the maximum price in dollars. Equation (8.7) reveals that the larger the variable unit costs are relative to the maximum price, the stronger the effect of the exchange rate is on the optimal price. If marginal costs are zero (e.g., for digital products), the exchange rate has no influence on the optimal price. Only the maximum price matters in that case.

In order to illustrate the consequences for profit, we look at a numerical example and set the parameters at $a = 200$ [units] and $b = 10$ [units/\$]. The maximum price is therefore $200 \div 10 = \$20$. The marginal costs are €5, and the exchange rate is 1.33 [\$/€]. According to (8.7), we get an optimal price of \$13.33. The company sells 67 units in the US market and gets a profit of $(0.75 \times 13.33 - 5) \times 67 = €334.83$. If the value of the dollar rises to parity with the euro, which would be the equivalent of a euro devaluation of 25%, the optimal price would fall to \$12.50, which is a decline of only 6.2%. The sales volume rises to 75 units. Profit likewise increases to €562.50, a gain of 68%. In other words, such exchange rate changes have a massive effect on profit.

Figure 8.2 shows the effects of exchange rate changes in a range of $w = \$2.00/€$ to $w = \$0.77/€$. The actual range of the dollar-euro exchange rate has extended from a high of \$1.59/€ in 2008 to a low of \$0.85/€ in 2002. In 2017, it stood at \$1.05/€ on January 1 and \$1.20/€ at the end of December.

The upper part of Fig. 8.2 shows how the optimal price in dollars and the sales volume behave as a function of the exchange rate. The price drops underproportionally as the value of the dollar rises. One also sees that the growth in sales volume is not a direct result of the change in exchange rate but rather a consequence of the lower price in dollars.

In the middle part of the figure, we see how profit develops in dollars and in euros. The profit in dollars rises underproportionally as the dollar gains in value. The profit in euros, however, rises overproportionally because of two effects. First, the sales volume grows, thanks to the lower price in dollars. But this growth is not accompanied by a decline in unit contribution margin, as one would expect from pricing in one currency. In fact, the opposite occurs. The price in euro and therefore the unit contribution margin (in euro) increase as the dollar gains in value. This occurs because the dollar price declines underproportionally. The price in euro increases linearly with the exchange rate, as the lower part of Fig. 8.2 shows. The combination of higher sales volumes and higher euro price (and thus unit contribution margin) explains the extremely strong profit increase on a euro basis.

American exporters will naturally face the opposite effects from exchange rate changes. Their optimal price in euros will rise, and the profit will decline with a higher dollar value.

Units, $ Exchange rate effects on price and sales volume

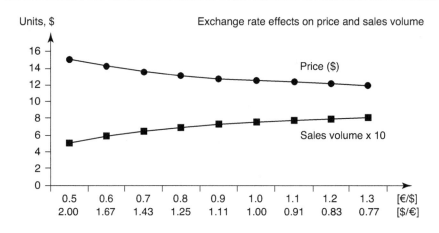

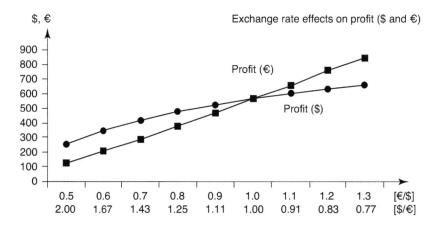

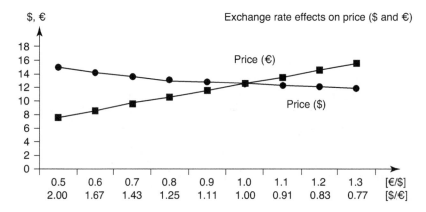

Fig. 8.2 The effects of exchange rate changes on prices, sales volume and profit

Overview

A company faces the following consequences when it sets prices in the currency of the target country and generates costs in the currency of the country of origin:

- The optimal price, denominated in the target country's currency, will decline as the exchange rate rises.
- The decline in price is underproportional.
- The profit in the currency of the country of origin responds sharply, because both sales volume and unit contribution margin effects increase.

We would like to stress that in this example we have changed only the exchange rate. In reality, there can be other consequences when the exchange rate changes. These can include higher costs (if some costs are denominated in dollars) or a shift in the price-response function. In such cases, it is not possible to make the kind of clear-cut statements as above.

Consequences of Sub-optimal Prices

What happens when a company makes sub-optimal price adjustments in the wake of an exchange rate change? We look at two such alternative adjustments:

- The price in dollars is held constant.
- The price in euros is held constant.

The argument for the first alternative is that US buyers and domestic US competitors are not interested in the exchange rate changes between the euro and the dollar. Put simply, this argument claims that if one wants to sell in the US market, one should behave in the same way as the local competition, which is not affected by exchange rate changes. Leaving the price unchanged preserves price continuity. Under this approach, the seller importing into the United States bears the entire exchange rate risk.

The second alternative is the equivalent of invoicing in euros, which means that one preserves price continuity in terms of euros and shifts the burden of the exchange rate changes to the customers abroad. That is equivalent to an American customer making a purchase in the United States but paying in euros. The customer bears the entire exchange rate risk.

We look at the numerical example from before, where $a = 200$, $b = 10$, and $k = €5$. We start with an exchange rate of 1.33 [$/€]. As we have seen, the profit-maximizing price is $13.33, sales volume is 67 units, and profit is €334.83. We assume that the price in Europe is €10, which corresponds to the dollar price at the prevailing exchange rate ($0.75 \times 13.33 = €10$).

Under the option "constant price in dollars," the company maintains the price at $13.33 despite the change in the exchange rate. Sales volume remains at 67 units.

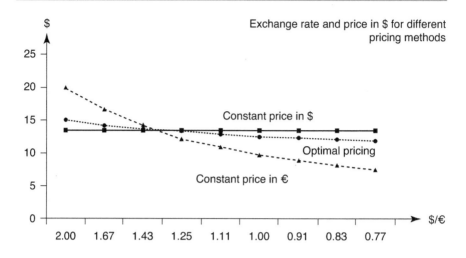

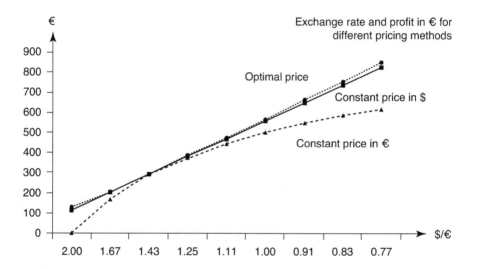

Fig. 8.3 The effects of sub-optimal behavior with changes in exchange rates

But the unit revenue in euros changes because of the change in the exchange rate. Under the option "constant price in euros," the company aims to keep its unit revenue constant at €10, so that every change in the exchange rate impacts the dollar price directly. Figure 8.3 shows the effects of the two alternatives compared to the optimal behavior according to (8.7).

The upper part of the figure depicts the resulting dollar price. Under the second option ("constant price in euros"), the reaction of the price in dollars is much more pronounced than under optimal behavior. This is synonymous with saying that the willingness to pay of American customers has been misinterpreted. It overlooks the fact that US customers calculate in their own currency and therefore end up paying less when the dollar gains in value. The additional decrease in the dollar price means the company sacrifices profit. The opposite holds true when the dollar experiences a devaluation. In that case, the dollar price rises too sharply. The US customers are incorrectly treated as if they were European customers.

The strategy of constant prices in dollars neglects the effects that exchange rate changes have on unit contribution margin. When the dollar is strong, a price cut on a dollar basis would be optimal because it would drive higher volumes and compound the effect that the unit contribution margin is much higher in euro terms. Keeping the price constant in dollar terms means the company fails to capitalize on this opportunity. The optimal dollar price lies between the prices of the two sub-optimal strategies. That is the case because optimal price setting accounts for effects which the other two options neglect.

Especially important is the clear finding in the lower part of the figure: the foregone profit opportunity from a constant euro price at a high exchange rate is much greater than the lost profit from keeping the price constant (in dollars). If the exchange rate were 1.67 [$/€], the profit sacrifice from keeping the euro price is 18.40%, but only 2.1% from keeping the dollar price constant.

One also observes that under the strategy to keep the euro price constant, an exchange rate of 2.00 [$/€] means that volume drops to zero. At a constant euro price of €10 and that exchange rate, the price in dollars would rise to $20 (10 ÷ 0.5 = 20$), which corresponds to the maximum price (200 ÷ 10 = 20$). That is the point where sales volume is zero. In the optimal scenario, one would set a price of $15 at that exchange rate and would still generate a profit of €125. The insistence on a constant unit revenue in euros can lead a company to "calculate" its way out of the market.

The popular practice in some euro countries of invoicing in euros, as we discussed above, is not identical with keeping unit revenue constant in euro terms, but it can be viewed similarly. The risk of sub-optimal behavior is particularly likely when the US customers are still invoiced at the same euro price as European customers, despite the change in the exchange rate. In line with what we described above, changes in exchange rates can make it wise, if not necessary, to invoice customers in different countries at different prices in euros. One therefore needs country-specific price lists in euros or country-specific discount rates in order to exploit the full profit potential in the individual countries.

Overview
Practices such as keeping prices constant in the target market or keeping the price constant in the currency of origin can lead to sub-optimal results when exchange rates change. Especially disadvantageous is keeping the price in the currency of the country of origin constant. When invoicing in the currency of the country of origin, one should make sure that the effects of the price on the customers in the target country have been adequately taken into account.

8.2.3 Parallel Imports

Parallel imports refer to a flow of goods between countries which is unwarranted by the manufacturer or seller. One also refers to such flows of goods as reimports, gray imports, or gray markets. Parallel imports occur when distributors, other middlemen, or end users try to take advantage of price differences between countries. They purchase a product in a low-price country, modify the product if necessary, and then ship it to a high-price country where the product is sold or consumed. Such modifications can include replacing the package inserts for a pharmaceutical product or altering a motor vehicle so that it complies with regulations in the high-price country.

In some industries, such as automotive or pharmaceuticals, there are companies which specialize in parallel imports. In other industries, such imports occur rather on an ad hoc basis. Parallel imports can reach very significant levels [18, 19]. Parallel imports had a market share of 10.2% of the German pharmaceutical market in 2012 [23]. The company Kohlpharma, one specialist in that area, posted revenues of around €621 million in its 2013/2014 financial year [24]. This line of business, however, is very volatile and subject to swings in exchange rates. CC Pharma, one of the leading importers, laid off almost 40% of its employees in the wake of the devaluation of the euro. That devaluation eroded a considerable portion of the price advantage which parallel imports rely on [25]. Parallel imports are in no way narrowly confined to specific economic areas or countries in close proximity to each other. "China's parallel auto imports speed ahead" was the headline of a report in the *Financial Times*, which said that the number of "gray import" cars grew sharply after these imports were permitted. One wholesaler alone imported 20,000 vehicles, which came primarily from America or the Middle East [26].

The following factors favor parallel imports:

- Persistent international price differences.
- Declining shipping costs.
- Improvements in international communications and information systems.
- International trade liberalization, which limits the possibilities for manufacturers to protect their national markets.
- The penetration of international and global brands. Such brands often have a uniform appearance in every market, and the use of the product is standardized.
- The increasing internationalization of consumers and the resulting increased acceptance of "foreign" products.

Products with a high value and relatively low arbitrage costs are best suited for parallel imports. Luxury goods or products which are easily transported fall into this category, as do branded and high-value industrial goods.

It is hard to reconcile a global brand and product strategy with a price strategy calling for sharply differentiated prices from country to country. The price differentiation cannot neglect the arbitrage costs. Many companies strive to prevent or eliminate parallel imports entirely. Purely from a pricing standpoint, such a rigorous position is not advisable. The overarching objectives of attempts to prevent parallel imports are to avoid conflicts in sales channels, avoid tarnishing the company's image, and to prevent internal conflicts. Parallel imports often cause friction between a company's own operating units in the respective countries. The local unit in the target market develops the market, pays for the advertising, and opens up the sales channels, but another business unit within the same company, but from another country, harvests a portion of that investment. Those units often hide behind gray market dealers and distributors. This puts the corporate headquarters in an awkward position.

In order to analyze the effects of parallel imports, we consider for simplicity's sake a two-country model with one high-price and one low-price country. Bucklin [27] used such a model to come to the conclusion that a failure to give parallel imports proper attention can lower a company's profits [28]. If prices are coordinated, i.e., the company reduces the price differential, the profit loss can be reduced to a tolerable level. If the producer is actually in a position to manage the prices of the imported products, then parallel imports can even lead to higher profits. Parallel imports in this sense are a method of price differentiation. In practice, however, a manufacturer's ability to control or manage the prices for parallel import goods is the exception, unless the manufacturer organizes the parallel imports itself.

Above and beyond the purely price-related measures, a number of tactics can come into play to increase arbitrage costs. The greater the difference in the isolated optimal prices across the countries, the more one should invest in such tactics. They include product differentiation, the use of different brands, national markings, or identification, and the use of sales volume commitments. One should keep in mind, however, that these measures cost money and that using them runs counter to economies of scale in production, logistics, and sales. Such differentiation is also not compatible with a uniform, global brand strategy.

8.2.3.1 International Price Corridor

It is becoming increasingly difficult to implement a strategy of price differentiation which calls for setting the optimal price in each country in isolation, in line with local conditions. How does one manage this situation? One extreme option is to lower all prices to the level of the lowest price. But such a strategy is generally not worth pursuing. It leads to drastic declines in profit. Alternatively, one could align all the prices with the highest prevailing price, but that strategy can result in big losses of market share. A solution between those two extremes would be to set a uniform international price which lies within the existing spectrum of prices. In general, neither of these three solutions offers an adequate answer, because customer preferences, competitive conditions, costs, etc. differ from country to country. This in turn means optimal prices should differ from country to country. The pressure to harmonize international prices should not lead to one uniform price for all countries, nor should it lead to isolated price optimization on a country-by-country basis. When price gaps between countries get too large, they facilitate gray markets and lead to difficulties with distributors and a company's local operating units. A uniform price,

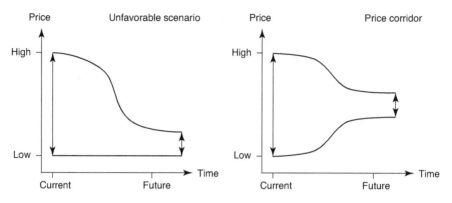

Fig. 8.4 Price corridor concept

in contrast, sacrifices considerable profit potential. It is estimated that profits in the automotive industry would be 25% lower if prices were harmonized at a uniform level within Europe [7, p. 160].

A better alternative is to raise some prices and reduce others to create an appropriate spread of prices. The goal is the simultaneous optimization of the individual country prices. This is achieved by a so-called price corridor comprising the prices of all countries. Figure 8.4 illustrates this concept graphically. The international price corridor represents a compromise between a uniform price and the independent, isolated price optimization by country. The corridor takes into account differences between countries and the pressure toward price harmonization. A price corridor must incorporate the size of the markets, their different price elasticities, gray imports, cost structures, and arbitrage as well as the competitive and sales situations in the individual countries. The width of the corridor should be defined in such a way that parallel imports and gray markets are contained, but not necessarily eliminated.

Important for setting the optimal corridor is the sensitivity with which parallel import volumes respond to international price differences. The higher this sensitivity is, the narrower the price corridor will be. It will also become clear how large the profit sacrifice would be if prices were uniform.

In practice, one sets the width of the price corridor right below the arbitrage costs in order to precisely achieve the desired goal to prevent parallel imports. In this sense, the arbitrage costs include the expected profits of the parallel importer. Preventing parallel imports, however, also creates opportunity costs. One must weigh this foregone profit against the advantages of preventing parallel imports, which are admittedly hard to quantify. We would like to emphasize here once again that the complete elimination of parallel imports is not always a sensible objective.

Introducing a price corridor, of course, has associated costs. It requires detailed information about the markets. But in our experience, these costs are more than offset by the suppression of gray markets and the improved profit situation. The price corridor tries to find a compromise between the desired price differentiation and the inevitable price harmonization. It at least partially exploits the opportunities for price differentiation. The price corridor follows the principle of "as much differentiation as possible, as much harmonization as necessary" in a systematic and quantified way.

The following example illustrates the effects of different approaches and the advantage of a price corridor. We assume two countries A and B with the following price-response functions:

Country A: $q = 100 - 1p$,
Country B: $q = 100 - 2p$.

The marginal costs in each case are $20. If we set the price at a uniform $60, there will be 40 units sold in Country A and none in Country B. The profit is $1600. If instead we optimize the prices for each country in isolation, we have the results shown in Table 8.4.

The maximum potential profit from both countries, achieved by separate price optimization, is $2050. But this leaves a price difference of 42% (relative to the higher price). If arbitrage costs were low (say, 20%), this situation could entice parallel imports.

Figure 8.5 shows the relationship between price differences and parallel imports estimated by experts. A price differential of 42% would lead to a share of parallel imports of 40%. The results under that assumption are shown in Table 8.5.

Profit falls by $400 due to the parallel imports, a level which is about 19.5% below the profit level without parallel imports.

Table 8.4 Isolated price optimization for both countries

	Price ($)	Sales volume (units)	Profit ($)
Country A	60	40	1600
Country B	35	30	450
Total	–	70	2050

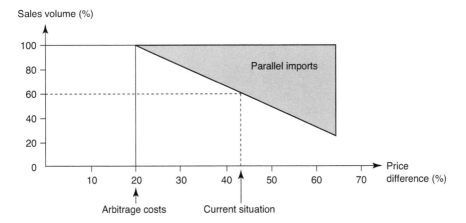

Fig. 8.5 Price differences and parallel imports

Table 8.5 Profit situation with parallel imports

	Sales volume share (%)	Sales volume (units)	Unit contribution margin ($)	Profit ($)
Official sales Country A	60	$(0.6 \times 40) = 24$	$(60 - 20) = 40$	960
Parallel imports Country A	40	$(0.4 \times 40) = 16$	$(35 - 20) = 15$	240
Total Country A	100	40	$(50 - 20) = 30$	1200
Country B	100	30	$(35 - 20) = 15$	450
Total A + B	–	70	–	1650

Table 8.6 Profit situation – price increase in low-price country

	Price ($)	Sales volume (units)	Profit ($)
Country A	60	40	1600
Country B	48	4	112
Total	–	44	1712

This prompts different price alternatives whose effects must be understood and compared. These alternatives are:

- Uniform price
- Price increase in the low-price country
- Price cut in the high-price country
- Price corridor

8.2.3.2 Uniform Price
This approach calls for setting a uniform price in both countries. In order to optimize this price, we add the price-response functions for both countries, which results in the following function:

$$q = 200 - 3 \times \text{uniform price}$$

The optimal uniform price works out to $43.33 with a sales volume of 70 units. The total volume remains the same, but the profit falls to $1633, a decline of 20.3% from the profit level without parallel imports. This profit decline originates from the fact that setting a uniform price does not take country-specific differences into account. On the positive side, the uniform price means there are no parallel imports.

8.2.3.3 Price Increase in the Low-Price Country
Under this scenario, we raise the price in country B from $35 to $48. This reduces the price difference between A and B to 20%, which would prevent parallel imports. Table 8.6 shows the consequences for profit. The sales volume in country B falls to almost zero, but overall profit improves by 3.7% to $1712 compared to the case with parallel imports. But compared to the starting situation in Table 8.4, profit is 16.5% lower. It is problematic, however, to completely abandon low-price markets.

Table 8.7 Profit situation with a price cut in the high-price country

	Price ($)	Sales volume (units)	Profit ($)
Country A	43.75	56.25	1336
Country B	35.00	30	450
Total	–	86.25	1786

Table 8.8 Profit situation with a price corridor

	Price ($)	Sales volume (units)	Profit ($)
Country A	55.88	49.12	1517
Country B	40.70	18.60	385
Total	–	67.72	1902

Table 8.9 Profit and relative profit decline for alternative price strategies

Price strategy	Profit ($)	Profit decline relative to the theoretically possible profit (in %)
Uniform price	1633	20.3
Price increase in low-price country	1712	16.5
Price cut in high-price country	1786	12.9
Price corridor	1902	7.2
Isolated price optimization (only theoretical; does not work in practice)	2050	0.0

8.2.3.4 Price Cut in the High-Price Country

The price in Country A would be reduced from $60 to $43.75. The difference once again is 20%, which is sufficient to stop parallel imports. Table 8.7 shows the results. Sales volume and profit both improve vs. the results shown in Table 8.6, but measured against the theoretical profit in Table 8.4, the situation remains unsatisfactory, with profit 12.9% lower.

The price corridor delivers better results. The price is reduced in Country A and raised in Country B. Consistent with our assumptions, parallel imports disappear when the price difference between the countries is at or lower than the maximum of 20%. If we allow a corridor at the maximum level of 20%, the optimal prices are $50.88 in Country A and $(1 - 0.20) \times 50.88 = 40.70 in Country B. Compared to the current situation with parallel imports, the sales volume is somewhat less. As Table 8.8 shows, the profit is only 7.2% lower than in the starting situation.

Table 8.9 compares the profits for the alternative price strategies. The strategy of a uniform price is the worst, while the price corridor offers the best practical alternative.

8.2.3.5 A Case from Practice

In the following case, we describe the creation of a price corridor for a pharmaceutical product which we call SYNOP. SYNOP is marketed by one of the leading pharma manufacturers in the world. In order to determine the optimal price strategy at the international level, an analysis was conducted in five countries: the United States, Great Britain, France, Italy, and Germany. Based on the results, the optimal

Price of daily dose ($)   Optimal prices for individual countries

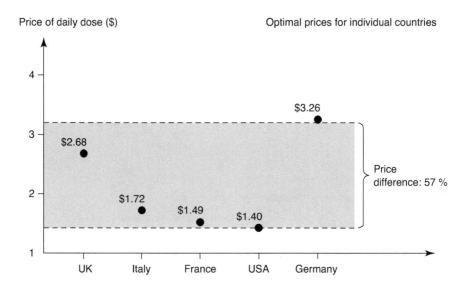

Price of daily dose ($)   Optimal price corridor

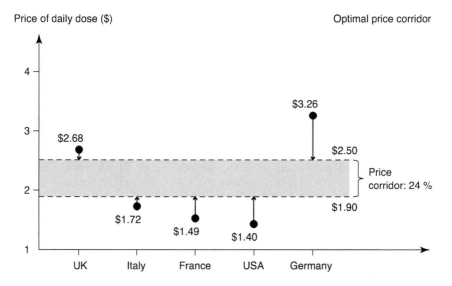

Fig. 8.6 Optimal prices for individual countries and the optimal price corridor for a pharmaceutical (Simon-Kucher & Partners)

prices for each country were determined, as shown in the upper portion of Fig. 8.6. These prices do not reflect any interdependencies among the countries, which means that these prices are optimal if the company succeeds in establishing effective fencing, i.e., barriers between the countries.

There were considerable differences between these isolated optimal prices. The optimal price in the United States was 57% below the German price and 48% below the optimal price in Great Britain. Barriers between countries would be overcome or evaded when price differences are that large. Fencing would not be effective, and the company should expect extensive parallel imports. The goal of the SYNOP project was to maximize profit, not to eliminate all parallel imports. Some importers should be allowed to overcome barriers, as long as their imports were consistent with the optimal prices. In a 1-day workshop with managers, price curves for parallel imports were created in accordance with Fig. 8.6. It turned out that around 32% of the sales volume in Germany would be covered by parallel imports from the United States, if the company were to launch SYNOP at the country-specific optimal prices. In contrast, parallel imports to Germany would not occur if the price difference were less than 20%.

We used the INTERPRICE (for INTERnational PRICE) system, developed by Simon-Kucher & Partners, to optimize the price corridor. The results are shown in the lower part of Fig. 8.6. The optimal international price corridor ranges from $1.90 to $2.50. Measured against the upper bound, the width of the corridor was 24%. All prices must be within the corridor. That means the isolated optimal prices for Germany and Great Britain will be reduced to $2.50, while the prices in Italy, France, and the United States will be raised to $1.90. With the price difference of 24%, Germany will experience parallel imports from France and the United States, but according to the price curves for parallel imports, they will remain under 5% of the market volume. This was viewed as tolerable.

We also looked at a uniform price for all markets, which would prevent parallel imports. The price corridor ranging from $1.90 to $2.50 and the toleration of parallel imports (to a certain extent) led to much higher profit than the uniform price strategy. Compared to the isolated optimal prices, which could not be implemented in practice, the profit sacrifice was acceptable. The price corridor also largely avoided frictions caused by parallel imports.

8.2.4 Price and Government Intervention

Forms of government intervention which affect price management play a much more important role in cross-border trade than they do in domestic markets.

8.2.4.1 Customs and Taxes
In addition to general corporate taxes – which can influence the choice of business locations, but which we will not consider here – governments have a direct influence over the prices customers pay when they impose value-added or other consumption-based taxes. The domestic gross price is the benchmark for a consumer's purchase decision.

On the one hand, a company faces the problem of adjusting country-specific prices to reflect local demand, and on the other hand, the company must coordinate the net price differences derived from the optimal gross prices. The European automotive market offers an example. From the German perspective, the gross price in Denmark, due to a higher value-added tax and a luxury tax, is much higher, but the net price is significantly lower than in Germany. Based on the EU principle of the free flow of goods, any resident of the European Union can import or export goods from one EU country to another. This applies equally to trade in automobiles [29]. Nonetheless, carmakers take advantage of various legal options to restrict cross-border trade [30]. Price differentiation on this basis results in significant additional profits for manufacturers and dealers.

High indirect taxes exert an influence on net prices. Against the backdrop of harmonization efforts in tax law (e.g., harmonization of value-added taxes), companies need to adjust their net price in order to take full advantage of available price latitudes.

8.2.4.2 Import Duties

Import customs and duties can be applied on a unit or a value basis and should be treated in the same way as taxes. A unit-based duty is essentially the equivalent of an increase in unit costs. The value-based duty is levied as a percentage of the value of the imported goods.

In order to demonstrate the effect of the value-based duty, we use the price-response $q = 100 - 10p$ and variable unit costs of 5. We look at value-based duties of 0%, 10%, and 20%. Table 8.10 shows the respective optimal prices and other key figures.

The optimal manufacturer selling price, or producer price, declines as the duty percentage increases, while the end consumer price rises. This results in a decline in sales volume. Lower unit contribution margins combined with declining sales volumes mean that higher duties sharply reduce profit.

The most important difference between duties and taxes is related to competition. While a tax affects all competing products in a country equally, the duty only affects imported products and thus worsens their competitive position relative to domestic products. These considerations shed light on possible consequences of the tariffs introduced by US President Donald Trump.

Table 8.10 Optimal prices for different value-based duties

Duty (%)	Optimal manufacturer selling price ($)	Duty per unit ($)	End consumer price including duty ($)	Sales volume (units)	Profit ($)	Duty revenue ($)
0	7.50	0.00	7.50	25.00	62.50	0.00
10	7.04	0.71	7.75	22.50	45.90	15.98
20	6.67	1.33	8.00	20.00	33.40	26.60

8.2.4.3 Antidumping Duties

Antidumping duties are a special kind of import duties. Dumping refers to the practice of selling at a price below the "normal export price," which incorporates specific costs and a profit margin, or below manufacturing costs in the country of origin. Dumping by its nature results in economic damage in the target country [19]. From a broad marketing perspective, this definition is not very compelling because there can be a whole host of reasons (dynamics, product line, nonlinear pricing, segmentation) which would make it optimal to charge prices abroad which are below prices in the country of origin or even below unit costs.

Companies which practice dumping run the risk of provoking antidumping duties. Such duties exist in the United States as well as in Europe. The dumping spread is typically the difference between the price in the country of origin and the price in the destination country. The antidumping duty affects price the same way as any other value- or unit-based duty. While in the 1990s, Japanese and Korean consumer electronics goods faced antidumping duties, nowadays such duties tend to target products from China and other emerging markets.

8.2.4.4 Quotas

Quotas are an additional form of government intervention to restrict imports. In general, a quota fixes an upper bound on volume, or a maximum volume, but occasionally quotas apply to market share. An example includes the import quotas agreed to by the United States and China on certain textile products. In the consumer area, there are fixed upper limits for many products which may be introduced depending on the country of origin. Examples include alcoholic beverages, tobacco products, coffee, and gasoline.

A maximum volume only makes sense when it is less than the import volume that would result from free trade. Under these conditions, it is optimal to set the price so that sales reach exactly the maximum allowable volume. To do this, one needs to know the price-response function. A well-known example is the group of maximum import quotas for Japanese automobiles in the US market. As a response, Japanese manufacturers set precisely those prices which would achieve the maximum allowable volumes. This kept the profit sacrifice within tolerable limits. There were also two unintended side effects. First, the quota had the effect of creating a quasi-cartel among the Japanese carmakers, because market shares were essentially fixed. On the other hand, it kept smaller, more price-aggressive Japanese manufacturers out of the US market, because those companies received only very small quotas on account of their weak starting position. With their sales potential limited in that way, it made no sense for them to establish an extensive sales network.

Minimum prices, as long as they are above prices that would result from free competition, have a similar function to maximum volumes. One would charge the minimum price. But in this case as well, one should know one's price-response function, in order to be sure that one's optimal price is not in fact above the minimum price. Such prices are most often set for entire product groups, not individual products.

8.2.5   Implementation in an International Context

In this section, we will discuss international implementation aspects such as delivery and payment terms and conditions, financing, location of price decision authority, transfer prices, and global strategy.

8.2.5.1 International Terms of Delivery and Payment Terms

Delivery and payment terms and conditions are generally part of the offer and negotiation process. In international business, standardized terms have been codified by the International Chamber of Commerce and are referred to as "incoterms." These terms govern the transfer of risk in international trade and specify which costs of the transfer (transportation, insurance) are borne by the seller and which by the buyer. The best-known terms of this kind include:

- Ex works
- FAS: free alongside ship
- FOB: free on board
- CFR: cost and freight
- CIF: cost, insurance, freight

Which price the international customer uses as a comparison basis is important, taking the incoterms into account. There can be consequences for competition depending on which form is agreed to.

8.2.5.2 Financing

The financial risks in international business are larger than those in domestic trade. On the one hand, currency fluctuations pose a risk which does not exist when business is conducted entirely in one currency. On the other hand, payment due dates in international business are lengthier. There are also greater political risks and judicial/legal risks in foreign markets. Companies can cover these financial risks to some extent through export insurance and by hedging against currency risk.

These risks, however, have nothing to do with price management as such. It is recommended, therefore, to keep the pricing and the financial functions separate and thus avoid dilution of responsibilities. Of course, the costs from covering risks should be considered in pricing. In general, these are variable costs related to an order. In the same sense, barter or other compensation deals are not a pricing problem. For price management, what ultimately matters is the resulting net proceeds.

8.2.5.3 Allocation of Price Decision Authority

The organizational location of price decision authority can be a touchy issue in the international context [31]. Business or operating units within a country generally have profit and loss responsibility. But if they are not permitted to set prices, they are left without an important profit driver. If, on the other hand, these local units have full pricing authority, the resulting international price differences could jeopardize overarching corporate objectives such as a global positioning or the avoidance of parallel imports. Prices are among the notorious causes of friction between head-quarters and foreign operating units, because these parties often have diverging interests. A solution which is completely satisfactory for all parties is difficult to find. The price corridor we introduced represents a compromise that has proven itself time and again in practice.

With ongoing globalization, we notice a tendency to centralize price manage-ment, while other functions such as sales or distribution are often decentralized. The centralization of price management is an inevitable consequence of lower trade barriers. A globally coordinated strategy is difficult to achieve without a certain centralization of pricing authority. But at the same time, businesses cannot take their eyes off the requirements of the local markets. Every company needs to determine its own degree of centralization and potentially differentiate by segment. Making sure the decentralized units get the right incentives is very important in this context.

Another facet of the relationship between the units of a multinational corporation is the question of *transfer prices* for intracompany deliveries. This is not primarily a question of price management in the spirit of this book, which focuses on the customer-facing prices. Factors determining transfer pricing include the optimal taxation of profits by country as well as the motivation effect for the respective country organizations.

Conclusion

Price management under consideration of the institutional and international context represents a multifaceted set of topics. Inflation and internationaliza-tion lead to the following recommendations:

- Inflation poses difficult challenges for price management. Decisive is how the net position of the company shifts. The extent of that shift in turn determines how much of the cost increase the company can pass on to customers.
- There are often major differences in prices for identical products in different national markets. Due to strong growth in international trade and the harmonization of markets, international price management continues to become more important.
- International markets are not homogeneous; they can in fact be markedly different from each other. This requires careful analysis of each individual country market. Relevant aspects include purchase behavior, competitive structure, distribution channels, costs, parallel imports, currency, and gov-ernment intervention.
- Exchange rate developments must be considered in price setting in different currency areas. Exchange rate changes exert considerable influence on optimal prices and profits.

(continued)

- The widespread practices of invoicing foreign customers in one's home currency or keeping prices constant in the target country are likely to be sub-optimal.
- One should keep a close eye on the balance between differentiation and standardization of international prices. The price corridor represents the best approach to setting profit-optimal prices across countries.
- Government intervention plays a much more important role in cross-border trade than it does within an internal market. Examples include different tax rates, import, and antidumping duties as well as quotas. These factors are to be taken into account in price setting.
- There are special delivery and payment terms and conditions for foreign transactions. Questions on financing, currency hedging, and legal aspects also matter.
- Finally, a company needs to manage the allocation of price decision authority between headquarters and foreign operating units. Increasing interconnection of markets is leading to stronger centralization of pricing authority.

Price management is becoming more challenging as globalization advances. The resultant greater complexity creates opportunities as well as risks. Companies which have a command of the theory, the tools, and the implementation of international price management will profit from this increasing complexity.

References

1. Bureau of Labor Statistics (2016). CPI Detailed Report – Data for October 2016. https://www.bls.gov/cpi/cpid1610.pdf. Accessed 15 December 2016
2. Simon-Kucher & Partners (2011). *Inflation – Secure Your Profits*. Bonn.
3. Simon-Kucher, & Partners (2011). *Global Pricing Study 2011*. Bonn.
4. Koll, W. (1979). *Inflation und Rentabilität*. Wiesbaden: Gabler.
5. Shapiro, B. P., & Jackson, B. B. (1978). Industrial Pricing to Meet Customer Needs. *Harvard Business Review*, 56(6), 119–127.
6. Beeck, S., Müller, J., Ehrhardt, A. (2014). *Pricing in der Deflation*. GDI Impuls (3), 70–74.
7. Simon, H. (2015). *Confessions of a Pricing Man*. New York: Springer.
8. Deutsche Bundesbank (2012). Monatsbericht Februar 2012, 18–21.
9. Apple Inc. (2015). http://www.apple.com. Accessed 7 December 2015.
10. Anonymous. (2012). Zara Prices Worldwide Comparative: Spain is the Cheaper. http://zaraforwarding.com/spain/zara-prices-worldwide-comparative-spain-is-the-cheaper/. Accessed 27 February 2015.
11. Eckert, W. (2012). Les Vignerons SWR1. http://www.swr.de/swr1/rp/tipps/2012-les-vignerons/-/id=446880/did=14928578/nid=446880/vr9jq9/index.html. Accessed 24 November 2015.

12. Chow, J. & Masidlover, N. (2015, March 18). Chanel Says Week Euro Worsens Gray Market. *Wall Street Journal*, p. 18.
13. Anonymous (2017, February 08). Wenn das Flugticket im Ausland billiger ist. *Frankfurter Allgemeine Zeitung*, p. 19.
14. European Commission (2017). Digital Single Market: EU negotiators agree on new rules allowing Europeans to travel and enjoy online content services across borders. http://europa. eu/rapid/press-release_IP-17-225_en.htm. Accessed 19 November 2017.
15. Skugge, G. (2011). The Future of Pricing: Outside-in. *Journal of Revenue & Pricing Management*, 10(4), 392–395.
16. Berndt, R., Altobelli, C. F., Sander, M. (2013). *Internationales Marketing Management*. Berlin: Springer.
17. Sarin, S. (2013). *Business Marketing: Concepts and Cases*. New Delhi: McGraw Hill.
18. Keegan, W., & Brill, E. A. (2014). *Global Marketing Management*. London: Prentice Hall.
19. Ghauri, P. N., & Cateora, P. R. (2014). *International Marketing*. London: McGraw-Hill.
20. Jones, C. (2015, August 19). Strong Franc Hits Swiss Retailers in the Pocket. *Financial Times*, p. 3.
21. Ritter J., & Soldt R. (2015, January 26). Rösti ausverkauft. *Frankfurter Allgemeine Zeitung*, p. 3.
22. McLucas, N. & Morse, A. (2015, January 20). "Euro Discount" Sales Draw Swiss Shoppers. *Wall Street Journal*, p. 3.
23. VFA – Verband forschender Arzneimittelhersteller (2012). Entwicklung des GKV-Arzneimittelmarktes. http://www.vfa.de/de/wirtschaft-politik/entwicklung-gkv-arzneimittelmarkt-2011.html. Accessed 28 February 2015.
24. Kohlpharma (2015). Der Grundgedanke. http://kohlpharma.com/de/import_arzneimittel/was_sind_import_arzneimittel. Accessed 24 February 2015.
25. Waschbüsch, H. & Hübner, M. (2015, July 25). Bittere Pille für 160 Mitarbeiter. *Trierischer Volksfreund*, p. 7.
26. Mitchell, T. (2015, January 19). China's Parallel Auto Imports Speed Ahead. *Financial Times*, p. 16.
27. Bucklin, L. P. (1990). *The Gray Market Threat to International Marketing Strategies*. Marketing Science Institute Working Paper Series. Report, Vol. 90/116. Cambridge: The Marketing Science Institute.
28. Xiao, Y., Palekar, U., Liu, Y. (2011). Shades of Gray – the Impact of Gray Markets on Authorized Distribution Channels. *Quantitative Marketing & Economics*, 9(2), 155–178.
29. Bundesamt für Verbraucherschutz und Lebensmittelsicherheit (2015). Grenzüberschreitender Handel. http://www.bvl.bund.de/DE/01_Lebensmittel/01_Aufgaben/05_GrenzueberschreitenderHandel/lm_grenzueberschrHandel_node.html. Accessed 26 February 2015.
30. Backhaus, K., & Voeth, M. (2010). *Internationales Marketing*. Stuttgart: Schäffer-Poeschel.
31. Cavusgil, S. T. (1996). Pricing for Global Markets. *The Columbia Journal of World Business*, 31(4), 66–78.

Implementation

9

Abstract

In the previous chapters, we have dealt with price strategy, analysis, and decision-making. But the mission is not accomplished. Price decisions need to be implemented, and this in turn requires that processes and responsibilities are clearly defined. In the first part of this chapter, we will examine questions regarding setup and process organization in price management. This will include a discussion of the CEO's tasks as well as the use of pricing software artificial intelligence and price consultants. The salesperson is central to successful price implementation. What pricing authority should salespeople have? How should a company set up its incentive systems, in order to achieve the desired objectives? Discounts, terms, and conditions likewise play a critical role. The effect of prices depends on the manner in which they are communicated. The topic of price communication therefore warrants a thorough treatment. The conclusion of the chapter will look at price monitoring and controlling. Ideally, this aspect should not be confined to price realization but include the overall pricing process. Throughout the chapter we will use real-life case studies from various industries to illustrate the respective topics.

9.1 Introduction

In the previous chapters, we have shown how optimal prices are determined. But we have not addressed aspects such as who makes the price decisions, how prices are communicated, how the salesforce implements the prices at the customer, or how the actual pricing behavior within the company is monitored.

In the last several years, we have observed that the awareness for implementation has grown significantly. As a result, price management is experiencing more attention at the highest leadership levels. In particular, we have observed that CEO's are becoming more involved in the pricing process. The ultimate contribution of price

© Springer Nature Switzerland AG 2019
H. Simon, M. Fassnacht, *Price Management*,
https://doi.org/10.1007/978-3-319-99456-7_9

management to a company's results depends at least as much on effective implementation as it does on the professionalism in the preceding phases of price strategy, analysis, and decision-making. The saying that "you can come up with the best strategy but implementation is 90 percent of it" also applies to price management.

This chapter will look at the following areas:

- Responsibilities
- Sales/salesforce
- Price communication
- Price controlling

9.2   Responsibilities in Price Management

Asking questions such as who sets prices or who ultimately makes the decisions on prices can trigger embarrassed looks within most companies. In many companies, who takes which price decision, who has the last word, or who has the responsibility over that decisive profit driver "price" is neither clearly defined nor managed. The literature is also reserved regarding this topic. Freiling and Wölting [1, p. 420] remark that: "We find only sporadic references to the need for the organization of price management." The works of Dutta et al. [2] as well as Wiltinger [3] look more deeply into this issue but are exceptions. When one considers the professional organization of all phases of the price management process as a capability which can generate competitive advantages (in the sense of a resource-based approach), it is astounding that the control and management of pricing responsibilities does not receive more attention [4].

Fundamentally speaking, the operational and organizational guidelines are there to ensure that the tasks which constitute the price management process are implemented efficiently and systematically on a recurring basis. Price decisions have to be made by clearly designated and defined leaders or team members. These decisions require a very wide range of information, which the respective responsible departments must provide.

The organizational structure defines and delegates the tasks and authority to employees and departments, demarcates the individual organizational units, and establishes how the departments interact with each other. The allocation of tasks should orient itself on the phases of the price management process. The process point of view takes into account the idea that the objective is not the isolated optimization of prices, but rather a value creation process which comprises planning, implementation, and monitoring of all activities related to price. The goal of the organizational structure must be the greatest possible integration of pricing authority while at the same time delegating the necessary decision-making latitude to employees or departments (e.g., foreign subsidiaries, sales force, etc.) which have direct contact with customers. The *delegation of price decision authority* effects a division of the price management process and the incorporation of several departments. The resulting problems need to be managed through clear rules of authority and if necessary through the creation of a coordinating function of a price manager or a pricing department.

9.2.1 Definition of the Tasks

The variety of tasks which price management must master is best illustrated from the process perspective. Figure 9.1 provides an overview of the four phases: strategy, analysis, decision-making, and implementation.

From the perspective of the object to be priced, the tasks listed in the figure can be broken down and expanded further, covering new product pricing, price mainte-nance for existing products, leasing prices, and prices for service contracts, replace-ment parts, etc. The price communication differentiates itself further into management of price lists, the handling of price requests, and price presentation in the context of advertising or point of sale. For all of these and many other tasks, the responsibilities must be clearly defined.

Figure 9.1 shows a generic price management process, i.e., the tasks listed come up in most businesses roughly in this form. But that is not sufficient for a specific case. Our experience shows that price management processes differ considerably by industry and can even be unique to a specific company. The generic perspective provides only a starting point for the deeper and more refined definition of tasks and roles. We illustrate this in Fig. 9.2 with a detailed price management process for a hotel chain.

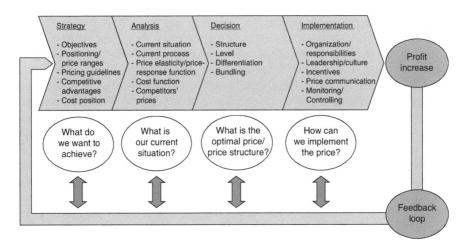

Fig. 9.1 Tasks in the price management process

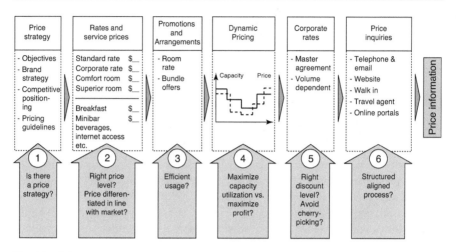

Fig. 9.2 Price management process for a hotel chain

In this case there are six basic sets of tasks which are typical for the hotel industry. Promotions (e.g., for weekends or holidays) play a significant role. The differentiation between business and private/leisure customers also exerts a strong influence on capacity utilization and profit. The manner in which prices are communicated and price requests are handled warrants high attention in the hotel industry. Generally speaking, booking systems such as booking.com or hrs.com require that particularly attractive prices are displayed on their sites. A deep immersion in the specific characteristics and nuances of a business is necessary in order to properly understand price management processes and to direct organizational measures accordingly. We expressly warn against a standardized, superficial treatment of this organizational issue.

Often, employees and departments are not even aware of the issue of clear *roles and responsibilities*, as the following case demonstrates. At a large software company, Mr. Smith (name anonymized), an employee at the third hierarchical level in the organization, was responsible for managing the company's complex price lists. Yet when we questioned the CEO, he told us that Mr. Smith had an administrative role and not a management role with decision-making authority. Then we asked the sales manager in the company's largest overseas market how prices are set. He explained to us that he could decide up to a certain level on discounts and special terms and conditions. Anything beyond that level of authority had to be approved by headquarters. Yet when we asked him who he contacts at headquarters for approval, his answer was Mr. Smith. Over three quarters of the company's business in this market was transacted under special terms and conditions which Mr. Smith had decided or approved. No one in the upper management was aware that this practice had been going on for many years.

9.2.2 Allocation of Price Decision Authority

Empirical findings on the allocation of price decision authority are sparse. Fassnacht et al. [5] have explored how consumer goods manufacturers organize their price management. The authors focused in particular on the question of the final level of price decision authority. They distinguished between *list prices, discounts,* and *price promotions* [5, p. 69, 6, p. 180]. In addition, Nelius [6] examined the roles different functions play in pricing. Table 9.1 shows the results of these studies for different major hierarchical levels.

The study confirmed that for consumer goods manufacturers, price decision authority and the participation in the price decisions are allocated primarily to senior management, with additional and significant participation of the market-facing functions of sales, marketing, and key account management. In most cases (73% of the companies), the final *price decision authority* rested with senior management, at least with respect to list prices. But for short-term pricing activities, the balance of authority shifts significantly in favor of marketing and sales. Senior management had final price decision authority in 52% of cases involving discounts. The picture was similar for price promotions, where senior management made final decisions in 43% of the companies. This stands in sharp contrast to the influence of the sales leadership, whose opportunities and latitude for decision-making significantly increase when the decisions are short-term, e.g., discounts and promotions. In 39% of cases, the sales leadership makes the final decision on price promotions. Although their final price decision authority is rather low, sales leadership is nonetheless involved in price decisions 81% of the time. These findings show a considerable discrepancy in the role of finance and controlling. People from finance and controlling take part in the price management process in half of all cases and exert a significant influence on price decisions but hold the ultimate price decision authority on list prices and discounts in only 1% of cases. Atkin and Skinner [7] came to a similar conclusion in their study of the final price decision authority in British industrial firms. Nelius [6] found that key account management participates in the price management process in 45% of cases. But key account managers rarely have price decision authority.

Table 9.1 Allocation of price decision authority [5, 6]

	"Final price decision authority"			
Function	List prices	Discounts	Price promotions	"Participation in the price decision"[a]
Senior management	73%	52%	43%	89%
Finance/controlling managers	1%	1%	<1%	50%
Marketing leadership	5%	3%	9%	66%
Sales leadership	15%	34%	39%	81%
Key account management leadership	<1%	5%	4%	45%

[a]Multiple responses possible

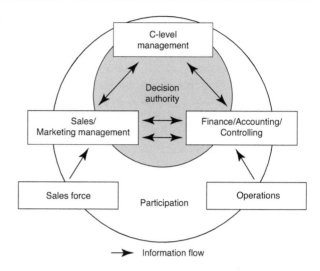

Fig. 9.3 Decision authority and participation in price decisions

The cooperation among market-oriented departments and internal functions such as production, controlling, finance, and accounting is critical for successful price management. Figure 9.3 shows these interconnections. The necessity for both sides to participate results from the fact that the determinants of the optimal price come from the cost side as well as the market side. In the figure, the arrows show the information flows.

The precise point in the hierarchy where both sides come together to arrive at the final price decision differs from company to company, as the studies we cited have shown. In general, the price decision authority should be at a higher level of the hierarchy:

• The more important a particular product is to the company.
• The better senior managers are informed about products and markets.
• The more homogeneous and less dynamic the markets are.
• The more critical the coordination of prices is in different segments.
• The less the culture and the behavior of lower hierarchical levels are focused on the overall goals of the company.
• The more important clear and consistent signals to competitors and customers are.

While the market-facing side looks more intensively at aspects such as increasing value-to-customer, the implementability of prices, and the price reaction of competitors, the margin- and cost-related information flows in from the finance side. Typically, the finance side favors higher prices than the market side. These opposing views should be used consciously and constructively for pricing rather than being viewed as a conflict.

In many multinational companies, the allocation of price decision authority between the *central* and *decentral units*, for instance, between headquarters and the foreign operating units, is a constant point of contention. Headquarters is interested in a certain level of control and coordination of pricing behavior; the subsidiaries want as much pricing latitude as possible. They justify this on the basis of their profit-and-loss responsibility and the local market characteristics, which can vary considerably by country or region. There is no simple solution for this problem. Depending on the situation (e.g., exchange rate fluctuations), the headquarters can and must assume greater pricing authority, or conversely it can grant greater authority to the local operating units. The problem is structurally similar to the delegation of pricing authority to the salesforce, which we will discuss below.

We will use three brief case studies to illustrate this problem.

In a logistics company which is active in more than 150 countries, the country managers held the price decision authority. An analysis revealed that the prices were "abused" primarily to manage volume and capacity utilization. We observed a strong tendency to use aggressive pricing practices to achieve the highest possible capacity utilization. As a result, there were extreme price differences both within and across countries. This behavior made a large share of deals unprofitable and threatened the company with a collapse of prices due to greater price transparency among global key accounts. The solution called for a centrally managed system of prices and discounts. This did not entail a complete harmonization of country-level prices. Rather, it ensured that prices were set using the same criteria. The firm also introduced centralized price monitoring, which led to the elimination of numerous loss-making deals. The company's return on sales increased by 1.5% points after these measures took hold.

For a mobile communications equipment manufacturer, offers and prices were worked out at the country level. Global customers became more important and compared prices across countries. This led to massive problems and made price concessions necessary in high-price countries. The solution involved establishing a central price department, which needed to review all offers for consistency and then decided whether to approve them. This procedure imposed constraints on the price decision authority of the individual countries, but it eliminated the inconsistencies and severe margin declines at internationally active key accounts.

The third case is about a supplier in a very fragmented industrial market. The company's divisions, located at headquarters, traditionally had the responsibility for pricing. The local operating units in each country had very limited room to offer discounts and had no further pricing authority. An analysis revealed extreme differences in the markets and competitive situations across countries. The managers at headquarters were too far away from the local circumstances to set optimal prices and to understand competitive reactions. The solution reallocated pricing authority to the local operating units. Headquarters limited its price setting to internal ex works or transfer prices. The change resulted in fundamentally sharper international price differentiation and had very positive effects on profit and on market share. Headquarters would only intervene when profits were too low or when parallel imports occurred.

These brief case studies show that the allocation of price decision authority between central and decentral units must be determined and managed on a case-by-case basis. We do, however, notice a trend toward greater centralization of price management. In the Global Pricing Study conducted by Simon-Kucher & Partners [8], some 39% of the 2713 respondents said that their price decisions had become more centralized in recent years, while only 11% reported greater decentralization.

9.2.3 Price-Related Organization

The increasing importance of price management has given rise to organizational structures designed with this function in mind. These structures include price managers and pricing departments. Some companies also practice Six Sigma pricing to eliminate deficiencies in their price management processes. In this context, we also discuss whether a company should deploy pricing software including artificial intelligence or use the services of price consultants.

9.2.3.1 The Price Manager

One answer to the coordination requirements we have described is the appointment of a *price or pricing manager*. This trend began in the United States in the 1990s. Today many companies all over the world have specialized price managers. On the website indeed.com in the United States, there were 71,090 job openings for pricing managers, while in Germany there were 782 postings. The more than 5000 members of the Professional Pricing Society, which offers seminars and conferences around the world, are primarily such price managers.

The job descriptions for price managers are not uniform; they vary from case to case. The advertisement in Fig. 9.4 shows what companies are typically looking for.

This job description lists the most important tasks of a typical price manager. Whether and to what extent the position offers the manager real price decision authority depends on factors such as the hierarchical level of the position. General Electric (GE) was a pioneer in placing the role of price managers at a high level in the organization. GE's role model led to similar initiatives at many other companies. This trend was accelerated by the professionalization of procurement on the customer side, which in turn requires correspondingly better price management skills on the seller's side.

9.2.3.2 The Pricing Department

For companies with large assortments (e.g., home improvement stores) and/or the need for frequent price decisions, the creation of a special *pricing department* is advisable. We see such departments today in telecommunication, pharmaceutical, automotive, and electronics companies as well as in retailers. The complex methods for price analysis and price setting which we describe in this book demand a high degree of know-how and a solid information base. These roles can only be filled by specialists. In the Global Pricing Study from Simon-Kucher & Partners [8], some 58% of respondents reported that their companies have a dedicated pricing function. The highest percentage was in the United States with 79%, while Germany was about average with 57%. The market-facing side is typically the bottleneck when a company sets up a price department. Employees who have mastered the full

Pricing Manager

Job Summary

The Pricing Manager will be in charge of pricing analysis, margin improvement across all customers, and the provision of actionable analysis of customer performance data. Furthermore, this position will be hold responsibilities of reporting, recommendation, and implementation for all products across our markets and be a part of the Product Marketing & Business Management team. We are looking for a high potential Manager with strong analytical skills, a deep interest in our products, business and strategy, solid communication skills, a leader mentality with an ability to build high-performance teams, and a powerful executive presence. The Pricing Manager collaborates with various groups and carries a very high level of exposure.

Key Qualifications

- 5 - 7 years of related experience in reviewing and building new pricing policies
- Excellent analytical skills and ability to identify and articulate the best course of action from the data
- Excellent communication skills - able to work at all levels within the business
- Exceptional problem solving skills, combined with statistical skills
- Passion for the ability to build and manage processes
- Strong direct and indirect influencing/leadership skills

Description

- Develop pricing strategies
- Formulate, present, and implement pricing proposals for various products and services taking into account volume and margin interdependencies and market conditions
- Partner with various teams to provide pricing analyses and recommendations
- Build a tactical framework, get internal alignment that may require coaching high-level stakeholders and develop a negotiation strategy, train customer facing sales/commercial personnel
- Collaborate very closely with Pricing Operations to ensure flawless and secure implementation of all required pricing actions
- Be an active participant in the Business Management team and handle special projects and requests
- Create and maintain a robust pricing analysis and reporting infrastructure

Education

Bachelor's degree or MBA in Finance, Engineering, or a related field

Fig. 9.4 Job advertisement for a price manager

spectrum of methods needed for pricing and who at the same time have sufficient market knowledge are rare and seldom to be found already within the company. The best but often the most time-consuming way to build up such a department is to hire people with advanced degrees in relevant fields. Another approach is to hire former consultants. Finding the right personnel on the controlling or cost side is generally less difficult. One problem is the continuity and retention of know-how. We have often observed that qualified and ambitious employees will only want to work in the pricing department for a limited time, in order to move on to the next step in their careers. Beyond the need for the right personnel, the availability of an information and software infrastructure is an indispensable prerequisite for a price department. This prerequisite should not be thought of in isolation, though. Having such an infrastructure would normally be part of any comprehensive information system on markets and competitors.

9.2.3.3 Six Sigma Pricing

Six Sigma is a process originally developed by Motorola and General Electric to minimize mistakes or deficiencies in manufacturing processes. It is an effective method to improve efficiency and quality. It was inevitable that Six Sigma would also be applied to price management [9]. The objective is to eliminate deficiencies in price management and their root causes, especially regarding implementation [10]. Such root causes or sources of failure include wrong decision rules, non-compliance with discount guidelines, exceeding the bounds of one's price decision authority, or using inadequate or outdated information. The opportunities for process failure are numerous. The ideal Six Sigma process encompasses five steps: define, measure, analyze, improve, and control, summarized in the acronym DMAIC. The goal is to eliminate all sources of process failure. Specially trained personnel known as Black Belts play a central role in implementing the Six Sigma process. We illustrate these steps using an example from a project conducted by Simon-Kucher & Partners.

Zalaxy Corporation (name anonymized) ranked as a US Fortune 500 company and generated around $7 billion in annual revenues across nine divisions. The pretax return on sales was 8.4%. The company had achieved continuous growth over decades in markets which had become very dynamic as well as technology-intensive and highly competitive. For the previous 5 years, Zalaxy had applied Six Sigma in its manufacturing processes and had assembled an internal team of more than 100 Black Belts. The company now wanted to apply its deep Six Sigma know-how to pricing processes.

The method was tested as a pilot project in the industrial components division, which had $1.25 billion in revenue. The reorganization of the pricing process according to Six Sigma led to a revenue increase of $75 million and an additional profit of $25 million, which represented an increase in return on sales of 2% points. Based on this result, the company assigned 18 Black Belts (on average, two per division) for one full year as part of a "Six Sigma Pricing" project. These 18 Black Belts devoted an entire year exclusively to the improvement of pricing processes. The Black Belts first attended a 1-week seminar on price management, after which they spent 3 months in their respective divisions diagnosing existing pricing practices, the three ensuing months developing solutions, and the next 6 months implementing them. Zalaxy's operating profit ultimately rose by $140 million, translating into an improvement of 2% points in return on sales. The improvements took hold within 2 years after the start of the Six Sigma Pricing process.

Though it was originally conceived for manufacturing processes, the application of Six Sigma holds considerable promise for price management. But there are limits to how well Six Sigma transfers to price processes. One constraint is information. In contrast to manufacturing processes, the range and quality of available information regarding pricing processes are limited or inexact (e.g., the true willingness to pay of customers, the content of competitive offers, and the behavior of intermediaries). Pricing questions from the external sales team are often addressed under heavy time pressure, without adequate time for a thorough validation of the answer. It is likewise difficult for an internal pricing department to cross-check the information it receives from sales representatives, who may consciously distort reality. In many cases, salespeople make price commitments to customers and then ask for approval after the fact. The Six Sigma process is not a panacea for all pricing problems, but it can lead to fundamental improvements in price discipline as well as the avoidance of major missteps.

9.2.3.4 Price Consultants

In light of the ever-increasing specialization, it is legitimate to ask to what extent price analyses should be conducted internally or commissioned to external specialists. For many companies, it does not make financial sense to keep personnel with the corresponding know-how on staff and busy on a full-time basis. One should keep in mind that in many companies, only important price decisions justify an investment in extensive analyses. Typical cases are the introduction of new products, a strategic repositioning, significant cost changes, or serious competitive reactions. Such analyses are more strategic in nature than routine market research and often warrant the use of external consultants. Having the entire spectrum of pricing methods in-house makes sense only for companies which have large assortments whose prices require frequent review or examination. In all other cases, companies should bring in specialized service providers when complex analyses are required.

Nowadays, there are specialized firms which offer price consulting but with considerable differences in competencies. Atkin and Skinner [7] determined in 1976 that external consultants should not be used for price decisions. One of the authors of this book experienced for the first time in 1979 that an individual called himself a "price consultant." The development of price consulting since that time is described in detail in an article we refer to [11].

We estimate that worldwide there are around 2000 consulting firms which specialize in pricing. The vast majority of these is made up of individuals and small firms. Assuming an average number of employees of five and average revenue per employee of $200,000, the global market for price consulting services totals around $2.1 billion, which represents a tripling of revenue over the last 10 years. The market is likely to continue to grow. The world market leader in price consulting is

Table 9.2 Example of a price management workshop

9:00–9:30 a.m.	Introduction of the participants Collection of the goals and expectations of the participants
9:30–10:45 a.m.	Pricing levers of the company • Discussion of the profit drivers and the effects of price changes • Prices and customer responses • Price and competition • In-depth analysis for a selected product
10:45–11:00 a.m.	Coffee break
11:00 a.m.– 12:30 p.m.	Price differentiation and innovative pricing methods: every customer gets its own price • Goals of price differentiation • Segmentation: concept and solutions • New price differentiation approaches for the company
12:30–1:30 p.m.	Lunch
1:30–2:30 p.m.	Ways to the right price • Information necessary for determining optimal prices • Price decision rules and guidelines • Computer-aided pricing
2:30–3:30 p.m.	Price decisions and implementation • Price stakeholders, goals, and conflict potential • Centralized and decentralized price decision authority • Implementation of prices in the marketplace • Organization of pricing activities
3:30–3:45 p.m.	Coffee break
3:45–4:30 p.m.	Optimizing discount policies, terms, and conditions
4:30–5:00 p.m.	Summary of results and creation of to-do lists

Simon-Kucher & Partners. With revenue of $300 million in 2017, its global market share is about 15%.

The services of price consultants range from brief workshops to projects lasting many months. Table 9.2 shows the program for a 1-day price management workshop for a company in the building materials industry. Preparation for this workshop included internal price analyses and a short customer survey. It also included five discussions with managers and sales representatives on the themes to be covered in the workshop. The goal was to familiarize the 15 workshop participants with the methods of modern pricing and draft specific to-do lists.

Consulting projects in price management can last many months. Figure 9.5 shows the schedule for a price consulting project for a private bank.

This project addressed all aspects of price management, from an analysis of the current situation to the development of a controlling system, and had a duration of 10 months. The work included an extensive customer survey.

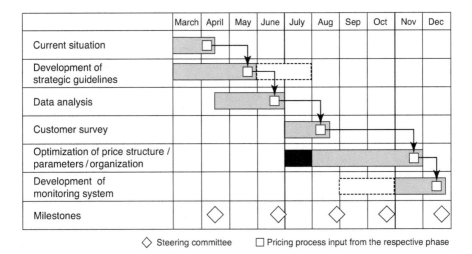

	March	April	May	June	July	Aug	Sep	Oct	Nov	Dec
Current situation										
Development of strategic guidelines										
Data analysis										
Customer survey										
Optimization of price structure / parameters / organization										
Development of monitoring system										
Milestones										

◇ Steering committee   ☐ Pricing process input from the respective phase

Fig. 9.5 Schedule for a price consulting project

9.2.3.5 Pricing Software

Because of the high complexity and the underlying processes, most companies use individually developed solutions for operational price management. Nonetheless, a range of standard pricing software packages have come onto the market since the 1980s. Over the last 10 years, software specialists have emerged to serve individual industries. Most of these software suppliers come from the United States.

The market breaks down into solutions for price optimization and management (POM) and solutions for "configure, price, quote" (CPQ). POM solutions offer functionality for analyzing prices, setting prices, and implementing discount and terms/conditions systems. They are used primarily in companies which need to make frequent price decisions, have large assortments, or have a large number of customers. CPQ solutions are used in sales to automate the process of generating and pricing complex offers, such as offers comprising a large number of diverse line items.

The market for pricing software is highly fragmented and lacks the formal standardization one sees in ERP or CRM solutions. Important vendors of POM solutions include PROS, Vendavo, and Zilliant. There are also several suppliers such as Navetti, Syncron, and Servigistics, which focus on aftermarket business. The market for CPQ solutions is even more fragmented. In addition to the large ERP suppliers such as SAP and Oracle, the market also includes notable vendors such as BigMachines and IBM Sterling.

One sector the POM vendors do not cover is retail, where competition-oriented pricing and the implementation and evaluation of price promotions are at the forefront. In that sector there are instead a range of specialists such as ProfitLogic, KSS Retail, Upstream Commerce, or Boomerang Commerce, which offer solutions for online retailers. Banking is similar, with specialized suppliers such as Nomis and Earnix.

Some of the POM vendors got their start with yield management software for airlines. One example is the US-based firm PROS, founded in 1985. Yield management is still one of the cornerstones of PROS, which has extended its systems to hotels, tourism, car rental, and similar sectors. Within these sectors, there are likewise focused specialists. Sabre Airline Solutions plays an important role for airlines, as do the internal IT departments of the respective airlines. IDeaS and Easy RMS focus on hotels. These firms work with methods drawn from operations research and management science. They are method- and technology-driven and also protect their software components with patents. PROS alone has 9 US patents and another 27 patents pending [12].

An important aspect of standard solutions is the integration with the comprehensive ERP systems from SAP or Oracle. There is a marketing partnership, for example, between SAP and the pricing software vendor Vendavo. Recently one has also observed integration into customer relationship management (CRM) systems such as Salesforce or Microsoft Dynamics CRM. This applies in particular to CPQ solutions which the sales force can use directly.

9.2.3.6 Machine Learning in Pricing

Artificial intelligence (AI) always generates considerable media excitement. The fundamental idea behind AI is simply to develop systems that automate analysis and decision-making processes normally carried out by human experts. One way to achieve this is through machine learning (ML), a set of algorithms that "learns" by itself, acquiring expert knowledge based on observed data, particularly historical data.

Machine learning has been studied academically and applied in business for quite some time. Amazon's well-established recommendation engines are a classic example. Systems for up- and cross-selling no longer need to be continually reprogrammed by an expert; they update themselves by analyzing consumer behavior. The list of potential areas of application in pricing, marketing, and sales is impressive. An ML algorithm could be used to automate lead scoring, calculate price elasticity, predict customer choice, estimate willingness to pay, recommend a discount, predict churn rates, assess the win likelihood for a deal at a certain price, and identify the best targets for a promotion, to name just a few.

While this sounds promising at first glance, companies must keep four major pitfalls in mind as they consider using ML:

- *Applicability*: Not all problems can be solved with machine learning. Machines can help solve problems that involve predicting a target variable, identifying patterns, classifying data items, or finding relationships. However, if the information that the machine needs to reach its conclusion cannot be observed in the data, ML will not provide any meaningful output. This pitfall is analogous to the use of econometric methods when the underlying situation has changed.

- *Expertise*: Even though more and more ready-to-use software packages and cloud services are appearing on the market, it still takes a data scientist to draw the best insights out of the vast amount of data a company collects. In addition to data aggregation, outlier detection, and data cleansing, human experts offer another vital capability called "feature engineering." That is the application of domain knowledge to recombine or reinterpret the variables to be used in training the machine. Small variations in how features are interpreted and fed into the machine can have large effects on the predictive value of a model.
- *Data availability*: In order to train an ML algorithm, the necessary data has to be available. Pricing-related problems usually require observations at a transactional level. For more specific problems, there is often a need for additional information which is not necessarily collected by default. For example, how can a company build a win/loss prediction model in B2B if it does not have any information on the price at which orders are lost? Furthermore, ML is often applied based on historical data, which presents two inherent problems. First, the trained model may only end up repeating past mistakes. Second, one cannot account for factors that make sense from a strategy perspective, but currently do not exist in the data. In practice, one would apply additional rules and guardrails to tweak the model to produce the desired outcome.
- *Long-term effects of automated price setting*: This is hard to assess. Will an immediate margin increase that exploits customers' willingness to pay lead to a reduction in customer loyalty or negatively affect the price image over the long run? Will salespeople accept discounts recommended by a machine? How will customers respond to frequent price changes in markets where they are accustomed to stable prices? To avoid negative side effects and long-term repercussions, it is important to test the system thoroughly, to establish a clear monitoring system that looks beyond the one or two core KPIs optimized by the system, to allow for manual intervention, and to deploy automatic price safeguards (e.g., price change limits) to prevent the machine from making pricing decisions that may cause long-term harm.

Many pricing software vendors offer machine learning as part of their solutions. We distinguish between two types of ML vendors. The first type offers dynamic pricing and promotion solutions based on machine learning. They often have an industry focus, such as retail, e-commerce, or yield management. Some examples are Boomerang Commerce, Blue Yonder, Smart Pricer, and Perfect Price. These firms provide data science services and create customized machine-learning models. The second type of vendor targets B2B industries by providing machine learning to calculate deal-specific price recommendations for sales teams. Examples include Zilliant, PROS, and Price f(X).

We observe varying degrees of transparency with regard to the algorithms and the quality of the predictions the machines make. A company could, of course, create a machine-learning model customized to its own pricing model. This grants the company more control and transparency, but its implementation requires significantly more expertise and effort.

9.2.4 The Role of the CEO

The primary task of the CEO is to maintain and increase shareholder value, an objective which is essentially synonymous with long-term profit maximization. Price is an enormously effective driver of shareholder value (see Chap. 2). It follows that responsibility for prices and their realization lies with the highest levels of management, and ultimately with the CEO. Of course it is obvious that the head of a large company cannot make the decision on every price; some companies have hundreds of thousands of prices. Likewise, the CEO cannot sign off on each and every price negotiation, never mind take part in it. What is the right role for the CEO in the context of price management?

The following points are the tasks of the CEO; this list is not exhaustive [13]:

- Generating awareness for the importance of price
- Setting clear goals
- Establishing strategy and price positioning
- Organizing a systematic pricing process
- Creating a culture which prevents price wars
- Establishing price leadership (if possible)
- Creating price discipline
- Using price in investor relations

In recent years we have seen a strong increase in both the interest and the involvement of CEOs in price management issues [14]. In the Global Pricing Study of Simon-Kucher & Partners [8], some 82% of respondents said that the participation of top management in pricing matters has increased in recent years. This percentage varied only slightly by country and industry. The key point, however, is that companies with CEO involvement in price management achieve an average operating EBITDA return of 15%, versus only 11% for companies which lack such CEO involvement. The pricing power and the success rate of price increases are also higher. Table 9.3 summarizes the findings.

One can say across the board that the involvement of the CEO in price management leads to better operational and financial results.

A pioneer in this area was Jack Welch, who served as CEO of General Electric from 1982 until 2001. He introduced a high-ranking price management role, the so-called Chief Pricing Officer. His successor, Jeffrey Immelt, continued that initiative. He told one of the authors that price discipline had increased significantly. The achievement of the predetermined price targets worked out better than before. The

Table 9.3 CEO involvement and results

Key indicator	With CEO involvement	Without CEO involvement
EBITDA return	15%	11%
High pricing power	35%	26%
Success rate for price increases	60%	53%

Chief Pricing Officers also took on a teaching and training role, which led to GE's salespeople being more thoroughly prepared for price negotiations. All in all, this pricing initiative exceeded expectations.

The statement of investor Warren Buffett—that "the single most important decision in evaluating a business is pricing power"—has directed the attention of investors and CEOs increasingly to the topic of price.[1] The former CEO of Microsoft, Steve Ballmer, echoed this sentiment when he said: "This thing called 'price' is really, really important. I still think that a lot of people underthink it through. You have a lot of companies that start and the only difference between the ones that succeed and fail is that one figured out how to make money, because they were deep in thinking through the revenue, price, and business model. I think that's underattended to generally." [15]

As part of this development, CEOs are speaking more frequently about the price management of their companies. The occasions include interviews, roadshows, trade fairs, and annual shareholder meetings. Likewise we have witnessed that top managers are expressing an increased interest in price-related consulting projects. Consistent leadership regarding price realization and the creation of the corresponding culture are among the tasks which a CEO cannot delegate. We bring this point to light through a range of quotes from top managers on the specific tasks and topics we mentioned above. The executives behind these selected all share one characteristic: they lead or led companies with a high market capitalization.

On goals, positioning, market share, and avoiding aggression:

- Norbert Reithofer, CEO of BMW from 2006 to 2015: "At no time are high discounts compatible with 'premium'. They are neither good for the brand nor good for the business. We have therefore decided to not defend our market share in Germany at any price. Profit comes before volume."
- Wendelin Wiedeking, CEO of Porsche from 1992 to 2009: "We have a policy of keeping prices stable to protect our brand and to prevent a drop in prices for used cars. When demand goes down, we reduce production volume but don't lower our prices." This remark is aligned with Porsche's strategy, positioning, and brand policies and provides the entire organization with clear guiding principles for price management. Porsche has firmly punished violations of these principles by dismissing the responsible managers (e.g., in the US market).
- Elon Musk, CEO of Tesla: "It is absolutely vital that we adhere to the no-negotiation and no-discount policy that has been true since we first started taking orders 10 years ago. This is fundamental to our integrity" [16].
- Soren Skou, CEO of Maersk Line (world market leader in container shipping): "We changed from 'growing more than the market' to 'growing with the market'. We hope that our competitors are content with this goal."

---

[1]From the transcript of an interview with Warren Buffett before the Financial Crisis Inquiry Commission (FCIC) on May 26, 2010

- The following citation expresses a desire to calm the market and create a more peaceful competitive atmosphere: "Toyota Chairman Hiroshi Okuda told reporters that Japan's auto industry needed to give Detroit 'time and room to catch a breath'. He even suggested Toyota might raise prices on cars sold in the US to ease competitive pressures on General Motors Corp. and Ford Motor Co., both of which have disclosed declining financial performance and market share recently. Some car-industry officials in Tokyo saw Mr. Okuda's comments as the latest in a long series of pre-emptive moves to keep tensions low" [17].

On price leadership:

- Johan Molin, CEO of Assa Abloy (world market leader in lock systems): "We are by far the market leader and a market leader's role is to help prices upwards" [18].

On pricing process and pricing discipline:

- Albert Baehny, former CEO (2005–2014) and current chairman of Geberit, the world market leader in sanitary technology: "Wherever there is active price management, a clearly defined pricing process, explicit rules of price determination, and well-defined responsibilities for price implementation and price controlling, margins may be increased significantly and sustainably. When pricing is delegated or—if worse comes to worst—left to the market, you will never get beyond mediocrity" [19].
- Jeffrey Immelt, CEO of General Electric from 2001 to 2017: "We're getting the sales force better trained and equipped with better tools and metrics. A good example is what we're doing to create discipline around pricing. Not long ago, an analysis of our pricing found out that about $5 billion of it is discretionary. Given all the decisions that sales reps can make on their own, that's how much is in play. It was the most astounding number I'd ever heard. We would never allow something like that on the cost side. When it comes to the prices we pay, we study them, we map them, we work on them. But with the prices we charge, we're too sloppy" [20].

We warn, however, against too much intervention by the CEO in concrete price decisions and the ongoing pricing process. In practice, it is not unusual to find examples where the CEO's behavior goes far beyond what we recommend, with negative consequences. Some case examples illustrate this. The CEO of a large logistics service provider made a habit of visiting the CEOs of his company's key accounts. These CEOs regularly brought up the topic of price and managed to extract additional price concessions from the logistic company's CEO. These meetings undermined the month-long efforts of his sales teams. Once the CEO stopped making these goodwill visits, his company's margins improved noticeably. In general, we find it advisable to keep the CEO and other senior managers out of *price negotiations.*

The CEO of a well-known car company once told us about a large discrepancy between the company's official objective of *achieving profit* and the company's actual behavior. The senior managers in that company would often emphasize the importance of profit. But when push came to shove, volume and market share goals always became priorities, resulting in price concessions which hurt the company's margins.

A large Japanese electronics group had achieved subpar margins for many years. In a meeting with senior managers in the company's Tokyo headquarters, there was unanimous agreement that the company needed to boost margins to satisfactory levels and charge higher prices to capitalize on the group's brand premium. Then the group's global chief marketing officer commented "if we do that, we will lose market share." The discussion immediately ground to a halt. Losing market share was taboo in this Japanese company, and any strategies or tactics which would lead to such a result were therefore out of the question. After posting losses in several subsequent years, the company's new CEO finally announced that from now on the firm will focus on "high value-added business instead of expansion of market share."

At the beginning of a project for a large European bank, the CEO told us that "we need a massive improvement in profits. So we are getting to work on optimizing our prices, but under one condition: we cannot lose any customers, not a single one. If something about losing customers appears in the newspapers, I will be in trouble with the board." It is clear amid such signals from the top of the organization that an optimal pricing strategy, which may in fact require some loss of unprofitable customers, is very hard to achieve. Admittedly, we can appreciate the CEO's dilemma to some degree. The real problem in this case lies with the board.

It is extremely important that senior managers act consistently with respect to pricing and refrain from sending conflicting signals to their employees. The specific goals may vary by region or market segment, but the goals must still be communicated not only clearly and consistently but also sustainably. Key to that last point is the alignment between price management and corporate culture. The term corporate culture refers to a company's value and goal systems, which employees see as their obligation to fulfill. Diller [21, p. 455] extends this concept and speaks of "price culture." The awareness of price-related values, goals, and priorities must be anchored deeply in the minds of employees; otherwise, contradictory behaviors will arise again and again. A premium or luxury price positioning is built on a different foundation of values and competencies than a low-price or ultra-low-price positioning. Management needs to live out the corresponding priorities and communicate them internally on a continual basis, so that they can take root in the organization.

An important task of the CEO and the Chief Financial Officer (CFO) is investor communication, which takes place in roadshows, regular reports, conference calls, and at the company's annual shareholder meeting. Price traditionally plays hardly any role in this context, which contradicts its importance as a driver of share price and enterprise value. The same holds true for analyst reports. The quote from Warren

Buffett which we cited above appears to have set a new orientation in motion. Nowadays, price is receiving more prominence in senior managers' communication with investors and analysts [22].

An important aspect which warrants attention in the context of leadership is the *pricing intelligence* of the organization. This refers to the knowledge level of each person involved in the pricing process: how well do they understand pricing-related interrelationships and to what extent have they mastered pricing methods? We often observe that price intelligence is low. Training and educational efforts are mostly limited to basic calculation methods and *price negotiation tactics*. A massive increase in price-related training and education is urgently needed in many companies.

9.3   The Role of the Sales Force

The sales force plays a central role in the implementation of prices [23]. In this section, we will use the terms sales, sales team, salespeople, sales force, and external sales interchangeably. In many companies, the act of selling takes place at the customer's location, which gives rise to the term "external" sales force. At the same time, many companies have an internal sales force or "inside sales," which is often involved in completing transactions and likewise exerts some influence on price implementation.

Selling through an external sales force is highly popular among B2B companies, whose prices are almost always subject to negotiation. While list prices are set by internal departments, the ultimate transaction price (the one which is relevant for profit) is the outcome of the sales process. List prices and transaction prices often deviate significantly. The resulting divergence between the ideal prices and the actual ones is often attributed to general price declines in the market, but the true underlying cause is sometimes a weak-performing sales force [3].

The *implementation* of list prices can fail for two reasons: first, salespeople use their price decision authority in their own interests rather than those of the company, because they have different objectives. This is a problem of will. In order to address this, a company needs either to constrain the decision authority of the salesforce or design its incentive plan in a way that harmonizes the sales team's interest with the company's [24]. Second, price implementation can suffer when the salespeople either lack the information they need or do not have the knowledge or training to perform effectively. This is a problem of ability. Companies can combat this with better information systems, improved communication, and appropriate training.

9.3.1   Price Decision Authority of the Sales Force

When prices are negotiated between salespeople and customers, it needs to be clear whether and to what extent the salespeople have decision authority over price [25]. In practice, we observe most often one of three alternatives:

- Salespeople have far-reaching and in some cases complete decision authority over prices.
- Salespeople have limited decision authority, i.e., they can decide independently on prices above a set lower limit. To breach this lower limit, the salespeople would require approval from a higher management level.
- Salespeople have no price decision authority at all, i.e., any price lower than a predetermined price requires approval by a higher management level.

The question of delegating price decision authority to salespeople is controversial. Kern [26, p. 44] describes it this way: "Letting the sales force set prices is about the same as hiring a fox to guard the hen house."

9.3.1.1 Qualitative Arguments

There are many qualitative arguments—pro and con—regarding the delegation of price decision authority to salespeople [26–29]. Arguments in favor of this delegation include:

- The status of the salespeople is enhanced, which improves motivation.
- The salesperson is in the best position to assess the willingness to pay of an individual customer and thus achieve optimal price differentiation [27, 30].
- The delegation eliminates the need for internal back and forth between the salespeople and headquarters. This avoids organizational delays and creates a high level of flexibility. The salesperson can react quickly to specific situations and changes in market conditions.
- Complex product and price questions often need to be resolved simultaneously in a negotiation. If the salesperson lacks decision authority and constantly needs to get approval from headquarters, it can make the negotiation process cumbersome.

The following aspects speak against the delegation of price decision authority to salespeople:

- The salespeople tend to be too acquiescent in the price negotiation, because in general they have a strong motivation to win the deal. This holds true even when they have a commission scheme based on contribution margin. "There is the temptation always to 'play it safe' to get the order." [31, p. 48]
- The centralization of price decision authority is a psychological relief for the salesperson. According to Zarth, "most salespeople have a fear of price discussions" [32, p. 111].
- Centralization also lessens the amount of pressure a purchaser can apply. "An old purchasing axiom is: Find out if the salesperson can reduce the price. If he can, insist that he does so." [28, p. 27]
- Centralization of price decision authority lessens or avoids the risk of creating price inconsistencies between individual customers or segments.
- In some circumstances a price decision demands complex cost, capacity, or competitive analyses which only a centralized team is capable of performing.

These pro and con arguments show that there is no generally applicable rule. The optimal solution depends on the circumstances of the individual case [33]. As Krafft [34] showed, the motivational structure of salespeople is extraordinarily complicated. We now shed some light on these aspects, first from a theoretical perspective.

9.3.1.2 Theoretical Arguments

Based on decision theory and the *principal-agent theory*, the delegation of full price decision authority to the salesperson is optimal when:

- The company and the salesperson behave in a profit-maximizing way.
- The salesperson's commission is proportional to the contribution margin.

For a commission rate of α, the company's profit (contribution margin) is defined as:

$$\pi = (1 - \alpha)(pq - C) \tag{9.1}$$

and the salesperson receives a commission P of:

$$P = \alpha(pq - C) \tag{9.2}$$

Because only the expressions in the second set of parentheses determine the maximum of the profit π and the commission P, and these expressions are equal, it means that the company and the salesperson have fully aligned goals. Because the salesperson can often estimate the price elasticity of the respective business partner better than senior management can, it makes sense to transfer full price decision authority to the salesperson [30]. Weinberg [35] has shown that this guideline remains optimal when the salesperson is not striving for absolute income maximization, but instead is pursuing a certain target income with minimal time commitment.

In contrast, the delegation of price authority is not optimal when the company pays a commission of β on revenue. In this case, the profit of the company, net of the commission, is:

$$\pi = (1 - \beta)pq - C \tag{9.3}$$

and the salesperson receives a commission of:

$$P = \beta pq \tag{9.4}$$

The salesperson is obviously interested in maximizing revenue. But the profit-maximizing price for the company, assuming marginal costs are not zero, is higher than the revenue-maximizing price. Delegating the price decision authority to the salesperson leads to prices which are too low from the company's perspective. When a company uses revenue-based commissions, it is advisable not to delegate price decision authority to the salesperson.

It is difficult to assess the extent to which the hypothesis that salespeople consistently want to maximize their income corresponds to reality. The validity of this hypothesis is critical for the theoretical considerations we have presented. In our experience, salespeople are often motivated to close a sale and not necessarily to maximize their income.

A number of works provide additional theoretical insights. Joseph [36] considers not only the better information which the salesperson has regarding the customer's willingness to pay but also takes into account the fact that a salesperson with price decision authority will substitute *price discounts* for *time and effort* in order to close the sale. It is easier to grant a discount than to devote more time to argumentation. The net effect of these two opposing forces can make the complete delegation of price authority, or even a somewhat limited form, the best strategy. Joseph [36] points out that in general, restricting price decision authority increases the amount of effort the salesperson needs to put in. As a result, salespeople will concentrate on the customers which offer the highest return. Bhardwaj [37] investigated the delegation of price decision authority from the vantage point that demand is a function of both price and the effort the salesperson puts forth. The competitive intensity on both dimensions determines when the pricing authority should be delegated to the salespeople. When price competition is strong, it is advantageous to delegate pricing authority. When there is intense competition with respect to the salesperson's effort, centralizing the pricing authority is the better choice [37, 38]. Based on contract theory, Mishra and Prasad [27] show that when the form of the contract is optimal, centralization is at least as advantageous as the delegation of price decision authority [39]. The contract must be constructed in such a way that the personal information of the salesperson is revealed.

In summary, we can say that theory offers no definite conclusion on the delegation of price decision authority to salespeople. The studies we mentioned deliver arguments both pro and con on the issue. One should therefore carefully examine the prevailing circumstances and make an appropriate decision. No matter what, commissions which are proportional to contribution margins are a necessary prerequisite for the delegation of price decision authority. Most recent theoretical works tend to favor a limit on the delegation of such authority to salespeople.

9.3.1.3 Empirical Findings

Existing empirical findings support that tendency. We often observe an enormous heterogeneity when we compare the revenue salespeople generate with the resulting contribution margin. Table 9.4 illustrates this using the example of a sanitation technology company.

The 33 salespeople had full price decision authority. On average they achieved a revenue of $810,775 and a margin of 11.1%. Salesperson 31 achieved a margin of 29.8%, far above average, but generated revenue of only $288,499. Salesperson 2 recorded the lowest margin (5.3%) but had the second-highest revenue ($1.78 million). In absolute terms, both have similar contribution margins ($85,972 vs. $94,193). Revenue and contribution margin have a correlation coefficient of −0.4, a significant negative correlation. In other words, margin tends to

Table 9.4 Revenue and contribution margin by salesperson—case study of a sanitation technology company

Salesperson	Revenue ($)	Contribution margin (%)	Salesperson	Revenue ($)	Contribution margin (%)
1	1,829,900	9.7	18	759,932	6.4
2	1,777,249	5.3	19	741,547	10.3
3	1,517,807	10.0	20	738,556	14.8
4	1,376,467	10.2	21	669,649	9.8
5	1,333,197	6.3	22	597,963	12.2
6	1,330,938	9.6	23	536,645	14.5
7	1,135,605	7.3	24	452,553	14.0
8	1,084,862	9.8	25	418,409	6.4
9	1,046,956	9.5	26	367,133	8.1
10	940,204	5.9	27	350,644	9.6
11	925,717	6.7	28	339,007	10.0
12	909,453	6.0	29	309,307	26.1
13	904,090	7.5	30	308,264	9.2
14	842,032	10.1	31	288,499	29.8
15	820,331	23.0	32	281,164	24.3
16	790,327	9.7	33	271,067	7.0
17	771,646	8.0	–	–	–
–	–	–	33 salespeople (∅)	810,775	11.1

decline as revenue increases. This suggests that the salespeople who produce the most revenue "sell on price" and the salespeople with lower revenues tend to "sell on value." This brings the discrepancy between profit orientation and revenue orientation to the forefront. In this case, it had clear consequences: the price authority of the salespeople was reduced and the incentive system restructured. Some "price sellers" were also replaced by "value sellers."

Stephenson et al. [28] explored the relationship between the price decision authority of the salesforce and the success of a company. Their sample covered 108 firms which sold medical products to hospitals. They categorized the companies according to the amount of price decision authority granted to the salesforce (none, limited, full) and then looked at each category across several performance indicators. Table 9.5 shows the results.

For all performance indicators except "revenue per salesperson," there was a negative relationship between the degree of the salesforce's price decision authority and the company's performance. Limited pricing authority showed the highest value only for revenue per salesperson. The results were remarkable because almost all of the companies in the sample paid commissions proportional to contribution margin, which fulfills a theoretical prerequisite for the delegation of pricing authority. The authors believe that the root cause of these findings lies in the *price acquiescence* we

Table 9.5 Relationship between price decision authority of the salesforce and company success [28, p. 24]

Price decision authority of the salesforce	No. of firms	Normalized performance indicators		Revenue per salesperson	Revenue growth	Margin (%)
		Contribution margin				
		Before selling costs	After selling costs	–	–	–
None	31	1.0570	1.0436	0.8697	1.3939	11.79
Limited	52	0.9827	0.9978	1.2116	0.9905	10.49
Full	25	0.9434	0.9537	0.7591	0.5605	9.65

mentioned above, which increases with pricing authority. The results indicate that the simple hypothesis of income maximization does not do justice to the complex motivation structure of salespeople [34].

Hansen et al. [40] could confirm empirically the theoretical considerations we described above, according to which the delegation of price decision authority is associated with the positive effect of salespeople's information as well as the suboptimal substitution (from the company's perspective) between discounts and effort. In a survey of 222 companies from different industries, they found that companies tend to have more centralized price decision authority when the risk is high that price discounts will be substituted for time and effort. Just as Stephenson et al. [28] did, they also found a strong heterogeneity among the companies with respect to their delegation of pricing authority. A study by Alavi et al. [41] in the B2C sector showed that salespeople who correctly assessed the importance of price from the customer's perspective granted significantly lower discounts. In another study, Wieseke et al. [42] found a positive effect of customer loyalty on discounts in retail price negotiations which is driven by customers' demand for a loyalty reward and their elevated perceived negotiation power.

In an empirical study of 87 large companies, Wiltinger [43] investigated the influence which various environmental factors have on the delegation of price decision authority. He found that more pricing authority will be delegated to the salesforce when:

- Customers expect to receive price information immediately.
- The financial weight of the individual customer is high.
- The salespeople have intimate knowledge of the customer.
- The salespeople identify strongly with their company's goals.

Blanket statements regarding the delegation of pricing authority to the salesforce have neither a theoretical nor an empirical basis. We urge caution with regard to this question. Far-reaching or full delegation of pricing authority to the salesforce is not advisable in our view. Limited delegation of price decision authority is sufficient to provide flexibility when necessary.

The education level of the salespeople should be viewed as closely related to the delegation of price decision authority. The better they understand the internal and external consequences of certain price decisions, the more readily a company can delegate price decision authority to them. Kern [26] reports a successful example of delegation which worked because the salespeople were trained intensively with the help of a computer simulation game.

9.3.2 Price-Oriented Incentive Systems

The incentives for the salesforce are decisive for ensuring price implementation in line with the company's goals. "In line with the goals" means that the incentivization—from the structure to the actual configuration of the *incentives*—is closely and consistently aligned with the strategic goals of the company. The most popular form in practice is a commission plan based on revenue. As we have shown, this form of incentivization does not make sense when combined with price decision authority. Such authority should be tied to a profit- or contribution margin-based incentive system. But this form presents problems in practice. First, revealing profit or contribution margin data to the salesforce runs the risk that such information gets into the hands of customers. That is generally not desirable. Second, customer-specific information on contribution margin is not as easy to compile as revenue data. It requires information systems which many companies do not have.

In order to get around these difficulties, there are proven systems which avoid the undesirable effects of a revenue-based commission and come close to replicating a contribution margin-based incentivation. Figure 9.6 illustrates the use of a *price implementation premium*. The basis of the variable compensation is still the revenue the salesperson generates. But the additional "price premium" rewards the price discipline which the individual salesperson demonstrates, as manifested in the realized price level relative to the target price level. Salespeople who sell while maintaining price discipline will be much better compensated than the notorious discounters. Our experience shows that such systems generate sustainable profit improvements.

The example in Fig. 9.7 illustrates another incentive option which likewise avoids the disclosure of actual contribution margins. In this case, the commission rate depends on the magnitude of the discount. The higher the discount the salesperson grants, the lower the commission rate (which otherwise still depends on revenue) will be. This is referred to as an "anti-discount incentive." In order to amplify the incentive's effect, the amount of the additional incentive can be calculated in real time and displayed on the salesperson's laptop. The salespeople immediately see how their incentive changes when they increase the discount from, say, 5–10%. The effect of this system had a resounding effect on the company's profit. Within 2 months, the average discount fell from 16% to 14%, without losses of customers or volume. This translates to a margin increase of 2% points, equivalent to a price increase of 2%.

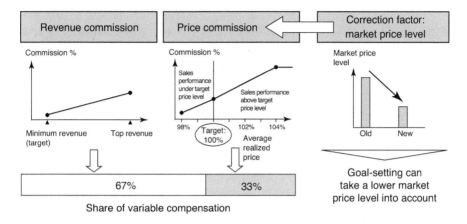

Fig. 9.6   Price implementation commission (Simon-Kucher & Partners)

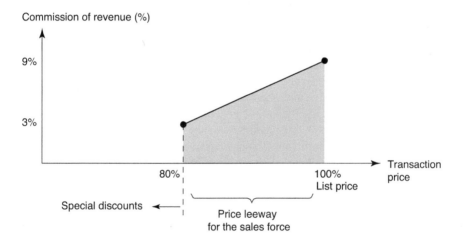

Fig. 9.7   Anti-discount incentive (Simon-Kucher & Partners)

Incentive systems for the salesforce should meet three criteria:

- Simplicity
- Fairness
- Equality

The simplicity ensures that the costs of maintaining the system remain reasonable and that the salespeople understand the effects of the incentives. Fairness means that the salespeople actually receive the financial rewards when they behave as the company desires. Equality means that comparable levels of performance will be rewarded financially the same way.

Even when a company adheres to these principles and crafts a contribution margin-based incentive system, it cannot rule out that goal conflicts will arise between the company and its salespeople. That risk always exists whenever the salespeople pursue the goal of maximizing their free time rather than their own income or when the salespeople behave in a very risk-averse manner [44, 45]. A salesperson with an affinity for more leisure time will be willing to sacrifice some commission dollars in order to gain more free time. As we showed above, having price decision authority allows salespeople to use price concessions to "buy" more free time or a lower mental/psychological effort. That behavior is not in the company's interest. The cause is that the salesperson—in his or her own utility function—ascribes higher value to free time or lower mental stress than to more income [46]. Extremely risk-averse salespeople also pose a problem from the company's perspective. They acquiesce to price demands because they fear losing the deal [45].

9.3.2.1 Management by Objectives

In this section, we suggest an approach which according to our knowledge is new. It is based on the concept of management by objectives (MBO). MBO was made popular by Peter Drucker in the 1950s but has older roots. It actually can be traced back to the so-called "mission-oriented control system" introduced in the Prussian army in the nineteenth century. The alternative is the "process-oriented control system" historically used in the American military. Mission-oriented or management by objectives means that the leader only gives a mission to the person who executes, but does not prescribe how this mission has to be carried out. Process-oriented, on the other hand, employs a diligent ex ante-analysis to devise a detailed process which the executing person is supposed to precisely follow. The most popular planning systems such as SAP-CO only allow for one combination of sales volume and price, i.e., one point on the price-response curve. If the manager and the salesperson agree on and commit to this point, the salesperson has no leeway for price decision authority and thus no opportunity to manage by objectives.

An alternative system could be constructed as follows. To illustrate it, we recall the numerical case from Fig. 1.2 with a price of $100, a sales volume of 1 million units, variable unit costs of $30, and fixed costs of $30 million. This base scenario yields a profit of $10 million. In the spirit of management by objectives, a manager could set profit objective of at least $10 million, but let the salesperson choose the means to achieve that objective. Figure 5.2 shows the options the salesperson has in terms of prices and volumes in order to achieve at least $10 million in profit. A price of $80, for example, would mean the salesperson would need to sell 2 million units, i.e., twice the volume shown in base scenario in Fig. 1.2, to achieve $10 million in profit. In contrast, a price of $120 would allow the salesperson to lose up to one third of the base volume. If the salesperson over- or underachieves the base profit, he or she would be incentivized or penalized accordingly. An important advantage of this system is that the person who decides on the price is the one who is closest to the customer and is thus best able to evaluate the customer's willingness to pay. At the same time, the agreed profit objectives alleviate the risk that the salesperson's actions will harm profits. MBO encourages the sales force to focus on profitable customers and discourages them from cutting prices. This incentive system is particularly useful if the salesperson is experienced, knows which selling activities are most effective, and is empowered by the company [47].

9.3.2.2 Non-monetary Incentives

In addition to monetary incentives, non-monetary incentives play an outstanding role in sales and can also be used for price management [48]. Concepts such as sales competitions, honorary awards, salesperson of the month, incentive trips, 100 percent clubs, etc. are used regularly in most sales organizations. With respect to price implementation, however, such incentives are rarely employed, even though there are interesting ways to start using them. One could offer awards for the highest price, for the lowest discount, the highest contribution margin, or the most creative pricing solution. Internal communication can also create or reinforce non-monetary incentives. At meetings or conferences for sales teams or sales management, it is common to discuss market price trends, current pricing problems, necessary price increases, and price strategy. Such opportunities can be used to grant incentives and awards for better pricing policies.

A study by Spiro, Stanton, and Rich [49] showed that non-monetary incentives can have a positive influence on price implementation. A medical technology firm improved its price realization after a new general manager introduced a reporting system which exposed instances where high discounts were granted. He commented: "When I began here a year ago, I demanded a daily printout of all deals with the lowest prices approved under our discount terms and conditions. In the first months, there were hundreds of line items on the list. Nowadays the printout has maybe ten such instances per day, and these are usually ones I signed off on myself. Despite this strict policy, we have lost very few customers while improving our profit significantly."

The fact that no salesperson wants to be identified as a "price loser" or a notorious discounter provides a strong motivation to defend prices.

Most companies have *systems of discounts, terms, and conditions*. These systems play a critical role in cases where the salesforce has limited or no price decision authority. The system's role is to ensure that individual customers are offered adequate prices. The flexibility, which would otherwise derive from the price decision authority of a salesperson, is built into the system. *Conditions* are mutually agreed, customer-specific modifications to the otherwise standard ways of measuring supplier performance and how that performance is rewarded by the customer. They are usually tied to criteria and find application in both spot transactions and in ongoing business relationships. Granting conditions reflects differentiated treatment of customers on the part of the sellers, and requesting certain conditions conversely reflects the customers' different treatment of sellers. Granting conditions helps the seller pursue two goals: extracting willingness to pay (which varies by customer) to the greatest extent possible and incentivizing customers to behave in a way which

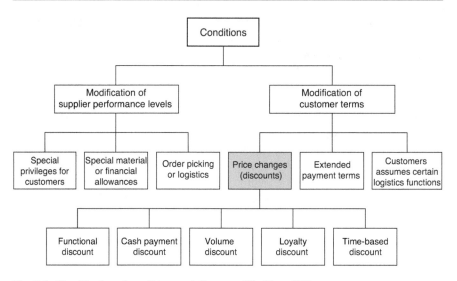

Fig. 9.8 Classification of conditions and discounts [50, 51, p. 577]

benefits the seller. Such customer behavior may include increasing volume and/or range of products and services purchased, longer lead times on orders, less frequent deliveries, or faster payment.

Figure 9.8 shows a classification of conditions and discounts. On the left side, the standard performance levels have been modified for a particular customer. This allows the seller to offer the customer special privileges such as exchange or return rights, provide the customer with material or financial allowances (e.g., product samples, advertising subsidies), or perform functions such as order picking or logistics. The right side shows how standard customer terms can be modified through discounts, extended payment terms, or having the customers assume certain logistics functions, e.g., picking up the product themselves.

Price modifications in the form of reductions are referred to as *discounts*. They are typically granted to the customer at purchase or on the invoice. Thus, discounts determine the *transaction price*, i.e., the actual price the customer ultimately pays. We can classify discounts according to the rationale for granting them:

- *Functional discounts* are offered to customers, in particular to intermediaries, in exchange for that party's performing functions on behalf of the seller, such as warehousing, product presentation, or consulting.
- *Cash payment discounts* are granted to customers who pay within a pre-defined period.
- *Volume discounts* are offered to customers who purchase a certain amount of a product. In general, the more units the customer buys, the greater the discount. Bonuses are a special form of volume discount. They are not granted at invoice, but retroactively on volumes purchased in a certain period.

- *Loyalty discounts* are offered to customers who purchase products or services predominantly or exclusively from one seller.
- *Time-based discounts* refer to the timing of the purchase or delivery and include advance, seasonal, introductory, or clearance discounts.

There are seemingly countless other types of discounts beyond these most common, frequently used forms. Pechtl [52] counts around 40 types of discounts and conditions. Manufacturers sometimes use more than 70 different terms, conditions, and rebates in dealing with intermediaries such as distributors or retailers. In practice, the discounts are typically offered in combined form within the framework of a *discount system*. In order to maintain internal transparency, the discount system should not be too extensive or complex. One central question regarding complex discount systems is whether a particular discount is truly necessary for the company to compete in its market. The diverse range of discounts a company offers is often not the outcome of rational planning but rather results from the accumulation of discounts over many years into a "discount jungle."

A typical indicator for such "jungles" is the continued presence of discounts originally granted to customers for functions which in the meantime are no longer performed. In other cases, one-time or special discounts evolve into standard practice for customers with which the seller has a long-standing relationship. These indicators are common enough that many companies have an opportunity to plug these revenue and profit "leaks" by applying a stricter "pay for performance" principle to the discounts they offer.

Most condition systems share a unique characteristic: at some point, no one in the company knows anymore why certain guidelines, special exceptions, and side agreements were created and implemented in the first place. The proliferation of discounts, combined with their increasing levels, results in intransparent systems which engender mistrust among customers and damage their belief in the fairness of the seller's prices. Because retailers rely on discount levels when making their own price calculations, they can lead to price erosion, lower margins, and lower profits. It is not unusual that budgets for discounts and conditions run in the tens or hundreds of millions of dollars. The conditions budget for a large building materials supplier represented more than 30% of gross revenues. Companies invest considerable time and expense in reducing their costs in order to improve their profits. But they underestimate the profit potential of a systematic optimization of their discount and condition systems. For the materials manufacturer just mentioned, reducing the average discount level by only 2% resulted in a profit increase of more than 15%. Tapping such potential requires a comprehensive overhaul of the price and condition system. How the new condition system should look will depend on the prevailing market situation of the company as well as the key pillars of its strategy. We suggest six ways a company can establish a consistent, goal-driven performance orientation for its conditions policies.

9.3.2.3 Reducing Price Competition by Limiting Discounts

A women's fashion manufacturer witnessed increasing price competition among retailers as a result of high and largely undifferentiated discounts. It was not unusual for these discounts to favor smaller retailers to such an extent that they could enter into price competition with larger, more powerful retailers. In this case, the goal of the redesign of the discount structure was to provide retailers with a firmer, more reliable calculation basis. The company achieved this through a differentiated discount structure which was based strictly on performance-oriented criteria and which did not discriminate against individual retailers.

9.3.2.4 Using System Bonuses to Defend Against Aggressive Competitors

A door manufacturer had two business areas (warehouse and project), both of which were invoiced via distributors. When the manufacturer felt threatened by an aggressive brand, its product advantages were enough to withstand the threat in the price-sensitive project business, but it needed to take action to bolster its warehouse business. In order to create the right balance between incentives and pressure, the manufacturer introduced a bonus system based on two components: warehouse revenue and overall revenue (warehouse plus project). The distributors with high overall revenue and a strong warehouse business were fully aligned with the manufacturer's goals and thus earned the highest bonuses. But the system also offered strong incentives for distributors who had a low overall level of revenue but a high share of warehouse business, as well as distributors with high overall revenue but a minimal warehouse business.

9.3.2.5 Using Value Bonuses to Reduce Price Pressure

Prices in a market can come under pressure when demand is weak. Distributors and retailers eagerly offer more affordable alternatives in order to generate revenue in any way they can. In order to increase the "revenue quality," a manufacturer needs to design incentives for these intermediaries to sell higher-value products. One leading manufacturer of automotive equipment incorporated a value bonus into its condition system, in order to counter the price pressures in its market. The value bonus is meant to spur sales of higher-value products.

9.3.2.6 Avoiding Abuse of Project-Based Conditions

Large projects usually require some form of price concession because of their sheer size. A fundamental problem with project business is its precise definition and its fencing from standard business. Too much ambiguity and room for interpretation can sometimes tempt intermediaries to abuse the system in an effort to get the more favorable project conditions to apply to standard business—e.g., by claiming that "my warehouse is my biggest project." It is not unusual for such deals to be in reality a sweetheart deal between the sales team and the intermediaries. To eliminate these opportunities for abuse, one manufacturer redesigned its conditions for the project business. A project commission would only be granted as such when it produced a specific, verifiable result.

9.3.2.7 Using a Partner Concept to Deepen Relationships with Strategic Customers

The redesign of the condition system is often driven by a desire to focus more on strategic customers. When this occurs, smaller established distributors fear they will lose their hard-earned privileges and come out worse under the new regime. Some may threaten to end their business relationship with the seller. A manufacturer of garden tools found itself in this situation. It was aiming for a better selection of strategically important distributors (with respect to revenue, regional position, and competence). Its objectives were to:

- Offer greater rewards to strategically important business partners.
- Reward distributors appropriately for the services they perform.
- Do joint planning with selected distributors.

A partner concept will only work when it follows clear guidelines and avoids watering down the prevailing condition system. In this case, the manufacturer instituted transparent budget guidelines for revenue eligible for a bonus.

The redesign of condition systems must be in line both with the manufacturer's internal requirements and the implementation needs of the trade partners. Even at the concept stage, it is important to get salespeople involved. In practice, their input usually proves to be very valuable, because they know the trade partners best. One should also involve selected trade partners in the concept development phase. In parallel, the company should analyze customer-specific data. This includes capturing the precise customer structure with respect to their interrelationships and not only with respect to their revenue and to the conditions which apply to them. These data can serve as the basis for computer simulations of the effects of a new set of trade terms and conditions. Such simulations will identify in advance which trade partners will be "winners" and "losers" under the redesigned system. This is the best way to develop individual measures for customers and communicate the new expectations to the "winners." The company can also show the "losers" the steps they can take and the behaviors they can change in order to improve their standing.

Clarifying the individual elements in advance and in close cooperation with the trade partners ensures that the new system meets minimal resistance in the market. The much greater challenge is to maintain the integrity and consistency of the system over the medium and long term. As soon as a company starts granting exceptions or making special allowances, it risks heading quickly back down the path to the discount jungle. Intensive training on the new condition system is essential. That is the only way to make sure the salespeople can communicate the new system convincingly and show each customer—within the context of the new system—how it can make improvements to its situation. Otherwise the salespeople may revert to reflexively granting exceptions.

9.3.2.8 Risk Sharing

Enercon, the global technology leader in wind power generation, practices a very successful pricing model which involves a new form of risk sharing. Under its

Enercon Partner Concept (EPC), a customer can sign up for maintenance, security services, and repairs at a price which depends on the yield of the Enercon turbine. In other words, Enercon reduces its customers' entrepreneurial risks by sharing those risks with the operator of the wind park. Customers have found the offer very attractive, and more than 90% of them sign an EPC contract.

As with all risk assumptions and guarantees, the provider needs to consider the potential costs. In Enercon's case, the costs are manageable because of its superior product quality. The absence of a gear (the number one cause of a breakdown) means that Enercon can guarantee its customer uptime of 97%; competitors typically do not guarantee more than 90%. In reality, Enercon products achieve 99% uptime. It costs Enercon nothing to guarantee uptime of 97%. This is an ideal example of optimal risk sharing between supplier and customer, which can noticeably lower a customer's resistance to buy. Enercon also assumes half of all service fees for the first half of the 12-year contract period. This provides substantial and much appreciated financial relief for the wind park investor, who is liable to be financially strapped in the few years it takes to ramp up a wind park.

9.4   Price Communication

In Chap. 4 on the psychology of price, we explained the important role that several processes—from perception to assessments to forming preferences—play in price management. The effects of prices depend in large part on how they are presented and communicated. This applies primarily to customers and to potential buyers, but price communication can also be directed at competitors and also to one's own employees.

The spectacularly successful 2012 Olympic Games in London demonstrate how intelligent price communication can be an essential element of price management. Paul Williamson [53], who was responsible for managing the ticket program, used prices not only as an effective revenue and profit driver but also as a powerful and targeted means of communications. The digits of the prices themselves were designed to send a message without any additional commentary. The lowest standard price was £20.12, the most expensive was £2012. The number "2012" appeared over and over again in the price points, and everyone knew immediately that such price points referred to the Olympic Games.

Just as creative was the idea to introduce a special price structure for children under 18. The motto was "Pay Your Age": a 6-year-old would pay £6, a 16-year-old £16. Seniors could also purchase lowered-price tickets. All of these measures helped the organizers remain true to their claim that the London Olympics would be "Everybody's Games" [54]. These price structures generated an extremely positive resonance; the media reported on it thousands of times. Even the queen and the prime minister publicly praised the "Pay Your Age" tactic. These prices were not only an effective means of communication but also perceived as very fair.

Another important feature of the price structure: there were absolutely no discounts. The management of the London Olympics remained firm about this policy, even when certain events did not sell out. This sent the clear signal about value: the tickets and the events were worth their price. The team also decided not to offer any bundles, a common practice in sports under which a team combines attractive and less attractive games or events into a single package.

The organization relied very heavily on the Internet both for communications and sales. Approximately 99% of tickets were sold online. With their ingenious price structure and communication campaign, Williamson and his organization generated ticket revenues of $824 million, which was 75% more than anticipated, and more ticket revenue than from the preceding three Olympic Games (Beijing, Athens, and Sydney) combined. This case clearly shows the potential power of strong price communication.

9.4.1 External Price Communication

Prices must be communicated to customers. Here the issue is not only the information about the price itself but also about influencing the customer's perception and assessment in such a way that the customer feels that the offered product or service is worth the money. Below we will discuss the available instruments and techniques for price communication.

The German company Teekampagne, the market leader for organically grown Darjeeling tea, exemplifies how effective intelligent external price communication can be. Through its complete and consistent price transparency, it shows how it derives its selling prices by revealing more than 300 individual line items from its accounting statements. For 1 kilogram of tea, cost of goods accounts for €16.94, overseas shipping costs €0.23, and €1.30 goes to insurance and taxes. The list goes on to include line items such as €1.31 for package filling, bags, and labeling, €0.52 for organic controls and certification, €1.23 for office costs and data processing, etc. All total, the company tallies up the items and comes to a price of €29.50/kg [55]. The listings constitute credible statements on the part of the company on what goes into its prices. This makes the selling prices transparent and understandable for customers.

9.4.1.1 Price Lists
The most elementary and most frequently used medium for price communication is the price list, which comes in several different forms. Gross price lists indicate the price to end consumers. Retailers, distributors, and other intermediaries receive a discount from the gross price. The discount represents their compensation for the function they perform. In industry sectors where fixed price agreements are still allowed, the intermediary is obligated to honor the gross price. Germany has some examples of this, even though fixed price agreements are generally forbidden. Exceptions are made for prescription medications, books, magazines, and cigarettes. In all other markets, the manufacturer is only permitted to suggest or recommend the

price for end consumers, but that price is not binding for trade partners. Practically speaking, the recommended price on a price list represents the highest or maximum price. This price forms an anchor for consumers, to the extent they know this price. Retailers usually charge a lower price than what the manufacturer recommends, in an effort to gain an advantage. But the reality for retailers often deviates from the intended model of pricing freedom. Manufacturers, especially those with powerful brands, are vigilant and exert pressure on retailers to stick to the suggested or recommended prices. This is in the interests of manufacturers of branded products, because uniform or at least consistent prices are an important element of strong brands. Difficulties in implementing list prices at retail have induced some manufacturers, luxury goods makers in particular, to establish their own sales channels, where they have complete control over prices. Luxury goods groups such as Richemont, LVMH, and Kering generate the bulk of their revenue through their own stores.

Net price lists contain the prices at which manufacturers sell their products. Their trade partners are then free to set their own selling prices. Some manufacturers have switched from gross prices to net prices, in order to avoid conflicts with trade partners. As a result, they surrender almost all their influence over the end-user price of their products. Of course there are also discounts to net prices. But these are not considered as compensation for the trade partner's role per se; rather, they are either volume or functional discounts, the latter reflecting some specific task which the trade partner takes on (such as picking up the goods at their own cost).

Additionally, a manufacturer needs to consider whether to make its price lists available to customers or keep them for internal use and reference only. When suppliers publish their price lists, they have effectively established a maximum price. Even if a customer's willingness to pay were higher, the supplier normally cannot charge a higher price than list. These upper bounds are sometimes breached in times of scarcity, though. In some large cities during rush hour, it is difficult if not impossible to get a taxi at standard prices (=list price). Drivers can demand a higher price and get it. The exact price is then a matter of negotiation. Price lists for internal use only, in contrast, allow for pricing latitude upward and downward. They serve primarily as guidelines to help employees quote prices, but this does not preclude charging prices in excess of list prices if circumstances warrant it (e.g., scarcity or when a customer likely has a higher willingness to pay). The leeway for lower prices is also greater. One can grant high discounts from published list prices, but the firm's credibility may suffer as a result. If the customers are not aware of the list prices, one can price lower without putting credibility at risk. In short, price lists for internal use offer greater possibilities for price differentiation than published price lists. Therefore, we recommend that firms use internal price lists rather than published ones in markets where price transparency is lower and the heterogeneity of customers is greater.

Traditionally list prices were printed in hard copy and—if used externally—distributed to customers. This was a rather costly exercise for companies with large assortments and many customers. Because of this, firms tended to adjust list prices only on an infrequent basis, usually semiannually or annually. The Internet caused a radical shift. When price lists are published primarily or exclusively online, this yields not only considerable cost savings but also the ability to change prices at any time. In many industries, though, printed and electronic price lists still co-exist side by side.

9.4.1.2 Price-Related Advertising

The positioning of a company finds its concrete expression in product, price, and communication. Just as premium suppliers rely on quality-dependent slogans in their advertising (e.g., Miele's "Forever Better" or Mercedes-Benz's "The best or nothing"), companies whose competitive advantage derives from its prices will put price-related slogans at the forefront of their communication. Constant repetition of these price-driven messages has a favorable effect on their price image. Retailers, and discounters in particular, make the most intensive use of price advertising. Chains such as Walmart and ALDI take out newspaper advertisements devoted largely to price advertising. The fashion retail chain H&M advertises with the slogan "fashion and quality at the best price." A price image depends on several factors, with the actual prices themselves at the top of the list. But price advertising also has a powerful influence on price image. One sees this in the way that some companies have succeeded in establishing an especially favorable price image, even though objectively speaking their prices are not necessarily the lowest. Their technique is the sustained, intensive use of price advertising.

- Examples of price-related advertising slogans companies have used for extended periods include:
  - "Unbeatable price" (Best Buy)
  - "Always low prices" (former Walmart slogan), followed by "Save Money. Live better"
  - "Expect More. Pay Less" (Target)
- Companies also commonly use price-related advertising slogans for specific, limited-time campaigns. Examples include:
  - "At these prices, you have to travel" (1-2-Fly)[2]
  - "Big wines. Small prices" (52weine.de)[3]
  - "Prices that make people happy" (Galeria Kaufhof)[4]
  - "Better prices for getting better" (Ratiopharm)[5]

Some businesses—such as Save-A-Lot, Dollar Tree, and Five Below—even express their favorable price image in their names. Online firms likewise use their names and URL's to communicate an attractive price image: cheapprices.com and megacheaphardware.com.au. Some popular terms and phrases in price

---

[2]Original German slogan: "Bei diesen Preisen muss man reisen"

[3]Original German slogan: "Große Weine. Kleine Preise"

[4]Original German slogan: "Preise, die glücklich machen"

[5]Original German slogan: "Gute Preise, gute Besserung"

communication literally shout the presence of low prices: "prices slashed," "dirt cheap," "we won't be undersold," or "insanely low prices."

These examples convey what we mean with price-related slogans. When the steady stream of advertising impressions remains sufficiently consistent with the actual prices over a long period, such slogans can effectively steer the firm's price image in the desired direction. One must be careful, however, not to cross the line where a "cheap" image begins to rub off on the consumers' perception of quality as well.

9.4.1.3 Price Guarantees

A less common form of price communication is the price guarantee. This goes beyond a pure communications measure, because it obligates a firm to accept a product return and reimburse the price, or pay the consumer the price difference, if the consumer finds the same product from another supplier at a lower price. Best Buy has used this form of communication: "We won't be beat on price. We'll match the prices of key online and local competitors" [56]. Via its new customer card in Europe, Shell guarantees that the current pump prices it charges for fuel will never be more than two cents above other gas stations in the area [57].

Price guarantees send a strong message. Even if consumers rarely take advantage of them, they transmit to customers a high level of perceived reassurance that the prices they pay will be affordable, if not less expensive than what competitors are offering. One risk for sellers is that its competitors target their price guarantees as a way to damage them. But in practice, competitors' ability to effect is limited, especially if a considerable portion of a seller's assortment is proprietary and therefore not stocked by the competitors. Price guarantees are usually advisable only for firms whose price levels are truly low.

9.4.1.4 Communication of Price Changes

The interests of a seller are asymmetrical when it comes to price changes. It wants customers to notice price reductions to the greatest degree possible, whereas a price increase should escape notice in order to keep negative effects on sales volume to a minimum. This asymmetry leads to important insights regarding price communication:

- Price cuts should be supported by intensive communication, with the advantage of the lower price at the forefront. The goal is to increase the price elasticity (in absolute terms).
- Price increases could be cushioned by enhanced communication efforts which emphasize product quality. The goal is to reduce the price elasticity (in absolute terms).

Using an example from a consumer goods brand, Fig. 9.9 shows that these effects really do occur.

In this case, a price reduction combined with a high level of advertising can lead to very strong volume growth. If the price reduction is not supported by advertising,

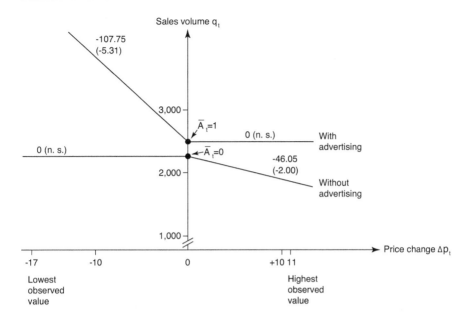

Fig. 9.9 Empirical findings on the influence of advertising on the price effect

however, the volume growth is not significant. Conversely, a price increase without advertising support has a strong negative effect on volume. If the firm accompanies the price increase by advertising, there is no noticeable decline in volume [58]. Such findings lead to the conclusion that both price increases and price decreases call for appropriate advertising support.

The following price communication from ALDI is insightful. Procurement prices for milk rose by €0.10 per liter in Germany after a strike by dairy farmers. ALDI took out full-page newspaper advertisements which proclaimed: "Procurement price increase of €0.10—retail price rises by *only* €0.07! ALDI does not pass along the full price increase onto you. Instead it assumes responsibility—also for the dairy farmers in our country." One suspects that consumers appreciate this kind of advertising; in this case, they had probably anticipated an increase of €0.10. Instead they are better off, in the spirit of prospect theory, because they have "saved" €0.03. In a similar vein, a service provider communicates that it passes on only 70% of wage increases. We would like to point out here that from the perspective of profit maximization, passing along the cost increase in full would not have been optimal. If we assume a linear price-response function, one should only pass along half of the cost increase, independent of the level of the price elasticity (see Chap. 5). With a consumer price increase of €0.07, ALDI is not far off from this theoretical optimum.

We observe strong effects on price elasticity in retail from the use of other communication instruments such as displays and posters. Supplementary advertising, special in-store placements, and in-store signage can amplify the effect of a price decrease on sales volume, compared to the use of a price decrease on its own without

Market share

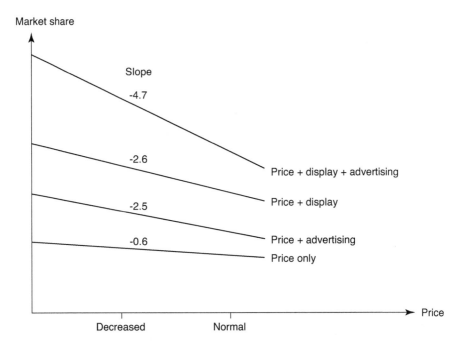

Fig. 9.10 Effect of different price communication instruments

such communication. Figure 9.10 illustrates this point [59]. A pure (unsupported) price decrease leads to an increase of market share of 0.6% points per price unit. If the price decrease is backed by advertising, the increase in market share improves to 2.5% points per price unit. If the price cut is accompanied by a display, the market share increase is 2.6% points, or roughly the same magnitude. If the firm combines the two instruments, the market share increase per unit of price cut is 4.7% points. In other words, the effect of a price decrease is eight times as high when the firm uses displays and advertising in combination, compared to making the price cut without support.

Another finding shows just how much perception and communication matter. Merely referring to a price as discounted—even in the absence of an actual, price cut—can stimulate sales volume. This trick is apparently not uncommon, but we warn that over time it can undermine consumers' trust in the retailer's discounting policies.

For price increases, companies have several instruments they can use to soften the perception and reduce the negative volume effects:

- Preference-building advertising: The price increase is accompanied by advertising which emphasizes quality. Newspapers and insurance companies regularly use this tactic when they announce price increases.

- Secrecy: A company conducts a "stealth" price increase in the hope that customers do not notice the change. This tactic works effectively for products which customers rarely purchase or whose prices they are not familiar with. In other cases, the company risks damaging its image and breaching customers' trust.
- Reduction in package size: This alternative comes into play when a company wants to avoid exceeding a price threshold or is bound by round prices (such as in vending machines). This tactic is common for products whose unit of usage varies from customer to customer or occasion to occasion (e.g., a container of ice cream, a roll of paper towels, a box of cereal) or which lack a clear standard package size (e.g., a bottle of fruit juice). Even the number of cigarettes is occasionally adjusted in order to keep the absolute package price constant. In 2015, Heinz raised the price for yellow mustard by reducing the package size from 9 ounces to 8 ounces. In 2016, Mondelez decided to change the shape of its Toblerone chocolate bar in the United Kingdom by lengthening the gaps between the chocolate "peaks" in its triangular packaging. The shape change slimmed the bars down from 170 g to 150 g, but the suggested retail price remained the same. Mondelez defended the action by claiming "higher production costs in Switzerland due to the high Swiss franc exchange rate, and higher raw materials costs" [60]. In 2015, Iglo, a frozen foods company in Germany, succeeded in using reductions in package sizes to effect real price increases of over 40% on some products [61].
- An example from a European drugstore demonstrates that the retail trade will not always be cooperative when a manufacturer reduces a package size. The chain used a sign to draw customers' attention to the fact that Colgate-Palmolive had reduced the amount of toothpaste in a tube but left the package price unchanged. This example was noteworthy because retailers traditionally do not inform their customers explicitly about such stealthy or hidden price changes.
- In 2016, Evian, which is part of Danone and one of the world's leading brands in water, reduced the volume of a popular bottle in Germany from 1.5 L to 1.25 L and, at the same time, raised the price. Evian was chosen as the "deceptive packaging of 2016" by Germany's most prestigious national daily newspaper [62].
- Improving reputation and trust: When a company raises price, customers normally do not ascribe a negative motivation to the company if it has an outstanding reputation and a strong basis of trust. If the company has focused on building and maintaining this level of trust, it can mitigate the negative perception which a price increase would trigger [63]. Nonetheless, a company should not abuse its goodwill.

9.4.1.5 Price Structure and Communication

Multidimensional and other complex price structures have a strong impact on the understanding of consumers and the effect of price. This creates opportunities as well as challenges for price communication. It applies just as much to multidimensional and non-linear price structures as it does to price bundling and similar structures. When the complexity reaches a certain level, the only way for a customer to make a reliable assessment of a price is to make some rather intricate calculations (e.g., the break-even point for the BahnCard, a return on investment, or life cycle costing).

It has been shown empirically many times that the presentation of the price (total price vs. breakdown of price components) exerts a strong influence on price perception. The booking of a cruise at a travel agent provides an example. Instead of quoting a one-dimensional price of $1500, the agents communicate multidimensional prices (e.g., $1350 for the trip itself and a $150 surcharge for port fees). This practice is also common among bargain airlines, for whom the various surcharges often add up to more than the price of the ticket itself [64]. Customers may see these multidimensional price presentations as more affordable—even when amounts are equal—and increase their demand accordingly. To counter this effect, the European Court requires that the ultimate (total) price must appear first when a customer books online [65].

Xia and Monroe [66] found that the effects of multidimensional prices follow a U-shaped progression. As the number of price components increases, customers view the offer as more and more favorable. But after a certain number of price parameters, customers start to view the offer as expensive. For products or services with two to four price components, the use of multidimensional pricing can make the offer seem less expensive. If the number of price components increases beyond that, customers will perceive the price structure as too complicated. The lack of transparency makes the price structure unattractive to them. One should therefore think carefully about the number of price components. There is no general rule on the optimal number; it varies from product to product. The number of price components in a mobile phone plan is far less than for an automobile, which could come with a wide range of individually priced options. The number of price components can also offer a point of differentiation from competitors. If all sellers use complex structures with multidimensional prices, a one-dimensional price can serve as an effective form of differentiation. Mobile operators and Internet service providers use that approach, e.g., with flat rates or triple play bundles.

An important aspect of multidimensional prices is the relative weighting of the price components. We observe two typical forms in practice. One form includes a primary price component which often constitutes more than 75% of the total price. The other form includes several components with roughly the same weight. In the first case, the price component with the significant weight is referred to as the base price. It corresponds to the most basic level of a product or service, such as for a cruise, where the price for the trip itself is the base price. That price is then supplemented by other charges/prices such as port fees. Empirical studies have shown that the existence of a base price has an anchoring effect. In other words, the customers make an assessment of the base price and then adjust that impression when they consider the less important price components [67]. The base price therefore plays a critical role in the customers' valuation of an offer. Only after the customers have made their assessment of the base price do the other price components come into consideration. In our previous example, if the customer perceives the port fee of $150 as too high, this affects the overall impression. An initial overall assessment of "very inexpensive," for example, can shift to simply "inexpensive." This sequential evaluation process lends a disproportionally high weight to the base price. Under such circumstances, it makes sense to set the base price as low as possible and make it the focus of communication.

Another form of communication is recommended when customers see several price parameters as important. Leasing contracts for cars, which have a one-time payment plus recurring monthly payments, fall into this category. In these cases, the price components do not flow sequentially into the customers' assessments; they are considered in parallel. For car leasing, Herrmann and Wricke [68] investigated the influence of monthly payments, one-time payments, and the length/duration of the contract. The monthly rate had a stronger effect on the overall assessment than the one-time payment. According to the authors, the reason was that customers view the monthly payment in the context of their monthly income and consider the proportional reduction of their discretionary income. The one-time payment is viewed as just that, a one-time expenditure which does not directly reduce their monthly purchasing power. These findings are aligned with what one would expect according to prospect theory, and mental accounting in particular (see Chap. 4). Leasing companies should therefore set the monthly rates lower and make them the thrust of their communication. The one-time payment can be higher and appear in the background in the communication.

Price bundling and the associated communication also open up opportunities. Products which comprise several or even numerous components push the limits when it comes to the communication of the individual components and their prices [69]. In contrast, bundles and their favorable prices can be advertised in a targeted manner. A classic example is the range of options for cars, which can include dozens of separate components. When these are grouped into bundles or special packages (sports, comfort, safety, etc.), however, they can be aimed effectively at target groups with messages which emphasize how advantageous the bundled price is relative to the individual prices. Special meals or combos at restaurants, such as the McDonald's meal combinations, work in a similar fashion, as do many software packages. The profit capture inherent in bundling (see Chap. 6) can be considerably enhanced through more effective communication of the bundle and its price.

Many countries have laws which define and restrict the limits of price communication. The idea behind these regulations is to ensure the integrity and clarity of the prices consumers pay for the merchandise or services they receive [70]. This depends, for example, on transparency, i.e., that the customer can unequivocally match a product to an offered price and vice versa. The US Federal Trade Communication has extensive guidelines which define deceptive advertising practices. These include the uses of words such as "wholesale," "free," and "limited" in price communication or practices which create the impression that an item is on sale when the price actually reflects normal levels [71]. The requirements on retailers to express both a total price and a unit price vary by country. Such guidelines are especially relevant for the comparison of discounted prices and reference prices. The latter is normally higher and could be based on the manufacturer's recommendation, previously asked prices, or competitors' prices. Many countries (e.g., the United States and Germany) expressly prohibit the use of artificially inflated prices to convey the impression that a prevailing price is a bargain.

9.4.1.6 Payment Terms

Payment terms are not primarily a communications instrument, but they have a perception-related and therefore a communicative component. A price offer split into installments, for example, can be perceived differently from the corresponding total price. The same applies for leasing rates. These effects occur even when the prices, from a financial accounting perspective, are comparable. These insights give rise to interesting opportunities for the design and communication of prices. The car industry recognized this long ago and offers seemingly countless financing and leasing options. They have learned that customers who finance their vehicles tend to order more options. Let us assume that an air conditioning unit for a vehicle costs $1200 if the customer pays upfront but only $20 per month if the customer leases the vehicle. One can assume that customers who lease their cars are more likely to purchase the air conditioning unit. From a communications standpoint, $20 looks like a much better deal than $1200.

As we know from Chap. 4, additional effects derive from the *timing and design of payment flows*. At a fitness center, customers who pay their annual fee in one lump sum at the start of the year use the facilities less and less frequently over time and have significantly lower renewal rates than customers who pay their membership dues monthly. Thus, it makes more sense for the club operator to promote monthly payment plans. In contrast to car leases, the emphasis here is on the effects on customer loyalty, not the (lower) level of the payment itself.

An additional effect which touches consumer behavior and price communication is the time gap between the moment of payment and the moment of actual consumption. Gourville and Soman [72] demonstrated this phenomenon for the purchase of theater tickets. Two people have tickets for a show. Person A purchased the ticket well in advance, while Person B's purchase took place on the day before the show. Let us assume that on the day of the show, bad weather would make travel to the theater very unpleasant. Person B has a strong motivation to attend the show despite the weather, because the payment for the ticket happened very recently. Person A, in contrast, bought the ticket weeks earlier. This person therefore perceives a much slighter negative impact from not using the ticket. This effect is known as *payment depreciation*.

Companies can capitalize on the effect of *payment depreciation* in several ways. One can influence the time of payment through appropriate communication and through additional price incentives (early booking discount, advance sale prices, etc.). Consumer goods manufacturers can offer larger package sizes, which increase the time lag between payment and full consumption and therefore reduce the perceived price sacrifice. An additional effect is that larger package sizes tend to result in increased consumption [73, 74]. The reverse effect occurs when the payment is due long after the consumption. In that case, the perceived value from the consumption diminishes over time, leading to a more negative perception of the price sacrifice. An example of this is invoicing by service companies long after they have performed the actual service. Service providers should avoid the practice of delayed invoicing or at least include some form of communication aimed at mitigating the negative effects.

The effects of stretching payment out over a long period and the effects of perceived value are therefore countervailing. Stretching out payments reduces the amount paid per unit of time. This can help a company tap into new customer segments. But it also means that the payment intervals are pushed back, often beyond the time of consumption. With regard to the perception of the value and the price sacrifice, this is an unfavorable constellation, especially concerning the chances of repeat purchase.

Another related aspect is the design and communication of prices with respect to the unit of time. Salesforce.com communicates monthly prices, but customers pay an annual fee. Gourville [75] recommends expressing the costs per day rather than per month, which makes the offering appear to be more of a bargain from the customers' perspective. The message "Drive a Porsche for only $40 per day" appears to be a better deal than the message of $1200 per month. The opposite applies when one is communicating savings. Saving $3650 per year sounds more impressive than saving $10 per day. These comparisons show that even when two payment amounts are objectively and mathematically identical, the way the amount is paid and the accompanying communication can have a strong influence on consumer perception and behavior.

9.4.2 Internal Price Communication

In addition to the outbound price communication, internal price communication warrants close attention. A firm should ensure that salespeople have up-to-date price information at all times. But this seemingly trivial requirement is not easy to meet when the firm has a large assortment and frequent price changes. In previous times, it was necessary to print and distribute price lists. Nowadays, the general practice is to make prices accessible online. These systems may also be used to communicate information beyond prices to the salespeople. Such information can include contribution margin, variable compensation, and online tools to support the salesperson. In a study conducted by the Professional Pricing Society, some 36% of companies said that a transaction's actual profitability, determined and communicated in real time, is one of the most important pieces of information for price implementation. Almost half of the respondents (42%) believe that the use of price management software improves price discipline among salespeople [76].

Companies should inform their salespeople how prices are determined and what the rationale is behind any price change. Such information motivates the salespeople and provides them with the ammunition they need to develop their selling arguments toward customers. In this regard, however, the communication and openness within many companies leave much to be desired. Salespeople are not always thoroughly informed about how prices come together, the role of each factor in price setting, and the underlying pricing process. These information deficits can lead to inadequate communication and price argumentation by the salesperson.

To facilitate the communication of prices and price changes, companies can provide their salespeople with *argumentation guidelines*. These guidelines cover a product's advantages from a price value perspective, as well as comparisons to individual competitors and to the overall market. They can help a premium supplier, for example, shift the sales negotiation toward value arguments and away from price arguments. Low-price suppliers should make sure that they not only communicate their favorable price position but also their ability to deliver acceptable product quality.

Modern price systems are becoming increasingly complex. Information technology helps reduce some of the complexity, but it still places heavier burdens on the salespeople. The result is a greater need for communication and for training. The salespeople must be in a position to deal with this complexity. Otherwise these complex price systems can overwhelm the sales organization and lead to internal chaos around prices. When we mystery shopped the same request at a logistics firm, we received six different price offers for the identical service. Even with access to IT support, the salespeople were not able to manage the complexity. They did not understand the price structures and could not defend or explain them to customers. The time required to explain a price system to one's salespeople and to the customers grows overproportionally with the complexity of the system. When one conceives and designs a price system, one should not only consider the challenge for the customers to understand it (and the communication required to support the understanding) but also the same potential (and communication requirements) for one's own sales team.

9.5   Price Controlling

Price controlling looks at every phase of the price management process. One also speaks of *price monitoring* in this context. A prerequisite for price controlling is that plans and price goals are formulated in explicit and measurable ways. In the ongoing business, controlling checks whether the plans and price goals have been achieved. In the case of deviations or discrepancies, one should identify the underlying causes and put countermeasures in place or consider more realistic objectives for the future. There is a wide range of what people understand under the term "controlling." In the broadest case, controlling assumes the full responsibility for all planning and monitoring activities. A narrower definition limits controlling to the review or audit of results. In this section, we will focus primarily on that latter definition, although we expressly acknowledge that controlling can play a role in the other phases of price management. This applies to content as well as process. One could even argue that controlling plays a particularly important role in price management, because the market-facing side of a company is not always in harmony with the internal corporate functions involved in pricing.

9.5.1 The Price Controlling Function

In detail, the price controlling function needs to answer the following questions:

- Were the planned prices and volumes achieved?
- How large are the deviations between list and transaction prices, and what explains them?
- Did the implementation of a planned price increase succeed?
- Why did we lose deals? What role did price and other factors play?
- Is the necessary information made available in every phase?
- Are price promotions and discounts achieving their desired effects?
- Are the learnings flowing into the subsequent rounds of pricing?
- Were the agreed goals and conditions adhered to?
- Are the incentive systems effective or were they undermined or "gamed"?
- Is there price-related friction between operating units, market segments, or countries?

The list of questions is only partial. Each company should create its own list and adjust it over time to address all relevant issues.

9.5.2 IT Requirements

The complexity of price controlling depends heavily on the specific business model. In many companies, the complexity and the resulting demands on information technology (IT) are very high. Several factors can be responsible for this:

- The assortment offered by retailers, spare parts suppliers, or service providers can include hundreds of thousands of units, if not millions. Airlines make millions of price changes over the course of a year. Travel agencies and tour operators not only need to set and monitor the prices for every hotel and every room category either on a per day or per week basis, or even based on departure city, but also the prices of add-on products and services, rental cars, etc.
- Price differentiation, individual price negotiations, and complex price structures mean that de facto every transaction has its own specific price.
- Discounts and conditions are responsible for large discrepancies between list prices and transaction prices.

It is clear that effective price controlling under these circumstances can succeed only if the corresponding IT requirements are met. The information system of a company should be able to provide comprehensive data on questions relevant for pricing. This requires a *pricing database*, the appropriate software, and qualified team members. Standard software from SAP and similar vendors already make a lot of price-relevant data available. CRM systems offer an ever larger spectrum.

Specialized pricing software delivers all the important information needed for standardized deals and transactions.

The following case examples illustrate how to achieve the necessary transparency in practice: a materials manufacturer had two sales channels. Their project business sold directly to large contractors. The rest of the market was served indirectly via the specialty trade. The list prices for each channel were differentiated, with significantly higher list prices in the specialty trade. Conditions played a prominent role in the trade, and there were almost no limits to the creativity of salespeople in inventing and hiding conditions. Determining the true transaction prices in each channel and finding a basis to compare them took a team of three employees 6 weeks. The company was very surprised to learn—contrary to its beliefs—that its margins in specialty trade were lower than in their project business.

A bank wanted to analyze the discrepancies between list and transaction prices as well as the granting of special terms and conditions, on a per-branch basis. Pulling together the necessary data proved so complicated that a two-person team needed 3 months to produce the numbers for the comparison. The best branch was only 15 basis points (0.15% points) under the list price (=base interest rate), while the worst-performing branch was 35 basis points below the base interest rate. This was completely new information for the bank's management.

The comparison of salespeople's revenues and margins in Table 9.4 was only possible after the sanitation technology company (whose numbers were the basis for the table) implemented new software. Prior to that installation, the company could not break down contribution margins to the level of an individual salesperson.

Ideally, all of the information mentioned in these cases above and the rest of this section should be available at the push of a button. The reality in most companies remains far from this ideal, but the situation is constantly improving.

9.5.3 Tools for Price Controlling

Because of the sheer number and the diversity of the questions involved in price controlling, companies require certain approaches and tools. In this section, we describe a selection of such tools which have proven themselves in practice.

9.5.3.1 Price Realization

The simplest and most fundamental question of price controlling concerns price realization. What transaction prices were actually achieved? This question can be broken down by product, customer, segment, sales channel, or region. Depending on the case, one then looks at deviations between the transaction prices and the list prices, target prices, average prices, or other benchmarks. Deviations from competitors' prices could also be of interest. One can perform the same set of analyses and comparisons for margins.

Figure 9.11 shows price realization by customer for a technology company. The comparison basis in this case is the average price. The bars indicate the difference from the average price.

Customer

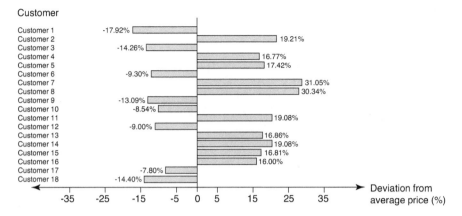

Fig. 9.11 Price realization by customer for a technology company (Simon-Kucher & Partners)

The discrepancies between the average price and the prices paid by individual customers are enormous. Customer 1 pays 17.92% less than the average price, while the prices paid by customers 7 and 8 are more than 30% above the average. Such price differences are not unusual at all in practice. The first step is to identify them in the first place and make them transparent. The second step is to investigate the causes of the discrepancies. The fact that price differences of this magnitude exist is something the responsible management should be aware of, but the discrepancies' existence alone says nothing about whether they make sense. In the spirit of this book's arguments, one must ask whether these discrepancies are appropriate with respect to price differentiation.

Table 9.6 shows the realization of prices by individual key accounts for a chemicals company. The comparison basis in this case is a target price set in advance. For 4 of the 11 customers, the company succeeded in achieving the target price. For two customers, the actual realized price was well below target at $0.42 and $0.36/kg, respectively. On average, the company missed the target price by $0.17/kg or by 7.5%. When the target margin is 18%, that deviation is very high. In this case, management had believed that its price realization was rather effective. It took only a few exceptions with very large price gaps to drag down the overall margin significantly.

Detailing and examining price realization by hand, as in the previous two examples, are only possible when the number of customers is small. For comprehensive assortments, large numbers of customers, or numerous price parameters, such an analysis requires either an aggregation of the price indicators or an automated process.

Figure 9.12 illustrates an aggregated *price realization analysis* for two regions for a company in the packaging sector. In this case, all customers and products in the two regions are summarized. The chart shows the trend in realized prices over time. The prices are shown on an index basis, with the index set at 100 for the first month in both regions.

		Target price	Realized price	Price gap
		$/kg	$/kg	$/kg
Table 9.6 Price realization by key account for a chemicals company (deviations from target price) (Simon-Kucher & Partners)	Customer A	2.07	1.65	0.42
	Customer B	2.19	2.16	0.03
	Customer C	2.12	2.11	0.01
	Customer D	2.51	2.15	0.36
	Customer E	2.53	2.53	0.00
	Customer F	2.47	2.43	0.04
	Customer G	2.52	2.52	0.00
	Customer H	2.34	2.18	0.16
	Customer I	2.33	2.16	0.17
	Customer J	2.55	2.55	0.00
	Customer K	2.47	2.47	0.00
	Total	2.28	2.11	0.17

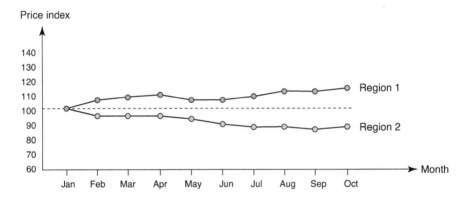

Fig. 9.12 Price realization trends in two regions

The realized prices in the two regions have followed vastly different paths. While the price in Region 1 rose by around 10%, the price in Region 2 declined by a similar percentage. In this case as well, the company needs to investigate the causes and take appropriate action. The effects on margins were dramatic.

An automated system is recommended when the price realization analysis covers several price parameters. A "traffic light" color scheme has proven to be an effective way to make the results of such a system easy to grasp at a glance. Green indicates that the situation is fine, yellow means "monitor," and red signifies that action, perhaps a renegotiation of prices, is necessary. Figure 9.13 shows an example of such a price traffic light. Continuous monitoring with respect to the revenue trends for each customer, deviations from price targets, and a profit cross-check help a company secure and maintain its profitability.

Customer number	Average revenue (last 3 Month)	Revenue trend	Check 1: Revenue trend	Same trend in the last 12 month ... times	Target revenue	Deviation from target	Check 2: Goal achievement	Same trend in the last 12 month ... times	Rate card Level	Rate card Profile	On top discount	Check 3: Profitability	Effective discount
14 123 234 4	0	-	○	-	1000	-	○	-	1	A	10%	●	22%
14 543 234 2	1520	-19%	●	8	1500	+1%	○	12	1	E	0%	○	19%
	4736	-4%	◐	5	5000	-5%	◐	4	3	C	0%	○	36%
14 646 332 1	5007	+11%	○	5	6500	-23%	●	6	4	B	5%	●	46%
14 564 454 6	-	-	○	5	1000	-	○	-	1	A	0%	○	23%
	6897	-27%	●	6	8000	-14%	●	6	4	A	5%	○	42%
14 878 676 4	582	+20%	○	4	2000	-71%	●	8	2	D	10%	●	31%
	2276	+3%	◐	2	2000	+14%	○	10	1	B	0%	●	24%
14 456 345 4	1157	+178%	○	2	3000	-61%	●	5	3	E	0%	●	39%
14 365 456 5	3786	-74%	●	1	4000	-5%	◐	10	3	A	5%	○	35%

○ green   ◐ yellow   ● red

Fig. 9.13   Price traffic light (Simon-Kucher & Partners)

9.5.3.2 Price Waterfall

The analyses described in the previous section offer no information on how the prices were realized, i.e., which parameters accounted for the discrepancies between realized prices and the list or target prices. If one follows the path from the list price to the final transaction price, it resembles an incrementally descending staircase or waterfall. The latter name is typically associated with such images. Figure 9.14 shows such a price waterfall for a consumer products manufacturer who sells into the food-and-grocery trade.

The price waterfall concept brings several aspects to light. First, it makes clear at a glance the number of price- and margin-reducing conditions involved, as well as their individual magnitudes. In our experience, in almost all cases, the totality of these price- and margin-reducing factors (or "profit leaks") is not known and certainly not transparent. In the present case, these effects summed up to 30%, which is an alarming magnitude. Second, a price waterfall indicates opportunities to reduce the profit leakage. As we indicated with respect to discount and condition systems, the principle of "pay for performance" needs to be applied more strictly. Prevailing terms or conditions originally granted on a one-off basis must be eliminated, when the customers no longer perform the activity or function which earned them the discount or terms in the first place.

9.5.3.3 Discount Jungle

Analyses of the relationship between customer or transaction size and discount levels are usually very eye-opening. All discount systems envisage some form of discount based on size or volume. But the reality in many cases looks much different. Figure 9.15 illustrates this using the case of a software company. There are clearly defined guidelines for volume discounts, as shown by the stepped, solid line. The actual granting of discounts in fact had little to do with these guidelines. First, almost all discounts were in excess of the prescribed magnitude. Second, there appears to be no correlation whatsoever between the purchase volume of the customers and the

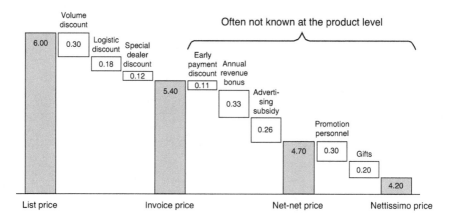

Fig. 9.14 Price waterfall (Simon-Kucher & Partners)

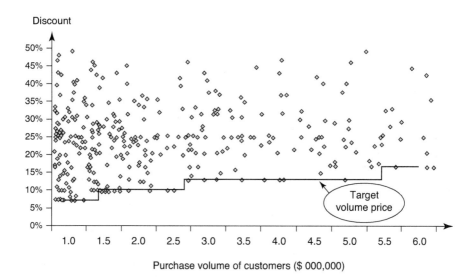

Fig. 9.15 Discount jungle of a software company

discounts they received. One can truly speak of a discount jungle. We observe similar situations in most companies, albeit not always to this extreme. The finding alone, however, says nothing about the extent to which these discounts make sense. Theoretically, each and every one of these discounts could have a sound justification. But that is highly improbable. Findings of this kind allow a company to derive concrete measures to improve price realization. Under normal circumstances, the smallest customers should not receive the highest discounts. Companies can often see significant margin improvement simply by reducing the discount levels which small customers receive.

Number of contracts

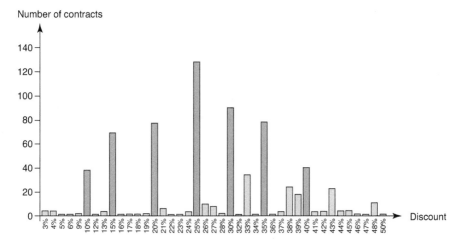

Fig. 9.16 Margin-reducing discounts resulting from rounding to the 0 or 5 (Simon-Kucher & Partners)

Figure 9.16 shows a typical pattern resulting from discounting, namely, the tendency to round off discounts. The example is drawn from an industrial service provider. Almost all discount levels are at round numbers such as 10%, 15%, or 25%. The discounts also cover a very wide range. If one attempted to target discount levels which were only a few percentage points less than the round numbers, it would have a dramatic effect on profit. Similarly, the company could also reduce the steps between the discounts within the context of negotiations. We often observe that discounts change in convenient intervals of 5 or 10% points. If a company succeeded in reducing the size of these intervals, it would generally lead to an overall lower discount level. Price controlling can and should bring such counterproductive practices to light so that the company can improve them.

9.5.3.4 Analysis of Responsibilities

The analyses described above reveal price realization and discounting—both their structures and distributions—at a customer and at a regional level. No less interesting are analyses which make the responsibilities for price realization decisions transparent. Figure 9.17 illustrates such a breakdown for a US-based industrial manufacturer. The data pertain to the US market. There are clear guidelines on who has what authority to grant discounts at or below a certain level. The discounting authority of the salespeople, for example, is capped at 10% of the list price. Beyond that, there are a series of escalation steps, all the way up to headquarters.

The analysis reveals that most discounts are granted (i.e., approved) by the regional sales managers or the national sales manager. The salespeople themselves grant relatively few discounts. The interpretation of this finding is anything but simple. Do the salespeople delegate most decisions up the chain of authority because

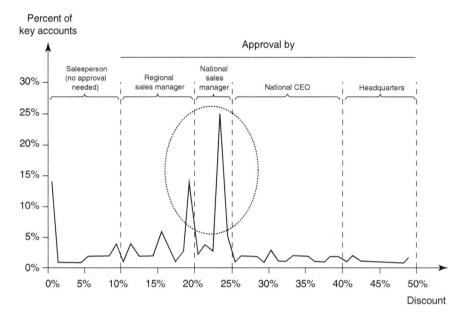

Fig. 9.17 Granting of discounts by role (Simon-Kucher & Partners)

their own authority limit is too low? Or are the sales managers too lenient and don't ensure that the salespeople make do with the authority they have? Should they be more adamant about rejecting the requests for higher discounts, either from sales-people or from customers? Since the national managing director and headquarters grant only a small number of all discounts, should they even be involved in the process at all? Or would it be better to give the national sales manager the last word and full decision authority on prices? A prerequisite for asking such qualified questions is the ability of price controlling to provide a clear, detailed, and factual view of the current situation.

9.5.3.5 Lost Deals

A very revealing yet problematic source of insights for price controlling is the analysis of *lost deals*. Of course, such analyses are not limited to price, but price plays a key role in almost any lost deal. Figure 9.18 shows the case of an engineering company which examined a large number of lost deals. This company had a "win rate" of 35% and conversely lost 65% of the deals they competed for.

In this case, the reasons behind the lost deals were determined using both an internal survey and an external (customer) survey. Price was at the top of the list of reasons for lost deals by a wide margin. That was the result of the surveys and should be taken into account. To determine whether this situation is acceptable, however, requires further evaluation. The company can tolerate this situation as long as it still wins a sufficient number of deals, even though many potential customers consider its prices to be too high. One could consider eliminating price-sensitive customers from

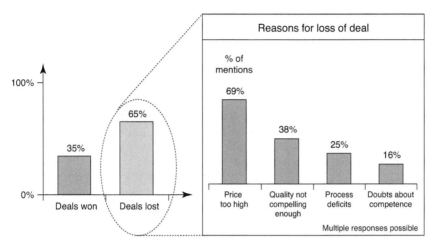

Fig. 9.18 Lost deal analysis

consideration early on and therefore avoid the cost and effort of making bids which have lower chances of success. One can also call the validity of these kinds of surveys into question. In both the internal and external surveys, respondents conveniently cite price as the reason for lost deals. An extensive investigation which truly gets to the bottom of the reasons for lost deals is warranted in such cases.

9.5.3.6 Complex Analyses of Variance

An implicit assumption in the above analyses is that the list or target prices are "optimal" and should therefore be adhered to. The company does not want any downward deviations, which are the only ones which occur in practice. But price controlling can challenge the assumption that the list prices are indeed optimal. To do this, it must obtain insights into the price-response function or price elasticity. A simple analysis of variance ("as is" vs. "should be") is no longer sufficient. These questions require a fundamentally more complex analysis of the actual price-volume combinations the company has achieved. Whether price controlling can conduct such an analysis is questionable. We will discuss this situation briefly using two cases. The first involves the Hilton Hotel in Chicago, a case we explore in greater detail in Chap. 12 in the context of yield management. On one night, some 13 of the 1600 available rooms were vacant. The question price controlling must answer is whether it would have been better to charge a higher price and accept a larger number of vacancies or should the hotel have cut prices slightly in order to fill the remaining vacant rooms? In the second case, a car maker introduced a new model whose demand in the first year far exceeds its manufacturing capacity. The company could have set a higher introductory price and still achieved full capacity utilization. Can and should price controlling estimate how much higher the introductory price should have been and how much profit was sacrificed at the lower price?

Similar challenges arise when market and competitive situations change or other exogenous factors compel a company to adjust its own prices. The same applies to internal operational factors. Changes to the marketing mix can influence the price response in such a way that the company can keep volume constant despite higher prices (and vice versa). In such situations, price controlling cannot take on the roles of marketing and sales management. Nonetheless, it is advisable to involve controllers already at the beginning of the price management process and take advantage of their competencies to improve the quality of the process. Well-managed companies have taken this step. Price controlling's role should not be limited to *ex post* analyses to identify mistakes in pricing policies. From the beginning of the pricing process onward, the controllers can contribute to the setting and implementation of optimal prices.

Conclusion
Success in price management ultimately depends on implementation. The tasks are to define price-related responsibilities clearly, to design incentive systems which align with corporate objectives, to communicate prices effectively, and finally to monitor price realization. We summarize our main insights as follows:

- A company should assign responsibilities for each of the diverse tasks and duties of the price management process.
- Each part of the process and each organizational unit should be tailored to the company's business model to the greatest extent possible.
- In general, it is advisable to allocate price decision authority rather high in the hierarchy. There are specific conditions under which this is even more strongly recommended.
- An absolute prerequisite for pricing is to ensure the cooperation and the smooth flow of information between market-facing and internal functions.
- More and more companies are creating the role of pricing manager, establishing pricing departments, and using the services of specialized price consultants.
- Specialized software and artificial intelligence (machine learning) are increasingly used in price management.
- The role of the CEO in price management is becoming increasingly important. The CEO must ensure that goals are met, that processes are optimally designed, and that the company fosters a profit-oriented culture with regard to pricing.
- Sales forces play a critical role in price implementation. The delegation of price decision authority to salespeople is highly controversial. One should err on the side of caution.
- If the salespeople do have price decision authority, their compensation system should not be based on revenue. Instead, commissions and other incentives should be based on contribution margin. Incentive systems

(continued)

should focus on how well salespeople implement prices and reward them accordingly.

- Discount and condition systems offer the necessary price flexibility even when the salespeople have little or no price authority. They allow price differentiation for managing and influencing customer behavior.
- The effect of price is highly dependent on price communication, because customers react according to their perception and evaluation of prices.
- There are numerous instruments, opportunities, and occasions for external price communication. These include price lists, price-related advertising, the use of complex price structures, and, in a broader sense, the definition of payment terms.
- Prices and what they are based on should also be communicated internally. This boosts the sales teams' motivation and enhances their ability to explain and defend prices.
- Effective price controlling is indispensable, but it requires first-class information technology.
- Companies have many proven tools at their disposal to investigate their price realization, price differentiation, discounting practices, price waterfalls, and roles and responsibilities.
- Ideally price controlling will be involved in the entire price management process, but responsible only for monitoring results.

Every strategy is only as good as its implementation. This statement also applies to price management. As the professionalization of price management continues, senior management should devote more attention to implementation. This includes organizational innovations such as pricing managers or pricing departments, goal-driven decision-making and incentive systems, and modern methods for price controlling and monitoring.

References

1. Freiling, J., & Wölting, H. (2003). Organisation des Preismanagements. In H. Diller, & A. Herrmann (Ed.), *Handbuch Preispolitik: Strategien – Planung – Organisation – Umsetzung* (pp. 419–436). Wiesbaden: Gabler.
2. Dutta, S., Zbaracki, M., & Bergen, M. (2003). Pricing Process as a Capability: A Case Study. *Strategic Management Journal, 24*(7), 615–630.
3. Wiltinger, K. (1998). *Preismanagement in der unternehmerischen Praxis: Probleme der organisatorischen Implementierung.* Wiesbaden: Gabler.
4. Kossmann, J. (2008). *Die Implementierung der Preispolitik in Business-to-Business Unternehmen.* Nürnberg: GIM.
5. Fassnacht, M., Nelius, Y., & Szajna, M. (2013). Preismanagement – nicht immer ein Top-Thema bei Konsumgüterherstellern. *Sales Management Review, 9*(2), 58–70.

6. Nelius, Y. (2011). *Organisation des Preismanagements von Konsumgüterherstellern – Eine empirische Untersuchung*. Frankfurt am Main: Peter Lang.
7. Atkin, B., & Skinner, R. (1976). *How British Industry Prices*. Old Woking: The Gresham Press.
8. Ehrhardt, A., Vidal, D., & Uhl, A. (2012). *Global Pricing Study*. Bonn: Simon-Kucher & Partners.
9. Sodhi, M., & Sodhi, N. (2008). *Six Sigma Pricing: Improving Pricing Operations to Increase Profits*. Upper Saddle River: Financial Times Press.
10. Hofbauer, G., & Bergmann, S. (2012). *Professionelles Controlling in Marketing und Vertrieb*. Erlangen: Publicis Publishing.
11. Simon, H. (2013). How Price Consulting is Coming of Age. *Journal of Professional Pricing*, 22 (1), 12–19.
12. PROS Holdings (2014). Annual Report 2014. http://investors.pros.com/phoenix.zhtml? c=211158&p=irol-reportsAnnual. Accessed 6 July 2014.
13. Mühlberger, A. (2013). Chefsache Preis. *Sales Management Review*, 12(1), 8–11.
14. Tacke, G., Vidal, D., & Haemer, J. (2014). Profitable Innovation. http://www.simon-kucher. com/sites/default/files/simon-kucher_ebook_profitable_innovation_2014.pdf.   Accessed 27 July 2015.
15. Sawers, P. (2014). Be all-in, or all-out: Steve Ballmer's advice for startups. http://thenextweb. com/insider/2014/03/04/steve-ballmers-advice-startups/#!za6rp. Accessed 6 July 2015.
16. Doyle, M. (2018). Elon Musk pricing strategy email to Tesla dealers – we all can learn from this email. https://www.linkedin.com/pulse/elon-musk-pricing-strategy-email-tesla-dealers-we-all-michael-doyle/?trackingId=BfNlN2X11WonSdTlP65w1g%3D%3D.   Accessed 10 March 2018.
17. Anonymous. (2005, April 27). *The Wall Street Journal*, p. 22.
18. Earnings Conference Quarter II 2011.
19. Anonymous. (2008). *Handelszeitung*, No. 27, pp. 2–3.
20. Stewart, T. A. (2006). Growth as a Process. https://hbr.org/2006/06/growth-as-a-process. Accessed 7 July 2015.
21. Diller, H. (2007). *Preispolitik* (4th ed.). Stuttgart: Kohlhammer.
22. Credit Suisse (2010). Global Equity Strategy, 18. Oktober 2010. Zürich.
23. Lehmitz, S., McLellan, K., & Schulze, P. (2015). Pricing's Secret Weapon: A Well-Trained Sales Force. McKinsey on Marketing and Sales. http://www.mckinseyonmarketingandsales. com/pricings-secret-weapon-a-well-trained-sales-force. Accessed 17 April 2015.
24. Stadie, E., & Clausen, G. (2008). B-to-B-Pricing-Excellence. *Marketing Review St. Gallen*, 25 (3), 48–51.
25. Fassnacht, M. (2009). Preismanagement: Eine prozessorientierte Perspektive. *Marketing Review St. Gallen*, 26(5), 8–13.
26. Kern, R. (1989). Letting your Salespeople Set Prices. *Sales and Marketing Management*, 141 (9), 44–49.
27. Mishra, B. K., & Prasad, A. (2004). Centralized Pricing Versus Delegating Pricing to the Salesforce under Information Asymmetry. *Marketing Science*, 23(1), 21–27.
28. Stephenson, P. R., Cron, W. C., & Frazier, G. L. (1979). Delegating Pricing Authority to the Sales Force: the Effects on Sales and Profit Performance. *Journal of Marketing*, 43(2), 21–28.
29. Walker, O. C., Orville, C., Churchill, G. A., & Ford, N. M. (1977). Motivation and Performance in Industrial Selling: Present Knowledge and Needed Research. *Journal of Marketing Research*, 14(2), 156–168.
30. Lal, R., & Staelin, R. (1986). Salesforce Compensation Plans in Environments with Asymmetric Information. *Marketing Science*, 5(3), 179–198.
31. Nimer, D. (1971). Nimer on Pricing. *Industrial Marketing*, 56(3), 48–55.
32. Zarth, H. R. (1981). Effizienter verkaufen durch die richtige Strategie für das Preisgespräch. *Markenartikel*, 43(2), 111–113.
33. Voeth, M., & Herbst, U. (2011). Preisverhandlungen auf Commodity-Märkten. In *Commodity Marketing: Grundlagen – Besonderheiten – Erfahrungen* (pp. 149–172). Wiesbaden: Gabler.

34. Krafft, M. (1999). An Empirical Investigation of the Antecedents of Sales Force Control Systems. *Journal of Marketing*, 63(3), 120–134.
35. Weinberg, C. B. (1978). Jointly Optimal Sales Commissions for Nonincome Maximizing Sales Forces. *Management Science*, 24(12), 1252–1258.
36. Joseph, K. (2001). On the Optimality of Delegating Pricing Authority to the Sales Force. *Journal of Marketing*, 65(1), 62–70.
37. Bhardwaj, P. (2001). Delegating Pricing Decisions. *Marketing Science*, 20(2), 143–169.
38. Roth, S. (2011). Koordination von Preisentscheidungen in konkurrierenden Wertschöpfungsketten. In H. Corsten, & R. Gössinger (Ed.), *Dezentrale Koordination ökonomischer Aktivitäten: Markt, Hierarchie, Hybride* (pp. 91–122). Berlin: Erich Schmidt.
39. Roth, S. (2006). *Preismanagement für Leistungsbündel*. Wiesbaden: Gabler.
40. Hansen, A.-K., Joseph, K., & Krafft, M. (2008). Price Delegation in Sales Organizations: An Empirical Investigation. *Business Research*, 1(1), 94–104.
41. Alavi, S., Wieseke, J., & Guba, J. H. (2015). Saving on Discounts through Accurate Sensing – Salespeople's Estimations of Customer Price Importance and Their Effects on Negotiation Success. *Journal of Retailing*, 96(1), 40–55.
42. Wieseke, J., Alavi, S., & Habel, J. (2014). Willing to Pay More, Eager to Pay Less: The Role of Customer Loyalty in Price Negotiations. *Journal of Marketing*, 78(6), 17–37.
43. Wiltinger, K. (1996). Der Einfluß von Umweltcharakteristika auf die Delegation von Preiskompetenz an den Außendienst. *Schmalenbachs Zeitschrift für betriebswirtschaftliche Forschung*, 48(11), 983–998.
44. Krafft, M. (1995). *Außendienstentlohnung im Licht der Neuen Institutionenlehre*. Wiesbaden: Gabler.
45. Schmidt, S., & Krafft, M. (2005). Delegation von Preiskompetenz an Verkaufsaußendienstmitarbeiter. In H. Diller (Ed.), *Pricing-Forschung in Deutschland* (pp. 17–28). Nürnberg: Wissenschaftliche Gesellschaft für Innovatives Marketing.
46. Albers, S., & Krafft, M. (1992). Steuerungssysteme für den Verkaufsaußendienst. *Manuskripte aus den Instituten für Betriebswirtschaftslehre*, No. 306, Christian-Albrechts-Universität zu Kiel.
47. Zoltners, A. A., Sinha, P., & Lorimer, S. E. (2006). *The Complete Guide to Sales Force Incentive Compensation: How to Design and Implement Plans that Work*. New York: Amacon.
48. Albers, K., & Krafft, M. (2013). *Vertriebsmanagement: Organisation – Planung – Controlling – Support*. Wiesbaden: Gabler.
49. Spiro, R. L., Stanton, W. J., & Rich, G. A. (2007). *Management of a Sales Force*. Boston: McGraw-Hill.
50. Meffert, H., Burmann, C., & Kirchgeorg, M. (2011). *Marketing: Grundlagen marktorientierter Unternehmensführung: Konzepte – Instrumente – Praxisbeispiele* (11th ed.). Wiesbaden: Gabler.
51. Steffenhagen, H. (2003). Konditionensysteme. In H. Diller, & A. Herrmann (Ed.), *Handbuch Preispolitik: Strategien – Planung – Organisation – Umsetzung* (pp. 576–596). Wiesbaden: Gabler.
52. Pechtl, H. (2014). *Preispolitik: Behavioral Pricing und Preissysteme* (2nd ed.). Konstanz: UVK.
53. Williamson, P. (2012). *Pricing for the London Olympics 2012*. Simon-Kucher & Partners World Meeting, Bonn.
54. Bertini, M., & Gourville, J. T. (2012). Pricing to Create Shared Value. Harvard Business Review, 6. https://hbr.org/2012/06/pricing-to-create-shared-value/ar/1. Accessed 17 May 2015.
55. Teekampagne (2017). Exclusive Darjeeling tea at an affordable price. https://www.teacampaign.com /Transparency/Exclusive-Darjeeling-tea-affordable-price. Accessed 19 February 2018.
56. Best Buy Price Match Guarantee (2016). http://www.bestbuy.com/site/clp/price-match-guarantee/pcmcat290300050002.c?id=pcmcat290300050002. Accessed 21 December 2016.

57. Stech, J. (2015). Bonner Unternehmen Simon-Kucher: Der Trick der Pizzabäcker. General-Anzeiger   Bonn.   http://www.general-anzeiger-bonn.de/bonn/wirtschaft/der-trick-der-pizzabaecker-article1677143.html. Accessed 12 July 2015.
58. Simon, H. (1992). *Preismanagement* (2nd ed.). Wiesbaden: Gabler.
59. Eskin, G. J. (1982). Behaviour Scan: A State of the Art Market Research Facility Utilizing UPC Scanning and Targetable Television. Paper presented at The European Congress on Automation in Retailing.
60. Chaudhuri, S. (2016). Mind the Gap: Toblerone Customers Feel Short-Changed by Shape Change. The Wall Street Journal. http://www.wsj.com/articles/mind-the-gap-toblerone-customers-feel-short-changed-by-shape-change-1478612997. Accessed 21 December 2016.
61. Verbraucherzentrale Hamburg (2015). Anbieter sparen – Verbraucher zahlen: Kleinere Menge zum gleichen Preis!. www.vzhh.de/ernaehrung/32535/Versteckte%20Preiserhoehungen.pdf. Accessed 7 July 2015.
62. Anonymous. (2017, January 21). Evian ist Mogelpackung des Jahres. *Frankfurter Allgemeine Zeitung*, p. 18.
63. Cox, J. (2001). Can Differential Prices be Fair?. *Journal of Product and Brand Management*, 10 (4/5), 264–275.
64. Winkelmeier-Becker, E. (2015, January 16). Reiseportale müssen bei Flügen stets den vollen Endpreis nennen. *Frankfurter Allgemeine Zeitung*, p. 23.
65. Bundesgerichtshof (2015). Preisdarstellungen bei Flugbuchungen im Internet. http://juris. bundesgerichtshof.de/cgi-bin/rechtsprechung/document.py?Gericht=bgh&Art=pm& Datum=2015&Sort=3&nr=71812&pos=0&anz=133. Accessed 9 September 2015.
66. Xia, L., & Monroe, K. B. (2004). Price Partitioning on the Internet. *Journal of Interactive Marketing*, 18(4), 63–73.
67. Morwitz, V. G., Greenleaf, E. A., & Johnson, E. J. (1998). Divide and Prosper: Consumers' Reactions to Partitioned Prices. *Journal of Marketing Research*, 35(4), 453–463.
68. Herrmann, A., & Wricke, M. (1998). Evaluating Multidimensional Prices. *Journal of Product and Brand Management*, 7(2), 161–169.
69. Huber, C., Gatzert, N., & Schmeiser, H. (2012). Price Presentation and Consumers' Choice. *Zeitschrift für die gesamte Versicherungswissenschaft*, 101(1), 63–73.
70. Völker, S. (2002). *Preisangabenrecht* (2nd ed.). München: Beck.
71. Government Publishing Office (2018). Electronic Code of Federal Regulations. https://www. ecfr.gov/cgi-bin/text-idx?SID=866b1c600a4f619ef31ce1d14ad49a2c&mc=true&tpl=/ ecfrbrowse/Title16/16cfrv1_02.tpl#0. Accessed 19 February 2018.
72. Gourville, J. T., & Soman, D. (1998). Payment Depreciation: The Behavioral Effects of Temporally Separating Payments from Consumption. *Journal of Consumer Research*, 25(2), 160–174.
73. Ailawadi, K. L., & Neslin, S. A. (1998). The Effect of Promotion on Consumption: Buying More and Consuming it Faster. *Journal of Marketing Research*, 35(3), 390–398.
74. Busch, R., Dögl, R., & Unger, F. (2008). *Integriertes Marketing: Strategie – Organisation – Instrumente*. Wiesbaden: Gabler.
75. Gourville, J. T. (1998). Pennies-a-Day. The Effect of Temporal Reframing on Transaction Evaluation. *Journal of Consumer Research*, 24(4), 395–408.
76. Professional Pricing Society, Atlanta 2007.

Price Management for Consumer Goods

10

Abstract

The most important aspect of price management for consumer goods is that manufacturers typically do not sell their products directly to the end consumers. Instead, retailers or other third parties are engaged as intermediaries. In order to set optimal prices, the manufacturers must take the behavior of the retailers into account in their price decisions. There are many forms for this, ranging from vertical price-fixing and resale price maintenance (under which the manufacturer sets both the wholesale price and the final price to consumers) to strategies for joint profit maximization. In general nowadays, the retailer can set the selling prices to consumers autonomously. When setting its own prices, the manufacturer needs to consider whether the retailer uses a cost-plus calculation to arrive at its selling price or behaves instead in a profit-maximizing way. The balance of power between manufacturers and retailers plays a key role in the implementation of prices. Different constellations and patterns of behavior can have strong effects on profit. We observe a pronounced trend toward multichannel strategies, facilitated by the Internet which poses unusual challenges for price management of consumer goods. These include price differentiation online vs. offline and the avoidance of channel conflicts.

10.1 Introduction

Chapters 1 through 9 looked at analyses, decisions, and implementation in price management in general terms. These chapters did not get into detail on the challenges facing industry-specific price management issues. This chapter and the next three are devoted to the special characteristics of the most important sectors. We will deal with pricing problems faced by suppliers of consumer goods, industrial goods, services, and retailers in a way befitting each sector. Naturally there is some overlap, but the price-related issues of focus are indeed distinct for each sector.

© Springer Nature Switzerland AG 2019
H. Simon, M. Fassnacht, *Price Management*,
https://doi.org/10.1007/978-3-319-99456-7_10

Consumer goods most closely resemble the general view we have taken so far. An important aspect of price management for consumer goods, and one we have not explored yet, is that consumer goods are typically not sold directly by manufacturers to end consumers but rather through retailers or other intermediaries. In such cases, the manufacturer must take the behavior of the retailers and other third parties into account. Increasingly we are observing that consumer goods manufacturers are selling directly to end consumers using a variety of sales channels. This multichannel approach gives rise to potential conflicts of interest which affect price management. The Internet allows manufacturers to contact consumers directly and enables new business models which affect price management.

10.2   Vertical Price Management

The previous analyses in this book were based on the assumption that the manufacturer sold directly to the end user and set the final selling price itself. This assumption corresponds to reality in many industries. In most cases it holds true for industrial goods as well as for skilled trades, banking, and insurance. Other industries have companies that sell products directly and/or indirectly, such as automobiles, furniture, household durable goods, and shoes. For consumer goods, selling through retailers is the *typical*, if not the only, sales form which matters. This is true, for example, for food and grocery, clothing, consumer electronics, and books. Such markets, in which there is an intermediary between the manufacturer and the end consumer, are referred to as *multi-level or multi-tier*.

This chapter will focus on consumer goods manufacturers who sell indirectly to end users. These companies need to understand how selling through intermediaries (e.g., retailers or other trade partners) will influence their own price strategies and tactics. Factors which determine the nature and extent of this influence include the:

- Effect of the *end (consumer) price* on sales volume
- *Pricing behavior* of the retailers
- Relative *balance of power* between manufacturer and retailer

Figure 10.1 provides a simple overview of the interdependencies in this system. The following scenarios are of interest:

1. The manufacturer determines both the *manufacturer's selling price* as well as the *end consumer price* and thus the *retailer's margin*. The ideal expression of this is the classic vertical price-fixing. This form of vertical or resale price maintenance is legally permissible only in a few sectors nowadays but is generally a per se violation of antitrust laws in many jurisdictions. The use of the manufacturer's suggested retail price corresponds to this model, if it is strictly enforced.
2. The manufacturer sets *only* its own selling price, but has no influence on the end consumer price. The retailer sets that price on its own.

Fig. 10.1 Interdependencies
when a manufacturer sells
through an intermediary

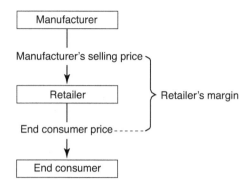

3. The retailer sets the manufacturer's selling price, leaving the manufacturer with the choice of accepting that price or not. This situation occurs in transactions between small manufacturers and large retailers. But the vast demand power behind retail means that even larger manufacturers may face the same situation. The manufacturer then has no independent price policy. The "price mandate" from the retailer leaves the manufacturer only with a "yes-no" decision. In that case the manufacturer definitely has no influence on the end consumer price.
4. Manufacturers and retailers pursue *joint profit maximization*. The distribution of the profits is managed via the manufacturer's selling price, which is negotiated in a subsequent step.

The manufacturer's balance of power can vary by retailer, so that several of the situations may apply simultaneously for the same product from one manufacturer. Customer management and *key account management* attempt to do justice to the resulting need for differentiation. The balance of power between manufacturer and retailer depends not only on sheer size (economies of scale) but also on the breadth of the assortment (economies of scope). A manufacturer with a broad assortment should generally have a stronger negotiating position than a company which offers only a small number of products and thus has a greater degree of dependency. Philip Kotler [1, p. 8] notes in this regard that "Procter & Gamble, which sells over a hundred different P&G products to supermarkets, has a distinct power advantage over companies that only sell one product to supermarkets."

Below we will deal with price optimization for a manufacturer who sells indirectly to the end consumer, i.e., via an intermediary. For consumer goods manufacturers, this intermediary or trade partner is generally a retailer. We will look only at those cases in which the manufacturer has the opportunity to exercise an active price strategy:

• The manufacturer determines both its own selling price and the price to end consumers.
• The manufacturer determines only its own selling price to retailers.
• The manufacturer and retailer aim for joint profit maximization, with the manufacturer's selling price negotiated as the means to distribute the total profit.

We limit ourselves to a static situation. There is only one level of distribution between the manufacturer and the end consumer. But the analysis is not fundamentally different for multiple sales levels or distribution tiers. Pricing in multitiered markets has been covered many times in the literature, e.g., [2–8].

10.2.1 The Manufacturer Sets Both Its Selling Price and the End Consumer Price

In this situation, the manufacturer has two action parameters at its disposal: the manufacturer's selling price p_M and the end consumer price p. Setting these prices also determines the retailer's margin s as defined by the equation $s = p - p_M$.

What matters for the decision as such is only the factual enforceability of the manufacturer's desired price. It does not matter whether the desired price is legally implementable, and in fact the strict practice of vertical price-fixing is forbidden in most countries. A non-binding suggested retail price, which is a price recommendation the retail trade *actually* follows, has a similar relevance for vertical (resale) price management. In some sectors, the intermediary in the selling system acts as the manufacturer's agent or sells on a commission basis. Such systems can be evaluated similarly, because the intermediary has no price decision authority. This applies, for example, to gas stations, which often serve as agents. The discussion around resale price maintenance has increased in recent years [9–11], as manufacturers of branded products try to defend themselves against the practice of retailers using their products as loss leaders. They fear that the practice damages the brand image. This has led to at least one lawsuit (Leegin Creative Leather Products, Inc. v. PSKS, Inc.) reaching the US Supreme Court, which ruled in favor of Leegin, the manufacturer. This scenario remains relevant in practice, as manufacturers (and large ones in particular) and retailers (especially smaller ones) attach a high importance to the manufacturer's suggested retail price (MSRP). Compliance is highest in specialty retail, while aggressive sales channels generally charge prices below the MSRP. E-commerce has exacerbated this.

There are two kinds of price recommendations. One is the retailer recommended price and the other is the consumer price recommendation. The *retailer recommended price*, under which the recommended price is known only to the retailer, but not to the end consumer, occurs more frequently than the *consumer price recommendation*, which is visible to the end consumer. Smaller retailers value the price recommendation as a support for their own price setting. Larger retailers, in contrast, see undercutting the price recommendation as an opportunity for additional customer acquisition ("moon price effect"). These different behaviors lead—from a competitive standpoint—to the price recommendations which rarely succeed in preventing price competition at the retail level. Nowadays that goal is achieved more effectively through selective distribution, i.e., the *refusal of delivery* to channels which price in an aggressive manner. Many manufacturers put a lot of effort into stabilizing and harmonizing prices across the retail tier, i.e., into getting their desired or recommended prices implemented.

In summary, one can say that scenarios under which both the manufacturer's selling price and the end consumer price are effectively set by the manufacturer still remain important in practice.

10.2.1.1 Optimization of End Price and Margin

Under the assumptions made above, the price-margin-response function for the manufacturer has the following form:

$$q = q(p, s) \tag{10.1}$$

with p as the end consumer price and s as the retailer margin.

The level of the end price drives the reaction of consumers, so that the price elasticity with regard to the end price is negative, as usual. The level of the margin determines the *effort of the retailer* for the product. The higher the margin is, the more intensive the retailer's effort will be. The effect of this effort on sales volume is *positive*. Analogously to the price elasticity, we can define a margin elasticity:

$$\gamma = \frac{\partial q}{\partial s} \times \frac{s}{q} \tag{10.2}$$

This formula expresses the percentage change in sales volume (assuming a constant end consumer price of p) when the retailer margin changes by 1%.

The margin and the end consumer price have *countervailing* effects. An increase in the end consumer price will cause a negative reaction among consumers, but it also increases the retailer's margin, assuming the manufacturer's selling price remains constant. That, in turn, spurs more activity by the retailer, which offsets the negative consumer reaction. It is intuitively clear that the optimal combination of end consumer price and retailer margin lies precisely at the point where these two opposite effects cancel each other out. The considerations below may also be applied analogously to the optimization of commissions for dealers, agents, or manufacturers' representatives.

In order to get to the profit-maximizing combination of end consumer price and retailer margin, we need to differentiate the profit function of the manufacturer

$$\pi = (p - s)q(p, s) - C(q) \tag{10.3}$$

with respect to p and s. After several steps we get:

$$p^* = \frac{\varepsilon}{1 + \varepsilon + \gamma} \times C' \tag{10.4}$$

$$s^* = \frac{\gamma}{1 + \varepsilon + \gamma} \times C' \tag{10.5}$$

C' is as usual the marginal costs, and ε and γ are the price and the margin elasticities. Because the manufacturer's selling price is the difference between the end price p and margin s, we get:

$$p_M^* = \frac{\varepsilon + \gamma}{1 + \varepsilon + \gamma} \times C'. \tag{10.6}$$

The optimality conditions for simultaneous optimization of consumer price and margin can thus be formulated in a way which is analogous to the Amoroso-Robinson relation (5.6).

From these conditions we can derive the following *ceteris paribus* statements:

- The smaller the price elasticity ε is in absolute terms, the higher the end consumer price p^*, the margin s^*, and the manufacturer's selling price p_M^*.
- The larger the margin elasticity γ is, the higher the end consumer price p^*, the margin s^*, and the manufacturer's selling price p_M^*. Regarding the end price p^*, the margin elasticity has the same effect as a lowering of the price elasticity.
- Selling through a retailer or intermediary leads to a *higher* end price, compared to direct sales, when the manufacturer sets both the end consumer price p and the dealer margin s, and the margin elasticity is positive. This statement assumes, however, that there are no variable distribution costs. These can be higher for direct sales than for indirect sales.
- As the price elasticity ε declines, the margin s^* rises more strongly than the manufacturer's selling price p_M^* and the unit contribution margin, assuming the margin elasticity is greater than one. For $\gamma < 1$ the opposite applies.
- As the margin elasticity γ rises, the margin s^* increases faster than the manufacturer's selling price p_M^*, assuming the price elasticity is greater than two (absolute value).

If the retailer has variable distribution costs of k per unit, then in the derivation above, one should replace the gross margin $(p - p_M)$ with the net margin $(p - p_M - k)$. The derivations then follow analogously, and the statements on the influence of price and margin elasticity do not change.

Table 10.1 summarizes the qualitative recommendations for end price and margin policies, if we consider the categories "high" and "low" for both price and margin elasticity.

To illustrate this, we assume constant elasticities, which result in a price-margin-response function of the form:

$$q = ap^\varepsilon s^\gamma. \tag{10.7}$$

Table 10.1 Qualitative recommendations on end price and margin policies of a manufacturer

Price elasticity	Margin elasticity	
	Low	High
Low	End price high Margin low	End price high Margin high
High	End price low Margin low	End price low Margin high

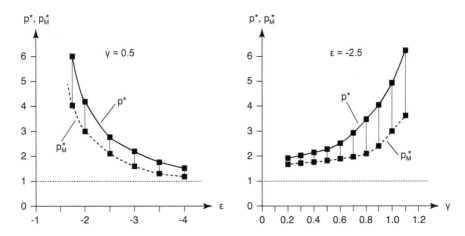

Fig. 10.2 Effects of changes in elasticity on optimal prices and margins

Assuming constant marginal costs C', the decision rules (10.4) and (10.5) can be applied directly. Figure 10.2 shows the optimal end consumer and manufacturer's selling prices as a function of the price elasticity ε and the margin elasticity γ. The difference between the two curves corresponds to the margin s^*. Using this figure, we can easily verify the statements above.

10.2.1.2 Manufacturer and Retailer Share

The question of how the optimal total margin $(p^* - C')$ gets divided between manufacturer and retailer is a fascinating one. The manufacturer's share of the total margin is $(p_M^* - C')/(p^* - C')$. If we plug in p_M^* and p^* from (10.6) and (10.4) and simplify, we get $1/(1 + \gamma)$ as the manufacturer's share and consequently $\gamma/(1 + \gamma)$ as the retailer's share.

The ratio of manufacturer and retailer shares is:

$$\frac{\text{Manufacturer's share}}{\text{Retailer's share}} = \frac{1}{\gamma} \qquad (10.8)$$

This relationship does not depend on the price elasticity. The manufacturer margin and the retailer margin are identical when the margin elasticity equals one. For $\gamma > 1$ the retailer keeps the larger share of the total margin $(p^* - C')$, and for $\gamma < 1$ the manufacturer gets a higher share. This result makes sense, because for $\gamma > 1$ a marginal reduction of the manufacturer margin is overcompensated by the incremental sales volume driven by the higher margin elasticity.

10.2.1.3 Margin as a Competitive Instrument

The retailer's margin can become an important competitive instrument in the typical situation where many products are competing at the retail level for shelf space and end consumer demand. This is particularly true in situations where the consumer has already made the fundamental decision to buy, but must still select which brand, and the retailer can influence that choice.

If price and quality of competing products are roughly similar—and in the latter case, the buyer is often unsure of his or her judgment—the retailer will recommend the product which yields the highest margin. All of the analyses above are transferable to the case of competition. Oligopoly theory regarding price can likewise be applied analogously to margin, which means one can define cross-margin elasticities as well as reaction functions. Because this involves the inversion of the insights derived for price, the transfer of insights from price to margin is relatively easy. A detailed treatment is therefore not necessary here.

In practice, store brands, generics, and no-names often have higher margins in percentage terms (and sometimes in absolute terms) than classic branded products. From a competitive standpoint, margin strategy differs from (open) price strategy with respect to transparency. Because margins can be managed with individually granted and therefore nonpublic rebates (often in the form of bonuses in kind), the manipulation of this instrument is less transparent for the competition than open, i.e., public, price changes. Margins thus offer a lucrative starting point for covert or discreet measures to increase one's own market share.

10.2.1.4 Empirical Aspects of Margin Elasticity

The theoretical considerations we have presented so far provide useful insights into the links between margin elasticity and optimal prices and trade margins. Practical implementation, however, requires numerical values for the margin effects. If one has specified a price-response function, the measurement of the respective parameters for the margin effects will not be difficult in principle. Similarly to price effects, one can use econometric methods or expert judgment to measure them. Customer surveys are not a useful option.

Econometric measurement, however, often proves difficult, because the margins the manufacturer sets only rarely show sufficient variation for analysis. One workaround can be estimating the elasticities for promotional budgets. The manufacturer can offer additional monetary incentives which have a similar effect to a margin increase, and thus one might expect the elasticities for such promotional budgets to be similar to a margin elasticity. In reality, it is not unusual for the trade to treat those promotional budgets the way they treat discounts, meaning they effectively serve as "margin" anyway. Promotional budgets have an added advantage, namely, that they tend to show wide variation. This helps with the measurement of the effects. The problem, however, can be the short-term nature of the promotional effects. Table 10.2 shows estimates of promotional and price elasticities for three consumer goods.

If we express the optimal margin s^* as a function of the manufacturer's selling price, the markups to the manufacturer's selling price p_M^* for the price and trade elasticities are as follows:

Table 10.2 Econometrically estimated promotional budget elasticities (as approximation for margin elasticities) and price elasticities

Product	Promotion budget elasticity	Price elasticity
A	0.742	−2.190
B	0.401	−4.130
C	0.363	−1.157

Table 10.3 Implicit values for margin elasticities for different price elasticities and markups

	Price elasticity		
Markup (s in % of p_M)	$\varepsilon = -2$	$\varepsilon = -3$	$\varepsilon = -4$
10	0.18	0.27	0.36
25	0.40	0.60	0.80
50	0.67	1.00	1.33
100	1.00	1.50	2.00

Product A: 51.2%
Product B: 29.3%
Product C: 45.7%

These markup percentages are realistic, which implies that the estimated elasticities in Table 10.2 appear to be plausible.

From our theoretical considerations, we can draw certain conclusions about the empirical values of the margin elasticities. Based on our optimality conditions, different price elasticities and different markups on the manufacturer's selling price p_M yield the implied margin elasticities shown in Table 10.3. They are calculated by expressing the trade margin as a percentage of the manufacturer's selling price, $s = -\gamma p_M/(\varepsilon + \gamma)$, and then solving for γ. In line with this, one would expect margin elasticities in practice to be in a range from around 0.2 to a maximum of 1.5. The values in Table 10.3 are all within this interval.

Overview

If the end consumer price and the retailer's margin are actionable parameters for the manufacturer (a situation which still corresponds to reality in some markets despite prohibitions on vertical price-fixing), one can state simple conditions for the simultaneous optimization of both parameters. The optimal values for price and margin depend on the price elasticity and the margin elasticity. The split of the overall margin between the end consumer price and the manufacturer's marginal costs is determined solely by the margin elasticity.

As a competitive instrument, margin has a lower transparency compared to the end price, which has implications for competitive response. The measurement of the margin elasticity is difficult, and empirical findings are shaky. Different lines of thought indicate that realistic values are no smaller than 0.2 and no larger than 1.5.

10.2.2 The Manufacturer Sets Only the Manufacturer's Selling Price

Since the prohibition of vertical price-fixing, the legal position—expect for special cases—is that the manufacturer can only set a legally binding manufacturer's selling price. The trade partners are then allowed to determine both their margin and their selling prices to end users autonomously.

10.2.2.1 Behavior of the Trade

In order to set a profit-maximizing selling price, the manufacturer needs information on:

- The price-response function for *end consumer demand*
- The *behavior of the trade partners* in setting their end consumer prices (as a function of the manufacturer's selling price)

Logically speaking, the decision-making here is equivalent to the situation in an oligopoly, because the manufacturer sets its price on the basis of a certain "reaction hypothesis" on how the trade will behave. The following "reaction hypotheses" warrant attention:

- The trade partner sets the end consumer price based on a rule of thumb, i.e., the trade partner applies a *fixed* percentage markup to the manufacturer's selling price (cost-plus calculation).
- The trade partner behaves in a profit-maximizing manner, i.e., the trade partner sets profit-maximizing end consumer price as a function of the manufacturer's selling price p_M and the end user price-response function.

In light of the widespread use of the cost-plus calculation in the trade, the first approach will be more common. The greater the degree of the trade partner's professionalism, the more likely one encounters the second situation.

10.2.2.2 Optimization of the Manufacturer's Selling Price When the Trade Partner Uses Cost-Plus Calculation

When the trade partner uses a cost-plus calculation, the end consumer price is defined as shown in (10.9), with α representing the markup factor and k representing the trade partner's variable cost:

$$p = \alpha(p_M + k). \qquad (10.9)$$

If we plug in the end price-response function $q = q(p)$ (10.9) for p, the manufacturer's profit function to maximize is:

$$\pi = p_M q\left[\alpha(p_M + k)\right] - C(q). \qquad (10.10)$$

After the usual steps, we get the optimality condition for the manufacturer's selling price as:

$$p_M^* = \frac{\varepsilon(\alpha)}{1 + \varepsilon(\alpha)}\left(C' - \frac{k}{\varepsilon(\alpha)}\right). \tag{10.11}$$

For distribution costs of $k = 0$, this formula corresponds to the familiar Amoroso-Robinson relation. The price elasticity, however, which we have expressed as $\varepsilon(\alpha)$, can depend on the markup factor α. In the special case of the iso-elastic price-response function $q = ap^b$ we get $\varepsilon(\alpha) = \varepsilon = b$, and the optimal selling price of the manufacturer does not depend on whether the manufacturer sells directly or via trade partners. This statement does not apply, however, to other forms of end price-response functions.

If we apply the markup rule (10.9) to the optimal manufacturer's selling price in (10.11), we get the following end consumer price:

$$p = \frac{\alpha\varepsilon(\alpha)}{1 + \varepsilon(\alpha)}(C' + k). \tag{10.12}$$

For an iso-elastic price-response function, the end consumer price is higher than the price when selling directly, assuming the same marginal costs for distribution, and as long as $\alpha > 1$.

Specific statements are possible for linear price-response functions. The resulting optimal values are as follows:

$$p_M^* = \frac{1}{2}\left(\frac{a}{b\alpha} + C' - k\right) \tag{10.13}$$

and

$$p = \frac{1}{2}\left(\frac{a}{b} + \alpha C' + \alpha k\right). \tag{10.14}$$

p_M^* is lower and p higher than the optimal price when selling directly, assuming distribution costs are the same. The higher the markup factor α is, the lower the manufacturer's selling price is, and the higher the end consumer price is.

Figure 10.3 shows the profit situation and the profit breakdown between manufacturer and trade partner for the case of a linear price-response function. The results are based on an end price-response function of $q = 100 - 10p$, constant marginal costs of $C' = 4$, and variable distribution costs of $k = 0$. We assume the trade markup is 25% ($\alpha = 1.25$).

The optimal end consumer price is $p^* = \$7.50$ and the optimal manufacturer's selling price is $p_M^* = \$6$. The manufacturer's profit is \$50, while the trade partner earns a profit of \$37.50. The maximum possible profit for both parties is *not* achieved.

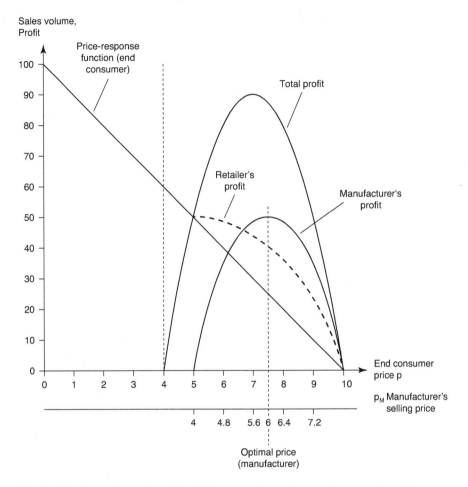

Fig. 10.3 Profit situation and profit breakdown when the retailer practices cost-plus pricing

The profit curves of the two parties show that there are serious *conflicts of interest*. To the right of $p = \$7.50$, both parties would be interested in price cuts, while to the left of this price, the interests of the two parties run counter to each other. The trade partner wants the lowest possible end consumer price, which, thanks to the trade partner's fixed cost-plus calculation, is only possible if the manufacturer's selling price is as low as possible. In such situations, the trade partner will apply considerable pressure on the manufacturer.

The countervailing profit effects for manufacturers and trade partners in the low-price area are due to the fact that the unit contribution margins—relative to the volumes—change in very different ways for manufacturers than for trade partners. At an end consumer price of $p = \$7$ (manufacturer's selling price of $p_M = \$5.60$), the trade partner and the manufacturer achieve unit contribution margins of $1.60 and $1.40, respectively. If p falls to $6 and thus p_M to $4.80, the unit contribution margin of the trade partner falls by $0.40 to $1.20 (−25%), while that of the manufacturer falls by $0.60 to $0.80 (−42.8%). Sales volume, due to the price decrease of $1, rises from 30 to 40 units, an increase of +33.3%. On a percentage basis, the volume increase is thus higher than the decline in unit contribution margin for the trade partner, who thus does better with the lower price. But the opposite is true for the manufacturer, whose unit contribution margin drops at a faster rate than the sales volume rises. This lowers the manufacturer's profit. This view is consistent with empirical observations that trade partners are strongly interested in high volumes.

10.2.2.3 Optimization of the Manufacturer's Selling Price When the Trade Partner Maximizes Profit

The trade partner determines the end consumer price, assuming distribution unit costs of k, in such a way that its profit

$$\pi_D = (p - p_M - k)q(p) \tag{10.15}$$

would be maximized, which means that the Amoroso-Robinson relation which applies in this case

$$p^* = \frac{\varepsilon}{1+\varepsilon}(p_M + k) \tag{10.16}$$

is fulfilled.

The manufacturer optimizes the manufacturer's selling price by differentiating the profit function with respect to p_M, in that (10.16) is inserted for p. That leads to the optimal manufacturer's selling price:

$$p_M^* = \frac{\varepsilon}{1+\varepsilon}\left(C' - \frac{k}{\varepsilon}\right). \tag{10.17}$$

This condition corresponds formula-wise to condition (10.11) for the optimal manufacturer's selling price when the trade partner uses a cost-plus calculation. For $k = 0$ and $\varepsilon = $ const., the manufacturer sets its selling price without considering the trade partner when the latter's goal is profit maximization. If distribution costs are positive and $\varepsilon = $ const., the manufacturer's selling price is higher.

Using (10.16) one gets the following end consumer price:

$$p = \frac{\varepsilon^2}{(1+\varepsilon)^2}(C' + k). \tag{10.18}$$

This price is *higher* than the optimal price when selling directly, assuming equal distribution costs. The intermediation of a profit-maximizing trade partner increases the end consumer price. We use a linear price-response function to derive results which can be easily interpreted.

The optimal manufacturer's selling price is:

$$p_M^* = \frac{1}{2}\left(\frac{a}{b} + C' - k\right). \tag{10.19}$$

For $k = 0$, p_M^* is identical to the optimal price for direct selling, so that the manufacturer, under these conditions, can set its price without considering the trade partner. If distribution costs are positive, the resulting optimal end consumer price is higher than the optimal price when selling directly, with the same distribution costs.

Figure 10.4 illustrates the situation for the linear end price-response function $q = 100 - 10p$, constant marginal costs of $C' = 4$, and variable distribution costs $k = 0$.

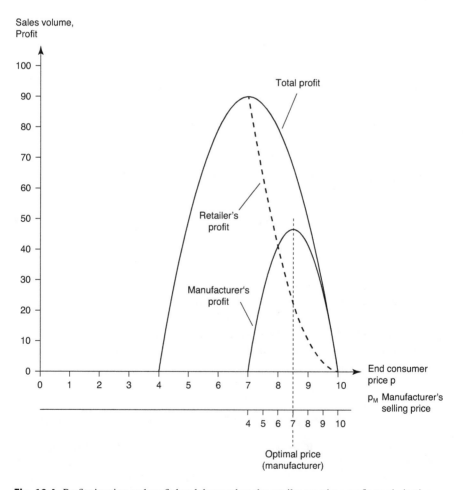

Fig. 10.4 Profit situation and profit breakdown when the retailer practices profit maximization

The optimal end consumer price from the manufacturer's perspective is p^* = $8.50 (with the optimal manufacturer's selling price at $p_M^* = \$7$). The manufacturer earns a profit of $45, while the trade partner needs to make due with a profit of $22.50.

There is a conflict of interest between manufacturer and trade partner when one looks to the left of the optimal end consumer price p^*. The causes are the same as those for the cost-plus calculation, but comparing the two numerical examples, the conflicts are more pronounced in the case of the numerical example for the profit-maximizing trade partner. The manufacturer needs to reduce its selling price by $2 in order to affect a reduction of $1 in the end consumer price. The manufacturer "sacrifices" twice as much unit contribution margin from a price cut as the trade partner does.

10.2.2.4 Comparison of the Two Situations

Using linear price-response functions, we can compare the consequences of the two forms of behavior on the part of the trade partner. Figure 10.5 illustrates the two situations. The solid line represents the respective price-response function with regard to the end consumer price, while the dashed line represents the price-response function with regard to the manufacturer's selling price. The parameters are $a = 100$ and $b = 10$, and the markup factor is $\alpha = 1.25$. The arrows indicate how the end prices are derived from the manufacturer's selling prices ($C' = 4$).

Simplified somewhat, the cost-plus calculation means that the trade partner uses a low markup when p_M is low and a higher markup when p_M is high. When the trade partner strives for profit maximization, it will behave in the opposite manner. In other words, the trade partner takes optimal advantage of the *difference* between the

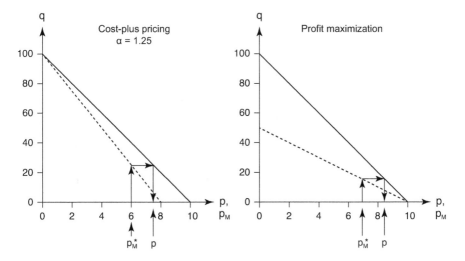

Fig. 10.5 Comparison of two retail pricing methods (cost-plus vs. profit maximizing)

price the manufacturer charges and the end consumers' willingness to pay. Table 10.4 shows the optimal prices and profits for variable distribution costs of $k = 0$ and $k = 1$.

In both examples, the trade partner and the manufacturer come out *better* when the trade partner uses the cost-plus calculation than when the trade partner pursues profit maximization. This statement does not apply universally, though. For higher markup factors (e.g., $\alpha = 2$), the cost-plus calculation would lead to a worse result. But one can say in general that the presence of an intermediary (trade partner) leads to higher end consumer prices and lower overall profit than when the manufacturer sells directly. This statement is true regardless of whether the trade partner uses a cost-plus calculation or seeks to maximize profit.

Overview

In order to set the manufacturer's selling price optimally, the manufacturer needs information on the price elasticity of the end consumer as well as information on which method the trade partner will use to set the end consumer price ("reaction function" of the trade partner.) The trade partner can use cost-plus calculation or profit maximization. In both cases, the activity of the trade partner leads to an end consumer price which is higher than the price would be if the manufacturer sold directly, assuming the same distribution costs. There can be situations (constant price elasticity, variable distribution costs of zero) under which the manufacturer does not need to pay attention to the behavior of the trade partner when it sets the manufacturer's selling price.

10.2.3 Manufacturer and Trade Partner Pursue Joint Profit Maximization

In light of the interdependencies between manufacturer and trade partner, it is self-evident that the two parties should join forces and aim for joint profit maximization. The decision process then breaks down into two steps which reflect the different interests of the respective partners.

The first step is to set the end consumer price which maximizes the joint profit. The interests of the two parties are aligned, because they should be motivated to make the total profit as large as possible. In the second step, the total profit must be shared between the manufacturer and the trade partner. In this second step, the interests of the two parties are *diametrically opposed*. Because the profit pool to distribute is fixed, the distribution is a *zero-sum game*. The more one party receives, the less the other gets. Practically speaking, the distribution is accomplished through the negotiation of the manufacturer's selling price.

Joint profit maximization is the most meaningful approach per se and, surprisingly, is even a favorable solution for the end consumer. But its relevance in practice is hard to gauge, and its realization faces a number of difficulties.

Table 10.4 Prices and profits for different trade partner behaviors as well as for direct sales

| | k = 0 | | | | | k = 1 | | | | |
| | | | Profit | | | | | Profit | | |
Behavior of the trade partner	p_M^*	p	Manufacturer	Trade		p_M^*	p	Manufacturer	Trade
Cost-plus, $\alpha = 1.25$	6	7.50	50	37.50		5.50	8.13	28.10	30.50
Profit maximization	7	8.50	45	22.50		6.50	8.75	31.30	15.60
Direct sales	–	7	90	–		–	7.50	62.50	–

Price Optimization

We assume no competitive influence in this scenario. Determining the optimal price (first step) is therefore straightforward. The revenue of the manufacturer, $p_M \times q$, appears in the function for the total profit π_G

$$\pi_G = p_M q(p) - C(q) + (p - p_M - k)q(p) \tag{10.20}$$

twice with opposite signs so that the two terms cancel each other out. The total profit π_G thus only depends on the end consumer price p. This is a straightforward price optimization, for which we can use the Amoroso-Robinson relation (including distribution costs k), that is,

$$p = \frac{\varepsilon}{1 + \varepsilon}(C' + k). \tag{10.21}$$

Logically p^* must be identical to the optimal price from a direct sale, assuming the same distribution costs. The optimal end consumer price under a joint profit maximization strategy is thus lower than the prices which result from the two forms of trade partner behavior we discussed previously.

Figure 10.6 shows the relations using an example with a linear end price-response function of $q = 100 - 10p$, constant marginal costs of $C' = 4$, and distribution costs of $k = 0$.

Under a joint profit maximization strategy, the resulting end consumer price is $7, and the joint profit is $90. Under isolated profit maximization of manufacturer and trade partner, the optimal end consumer price is $8.50 and the profit significantly lower at $67.50 (see Table 10.4.) The price is also higher and the profit lower for a cost-plus calculation by the trade partner and profit maximization by the manufacturer. The price rises, but the total profit declines with the higher trade markup. Cooperation in the spirit of joint profit maximization by the manufacturer and the trade partner, under these assumptions, achieves a better outcome for the two selling parties together (though not necessarily individually) and for the end consumer than when the manufacturer and trade partner act in isolation.

10.2.4 Distribution of Profit

While the interests of the manufacturer and trade partner are aligned in the first step, they are diametrically opposed with regard to profit distribution between them. The optimal price says nothing about the profit distribution, because in the optimization of the total profit, the manufacturer's selling price is merely a pass-through term. The profit distribution is typically determined by the negotiation of the manufacturer's selling price. This price determines how well each party does profit-wise in the transaction. The negotiation problem has the structure shown in Fig. 10.7. One partner can only improve its outcome when it makes the other party worse off by the same amount. This is a zero-sum game.

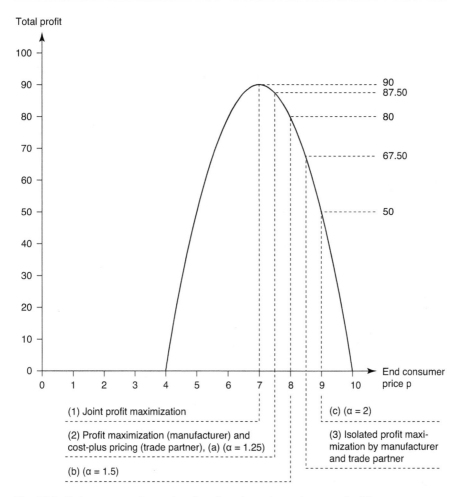

Fig. 10.6 End consumer prices and total profit under various price strategies [5]

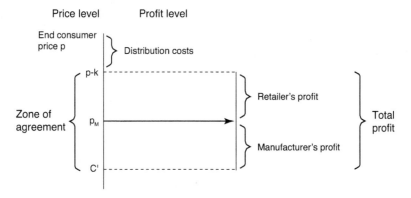

Fig. 10.7 Problem structure of profit distribution

A general conclusion can only be drawn about the potential zone of agreement. The boundaries of this zone are determined by the points where either the manufacturer or the trade partner would suffer a loss and thus have no interest in the deal. The lower bound therefore lies at the marginal costs of the manufacturer in the short term (and fully loaded costs in the long term). The upper bound lies at the net revenue of the trade partner ($p - k$). These boundaries are referred to as the "exploitation points" [12, p., 417].

The relative balance of power between the manufacturer and the trade partner as well as personal traits—such as negotiation savviness or the readiness to make concessions—determines which price will be negotiated between the two parties within the zone of agreement.

10.2.4.1 On the Relationship Between Manufacturer and Trade Partner

Our considerations have clearly brought to light the *fundamental* and intractable conflicts of interest between manufacturer and trade partner. The phenomenon does not only occur with joint profit maximization but whenever the available profit is known and the only question is how to divide it up.

This is the root of the fundamental conflict of interest between manufacturer and trade partner. The shifting balance of power to the detriment of consumer goods manufacturers has led many to complain about this situation. The loss of leverage by the manufacturers, and the corresponding reciprocal gain in power of retailers, is a consequence of two developments. One is the increasing concentration in retail (read: demand-side power) and the fact that selling and not manufacturing has become the bottleneck in many highly developed and contested markets.

If a manufacturer wants to achieve a better outcome in this "natural" conflict, it needs to improve the balance of power in its favor (e.g., through better positioning of its brand, innovation, or more effective pull communication.) The trade partner ultimately depends on the attractiveness of the products to the end consumer. The stronger this attraction, the better the chances of the manufacturer to get its prices accepted by the trade.

In practice, the predominant form of the negotiation process is an annual agreement which comprises prices and volumes. The negotiations often involve the top management of the manufacturer, which reflects what is at stake. In recent times "the only topic of discussion is prices and conditions, and there are constant renegotiations with the retailers demanding absurd discounts ..." as well as ludicrous conditions which effectively become a component of the price. It has also been reported [13] that retailers have demanded "wedding bonuses" when they merge their chains, investment support when they open new stores, and even junior bonuses when young managers join the company. "That is money which they demand without offering anything material in return" [13].

The haggling over "discounts" and "conditions" has become so rough that one brand consultant [14] describes it as "psychological warfare," a mix of brutality and humiliation. The following comment conveys the tense situation between manufacturers and trade partners during the battle over price: "The managers have barely taken their seats when the window blinds were closed. On the front wall, a film plays which urgently displays the unbelievable strength of the grocery store chain. Intense music, drum rolls, and then at the end a spokesman proclaims: 'we set the tone'" [14]. Only manufacturers with strong brands can hold their own against such brazen negotiation methods, because "no retailer can afford to delist Nutella or Tide," according to one retail expert [13]. The "annual agreements" are not merely negotiations, but rather a "power struggle with millions at stake and not exactly for the weak or sensitive" [15].

In reality, all of these battles are ultimately about *profit distribution*. It makes no difference from an economic standpoint how this distribution is "packaged" into prices and conditions. The significance of conditions appears to be better explained as psychological, driven either by negotiation tactics or oligopolistic motivations (nontransparency, masking true prices.)

10.2.4.2 Practical Aspects of Joint Profit Maximization

Given that joint profit maximization leaves the manufacturer and trade partner in the best overall position, and at the same time is favorable to the end consumer, it is worth exploring the odds of realizing this approach in practice.

The simultaneous agreement on prices and volumes in the annual negotiations indicates that reality does not diverge all that much from this form of behavior. But at the same time, the idealized approach we have described faces a number of barriers:

1. *Time/resource allocation:* An intensive, joint treatment of the respective specific pricing problems is required. However, because the manufacturer has a large number of customers, it can only have that kind of cooperation with key accounts. At the same time, the trade partner has a large, comprehensive assortment, which means the time it can devote to an individual product or category is limited.
2. *Data:* A prerequisite for joint profit maximization is that the manufacturer and trade partner have similar estimates of price elasticities. The elasticities can vary sharply, however, by store, and assessing local differences can prove difficult.
3. *Objectives:* Interests can diverge, for example, when the trade partner's strategy warrants the use of a product as a loss leader, while the manufacturer wants to keep the price at a high level for image reasons.
4. *Trust:* Joint profit maximization requires a high degree of trust in the cost figures provided by the other party. The temptation to bring exaggerated cost figures into the optimization effort is high.

An example illustrates that last point. Let's assume the price-response function is $q = 100 - 10p$, the manufacturer has marginal costs of $C' = 4$, and the trade partner has distribution costs of $k = 1$. The agreed profit split is 50:50. According to formula (10.21), the optimal end consumer price is $p^* = \$7.50$. The resulting total profit is \$62.50 and each party receives \$31.25. If the manufacturer does not reveal its true marginal costs of $C' = 4$ and instead claims costs of \$5, the optimal price is $p^* = \$8$, and the "official" joint profit is \$40. The manufacturer's share of this is \$20, but the manufacturer earns an additional "hidden" profit of $20. This leaves the manufacturer clearly better off than if it had revealed its true marginal costs. The same applies analogously for the trade partner and its distribution costs. There is an incentive to claim costs which are excessive. Despite being potentially advantageous for both parties, the pursuit of joint profit maximization does not always meet all the prerequisites. Nonetheless, this form may not deviate too much from the actual behavior for large manufacturers and trade partners.

Overview
The first of two steps in the joint profit maximization by the manufacturer and the trade partner is to determine the optimal end consumer price. The distribution of the profit follows in the second step and is implemented through the negotiation of the manufacturer's selling price. The optimal end consumer price under a joint profit maximization strategy is lower than when the parties set prices separately or under resale price maintenance by the manufacturer. In general, one can determine only the boundaries for the potential area of agreement when the parties negotiate the division of profits. The lower bound is the manufacturer's marginal cost, while the upper bound is the net revenue of the trade partner. Within this zone, the solution depends on the balance of power between the two parties as well as their negotiating skills. Prerequisites for joint profit maximization are a high degree of information sharing and mutual trust. The result can be advantageous for all participants (manufacturer, trade, partner, and end consumer.) In practice, the manufacturer and trade partner tend to approximate it rather than achieve it in pure form.

10.3   Multichannel Price Management

In addition to sales through trade partners, there have always been alternative channels for selling consumer goods. But these have tended to be exceptions. Companies such as Avon and Tupperware have practiced direct sales for decades. Dell was built around a direct-selling model from day 1. Traditional bakeries and butchers have generally sold their products directly to consumers. There are also numerous examples of companies who use a mixture of direct and indirect sales channels. Germany's Tchibo started as a direct mail-order firm for coffee but later opened its own stores and sold its products through other stores. Clothing and fashion firms often practice factory selling, meaning that consumers meet their needs "in the factory." The cutlery and cookware manufacturer WMF has always had its own stores while also selling its wares through the specialty retail trade. But, by and large, direct sales traditionally have not played an important role for consumer goods manufacturers.

This situation has changed dramatically in recent years for a number of reasons. Many brand-name manufacturers have opened their own stores, which offer the potential for higher margins. Apple confirms this: "The Company's direct sales generally have higher associated gross margins than its indirect sales through its channel partners" [16].

Manufacturers have greater control over merchandising and prices in their own stores. They also extend their value chain, because they now capture the revenue share that would otherwise fall to a third-party retailer. This forward integration is used by many manufacturers as a growth strategy. This phenomenon is particularly pronounced for luxury goods and fashion. Hugo Boss, for example, is focusing increasingly on direct sales through its own stores, outlets, and the online channel. In 2016 the company generated 62% of its total revenue from direct sales, 2% more than in the previous year. In contrast, the indirect sales through retailers declined by 3% [17]. The fragrance chain Douglas is achieving a steadily growing share of its total revenue from direct sales (e-commerce); in 2017 that channel accounted for 14% of the company's revenue (compared to 10% in 2015). In parallel, Douglas is building up its omni-channel retail through the introduction of cross-channel services such as Click & Collect, the Douglas Card on smartphones, and the mobile measurement device "Douglas Color Expert" [18]. Retailers of all kinds are adding channels to their distribution systems. Walmart, the world's largest retailer, acquired Jet.com for $3 billion and has added a number of smaller e-commerce companies to its portfolio. Amazon, the leader in e-commerce, went in the opposite direction by acquiring Whole Foods Market for $13.40 billion. Some firms such as Louis Vuitton, Tesla, or Nespresso focus exclusively on direct sales and thus have full control over the merchandising and pricing of their products. The price they pay for this advantage, however, comes in the form of higher fixed costs, which can become a burden in downturns or crises.

The growth of factory outlet centers has mushroomed in recent years. This distribution channel is clearly no longer limited to ex-factory sales, as the name would imply. This channel was traditionally used for closeout merchandise but is now increasingly employed to sell products from current selections and assortments. Because access to consumers can be a bottleneck in most markets, many manufacturers are relying more on a multichannel strategy. It is not unusual anymore for a manufacturer to use *all* relevant channels in order to reach the end consumers. In that case one speaks of an omni-channel strategy.

The most important cause behind this shift is the Internet, which has made it so much easier and less expensive for manufacturers to bypass the traditional intermediaries. In principle, every manufacturer can reach and serve its consumers directly nowadays, without the need for an intermediary. This development is still in its early stages. Nonetheless, B2C e-commerce has already reached a market volume of $409 billion in the United States, with double-digit growth rates expected in the coming years [19]. The shift has been the greatest in markets where digital products have replaced physical ones. Netflix's Internet platform for streaming has made the traditional video-rental store all but obsolete. E-books pose a strong competitive threat to printed books.

The Internet also opens a direct path for artists, authors, and other creative service providers to reach their end customers directly. In the traditional book business, an author seeks out a publisher which not only promotes the book but also decides on its price. The printed book then goes via wholesalers to the book stores, where the reader can purchase it. With the advent of modern self-publishing, the authors take publication and marketing into their own hands. They offer their works either as e-books or print at their own expense and then sell the printed books via Amazon or similar e-commerce channels. The authors are solely responsible for generating the "pull effect" for their books. This can make publishers, wholesalers, and the book trade superfluous. It also leads to a radical change in the way prices are calculated. The author can offer the book at a low price and still enjoy a higher margin than with the traditional publishing model. We know of several authors who have used this form of direct marketing at significantly lower prices to achieve sales volumes beyond 100,000 units, compared to a volume of around 10,000 units when they followed the traditional publishing model. These self-publishers lean heavily on social media such as Facebook, Twitter, and LinkedIn to generate the "pull effect."

In a similar manner, music producers, filmmakers, artists, and journalists can reach their customers directly, without needing a publisher as intermediary. In the music industry, 18 superstars have combined forces under the name Tidal in order to reach their fans directly. The reason is that these stars are not satisfied with the pricing policies of Spotify, particularly the low royalties for the free offer. Tidal offers both product and price differentiation. The price of its standard offer matches that of Spotify's paid subscription, which is $9.99 per month. But Tidal also offers a premium version with higher quality for $19.99 per month [20]. We are also familiar with several knowledge providers who generate notable revenues through paid blogs.

Companies which in the past have focused on third-party distribution are trying to find their way directly to end consumers. One example is Foxconn, which is the world's largest contract manufacturer of electronic goods and manufactures the majority of Apple iPhones and iPads. Foxconn's products have been sold to end consumers through various, often multi-tiered, distribution channels by brand owners such as Apple. In other words, Foxconn was an upstream producer, a long way from the end consumer. Together with partners, among them the retail group Metro, Foxconn attempted to operate its own stores, but these were unsuccessful and have since closed. Foxconn opened the e-commerce site flnet.com, on which it sells its own products as well as branded products [21]. Foxconn also has a stake in the Indian e-commerce company Snapdeal [22]. Each of these moves represents an attempt by Foxconn to claim a larger part of the value chain and exercise more effective control over downstream marketing activities and over prices.

What price management problems do manufacturers face when they decide to address end customers directly after previously selling their products through trade partners? The first problem is that these manufacturers have no experience with end consumer pricing. They need to acquire the respective competencies, such as economic and psychological analyses, price decision-making, and implementation. At the same time, they are not starting from scratch. They have learned from their experiences working together with retailers and intermediaries and in some cases have studied end consumer markets. "Downstreaming" along the value chain and in a multichannel approach means that pricing organizations and processes need to be restructured. The most important difference is that direct sales gives the manufacturer full autonomy over the end prices of its products. A manufacturer which markets directly to end consumers can take full advantage of tactics such as price promotions, price differentiation, price bundling, or non-linear pricing. This, in turn, requires the appropriate know-how or external advice.

Multichannel and omni-channel strategies pose difficult coordination problems for price management. Customers tend to show lower willingness to pay on the Internet than they do in brick-and-mortar stores [23]. Consumers expect lower prices online and think that only low prices are "fair" [24]. The Internet creates higher price transparency, which means consumers can make price comparisons with less effort. This gives rise to competition among different sales channels. When a manufacturer sells directly, it enters into competition with its own trade partners. Prices then become a flash point for conflicts. This leads to a difficult question: should one strive for prices which are as uniform as possible across the different channels or consciously allow different prices?

Without a doubt, the Internet makes price differentiation easier. In the offline world, the customer must first find a store but can then acquire the product with no time delay. The online world, in contrast, offers the advantages of convenience, but the buyer does not have immediate access to the product. Customers can select their preferred price-channel combination. This is a case of second-degree price differentiation. Unterhuber [25] has found that online price differentiation with higher prices has a negative effect on the perception of price fairness, on purchase intent, and on customers' word of mouth. Even a price discrepancy as small as 5% above offline prices is sufficient to trigger strong negative reactions. A similar effect occurs offline when the price difference is 15% higher than online prices. Another finding is that customers use their implicit assumptions about selling costs in the individual channels when they evaluate different price levels. In general, the offline channel is seen as costlier for the selling party, which means that higher offline prices are more likely to be accepted. Customers who see the two channels as similar with respect to costs only accept a price difference of 5%. Price differences between online and offline channels should therefore be handled carefully, because they can trigger strong reactions among customers [26].

In reality we observe a lot of variations. First, an increase has been observed in online vs. offline price differentiation [27]. Higher online selling costs (e.g., because of packaging materials or shipping) can lead to higher prices [28, 29]. One study showed that 91% of retailers who differentiate their prices across channels set higher prices online [27]. One European drugstore chain, in contrast, guarantees the same everyday low prices online and in its stores. Higher shipping costs are recouped through a surcharge of €4.95 [30]. The CEO explained the strategy as follows: "We don't hide our logistics costs in higher prices, as some competitors do. Instead we pass along the actual shipping costs to customers in a fair and transparent way" [30]. The British supermarket chain Tesco uses a similar approach [31]. Other online suppliers waive the shipping cost surcharge above a minimum order level.

Apple follows a broad-based multichannel strategy but points to potential risks: "Some resellers have perceived the expansion of the Company's direct sales as conflicting with their business interests as distributors and resellers of the Company's products. Such a perception could discourage resellers from investing resources in the distribution and sale of the Company's products or lead them to limit or cease distribution of those products" [16]. Price differentiation across different channels can lead to confusion and frustration of customers and to cannibalization of one's own sales channels [32]. In this way, multichannel strategies can limit a company's price autonomy. Some firms practice "self-matching" in a multichannel context. If the customer can prove that the product is offered in another channel at a lower price, then the sale is made at that price [33]. Self-matching resembles the price guarantee we discussed in Chap. 9, so it carries some price risk and should therefore be used with caution.

Conclusion

The special characteristics of price management for consumer goods result from the distribution structures. We summarize the most important insights:

- Consumer goods manufacturers traditionally sell their products primarily through retailers or other intermediaries. Therefore they must take the behavior of these trade partners into account when setting prices.
- Under the model of vertical price-fixing, which is generally prohibited and in its strictest form only applies to a few industries nowadays, the manufacturer decides its own selling price as well as the selling price to end consumers and thereby defines the trade partner's margin at the same time. In making these decisions, the manufacturer must take the price elasticity of end consumers and the margin elasticity of the trade partner into account.
- If the manufacturer can determine only its own selling price, it must consider which method the trade partner uses to set its prices for end consumers. The optimal manufacturer's selling price is different when the trade partner uses a cost-plus calculation than when it behaves in a profit-maximizing way.
- If the manufacturer and trade partner pursue joint profit maximization, they proceed in two steps. In the first step, the price to end consumers is set at the level which maximizes total profit. In the second step, the two parties must agree on how to divide up the total profit. This is usually done through the setting of the manufacturer's selling price. There is no concrete solution for how to do this; only the upper and lower bounds of the price range can be determined with certainty.
- Consumer goods manufacturers are turning increasingly to direct sales and multichannel strategies. The motivations for these moves include a desire to expand along the value chain, to generate additional growth, and to exercise

(continued)

more effective control over the merchandising and pricing of their brands. Luxury goods makers and fashion companies in particular are operating their own stores, which implies a shift in cost structure from variable costs to fixed costs and consequently changes a company's risk profile.
- The Internet has created opportunities for manufacturers to bypass intermediaries. It is becoming the most important driver of direct sales for manufacturers. The advantages are most significant for suppliers of products which can be offered in digital form, such as books, films, music, insurance, and similar products.
- This expansion of channel options creates new challenges and potential conflicts to price management for manufacturers. Direct sales expands the range of instruments a manufacturer can use, including price promotions, price differentiation, and price bundling. This in turn demands new competencies in end consumer pricing. Multichannel and omni-channel strategies generally exhibit not only competition among different trade partners but also competition between the manufacturer and its own trade partners. Prices become a main point of conflict. Price management needs to handle the delicate balance with caution and help avoid conflicts.

The distribution of consumer goods and the resulting opportunities and risks for price management are in a state of rapid flux. In that sense, this chapter offers more of a snapshot than a sound forecast for the future. Companies should keep their eyes open and remain flexible. The future will bring many more changes to price management for consumer goods.

References

1. Kotler, P. (2015). *Confronting Capitalism*. New York: Amacom.
2. Baligh, H. H., & Richartz, L. E. (1967). *Vertical Market Structures*. Boston: Allyn and Bacon.
3. Jeuland, A. P., & Shugan, S. (1983). Managing Channel Profits. *Marketing Science*, 2(3), 239–272.
4. Coughlan, A. T. (1982). *Vertical Integration Incentives in Marketing: Theory and Application to International Trade in the Semiconductor Industry*. Dissertation. Stanford University.
5. Coughlan, A. T. (1985). Competition and Cooperation in Marketing Channel Choice: Theory and Application. *Marketing Science*, 4(2), 110–129.
6. Gabrielsen, T. S., & Johansen, B. O. (2015). Buyer Power and Exclusion in Vertically Related Markets. *International Journal of Industrial Organization*, 38(C), 1–18.
7. Martin, S., & Vandekerckhove, J. (2013). Market Performance Implications of the Transfer Price Rule. *Southern Economic Journal*, 80(2), 466–487.
8. Herweg, F., & Müller, D. (2013). Price Discrimination in Input Markets: Quantity Discounts and Private Information. *The Economic Journal*, 124(577), 776–804.
9. Bilotkach, V. (2014). Price Floors and Quality Choice. *Bulletin of Economic Research*, 66(3), 231–245.
10. Rey, P., & Vergé, T. (2010). Resale Price Maintenance and Interlocking Relationships. *The Journal of Industrial Economics*, 58(4), 928–961.

11. Olbrich, R., & Buhr, C.-C. (2007). Handelskonzentration, Handelsmarken und Wettbewerb in der Konsumgüterdistribution – Warum das Verbot der vertikalen Preisbindung abgeschafft gehört. In M. Schuckel, & W. Toporowski (Ed.), *Theoretische Fundierung und praktische Relevanz der Handelsforschung* (pp. 486–505). Wiesbaden: DUV.
12. Krelle, W. (1976). *Preistheorie*. Tübingen: Mohr-Siebeck.
13. Amann, S. (2010, April 03). Geradezu verramscht. *Der Spiegel*, pp. 66–67.
14. Braun, C. (2010). Genug ist genug. http://www.brandeins.de/archiv/2010/irrationalitaet/genug-ist-genug/. Accessed 02 July 2015.
15. Geisler, B. (2015). Der Nivea-Zoff. http://www.welt.de/print/die_welt/hamburg/arti cle138275809/Der-Nivea-Zoff.html. Accessed 02 July 2015.
16. Apple (2014). K-10 Annual Report. http://investor.apple.com/secfiling.cfm?filingid=1193125-14-383437&cik=. Accessed 4 July 2015.
17. Hugo Boss (2016). Annual Report 2016. http://group.hugoboss.com/files/user_upload/Inves tor_Relations/Finanzberichte/Geschaeftsbericht_2016.pdf. Accessed 01 March 2018.
18. Douglas (2017). FY 2016/17 Financial Results. https://ir.douglas.de/websites/douglas/English/9999.html?filename=FY2016-17_Investor_Update.pdf. Accessed 01 March 2018.
19. Statista (2016): Annual desktop e-commerce sales in the United States from 2002 to 2014. https://www.statista.com/statistics/271449/annual-b2c-e-commerce-sales-in-the-united-states/. Accessed 19 December 2016.
20. Anonymous. (2015, April 01). Eine musikalische Unabhängigkeitserklärung – Popstars wie Madonna, Rihanna und Jay-Z fordern digitale Musikdienste mit einem eigenen Angebot heraus. *Frankfurter Allgemeine Zeitung*, p. 15.
21. Luk, L. (2015, March 05). Foxconn Takes on Giants of E-Commerce in China. *The Wall Street Journal Europe*, p. 19.
22. Luk, L., & Machado, K. (2015). Alibaba, Foxconn in Talks to Invest $500 Million in India's Snapdeal. http://www.wsj.com/articles/alibaba-foxconn-in-talks-to-invest-500-million-in-indias-snapdeal-1434444149. Accessed 14 July 2015.
23. Kacen, J. J., Hess, J. D., & Chiang, W. K. (2013). Bricks or Clicks? Consumer Attitudes toward Traditional Stores and Online Stores. *Global Economics and Management Review*, 18(1), 12–21.
24. Jensen, T., Kees, J., Burton, S., & Turnipseed, F. L. (2003). Advertised Reference Prices in an Internet Environment: Effects on Consumer Price Perceptions and Channel Search Intentions. *Journal of Interactive Marketing*, 17(2), 20–33.
25. Unterhuber, S. (2015). *Channel-Based Price Differentiation – Literature Review and Empirical Consumer Research*. Frankfurt am Main: Peter Lang.
26. Fassnacht, M., & Unterhuber, S. (2016). Consumer Response to Online/Offline Price Differen-tiation. *Journal of Retailing and Consumer Services*, 28, 137–148.
27. Wolk, A., & Ebling, C. (2010). Multi-Channel Price Differentiation: An Empirical Investigation of Existence and Causes. *International Journal of Research in Marketing*, 27(2), 142–150.
28. Yan, R. (2008). Pricing Strategy for Companies with Mixed Online and Traditional Retailing Distribution Markets. *Journal of Product & Brand Management*, 17(1), 48–56.
29. Zhang, J., Farris, P. W., Irvin, J. W., Kushwaha, T., Steenburgh, T. J., & Weitz, B. A. (2010). Crafting Integrated Multichannel Retailing Strategies. *Journal of Interactive Marketing*, 24(2), 168–180.
30. Anonymous. (2015, July 17). dm will Verluste im Netz in Grenzen halten. *Lebensmittel Zeitung*, p. 8.
31. Anonymous. (2015, July 17). Tesco erzürnt seine Online-Kunden. *Lebensmittel Zeitung*, p. 8.
32. Pan, X., Ratchford, B. T., & Shankar, V. (2004). Price Dispersion on the Internet: A Review and Directions for Future Research. *Journal of Interactive Marketing*, 18(4), 116–135.
33. Nalca, A., Boyaci, T., & Ray, S. (2010). Competitive Price-Matching Guarantees under Imperfect Store Availability. *Quantitative Marketing and Economics*, 8(3), 275–300.

Price Management for Industrial Goods

11

Abstract

Price management for industrial goods involves numerous special aspects. Overall, it is characterized by a wide variety of price models and pricing approaches. Because of these special aspects, analysis demands a thorough understanding of the specific case. That includes the role of individual people as well as groups, the so-called buying centers. Many industrial suppliers see themselves up against "derived demand" which has consequences for price management. For the price decision, very different processes come into play. Depending on the project, these can be driven more by value-to-customer, which is often quantifiable for industrial goods, or more by costs. Auctions play an important, and thanks to the Internet, growing role. Important aspects of implementation are skills and savvy in the protracted and tedious price negotiations and the contractual hedging of price risks.

11.1 Introduction

Industrial goods are defined as products and services which are not purchased by end consumers but rather by organizations (industrial manufacturers, public institutions, government bodies) to produce other products or services, which in turn are sold directly or indirectly to end consumers [1, p. 3, 2]. Industrial goods cover an extremely wide spectrum, from complex installations such as power plants or railroad systems to standard products such as screws or office supplies. Fittingly, the range of pricing problems and processes is very diverse. Products can have overlaps with consumer products, as some products can be consumed or used in production. One example is food, which is purchased by end consumers and by large cafeterias, restaurants, caterers, etc. In most cases, though, the presentation form, the package size, and the prices are different for consumers than for companies.

© Springer Nature Switzerland AG 2019
H. Simon, M. Fassnacht, *Price Management*,
https://doi.org/10.1007/978-3-319-99456-7_11

Generally speaking, any products which are sold to organizations or companies are considered industrial products. One also speaks of business-to-business marketing (B2B marketing).

Research into marketing for industrial goods has paid relatively scant attention to price. Aspects such as organizational buying behavior, strategy, or planning are at the forefront [3, 4, p. 9]. Price-related aspects such as economic value analysis, bidding processes, auctions, or price negotiations will be the focus of this chapter. We will look at the special characteristics of pricing for industrial goods according to a typology of the business or business transaction involved. Then we explore the analysis, decision, and implementation phases in depth.

A familiar typology of industrial goods classifies the transactions according to the "intensity of the business relationship" and the "individuality of the offer" [1, p. 195, 5, p. 842, 6, p. 1058]. This classification is shown in Fig. 11.1. The *product/spot business* shows a certain similarity to classical consumer goods marketing. Standardized products (e.g., office supplies, screws, or computers) are sold to numerous customers. Homogeneous goods are suitable for auctions. In other instances, value-based pricing is possible. In the *plant and project business*, the offer is tailored to the individual client. Because there is often no market price, one uses special costing procedures, or the buying firm conducts a bidding process. In a *systems business*, the first purchase initiates a stream of subsequent purchases of consumables, replacement parts, or maintenance services. Most forms of B2B business or transactions involve some type of price negotiation.

Industrial goods markets share the following characteristics [1, pp. 7–10, 7, p. 161, 8, pp. 30–32]:

Fig. 11.1 Classification of business types in the industrial goods sector [6, p. 1058]

- The purchase decision involves a buying center comprised of several people with different interests.
- Buyers in most cases have a good information basis for their purchase decisions, based on thorough supplier analysis. The performance of industrial products is often easier to quantify than the performance of consumer goods.
- Large projects are often multi-organizational, meaning they involve banks, other companies, or external consultants.
- Many projects are unique and executed to customer specifications.
- Purchase or procurement generally adheres to a formulized process and often award contracts only after a bidding or tender process.
- Some industrial goods suppliers feel subject to derived demand and should in these cases take into account the activities further down the value chain (i.e., the customers of their customers) in their pricing.
- There are often only a small number of firms on the supply and the demand side (bilateral oligopoly). For example, there are only a few recognized suppliers of pistons for automobile engines.

11.2 Analysis

Because the customers for industrial goods are organizations, their buying behavior—how they make their purchase decisions—must be investigated and understood. The concept of the *buying center (BC)* plays a central role. The BC comprises all people who participate in the purchase decision. These people evaluate the various proposals according to their own criteria, often have different levels of risk tolerance, and often follow their own goals. In order to provide an appropriate price-value offer and to communicate it adequately, one must identify the members of the BC and understand their respective preferences and roles. These roles could be initiator, user, buyer, information screener, or decision-maker. This analysis gives the supplier important insights for configuring its offer in terms of price and value. The price response of the BC members can vary, because the individual components of the offer may be perceived or valued differently. In order to achieve the highest possible price in the course of a price negotiation, it can be advisable for a supplier to emphasize different aspects of its offer, depending on the respective negotiating partner at the time.

Ahead of the negotiation, it is critical to know how the members of the BC think about value. Furthermore, one should know how the proposals or offers from different suppliers will be evaluated. A supplier may have different latitude for setting prices, depending on the evaluation process the buyer uses. Knowing the evaluation scheme is indispensable if a supplier wants to set an optimal price. Forbis and Mehta [9, p. 50] make the following remark on this topic: "The value customers perceive depends so heavily on the way they evaluate it that management ought to be

keenly concerned about how well and thoroughly these evaluations are made."
These insights can obviously be used for negotiations and in communication, not
just in preparing the offer.

Derived Demand

Many suppliers feel that they are subject to a situation referred to as "derived
demand." To explain this concept, we use an example of an automotive industry
supplier which makes components such as side mirrors. The sales volume for such
components depends entirely on the sales of the respective car model which contains
that component. In the case of side mirrors, every automobile sold needs two and
only two. The price of such individual components, however, has no significant
influence on either the end price of that automobile or the number of cars sold. In
other words, the supplier of side mirrors is faced with a production volume requirement it has no influence on. For the supplier, the sales volume is a given. This
situation is shown in Fig. 11.2. For simplicity's sake, we assume that the supplier is
the sole supplier, i.e., that this is a case of single sourcing.

The price-response function runs horizontally, i.e., the sales volume does not
depend on the price of the component. Whether the supplier gets the contract,
however, does indeed depend on the price it offers. The contribution margin (and
thus the profit as well) rises linearly with the price. This happens because the sales
volume is fixed. The supplier's challenge is to realize the highest (maximum) price.
The negotiating tactics must therefore be directed at driving up the customer's
willingness to pay. Naturally, competitors' prices will play an important role.
However, when the customer chooses only one supplier, the sales volume of the
component does not depend on its price. No matter how high or low the price is, the

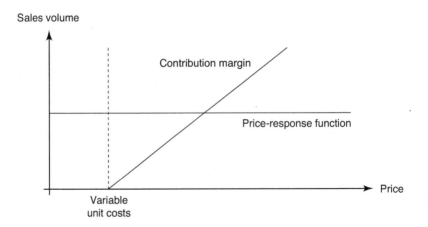

Fig. 11.2 Derived demand

demand is fixed: the automotive manufacturer will need only a set number of side mirrors.

The situation is somewhat different when the buyer intends to spread its total demand across several suppliers. In order to reduce supplier risk and exert greater pressure on prices, many industrial customers practice this multisourcing. In most cases the demand is allocated according to fixed percentages, e.g., 70–30. Within these shares, the situation resembles the situation we described above for single sourcing.

The situation is different in the aftermarket, i.e., the sale of replacement parts. This is particularly true when there is competition, i.e., the availability of spare parts from companies other than the OEM. In this case, the component faces a price-response function with a negative slope, which in turn can lead to a "normal" profit function.

11.3 Decision

Value-based pricing, cost-oriented pricing, and auctions are important regarding the price decision. We introduce each of these in the following sections.

11.3.1 Value-Based Pricing

The use of objective, value-based pricing is more relevant for industrial goods than for consumer goods because the performance (and thus the value) of industrial goods is often better quantifiable. "Value-based" in this context refers to a form of pricing by which measured performance or a value index is used as a guideline for the price decision.

The concepts of value-to-customer and performance in industrial goods, however, should not be limited merely to functionality. In addition to the perceived security of employees ("nobody ever got fired for buying IBM"), the internal and external presentation (symbolic performance) also matters for industrial goods. Even aesthetic points (emotional performance) can be relevant.

The measurement of value as the basis for pricing plays a critical role. Table 11.1 introduces selected methods for value measurement [10, pp. 6–11].

Value measurements through focus groups and importance ratings are frequently used. Economic value analysis is an established, tried-and-tested method for estimating pricing latitude. For this purpose, an actual economic value analysis of the customer must be made. A simple example illustrates this: Compared to an existing pesticide, a new product improves wheat yields by an additional 100 kg/ha. At the same time, the spreading of the pesticide costs an additional $5 per hectare. With incremental revenue to the farmer of $15/100 kg, the upper bound for the price

Table 11.1 Methods of value measurement for industrial goods

Name	Description of the method
Internal evaluation by company's own employees	• Internal estimate of value through tests • Very good knowledge of product usage/application and production processes is necessary
Economic value analysis	• Doing customer interviews and compiling an exhaustive list of all cost components of the offer • Comparison of the calculated costs with those of the product that the customer currently uses (product life cycle costs) • Estimation of pricing latitude
Evaluation by focus groups	• Discussion of offers (real or conceptual) within a focus group • Survey of specialists or experts (customer's employees, consultants, other experts) regarding the willingness to pay
Importance ratings	• Survey (primary research) on the importance of certain aspects or features of the offer • Evaluation of the supplier regarding its performance along those same aspects or features
Conjoint measurement	• Survey (primary research) on purchase preferences for different product offerings • Systematic variation of the performance attributes • Calculation of various part-worth utilities for different attributes and their levels

of the new pesticide is $15 − $5 = $10 higher than the old product. One should set the price below this upper bound, however, in order to incentivize the farmer to use the new product.

For durable goods, i.e., products which are expected to remain in use for several years, such considerations are more complex. The economic value analysis in this case compares the revenue inflows with the cash or expenditure outflows. The knowledge of the customer's economic value analysis is of paramount importance. Let us use the purchase of a commercial truck as an example. The customer makes its decision based on the net present value (NPV) which is defined as follows:

$$\text{NPV} = -a_0 + \sum_{t=1}^{T} \text{CF}_t (1 + i)^{-t}. \tag{11.1}$$

The price to be determined for the truck influences multiple variables:

- The payment to purchase the truck a_0
- The cash flow CF_t (through depreciation and financing costs)

The following numbers are used for calculating the net present value for the main competing product (Truck A):

Number of days used (per year)	200	Days
Revenue per day of use	500	$
Operating costs per day of use	250	$
Purchase price a_0	100,000	$
Product life	5	Years
Residual value	0	$
Equity invested	50,000	$
Cost of capital (interest rate)	10	Percent per year

Repayment of the loan would be after 5 years in a lump sum.
The cash flow per year is calculated as follows:

Revenue per year	100,000	$
Operating costs	−50,000	$
Interest payments	−5000	$
Depreciation	−20,000	$
Pre-tax profit	25,000	$
After-tax profit	12,500	$
Cash flow (after-tax profit + depreciation)	32,500	$

The sum of the discounted cash flows over the 5-year period is $123,200; the net present value (NPV) therefore comes to $23,200 ($123,200 minus the purchase price).

The new truck (Truck B) breaks down less often and at the same time costs less to operate, so that the operator can achieve 210 days of use with operating costs falling to $225 per day of use.

In this example, the net present value on Truck B can be expressed as a linear function of the truck price:

$$NPV = 118,936 - 0.8105p. \tag{11.2}$$

The price that is NPV neutral to the competitor's product is $118,120. At this price, the same net present value of $23,200 would be achieved as for Truck A. If the price for Truck B was below $118,120, it would be less expensive than Truck A (and vice versa).

This statement, however, applies only when the net present value is the customer's decision criterion. The competition-neutral price level is different if the customer makes the investment decision based on other criteria. Table 11.2 provides an overview of competition-neutral prices for the criteria return on equity (ROE), return on assets (ROA), and payoff period, as well as for NPV. It becomes clear that the price latitude available to manufacturer B depends on the customer's decision criterion for this investment. The competition-neutral prices lie in a range between $114,010 and $125,833.

Table 11.2 Competition-neutral price for different investment decision criteria

Criteria	Value for Truck A	Competition-neutral price Truck B
Return on equity (ROE)	25.0%	$125,833
Return on assets (ROA)	12.5%	$114,010
Pay-off period	3.08 years	$114,225
Net present value (NPV)	$23,200	$118,120

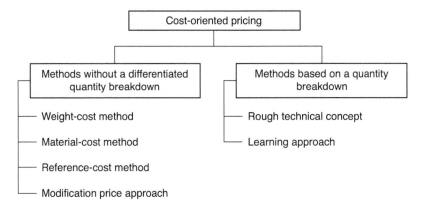

Fig. 11.3 Cost-oriented pricing methods

This simple case illustrates how important it is for an industrial goods manufacturer to have exact knowledge of its customers' economic value analysis. These lines of thinking also offer starting points for both sales negotiations and customer training. If a customer previously used the payoff period as its decision criterion, and the manufacturer succeeds in convincing this customer that the NPV method is a more adequate approach, then the manufacturer can justify a higher price difference of $3895.

11.3.2 Cost-Oriented Pricing

Cost-oriented pricing is very popular for industrial goods. For specific projects and customized offers (e.g., for a plant or facility), there is generally no market price. Rather, an individual quote is necessary. There are different methods for making such individual quotations [11, 12]. One first uses internal data in order to come up with an initial idea for the price. We show the most common methods below and describe them briefly. There are some methods which do not use a volume metric and others which explicitly use one (see Fig. 11.3).

The *weight-cost method* uses experienced-based cost values per "kilogram of plant" to calculate the offer price [13, p., 129]. Of course, this approach is not limited to weight-based metrics. One can also use "cubic meters of enclosed space" (customary in the construction industry) or "length of production line" in order to get to a rough price guideline for the offer.

The *material-cost method* assumes a constant relation between material, labor, and other costs. If this relation is known from previous projects, the manufacturing costs may be estimated on the basis of anticipated material costs.

In contrast to these simple methods, which draw on only one cost variable to calculate the offer price, one can use multiple cost functions. The first step is to identify the potential reference variables for cost (*reference-cost method*). These are then entered as independent variables in a multiple regression analysis in order to estimate the relationships and the strength of the influence between the independent variables and the manufacturing costs. With the help of the regression equation, the cost of the new project can then be estimated.

Under the *modification price approach*, similar projects which have been completed are used as calculation basis. The actual total costs for the current project are estimated, taking different modifications and correction factors into account (e.g., for special characteristics of the project such as geology, climate, inflation rate, etc.).

Another approach, the *rough projections*, uses a rough technical concept, with the individual components evaluated according to the anticipated costs. To the resulting base price, one then adds the particular one-off costs (e.g., travel costs, transportation, insurance) to determine a customer-specific base price. Furthermore, if special delivery or payment conditions (financing costs, warehousing, or other storage costs) are taken into account, one speaks of the "adjusted base price" which represents the starting price for placing a bid.

The basic idea behind the *learning approach* is that one has captured and itemized previously completed projects systematically in a database. For a new project, one can access the individual parts or components and the associated cost information and use this information to develop the quotation. One can distinguish between the analytical learning approach and the search calculation [14]. Under the analytical learning approach, one relies on existing technical solutions and a successively expanding pool of data. Under the search calculation, one looks for similar features in order to identify similar projects. These then serve as the basis for the quotation of the new project.

The criticism of cost-plus pricing also applies to the costing methods described above. In addition, these methods do not adequately take into account the special characteristics of a service-based offer [1, pp. 383f.]. This is important nowadays, as suppliers of facilities and plant equipment are increasingly becoming service providers as well (i.e., by offering training, consulting, financing, and operational or maintenance services).

11.3.3 Auctions

Contracts for industrial goods are often awarded as the result of tenders and auctions. The use of auctions, especially online auctions, has increased dramatically since the advent of the Internet.

11.3.3.1 Tender Processes

Tenders or bidding processes are a special form of auction in which potential suppliers are requested by the customer to submit written bids for the performance or fulfillment of a specified task. Tenders are commonplace in many markets for industrial goods and legally mandated in others (e.g., for providing goods and services to government institutions or organizations).

From the supplier perspective, we can distinguish between two decision problems:

- Selection of potentially worthwhile tenders or requests for proposal, i.e., the fundamental decision on whether to participate in a tender process
- Setting the offer price, assuming the company decides to participate ("competitive bidding")

In this section we focus on the second decision problem: the setting of the offer price. The starting point is a detailed description or specification of the desired goods and services. This description establishes the price as the sole decision criterion to evaluate the various bids and thus reduces the competition only to price.

Due to the intensive effort required by the bidders and the fact that contracts for very large projects are awarded through such tender processes, winning or losing the bid can have a strong influence on the financial situation of a supplier. Determining the optimal offer price is therefore of utmost importance. In principle, the objective is to find the highest possible price which is still below the price of the next-lowest competitor.

A bidder, however, will generally know neither the number of other bidders nor the level of their individual bids. Under so-called "sealed bid, first-price" tenders, a supplier may submit one and only one bid; it is not possible to make adjustments after submission. If the supplier wins the bid, the contract and the price are binding. However, additional bidding rounds or follow-up negotiations are not uncommon [15].

To determine the optimal price, fundamental game theory approaches or decision theory approaches come into play [1, pp. 393–396, 16, pp. 1064–1075, 17, p. 198, 18, pp. 21f].

Game theory models are regularly deployed in the awarding of licenses in sectors such as mobile telephony, energy, toll systems, etc. These efforts generally follow a comprehensive set of objectives. One therefore also speaks of "market design." We refer to specialized literature [16, p. 1074, 18, pp. 21f].[1]

---

[1]For further game theory literature, we refer the reader to [15, 19, 20].

We will concentrate here on *decision theory models*. For pricing of tender submissions, we assume that the bidding circumstances—including the behavior of the other bidders—are independent of one's own actions and that the decision will be made rationally [16, p. 1064].

Friedman [21] suggested a quantitative model for the pricing of tender submissions. Several expansions trace their roots to his work [22, 23]. The following factors are critical for the decision on which price to offer:

- The objective function of the supplier
- The costs for the project and for the preparation of the bid
- The behavior of the competitors
- The criteria the potential customer uses to award the contract

It is entirely conceivable that the various bidders will have different objectives [21, p., 105]. These include the minimization of an expected loss, or winning the bid, even if it results in a financial loss, in order to maintain capacity utilization. Of course, these different objectives lead to different solutions. In general, however, the goal is to maximize the expected value of the profit [24, p., 315].

The basic model of competitive bidding is to maximize the expected value of the contribution margin $E(\pi)$ from the project. We neglect fixed costs here.

$$E(\pi) = (p - k - C)\text{Prob}(p < \bar{p}) - C[1 - \text{Prob}(p < \bar{p})] \qquad (11.3)$$

where
$p =$ offered price,
$k =$ variable costs of the project,
$C =$ costs to prepare the offer, and
$\text{Prob}(p < \bar{p}) =$ probability that the firm will win the bid at the price p.

Table 11.3 shows a numerical example where $C = \$500,000$ and $k = \$10$ million. Contribution margins are calculated for the alternative prices, and success probabilities are estimated. Then the respective probabilities and contribution margins are multiplied and the costs in the case of a lost bid subtracted. The last column shows the expected contribution margin for the various bids. In this case, a bid of $30 million achieves the greatest expected profit.

Table 11.3 Expected profit for different bids (in millions of dollars)

Price offered p ($ millions)	Contribution margin $(p - k - K)$ ($ millions)	Probability of winning $\text{Prob}(p < \bar{p})$	Expected costs (without winning) $K[1 - \text{Prob}(p < \bar{p})]$ ($ millions)	Expected contribution margin ($ millions)
40	29.5	0.24	0.38	6.7
35	24.5	0.32	0.34	7.5
30	19.5	0.44	0.28	8.3
25	14.5	0.50	0.25	7.0

This procedure is simple in theory but faces problems in practice. First, there can be extreme variations in cost. Winning the bid may require a capacity expansion (resulting in a step change in fixed costs), or one must take opportunity costs into account because winning this bid would mean forgoing other worthwhile projects. On the other hand, it is difficult to estimate the probabilities of winning the bid. Doing so essentially involves estimating the probability distribution for the prices the competitors will offer. One usually draws on values from past experience to do this [16, pp. 1065–1068].

Competitive bidding often results in the so-called *winner's curse* [25, pp. 50–62]. Even when the methods described here are used to find an optimal bid price, the winner of the bid often suffers a loss. Ask the simple question: "What does it mean when I am the lowest bidder?" and there are two likely answers. It can mean that one is ready to sacrifice profit, or it can mean that one has underestimated the costs. The latter holds true in many cases, even when the costs of the project have been correctly assessed on average by all the bidders (based on the results of previous bids) and one has built in an upcharge to account for a profit. The primary reason for this is that winning bids are not a random sample of all bids. One tends to get awarded those projects for which one has underestimated the costs. The resulting profitability after winning the project tends to be lower than what was expected prior to winning. What is worse is that the more bidders are participating, the greater the chances of the winner to suffer a financial loss.

11.3.3.2 Online Auctions

According to a study by Frost and Sullivan [26], global B2B e-commerce will continue to grow strongly and is expected to reach $6.7 trillion by 2020, which is roughly twice as high as B2C e-commerce. The Internet has resulted in far-reaching changes in the practice of procurement. Price transparency has dramatically increased [27, p. 113]. This gave rise to expectations that completely transparent markets would emerge, turning nearly every project into a commodity case. This development, however, has not occurred [28, p. 8].

Online auctions have become very popular. For an overview of the potential forms and uses of auctions, we refer the reader to [15, pp. 104–124, 29, 30, p. 158, 31, 32, p. 104] and Chap. 3. Homogeneous products are particularly well suited for auctions. In such cases, the price is often the most important purchase criterion, if not the only one. Larger companies conduct such auctions on their own. General Electric (GE) was a pioneer in this area. Back in 1995, GE had already started its own in-house auction site. There are numerous purchasing co-ops and marketplaces such as Alibaba, eBay business, or ThomasNet, which use auctions for procurement.

The supplier is in a tricky situation here, as with every auction. If the auction is a pure price auction, then only the supplier's price will determine whether it wins the contract. In the industrial procurement market, *Dutch auctions* are common. The auction is initiated by the buyer ("reverse auction"). This has parallels to a traditional tender process. The customer (alone or as part of a buying cooperative) signals a

Table 11.4 Advantages and disadvantages of online auctions (from supplier perspective)

Advantages	Disadvantages
• Larger market	• Stronger competition
• Possibility to name a price at which the buyers buy immediately (buyout pricing)	• No personal contact
• Transactions in real time	• Fees for intermediaries
• Reduced transaction costs	–

need for goods and/or services which it specifies in a request for bid. In contrast to tenders or a "sealed bid, first price" or "sealed bid, second price," there is a sequence of offers. The prices drop step by step, and ultimately the lowest price wins the bid.

Table 11.4 lists the *advantages and disadvantages of online auctions* from the perspective of the supplier [27, p. 113, 32, p 105]. An important decision is whether to take part in the auction at all. If the supplier does decide to participate, it should attempt to exert some influence on the auction conditions. A premium supplier can, for example, try to receive a price premium. Such differentiation is observed more often in practice [15]. Internally, a supplier should also ex ante set a price at which it will no longer place any more bids.

There is a risk that the bidders get drawn into a downward spiral in which they continually underbid each other. The following real-life example illustrates this. The supplier of an industrial maintenance contract for power plants took part in an online auction in an intensely competitive market. Figure 11.4 shows the bid progression for this particular supplier. The last bids were significantly below the lower price bound initially set. Nonetheless, the contract went to a competitor. It became known which company received the award (another large competitor), but not at what price. In this case, there were a total of 20 bidding steps.

One of the reasons why the original lower bound was breached is the dynamic of the bidding process. Within 4 h, each supplier had to make numerous decisions. In such situations, a bidding supplier needs to remain level-headed and continually keep its preset lower limit in mind. There are also situations in which, after a certain point, a competitor may continue to undercut bids in order to drive other suppliers' prices lower, in an effort to damage the winning competitor. This is of course a very risky tactic because the aggressive bidder may actually win the contract itself at a low price and fall victim to the winner's curse.

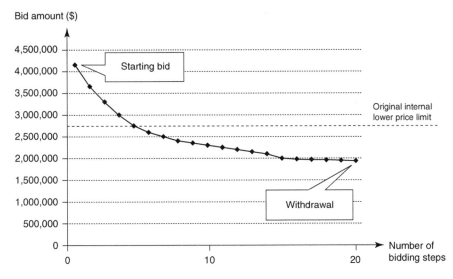

Fig. 11.4 Bid progression of an online auction (Simon-Kucher & Partners)

11.4   Implementation

Price negotiations and price contracts play an important role for industrial goods.

11.4.1 Price Negotiation

A sales contract in industrial goods markets is reached in most cases as a result of a negotiation. The negotiation potentially covers all aspects of the transaction. In addition to the technical solution, the negotiation may address the price, the payment terms, and the financing. Negotiation skills are a critical success factor.

We distinguish between theoretical and management-based approaches [33]. The theoretical approaches include game theory and behavioral economics. The approaches from game theory are aimed at analyzing and optimizing negotiation outcomes. Behavioral economics approaches attempt to answer questions on how the conditions of the negotiations should be arranged in order to steer the negotiation outcome in the desired direction. These approaches focus less on the actual negotiation process itself. *Management-related approaches* emphasize the negotiation process and attempt to derive specific strategic and tactical recommendations for the negotiation.

To illustrate the *game theoretical approaches*, we consider a negotiation between an industrial goods supplier and an industrial customer. Both supplier and customer need to reach an agreement on price and sales volume under circumstances in which the two parties have some opposing interests. This is another example of a zero-sum

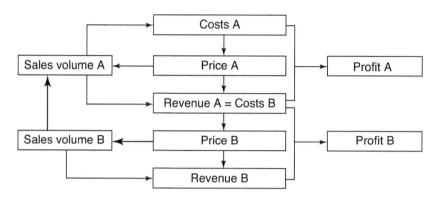

Fig. 11.5 System interrelationships within bilateral monopoly

or constant-sum game: what the seller gains in terms of additional revenue at a given volume represents a corresponding incremental loss for the buyer.

Supplier A negotiates with Customer B who in turn sells its products to a number of end consumers. A and B form a bilateral monopoly, meaning they are the only players involved in this transaction. The revenue of A represents the costs of B, whose sales volumes in turn determine the volume of A. The negotiations are confined to the sales volume of $B(q_B)$ and the price of $A(p_A)$. Alternatively, the negotiation could be about p_B instead of q_B, because p_B and q_B are clearly related via the price-response function. All other terms (q_A, R_A, π_A, R_B, π_B) are either given or can be calculated by formula once q_B or p_B are fixed. Figure 11.5 shows the interrelationships.

The revenue of A is merely a pass-through item and therefore has no influence on the joint total profit. This profit depends only on p_B and q_B, respectively. If the negotiating partners behave rationally, they should reach an agreement in two steps:

1. Determination of p_B (or q_B) in such a way that the total profit is maximized (assuming there is honesty between the partners and no conflict of interest)
2. Negotiation of p_A which determines the distribution of the profit between the two parties (countervailing interests)

The profit functions for the two companies are as follows (assuming a linear cost function):

$$\pi_A = (p_A - k_A)q_A \qquad (11.4)$$

and

$$\pi_B = (p_B - p_A - k_B)q_B. \qquad (11.5)$$

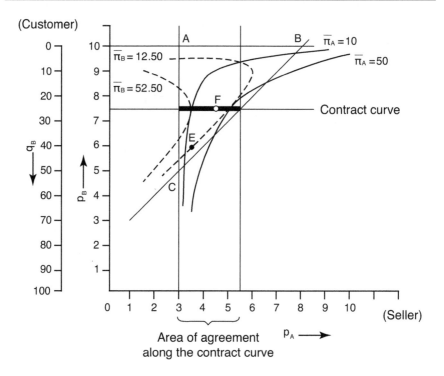

Fig. 11.6 Negotiation situation as iso-profit lines system

The volume units of A are defined such that each unit of B contains exactly one unit of A ($q_A = q_B$). The joint profit π_T then is:

$$\pi_T = \pi_A + \pi_B = (p_B - k_B - k_A)q_B. \qquad (11.6)$$

One sees that π_T is not dependent on p_A, so that the optimal price of B can be determined independently of p_A (Step 1).

We use a numerical example with a linear price-response function to illustrate this negotiation situation:

$$q_B = 100 - 10p_B. \qquad (11.7)$$

Supplier A has constant marginal costs of $k_A = 3$, while the marginal costs of B are $k_B = 2$. This is shown in Fig. 11.6. The vertical axis displays price p_B and the corresponding volume q_B (according to the price-response function), and the horizontal axis shows price p_A.

An agreement will only be reached if neither party incurs a loss. The prerequisite is met within the triangle A-B-C. Along the line A-B, there are no sales, because $q_B = 0$. Along the line A-C, supplier A earns no profit ($p_A = 3 = k_A$). Along the line B-C, customer B comes up empty profit-wise ($p_B = p_A + k_B$).

In order to localize the area of agreement, we look at point $E(p_A = 3.5; p_B = 6)$. Point E lies within the triangle A-B-C and in principle allows for a potential agreement. This price combination results in the following profits:

$$\pi_A = 20, \pi_B = 20, \pi_T = 40.$$

The companies can improve on this situation, however, by raising the price p_A to 4.5 and p_B to 7.5. That would result in profits of $\pi_A = 37.5$ and $\pi_B = 25$, for a total profit of $\pi_T = 62.5$.

Beyond point F, however, there is no further possibility for simultaneous profit improvement of both parties. This is the point where the price p_B (or the volume q_B) maximizes the joint profit π_T.

One can check this arithmetically, by determining p_B^* and q_B^* for the joint profit function.

$$p_B^* = \frac{1}{2}\left(\frac{a}{b} + k_A + k_B\right) = 7.5 \tag{11.8}$$

$$q_B^* = \frac{1}{2}(a - bk_A - bk_B) = 25 \tag{11.9}$$

These are precisely the values of point F. The line parallel to the p_A-axis with $q_B = q_B^*$ (or $p_B = p_B^*$) is the line of maximum total profit and is referred to as the contract curve. Along the contract curve, neither party can improve its situation without worsening the other party's situation by the same amount. This characteristic is known as pareto-optimal.

However, only a portion of the contract curve comes into play as the basis for an agreement. That is the section which lies within the general area of agreement defined by the triangle A-B-C. The upper bound of this interval is $p_A = 5.5$ (because $p_B = 7.5$ and $k_B = 2$). At this point, B's profit is zero. The lower bound is determined by the marginal costs of A and lies at $p_A = 3$. At either bound, one of the partners earns no money.

If the two parties behave rationally, they will strike an agreement between $3 \leq p_A \leq 5.5$. This restricts the negotiation problem to a comparatively small range. The result of the negotiation depends on the further assumptions about the behavior of the partners.

Behavioral economics approaches offer some helpful insights in this regard. Among other things, these approaches explore the effects of situational or contextual variables on the negotiation result [33, p. 1025]. Such variables include the number of people involved in the negotiation [34], time pressure [35], the presence of third parties [36], anger and stress [37], conflict situations, or cultural differences. Situational variables are specific and usually cannot be influenced, which means one cannot derive concrete recommendations from them for conducting negotiations. One can, however, gain some insights into making a better assessment of the existing situation [33, p. 1025, 38, p. 281].

We elaborate on this using a balance-of-power example between buyer and seller. The balance of power can have an influence on either party's room for maneuvering [39, p. 76, 40, p. 308, 41]. Whether a buyer or seller can be characterized as strong or weak, i.e., whether either has pricing power, depends on many factors. The power of the buyer is driven by factors such as size, past purchase volumes, anticipated level of future orders, and creditworthiness. The strength of the seller is determined by the level of performance the seller offers (quality, image, after-sales service) and the substitutability of its products and services. These factors can be weighted, and a score can be calculated to assess the power of the buyer and the seller (scoring model). Through this approach, one can gain valuable insights on whether and to what extent there is room to maneuver in terms of pricing.

Such analyses can be conducted using data from previous transactions. One quantifies the balance of power—from the seller's perspective—on the basis of the relevant factors and then juxtaposes that result with the actual outcome of the negotiation (e.g., the achieved price or volume). This allows the seller to define concrete benchmarks for the negotiating outcome it is seeking. Simon-Kucher & Partners uses this method regularly. The negotiation skills of one's own team have significant effects on the result. In numerous projects, Simon-Kucher & Partners has quantified the skills and competencies of different negotiating teams within the same company and then compared them to the achieved negotiation results. The correlations were highly significant.

The nature of the customer relationship also influences the room to maneuver. In practice, we can distinguish between two forms of customer relationships. In the first case, there is a common basis for trust, and the negotiations tend to be conducted fairly. In the second case, the relationship is tense and the negotiation is a struggle. The first case is typically characterized by continuity among personnel, while the second case features frequent personnel changes and aggressive goals on the buyer's side. A fair relationship does not preclude tough negotiations, but such negotiations are generally not perceived as unpleasant. One observes time and again that customers try to gain additional concessions by speaking directly to the supplier's CEO. This appears in general to be a soft spot. Suppliers should therefore avoid, to the greatest extent possible, letting the CEO get involved in price negotiations. The reverse may be true for buyers.

Within the actual negotiation process (*management-based approach*), *psychology and tactics* play a role. The achievement of a desired price ultimately depends on psychological and tactical negotiation talents. Beyond the relatively few articles which deal concretely with price negotiations [42, 43], there is an extremely vast literature on general negotiation tactics [44–46]. Below we describe some of the proven tips and tricks.

For very complex products or services, it is often advisable for the seller to educate the customer about the advantages of the product in the greatest possible detail. The focus should first be steered toward the performance, before one turns to price. The intensive discussion with the customer helps experienced sales people to better estimate the individual customer's willingness to pay (maximum price). As a result, the price which the one brings up at a later point in the negotiation is ideally higher than the price the one would have offered at an earlier point. The potential drawback to naming one's price at a later stage in the negotiations is that one has invested a lot of time and effort in obtaining information or preparing a proposal for customers whose willingness to pay turns out to be too low. Thus, the timing of the first specific naming of a price, coordinated with the exploration of the customer's willingness to pay, is critical. A company often incurs considerable costs before recognizing that a customer's willingness to pay is too low.

The objective of a negotiation is to close a sale at a reasonable price level. Two fundamental negotiation tenets are the principle of mutual interest and the "tit-for-tat" principle. Under the *principle of mutual interest*, one tries to emphasize the common interests of the parties and to focus on these [45, 47]. The *tit-for-tat principle* calls for making concessions only when one gets something of corresponding value in return [48, p. 53, 49].

No two negotiation situations are the same, which means there is no single tried-and-true negotiation technique [50–52]. However, one should not limit the content of the negotiation solely to the price. The deciding factor is always the price-value ratio. When price is the only object of the negotiation, one should not be surprised that price becomes the dominant, if not the sole decision criterion for the buyer: "Successful negotiators, acknowledging that economics aren't everything, focus on important non-price factors. Wise negotiators put the vital issue of price in perspective and don't straight-jacket their view of the richer interest at stake" [47, p. 90f].

The customer must see the value in the features and characteristics. A cost-benefit analysis helps to clarify the value of the offer. This method is not often employed, however, for a couple of reasons. First, it is relatively costly, and second, suppliers are leery of documenting specific cost savings and/or productivity improvements. Such documentation conveys an expectation which can be construed as an implied commitment. This risk can be minimized, though, if the supplier provides careful estimates and clears up with the customer in advance whether the underlying assumptions and the numbers used reflect reality.

Additional supportive techniques include the subtraction technique and the division technique. Under the *subtraction technique*, one withdraws a component from the original offer when the buyer asks for a lower price. In this manner, the seller gets a feeling for whether the purchasing side is trying only to wring price concessions or whether the customer truly does not value some parts of the offer.

Under the *division technique*, the seller breaks down the costs into smaller units corresponding to the customer's production process. Let us say the company offers a production facility for $2.04 million, which is 2% more expensive than the competitor's product. The seller could make the following argument:

1. The customer's production volume is 5000 units per day.
2. Each unit is sold for $40 and has a 50% profit margin.

Assuming that the average useful life of the facility is 360 days, then the cost of the plant per piece would be only $1.13. Thus, the price difference per unit is only around $0.02 ($2.00 million/(360 × 5.000) = $1.11), and this would be more than compensated for if the new plant can "save" 1 production day. Losing 1 day of production would cost $100,000 (5000 × $20) in profit. This focuses the negotiation on the ultimate value and demonstrates to the customer that the price difference—compared to the risk of downtime or other disadvantages—is negligible.

In addition, it can be advisable for the seller to adjust its behavior and its selling strategy in order to respond to the negotiating partner's requirements. Such an adjustment, referred to as *adaptive selling* [52, 53], may occur during the talks with the same partner, in talks with different partners, or during different phases of the negotiation. The significance of individual features often changes in the course of the negotiating processes, or the features are perceived differently by individual members of the buying center. The selling party must take this into consideration.

To conclude this section, we examine discounts and other terms and conditions within a price negotiation. *Granting a discount* is not always equivalent to negotiating prices, but many discounts for industrial goods are negotiable. List prices are often merely the starting point of a price negotiation.

Making substantial price reductions is common in practice. What matters are the effects that different combinations of list prices and discounts will have on sales volumes and profits. The same net price can be achieved in different ways. It is conceivable that a seller sets a high list price and offers a high discount or sets a low list price combined with a low discount. These two scenarios can draw different reactions from customers, even though the net price is the same. Industrial customers are in no way immune to the effects we discussed in Chap. 4 on the psychology of price. These reactions can be caused by different price perceptions or by the purchaser's incentive system. The influence of discounts is particularly strong when the purchaser is evaluated or even compensated based on the level of discount negotiated. We know of cases where the purchaser suggested a higher starting price, in order to be able to show a higher discount. A higher starting price combined with a higher discount is the obvious answer in such situations [1, 54, p. 511].

11.4.2 Price Contracts and Price Hedging

There are three fundamental types of risks for long-term contracts or durable investment goods: functional risk, delivery risk, and cost risk. An important decision involves how to allocate these risks among the parties to the contract. The supplier has an opportunity to improve its competitive position by assuming more risk.

Functional or technical risk can be reduced through guarantees or through the right to exchange the product. An innovative approach for risk reduction for the customers is an agreement on performance-based pricing: this can take on many forms [55, p., 54–57]. The level of purchase price is determined according to the extent to which performance parameters—which the two parties agree to in advance—are fulfilled. If the agreed level is met, the customer pays the agreed price. The price will rise (or drop) depending on whether the product over-performs (or underperforms) against the targets. Potential parameters for performance-based prices are time-based (ramp-up times, maintenance times), quality-related (level of quality, production tolerance, number of customer complaints), and volume- or value-based (operational activities; output; revenue or contribution margin shares; cost changes in consumables, fuel, or energy; or personnel costs).

Instruments for Price Hedging

For long-term contracts, it is necessary to have agreements to adjust for potential cost fluctuations. Price fluctuations in commodity or raw material prices or in labor costs make cost forecasts uncertain and therefore price setting difficult. Such fluctuations can have a strong effect on the profitability of a project. The supplier has several instruments to deal with these risks: fixed prices, conditional prices, open billing, or sliding-scale price clauses.

For *fixed-price offers*, a fixed upcharge (e.g., 5%) is often added to the bid to account for potential future price increases. Once agreed, this price is no longer subject to change, meaning that the customer no longer bears any price risk. If future cost changes are underestimated, the supplier has to cover the difference. If the costs are overestimated, the supplier realizes an additional profit.

Agreements with prices subject to change, or *conditional prices*, allow the supplier to pass along documented incurred costs to the customer. Depending on how the agreement is structured, the customer in this case bears partial or full risk. An example is the so-called force majeure clause which allows a supplier to nullify contractually agreed-upon prices in the event of circumstances beyond the parties' control (e.g., a natural disaster) and negotiate new prices which reflect the changed circumstances. In one case, when a supply shortage occurred for LDPE (low-density polyethylene), many chemical suppliers enforced force majeure clauses in their contracts and declared themselves unable to honor delivery commitments. This drove the average price of LDPE up by roughly 20% within a 4-month period [56].

Under an *open account*, the customer alone bears the risk of a cost increase. The supplier and the customer agree during the course of the production process on what the supplier has delivered and what the actual costs are. This type of billing is used for those portions of the supplier's service or delivery whose costs could not be reliably estimated during the negotiations. The two parties can agree to cap the amount in order to limit the customer's risk.

A *sliding-scale price clause* permits the development of certain underlying costs (e.g., labor, materials) to be reflected in the customer's final price. A standard price formula for this comes from the United Nations Economic Commission for Europe (ECE) [1, pp. 398f].

$$P = \frac{P_0}{100}\left(a + m \times \frac{M}{M_0} + w \times \frac{W}{W_0}\right) \qquad (11.10)$$

where
  P = final price,
  P_0 = price at the start of the billing period,
  a = nonadjustable share of the price,
  m = share of material costs in the price,

w = share of labor costs in the price,
M_0 = material costs (start of billing period),
M = material costs (end of billing period),
W_0 = labor costs (start of billing period),
W = labor costs (end of billing period), and
$a + m + w = 100$.

Implementing this approach requires determining the weightings and the starting values as well as monitoring the individual elements [1, pp. 398–402]. These data, such as the share of labor costs in the price, are often insufficiently known. One therefore tends to fall back on traditional industry averages. Because sliding-scale price clauses also create planning uncertainty, many customers insist on fixed-price contracts instead. Another problem is the demand for transparency which these clauses can place on the supplier. Customers often demand comprehensive breakdowns in the price formula, but suppliers generally do not want to expose all of their costs in such fine detail. Rental agreements often have price index clauses, which generally use the consumer price index (CPI) as the indicator. The rent is adjusted partially or in full after a certain period of time or when the index exceeds a pre-agreed value.

Conclusion
Price management for industrial goods has many special characteristics. With respect to the different phases of the price management process, one should observe the following aspects:

- In the analysis phase, an objective is to understand the *buying center* (BC). The BC comprises all people who have influence on the buying decision. Depending on their role or level of influence within the BC, the individual members will be motivated by different considerations. These should be taken into account both in the form of the offer and in how the supplier conducts the negotiations. Knowledge of how the BC will evaluate an offer (i.e., evaluation scheme or criteria) is helpful in optimizing the price offered.
- In the price decision phase, value-based pricing, cost-oriented pricing, and auctions come into play. In *value-based pricing*, the supplier uses a performance or value index as a guideline for price setting. In order to measure value, the supplier can draw on assessments from its own employees, economic value analyses, evaluations by focus groups, or conjoint measurement.
- For specific projects and customized offers, one uses *cost-oriented calculations* to set prices. Methods which rely on one variable include weight-cost method, material cost method, and the modification price approach. Other methods such as the rough projections and the learning

(continued)

approach rely on multiple variables drawn from reference projects and existing data or estimates.

- In many industrial sectors and in the public sector, auctions are used to award contracts. Based on a set of specifications or a request for proposal (RFP), several bidders submit their price offers. The supplier who offers the lowest price generally wins the bid. In principle, the task of the suppliers (from their perspective) is to find the highest possible price which is still below the price of the lowest-priced competitor. One can apply game theory and decision theory models here. Formally speaking, a decision theory model is meant to maximize the expected value of the profit, taking the probability of winning the bid into account.

- *Online auctions* are very common in industrial procurement. They are primarily used for homogeneous products and services. The advantage from the seller's perspective is that these auctions offer an opportunity to serve a larger market or the ability to reduce transaction costs. At the same time, because of the natural dynamics of the bidding process, there is a risk that a bidder undercuts lower thresholds that it had set for itself ex ante.

- In the implementation phase, price negotiations and price contracts, or price hedging, are of great relevance.

- The research into price negotiations distinguishes between theoretical approaches (game theory and behavioral science) and management-based approaches.

- According to the theory of price negotiation (*game theory*), the negotiation between rational parties in the simplest case (bilateral monopoly) comprises two steps. First, the volume is determined in a way that maximizes the joint profit (common interests). The second step involves the distribution of that joint profit among the partners (conflicting interests). The profit distribution is worked out via the price. The potential area of agreement results from the segment of the contract curve bounded by the points at which the profit of one of the partners is zero. The ultimate choice of the point on the contract curve depends on the balance of power between the partners.

- *Behavioral science approaches* and systematic quantification (based, among other things, on historical data) can provide guidance for estimating the balance of power between the partners.

- *Management-based approaches* focus on the negotiation process itself. The two fundamental negotiation tenets are the principle of mutual interest and the tit-for-tat principle. Additional supporting tools include the subtraction technique and the division technique. In the subtraction technique, one removes certain components from the original proposal if the customer demands a lower price. In the division technique, the costs are broken down into smaller units in order to make the price difference to the competition appear smaller.

(continued)

- For long-term contracts, measures to *hedge prices* are necessary. In the end, these revolve around how the supplier and customer will share the risks of future cost changes. Fixed-price offers, conditional prices, open accounts, and sliding-scale price clauses are alternatives.

In summary, the industrial goods area is characterized by a wide variety of price models and approaches. Finding the optimal solution requires a deep understanding of the respective situation.

References

1. Backhaus, K., & Voeth, M. (2014). *Industriegütermarketing* (10th ed.). München: Vahlen.
2. Engelhardt, W. H., & Günter, B. (1981). *Investitionsgütermarketing*. Stuttgart: Kohlhammer.
3. Kossmann, J. (2008). *Die Implementierung der Preispolitik in Business-to-Business-Unternehmen*. Nürnberg: GIM-Verlag
4. Reid, D. A., & Plank, R. E. (2000). Business Marketing Comes of Age: A Comprehensive Review of the Literature. *Journal of Business-to-Business Marketing*, 7(2–3), 9–186.
5. Plinke, W. (1992). Ausprägung der Marktorientierung in Investitionsgütermärkten. *Schmalenbachs Zeitschrift für betriebswirtschaftliche Forschung*, 44(9), 830–846.
6. Homburg, C. (2015). *Marketingmanagement – Strategie – Instrumente – Umsetzung – Unternehmensführung* (5th ed.). Wiesbaden: Gabler.
7. Barback, R. H. (1979). The Pricing of Industrial Products. *European Journal of Marketing*, 13 (4), 160–166.
8. Forman, H., & Lancioni, R. (2002). The Determinants of Pricing Strategies for Industrial Products in International Markets. *Journal of Business-to-Business Marketing*, 9(2), 29–64.
9. Forbis, J. L., & Mehta, N. T. (1981). Value-Based Strategies for Industrial Products. McKinsey Quarterly, 2, 35–52.
10. Anderson, J. C., Jain, D. C., & Chintagunta, P. K. (1993). Customer Value Assessment in Business Markets: A State-of-Practice Study. *Journal of Business-to-Business Marketing*, 1(1), 3–30.
11. Feller, A. H. (1992). Kalkulation in der Angebotsphase mit dem selbständig abgeleiteten Erfahrungswissen der Arbeitsplanung. Karlsruhe: Institute for machine tools and industrial engineering at the Karlsruhe Institute of Technology.
12. Funke, S. (1995). Angebotskalkulation bei Einzelfertigung. *Controlling*, 7(2), 82–89.
13. Plinke, W. (1998). Erlösgestaltung im Projektgeschäft. In M. Kleinaltenkamp, & W. Plinke (Ed.), *Auftrags- und Projektmanagement* (pp. 117–159). Berlin: Springer.
14. Nietsch, T. (1996). *Erfahrungswissen in der computergestützten Angebotsbearbeitung*. Wiesbaden: Deutscher Universitäts-Verlag.
15. Berz, G. (2014). *Spieltheoretische Verhandlungs- und Auktionsstrategien* (2nd ed.). Stuttgart: Schaeffer-Poeschel.
16. Alznauer, T., & Krafft, M. (2004). Submissionen. In K. Backhaus & M. Voeth (Ed.), *Handbuch Industriegütermarketing: Strategien – Instrumente – Anwendungen* (pp. 1057–1078). Wiesbaden: Gabler.
17. Näykki, P. (1976). On Optimal Bidding Strategies. *Management Science*, 23(2), 198–203.
18. Römhild, W. (1997). *Preisstrategien bei Ausschreibungen*. Berlin: Duncker & Humblot.
19. Holler, M. J., & Illing, G. (2009). *Einführung in die Spieltheorie* (7th ed.). Berlin: Springer.
20. Milgrom, P. (2004). *Putting Auction Theory to Work*. Cambridge: Cambridge University Press.

21. Friedman, L. (1956). A Competitive Bidding Strategy. *Operations Research*, 4(1), 104–112.
22. Edelman, F. (1965). Art and Science of Competitive Bidding. *Harvard Business Review*, 43(4), 53–66.
23. Willenbrock, J. H. (1973). Utility Function Determination for Bidding Models. *Journal of Construction*, 99(1), 133–153.
24. Slatter, S. S. P. (1990). Strategic Marketing Variables under Conditions of Competitive Bidding. *Strategic Management Journal*, 11(4), 309–317.
25. Thaler, R. H. (1992). *The Winner's Curse: Paradoxes and Anomalies of Economic Life*. New York: The Free Press.
26. Kaplan, M. (2015). B2B Ecommerce Growing; Becoming More Like B2C. http://www. practicalecommerce.com/articles/85970-B2B-Ecommerce-Growing-Becoming-More-Like-B2C. Accessed 5 July 2015.
27. Lancioni, R. (2005). Pricing Issues in Industrial Marketing. *Industrial Marketing Management*, 34(2), 111–114.
28. Lichtenthal, J. D., & Eliaz, S. (2003). Internet Integration in Business Marketing Tactics. *Industrial Marketing Management*, 32(1), 3–13.
29. Skiera, B., & Spann, M. (2004). Gestaltung von Auktionen. In K. Backhaus, & M. Voeth (Ed.), *Handbuch Industriegütermarketing: Strategien – Instrumente – Anwendungen* (pp. 1039–1056). Wiesbaden: Gabler.
30. Daly, S. P., & Nath, P. (2005). Reverse Auctions for Relationship Marketers. *Industrial Marketing Management*, 34(2), 157–166.
31. Lucking-Reiley, D. H. (1999). Using Field Experiments to Test Equivalence between Auction Formats: Magic on the Internet. *American Economic Review*, 89(5), 1063–1080.
32. Sashi, C. M., & O'Leary, B. (2002). The Role of Internet Auctions in the Expansion of B2B Markets. *Industrial Marketing Management*, 31(2), 103–110.
33. Voeth, M., & Rabe, C. (2004). Preisverhandlungen. In K. Backhaus, & M. Voeth (Ed.), *Handbuch Industriegütermarketing: Strategien – Instrumente – Anwendungen* (pp. 1015–1038). Wiesbaden: Gabler.
34. Marwell, G., & Schmitt, D. R. (1972). Cooperation in a Three-Person Prisoner's Dilemma. *Journal of Social Psychology*, 21(3), 376–383.
35. Pruitt, D. G., & Drews, J. L. (1969). The Effect of Time Pressure, Time Elapsed, and the Opponent's Concession Rate on Behavior in Negotiation. *Journal of Experimental Social Psychology*, 5(1), 43–60.
36. Pruitt, D. G., & Johnson, D. F. (1972). Mediation as an Aid of Face Saving in Negotiation. *Journal of Social Psychology*, 14(3), 239–246.
37. Gomes, M., Oliveira, T., Carneiro, D., Novais, P., & Neves, J. (2014). Studying the Effects of Stress on Negotiation Behavior. *Cybernetics and Systems*, 45(3), 279–291.
38. Bazerman, M. H., Curhan, J. R., Moore, D. A., & Valley, K. L. (2000). Negotiation. *Annual Review of Psychology*, 51(1), 279–314.
39. Jain, S. C., & Laric, M. V. (1979). A Framework for Strategic Industrial Pricing. *Industrial Marketing Management*, 8(1), 75–80.
40. Laric, M. V. (1980). Pricing Strategies in Industrial Markets. *European Journal of Marketing*, 14(5/6), 303–321.
41. Marwell, G., Ratcliff, K., & Schmitt, D. (1969). Minimizing Differences in a Maximizing Difference Game. *Journal of Personality and Social Psychology*, 12(2), 158–163.
42. Detroy, E. N. (2009). *Sich durchsetzen in Preisgesprächen und Verhandlungen* (14th ed.). Zürich: Moderne Industrie.
43. Zarth, H. R. (1981). Effizienter verkaufen durch die richtige Strategie für das Preisgespräch. *Markenartikel*, 43(2), 111–113.
44. Bänsch, A. (2013). *Verkaufspsychologie und Verkaufstechnik* (9th ed.). München: Oldenbourg.
45. Lewicki, R., Saunders, D. M., & Barry B. (2014). *Negotiation* (7th ed.). Burr Ridge: McGraw-Hill.
46. Nirenberg, J. S. (1984). *How to Sell Your Ideas*. New York: McGraw Hill.

47. Sebenius, J. (2001). Six Habits of Merely Effective Negotiators. *Harvard Business Review*, 79 (4), 87–95.
48. Sidow, H. (2007). *Key Account Management: Wettbewerbsvorteile durch kundenbezogene Strategien* (8th ed.). Landsberg am Lech: Moderne Industrie.
49. Jensen, O. (2004). *Key-Account-Management: Gestaltung - Determinanten - Erfolgsauswirkungen* (2nd ed.). Wiesbaden: Deutscher Universitäts-Verlag.
50. Thompson, J. W. (1973). *Selling: A Managerial and Behavioral Science Analysis*. New York: McGraw Hill.
51. Weitz, B. A. (1979): A Critical Review of Personal Selling Research: The Need for a Contingency Approach. In G. Albaum, & G. A. Churchill Jr. (Ed.), *Critical Issues in Sales Management: State of the Art and Future Research Need* (pp. 72–126). Eugene: University of Oregon.
52. Weitz, B. A., Sujan H., & Sujan, M. (1986). Knowledge, Motivation, and Adaptive Behavior: A Framework for Improving Selling Effectiveness. *Journal of Marketing*, 50(4), 174–191.
53. Pettijohn, C. E., Pettijohn, L. S., Taylor A. J., & Keillor, B. D. (2000). Adaptive Selling and Sales Performance: An Empirical Examination. *Journal of Applied Business Research*, 16(1), 91–111.
54. Voeth, M. (2015). Preispolitik auf Industriegütermärkten - Ein Überblick. In K. Backhaus, & M. Voeth (Ed.), *Handbuch Business-to-Business Marketing: Grundlagen, Geschäftsmodelle, Instrumente des Industriegütermarketing* (2nd ed.) (pp. 499–516). Wiesbaden: Gabler.
55. Hüttmann, A. (2003). *Leistungsabhängige Preiskonzepte im Investitionsgütergeschäft: Funktion, Wirkung, Einsatz*. Wiesbaden: Deutscher Universitäts-Verlag.
56. Anonymous. (2015, May 13). Mit höherer Gewalt zu höheren Preisen. *Frankfurter Allgemeine Zeitung*, p. 30.

Price Management for Services

12

Abstract

In highly developed economies, services typically account for more than three quarters of the gross domestic product (GDP). Services have a range of special characteristics which are very important for price management. Price management for services has to cover a very broad spectrum, from the complex yield management systems used by airlines to the straightforward, everyday price setting in many sub-sectors. This chapter deals with service-specific problems in price management and follows the pricing process of analysis, decision-making, and implementation. The characteristics of services relevant for price management include intangibility, the integration of customer resources, the ratio of fixed to variable costs, the lack of transferability from one customer to another, the importance of experience and trust, and the local nature of services. Price differentiation for services is more powerful and rewarding than for material goods because many services are highly customized. Furthermore, differentiated prices can be implemented more effectively and tend to be accepted by customers more readily. Services have not escaped the effects of the Internet. Price transparency as well as price and value competition have been increasing dramatically.

12.1 Introduction

Services have numerous special characteristics and considerable potential for pricing improvements. We first discuss these special features and the resulting implications for pricing. Package tours, concerts, sports events, insurance, and banking are all services; law firms, consulting firms, hospitals, hair salons, fitness clubs, professional sports teams, and cleaners are all service providers. Services include call centers, software as a service (SaaS), and Internet entertainment from the likes of Spotify, Apple Music, and Netflix. The extremely diverse services sector in modern

© Springer Nature Switzerland AG 2019
H. Simon, M. Fassnacht, *Price Management*,
https://doi.org/10.1007/978-3-319-99456-7_12

economies contributes three quarters (or more) to the gross domestic product (GDP) in highly developed countries.

One often uses alternative terms for "price" regarding services. Common expressions include honorarium, commission, fee, tariff, premium, dues, or rates. But in every one of these cases, these words are nothing more than prices by another name. These "prices" are calculated according to special rules: by time spent by an individual person (honorarium), by event (entrance into a sports match or game), by time for the use of a material good (rent), by access to certain resources (membership or monthly dues), or by a percentage of the value of another good (commission, brokerage fee).

Services share the following special characteristics:

- They are *intangible*, a fundamental criterion which has effects on perception as well as willingness to pay. The customer is normally not in a position to assess with confidence the quality of the service prior to the purchase. The customer in essence buys a promise of performance. That applies to a haircut as well as to a complex consulting project. Reputation, references, and price play an important role as ex ante quality indicators. Because of their intangibility, it is not possible to physically store or transport services.
- While material goods are produced in advance without the participation of the customer and then later sold, most services can only be performed with the participation of the customer or the customer's property, the so-called customer resources. We speak of the *integration of customer resources*. These could be in the form of people (e.g., for a haircut or medical treatment), objects (e.g., a car), rights, information, or financial assets. This means that the identity of the recipient of the service can be checked and verified, which in turn implies that differentiated prices can be implemented more effectively than for material goods.
- The inseparability of consumption and production is referred to as the *uno-actu principle*. Examples include education services, medical examinations, or attending a play or a concert. Services involve not only the integration of people but also objects, information, and rights. Thus, the attribute "inseparability" applies not only to the customer but also to the customer resources involved. The temporal coincidence of consumption and production makes it impossible to undermine the existing price differentiation through arbitrage.
- The *heterogeneity of customer resources*, an external factor in the provision of a service, almost inevitably induces a greater heterogeneity in the outcomes. Cars in need of repair are different, as are the illnesses of medical patients and the legal matters handled by lawyers. Therefore, both the process of providing the service and the actual results will differ from customer to customer.
- Manufacturers of material goods can determine on their own and independently of customers when and how to operate their manufacturing capacity. That does not apply to service providers. If a hotel room remains vacant on a given night, the revenue opportunity for that night is lost for good.

Table 12.1 Fees for checking account management and for transactions with a paper receipt [1]

Institution	Account	Account management fee (euros per month)	Transaction with paper receipt (euros per transaction)
Volkswagen Bank	Checking account	0.00	2.00
Berliner Sparkasse	Checking account	2.00	1.90
Ostsächsiche Sparkasse	Saxx tempo	3.00	1.50
Deutsche Bank	AktivKonto	4.99	1.50
Hamburger Volksbank	VR-NetKonto	3.95	1.50
Postbank	Giro plus	0.00	0.99
Stadtsparkasse Wuppertal	Giro Klassik	5.25	0.75

- Even an apparently simple or standardized service can include very different performance and price parameters, which makes comparisons difficult. An example is a checking account, which is the most basic banking product. Yet as one expert notes, "Checking accounts are relatively hard to compare because they contain a whole bundle of services and therefore have a bundle of different prices" [1]. It is no surprise then that one observes enormous price differences in the individual components of checking accounts. Table 12.1 shows these differences for selected banks, comparing the monthly charge for the account and the costs of making a transaction with a printed receipt. The highest price for a transaction with paper receipt is 167% higher than the lowest one.

The more intangible, integrative, and individualized a service is, the greater the behavioral uncertainty is on the part of the customer. For such services, the supplier cannot standardize its offer as easily and is obliged to provide the customer an individually customized service. Typical cases of this include professional services such as those performed by management consultants, lawyers, or psychiatrists.

Because the customers derive value not only from the actual outcome but also from the process itself, we distinguish between service potential, service process, and service outcome .

The *service potential* comprises the supplier resources and is a prerequisite for performing the service. These include buildings, personnel, machines, and other resources of the supplier. Such visible features often affect the customers' decision when they select a supplier. The service potential remains unused until it is activated by the customer or by the integration of customer resources. An activation of the potential takes place, for example, when a customer enters a restaurant (person), brings a suit to the dry cleaner (object), or sends an email which prompts the supplier to initiate work (information). The integration of the customer triggers the *service process*, which the customer actively experiences. The fact that the service process depends on the customer resources, and that unused production capacity is perishable, has significant consequences for price management.

A typology of services allows us to recognize starting points for pricing. We classify services into three categories: capital-intensive, technology-intensive, and labor-intensive.

For *capital-intensive services*, fixed costs far exceed variable costs. Often these services are collective services, meaning they are provided simultaneously to a number of customers. This in turn requires fixed capacity. Examples of capital-intensive services include hotels, airlines, cinemas, and theaters.

Technology-intensive services are characterized by relatively high (fixed) costs compared to variable costs. Examples include online accounts, automated ticket machines, and mobile telecommunications. Technology-intensive services tend to be used individually. Individual customers do not use the services at the same time. Although the demand can fluctuate, the capacity is in most cases fixed due to the technical requirements (e.g., the number of ticket machines, the server capacity of the bank, or the network capacity of the mobile operator). The supplier therefore puts enough capacity in place to cope with maximum utilization.

For *labor-intensive services*, the work performed by people is at the forefront. Personnel costs generally exceed fixed costs. These services are often individualized services, i.e., performed for one person (such as a doctor's consultation, advisory services, or tutoring), usually by appointment. Whether the labor costs for the services performed are considered fixed or variable depends on the nature of the employment contract. Taxi drivers are often paid based on the revenue they generate, meaning the compensation they receive is entirely variable.

The differences between capital-, technology-, and labor-intensive services are very important for pricing. For capital-intensive services, the capacity (e.g., the number of beds in the hotel) is a fixed number. The task of price management is to smooth the demand over time, so that as little capacity as possible remains unutilized. The demand can be managed with the help of differentiated prices. Yield or revenue management serves the management of capacity and thus the goal of profit maximization.

The infrastructure for technology-intensive services is built for a utilization level which is well above average. If the supplier, for example, could use appropriate price management techniques to spread the demand for tickets more evenly throughout the day, the supplier would need fewer ticket machines. The attempts of suppliers to align their demand more smoothly with capacity are reflected in time-based price differentiation (time of day, day of the week) practiced by telecommunication firms and electric utilities. Nonetheless, a different strategy is on the rise, namely, the use of flat rates [2]. One can see the justification for flat rates in the high fixed and low variable costs. Flat rates boost capacity utilization, because the "marginal price" for the user is zero. At the same time, the flat rate for a technology-intensive service poses no major risk for the supplier, because its marginal costs are low or are close to zero.

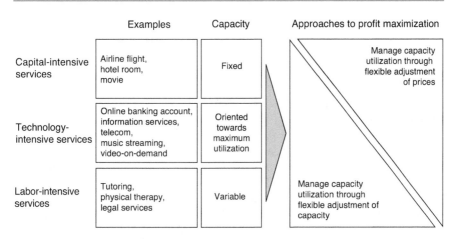

Fig. 12.1 Profit maximization for different types of services

For labor-intensive services, the supplier can in principle adjust its retained personnel capacity according to demand. The management of capacity utilization can therefore be accomplished to some degree by adjusting or reallocating the level of capacity itself. For example, a significant portion of legal advice involves the preparation work before and after the consultation itself. Lawyers can plan this time flexibly, in order to take advantage of staff capacity outside of the consultation. But when the external resources are not primarily information, but rather other people, it is difficult to allocate staff as effectively. In periods of low demand, a dentist could put his staff to other uses, such as administration. But because the dentist's service primarily involves the external resource "patient," the dentist's ability to reallocate capacity amidst low demand is much more limited than a lawyer's. Capacity adjustments can be realized either according to a plan or on an ad hoc basis. A restaurant, for example, could keep wait staff on call. A business offering labor-intensive services can achieve profit maximization through capacity adjustments as well as through demand management by differentiating prices. The more difficult it is to manage and adjust capacity, the more important the role of price management becomes—similar to capital- and technology-intensive services. Figure 12.1 shows the three types of services and the implications for profit maximization and for price management.

12.2 Analysis

In Chap. 3 we looked at companies, customers, and competitors as influencing factors on price. All three factors are relevant for services as well.

12.2.1 Company Information

An important characteristic which is relevant for the pricing of services is cost analysis. For services, the variable costs often cannot be determined with certainty ex ante because of the involvement of customer resources and their heterogeneity [3]. For example, a reliable itemization of the costs and the outputs of legal support for a court case is almost impossible to make in advance [4]. Experience-based estimates could potentially help put the customer at ease regarding the extent of the costs. But the unpredictability of the service process can lead to considerable deviations from the anticipated costs. Billing based on an hourly rate, on the other hand, exposes the customer to price risk. The same applies to a medical operation, because some problems and complications do not come to light until the operation is already underway.

Distinguishing between fixed and variable costs is central to services pricing. Among other things, this information serves to set the *lower limit for price*, i.e., to determine the lowest price at which a job or a contract can be accepted. Setting a lower limit for price at the variable unit costs, however, requires that the service can be offered individually on the market. That is not always the case. Let us look at the example of a capital-intensive service business such as an airline. Airlines incur variable costs for crew, jet fuel, landing fees, etc. These variable costs are rather independent of the number of seats sold and depend mainly on the number of flights. Thus, the variable costs are incurred on a per-flight basis and not per passenger. Because the capacity is fixed, the variable costs of an unsold seat are regarded as sunk costs. One can therefore see the nearly negligible marginal costs of a seat as the lower limit for price. Even a very low price for a seat generates a contribution margin.

Charging a price close to zero, however, carries considerable risks. If one sets the lower limit for price for such collective services at the marginal costs and uses that latitude to make price cuts, the effects can be devastating. First, such a move can lead to massive resentment among customers who paid full price. Second, one must consider the long-term consequences of setting prices in that manner. The regular availability of last-minute prices teaches customers that it is worth waiting for lower prices. But as the low-cost airlines have demonstrated, there are other methods to offer very low prices in such a way that the company can still achieve acceptable or even good financial results.

A cost accounting method which is especially well suited for services is *activity-based costing* [5]. Activity-based costing allocates the shared costs across process steps or discrete activities rather than units of volume [6]. This makes it possible to assign costs more equitably to their true causes rather than blanket them over all cost sources. Activity-based costing has proven itself to be a valuable management tool, finding use predominantly in industry but also at service providers such as banks, insurance companies, and public administration [7]. Nonetheless, activity-based costing remains essentially a form of fully loaded cost accounting with all its associated pitfalls.

Another piece of company information which is very important for pricing is the objective function. In the previous chapters, we have shown that profit maximization is the only appropriate objective function. Only this function takes revenue and costs into account in the logically correct way. But with services there is often an inherent conflict between profit maximization and capacity utilization. The causes lie in the cost structures we have described as well as in the uncertainty around the price-response function.

An example illustrates this. The revenue manager at Chicago's landmark Hilton Hotel described the following situation at a conference. The hotel has 1600 rooms, and on the previous night, 13 of those rooms remained vacant. That is 13 rooms too many, the manager explained. Obviously, when rooms are unsold, the revenue opportunity from them is untapped and gone for good. That is a "hard" number. What the revenue manager did not address in his line of argument, however, is the untapped willingness to pay, which is a "soft" number. Let us assume that the guests had paid $100 per room. The revenue for that night would have been $100 × 1,587 = $158,700. If the hotel had charged $10 more per room that night and tolerated 50 empty rooms (instead of 13), the revenue would have been $110 × 1,550 = $170,500, a significantly better result. In order to make a robust comparison between the two alternatives, one would need precise knowledge of the price-response function or the price elasticity. A fixation with capacity utilization, which is common among service providers, can be misleading from a profit perspective.

12.2.2 Customer Information

The price-response function captures the customers' response to alternative prices, with the implicit assumption that the function has a certain level of stability over time. It is also assumed that the service in question maintains a consistent, if not constant, level of quality. But this constant level of quality applies only to a very limited extent for many services. As we have explained, the customer resources required for providing the service are by definition heterogeneous, which often has a direct effect on the outcome. For labor-intensive services, factors such as the employee's experience, empathy, or state of mind can lead to considerable fluctuations in quality, so that one often cannot expect a stable price-volume relationship.

For highly standardized services, which are typically more technology-intensive (e.g., mobile telecom) or capital-intensive (e.g., cinemas), the price-response function is a useful instrument for determining the optimal price. For labor-intensive, highly individualized services, however, one should use such systematic price-volume relationships with caution. The prices for such services, however, can be more individualized. Much like the trader at an Oriental Bazaar, the service provider can try to estimate the individual customer's willingness to pay and adjust its price accordingly.

The intangibility of a service offering, and the fact that the service is not yet available at the time of purchase, makes it difficult for customers to evaluate services. A service such as a session with a personal trainer or a doctor's visit cannot be observed or tried out in advance, and therefore cannot be reliably evaluated ex ante. For experience goods, such as driver education lessons, the customer can at least evaluate the result after the fact. But for a consulting project, the customer's ability to make a valid assessment even ex post is limited. In fact, the competence gap between customer and service provider is often so large that a sound assessment of the outcome eludes the customer. One example is a complex medical diagnosis. As a result, the customer cannot judge whether the price-value relationship is appropriate. Because particularly labor-intensive services, such as legal advice, are often experience and confidence goods, price takes on a prominent role as a *quality indicator*. While the quality of experience goods can only be assessed after they have been purchased and consumed, the quality of confidence goods cannot be validly assessed either before or even after the purchase. The seller always knows more about the performance than the buyer, which means an information asymmetry exists. Collecting the corresponding information in advance takes considerable effort and expense (information costs). This increases the uncertainty and also the risk of making a mistake. Trust and confidence in the service provider play a critical role in the initial purchase decision. Follow-up or repeat purchases are then based on the experience the customer has with that first purchase. As we explained in Chap. 4, customers tend to perceive a positive correlation between price and quality and thus often see a high price as a sign of good quality. A price of $30 for a haircut signals a higher level of quality and competence than a haircut for $12. The same applies to restaurants and hotels.

In contrast to material goods, the limited ability to store services prevents a customer from buying larger amounts when prices are low. While one can stockpile laundry detergent or paper towels and buy more when prices drop, this is neither sensible nor possible for flights, hospital stays, or workouts. Suppliers can nonetheless offer price structures which contain incentives to buy more. Examples include multiple-visit passes for a fitness studio, coupons, or stamp cards for frequent restaurant visits, or season tickets to sports events.

One must distinguish here between the individual and the aggregated price-response function (see Chap. 3). Services are often "yes-no" cases rather than "variable-quantity" cases. In other words, customers generally purchase exactly one unit of a service (e.g., one medical checkup), or they buy none. The individual price-response function and the aggregate price-response function have the forms shown on the left-hand side of Figs. 3.3 and 3.4. This means that discounts or low prices can lead to higher volumes for services just as they can for material goods. This additional volume, however, does not come about because an individual customer buys more, but because more customers purchase one unit (e.g., a medical checkup). In this sense, some services are similar to durable goods, rather than consumables.

Making distinctions among target groups is necessary and offers many opportunities for price differentiation. One example is education, which is showing strong global growth with private suppliers playing an increasingly significant role. This has in turn led to the greater penetration of prices into the field of education. Education services which the government used to offer for free are now provided by private, profit-oriented companies for a price. The largest global supplier with revenue of £5 billion is the British firm Pearson PLC. Pearson's target groups comprise individuals who pay for their education on their own, companies who finance training for their employees, and government-run education programs, such as in the United States, where thousands of schools use testing materials produced by Pearson. The willingness to pay and the purchase processes for these target groups are completely different. Pricing has to acknowledge and reflect these differences.

In Chap. 3 we demonstrated *conjoint measurement* as a method to determine the price-response function and the price elasticity. There are several special aspects when this method is applied to services. Conjoint measurement is well suited for services which comprise easily quantifiable attributes. Examples include bank accounts (technology-intensive service) as well as flights and car rentals (capital-intensive services). The method is less suitable for labor-intensive services, because aspects such as friendliness or personal appearance are difficult to describe or generalize. In the service process, there is regular interaction between employees and customers. These "moments of truth" have a decisive influence on both the perception of quality and the willingness to pay. That applies to the customer orientation of a consultant as well as to the friendliness of a caretaker. These "soft" components of value can strongly impact overall value perception but are difficult to define precisely and to quantify. Their contribution to value is thus hard to measure with conjoint measurement. A similar problem exists with the ambience for services. The arrangement of a hotel room or the atmosphere in a restaurant defies description in simple terms or numbers, making it less suitable for use in conjoint measurement. One can build models, show a film or video, or describe the ambience in a brief text. The information value of such stimuli, however, is still limited.

Target pricing involves the determination of willingness to pay and the assessment of the value attributes prior to the conception of the service. Target pricing is suited for standardized capital-intensive or technology-intensive services. For the development of an entrée for a fast food restaurant, it can make sense to set a target price for the product which must not be exceeded. Target pricing also comes into consideration for standardized maintenance, repair, or advisory offerings. Examples include car inspections, dry cleaning, installation of an Internet connection, or standard tax services. Although this method is popular and proven for material goods, the opportunities for target pricing for services have not been fully exploited. Target pricing not only has effects on price; it can also require a redesign of the service provision processes. There is significant improvement potential for many services in this regard.

12.2.3 Competitor Information

The intensity of competition is an important determinant of the price elasticity of a service. The fewer search and experience features and the more trust and confidence features a service comprises, the more one can expect demand to be price-inelastic. Examples are personalized services with intensive interaction and significant heterogeneity such as those of a doctor or a lawyer. For such services, customers tend not to respond to price changes by switching suppliers, as they might for very homogeneous markets such as mobile telecommunications. In the latter markets, the features of the competitors are easy to compare and assess, and the competitive offerings are similar in terms of performance. Price therefore becomes the decisive factor for many customers.

Many services confront a potential buyer with a "make or buy" decision. Either the customers perform the task themselves or purchase the service externally. Examples include gardening and landscaping, food service, cleaning, home renovation, or tax return preparation. The customers become potential competitors to the service provider. The decision whether to purchase the service or perform the work oneself depends on the price, the customer's purchasing power, personal preferences, and the opportunity cost of time. When a company makes a competitive analysis, it must not only take competing service providers into account but also the costs of the customers' doing the work on their own.

12.3   Decision

12.3.1 Decision-Support Methods

Cost-plus pricing, break-even analysis, and competition-oriented pricing can all be applied to services. A special aspect of *cost-plus pricing* is that the costs for a service cannot always be reliably estimated in advance because of the integration of customer resources. That is why there are services, such as a contract with a craftsman, which start with a cost estimate. These estimates may eventually become a binding contract, in which case the supplier bears the complete risk for any cost overruns. The estimate could also remain non-binding, with an agreement that the estimate will be corrected later to align the bill with the actual costs incurred.

When using a *break-even analysis* for services, the ratio of fixed costs to variable costs is what matters. Figure 12.2 shows typical structures for the three categories of services. Let us assume that fixed costs for a capital-intensive service are $200 and the price is $2. The variable unit costs are zero. This makes 100 the break-even volume. The profit rises sharply right of the break-even volume, because the cost curve remains at a constant level. For the technology-intensive service, we assume that the fixed costs are $100, and the variable unit costs are $1. The break-even volume in this scenario is likewise 100 units. But the rise in volume beyond the break-even point results in a much smaller profit rise than in the case of the capital-intensive service. For the labor-intensive service with fixed costs of $50 and variable

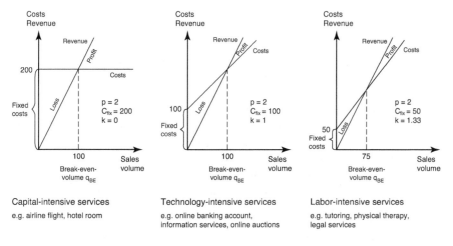

Fig. 12.2 Break-even volumes and profit effects for different types of services

unit costs of $1.33, the break-even point at a price of $2 will already be reached at a volume of 75 units. The profit increase after the break-even point is much smaller, however. For every additional unit of volume, the profit rises by $2 for the capital-intensive service, by $1 for the technology-intensive service, and only by 67 cents for the labor-intensive service.

Because of these differences, capacity utilization for capital-intensive services is an extremely important issue. The goal of the highest possible capacity utilization at the highest possible price is the objective of yield or revenue management, which we will discuss in more detail below.

The break-even analysis is often used as a decision-support tool in the tourism and in the education sectors. A bus company, for example, would calculate how many seats it needs to sell to break even. In the process the company would look at different prices and then select the price which gives the highest probability that the break-even point will be exceeded. In some cases, the tour operator reserves the right to cancel the trip if it does not achieve a minimum number of travelers. The same applies for seminars.

Competition-oriented pricing is also very common for services. Numerous services are priced by the hour, with suppliers often orienting their prices on what the competition charges. This applies likewise for quantity-based prices, e.g., for a haircut. Many salons post readily visible information on their prices. This makes it easy for competitors to compare prices and use them as orientation for their own pricing. The criticism on this approach applies to services as it does to material goods.

12.3.2 Price Differentiation for Services

The most important special aspect of services pricing is *price differentiation*. The basic idea behind price differentiation is that customers have different levels of willingness to pay and that these differences can be captured through differentiated prices. Services offer promising opportunities for all forms of price differentiation and for complex price structures.

12.3.2.1 Time-Based Price Differentiation

Examples for time-based differentiation can be found in sectors such as personal transportation, hotels, vacation, parking garages, restaurants, telephony, energy utilities, and movie theaters. Time-based differentiation reflects the different price elasticities of customers at various times. Because these services are perishable (they cannot be stored), arbitrage over time is not possible. The customer can, however, postpone or push back his or her demand, which means that the price in a particular time period can have an influence on demand in another time period. Typically, there is a substitutive relationship. Thus, the cross-price elasticity between the time periods is positive. Structurally speaking, this challenge is identical to pricing for a product line. The conclusions we drew in Chap. 6 on that topic apply analogously here.

It is also easy to explain why *last-minute* or *standby offers* always lead to increased profit in an isolated view of a category (the number of "lost seats" is minimized) but cannot possibly be optimal when viewed in a broader context. Last-minute offers can siphon off so much normal demand (i.e., the cross-price elasticity could be very high), that the supplier is no better off on a net basis, and could even be worse off.

One may get the impression that the primary objective of time-based differentiation is to smooth out capacity utilization. This is mistaken! The pricing objective is *profit maximization* and not capacity utilization. Prices oriented on price elasticity will nonetheless result in a smoother capacity utilization. For cases in which the price elasticity is low in times of lower demand (e.g., the demand for taxi services between 2 a.m. and 6 a.m.), it makes no sense to reduce prices. The critical point for time-based price differentiation is not whether demand is high or low in a certain period but rather how demand *responds* to price changes within that period, i.e., how high or low the price elasticity is.

Peak-load pricing deals with a special problem of time-based price differentiation for services. A central question is what the cost basis for pricing should be in periods of peak output or in periods of relatively low output. Joskow describes the procedure used in the United States [8, p. 198]: "The generally accepted result has been that peak users should pay marginal operating plus marginal capacity costs and off-peak users should pay only marginal operating costs." This means that users in peak periods will be charged on a fully loaded cost basis, while users in the softer periods will be charged on a marginal-cost basis. This method is justifiable to the extent that the capacity costs are variable from a long-term perspective. But this method does not explicitly take price elasticities at different points in time into account. In order to reach a true optimum, one must also consider the differences in price elasticity across time as well as the cross-price elasticities. The resulting dynamic price optimization problem resembles the problem a multi-product firm faces (see Chap. 6).

One effect which can occur when a company miscalculates the price elasticities is the so-called peak reversal. This phenomenon has been observed at certain times in the German as well as the US telephone systems. When "moonlight" prices were too inexpensive relative to normal prices, it created capacity bottlenecks at a time when capacity should theoretically be underutilized. The solution in such cases is to raise off-peak prices so that demand falls back under available capacity.

12.3.2.2 Regional Price Differentiation

Services enjoy a wide range of options for regional price differentiation. The inability to store or ship a service essentially rules out the possibility of arbitrage. Exceptions are services which can be provided by telecommunication, by Internet, or via post, which makes such services available anywhere, independent of the place where the service is performed. Examples of such services include databases, remote maintenance, consulting or advisory services, and call centers. They also include software as a service (SaaS) as well as essentially any services offered online, because in principle these are not confined by location. There has been government intervention in this area, however, which has led to a geographic separation of certain markets. Numerous Western Internet services, for example, are not permitted to operate in China.

Generally speaking, price differences for regional pricing should not be larger than the *arbitrage costs*. Otherwise there may be a flow in one direction or the other, such as when someone seeks a medical operation in another country. Sectors which exhibit significant regional price differences include hotels, airlines, car rental services, trades, and medical/health-related services.

12.3.2.3 Person-Based Price Differentiation

Person-based price differentiation occurs when a firm charges people different prices for more or less the same service, based on personal characteristics such as age, education status, or profession. What is interesting is that buyers seem more tolerant of large price differences for services than for products. As Mönch writes [9, p. 236]: "People have no issue with a 50-percent discount on a travel ticket for a senior citizen with no further social justification. But it is hard to imagine that they would show the same tolerance if the same kind of price discrimination occurred for a material good." This acceptance facilitates the implementation of person-based price differentiation.

There is an important difference between services and products. When a product is purchased, the purchase itself can be controlled, but what happens to the product after the purchase is beyond the seller's control. For services, the integration of the customer into the service process makes it very difficult to transfer the service to someone else. The following example illustrates this. A club can control access at the door, e.g., by admitting only those 18 and older or offering free admission to women. The club may impose similar rules for the sale of alcoholic beverages (e.g., 21 and over, discounts or free drinks for women) but faces a more difficult challenge in enforcement because a drink, once purchased, can be given to another person.

12.3.2.4 Performance-Based Price Differentiation

Often it is advisable to support price differentiation through a differentiation of performance. Typical examples are the passenger classes on an airplane or a train. The price differentials can be enormous. Let us look at flights between New York and London. The least expensive economy ticket for American Airlines flight 6143 on March 4, 2017, was $881. The price for first class, in contrast, was $7168.[1] The most expensive ticket costs 8.1 times more than the cheapest. Granted, traveling in economy class and first class does not provide the same experience, but passengers in both classes fly in the same plane and arrive at the same time. The basic performance, air transportation, is identical. Until 1907, trains in Germany had four classes, and the price gap at that time was around ten times, similar to air travel today.

Critical for the success of performance-based price differentiation is that the perceived value differences between the "classes" are sufficiently large. Theoretically, the implementable price difference cannot be larger than the difference in value. In the early days of railroads, the lowest-class cars had wooden benches and no roof. A quote from the year 1849 explains why: "It is not because of the few thousand francs which would have to be spent to put a roof over the third-class carriages or to upholster the third-class seats that some company or other has open carriages with wooden benches. What the company is trying to do is to prevent the passenger who can pay the second-class fare from travelling third-class; it hits the poor, not because it wants to hurt them, but to frighten the rich. It is for the same reason that the companies, having proved almost cruel to third-class passengers and mean to second-class ones, become lavish in dealing with first-class passengers. Having refused the poor what is necessary, they give the rich what is superfluous" [10, p. 216]. One needs a sufficiently large gap in value in order to be able to position additional classes with noticeably higher value. Whether the second-class coaches of modern trains fulfill this requirement is an interesting question. They offer a similar level of functional comfort to first-class coaches, though not necessarily the same value in terms of status. If the value "gap" between classes is too small, it can encourage passengers to trade down to the lower class. This phenomenon occurs regularly on short-haul flights. Business class is practically empty, while economy class is rather full. For long-haul flights, the situation is different. The lack of legroom and other restrictions in economy class are enough of a deterrent to business travelers on long-haul flights to induce them to book seats in business class or even first class. Performance-based price differentiation is also observed among SaaS suppliers and their service contracts. Comparisons of cloud service suppliers show

---

[1] Airfare quoted on December 21, 2016, on aa.com; lowest main cabin fare for an inflexible ticket; highest first-class fare for a flexible ticket.

that the companies not only take different approaches in their pricing models but also in the associated contractual terms, billing cycles, cancellation periods, and scalability. Nonetheless, the price differentiation is decisive.

12.3.2.5 Volume-Based Price Differentiation

Volume-based price differentiation can take on a variety of forms. Implementation of these forms is easier for services than for products. First, a transfer of the service from one person to another is normally not possible; second, the actual use of the service can be easily controlled. Both aspects are closely related, but not identical. In addition to prices which are directly volume-dependent, frequent flyer programs and bonus programs represent forms of volume discounts. Examples of volume-based price differentiation for services include:

- Subscriptions for large customers
- Amazon Prime and BahnCard
- Multi-part fees at banks
- Taxi fares, which combine a base fare plus a charge per distance driven
- Online flat rates, such as for music or video streaming services

Conjoint measurement is an ideal instrument for optimizing multidimensional prices or block tariffs. Such price structures lend themselves well to a conjoint measurement design, so that one can expect valid results.

12.3.2.6 Price Bundling

Price bundling refers to the combination of several components—which can be products or services—into one package or bundle. The bundle is typically offered at a price which is lower than the sum of the prices of the individual components of the bundle. Price bundling enables a firm to extract consumer surplus and thus increase its profits. The bundling can be done in pure form (only the bundle is offered) or in mixed form (the bundle as well as some or all of its individual components are available for purchase).

Several authors comment on bundling of services:

- "Bundling is more popular for services than for products" [11, p. 228].
- "The use of bundling appears to have been expanding, especially for consumer services" [12, p. 74].
- "Services or goods with high development costs—such as high-tech products or software—generally have more to gain from price bundling than do goods with high marginal costs, such as consumer durables or industrial goods" [13, p. 70].

In addition to arguments which apply generally to bundling, there are specific reasons why bundling for services can be advantageous:

- The individual service components are often complementary (e.g., flight, car rental, and hotel; banking services such as checking account, savings account, and investment advice; various forms of insurance; auditing and tax advice).
- Many service firms expand their product lines, so that they have more opportunities to bundle (e.g., accounting firms enter into management consulting; hotels establish fitness centers).
- A high share of fixed costs speaks for having the widest possible basis to allocate the fixed costs.

Some firms use the sheer breadth of their offering as a distinguishing feature of their positioning. An example is Club Med, whose package trips include travel, lodging, meals (including drinks), and entertainment. Price bundling has become widespread for telecommunication services. An example is the package offered by AT&T, which allows the customer to receive an Internet flat rate, a telephone flat rate, high-definition DVR, and HDTV service in one bundle.

The bundling of services offers interesting opportunities to create and market well-defined "brands." This is especially promising when it is difficult for a customer to get a handle on the value and price of the individual components because of their diversity or their complexity. The bundle represents a simplification for customers and at the same time reduces their ability to make price comparisons with competing offers. A good example of this is a bundle of insurance coverage. A travel insurance package offered by Allianz, the world's second largest insurer, includes a range of diverse coverages such as overseas health insurance, luggage insurance, insurance to cover the cancellation or interruption of travel, and a 24-h hotline.

An opposing approach, meant to make the core of the services stand out, is unbundling (see Chap. 6). This describes the stripping out of certain components from the bundle and offering those services separately for a price. Ryanair has practiced unbundling for many years. It began with charging separately for in-flight snacks and beverages. Then came charges for booking with a credit card and for checking luggage [14]. This price structure enables the passengers to decide which individual services they want to pay for.

12.3.3 Yield Management

Yield or revenue management is very common in capital-intensive services such as passenger transportation, air freight, car rental, and hotels. Robert L. Crandall, the former CEO of American Airlines, summed up the essence of yield management as follows: "If I have 2,000 customers on a route and 400 different prices, then obviously I'm short 1,600 prices." The objective is to offer price-sensitive customers a performance variant at lower prices and offer less price-sensitive customers such as business travelers a performance variant at higher prices. Yield management is the use of price and capacity management in order to deploy available (and in most cases fixed) capacity in a profit-maximizing way. Capacity is allocated to different prices at different points in time or under specific conditions. Each price has certain restrictions attached to it [15]. Because of the low variable costs (often zero), the typical goal of yield management is revenue maximization, which corresponds to profit maximization when marginal costs are zero. Yield management has proven to be a very effective profit driver. Companies which have implemented it report revenue improvement of 2–5% [16]. Dynamic pricing is used in a similar way to yield management but can also simply mean time-based price differentiation. As an optimization system for capacity management, yield management represents one of the innovative concepts in the service sector. Airlines are not the only companies which employ this tool. Hotels, cruise lines, car rental firms, and online service suppliers also use this strategic instrument [17].

On the supplier side, prerequisites for yield management are:

- The service supplier's capacity is fixed.
- The variable costs of performing the service are low, and the fixed costs for a capacity expansion are high.
- The capacity is perishable, i.e., it expires if unused.

On the demand side, prerequisites for yield management are:

- The service is purchased in advance.
- The demand can be divided into separable market segments, i.e., fencing is possible.
- The demand is uncertain.
- The demand fluctuates.

The supply-side prerequisites, especially the fixed capacity, have the consequence that the opportunity costs for an unused unit of capacity are very high. A hotel room not used on a given night is an opportunity lost forever. The demand-side prerequisites are equally important in order to smooth out demand and improve capacity utilization by making segment-specific adjustments to the offer, i.e., to the price classes. Finally, yield management addresses the classic question a hotel manager faces: "Should I rent this room today at a reduced price, in order to avoid that it remains vacant, or do I wait in the hope that another customer comes and pays a higher price?"

A highly developed information and data basis is necessary for effective yield management. To the extent that this data involves pricing-related parameters, the entire suite of instruments we have discussed can be applied to customer segmentation, to the definition of performance variants, and to the calculation of price elasticities. The statement that "it wasn't unusual to see thousands of fare changes for our airline alone during a single release on a busy day" [18] is a fitting description of how quickly the highly developed tools of the airlines analyze the data and determine new prices on that basis. Yield management is not limited to price-related parameters, however; it also optimizes the capacity offered (e.g., the type of aircraft), incorporates the distribution system, and communicates in a targeted way to potential customers. When services are perishable, time and speed play a critical role. Yield management is not a pure pricing tool but rather a comprehensive marketing and competitive instrument.

The upper limit for price is determined by the value-to-customer and the competitors' price for a comparable level of performance, with the lower of the two values applying. The lower limit for price is determined by the marginal costs (short term) and the fully loaded unit costs (long term). For capital-intensive services, the marginal costs and therefore the short-term lower limit for price is very low, often close to zero. In order to utilize capacity, one can offer low prices which appeal to the most price-sensitive customers. At the same time, one attempts to tap the willingness to pay of the price-insensitive customers and tries to charge prices near the upper limit. This differentiation can only work, though, when the company succeeds in *fencing* off the two segments, i.e., the two segments must be kept separated from each other.

This kind of behavior can be observed in travel bookings. Trips booked short term are more expensive than trips booked long in advance. This is based on the belief that both urgency and willingness to pay are greater when the booking is done close to departure date. Business travelers are either unable or unwilling to make a commitment far in advance and show a higher willingness to pay. One refers to "commitment costs" [19] in this context. These arise when one needs to make a commitment to a particular date well in advance. Business travelers try to avoid commitment costs and instead accept higher prices when they book. People traveling for personal reasons tend to be more price-sensitive and book further in advance.

Making an early commitment and the associated commitment costs can be advantageous to a customer. An example from professional sports illustrates this. When the soccer season began in Germany's Bundesliga on August 24, 2012, FC Bayern Munich announced that it had already sold out all of its home games for the season. Apparently the prices for the tickets were too low relative to the attractiveness of the team. Pricing tickets so affordably would have only made sense if one anticipated a weak season, accompanied by declining interest in the team over the course of the season. The 2012–2013 season turned out very well for Bayern Munich, however, as the team won the Bundesliga championship. The early commitment of ticket buyers certainly paid off in this case, especially in light of the prices observed later on the black market. As much as the fans may have enjoyed the low ticket prices, the club's management should give some thought to its pricing policies. However, paying in advance is not always as worthwhile. There are numerous examples of customers who have paid in advance only to see the companies declare bankruptcy (such as the suppliers of inexpensive electricity in the German market). One should heed this saying: "If you want to get annoyed, pay in advance."

Budget airlines have their own particular systems for optimizing their capacity utilization. The price tends to increase as the departure date approaches. In contrast to the advance-booking periods of the classic airlines (e.g., 7 days or 21 days), the

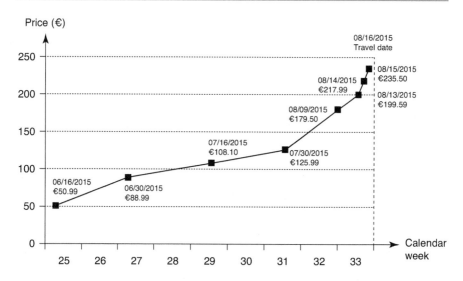

Fig. 12.3 Price changes over time for one specific flight from Frankfurt-Hahn to Dublin [20]

customers for the budget airlines have no transparency into when and by how much the prices may increase. Figure 12.3 shows how prices changed for one Ryanair flight from Frankfurt-Hahn to Dublin. Every price point shown applies to the same flight departing on August 16, 2015. The price savings between booking 2 months in advance and booking the day before travel was €184. The passenger would have actually paid more than the quoted prices shown here, due to taxes and fees. The way prices behave differs by airline and by time.

The key consideration and the optimization problem for yield management is whether a unit of capacity (an airline seat, a hotel room, a production opportunity) should be sold early at a low price or whether the supplier should wait for a customer who buys later and has a higher willingness to pay. Prior to the existence of yield management, the best way to solve this kind of optimization problem was to rely on the experience of hotel or airline employees. With the emergence of information technology and highly evolved methodologies and algorithms, we now have much greater ability to replace experience-based decision-making with empirically and quantitatively based decisions.

Taking advantage of opportunities to optimize capacity utilization requires a *data basis* as well as a *forecasting* and an *optimization* module. The data basis contains the following information:

- Historical data on the demand structure
- Historical data on booking patterns over time
- Price elasticities, disaggregated by time and segment
- Historical data on cancellations and "no shows"
- Data on events (e.g., conferences) which generate demand
- Data on the competition (offers, capacities, prices, etc.)

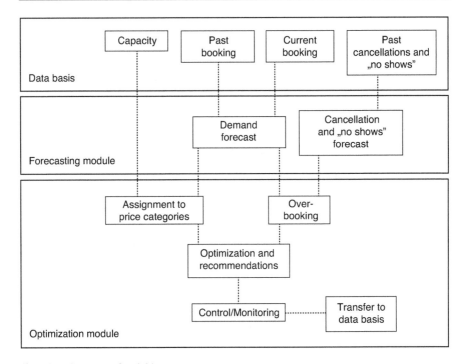

Fig. 12.4 Structure of a yield management system

A range of statistical methods is available to analyze this data and distill information relevant for decision-making. "The more regular patterns the yield management system can discern in demand data, the more accurately the supplier's prices can be tailored to every conceivable situation" [21, p. 250]. Building up the historical data basis means that it takes several years to introduce a comprehensive and reliable yield management system. Standardized software is available on the market. Figure 12.4 shows the basic structure of a yield management system. This is also an area where artificial ingelligence and machine learning hold big potential.

The profit optimum is characterized by the fact that the marginal profit of an additional unit of volume sold is identical in the different price categories. But the price-volume optimization derived from the *optimization module* is counteracted in reality by "no shows" and late cancellations. That means a customer who has booked a unit (a seat, a hotel room, etc.) either does not show up or cancels so late that a resale of that unit is not possible. This results in idle costs for the supplier, who tries to avoid such costs through overbooking, i.e., through selling more capacity than one actually has. The forecasting module of the yield management system is critical for optimizing this process. One must forecast as precisely as possible how many "no shows" and late cancellations will occur. If the forecast is correct, the capacity will be utilized in a profit-optimal way. If the forecasts are inaccurate, the firm can expect two consequences: if too much empty capacity was forecast and then overbooked, some customers with confirmed bookings will be denied service (no seat, no hotel room). That in turn has two consequences, namely, that the customers will be outraged and that the firm will incur additional costs for alternative lodging, rebooking premiums, or other compensation [22]. The other consequence from an inaccurate forecast is that the firm mistakenly expects too little excess capacity and thus does not overbook sufficiently. This costs the firm potential revenue [23]. One positive side effect is that such information will flow back into the database and help improve future forecasts.

Despite its popularity, there are some sectors in which yield management is still hardly used at all. One example is parking garages, especially in areas where finding a parking space is critical, such as at an airport or a train station. Yield management would mean that there is no fixed price per unit of time (e.g., per hour or per day). Instead, the price would be a function of spaces still available. Such a system is in use at London's Heathrow Airport as well as other garages in England. It is also employed in US cities, e.g., in Chicago and San Francisco. The price is managed in such a way that a customer with corresponding willingness to pay always finds a parking spot. One of the authors of this book has missed flights on two occasions because he could not find a parking spot at the airport. His willingness to pay in this situation was extremely high, but because the airport's parking garages had uniform prices, they were full. This is not a good outcome for the parking garages either, because they miss out on a substantial amount of profit. Yield management in such cases would have provided a greater benefit to both the customer and the garage operator.

It is not unusual for the concept of dynamic pricing to be misunderstood. In a downtown parking garage in a major city, 1 h of parking costs $2.50 on weekdays. On Sunday the price is only $1 per hour. Nonetheless, the garage is empty on most Sundays. Where is the mistake? The garage operator has mistaken low demand as high price elasticity. The garage is not empty on Sunday because the price of $2.50 per hour would have been too high. It is empty because very few people drive into the city on Sundays. The price cut makes no sense. The operator is only sacrificing profit.

In a project for a large movie theater chain, Simon-Kucher & Partners discovered similar misinterpretations. On certain weekdays and at certain times of day, the chain offered discounts of up to 25%, without any material increase in demand. The price structure Simon-Kucher suggested systematically captures profits in periods of high demand. There are discounts only on 1 day, advertised as "Cheap Day," but the discounts are just sufficiently high to fill the theaters. Before its introduction, the new system was tested at several locations. Overall attendance fell slightly, but profits saw a massive increase.

For a more thorough treatment of the complex methods and challenges of yield management and dynamic pricing, we refer the reader to specialized literature [24–27]. Yield management draws on highly developed processes from operations research. Its use has been increasingly expanding into other sectors such as industrial contract manufacturing. Fundamentally speaking, yield management is applicable in any industry or sector where the supply-side and demand-side prerequisites we described above are fulfilled. There are several specialized suppliers of systems for yield management. Many of them have their origin in the airline industry. Yield management can help service providers increase their revenue and profit. It extends beyond pure pricing initiatives.

12.4   Implementation

With respect to the implementation of pricing measures for services, the following topics are relevant: implementation of differentiated prices, case-specific prices vs. fixed prices, and price communication.

12.4.1 Implementation of Differentiated Prices

Perhaps the most important special aspect of services is the more effective implementation of differentiated prices. This applies to all forms of price differentiation. The incorporation of customer resources—whether it is the customers themselves (e.g., patients, passengers) or objects (e.g., a car to repair, a heater or furnace to maintain)—makes precise controls possible. The person who receives the service is the one who purchases it or pays for it. Interpersonal arbitrage is not possible. Fencing, i.e., the ability to keep customer segments separate, works better for services than for material goods, which one person can buy but another may consume. The effectiveness of price differentiation is high both for time-based and regional differentiation. Customers often lack the ability to shift their demand freely across time periods or locations. Families with school-aged children, for example, can only take vacations when the children are not in school. Business travelers do their utmost to keep their scheduled appointments. Wellness services can only be performed when the customer actually shows up. Online communication and interaction such as videoconferencing and teleshopping, however, have weakened these ties to time and location to a certain extent. This can make it harder to implement differentiated prices. Research, bookings, call center services, radiological diagnoses, and remote maintenance can be performed independent of the customer's location. That helps explain why the provision of many of these services has moved to Eastern Europe or India.

Customers accept greater price differentiation for services than they do for material goods. That also applies to price increases. In many markets for material goods, price increases encounter heavy resistance. This kind of resistance is less pronounced for services. In line with this, some prices are constantly being changed. Major airlines report that they may make millions of price adjustments in a single day. But price increases can meet with resistance when prices have remained constant for long periods, such as they do regularly for train travel or for postage. One reason is that prices which have been stable for longer periods become anchored in the minds of customers. The anchor effect comes into play and engenders the corresponding negative price-change effect.

12.4.2 Fixed Prices or Case-Specific Prices

For services, should a supplier offer the customer a fixed price in advance or charge a case-specific price ex post? Examples of services normally offered at a fixed price include tutoring, car washes, maintenance agreements, or a visit to a fitness center. The second form, under which the price is calculated ex post on the basis of the actual time devoted to the service, is the predominant form for car repairs, database usage, work performed by skilled tradesmen, or tax advisory services. In some industries both forms exist alongside each other or are offered as alternatives by the same supplier. Apple, for example, offers its "AppleCare Protection Plan" which allows the customer to receive free hardware service for the MacBook as well as direct access to Apple technicians. The plan costs $249 for 3 years. This maintenance contract, which works out to $6.90 per month, probably seems more favorable to the customer than a case-specific repair. For maintenance-intensive products, the customer can often choose between a maintenance contract whose fixed price covers all their risks and opt for case-by-case billing.

The parties' interests are obvious. The fixed price means that the supplier bears the entire price risk because it receives only the fixed amount, determined in advance, regardless of the actual time the supplier ultimately devotes to that client. The customer, however, faces an increased quality risk, because the service provider is motivated to minimize its time. For case-specific pricing, the situation is reversed. The customer bears the full price risk, but the quality risk is lower because the service provider has no incentive to minimize its time. In fact, the opposite is often true. The fixed-price system seems better suited to standardized services. The more specific and individualized the requirements are, the more appropriate the use of case-specific pricing would be. Both forms should also be assessed differently from a marketing perspective. Standardized services can be marketed similarly to classical branded products, which have clearly defined fixed prices.

Many services undergo an increasing standardization over their life cycles, much as products do. Standardized services with fixed prices are becoming more common for service providers such as tax advisors, lawyers, medical practices, and hospitals. The determination of the optimal fixed price for a standardized service differs little from price optimization for products. Above all, the price-response and cost functions must be determined, and all established methods can be applied. The case-specific pricing, in contrast, more closely resembles cost-plus thinking, because the cost aspect dominates and the customer's willingness to pay is not explicitly taken into account. At the same time, one must recognize that the time requirement to perform a service is often the most reliable starting point for setting a price, regardless of whether it is ex ante for an estimate or ex post for billing purposes. It is appropriate here, however, to warn about the dangers of using a fully loaded cost basis. Low capacity utilization means that fixed costs are allocated across a smaller volume, and this in turn can lead to higher unit prices. One should therefore use assumptions about normal or standard capacity utilization when setting hourly rates, and not allow short-term fluctuations to influence those rates.

12.4.3 Price Communication

For the purchase of a product, the purchase act and the *price communication* or
rather the agreement on price often occur simultaneously. For services, the situation
is typically different. Some services are provided (from the supplier's viewpoint) or
utilized (from the customer's viewpoint), without an advance agreement on price. In
many cases, a patient does not ask a doctor in advance how much an exam or
treatment will cost. On the other hand, it can be difficult to estimate in advance how
much time and effort a service will require (e.g., diagnosing and repairing a defective
heating unit or computer). In practice, because of these relationships, one observes
very diverse forms of price communication. Price communication by service
providers may not only take place publicly on the provider's own homepage but
also in covert ways. When discounts to individual customers are higher than the ones
offered on one's own website, it is advisable to conduct such actions as discreetly as
possible to avoid angering one's regular customers [28].

Some service providers will advertise the price of a particular service on boards,
in brochures, or online. This can occur voluntarily or due to regulatory requirements.
Examples are hotels, restaurants, and car washes. Other service sectors work with
hourly, daily, or monthly rates. The price of the service is then a function of time
spent, as shown on the invoice. Examples here are tradesmen, lawyers, and
consultants. Another model is success-based pricing. In such cases, the price
depends on other variables. Forms of success-based pricing include commissions
for real estate agents and also include the Enercon Partner Concept, under
which the maintenance price for wind turbines depends on their yield [29] (see -
Chaps. 9 and 14).

The Internet has had massive effects on price communication and price comparison for services. For standardized services such as flights or vacations, hotels, and
rental cars, online price comparisons and purchases dominate. Crowdsourced service
portals such as Yelp allow potential buyers to compare and evaluate local businesses
and contractors. Amazon offers "Amazon Home Services," an online portal for
services. Such offerings increase price transparency and heighten price competition.
They also improve value transparency, thanks in large part to their review systems.
We will look at this topic more deeply in Chap. 14. The effect of the price of a
service depends significantly on communication. Therefore, this aspect warrants
considerable attention.

Conclusion

In this chapter we examined the special aspects of price management for
services. We summarize the following key points:

- The special aspects of services relevant for price include intangibility, the
  integration of customer resources, the relationship between fixed and variable costs, the inability to transfer services from person to person, the
  experience- and trust-based nature, as well as the local nature of services.

(continued)

- Services are extremely heterogeneous, a fact which is reflected in a very diverse range of pricing practices.
- The integration of customer resources (customers themselves or their objects) influences both the cost and the outcome of the service. This integration therefore contributes to the individualization of services and their prices.
- Because of this integration, the interpersonal transfer of a service is not possible (unless tolerated by the service provider). This feature makes person-based price differentiation better implementable and more effective.
- The inability to store a service (i.e., its perishability) facilitates time-based price differentiation.
- Price is well suited as a tool for capacity management in conjunction with fixed capacity, which is common for capital- and technology-intensive services.
- The local nature of services favors regional price differentiation. New technologies, however, can weaken or overcome the local nature of a service.
- Services offer good opportunities for non-linear, multidimensional, and similarly complex price structures, as well as price bundling.
- Yield management is recommended when certain supply-side and demand-side conditions are fulfilled (e.g., fixed capacity, low variable costs, heterogeneous customers who book in advance). This approach extends beyond pure pricing measures. It aims at profit-maximizing capacity utilization. Yield management requires a comprehensive data basis as well as sophisticated forecasting and optimization models.
- Service providers are able to implement price differentiation more effectively than sellers of material goods. One reason is that customers tend to accept larger price differences than they would for material goods.
- When deciding on whether to offer a fixed price in advance or a case-specific price ex post, one should pay close attention to the perception and sharing of risk between supplier and customer.

In the service sector, differentiated and sophisticated price management opens up enormous opportunities for higher profits. Taking advantage of these opportunities, however, requires that the supplier has a deep and thorough understanding of the complex interrelationships. In many service sectors, price management is less well developed than in manufacturing sectors. This stands in stark contrast to the fact that services make up three quarters of the economic output in highly developed economies. Improving price management for services has vast potential for value creation and profitability.

References

1. Atzler, E. (2015, February 06). Besser Online überweisen. *Handelsblatt*, pp. 36–37.
2. Meffert, H., & Bruhn, M. (2012). *Dienstleistungsmarketing, Grundlagen, Konzepte, Methoden* (7th ed.). Wiesbaden: Gabler.
3. Corsten, H. (1985). *Die Produktion von Dienstleistungen: Grundzüge einer Produktionswirtschaftslehre des Tertiären Sektors*. Berlin: Erich Schmidt.
4. Weber, J., & Schäffer, U. (2001). Controlling in Dienstleistungsunternehmen. In *Handbuch Dienstleistungsmanagement: Von der strategischen Konzeption zur praktischen Umsetzung* (pp. 899–913). Wiesbaden: Gabler.
5. Corsten, H., & Gössinger, R. (2007). *Dienstleistungsmanagement*. München: Oldenbourg.
6. Franz, K.-P. (1990). Die Prozesskostenrechnung: Darstellung und Vergleich mit der Plankosten- und Deckungsbeitragsrechnung. In D. Ahlert, K.-P. Franz, & H. Goppel (Ed.), *Finanz- und Rechnungswesen als Führungsinstrument, Festschrift für H. Vormbaum* (pp. 109–136). Wiesbaden: Gabler.
7. Remer, D. (2005). *Einführen der Prozesskostenrechnung: Grundlagen, Methodik, Einführung und Anwendung der verursachungsgerechten Gemeinkostenzurechnung* (2nd ed.). Stuttgart: Schäffer-Poeschel.
8. Joskow, P. L. (1976). Contributions to the Theory of Marginal Cost Pricing. *The Bell Journal of Economics*, 7(1), 197–206.
9. Mönch, C. T. (1979). Marketing des Dienstleistungssektors. In U. Dornieden (Ed.), *Studienhefte für Operatives Marketing* (Vol. 5, pp. 217–255). Wiesbaden: Gabler.
10. Philips, L. (1983). *The Economics of Price Discrimination*. Cambridge: Cambridge University Press.
11. Dolan, R. J. (1987). Managing the Pricing of Service-Line and Service-Line Bundles. In L. K. Wright (Ed.), *Competing in a Deregulated or Volatile Market*, MSI Report, (Vol. 87-1111, pp. 28–29).
12. Guiltinan, J. P. (1987). The Price Bundling of Services: A Normative Framework. *Journal of Marketing*, 51(2), 74–85.
13. Stremersch, S., & Tellis, G. J. (2002). Strategic Bundling of Products and Prices: A New Synthesis for Marketing. *Journal of Marketing*, 66(1), 55–72.
14. van Spijker, B. J. (2015). *Enhancing Profits Through Service Monetization. Achieving TopLine Power*. Baarn: Simon-Kucher & Partners. 10/11/2015.
15. Phillips, R. L. (2005). *Pricing and Revenue Optimization*. Stanford: Stanford University Press.
16. O'Connor, P., & Murphy, J. (2008). Hotel Yield Management Practices Across Multiple Electronic Distribution Channels. *Information Technology & Tourism*, 10(2), 161–172.
17. Jallat, F., & Ancarani, F. (2008). Yield Management, Dynamic Pricing and CRM in Telecommunications. *Journal of Services Marketing*, 22(6), 465–478.
18. Hobica, G. (2009). Confessions of a Fat Fingered Airline Pricing Analyst. http://www.airfarewatchdog.com/blog/3801877/confessions-of-fat-fingered-airline-pricing-analyst/. Accessed 23 June 2015.
19. Pechtl, H. (2003). Logik von Preissystemen. In H. Diller, & A. Herrmann (Ed.), *Handbuch Preispolitik: Strategien – Planung – Organisation – Umsetzung* (pp. 69–91). Wiesbaden: Gabler.
20. Ryanair (2015). www.ryanair.com, Access Dates: 16/06/2015, 30/06/2015, 16/07/2015, 30/07/2015, 09/08/2015, 13/08/2015, 14/08/2015, 15/08/2015.
21. Enzweiler, T. (1990). Wo die Preise laufen lernen. *Manager Magazin*, 20(3), 246–253.
22. Tscheulin, D. K., & Lindemeier, J. (2003). Yield-Management – Ein State-of-the-Art. *Zeitschrift für Betriebswirtschaft*, 73(6), 629–662.
23. von Wangenheim, F., & Bayon, T. (2007). Behavioral Consequences of Overbooking Service Capacity. *Journal of Marketing*, 71(4), 36–47.
24. Klein, R., & Steinhardt, C. (2008). *Revenue Management*. Berlin: Springer.
25. Cross, R. G. (1997). *Revenue Management*. New York: Broadway Books.

26. Tscheulin, D. K., & Helmig, B. (2001). *Branchenspezifisches Marketing*. Wiesbaden: Gabler.
27. Sölter, M. (2007). *Hotelvertrieb, Yield-Management und Dynamic Pricing in der Hotellerie*. München: Grin.
28. Scherff, D. (2015, February 15). Wie günstig sind die Spezialtickets der Bahn? *Frankfurter Allgemeine Sonntagszeitung*, p. 24.
29. Enercon GmbH (2010). http://www.enercon.de/p/downloads/Enercon_EPK_2010_deu.pdf. Accessed 29 January 2015.

Price Management for Retailers

13

Abstract

This chapter addresses the special characteristics of retail price management. For many retailers, price is the most important and most effective competitive instrument. Price differences in retail have a greater impact on profit than they do for industrial goods or services because of the low profit margins. The priority for retailers is their price positioning in terms of setting the overall price ranges for a store or outlet as well as for individual product categories. The price image of a retailer is extremely important and must be carefully managed. Because of the large assortments, consumers normally do not know each individual product price and therefore rely on the store's price image for guidance. Retailers often have more information about consumers than manufacturers, but they only use this information to a limited extent for price setting. Information on competitors' prices is easier to acquire in retail channels than in other sectors. Standard price strategies such as everyday low prices (EDLP) or Hi-Lo are common. Discounts have complex effects which are only partially understood and which are not completely measurable. Assortment effects play an important role in price setting for retailers but are also difficult to quantify.

13.1 Introduction

For many retailers, price is the most important competitive instrument. The penetration of e-commerce has made price even more important as online retailers pass on their cost advantages to consumers in the form of lower prices. In order to fuel their growth and drive up their number of consumers, these retailers have focused on low prices and forgone profits for years. Amazon is a prime example, having posted no significant profits from its founding in 1994 through 2015. Despite the critical importance of price, retailers tend to set prices primarily either by using intuition, experience, and rules of thumb or by orienting themselves around what competitors

© Springer Nature Switzerland AG 2019
H. Simon, M. Fassnacht, *Price Management*,
https://doi.org/10.1007/978-3-319-99456-7_13

do. The CEO of one major grocery retailer told us that the prices for several hundred key value items—which represented about a quarter of overall revenue—are based on the prices of ALDI, one of the world's leading discounters. This company has essentially delegated the bulk of its pricing sovereignty to ALDI.

The price management environment for retailers is complex and challenging. First and foremost is the sheer size of assortments, which can include tens of thousands of items. That applies just as much to B2C retailers and B2B dealers as it does to specialty retailers or wholesalers. A price decision must be made for each item in these huge assortments. Major retail chains need to set almost half a million prices per season. Individual managers may have the responsibility for setting prices for more than 15,000 items. It is obvious that estimating the price-response function and price elasticity for each and every item under such conditions is not feasible. Another special aspect of the retail trade is that consumers often buy several items in one shopping trip or visit. The consumers concentrate their purchase activities in terms of time and place; we call this one-stop shopping. These interconnections within the assortment must be considered in price setting. They create major opportunities for price management in retail, but at the same time, they increase the complexity. For a department store with multiple checkouts on several floors, the only way to discover these interrelationships for an individual consumer is through consumer personalization, often with the help of an instrument such as a customer card. When a consumer makes only one trip for a basket of goods, such as to a supermarket, it is easier to track the purchases and their interrelationships. Both company-specific and multi-company customer cards such as Plenti in the United States or its European counterpart PAYBACK are building up impressive databases whose potential for price management has barely been tapped yet. In e-commerce, it is relatively easy to group the purchases of one consumer together and to analyze the effects of interrelationships among items because a consumer must tie personal identifying information to these purchases.

The price image of a retail or online store plays an important role. Many consumers choose their place to shop not because of the price of an individual article but rather based on an assessment of the overall price level at the store.

In retail, there are two basic price strategies. Under one strategy, the store or chain intermittently offers discounts and price promotions. This is referred to as a "Hi-Lo" strategy, whose name derives from "High-Low." Advertising flyers or circulars for a given week or period are often delivered by email or even in physical form via post or as supplements in newspapers. Consumers can also view the flyers on the respective store's websites or on aggregated sites such as www.befrugal.com. The alternative is known as the EDLP strategy, an acronym for "Every Day Low Prices." Price promotions play little or no role under the EDLP strategy [1]. In the luxury goods sector, there are stores which as a matter of principle never offer discounts or close-out sales. Instead, these stores ship close-out seasonal merchandise to special outlet stores.

The penetration of e-commerce has transformed the world of retail and will continue to do so. The various retail sectors have been affected in different ways. These changes are in no way limited to price, but price has played a prominent role.

Inescapable is the question of how a retail chain should manage its brick-and-mortar and online business together. Even Amazon has opened brick-and-mortar stores in several US states as well as "pop up" stores co-located in other department stores [2]. It also acquired the upscale Whole Foods grocery chain for $13.40 billion. Whole Foods operates 460 physical stores in the United States, Canada, and the UK [3]. Moving in the opposite direction, Walmart entered into a cooperation with Google.

We will now look at price strategy, i.e., price positioning and price image. As usual, we will follow the established flow: analysis, decision-making, and implementation.

13.2   Strategy

13.2.1   Price Positioning

Similar to companies in other industries, retailers also need to define their fundamental price strategy and price positioning. ALDI and Walmart have a lower price position than Kroger or Safeway.[1] In fashion, chains such as H&M or Zara compete in a different price segment than the classic fashion trade. IKEA is very price aggressive in the furniture trade. The same applies to online furniture retailers, who are making life difficult for their brick-and-mortar counterparts.

However, the ideal typical price positioning in the retail trade often does not occur in its pure form. Even some retailers with a high-price positioning typically offer some key value items at lower prices. Low-price retailers, on the other hand, need some higher-priced products in their assortments in order to achieve an adequate overall margin. Thus, it is appropriate that retailers formulate their desired price positioning at the corporate level, the category level (e.g., child care or cleaning), and the product category level (e.g., baby wipes or dishwashing liquid). Prices are also tailored by location. The same basket of groceries in the same chain can cost $100 more in an urban area such as San Francisco than in a rural area. This price positioning across multiple levels forms the fundamental basis for the company's orientation and actions.

When we look at how retail has developed over the last decades, we see three competitive constellations:

- Traditional retailers vs. discounters
- Urban retailers vs. suburban or greenfield retailers
- Brick-and-mortar vs. online retail

---

[1]ALDI has two operating units, ALDI North and ALDI South. In the United States, the former operates under the ALDI name, the latter under Trader Joe's.

There is partial, even increasing overlap across these categories. Price plays a key role in all three constellations.

13.2.1.1 Discounters

Discounters and hard discounters have continually increased their market shares over the years. Traditional retailers have responded to this aggressive price strategy with their own price cuts but without having the corresponding low costs that the (hard) discounters enjoy. Typically, these actions spark price wars and lead to a serious deterioration of profits. A prominent case is the US-based retail chain Kmart, which relied too heavily on discounts in its competition with Walmart and its efforts to attract consumers. Kmart, however, lacked the necessary cost position to make such heavy discounts sustainable. Kmart eventually filed for bankruptcy. Market exits have also occurred; even powerful and financially strong chains such as Walmart have withdrawn from important markets such as Germany and South Korea.

Often, the reason behind such setbacks is tactical behavior which is inconsistent with the company's fundamental strategy and price positioning. If a traditional retailer, despite its higher costs, enters into price competition with a discounter that has optimized its cost basis, the chances of success are bleak from the outset. It is more promising to emphasize other advantages, such as a positive shopping experience, which according to one study is largely independent of the attractiveness of the retailer's price positioning [4].

A few basic considerations attest to the problems involved in changing a price position. We use a break-even analysis to show the changes a traditional retailer would need in either costs or volume to compensate for price reductions, in order to prevent a decline in profits [5]. Let us assume a gross margin of 25% and operating costs of 24%, which leaves a net margin of 1%. That is a low but rather typical net margin level for many food and grocery retailers [6].

As Fig. 13.1 shows, a price reduction of 7% would require a volume increase of 39% to avoid a decline in profit, assuming that costs remain constant. This implies a very high price elasticity of 5.60. If such a sharp increase in volume is not achieved, the company would need to make drastic cost cuts. If the volume increased by only 10%, for example, which reflects a price elasticity of 1.42, the operating costs would need to be reduced by around 20%. This simple calculation shows how difficult and dangerous a downward price repositioning can be for a traditional retailer.

In contrast to a traditional retailer, discounters enjoy lower procurement costs. One reason is their conscious focus on a limited number of suppliers and as a result, their greater purchasing power. Furthermore, they enjoy lower logistics and labor costs than traditional retailers and in most cases invest less in advertising (as a percentage of sales). Traditional retailers should keep in mind that discounters such as ALDI and LIDL have much smaller assortments and achieve significantly higher revenues per item. In contrast, traditional retailers carry a wide assortment of items, some of which are listed for image reasons and are unprofitable. Table 13.1 shows a

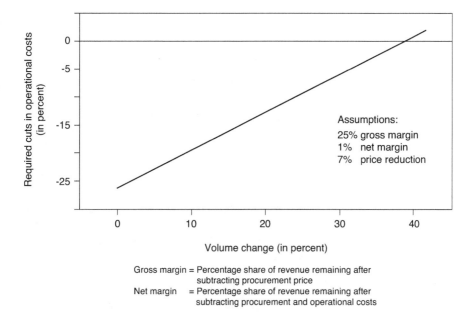

Fig. 13.1 Break-even analysis to assess a price cut by a retailer [5, p. 23]

Table 13.1 Comparison of selected key indicators for a discounter vs. a supermarket [7, 8]

Key performance indicator	Discounter	Supermarket
Store size (square meters)	400–1,200	400–2,500
Net revenue ($-000 per year)	$3,420	$7,500
Number of items	2,000	10,100
Revenue/item	$1,716	$744
Items/m^2 retail space	2.7	9.9
Number of employees	6.9	27.5
Revenue/employee	$495,000	$272,760
Consumers/day	880	1,531

comparison of key performance indicators (KPIs) between ALDI and a traditional supermarket.

This KPI comparison shows very clearly that the two retail formats reflect two fundamentally different strategies. These differences must inevitably be manifested in the prices in the stores. Once established, it is difficult for a retailer to change its strategy and price position. Traditional retailers have almost no chance of succeeding, never mind surviving, against a discounter solely on the basis of price competition. Instead they need to differentiate themselves in terms of product quality, shopping ambiance, location, services, convenience, etc. In recent years, European supermarket chains have taken this insight to heart and have enhanced both their stores and their assortments. This helped to stem further growth of the discounters. METRO Cash & Carry offers a variety of additional services such as financing and leasing, insurance, and parcel shipping. In the United States, Whole Foods (now part of Amazon) has succeeded against Walmart by offering an upscale, health-oriented assortment [9].

13.2.1.2 Suburban/Greenfield vs. Urban Locations

With respect to price-based competitiveness, what applies for competition with discounters also applies essentially to the relationship between greenfield locations and central urban locations. Here, we are thinking primarily of traditional specialty retailers with urban locations. The infrastructure costs for an urban location are significantly higher so that there is no way to compete on price with a greenfield location. The greenfield location also offers advantages such as convenience, parking, assortment size, and one-stop-shopping. An urban or city center location likewise has advantages, which include shopping experience, a broader range of stores, proximity to work or home, and often specialized personnel. In general, however, the retail trade in cities has declined over the years. This has primarily hurt the specialty retailers who have lost ground to large chains which are often aggressive on price.

A rather recent and rapidly expanding greenfield variant is the so-called factory outlet center (FOC). An alternative term which describes this concept more accurately is "Organized Outlet Agglomerations" (OOA). These agglomerations can have 100 or more stores of substantial size. They are usually located close to highway intersections. The United States has over 200 FOC/OOAs, while the UK has 36 and Germany has 14 [10]. The prices are at least 25% lower than the respective prices at central urban stores. While not as threatening as e-commerce, the FOC/OOAs have the power to grab significant market share from urban locations [11].

13.2.1.3 E-Commerce

In 2017, about 9% of retail sales were online sales. Forecasts from trade associations and research institutes predict that the share of online retail sales will rise to 12.5% by 2020, with strong variation by sector [12]. Considering both formats of books, physical and e-book form, the online share in the United States' book market is already at 40% [13].

In the 2016/17 business year, Walmart ranked as both the world's largest retailer and largest corporation with revenues of $485.90 billion [14]. Walmart employs 2.3 million people. The largest e-commerce retailer, Amazon, achieved revenues of $177.87 billion in 2017 [15], or roughly one third of Walmart's revenue, with 566,000 employees. This makes the employees of Amazon roughly 1.5 times as productive as Walmart's, based on revenue per employee. The growth rates, however, look much different. From 2011 to 2017, Amazon grew by 24.4% per year, while Walmart grew by only 1.4% annually. If these two retail giants continue to grow at these rates in the coming years, Amazon's revenue would reach around $1 trillion in 2025, making it significantly larger than Walmart, whose sales will have reached $543 billion by then. Many experts believe that Amazon will assume the title of world's largest retailer much sooner than that. The Chinese e-commerce company Alibaba experienced a tremendous start on the New York Stock Exchange in 2014. Its revenue stood at only $8.58 billion or roughly a tenth of Amazon's, but in the previous 4 years, it had grown by 63% on average. In 2017, it posted sales of $25 billion. Should this growth rate continue, Alibaba's revenue would be well above $1 trillion in 2025, much greater than either Amazon's or Walmart's. It remains to be seen whether these forecasts come true. But either way, the current numbers show the magnitude that e-commerce has already reached, as well as the much greater volumes which may be sold via e-commerce instead of traditional channels in the future.

The e-commerce numbers for traditional retailers are likewise interesting. Walmart's e-commerce revenue totaled $14.60 billion in 2017, which is not small in absolute terms but represents a mere 3% of Walmart's overall revenue. Germany's Otto Group, once the world's largest catalog retailer, posted online sales of €7 billion in its 2016/17 business year, more than 56% of the group's total sales. The e-commerce growth rate was 7.6% versus only 5% in the previous year [16].

The business models of Walmart, Amazon, and Alibaba are fundamentally different, a fact most clearly visible in the financial returns of the respective companies. Walmart had an after-tax profit of $13.60 billion in 2016/17, which is a good return on sales of 2.8%. Amazon's profit in 2013 was $276 million, followed by a net loss of $241 million in 2014, a profit of $596 million in 2015, and then a profit of $2.40 billion in 2016. Nonetheless, from the time it entered the market in 1994, Amazon has used aggressive pricing to fuel its revenue growth. In contrast, Alibaba is extremely profitable. It earned a profit of $6 billion in 2017 on revenue of $23 billion, which translates into an amazing return on sales of 26% [17]. Relative to its costs, Alibaba also has a high-price position—essentially the opposite price position of Amazon.

But e-commerce and the associated price management do not only play at this global level. They also have a transformative effect in localized retail sectors. The following case, which has been anonymized for confidentiality reasons and will simply be called "Furniture Store", illustrates this impressively. Furniture Store had achieved an annual sales revenue of around $5 million per year with its traditional brick-and-mortar store in a rural area. Management recognized the potential of the Internet at a very early stage and reserved a domain name which conveyed—with no further explanation—that their offerings sell at very attractive prices. The company launched its e-commerce business in 2004. At that time, most experts believed that the online channel would remain irrelevant for the furniture sector. How mistaken those experts were! Furniture Store now has annual online revenue of $50 million per year, which is ten times more than its previous revenue from the brick-and-mortar store. The consumer orders online. A contract shipping service then picks up the merchandise directly from the manufacturer and delivers it to the consumer's door. Because they can serve consumers directly without any floor space, warehousing, or the accompanying personnel costs, they save about 40% of the costs vs. a traditional model. These savings allow Furniture Store to position itself in a much lower price range. The company passes on roughly half of the cost savings to consumers in the form of lower prices, yet still achieves profit margins which are higher than in the brick-and-mortar business. The original store in the rural area could serve only a limited geographic area. There are no such limitations for e-commerce; consumers originate from around the country. In the meantime, the company has built up a competent team of e-commerce experts. Furniture Store is living proof of the enormous potential of e-commerce even in a very traditional sector—if a company meets the needs of consumers and strikes early.

One may ask where consumers had an opportunity to first view the furniture which they ultimately bought from Furniture Store. The most likely place is a brick-and-mortar store. Furniture Store benefits from the so-called "showrooming" effect, which can be defined as follows: "One goes into a store, takes one's time to try out a product or try on some clothes, and then leaves the store without having purchased anything" [18].

According to a current study, three fourths of consumers have informed themselves by visiting a store and then purchased a product online; some 14% made the purchase immediately via their smartphone. Showrooming is nothing new. There have always been consumers who have sought out a consultation at a specialty retailer and then bought their chosen product later at a lower price at another store (often a greenfield or suburban store). The Internet has greatly multiplied the effect of showrooming [19]. Thus, the cross-price elasticity between brick-and-mortar and online retail is increasing sharply. One possibility to circumvent the problem of lost revenue through showrooming is to create a more-engaging experience for consumers. The sporting goods retailer Sports Basement Inc. is a good example for how to make consumers purchase goods while they are in the store. Sports Basement Inc. provides consumers with the possibility to use a mobile app to scan merchandise in the store and search online prices. If a consumer finds a lower price, the retailer will match it. In this way, consumers get the best deal in the store, which increases their loyalty and builds on a trust relationship [20].

The flipside/opposite of showrooming is webrooming. Webrooming means that consumers research products and information online before shopping in-store. It is still the shopping preference of many consumers. Consequently, online-only retailers increasingly expand their operations and open up brick-and-mortar locations [21].

13.2.2 Price Image

As previously indicated, consumers rarely choose a store on the basis of the price of an individual item. Rather, consumers make the choice based on a general perception of the store's price level, i.e., the store's price image. Nyström [22] defines price image as an individual consumer's assessment of the price level of a store. The price image in this sense represents a composite of a shopper's price impressions [23]. It therefore plays a central role in retail price management because the sheer size of a retailer's assortment generally does not allow the consumer to remember many, never mind all, of the prices of the products which are relevant to him or her. If the consumer considers buying an item whose price is unfamiliar, the price image of the store will influence that consumer's decision on where to shop. This is a simple and relatively efficient process for a consumer who would otherwise have to research and explicitly compare the prices in individual stores (a much more tedious process). When a chain such as ALDI follows an EDLP strategy and keeps prices more or less constant, the consumers expect to find a relatively low price. But even EDLP stores can occasionally be undersold by a chain which pursues a Hi-Lo strategy and offers alternating price promotions. But in order to learn the availability of such lower prices, the consumer must first have the necessary information.

The costs of laborious information collection can outweigh the benefits, which means that using the price image to generalize about the price of a specific item can definitely be rational. The essential role of the price image has not been eliminated by the Internet but changed depending on the retail sector. Easy access to the prices stores charge for individual products creates an objective information basis which alleviates the need to rely on the price image. With the help of the Internet, a potential consumer can find an attractive price at a retailer whose price image is not typically considered favorable and vice versa, i.e., notice that an item may be offered at a higher price than one would have expected based on a store's price image. For price research, consumers prefer to use Google, Amazon, or one of many familiar price search engines such as nextag.com, pricegrabber.com, and pricewatch. com. For many consumers doing initial research into general or popular products, Amazon provides a price benchmark. Consumers are particularly active in searching for prices for electronics (around 68% of users have made at least one price comparison), household items (59%), and clothing and shoes (50%) [24]. The Internet makes price information more objective and diminishes the influence of price image.

One must not forget, however, that nowadays prices are changing frequently, and at shorter intervals, thanks to *dynamic pricing*. Online retailers can react in a matter of seconds to fluctuations in demand and change prices several times per day in order to maximize profit. Amazon openly admits to this practice [25]. The day of the week, not just the time of day, can also play a role [26]. This can lead to uncertainty and frustration among consumers who paid a high price and thus have a negative impact on a retailer's price image. Figure 13.2 illustrates, based on the example of a digital frame sold at various retailers, how significantly prices can vary within 10 days. Especially, the medium-priced segment is highly competitive, and retailers try to find the "right" price. The Media Markt online shop, however, has the highest price for the product and shows a stable price.

Price image and actual price level do not need to coincide. Figure 13.3 shows such deviations for large French retailers. While price image and price level are aligned in the case of Leclerc, Intermarché is the most expensive supplier but has the perceived affordability of Auchan and Carrefour. One observes similar phenomena in Germany. In the area of consumer electronics, Media Markt and Saturn advertised for many years to create the perception of being the least expensive stores. They were able to maintain this price image even though online retailers offered lower prices.

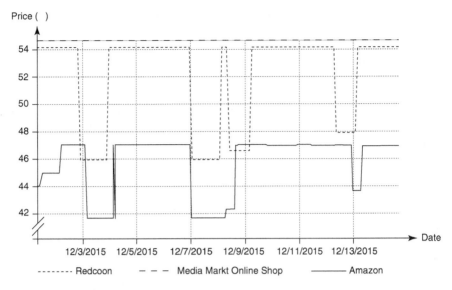

Fig. 13.2 Pricing of a digital frame at selected retailers [27]

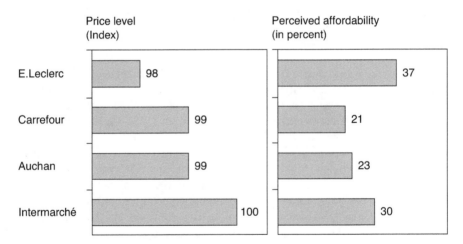

Fig. 13.3 Objective price level and price image for selected French retailers

There are two competing hypotheses for how a retailer's price image originates:

- Hypothesis 1: The price image is derived from the prices of a small number of items, especially the so-called key value items (KVIs), as well as from the prices of discounted products and items featured prominently in the firm's advertisements.
- Hypothesis 2: The consumers orient themselves on their actual purchases and take the prices of many items into account when they form their price image.

Hypothesis 1, which is also called the key value item hypothesis, postulates that certain products or product categories contribute more strongly to the overall price perception than others [28, pp. 125–128]. Such products include manufacturers' brands (as opposed to store brands) as well as products with a high purchase frequency [29, p. 238]. In this context, it is interesting to mention that Amazon, a retailer that believes that offering low prices to its consumers is crucial for success, indeed offers lower prices than other retailers do for its 100 top-selling products, the key value items. However, for the rest of the assortment, Amazon has higher prices. Nonetheless, Amazon is perceived as e-commerce price leader [30]. Under the prerequisite that the key value item hypothesis is valid, Müller [29, pp. 235–254] identified points on which to build a positive price image. In order to achieve a favorable (affordable) price image, one must not only reduce prices but also envision changes to price-value relationships. Diller [31, pp. 505 f.] describes the price-value relationship as both a primary and before-the-fact level of perception. Not only price but also other attributes such as outward appearance, advertising, assortment, operating principles, services, and the physical appearance of the stores contribute to the price-value image. This is how a retailer of affordably priced clothing lost a portion of its core consumers after it modernized one of its stores. The more chic setup of the store conveyed (inaccurately) the impression that prices were now higher.

The price image is one aspect of a more comprehensive perceptual construct. One should make selective price reductions for those items which have a strong influence on the price image in order to positively affect the perceived price-value relationship. The resulting lower margin represents an investment in the price image [29]. Kenning [32, p. 240] investigated the influence of selected product categories on the price image of a warehouse store. He found that personal hygiene products, candy/sweets, and dairy products had a significantly stronger influence than textiles, consumer electronics, and beverages. In this light, it makes sense for a retailer to make an investment in its price image by lowering prices for the more influential products. This can, however, lead to conflicts with manufacturers. In contrast, retailers can view items which have a lesser influence on the price image as opportunities to implement relatively higher prices to bolster their margins.

Discounters face the problem of reconciling their price image with the necessity of having a sufficient number of higher-priced items. While the classic retailer predominantly charges high prices, and uses lower prices selectively, in order to foster a favorable price image, discounters have predominantly low prices. At the same time, they need items with higher prices in order to earn an overall reasonable margin. Figure 13.4 uses an example from Trader Joe's to show that price differentiation and the mixed calculations which support it really do exist in practice.

In other words, even discounters should not operate without having some higher-margin products in their assortments [34]. For this reason, they are making greater use of higher-priced premium store brands such as the "Gourmet" line at ALDI or the "Deluxe" line at LIDL. Relative to basic store brands, these premium brands offer consumers more indulgence and better quality, as well as emotional and

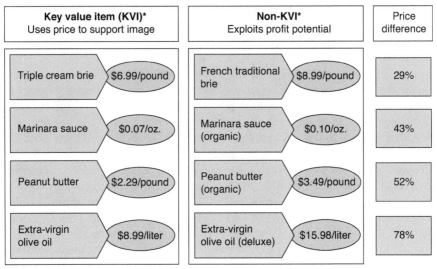

Key value item (KVI)* Uses price to support image		Non-KVI* Exploits profit potential		Price difference
Triple cream brie	$6.99/pound	French traditional brie	$8.99/pound	29%
Marinara sauce	$0.07/oz.	Marinara sauce (organic)	$0.10/oz.	43%
Peanut butter	$2.29/pound	Peanut butter (organic)	$3.49/pound	52%
Extra-virgin olive oil	$8.99/liter	Extra-virgin olive oil (deluxe)	$15.98/liter	78%

*all products carry the Trader Joe's brand

Fig. 13.4   Price differences between key value items (KVI) and higher-end items at Trader Joe's [33]

symbolic benefits. This has helped the market share of such brands in Germany grow from 9.2% to 14% in the years from 2007 to 2017, mostly at the expense of established brands, which have steadily been losing market share [35, 36].

However, one should be careful when using discounts to improve one's price image. There is a risk that consumers' views on price and affordability will diverge when the discrepancies between the discounts and the normal prices get too large. A store may be perceived as particularly inexpensive or affordable on the temporarily discounted products, but not very affordable or attractive on items at normal prices. Such stores become preferred targets for bargain hunters. Empirical results support this presumption and the associated risks [28, pp. 134–137, 37].

In retail practice, the role of key value items is almost universally accepted as a guideline for pricing. As a result, there are three distinct kinds of items within an assortment, each of which is handled differently from a pricing standpoint. *Key value items* or *focus items* have a high influence on price perception. They are subject to price comparisons and influence consumer purchase frequency. Pricing for these articles therefore orients itself strongly on what competitors do. The critical factor in pricing these products is exact knowledge of competitors' prices, near real-time responses to price changes by competitors, and regional/local differentiation of prices based on the competitive situation in the territory served by the individual store. A typical example of these articles is milk: with the exception of some branded items, the bulk of revenue from milk is achieved at a uniform price. Similar to gasoline, which shows regional differences in price levels at gas stations, a retailer cannot afford to have its price for milk be noticeably out of line with competitors' prices in its local area. The more the product in question resembles a commodity, the greater the pressure is for uniform prices. In other words, it is very hard to differentiate milk. The product is standardized, regulation ensures uniform quality, and even the packaging is virtually identical.

For *fixed-price items* the price decision is taken by the manufacturer. The retailer does not have to deal with price-setting anymore. These include items which are governed by fixed-price guidelines or for which the retailer follows the manufacturer's suggested retail price (MSRP). Depending on the jurisdiction, fixed-price guidelines cover newspapers, magazines, books and cigarettes, as well as prescription medications. The category also includes items on which a branded manufacturer has pre-printed or pre-tagged the price (e.g., the price printed on the back cover of a book). This methodology saves the retailer some handling effort and is common for branded products in fashion retail. One must be careful, however, not to violate a retailer's rights to set prices independently because fixed-price arrangements can run afoul of antitrust or competition law [38]. In order to avoid this, it is recommended that the retailer explicitly asks the manufacturer for the price tag so that an unlawful restraint or restriction by the manufacturer can be ruled out. Nonetheless, the price tag should make reference to the price as being suggested or recommended, not binding.

The rest of the assortment comprises *skimming products*. These items have minimal influence on the price perception of the consumers and are difficult if not impossible to compare. The latter applies to a retailer's own brands or exclusive products. One should take price-volume relationships into account when setting prices for categories with a large number of items across many retail formats. This helps the retailer systematically extract willingness to pay.

13.3 Analysis

For the analysis, we distinguish between company, consumer, and competitor information. We limit ourselves to the specific aspects which are relevant for retail.

13.3.1 Company Information

Our general remarks on goals and costs apply to retail just as they apply to other sectors. Given the size of the assortments, an allocation of all costs—including costs such as sales or consulting/advisory costs—in the spirit of methods such as activity-based costing is unrealistic. For this reason, retailers generally use procurement costs for calculation. Because cost-plus pricing is in widespread use, the costs of goods play a key role in pricing for retailers. If the cost burden varies widely across products or categories, perhaps due to shipping, storage, advisory, or other operational costs, then it is recommended that these costs should be captured and included in the price calculation for the respective products or categories. This also applies to services which are not explicitly invoiced. When, for example, a pharmacy delivers a low-price medication to a patient's house, this particular transaction may not yield any profit. It needs to justify itself in terms of consumer value. Charging separately for services offers an important starting point for profit improvement in retail. A beverage supplier could, for example, consider charging for delivery. E-commerce for food and groceries with home delivery will probably not be economically viable without separate charges for delivery. In light of the low profit margins in retail, even small amounts of profit in return for those services can make a difference. Whether the payment for such additional services is made via higher prices for the items purchased or as an extra charge for the service is a question of consumer perception. Many suppliers shy away from charging a separate price for such services because this makes the costs more transparent to consumers in a price comparison vs. a "hidden" charge for the service in the form of a higher item price. More often than not, however, the opposite may apply. Hiding the service costs within the price of an item can turn into a competitive disadvantage when the comparing consumer focuses only on the price for the item itself and ignores the separate charges they would incur procuring the service from another provider.

When allocating costs, one needs to keep an eye on the split of costs into fixed and variable components. In the example of the pharmacy, personnel costs could be fixed, but the costs for the car trip to deliver the medication would be variable. The car-related costs would therefore be included in the cost accounting basis under an activity-based approach, but the personnel costs would not be. Yet this simple example illustrates that a complete and activity-based allocation of costs is hardly feasible in practice.

A thorough and comprehensive analysis of the margin and profit situation is extremely important. In light of the large assortment and differing margins, it is imperative that the store knows how much it earns from each product category and item. This information is not only important for price management but also relevant for assortment decisions, floor space allocation, and similar aspects. In this regard, many retail chains have made radical improvements over the last decades, thanks to innovations such as scanner cash registers, customer cards, RFID tags, and closed merchandise management systems [39]. This is especially true for e-commerce, which allows the capture of far more data than older systems. The emergence of Big Data has enabled even broader and deeper analyses of consumer behavior. Nonetheless, when it comes to price management, most retailers have not come close to tapping into the potential of the available data. The analytical capabilities of many retailers have not yet caught up with the technical possibilities.

13.3.2 Consumer Information

The methods described in Chap. 3 for determining price-relevant consumer infor-mation also apply to retail and thus do not require a fresh treatment here. Chapter 3 referred to several applications which originated in or saw primary usage in retail, including the determination of price-response functions using scanner or online data or price tests conducted by mail-order companies using test catalogs. When we distinguish between external consumer information (normally collected for a specific purpose) and internal consumer information (derived from the data the company has collected in the course of its normal business), the latter category plays a much more important role for retailers. In contrast to manufacturers, who often do not deal directly with end consumers, retailers deal directly with end consumers and therefore have more information about their behavior. In detail, what they can do depends on the concrete kinds of data they collect.

13.3.2.1 Scanner Registers

Scanner registers and similar point-of-sale systems make it possible to track and capture each and every sale, yielding a set of data a company can use to make very detailed analyses of consumer behavior with respect to price influence, reaction to price promotions, time-based behavioral patterns, and associated purchases. These analyses all fall under the overarching concept of "shopping basket analysis." But if the individual consumer cannot be identified via a customer card, shopping basket analysis cannot provide any meaningful insights into dynamic purchase patterns at the individual consumer level. However, they are useful for analyzing relationships across the purchase of certain items during one shopping trip. Such data permit the optimization of cross-selling activities at the item level. One can also draw conclusions applicable to price bundling, promotions, placement, and similar actions. But because the relevant receipt or shopping basket represents only one isolated shopping trip, one cannot draw conclusions about substitution effects, pull-forward effects, or other effects across time periods.

13.3.2.2 Customer Cards

Customer cards enable a retailer to track purchase behavior of consumers over time. They allow for a much deeper and richer analysis than scanner data alone. Customer card data provide the retailer with insights into consumer loyalty, consumer value, the effects of loyalty bonuses, etc. Combined with the data on the purchases of individual items, e.g., through scanner data, one can analyze associated purchases and shopping baskets at the individual consumer level. Based on these data and insights, a retailer can optimize prices across multiple products and promote cross-selling.

Figure 13.5 shows an application. Consumer A has previously only bought product groups one and two (PG1, PG2). An analysis of other consumers who also bought from PG1 and PG2 revealed that they buy particularly often from PG7 (50%) and PG6 (28.6%). One can therefore suspect that there is a high affinity between the buyers of PG1/PG2 and the cross-selling potential for PG6/PG7. On the next shopping trip, consumer A was offered products from PG6 and PG7 at very attractive test prices. The action was extremely successful. Customer cards have a high potential to support segmentation and price differentiation efforts. If a company succeeds in combining sociodemographic data with behavioral data such as purchases of an item within a certain price range or reactions to price changes, one can determine segments which can be targeted directly with price actions.

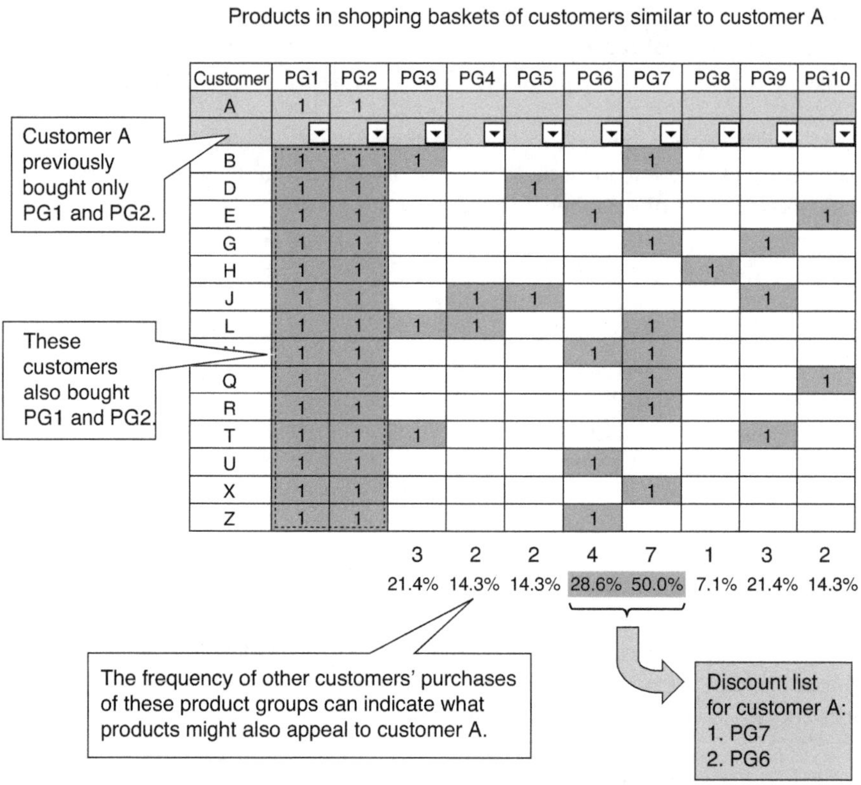

Products in shopping baskets of customers similar to customer A

Customer A previously bought only PG1 and PG2.

These customers also bought PG1 and PG2.

Customer	PG1	PG2	PG3	PG4	PG5	PG6	PG7	PG8	PG9	PG10
A	1	1								
	▾	▾	▾	▾	▾	▾	▾	▾	▾	▾
B	1	1	1				1			
D	1	1			1					
E	1	1				1				1
G	1	1					1		1	
H	1	1						1		
J	1	1		1	1				1	
L	1	1	1	1			1			
	1	1				1	1			
Q	1	1					1			1
R	1	1					1			
T	1	1	1						1	
U	1	1				1				
X	1	1					1			
Z	1	1				1				
			3	2	2	4	7	1	3	2
			21.4%	14.3%	14.3%	28.6%	50.0%	7.1%	21.4%	14.3%

The frequency of other customers' purchases of these product groups can indicate what products might also appeal to customer A.

Discount list for customer A:
1. PG7
2. PG6

Fig. 13.5 Identification of cross-selling potential using customer cards (Simon-Kucher & Partners)

13.3.2.3 E-Commerce

As discussed, e-commerce offers the greatest data and information potential. Online retailers such as Amazon or Zalando know exactly what their consumers buy. With little effort, they can conduct price tests in order to optimize prices. The possibilities from combining such consumer-specific data with the data from social networks such as LinkedIn, Facebook, or Twitter are nearly limitless. The efforts in e-commerce currently concentrate more on targeted messaging, advertising, and active sales than on price management. This is astounding because a reliable information basis for price management is rather easy to establish. One must, however, be able to conduct targeted price tests. The large assortments are a limiting factor. Even in e-commerce, one cannot realistically test the price elasticity for hundreds or thousands of items. Furthermore, the analysis of historical data on volume and price is subject to the limitations we discussed in great detail in Chap. 3. One idea would be to automate the measurement of price elasticities and the subsequent price decisions. In theory, this approach is feasable for e-commerce, but it also carries risks, because the data analyses may occasionally yield price elasticity values which are nonsense. In other words, testing the results for face validity is still necessary. It remains to be seen whether the automated analysis of price effects, in whole or in part, becomes a widespread practice.

13.3.2.4 Analysis of Price Promotions

Because price promotions play such an important role in retail, a deeper analysis of this phenomenon is required. Price promotions include discounts as well as numerous other forms of temporary price reductions. An analysis of the effects of price promotions and discounts poses questions such as:

- How do discounts work?
- Which items are suitable for discounting?
  - Familiar or less well-known brands?
  - New or mature/established brands?
  - Perishable or stock-up products?
  - Consumables or durable goods?
- What range should the assortment of discounted products cover?
- How much should the prices be reduced?
- When should the discount period begin and how long should it last?
- How frequently should discounts be used?
- When should discounts be used within a season?
- Should discounts be offered in the same channel or in separate channels?

For most of these questions, there are no general, empirically validated answers. A comprehensive assessment of discounts is difficult because the overall effect results from a variety of hard-to-capture partial effects created by the interplay across three types of items:

- The items offered at the discounted prices
- The other items in that category (substitutes)
- The rest of the assortment (potential for associated purchases)

To get an overall assessment, one must not only focus on the effects in the discount period but include the dynamic effects which influence behavior in subsequent time periods. "It is very important for retailers to track post-promotion movement of items for at least two weeks. Some items do very well on promotion but then tend to drop off more sharply than others," one author explains. Consumers learn to anticipate when discounts will occur and limit their new purchases to those periods. Consumers use these opportunities to stock up ("pantry filling"), which makes a volume decline in the periods right after the discount almost inevitable [40]. Furthermore, it makes sense to differentiate between normal consumers (the ones who come to the store regardless of discounts) and bargain hunters, who are only attracted to the store when items they want are on discount. Summarizing these effects results in the system shown in Table 13.2.

The signs in the top row for each item category symbolize the volume change, when Item A is on discount. The signs in the bottom row for each item category

Table 13.2 System of short- and medium-term effects of discounts

Item category	Normal consumers		"Bargain hunters"	
	Discount period t	Subsequent period $t + \tau$	Discount period t	Subsequent period $t + \tau$
Discounted item(s)	+/0	+/0	+	+
	+	−	+	0
Other products from the discounted item's category (substitutes)	0	0	0	+
	−	−	0	0
Rest of the assortment	0	0	+	+
	−/0	0	0	0

apply analogously to Item B, when it is offered on discount ("+" means volume growth, "0" no change, "−" volume decline). A and B show very different patterns.
Item A:
Offering Item A on discount causes the following effects:
Normal consumers:

- Buy the same amount or more of A in discount period t and in subsequent periods $t + \tau$ (positive carryover).
- Increased purchases of A are not at the expense of substitutes.
- The rest of the assortment is unaffected.

Bargain hunters:

- Buy A in t and $t + \tau$.
- Also buy substitutes in $t + \tau$ because they become regular consumers.
- Buy the rest of the assortment in t (associated purchases) and $t + \tau$ (as regular consumers).

Item B:
In contrast, the following effects occur when Item B is sold on discount:
Normal consumers:

- Buy more of B in t and less in $t + \tau$ (purchases are "borrowed" from the future, Item B will be stored, negative carryover).
- Increased purchases of B occur at the expense of substitutes in t and $t + \tau$.
- The rest of the assortment is unaffected, or rather, in t purchasing power will be shifted in favor of the increased purchases of B.

Bargain hunters:

- Buy only B in t (bargain hunting); there are no associated purchases in t, nor do these buyers become regular consumers.

It is apparent that A and B are extreme opposites in their suitability for discounting. The overall effects of the discount for Item A are positive, while Item B is very poorly suited to be offered on discount. The two opposite cases make clear that the effects of discounting a product are complex.

In addition to the short- and medium-term effects, one must consider the long-term influence that discounts have on the price image of the retailer. It is an illusion to think that one can analytically quantify all these effects with precision. With the help of scanner and e-commerce data, one can at least measure some of the major effects, e.g., the sales volume of the discounted item in the discount period and in subsequent periods. The table provides a useful structure for analyzing these complex effects. One should at least consider these effects in qualitative form.

13.3.3 Competitor Information

As explained, competitors' prices play a preeminent role in retail. This is true to such an extent that a large part of the price decision authority is de facto delegated to competitors. In other words, many retailers more or less strictly follow the price setting of certain competitors who are recognized as price leaders. This applies at least for key value items. For skimming items, for which one uses less strict pricing policies, retailers may still closely monitor their competitors' prices in a timely fashion.

In consumer retail, it is rather easy to acquire price-related information on competitors. That applies to brick-and-mortar retail and especially to online retail. Because consumers have access to prices, competitors can slip into the "consumer" role and gain access to the same information. One refers to "mystery shopping" in this context. For online retail, the competitors' mystery shoppers do not even need to leave their offices. Collecting competitors' prices requires a certain level of diligence, speed, and care, but the task does not rise to the level of a covert intelligence operation. One can also turn to market research agencies or apps which have specialized in retail prices and collect such information on a regular basis. Diffbot.com is a major innovation in this area. It uses artificial intelligence to collect information on competitors' prices. Diffbot.com crawls sites and then extracts the complete data in a structured form from the web page. This can be done automatically or manually.

But situations still arise in which it is difficult to collect information on prices and/or discounts. A typical example is the automotive sector, where the actual, agreed-to discount levels are not fully transparent. Even when market researchers conduct mystery shopping for a car and negotiate a discount with a dealer, the results they achieve and the information they acquire have limited validity. Acquiring information on competitors' prices is even more difficult in B2B retail, where prices are often negotiated. Buyers can be reluctant to share price information or may even intentionally cite incorrect (misleading) prices.

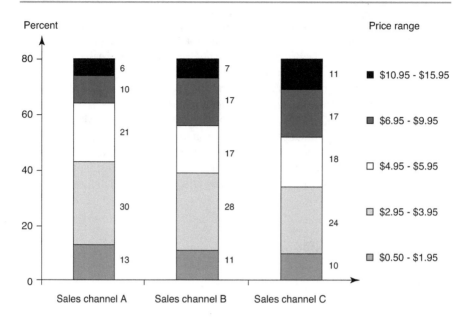

Fig. 13.6 Price ranges for three sales channels (Simon-Kucher & Partners)

13.4   Decision

Retail-specific aspects of price decisions cover the setting of price ranges and prices for individual items, pricing for associated products, as well as price promotions.

13.4.1 Setting Price Ranges

The starting point for a price decision in retail is the setting of a price range and its architecture. Figure 13.6 shows a case for an American retail chain which operates in three channels, each with a different positioning. A is the lowest priced with an average price per item of $3.72, while B lies in the medium range at $4.02. Channel C has the highest price position with an average price per item of $4.66.

Beyond the average price, however, there is an insufficient level of differentiation in this case. The distribution of the individual price ranges in all three channels is similar. The lack of differentiation cannot be alleviated solely through price levels; it requires further-reaching measures such as a redesign of the stores and/or shifts in the assortments.

The chosen price range lends structure, clarity, and transparency to the assortment a retailer offers. This makes it easier for consumers to orient themselves and form a price image. A good price range architecture assures better assortment controlling and reduces the complexity of retail price management, because the price ranges manifest the retailer's desired price position. But there are also risks. When a retailer adheres too rigidly to a pre-defined price range, it reduces flexibility vs. the competition. On the other hand, too many exceptions will render the price range architecture ineffective. One should also be careful not to allocate too many items into one price range. In one European supermarket, some 70% of the jams and jellies cost around €2, while only 10% cost around €1 and 20% around €3. Too large a "bulge" at €2 delivers hardly any added value to the consumers. Reducing the size of that "bulge" would improve the array of choices for the consumers [41].

One must take the consumers' willingness to pay into account when building a price range architecture. One starts by setting the price thresholds, determined either through consumer surveys or internal analyses. If the price ranges are considered in line with market conditions, then costs must be adjusted to fit them. That means that in the spirit of target costing with a desired target margin, the retailer should only procure those items which achieve target profitability. Several retailers use target prices as guidance for positioning their store brands, which have a different price position than manufacturer-branded products. The British food and grocery retailer Tesco offers the store brands Tesco Value, Tesco Standard, and Tesco Finest with two objectives in mind: to signal its own affordability in competition with discounters and at the same time to offer its consumers premium products.

13.4.2 Price Decisions for Individual Items

Rules of thumb are the dominant method used by retailers when setting prices for individual items. The quantification of price elasticity is the exception to the rule. Pricing software can measure price elasticities in some instances in rudimentary form. The elasticities are sometimes calculated automatically, e.g., based on scanner data, and should be viewed skeptically with respect to their validity.

13.4.2.1 Rules of Thumb
Pricing in retail is characterized by rules of thumb and cost-plus pricing to an even greater extent than in other industries. The basis for the markup is generally the cost of goods, plus additional operating or trading costs in some cases. Normally the markups in retail do not follow a uniform scheme. Instead, they are differentiated according to experienced-based criteria. In practice, the rules of thumb for differentiation include, among others [31, 42–46]:

- Rule 1: The lower the price is in absolute terms, the higher the markup percentage should be.
- Rule 2: The markup factor should be lower, the greater the velocity of inventory turns is.
- Rule 3: For products for which consumers have a particularly strong price perception (key value items such as bread, milk, butter, or gasoline), the markup factors should be very low.

- Rule 4: The markups for mass merchandise should be lower than those for specialty products.
- Rule 5: The markups should be oriented on the competition.

13.4.2.2 Theoretical Considerations

The pricing for an individual item is a classic one-product case, for which the optimal price is determined by the Amoroso-Robinson relation (5.6):

$$p^* = \frac{\varepsilon}{1 + \varepsilon} C' \tag{13.1}$$

In other words, the optimal price results from a markup on marginal costs. The markup factor depends on the price elasticity. The formula—and thus the cost-plus pricing approach—is an optimal decision-making rule of thumb when the price elasticity ε and the marginal costs C' are constant. Within a narrow interval, the Amoroso-Robinson relation can be seen as a useful and theoretical basis for cost-plus pricing in retail.

One can indeed find convincing arguments to justify the rules of thumb described above:

- Rule 1: Higher markup factors on (absolute) low prices. This rule follows directly from the fact that the price elasticity rises with the absolute level of the price, i.e., price changes on higher prices (in absolute terms) tend to have a greater effect on volume.
- Rule 2: Lower markup factors for higher velocity of inventory turnover: Higher inventory turnover tends to be synonymous with more frequent purchases by an individual consumer. The assumption is that a buyer knows the prices better for items they purchase more frequently and would react more sensitively to price changes on those items than they would on items they purchase less often. It follows that the price elasticity would be higher (in absolute terms).
- Rule 3: Lower markup factors on key value items. In this case, the higher price elasticity results from the strength of the consumers' price perception.
- Rules 4 and 5: The justification for these rules of thumb is self-evident.

One should be careful, however, when passing along the full amount of a cost increase to consumers. If the price-response function is linear, it is not recommended to pass along the full amount. When the wholesale price of milk in Germany rose by €0.10, ALDI raised its retail prices by only €0.07 (see Chap. 9). ALDI [47] promises: "Whenever we have the opportunity, e.g. when raw materials prices fall, we pass along these savings to our customers right away through lower prices."

Because of the extent of the assortment, an exact measurement of price elasticity and the price-response function come into play at best for important items. But retail managers generally have a rather concrete idea of approximate price effects and price elasticities. An explicit, elasticity-oriented calculation method is foreign to the retail sector; instead, it is practiced without the theory in mind and is implicitly expressed in the rules of thumb we have discussed above.

The elasticity-oriented markup calculation can offer a starting point for pricing which is decentralized by category. In such systems, senior management sets average markup factors by category for the department heads. These factors reflect the respective "category elasticities." Within a category, the price calculator can determine the markups according to assumed item-specific price elasticities, as long as the markups are in line with the prescribed averages. In order for this method to be feasible, the retailer's team must understand the basic principles of professional price management.

The purchasing departments of retailers, however, often lack precise knowledge about consumers' willingness to pay. This stems from the predominant division of labor between purchasing and warehouse management. Purchasing sets the prices; the warehouse manager is responsible for acquiring the necessary goods. Once the price is set, the volume is essentially determined by the planned revenue.

A prerequisite of professional price management is that these separate ways of thinking are bridged. The buyer must understand that the price should be set as a function of the achievable volume, and not the other way around. Implementing this way of thinking requires a systematic, incremental trial-and-error approach to finding the optimal price: the buyer estimates the sales volume for different end consumer (retail) prices for an item, and then the contribution margin should be calculated for each price-volume estimate. This helps the buyer determine the profit-maximizing price.

Of course, the buyer's price decisions should be supported by making all relevant information available. This can include additional sales volume and price data for reference items. Reference items are items which exhibit similar price-volume behavior. One should also tap into external databases which contain information on competitors' prices and sales volumes. Price tests make sense in exceptional situations, in order to get a thorough evaluation of the fundamental interrelationships within an assortment. The results of price tests serve as a means to validate the buyer's estimates and the resulting optimal prices. At the same time, the buyers can learn from the test results by comparing their own estimates with the test results and using the latter as guidance for future estimates. The difference between this approach and more automated software-driven approaches is that the information systems support the buyers in their decision-making, but do not replace them. The subjective knowledge of the buyers is fully reflected in the ultimate estimates.

If elasticities are estimated, one can derive indications or hints for price increases or decreases for individual items. The price elasticities and the profit margins are captured at the category level. One should reduce the prices of products which have high elasticities at the category level and medium to high profit margins. In contrast, one should raise the prices of products with a low category price elasticity. Figure 13.7 illustrates the respective categories. With the help of this differentiated process, retailers and other businesses with similarly large and extensive assortments can achieve significant profit improvements.

Fig. 13.7 Pricing
recommendations depending
on price elasticity and profit
margin

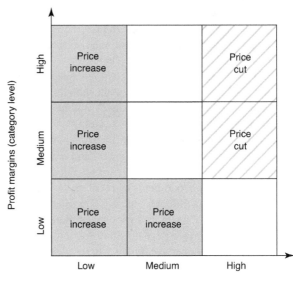

Price elasticity (category level)

The elasticity-oriented pricing applies primarily to skimming items, less so for fixed-price items or key value items. Competition-oriented pricing dominates for key value items. What counts is the assortment effect and not the contribution margin of the individual item. Key value items, similar to discounted items, are supposed to attract consumers into the store, i.e., they serve as traffic builders. Their direct profit contribution is secondary.

13.4.3 Price Decisions and Assortment Effects

As explained at the beginning of this chapter, it is advantageous for consumers to purchase many different items at one location ("one-stop shopping") because it reduces their search and acquisition costs. This is especially true for food and grocery shopping, but related or associated purchases also play an important role in other retail sectors such as clothing/fashion, gas stations, and home improvement stores.

One consequence of such associated purchases is that the cross-price elasticities between many items are not zero. A price cut for item j attracts new consumers, who buy not only that item but other items as well. These assortment effects in retail are often complementary, even if a strict technical- or usage-based complementarity does not exist between the products. Instead, the complementarity is induced by the shopping trip itself.

We discussed the case of complementary volume relationships in Chap. 6 and can draw on the respective conclusions and statements on price optimization from that chapter. The overall optimal price p_j relative to the isolated optimal price, which does not take assortment effects into account, will *ceteris paribus* be lower:

- The greater the number of products which are complementary
- The greater the cross-price elasticities of the complementary items are (in absolute terms)
- The larger the contribution margins of the complementary items are
- The closer the direct price elasticity of product j is to 1
- The greater the ratio of the sales volumes of complementary items i and j is

Interpreted in a simple way, these statements mean that the more an item contributes to the overall sales volume and to the profit of the assortment, the lower its price should be. The condition is a mathematically precise formulation of the retail pricing policy known as mixed calculation. In retail stores, as is generally true for multi-product companies, the goal is not to maximize the profit of each individual item, but rather to achieve the largest possible profit for the assortment as a whole. That means that the optimal price of an individual item might even be below marginal costs or theoretically even be negative [48]. We call these products "loss leaders."

Here, we will use a simplification of the optimality condition (6.8). This simplification is based on observable combined purchases. If there are on average a_{ij} units of i purchased when a consumer buys item j, and j is the reason for the purchase of i (i.e., the consumer would not have bought i without having bought j), we can describe the optimality condition as:

$$p_j^* = \frac{\varepsilon_j}{1 + \varepsilon_j}\left(C' - m_j\right) \tag{13.2}$$

with

$$m_j = \sum_{\substack{i=1 \\ i \neq j}}^{n} a_{ij}\left(p_i - C'_i\right) \tag{13.3}$$

m_j reflects the sum of the contribution margins from other products whose sales/purchases were caused by the purchase of j. This contribution margin is equivalent to a reduction of item j's marginal costs. The greater the extent that item j drives sales of other items, the lower the optimal price of j is.

An example illustrates these interrelationships. In a clothing store, a consumer who buys a suit also purchases on average two shirts and 1.33 ties. The average contribution margin per piece for shirts and ties is $15. The price-response function for suits is estimated as follows:

$$q = 1,000 - 2p \tag{13.4}$$

which results in a maximum price of $500. If marginal costs are $200, the optimal price for a suit is $350 without taking associated purchases into account. The price elasticity is -2.33. The markup factor according to the Amoroso-Robinson relation is 1.75 ($200 \times 1.75 = 350$). The store sells 300 suits. These sales induce additional sales of 600 shirts and 400 ties. The resulting contribution margins are:

- $45,000 for suits
- $9000 for shirts
- $6000 for ties
- $60,000 all total

If one incorporates the associated purchases into the pricing for suits, the marginal costs of a suit should be reduced by $(2 + 1.33) \times 15 = \$50$. The new optimal price for a suit would be $325 or $25 less than the isolated optimal price of $350. The store sells more units of all three products: 350 suits ($+50$), 700 shirts ($+100$), and 466 ties ($+66$). The new contribution margins are:

- $43,750 for suits
- $10,500 or shirts
- $6990 for ties

The total contribution margin is $61,240, which exceeds the isolated optimization by $1240 or 2.07%. The store earns $1250 less in contribution margin from suits, but this decline is more than offset by higher contribution margins from shirts and ties.

As we described in the analysis section, one can measure these complementary coefficients without much effort using the data from scanners, customer cards, or e-commerce. The relationships revealed can provide retail managers valuable decision support.

13.4.4 Decisions on Price Promotions

Price promotions involve temporary, short-term price reductions for selected items. They can come in many forms, including discounts, special package sizes, loyalty discounts, coupons, or refunds. We already pointed out that these tactics are not backed or supported by corresponding, robust knowledge about the direct and indirect effects of price promotions. Many of the rules which are accepted in practice have neither a theoretical nor an empirical foundation. We will concentrate here on the most common consumer-focused price promotions in retail. These can be initiated by the manufacturer or by the retailer. The consumer generally does not know which party was the initiator.

13.4.4.1 Forms of Price Promotions

With respect to the required decisions, we describe the forms of price promotions as follows:

- Discounts mean that the price is reduced temporarily on a product which remains otherwise unchanged. The decision on discount involves the level, the duration, and the frequency. Discounts are often supported by special advertising. The discounted price can be above, at, or below the retailer's cost of goods. The consumer will often orient themselves toward the amount of the discount relative to the normal price, which serves as the price anchor. In some countries, selling below the cost of goods is forbidden for companies with a dominant market position, unless the sales are occasional/infrequent or have an objective business justification. One discounter in Germany violated this law when it offered various dairy products at 40% below the respective cost of goods. Germany's competition authorities made the provisions of the law more precise in this regard by stating that the limits for "occasional/infrequent" are exceeded when such an offer occurs for more than 3 weeks in a half-year period [49].
- Special package sizes mean that the package size is changed. The absolute price may actually remain the same, but the unit price (per kilo, liter, ounce, pound, gallon, etc.) changes. The most common form is an increase in the actual package size. Gillette regularly carries out this approach with shaving cream. One can also offer several packages of the same product at a reduced total price. Another common approach is to offer a free unit of a product when the consumer buys one (or several) units, which is known in retail as "buy one, get one" or BOGO. The key decisions are how much larger the special package has to be made.
- Loyalty discounts offer consumers a reduced price if they make repeat purchases. The key decisions are the level of the discount and the conditions. The drugstore and warehouse chain Müller employs a special form of loyalty discount. On the consumers' receipts, they print a coupon for 3% off the entire next purchase.
- Price advantages mean that certain consumer groups receive preferential lower prices. A special aspect of this approach is the communication of the price advantages. They are also visible to those consumers who are not in the preferred group and therefore need to pay regular prices. The drugstore chain Rite Aid offers many products at permanently reduced prices to consumers who are members of the points program Plenti, which is similar to PAYBACK in Europe. The price tags at the shelf inform consumers about the regular price as well as the reduced price. Its competitor CVS does the same, posting different prices based on whether the consumer has a CVS card. The objective of the open communication is to motivate consumers who are not in the store's program to join and therefore gain access to the lower prices.
- Couponing involves the distribution of discount or other coupons via newspapers, in-store displays, the Internet, or other media. The consumer can redeem them at the point of sale to receive a product for free or purchase it at a reduced price. The decisions here are the face value of the coupon and its terms and conditions. Couponing is well established and extremely popular in the United States, but the

practice is not nearly as widespread in other developed countries. A growing area within couponing is check-out couponing. Upon checkout, the consumer receives special coupons whose products and amounts are based on an automated analysis of the goods just purchased. When someone buys two bottles of wine, for example, the store may offer a coupon which the consumer can redeem the next time and get a lower price. If someone buys beer brand A, the store may offer a discount coupon for brand B or store brand C. Many stores use this opportunity to distribute coupons for complementary products. The purchase of tortilla chips may trigger the issuance of a coupon for salsa, or the purchase of diapers may trigger a coupon for the purchase of baby wipes. This method is quite effective and can be personalized when a customer card allows to access the consumer's purchase history. On the basis of such customer card information, the UK retail chain Tesco sends its consumers individualized coupons via email. Another retailer in Europe applies a similar approach in-store. After the customer's card is scanned, the store prints coupons at the register which reflect not only the immediate purchase but also the consumer's overall purchase behavior, as recorded via the card [50]. This method fits the mold of what we described as cross-selling mechanisms in the analysis section. It can serve to drive higher sales and also to attract consumers to other products. Compared to conventional couponing, the scatter loss is low, and an exact measurement of success is possible [50]. An inherent advantage of couponing is that it does not represent a blanket price reduction which benefits all consumers. In the spirit of price differentiation, the only ones who benefit from the coupons are those consumers who meet the conditions and actually redeem the coupon. The price remains unchanged for all other consumers. Because of these advantages, one can expect an increase in the use of coupons.

- Another form of retail price promotion which should gain traction in the future is the rebate. In the past, the consumer needed to go through the tedious process of sending their purchase receipt to the manufacturer in order to receive a partial refund on the price paid. This process has become simpler with the advent of the smartphone. The cash-back mobile apps SavingStar, Scondoo (Germany), and Checkout51 (Canada) offer numerous actions which enable the consumer to get an immediate rebate after buying products. The consumer takes a picture of the receipt with a smartphone and uses the respective app to upload the photo. The money is then disbursed or put into an account. The advantage for the manufacturer is that it eliminates the intricate coordination process with retailers and allows rebates across all participating retailers.

Most retailers use price promotions. This observation seems to speak for their effectiveness. Studies on the effectiveness of price promotions, however, show that such actions are often not profitable for the retailer [51]. Studies revealed that certain retail managers devote 80% of their time to the management of promotions, although these actions only contribute 20% of revenues [52]. Against this background, it is no surprise that some retailers have virtually eliminated discounts in favor of an EDLP approach, e.g., the German drugstore chain dm [53]. Walmart is operating likewise.

Making a comprehensive assessment of the profit effect of price promotions remains difficult. No general or simple rules of thumb have emerged despite a large number of scientific studies [1]. Distinguishing between short-term and long-term effects is essential.

13.4.4.2 Short-Term Effects

Typically, discounts in retail generate significantly higher sales volumes during the promotional period. The short-term price elasticities of discounts are typically higher (in absolute terms) than the elasticities based on normal price changes [54]. Discounting is therefore an effective method when the objective is to drive sales volume in the short term, e.g., to clear a warehouse or sell off excess inventory.

Volume increases of several hundred percent can occur when the discount offers are supported by displays, handouts, and flyers, or through in-store media such as video monitors or public address announcements [55]. According to one study, some 41% of price promotions were enhanced and supported with additional measures [56]. Maximum purchase limits in conjunction with price reductions can also induce higher sales volumes [57]. Time restrictions, such as those built into limited time offers, likewise drive short-term sales volumes higher.

Ivens [58] criticizes correctly that the assessment of price promotions typically overemphasizes the short-term volume effects. The reason is that these are easy to measure. Yet short-term increases in volume do not necessarily lead to higher profits. Often the opposite is the case, and the company experiences a decline in profit. The primary reason for this is that the additional volume is not sufficient to compensate for the lower unit contribution. Let us assume that the gross margin is 25% and the discount will be 20%. In that case, volume would need to increase fivefold in order to increase profit. That implies a price elasticity of 20 (400% more volume/20% price reduction). Such a high price elasticity is extremely rare, even for discounted items.

The pull-forward effect of promotions occurs frequently, meaning that the short-term increases in volume are actually advance or stock-up purchases ("pantry filling") by consumers. Consumers buy more packages of Tide when it is on sale, but they do not increase their overall consumption. According to one study [50], using the data from the US drugstore chain CVS, some 10% of the volume increase from price promotions results from pantry filling and 45% from brand-switching within the store. Instead of buying cream from Nivea, for example, the store's regular consumer buys L'Oréal when the latter is on sale. But from the retailer's perspective, in contrast to the manufacturers', it does not matter whether the revenue of the promoted or discounted item rises. What matters is the revenue and profit performance of the entire category in that store [59].

More important for the retailer is the question of whether the short-term volume increase is attributable to more consumption from existing consumers or to purchases from consumers who have switched stores. According to the study using the data from CVS [51], some 45% of the total volume increase represents a "true" volume increase, i.e., higher consumption from existing consumers or acquisition of new consumers. Next to consumer retention, getting consumers to switch stores is the primary goal. The idea is to attract new consumers to the store in the hope that those consumers purchase other products with higher margins. The closer other competing stores are nearby, the greater the probability of store switching [60]. Price promotions with volume or size advantages—i.e., price promotions based on the purchase of larger package sizes or a larger number of packages—often lead to a true increase in consumption [61]. "Once it is in the fridge, the kids take care of it," a marketing executive at Coca-Cola said.

Premium and luxury goods stores deserve special mention regarding price promotions. As argued in Chap. 2, discounting and similar price actions are rather incompatible with a premium price position. This is even more true for a luxury price position. Even these price segments, however, cannot escape the fact that fashion items lose value when they are out of season and can only be sold at deep discounts (often 50%). Luxury goods sellers, however, try to avoid such sales side by side with their current seasonal lines. The discounted goods are often removed from the high-priced retail stores and sold in separate outlets located in a significant distance away from the front-line stores. Another way to address this issue is to invite selected consumers to a sales event otherwise closed to the public. The luxury retailer Quartier 206 in Berlin takes this approach, as do luxury jewelers and high-end fashion houses in the United States.

Online price promotions have the advantage that a retailer can address individual consumers directly. This allows them to achieve more specific price differentiation across consumer segments [56]. We therefore expect online price promotions to become significantly more widespread and frequent.

13.4.4.3 Long-Term Effects

The long-term effects of price promotions can be positive or negative, but the quantification of these effects is more difficult than for short-term ones. The focus of interest relates to the effects on brand, shopping location, and price image.

On the one hand, retailers hope that the consumers they have attracted through the discounts become accustomed to using their brand or their locations and continue to prefer them. This can be seen as the "carryover" or loyalty effect which we described in Chap. 7. On the other hand, there is a risk that consumers grow accustomed instead to the regular promotions, which condition them to buy only when products are on sale. Consumers adjust their buying behavior to the promotional cycles of the retailers [62]. Lodish and Mela [63, p. 6] note that: "Consumers now lie in wait for a deal. If they are lying in wait for the next deal, they are not buying at the normal price."

Thanks to the internet, getting information about available discounts has become dramatically easier. One can assume that this will only strengthen consumers' discount "habit" and enhance their systematic searching for discounted offers.

Discounts can have a negative effect on future buying decisions when consumers associate the lower prices with lower quality [64, 65]. Discounts also create lower price anchors and reference prices, so that the absence of a discount leads consumers to perceive that the products are too expensive. Interestingly, according to the results of one study, this applies to a lesser extent when the item is offered as a "buy one, get one" than when the item is offered at a discounted price [66]. In general, price promotions carry the risk—independent of the shopping location or the brand—that they reduce consumers' loyalty to products or locations in favor of loyalty to price promotions [67].

Ambivalent effects are possible with respect to the price image of a retailer. On the one hand, discounts do contribute to a favorable or affordable price image and have an effect in this regard similar to everyday low prices. On the other hand, they may lead to an inconsistent or diffuse price image, with the inexpensive discount items sharing the aisles with more expensive, normally priced items. In extreme cases, this can lead to a split price image: "this store has low sale prices, but other items are expensive."

All in all, it is not possible to make general statements on whether discounts are advantageous in either the short or the long term. Retail managers need to realize that discounts may have a negative impact on consumers' future buying decisions, despite the increased sales volumes in the short term. The use of price promotions and discounts must be in harmony with the price strategy and the fundamental price positioning. Retailers who strive for a premium position should use discounts sparingly. Discounts are indispensable, however, for mass market retailers. Even Walmart, which adheres very strictly to its EDLP strategy and communicates that to its consumers, makes use of discounts ("roll back" actions). Retailers should also be very careful when they select which items and categories to discount.

13.5 Implementation

Regarding implementation, we will limit our discussion to retail-specific aspects of organization and monitoring.

13.5.1 Organizational Aspects

The price decision is allocated relatively high up (senior management level) and centralized in many retail organizations. In line with this top-down approach, senior managers develop guidelines for pricing together with the department leaders and set the revenue and profit targets. They also determine the price ranges for individual product categories and product groups. Figure 13.8 shows a typical organizational structure for a retailer.

On the basis of the predetermined goals and guidance, the purchasing department develops operational goals for the respective planning period. Price ranges are set for individual product groups. The planned sales volumes are based on historical sales volume data and market assessments.

Finally, using the targets for sales volume, price range, revenue, and profit as a basis, the purchasing department procures the merchandise. The selling prices tend to be determined prior to the procurement of the goods. One refers to this process as price-based target costing, which means that the selling price determines the

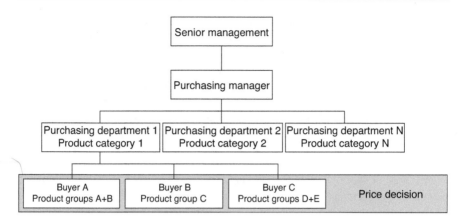

Fig. 13.8 Typical organizational structure and pricing responsibilities for a retailer

procurement price [68]. This process is typical for retail and explains why retailers respond to changes in demand by volume adjustments rather than price changes. During the World Cup soccer tournament in Brazil in 2014, retailers responded to the higher demand for soccer balls by increasing volumes, not by raising prices. Retailers tend to take prices within a certain range as given and react instead with volume adjustments. That behavior is different, for example, from what hotels do during peak demand periods such as trade fairs. Hotels often react by raising prices to multiples of normal prices (see Chap. 6). The reason for the difference is that the hotels have fixed capacity, while retailers can adjust their volumes as long as they have sufficient lead time.

The associated relationships we have already discussed must be considered in the retailer's organizational structure and goals. Key value items or loss leaders should be assessed according to different criteria than normal products. This affects incentives. An incentive system based solely on product groups can be disadvantageous for overall profit when individual product groups are particularly well suited to serving as key value items or loss leaders.

A difficult topic is the allocation of price authority between centralized and decentralized units. As mentioned, price decision-making shows a relatively strong centralization in retail. At ALDI, for example, price decisions are made centrally except in special cases such as for perishable goods. In the gas station business, headquarters generally set prices as well. Some retailers do not permit any regional price differentiation, which means practically all decisions are taken centrally. At one large European retailer, privately owned stores have some latitude in setting prices, with the exception of store brands. The more common situation, though, is that most prices are set centrally, but the decentralized managers, usually the district or store managers, do possess a certain level of pricing authority. This could apply to regional products, close-out merchandise, perishable goods, seasonal clearance sales, and similar categories. It can make sense to allow a store manager to take local circumstances and consumer needs into account in price setting. The local

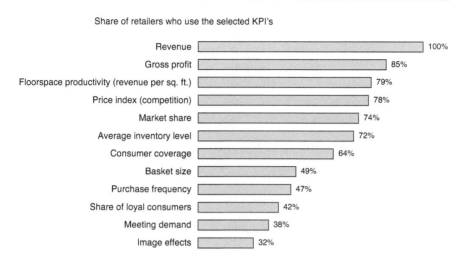

Fig. 13.9 Importance of key performance indicators for monitoring/controlling in retail [69, p. 7]

operations managers for Media Markt and Saturn, two large electronics retailers in Europe, hold shares in their stores and can set prices independently. In many cases, a more pronounced decentralization of price authority is worth considering. However, it must be supported by the right incentive system as well as proper training for the decision-makers.

13.5.2 Controlling

Controlling—in the sense of monitoring realized prices and profit margins—is, due to complexity, an extremely important task in retail. Senior management must know what prices and margins have been achieved in which stores and when. Retailers must also keep a constant watch on prices relative to competitors' prices. Figure 13.9 shows the importance of key performance indicators which managers at leading retailers use for ongoing monitoring.

Only three of these KPIs—the revenue, the gross profit, and the price index of competitors—have a direct relation to price. Price-based KPIs or benchmarks, such as relative prices for the business overall or for product categories, price and cross-price elasticities, data on price positioning, and the frequency and extent of price promotions did not appear in this study. This finding confirms our suspicion that most retailers still have a long way to go in the professionalization of price management.

13.5.3 Price Communication

There are retail-specific aspects to consider in price communication. These include price image communication, price presentation at the point of sale, and the advertising of price promotions.

Many retailers focus their advertising consistently over long periods on their price image. Well-known examples from around the world include:

- The eyewear chain Fielmann (market leader in Europe): Their slogan "My dad didn't even need to pay a single penny" has evolved into "glasses at no cost." If a consumer purchases insurance for €10 per year, he or she receives a new pair of glasses free of charge every 2 years. Both slogans express the idea that Fielmann sells glasses without any payment beyond what health insurers' cover, meaning that the price for consumers is truly zero.
- The discounter Walmart used the slogan "Always low prices. Always." then changed it later to "Save Money. Live Better."
- More and more retailers are combining a price message with a performance aspect, preferring expressions of quality and service. The fashion retailer H&M uses the slogan "fashion and quality at the best price" and Best Buy (US) uses "Expert Service. Unbeatable Price."
- The German drugstore chain dm practiced a very unusual communication related to price image. Colgate-Palmolive reduced the package size of the toothpaste brand Dentagard from 100 to 75 ml but kept the price constant. That corresponds to a massive, disguised price increase of 33.3%. The drugstore chain reacted by leaving the shelf space for Dentagard empty except for a sign with the headline "Same price for less product: we protest!" and an accompanying explanation [70]. On the one hand, a retailer's calling out a manufacturer so publicly is unusual. Normally such conflicts between manufacturers and retailers play out behind the scenes, out of sight of the consumers. On the other hand, the retailer assumes the role of watchdog or advocate for the consumer and attempts to enhance its price image, in the spirit of "we pay attention to low prices and keep manufacturers from playing tricks." This highly visible and public incident was negative price communication for Colgate-Palmolive and the Dentagard brand.

In these cases, the retailers achieved the intended effect, namely, to convey an affordable price image. The length, consistency, and frequency all play a role in the success of these kinds of campaigns. The fact that the retailers changed the content of the campaign after several years leads us to suspect that the power of such pure price-related messages wanes after a certain amount of time. At the same time, a purely price-driven image campaign can backfire. The example of the German home improvement chain Praktiker illustrates this. Praktiker used the slogan "20 percent off everything" for many years, but eventually had to file for bankruptcy.

Price communication at the point of sale is very important. The instruments range from a gas station's large price displays (visible from passing cars) to price tags at the shelf or on the item itself. There can be no doubt that the prominent, easy-to-understand price communication constrains the pricing latitude of neighboring gas stations. Regarding the price tags or displays for individual items, Wi-Fi-enabled electronic shelf labels or ESL have brought important changes. They enable retailers to change prices electronically in seconds from a remote location (e.g. from head-quarters) or from within the store. This saves on personnel costs because the retailer no longer needs to change shelf labels by hand for each promotion. On the other hand, retailers can now conduct promotions more flexibly and on shorter notice, e.g. to respond to larger price fluctuations from online retailers. This is especially important for key value items as most retailers respond immediately to price changes made by their close competitors.

Price promotions and discounts are often supported by advertising. Many discounters take out full-page newspaper advertisements on a weekly basis, while others distribute flyers or supplements. Radio and television are also used for advertising special offers. The price is at the forefront of these campaigns. The advertisements often show the regular prices crossed out; this is especially true at point of sale where the discounted price appears with the crossed-out normal price, often with the discount expressed in percentage terms as well. Such messages use the price anchor effect which we discussed in Chap. 4. The form and intensity of price communication have a strong influence on the effects of a discount.

The combination of offline and online is becoming more common for price promotions. Consumers who are near a particular store location can be recognized through geo-fencing and lured into the store via an exclusive offer sent to their smartphones. Beacon technology can find the exact location of a registered smartphone user within a store. If a consumer is standing, say, in front of the laundry detergent shelf, the store can immediately send out a discount for detergent via a smartphone app. Upon payment, the consumer must let the app discount be scanned in, which provides the retailer with additional information about the entire basket the respective consumer just bought. The retailer can then use this information to make even more precise and individualized offers in the future. The app Shopkick follows a different concept: the consumers receive points—or so-called kicks—when they enter a particular store or use their smartphones to scan in a product there. The consumer can then redeem the kicks they collected in exchange for coupons. Consumers in the United States who have downloaded and used Shopkick spend on average significantly more money than before in the respective stores [71].

When communicating online price promotions, one should be careful not to overload consumers with too much information. While consumers process informa-tion about offline price promotions relatively quickly, they have more difficulties with online promotions because of the more limited possibilities to render the communication on the screen of a laptop, tablet, smartphone, or smartwatch.

For exclusive items, online retailers in some cases do not publicize the prices at all. An online furniture store allows consumers to choose from a variety of pieces with different accessories and configurations in order to create their desired product. In response, the consumer receives an individualized offer for the desired item or items. This gives the retailer opportunities for price differentiation which it would not have with *ex ante* price communication. This is particularly interesting in the case of regular consumers, whose previous purchases provide clues about their willingness to pay. There is also the possibility to practice consumer-driven pricing, by which the consumer suggests a price to the retailer and the latter decides whether to accept the transaction at that price [72, p. 141].

An extreme approach to competition-oriented pricing is *price matching*: If the consumer finds an identical item at a lower price at a competitor's store, the consumer may either purchase the product at the competitor's lower price or receive the difference as reimbursement. This essentially offers a price guarantee under which the consumers can always expect to receive the most favorable price. While some brick-and-mortar retailers consider only the prices from other brick-and-mortar retailers, others take the prices of online competitors into account. At the German retailer Bauhaus, for example, consumers who find the identical article at a lower price at another brick-and-mortar retailer within 14 days after purchase are entitled to receive the difference between the two prices plus 12% of the lower price as reimbursement [73]. Some electronics retailers honor the prices of the most important online retailers such as Amazon or redcoon.de when the consumer shows proof of them. It is evident that this strategy can have an immense impact on the margins of brick-and-mortar retailers.

Conclusion

There are numerous special aspects to price management in retail. These include the large number of prices to set, associated purchases, the role of the price image, and the intensive use of price promotions. We summarize the key points as follows:

- The balance between traditional, urban or in-town retailers, discounters, suburban or greenfield stores, and e-commerce has shifted massively in the last few decades. Price has played a central role in this shift. Everything speaks for these shifts to continue, with e-commerce seeing disproportionately larger growth.
- In light of their cost structures, many traditional retailers are not prepared for the price competition with discounters and online retailers. They need to fundamentally rethink their business models and potentially change them. This can include a combination of brick-and-mortar and online retail, although this combination has yet to show its advantage.
- The price image of retail stores has a strong influence on the consumer's decision where to shop. The image must be understood, controlled, and communicated in a deliberate fashion.
- In addition to typical standard price strategies such as EDLP (everyday low prices), Hi-Lo (price promotions on a regular basis), and premium/luxury, mixed strategies and mixed price positionings are in widespread use. It is important that a retailer has a clear strategic framework for its price

(continued)

strategy. It should not deviate from this strategic framework without good cause.

- Activity-based cost allocation of all costs onto every individual item in an assortment is a practical impossibility in retail due to the sheer size of the assortment. For this reason, the cost of goods is generally used as the basis for setting selling prices.
- Scanner checkouts, RFID, and consumer data acquired through online purchases (notebook and smartphone) can be used to capture price-related consumer information. But in practice, retailers have not adequately tapped this potential.
- In B2C retail, it is comparatively easy to get information on competitors' prices. Retailers should take advantage of this because the relation between competitors' prices and one's own price is a critical success factor. In B2B retail, it can be difficult to get reliable information on competitors' prices because prices are often negotiated.
- Rules of thumb play a predominant role in price decisions for individual items. In practice, these tried-and-true recommendations are rather in line with theoretical rules for optimization. Purchasers should get up to speed on price management in order to better take price-volume relationships into account when setting prices.
- Associated purchases within an assortment are very important for price decisions at retailers. The optimality condition leads to the result that the greater the positive influence an item has on the sales volume of other items, and the greater the unit contribution margins of those other items are, the lower the price of that influencing item should be.
- Price promotions are very popular on the one hand; on the other hand, their overall effect is hard to assess. The short-term effects are generally strong, but the effects on profit and long-term sales performance are dubious. We advise against excessive use of price promotions with respect to the discount levels, the number of items on promotion, and the frequency of the promotional activity.
- In retail, the purchasing department is responsible for price decisions. There is an inclination in retail to centralize pricing. A stronger decentralization is worth considering for many retailers, as long as they have the appropriate incentive systems and training.
- Price factors are not sufficiently monitored in retail.
- In general, the Internet and the ubiquity of smartphones have created a wide range of new possibilities for retail price management. We expect major changes in this area.

Price is by far the most important marketing instrument for many retailers. Because of the tight margins in retail, it is also the strongest profit driver. In

(continued)

practice, however, pricing in retail clings to traditional methods in most cases. The profit improvement potential through a professionalization of price management is therefore especially high.

References

1. Fassnacht, M., & El Husseini, S. (2013). EDLP vs. Hi-Lo Pricing Strategies in Retailing – A State of the Art Article. *Journal of Business Economics*, 83(3), 259–289.
2. Anonymous. (2015, November 4). Amazon eröffnet ersten eigenen Laden. *Frankfurter Allgemeine Zeitung*, p. 19.
3. Wingfield, N. and de la Merced, M. J. (2017). Amazon to buy Whole Foods for $13.4 Billion. https://www.nytimes.com/2017/06/16/business/dealbook/amazon-whole-foods.html. Accessed 28 February 2018.
4. Schuckmann, E. (2015). *Shopping Enjoyment: Determinanten, Auswirkungen und moderierende Effekte*. Frankfurt am Main: Lang.
5. Hoch, S. J., Drèze, X., & Purk, M. E. (1994). EDLP, Hi-Lo, and Margin Arithmetic. *Journal of Marketing*, 58(4), 16–27.
6. Haucap, J., Heimeshoff, U., Klein, G. J., Rickert, D., & Wey, C. (2014). Wettbewerbsprobleme im Lebensmitteleinzelhandel. In P. Oberender (Ed.), *Wettbewerbsprobleme im Lebensmitteleinzelhandel* (pp. 11–38). Berlin: Dunckler & Humblot.
7. EHI Europäisches Handelsinstitut. (2010). Handel aktuell 2009/2010. Köln: EHI.
8. Lademann, R. (2013). Wettbewerbsökonomische Grundlagen des Betriebsformenwettbewerbs im Lebensmitteleinzelhandel. In H.-C. Riekhof (Ed.), *Retail Business. Perspektiven, Strategien, Erfolgsmuster* (3. ed., pp. 3–30). Wiesbaden: Gabler.
9. Kowitt, B. (2014, April 28). Whole Foods Takes Over America. *Fortune*. pp. 28–35.
10. Humphers, L. (2015). Betting on outlets – 2015 State of the Outlet Industry. https://www.icsc.org/vrn/uploads/2015_VRN_State_of_the_Outlet_Industry_story.pdf. Accessed 28 February 2018.
11. Mueller-Hagedorn, L. (2017, August 28) Outlet-Center fordern Innenstaedte heraus, Frankfurter Allgemeine Zeitung, p. 16
12. Statista (2016). Online Anteil am Umsatz im Einzelhandel in den USA. https://de.statista.com/statistik/daten/studie/379363/umfrage/online-anteil-am-umsatz-im-einzelhandel-in-den-usa/. Accessed 28 December 2016.
13. Anonymous. (2015, February 19). Ich glaube an das gedruckte Buch. *Frankfurter Allgemeine Zeitung (FAZ)*, p. 11.
14. Walmart (2017). Annual Report 2017. http://s2.q4cdn.com/056532643/files/doc_financials/2017/Annual/WMT_2017_AR-(1).pdf. Accessed 28 February 2018.
15. Statista (2018). Net sales revenue of Amazon from 2004 to 2017 (in billion U.S. dollars. https://www.statista.com/statistics/266282/annual-net-revenue-of-amazoncom/. Accessed 28 February 2018.
16. Otto Group (2017). Annual Report 2016/17. https://www.ottogroup.com/media/docs/en/geschaeftsbericht/Otto_Group_Annual_Report_16_17_EN.pdf. Accessed 13 March 2018.
17. Alibaba Group (2017). Alibaba Group Announces March Quarter 2017 and Full Fiscal Year 2017 Results. http://www.alibabagroup.com/en/news/press_pdf/p170518.pdf. Accessed 13 March 2018.
18. Kilian, K. (2015, January). Showrooming. *Absatzwirtschaft*, p. 9.
19. Fassnacht, M., & Szajna, M. (2014). Shoppen ohne einzukaufen – Der Trend Showrooming im Einzelhandel. In R. Gössinger, & G. Zäpfel (Ed.), *Management integrativer*

Leistungserstellung. Festschrift für Hans Corsten. Betriebswirtschaftliche Schriften (Volume 168, pp. 287–304). Berlin: Duncker & Humblot.
20. Spivey, S. (2016). Consumers have spoken: 2016 is the year of "webrooming". https://marketingland.com/consumers-spoken-2016-year-webrooming-180125. Accessed 13 March 2018.
21. Graham, S. (2017). Using Competitive Online Pricing to Drive In-Store Sales. https://www.growthmattersnetwork.com/story/using-competitive-online-pricing-to-drive-in-store-sales/?source=social-global-voicestorm-None&campaigncode=CRM-YD18-SOC-GETSOC. Accessed 13 March 2018.
22. Nyström, H. (1970). *Retail Pricing – An Integrated Economic and Psychological Approach.* Stockholm: Economic Research Institute, Stockholm School of Economics.
23. Hamilton, R., & Chernev, A. (2013). Low Prices Are Just the Beginning: Price Image in Retail Management. *Journal of Marketing, 77*(6), 1–20.
24. GMI Global Market Insite (2014). Internet World Business: Wer den Cent nicht ehrt. http://heftarchiv.internetworld.de/2014/Ausgabe-14-2014/Wer-den-Cent-nicht-ehrt2. Accessed 10 March 2015.
25. Anonymous. (2015, November 02). Amazon lässt die Preise schwanken. *Frankfurter Allgemeine Zeitung*, p. 26.
26. Riedl, A.-K. (2015). Studie zeigt: Preise bei Amazon schwanken um bis zu 240 Prozent. The Huffington Post. 25.02. http://www.huffingtonpost.de/2015/02/25/zockt-uns-amazon-ab_n_6749748.html?utm_hp_ref=germany. Accessed 20 March 2015.
27. ZDF WISO (n.d.). Preis € Wert – So dynamisch sind die Preise im Netz. http://module.zdf.de/wiso-dynamische-preise-im-netz/. Accessed 13 March 2018.
28. Schindler, H. (1998). *Marktorientiertes Preismanagement.* St. Gallen: Schindler.
29. Müller, I. (2003). *Die Entstehung von Preisimages im Handel.* Nürnberg: GIM.
30. Fishmann, J. (2017). Amazon, the Price Perception Leader. https://www.gapintelligence.com/blog/2017/amazon-com-the-price-perception-leader. Accessed 13 March 2018.
31. Diller, H. (2008). *Preispolitik* (4 ed.). Stuttgart: Kohlhammer.
32. Kenning, P. (2003). Kundenorientiertes Preismanagement: Ein Beitrag zur Renditenverbesserung im Handel. In D. Ahlert, R. Olbrich, & H. Schröder (Ed.), *Jahrbuch Vertriebs- und Handelsmanagement* (pp. 85–102). Frankfurt am Main: Deutscher Fachverlag.
33. Authors' own study, prices as of December 6, 2017.
34. Fassnacht, M. (2003). *Eine dienstleistungsorientierte Perspektive des Handelsmarketing.* Wiesbaden: Deutscher Universitäts-Verlag.
35. Adlwarth, W. (2014). No-Names drängen stärker in die "Feine Welt". Lebensmittelzeitung.net. http://www.lebensmittelzeitung.net/business/themen/maerkte-marken/protected/Handelsmarken-_130_15510.html?dossierid=130&tid=104958&page=1 (Created 16 May). Accessed 11 March 2015.
36. Statista (2018). Marktanteile von Hersteller- und Handelsmarken in Deutschland in den Jahren 2012 bis 2017. https://de.statista.com/statistik/daten/studie/205728/umfrage/marktanteilsentwicklung-von-mehrwert-handelsmarken/. Accessed 13 March 2018.
37. Novich, N. S. (1981). *Price and Promotion Analysis Using Scanner Data: An Example. Master's Thesis.* Sloan School of Management. Massachusetts Institute of Technology.
38. Haucap, J., & Klein, G. J. (2012). Einschränkungen der Preisgestaltung im Einzelhandel aus wettbewerbsökonomischer Perspektive. In D. Ahlert, P. Kenning, R. Olbrich, & H. Schröder (Ed.), *Vertikale Preis- und Markenpflege im Kreuzfeuer des Kartellrechts* (pp. 169–186). Wiesbaden: Springer Gabler. Forum Vertriebs- und Handelsmanagement.
39. Pezoldt, K., & Gebert, R. (2011). RFID im Handel – Vor- und Nachteile aus Unternehmens- und Kundensicht. In N. Bach, G. Brähler, G. Brösel, D. Müller, & R. Souren (Ed.), *Ilmenauer Schriften zur Betriebswirtschaftslehre* Volume 8/2011 Ilmenau: VERLAG proWiWi e.V.
40. Talukdar, D., Gauri, D. K., & Grewal, D. (2010). An Empirical Analysis of the Extreme Cherry Picking Behavior of Consumers in the Frequently Purchased Goods Market. *Journal of Retailing, 86*(4), 337–355.

41. Preuss, S. (2015, July 18). Kaufland will lokalen Anbietern eine Chance geben. *Frankfurter Allgemeine Zeitung*, p. 25.
42. Gabor, A. (1988). *Pricing: Concepts and Methods for Effective Marketing* (2 ed.). Hants: Gower.
43. Holdren, B. R. (1960). *The Structure of a Retail Market and the Behavior of Retail Units*. Englewood Cliffs: Prentice-Hall.
44. Holton, R. H. (1957). Price Discrimination at Retail: The Supermarket Case. *Journal of Industrial Economics*, 6(1), 13–32.
45. Monroe, K. B. (2003). *Pricing: Making Profitable Decisions* (3 ed.). Boston: McGraw-Hill.
46. Preston, L. E. (1963). *Profits, Competition and Rules of Thumb in Retailing Food Pricing*. Berkeley: University of California.
47. ALDI Süd (2015). Aldi Süd Philiosophie. https://unternehmen.aldi-sued.de/de/ueber-aldi-sued/philosophie/ (Created 23 February). Accessed 09 March 2015.
48. Simon, H. (2016). Negative Prices – A New Phenomenon, *The Journal of Professional Pricing*, Fourth Quarter 2016, pp. 18–21
49. Anonymous. (2007). Pressemeldung des Bundeskartellamtes vom 30.10.2007: Bundeskartellamt setzt klaren Maßstab für das Unter-Einstandspreis-Verbot. http://www.advokat.de/infodienst/startseite/marken-und-wettbewerbsrecht/marken-und-wettbewerbsrecht/datum/2007/11/04/bundeskartellamt-setzt-klaren-massstab-fuer-das-unter-einstandspreis-verbot/. Accessed 27 May 2015.
50. Rode, J. (2014). Kaiser's testet individuelle Coupons. Lebensmittelzeitung.net. http://www.lebensmittelzeitung.net/news/it-logistik/protected/Kaisers-testet-individuelle-Coupons_105434.html?id=105434 (Created 12 June). Accessed 5 May 2015.
51. Ailawadi, K. L., Harlam, B. A., César, J., & Trounce, D. (2007). Quantifying and Improving Promotion Effectiveness at CVS. *Marketing Science*, 26(4), 566–575.
52. Bolton, R. N., Shankar, V., & Montoya, D. Y. (2006). Recent Trends and Emerging Practices in Retailer Pricing. In M. Krafft, & M. K. Mantrala (Ed.), *Retailing in the 21st Century: Current and Future Trends* (pp. 255–270). Wiesbaden: Gabler.
53. dm (2015). Der günstige dm-Dauerpreis. http://www.dm.de/de_homepage/services/service_erleben/dm_dauerpreis_garantie/. Accessed 04 May 2015.
54. Hanssens, D. (Ed.) (2015). *Empirical Generalizations about Marketing Impact*. Cambridge, MA.: Marketing Science Institute.
55. Kaiser, T. (2014). *Direct-Mail-Couponing: Eine empirische Untersuchung der langfristigen Absatzwirkung*. Wiesbaden: Springer Gabler.
56. Fassnacht, M., & Königsfeld, J. A. (2015). Sales Promotion Management in Retailing: Tasks, Benchmarks, and Future Trends. *Marketing Review St. Gallen*, 32(3), 68–77.
57. Wagner, U., Jamsawang, J., & Seher, F. (2012). Preisorientierte Aktionspolitik. In J. Zentes, B. Swoboda, D. Morschett, & H. Schramm-Klein (Ed.), *Handbuch Handel* (pp. 585–607). Wiesbaden: Springer Gabler.
58. Ivens, B. (2013). *Geleitwort zu: T. Kaiser. Direct-Mail-Couponing: Eine empirische Untersuchung der langfristigen Absatzwirkung*. Wiesbaden: Springer Gabler.
59. Fassnacht, M., & Königsfeld, J. A. (2014). Wertschöpfung im Handel durch Preismanagement. In W. Reinartz, & M. Käuferle (Ed.), *Wertschöpfung im Handel* (pp. 62–83). Stuttgart: Kohlhammer.
60. Gedenk, K. (2003). Preis-Promotions. In H. Diller, & A. Herrmann (Hrsg.), *Handbuch Preispolitik: Strategien – Planung – Organisation – Umsetzung* (pp. 597–622). Wiesbaden: Gabler.
61. Chandon, P., & Wansink, B. (2011). Is Food Marketing Making Us Fat? A Multi-Disciplinary Review. *Foundations and Trends in Marketing*, 5(3), 113–196.
62. DelVecchio, D., Krishnan, H. S., & Smith, D. C. (2007). Cents or Percents? The Effects of Promotion Framing on Price Expectations and Choice. *Journal of Marketing*, 71(3), 158–170.
63. Lodish, L., & Mela, C. F. (2008). *Manage Brands over Years, not Quarters. The Pricing Advisor*. Marietta: Professional Pricing Society.

64. Xia, L., & Monroe, K. B. (2009). The Influence of Pre-Purchase Goals on Consumers' Perceptions of Price Promotions. *International Journal of Retail & Distribution Management*, 37(8), 680–694.
65. Yoon, S., Oh, S., Song, S., Kim, K. K., Kim, Y. (2014). Higher Quality or Lower Price? How Value-Increasing Promotions Affect Retailer Reputation Via Perceived Value. *Journal of Business Research*, 67(10), 2088–2096.
66. Palmeira, M. M., & Srivastava, J. (2013). Free Offer ≠ Cheap Product: A Selective Accessibility Account on the Valuation of Free Offers. *Journal of Consumer Research*, 40(4), 644–656.
67. Dubey, J. (2014). Personal Care Products: Sales Promotion and Brand Loyalty. *Journal of Contemporary Management Research*, 8(1), 52–71.
68. Swenson, D., Ansari, S., Bell, J., Kim, I.-W. (2003). Best Practices in Target Costing. *Management Accounting Quarterly*, 4(2), 12–17.
69. Universität Essen, & Mercer Management Consulting (2003). Retail-Studie – Preis- und Sortimentsmanagement als Erfolgshebel im Einzelhandel. https://www.cm-net.wiwi.uni-due.de/fileadmin/fileupload/BWL-MARKETING/Management_Summary_Retail_Studie_1_.pdf. Accessed 28 April 2015.
70. Reimann, E. (2015, August 27). dm boykottiert Mogelpackungen. *Generalanzeiger Bonn*, p. 6.
71. Happel, S. (2015). Nun wird der Kunde ferngesteuert und vermessen, Wirtschaftswoche. http://www.wiwo.de/unternehmen/handel/smartphone-app-shopkick-nun-wird-der-kunde-ferngesteuert-und-vermessen/11223624-all.html (Created 15 January). Accessed 16 March 2015.
72. Schröder, H. (2012). *Handelsmarketing: Strategien und Instrumente für den stationären Einzelhandel und für Online-Shops* (2. Aufl.). Wiesbaden: Springer Gabler.
73. Bauhaus (2015). Bauhaus Garantien. http://www.bauhaus.info/service/leistungen/garantien. Accessed 27 March 2015.

Innovations in Price Management

14

Abstract

Price management has been a field of sporadic innovation. Auctions, nonlinear pricing, and bundling precede our current era. Innovations in pricing used to be rare and slow to spread, but we have seen rapid, widespread pricing innovations, thanks in large part to the Internet. Measurement technology (allowing precise price metrics), more powerful computers (enabling the analysis of Big Data), and creative business models all contribute to price management innovations. The Internet simplifies price comparisons, which results in higher price transparency. Over the long run, however, the increase in "value transparency" may prove to be more important. Innovations such as flat rates, freemium, name-your-own-price, and pay-what-you-want enable companies to tap more profit potential. Companies should be careful when opting for a new pricing model. Each tactic carries considerable risks when not used properly. Two-sided price systems, allowing companies to generate revenue from two sources, are becoming more common. Perhaps for the first time, we observe negative prices in some markets. Marginal costs of zero and the sharing economy are influencing price decisions and disrupting established business models. New payment systems and new forms of money such as bitcoin may have hitherto unknown effects on price management.

14.1 Pricing Innovations: A Historical Overview

Many of the price tactics and strategies which we view today as highly developed and refined are not new. They have been used for a long time. But the sophistication of the tactics and strategies in use today, compared to the predominantly rudimentary level of those employed in history, means today's processes and methods have little overlap with those of earlier times.

© Springer Nature Switzerland AG 2019
H. Simon, M. Fassnacht, *Price Management*,
https://doi.org/10.1007/978-3-319-99456-7_14

In ancient markets, there were generally no fixed prices. The traders at a bazaar tried to gauge the willingness to pay off a customer and exploit it to the greatest extent possible through haggling. They were practicing first-degree price differentiation (see Chap. 6), and if their assessments of willingness to pay were correct, they would extract the entire consumer surplus. We refer to this as perfect price differentiation. The same practices prevail at contemporary flea markets.

Auctions have likewise been popular from time immemorial, especially in agricultural markets. One of the most famous examples of all time are the auctions for tulips in the Netherlands in the seventeenth century. There were spot markets, futures contracts, and even short selling. One speculative bubble, known as the tulip mania, ended in a price collapse. Whether Germany's most famous poet Johann Wolfgang Goethe invented the Vickrey auction (see Chap. 3)—under which the highest bidder wins, but pays the amount of the second highest bid—is not known with certainty. But he used this clever process when he auctioned off his manuscripts to publishers. What makes a Vickrey auction special is that it incentivizes bidders to reveal their true willingness to pay [1].

When a customer buys on installment, the purchase price is not paid in one lump-sum upfront, but over time in several incremental payments. Installment payment plans have essentially been around forever, just in unsystematic, individualized forms. Customers received credit from a dealer or trader and paid off the debt in several tranches. Systematic installment payment offers came about in the nineteenth century. Their inventor is considered to be Edward Clark, who deployed the installment payment system to promote the sales of sewing machines.

From the perspective of payment flows, leasing is similar to an installment purchase. Both methods are characterized by significantly smaller monthly payments instead of a high, onetime price. The key difference between a lease and an installment plan is that the customer purchases the product under an installment plan but does not acquire and own the product under leasing—the customer must pay the balance or return the used product at the end of the lease. Real estate rental is a special, enduring, and common form of leasing. The spiritual father of leasing might actually be Aristotle (384–322 BC). He noted that the value of a good lay in its use, not in its possession. In general, the financing aspect plays an important role in leasing. Financial and tax advantages of leasing have driven its strong growth. But the price aspect remains important. One can plan around a fixed monthly rate. Relative to the purchase price, a leasing rate is manageable. The first systematic leasing offer was introduced by the American telephone manufacturer Bell, which started leasing telephone equipment in 1877 rather than selling it. IBM was also a pioneer in leasing. Starting in the 1920s, IBM leased punch-card machines and practiced price bundling (see Chap. 6). Customers of tabulating machines (the so-called Hollerith machines) had to use IBM punch cards. Leasing has now reached a huge volume, with some estimates putting the global leasing business at over $1 trillion per year.

A notable innovation in price bundling was "block booking," which was introduced to the film industry by producer Adolph Zukor in 1915 and adopted by the entire sector in the ensuing decades. Cinema operators were not offered individual films, but rather packages or bundles of films. These packages comprised a mix of attractive and less attractive titles. In some cases the cinema operators could not even check the films beforehand, which was called "blind booking." Block booking was eventually forbidden by the US Supreme Court in 1948. Only later was the theoretical foundation for the advantages of price bundling worked out (see Chap. 6). Coase [2] and Demsetz [3] argued with cost advantages to justify the tactic. An approach by Burstein [4] relied on the complementarity of products. It was Adams and Yellen [5] who first provided the more important explanation that the consumer surplus of heterogeneous customers can be better exploited through price bundling than through separate pricing for each product. Real-world, time-tested pricing practices have preceded explanatory attempts of theory in other cases as well. This gap between theory and established practice also arose in nonlinear pricing, which has been used in practice seemingly forever. The theoretical basis, Gossen's Law of diminishing marginal utility, dates back to 1854. The expansion of this theory to heterogeneous markets did not come until the work of Oren, Smith, and Wilson over 100 years later [6].

The idea that one could rent or lease a car for a period of time once seemed far-fetched. The suspicion was that someone who did not own the car would not treat it well, thus shortening the vehicle's useful life. Car rentals for short periods have existed in the United States since 1904. The predecessor of the car rental firm Hertz was founded in 1918 by Walter L. Jacobs.

Flat rates have also been around for a very long time. Private water consumption was originally calculated based on the number of people in a household. It was not possible to track the actual consumption and charge for it until the introduction of the water meter, which allowed utilities to charge a price per cubic meter. In this case one can speak of the introduction of a new "price metric," a topic which we will discuss in detail below. Another radically new business model was the "all-you-can-eat" offer, which gained popularity in the United States in the 1960s and 1970s. Such flat rate prices for food make sense only beyond a certain threshold of prosperity. If incomes are too low, the willingness to pay will be too low and the consumption too high, which leaves the restaurants with an insufficient profit margin.

Price Management and Music

The history of price management innovations in music is extremely dynamic and instructive. For that reason we explore the historical development of the industry's business and price models in greater detail. Until the end of the nineteenth century, the only way to experience music was through live performance. Interestingly, this form of marketing music has seen a resurgence in the Internet era. The phonograph record, based on a patent originally awarded to Edison in 1877, made it possible for the first time to market music in a stored form on a broader basis. Later, recordings of individual songs were sold as "singles." The prevailing price model in the industry was simple and one-dimensional: one piece of music for a price of x.

When Columbia launched long-play (LP) vinyl albums in 1948, it became possible to pack a larger number of songs on a single record. The LP generally held between 12 and 14 songs and was sold as a package for a price of y. The industry used this technological breakthrough to introduce a new price model, price bundling. With the exception of a few singles (known as 45's for the 7 in. disc's 45 rpm speed on a turntable), consumers could no longer buy any song individually. Similar to the "block bookings" for films, music companies packaged attractive and less attractive songs together in one bundle. In this manner, excess willingness to pay for the more popular titles was transferred to the less popular ones. This price model remained in place after the transition to the compact disc (CD), a format which brought the industry almost two decades of massive revenues and profits. But many customers hated being forced to buy 14 songs in order to get the two or three songs they really wanted. Pent-up dissatisfaction and openness for an alternative business model grew among music fans.

The dam broke when the Internet emerged. Users began to exchange music among themselves. The largest file-sharing exchange napster.com operated on a peer-to-peer platform. In January 2001 alone, more than two billion songs were shared among Napster users, all for a price of zero. Napster was eventually shut down when courts declared the file sharing on Napster to be illegal. Today, Napster is a brand owned by Rhapsody and offers music at a monthly flat rate of $9.99. To this day, the music industry continues to lose vast sums of potential revenue to illegal copying or "pirating" on song recordings. The same holds true for films and other content.

In the early 2000s, the time was ripe for an innovative price model. Apple filled that need when it launched the iTunes Store in 2003. Each recording could be purchased separately, as in the era of the single. In our terminology, this is referred to as unbundling. Steve Jobs is said to have visited the CEOs of the five leading music labels personally in order to acquire the music rights for iTunes and the permission to unbundle albums. This was a revolution for the music industry. The iTunes assortment now boasts over 45 million separate items, including songs, e-books, movies, and apps. Songs are available for $0.69, $0.99 cents, or $1.29. For other items, iTunes offers different price categories and also offers weekly specials. Apple has increased its revenue from iTunes and additional services from $18.1 billion in 2014 to $30.0 billion in 2017 [7]. The spectacular success of iTunes was due to its innovative price model, which at the time might have seemed like "the end of price innovation" in the music industry.

Such thinking, however, would have been a mistake. Music streaming services underwent explosive growth. The pioneer in this area was Pandora, which was founded before iTunes, but Spotify became the market leader in 2015. Streaming services offer music via a freemium model and threaten to make iTunes and similar services obsolete. Spotify offers a selection of over 30 million songs and, in 2017, had about 159 million users, over 40% of whom pay a flat rate of $9.99 per month for Spotify's premium offering. Although Spotify has only posted losses so far, the company went public in April 2018 via a direct listing on the New York Stock Exchange and had a market capitalization of $28.7 billion [8]. It took 9 years after the launch of Spotify for Apple to respond to declining revenues on iTunes by launching its own streaming service called Apple Music. To reach the same level of revenues generated by iTunes, however, Apple Music would need to attract twice as many users as Spotify has since its inception [9]. In contrast to Spotify, Apple does not use a freemium model, which in this case means offering free content interrupted by regular advertising, in order to entice users to switch to a paid or premium membership with no ads. Instead, Apple offers its new customers 3 months of free services when they sign up. Apple also offers a "Family Plan," which allows up to six users to share the same account for $14.99 per month [10]. Amazon offers Amazon Music Unlimited, which has about 16 million paid users who can access 40 million songs. It also offers its Prime customers a limited music streaming service whose price is included in the cost of a Prime membership.

Whether streaming services such as Spotify or Apple Music now represent the "end of price innovation" in the music industry is doubtful. The music industry in general and many superstars in particular are dissatisfied with the royalty payouts they receive from streaming services. Spotify states that the average per-stream payout to rights holders lies between $0.006 and $0.0084. For superstar artists, withholding albums from streaming services can be a way to increase traditional sales in an era when physical purchases and digital downloads are shrinking. One well-known example of this is the singer Adele, who did not make her album "25" available to streaming services until 7 months after its release [11, 12]. Blockchain technology enables artists to distribute their own content and thereby reduce the influence of streaming platforms and labels. In future, this technology could lead to another industry transformation.

The overall revenue of the music industry has declined from more than $25 billion in 2002 to $15 billion in 2015. The share of digital sales (45%) exceeded the share of revenue from physical formats (39%). At over 100 million, the number of consumers who paid for a music subscription in 2017 still seems very low. But it is nonetheless more than 12 times greater than in 2010, when there were 8 million paying subscribers [12]. Paid subscription has rekindled strong growth in the US music industry. Revenues grew by 16.5% in 2017 to $8.72 billion, after having already grown by 11.5% year-on-year in 2016 [13].

Overview

This brief historical overview shows that there has always been innovation in price management but also that these innovations have been few and far between and took a long time to spread. Both of these aspects, however, have changed radically over the last two decades with the advent of the Internet. We are experiencing a wave of innovations in price management. But this wave is not entirely due to the Internet. Behind these efforts are other factors such as a keener awareness of price management among senior executives, more systematic thinking about business models, and technological developments such as sensors which allow more valid measurement of the duration of usage, consumption, or actual value delivered. Think again of the invention of the water meter. The price system for Google AdWords fits in this

(continued)

context. While traditional media sets prices of advertisements as a function of placement, Google uses the number of clicks, a metric which measures the actual reaction of potential customers. In the following section, we will look at many innovative approaches and discuss their current and future significance for price management.

14.2   Changes in the Price-Response Function Due to Increased Transparency

One of the most immediate and most important effects of the Internet is the radical increase in transparency. In former times, making a thorough comparison of price and value was a tedious, expensive, and time-consuming process. Nowadays, we get such comparisons instantaneously on a notebook or smartphone. This information is available anywhere at any time. Price comparisons are the innovation with the broadest impact. At the same time, one should ask the question whether value comparisons are even more important, or will become more important in the future, than pure price comparisons.

14.2.1 Price Transparency

In the pre-Internet era, collecting price information meant one needed to call up several suppliers, visit different shops, get alternative offers, or find and peruse printed test reports and catalogs. Because of these necessary efforts, customers' level of information on the prices of different suppliers was generally low. Nowadays, a large number of online services such as nextag.com, pricegrabber.com, or pricewatch.com offer price comparisons across industries. In addition, almost every industry or sector has specialized services which track prices. Carrentals. com helps finding the lowest-priced rental car. Pages such as cheaphotels.com, kayak.com, or booking.com enable price comparisons for trips. Bankrate.com shows prices for banking services. LendingTree offers tailored price comparisons for consumer loans. The app Gas Guru provides information on the prices at individual gas stations in near real time. The app draws its gas price information from the Oil Price Information Service, so the prices are always up to date [14]. Today a majority of consumers use online price comparisons, with men between the ages of 20 and 59 the most active. The most frequent comparisons are for vacations (48%), followed closely by electricity and gas (47%), electronics and household goods (45%), insurance (42%), mobile phone contracts (39%), flights (35%), and hotels (32%) [15].

Price transparency takes on a very concrete, local dimension, thanks to smartphones and other mobile devices. With the right apps, such as the iPhone app "ShopSavvy," one scans the barcode of a product in a store and immediately receives information on what the exact same product costs in nearby stores. This places tight restrictions on regional and time-based price differentiation, which were traditionally well suited for fencing. It becomes more difficult to realize differentiated prices for identical products or services. The customers are simply too well informed and when in doubt will purchase from the lowest-priced competitor. In Brazil, a start-up with the name Premise has established itself with a smartphone app which allows users to share pictures of food and price information with other users. Using the collected data, the company can determine a consumer price index for food for the Brazilian market some 25 days before the government publishes the official data [16].

According to a recent study, 40% of all consumers worldwide have already used their mobile phone in a store to make a price comparison. The South Koreans (59%), Chinese (54%), and Turks (53%) use their smartphones the most to compare prices [17]. Social networking also promotes more active price transparency. When McDonald's tried to raise the price of a cheeseburger by $0.39, it met with vehement resistance from customers. Within 48 h, some 80,000 Facebook followers posted negative feedback to the price increase. The move compelled McDonald's to rescind the increase [18].

There are websites which allow users to not only call up "passive" price comparisons but actively inform users when price conditions they set have been met. This can occur, for example, when the price for a product has fallen below an amount pre-defined by the user. Websites such as pricegrabber.com or onlinepricealert.com offer users the option of a price alarm which informs immediately when prices have dropped for one or more products they have selected. While hotel platforms such as hrs.de or booking.com offer the lowest price at the time of the search, trip-rebel.com follows the price for a booked hotel room. If the price drops ahead of the date, the original booking is cancelled and replaced with one at the prevailing lower price. The customer can therefore assume that at any time after the initial booking, he or she will get the lowest price for that room. This process erodes the basis of yield management. Price transparency will increase further as search engines and programs become more refined. In other words, the price information which consumers have is constantly improving. The effects of increased price transparency on the price-response function are shown in Fig. 14.1.

Increased price transparency can lead to an increase or decrease in volume even in the absence of a price change. This is shown by the vertical arrow with the question marks. We can make clear statements, however, on what happens when there are price cuts or changes to the relative difference between one's own price and competitors' prices. Price cuts which undercut competitors' prices lead to a stronger volume increase than when price transparency is lower. The opposite is true for price increases or larger gaps to competitors' prices; volume declines more sharply.

Fig. 14.1 Effects of higher price transparency

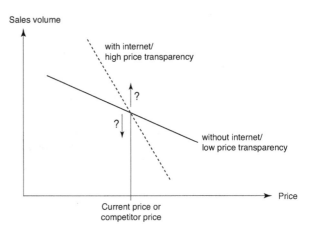

14.2.2 Value Transparency

The increase in price transparency is the most pronounced effect of the Internet on price management to date. We consider the hypothesis, though, that the increase in value transparency has the potential to be the more powerful effect over the longer term. As pointed out by the book *The Cluetrain Manifesto* [19], revolutionary when it was published in 2000, the Internet enables customers to inform and speak with each other to a previously unimaginable extent. Both good and bad reviews of a supplier or a product become transparent and accessible to anyone who is interested. Domizlaff [20] distinguished in 1939 between the "county fair salesman" and "the local merchant." The county fair salesman appears once a year and then disappears. He sells his customers poor quality at inflated prices. When the customers notice the poor quality the next day, the county fair salesman is long gone. When he reappears the following year, the customers no longer remember him and fall for his tricks again. The local merchant acts differently; he cannot afford to behave the way the county fair salesman does. Word will spread quickly in town if he delivers poor quality at high prices, and customers will soon shun him. He needs to try to "retain customers by winning their trust" and viewing "a commitment to quality as a prerequisite for a profitable and enduring business" [20, p. 61].

Somewhat oversimplified, we can say that no seller of the "county fair" type will last long on the Internet; there will only be suppliers of the "local merchant" type. Poor reviews—whether it is a seller on eBay, a hotel operator on booking.com, a driver on Uber, or a service provider on Yelp—can hardly be offset through low prices. This range of information on quality, trustworthiness, and reliability used to be available and communicated only at the local level. Now that same range of information is universally available online. Scammers and suppliers of sub-par quality goods and services at inflated prices will find it difficult, if not impossible, to establish a lasting successful online business. The opposite applies to merchants who offer a good price-value relationship; the Internet enhances their value because the advantages they offer can be communicated independent of place and time. Of course one cannot entirely rule out the manipulation of online feedback and reviews, but greater dissemination and higher numbers of reviewers make such manipulation more difficult. Furthermore, online suppliers and their website managers attempt to prevent such manipulation by deploying the appropriate monitoring software. The form of the reviews and evaluations is also becoming more differentiated, moving beyond the "star" system or other one-dimensional scales.

So-called trust marks play an important role in value transparency. In spirit, these are nothing new. Older American readers will certainly be familiar with the "Good Housekeeping Seal of Approval," a trust mark first used in 1909 and still actively awarded today. Such seals of approval are awarded by "Good Housekeeping" or by services such as Europe's "TrustedShops" after a careful examination of a supplier. They provide consumers with a level of emotional security and are sometimes combined with a formal guarantee. Trust marks offer lesser-known online firms an opportunity to gain acceptance among potential customers and to charge higher prices. A common example today is the "Non-GMO Project Verified" seal on many grocery items, denoting products made without the use of GMOs (genetically modified organisms). For larger suppliers who have a well-established and trusted brand name, a trust mark is less important [21].

Figure 14.2 illustrates the sales volume effects of increased value transparency. These effects differ fundamentally for offers which are evaluated favorably and unfavorably online and are asymmetrical. At first, one should expect that—similar to Fig. 14.1—at a given price or a given gap to competitors' prices, volume will increase for products with favorable evaluations and decline for those with unfavorable ones. If a product generally has negative evaluations, the impact of a price cut will be weaker compared to situations when value transparency is lower. The same applies when one undercuts competitors' prices. In contrast, price increases or larger upward deviations from competitors' prices have a stronger negative effect on sales

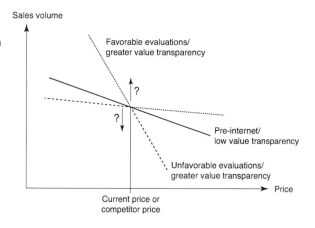

Fig. 14.2 Structural effects of greater value transparency on the price-response function

volumes than when transparency is lower. The opposite holds true for offers which are positively viewed online. Price cuts have a stronger positive effect on sales volumes, and price increases have a weaker effect than when transparency was lower.

The consequences for the optimal price depend on the change in the slope of the price-response function and are complex. Let us first look at the case with mostly favorable customer feedback. If the slope to the left side is very steep, it can be optimal to cut the price. If the slope to the right side is very flat, it can be optimal to raise the price. Also, as in the case of the Gutenberg function (see Chap. 3), two local profit maxima can occur. Then one has to find out whether the maximum profit is attained at a lower or at a higher price. In the case of mostly unfavorable feedback, the most likely outcome is that the price sticks at the former level, because a price cut does not increase volume significantly and a price increase leads to a strong volume decline. This phenomenon resembles the effects of advertising on the price-response function, which we showed in Fig. 9.9. The basic difference is that the supplier can manage the effect shown in Fig. 9.9 through its own decisions on advertising, while it is at the mercy of the market regarding the effects shown in Fig. 14.2. A supplier can influence the latter situation in Fig. 14.2 only by improving its products and services, which is generally a difficult and protracted process.

14.3   Innovative Pricing Models

Innovations in price management can be driven by new business models or technology. In some instances, both drivers manifest themselves. The term "business model" defines the manner in which a company offers its products or services and monetizes the value in the form of a price [22–24].

14.3.1 Flat Rates

Under a flat rate, customers pay a fixed price per occasion or time period and can use the acquired goods or services as much as they choose. Classic forms of flat rates include monthly bus or train passes and memberships in fitness studios or similar organizations. Generally speaking, a flat rate means that the majority of less intensive users subsidizes a minority of heavy users [25]. Flat rates are very popular today in telecommunications and Internet access. Cable television's monthly flat rates allow subscribers access to all available channels, which they can watch as much as they like. The BahnCard 100 of the German Railroad Corporation is a flat rate offer. The cardholders can ride the trains as far and as often as they like for a period of 1 year. The flat rate is a very effective instrument for price differentiation. Intensive or heavy users receive a high discount from a flat rate. When someone in Germany travels by train so often that they would pay €20,000 at normal prices, they receive a discount of 79.6% with the BahnCard 100 for second-class travel.

Flat rates rank among the most frequent innovations in the pricing landscape. At McDonald's, customers who buy a menu receive a cup which they can fill repeatedly with soft drinks as long as they remain in the restaurant. As the slogan "all-you-can-eat" implies, buffets are also flat rate systems. The person who eats three steaks does not pay more than the person who consumes one steak. The risk for the restaurant owner is limited, because guests can only eat or drink up to certain personal limits anyway. In Japanese restaurants, a popular price model is a flat rate which allows guests to eat and drink as much as they want during a certain period. The prices range from ¥1,500 yen for 1 h to ¥2,500 for 2 h and to ¥3,500 for 3 h. These flat rates are popular among Japanese students. The time limits help reduce the owners' risks. According to reports, service is also noticeably slower for flat rate guests. Flat rates in the form of "all-inclusive offers" are also popular in tourism. Such offers include a combination of flat rate elements (e.g., for meals and drinks) as well as price bundling (e.g., flight, hotel, and car rental). One expert in the tourism industry has said that at destinations "such as Turkey or the Dominican Republic, well over 90 percent of offers are all-inclusive" [26, p. 8].

In addition to the music streaming services we have already mentioned, there are also film and video streaming services offered at flat rates. The most popular of these is Netflix. For a fixed monthly fee, the subscriber receives unrestricted use of the service. Netflix charges between $7.99 and $13.99 depending on the type of subscription [27]. Netflix had 109 million subscribers worldwide in 2017. It now produces its own wide range of popular programs such as "Stranger Things," for which it releases an entire season (multiple episodes) all at once [28]. Amazon also offers a video streaming service for its Amazon Prime members [29].

The introduction of a flat rate confronts a supplier with risks and potential disadvantages. Developments in telecommunications and Internet businesses illustrate these dangers. Intensive users of a service will increase pressure on the supplier to introduce a flat rate because they stand to gain the most. Contracts for mobile Internet access, which also include voice and text, show that a price model is neither good nor bad per se but instead can either be considered appropriate or inappropriate. In the early stages of the mobile Internet, customers were very skeptical. Hardly anyone could figure out what a megabyte of data volume meant. In order to alleviate consumers' fears of unpredictable or incalculable fees, suppliers increasingly introduced data packages and data flat rates. These price metrics stimulated the acceptance of mobile Internet services in the early phase, eliminated fears of so-called bill shock, and increased penetration.

Induced by competition, the Internet flat rate became the market standard. But the Internet flat rate became a problem as market saturation neared and data volume per user kept increasing: 10 % of users were responsible for 80% of total data usage. Increased costs to maintain network quality, combined with a lack of improved revenues per customer, called the revenue model into question. At the same time, flat rates enabled Internet start-ups to offer new services on the infrastructure of the telecom companies and cannibalize their offerings. WhatsApp, WeChat, and iMessage, as well as Skype and FaceTime made free texting and voice communication possible, in some cases with higher quality. These services are also easier to use and have multimedia functionality. Revenues for classic services of the telecom companies, such as text and voice, dropped significantly. One potential solution for the telecom companies would be to sell only data packages instead of unlimited data flat rates. Currently the telecom companies offer flat rate contracts which call for a reduction of data transmission speeds as soon as certain data volume levels are exceeded. This is meant to encourage customers to either reduce their data usage, buy additional capacity, or upgrade their contracts. In this manner, the telecom companies are trying to strike a compromise between billing by the megabyte (unpredictable, risk of bill shock, consumer resistance) and billing at a flat rate. But they also launched flat rates for text and voice, an obvious and superficial attempt to shore up these two dying pillars of their business. Nonetheless, the business continues to shift more and more to WhatsApp, etc. Whether telecom companies can succeed in generating more revenue through a higher price level is questionable, because of the competitive intensity. In this regard, shoring up the legacy services such as text and voice using a flat rate price model makes sense.

Many customers desire flat rates for electricity, but only 5% of companies currently use this price model. One concern is the change to much higher electricity consumption as electric cars become common and customers regularly charge them at home. This may lead to a doubling of household electricity consumption, according to some observers [30].

Flat rates have many advantages from the perspective of consumers. Some consumers purchase a flat rate even though it is not the least expensive plan for them. This is the so-called flat rate bias. It means that customers prefer a flat rate even though a usage-based plan would be less expensive. This can happen for the following reasons:

- Insurance effect: The customers want to avoid fluctuations in their monthly bills.
- Taximeter effect: Usage is more enjoyable under a flat rate than on a usage-based plan because the "taximeter" is not running constantly.
- Convenience effect: Customers opt for a flat rate to save time and avoid search costs.
- Overestimation effect: Customers choose a flat rate because they overestimate how much they will use a service.

From the perspective of prospect theory, every phone call or online interaction provides a positive value. We have these experiences daily, and their sum is greater than the negative utility of the flat rate, which we pay once a month.

An important prerequisite for offering a flat rate is a marginal cost level of zero or near zero. Jeremy Rifkin [31] devoted a book, *The Zero Marginal Cost Society*, to this phenomenon and its consequences. Marginal costs at or near zero are indeed a new phenomenon of the Internet age, at least on a broad basis. We are, however, somewhat skeptical about this point. Within certain limits or ranges, marginal costs may actually be near zero. But if demand explodes, a company faces a step change in fixed costs due to the required capacity expansions. It means that marginal costs are at or near zero only when one considers an individual user or a small number of users, but not for larger numbers of users. We will take a closer look at the problem of zero marginal costs below.

If consumption or usage is not constrained by some natural or artificial limits, companies should be very careful with flat rates. It is critical to have detailed information about the distribution of light vs. heavy users and to run rigorous simulations. Otherwise, one can experience a nasty surprise with flat rates. If the number of heavy users is large, flat rates put profits at considerable risk. This explains why the US-based online book subscription service Scribd switched from an unlimited service to one with a restricted selection of titles subscribers can access for $8.99 per month. Scribd has to pay publishers a licensing fee for every download, and readers downloaded so many books that the service became unprofitable for Scribd [32]. One should be careful, though, when marginal costs are truly zero. Pricing is ultimately about extracting customers' willingness to pay and not only about marginal costs.

14.3.2 Freemium

Freemium is a pricing innovation which is in widespread use online. Freemium derives from the words "free" and "premium" and refers to a price strategy under which customers can use a basic version of a product or service free of charge or pay a fee to use a higher-value premium version of the same product or service. For a freemium model, it is even more important than for flat rates that marginal costs are at or near zero, at least for the basic version. This ensures that the free basic option will not become an undue burden for the supplier. "Freemium-like" models also exist in the offline world. Banks lure customers in with free checking accounts, but if the customers want anything beyond basic services, they must pay. The free offers for a basic bank account often came with conditions, such as a minimum balance requirement. But such offers only look like freemium models. The customer pays because they earn little or no interest on their deposits. A similar hidden payment occurs with "zero-percent" financing offers from retailers or car dealers. The financing costs are hidden in the purchase price [33].

The goal of freemium models is to use the free version to attract the largest number of potential customers. One author who is critical of freemium services described the process as "fattening up the customer with free goods and then milking them later" [34]. The company hopes that if the users become comfortable with the basic functionality, they will have a growing interest in paying for a version which is more powerful, more advanced, or offers additional functionality. Freemium fits very well to experience goods, whose full value only becomes apparent when customers have had a chance to use the good. In these cases, one could interpret freemium as a specific form of penetration strategy.

Freemium models are experiencing a growing popularity. Typical uses are in software (e.g., Skype), media and entertainment (e.g., Spotify), games (e.g., Farmville), apps (e.g., Angry Birds), social networks (e.g., LinkedIn), or web services. One form of differentiation is whether the free version will be combined with advertising. For many freemium services, the free offer is truly "free," i.e., there are no advertisements. An example is the smartphone and tablet version of Microsoft Office, whose basic version is made available to customers free of charge [35]. The user "pays" however with his or her data. LinkedIn is another example. For other freemium services, users of the free basic service must accept advertisements which accompany or interrupt the service. Spotify is an example. The users who pay $9.99 for the premium version receive their music with interruption from ads, while users of the free version have an experience similar to AM/FM radio: songs with occasional advertisements in between. In that case, the users "pay" with their attention. The dictionary leo.org offers its services for free but shows advertisements. If someone tries to block the ads, the site asks the user for a donation. This could be interpreted as a variant of the pay-what-you-want model, which we will elaborate on below.

LinkedIn goes a step further with its premium offer and differentiates its prices according to the user's needs. The version designed around "Land your dream job" costs $29.99 per month. The premium page "Select and nurture your network" costs $59.99 per month, and the "Unlock sales opportunities" has a price of $79.99 per month. Apparently LinkedIn feels that job seekers, networkers, and salespeople have significantly different willingness to pay for its service. In addition, each offer comes with a discount of around 20% if the user books in advance for 1 year. The communications software Skype offers complete functionality but limits free calls to within its own network. Once users grow accustomed to the intuitive user interface, they are presumably ready to pay a price to make calls into cellular or fixed-line networks. At the outset, Skype focused on selling talk time in minutes. Later, it changed its offer to one structurally similar to what classic telecom companies use. The current paid offers include minute packages or flat rates for selected national networks.

The key success factors for freemium models are:

1. An attractive basic offer, which brings in many users
2. The proper fencing between the basic and premium versions, in order to convert enough first-time buyers
3. A concept which turns the free users into loyal repeat buyers with the highest customer lifetime value

There is a trade-off relationship between 1 and 2. If the basic offer is too attractive, it will make it hard to construct a premium offer. The company acquires a large number of users, but only a few of them will upgrade to the premium version. If the basic offer is too thin and not sufficiently attractive, the company fails to attract enough free users to convert. The company may have a high conversion rate to the premium version, but the overall total number of paying customer remains low. The fencing between the basic and premium offers is achieved through features, product versions, or differences in usage intensity.

Newspapers have started to embrace freemium models as well, after years of living in the "free culture" for digital content. In past years, most online versions of newspapers generated their revenue exclusively through advertising. In order to get money directly from readers, many publishers implemented paywalls. The main instrument for fencing in this case is not a higher-value version but rather the usage intensity. *The New York Times* allows a reader to view up to ten articles per month free of charge [36]. If readers want to read more articles, they need to pay. Subscribers to the print version receive free access to the online version of the newspaper. It is interesting to note that the digital monthly subscriptions to *The New York Times* are available from $0.99 cents per month, while the list price would be between $15 and $35. The Kindle version of *The New York Times* has a monthly price of $19.99.

Bridging the "penny gap" is the biggest hurdle which freemium offers face. For publishers, the challenge lies in weaning customers off of the "free culture" and establishing the digital content as a paid service. The IBM manager Saul Berman [37] named that "the challenge of the decade"—how do publishers get their readers to pay for online content? The situation may get worse for publishers, as the following comment implies: "Subsequent generations will have forgotten how to spend money on content because they perceive content as something freely available and only a mouse click away. An entire generation is coming of age which can no longer judge the value of cultural events." The same applies to apps: "Barely one percent of all apps have a price at the time of download." [34]

So far very few media companies have tried to achieve revenues solely from their journalistic work. One example is the French investigative and opinion newspaper *Mediapart*, led by former *Le Monde* editor in chief Edwy Plenel. Available purely online, *Mediapart* charges a monthly subscription fee of €11, has 140,000 subscribers, and generates revenue of €11 million. It is now the third largest French newspaper after *Le Monde* and *Le Figaro* and, even more amazing, is highly profitable with a return on sales of 16% it [38]. *Mediapart* accepts no advertising.

At the start of one of our projects for a social network using a freemium model, only 8% of its users were premium customers. Using online price tests, we found out that price changes would barely affect revenue. Because the company faced many comparable competitors—some with completely free offers—the number of premium users fell quickly in the tests after a price increase. Price cuts, in contrast, did not attract many new customers. The price elasticities were roughly -1. That means that price changes would be more or less revenue-neutral, as volume changes tended to balance them out. What did an effect have, however, were changes to the portfolio and to the offers themselves. On the strength of better, more content-rich offers, the share of premium customers rose from 8% to 10%. That represents a growth of 25% and corresponded exactly to the increase in revenue. It was the network's most successful project ever, and it confirms the central role that usage plays. The value difference between "free" and "paid" must be large enough to get customers across the penny gap.

In online gaming, the freemium model has become so popular that even classic game manufacturers have started to offer many games online for free, with the goal of earning money with individual features. Based on its popular "Need for Speed" racing game, Electronic Arts has developed a freemium product called "Need for Speed World." The player can use real money to purchase play money, which he or she can then use to buy additional cars or optional equipment to improve their cars' performance. Micropayments play a major role in such offerings. Small amounts paid by many users can add up to considerable sums. Super Mario Run, Nintendo's first complete mobile gaming app, can serve as an example. The game costs $10, but one can play the first three levels for free. After the introduction of the gaming app in December 2016, Nintendo's share price fell by 11%. This is attributable to what turned out to be an unsuccessful freemium model: users complained massively that they played through the free levels too quickly and that the price for the complete game was too high [39].

From a company's perspective, whether a freemium model is better than a conventional price structure or scheme depends on the competition, the target customers, and the product features [40]. The key metrics are conversion and the customer lifetime value of the premium customers. A company can get several hundred dollars from such customers, whereas users of the basic product generate no revenue at all. A systematic optimization of price and product using a freemium model typically increases revenues and profits by up to 20%, according to our project experience.

Media companies, however, can do very well without pursuing a freemium model, as we learned from a project for a leading magazine in the United States. Under the new price system, the print and online editions were both offered separately at annual subscription prices of $118. The price for the bundle of print and online was $148, a discount of 37% against the combined price of $236, which is the sum of the two individual prices. After implementation, the average revenue per subscriber rose by 15%, with no relevant loss of subscribers. One should note, however, that this magazine enjoys a very strong reputation. Customers are obviously willing to pay for it, and they perceive the combined access to the print and online versions as true added value.

The electric car manufacturer Tesla offers its customers a free service, not a freemium service. Customers who bought a car before 2017 could recharge their batteries at any time and at no cost at any supercharger station installed by Tesla. But customers who buy their cars starting in 2017 will only receive 1000 miles of free charging before they will need to pay to recharge batteries. The original idea from Tesla founder Elon Musk was that he could get the electricity for the stations at a marginal cost of zero from the solar power firm Solar City, which was founded by Musk and later bought by Tesla [41]. In the best case, that model would work well in the United States and only at times when the electricity costs are essentially zero. By the end of 2017, Tesla has installed 8250 supercharger stations around the world [42]. One article [43] calculated that the value of the electricity consumed by Tesla drivers at the charging stations in Germany in 2014 was more than €500,000. In addition to the cost of the electricity, Tesla incurred estimated installation costs of

€2.6 million for the charging stations. Offering a good at a price of zero after one has incurred costs for it, or has marginal costs greater than zero, is not a promising long-term business model. The more cars Tesla sold, the riskier this free model would be—hence the transition to a fee-based model once the introductory allowance has been consumed for cars sold in 2017 or later.

14.3.3 Interactive Pricing Models

Under interactive price models, the price is determined through an interactive process between the buyer and the seller. Historically speaking, interactive price models have dominated commerce. At the bazaar, prices were always negotiated, just as they are today at flea markets. The Internet has made it easier for buyers and sellers to interact and breathed new life into this kind of pricing model. Acceptance and success, however, have been mixed.

14.3.3.1 Name-Your-Own-Price
During the first Internet wave, there were high expectations for a price model under which the customer offers a price and the seller then decides whether or not to accept that price. "Name- your-own-price," also known as customer-driven pricing or reverse pricing, is a process which the seller expects will encourage the customers to reveal their true willingness to pay. The customer's price is binding, and payment is secured either through a credit card number or an Automated Clearing House (ACH) process. As soon as a customer's offer exceeds the seller's minimum price (known only to the seller), that customer wins the bid and pays the price he or she named. Such binding price offers form a "real" price-response function. We refer to Fig. 3.13, which shows such a function for a notebook.

The US firm Priceline.com is considered to be the inventor of the name-your-own-price model, but this model was not confined to the United States. In Germany there were several competitors including ihrpreis.de and tallyman.de. In the early years, the sites offered a wide assortment of products, although electronics and services (travel, hotels) were at the forefront. It turned out, though, that most customers submitted unrealistically low price offers. Either the name-your-own-price sites only appealed to bargain hunters or consumers shied away from revealing their true willingness to pay in an attempt to acquire products at extremely low prices. Eventually, the name-your-own-price model proved unsuccessful. Priceline.com did survive but with a different business model. Today, Priceline.com is a major Internet marketer with $9.2 billion in revenues and a market capitalization of $70.5 billion. The largest contributor to these numbers is the site booking.com, which originated in the Netherlands. The name-your-own-price tool, in contrast, contributes only a tiny amount to Priceline revenue. That platform sells overstock or excess capacity to extremely price sensitive customers who do not mind putting up with inconveniences in exchange for a low price, such as having multiple connecting flights on a single trip. The homepage of Priceline.com [44] says: "The Name Your Own Price® service uses the flexibility of buyers to enable sellers to accept a lower price in order to sell their excess capacity without disrupting their existing distribution channels or retail pricing structures." Despite its theoretically interesting potential with respect to customers revealing their true willingness to pay, the name-your-own-price model has not fulfilled expectations so far. But this does not rule out a future comeback or its suitability as a means to dispose of overstock or excess capacity.

14.3.3.2 Pay-What-You-Want

A variant of customer-driven pricing is the pay-what-you-want model. In this case the customer pays what he or she wants, without the seller being able to turn down the offer. The pay-what-you-want model is attracting some attention. The amount the customer decides to pay depends on social preferences regarding a fair sharing of the estimated value between buyer and seller. The desire to support the supplier and keep it in the market over the long term can play a role [45]. Under the motto "pay as much as you like," a zoo conducted several marketing actions which led to a fivefold increase in visitors and a doubling of revenues. It turned out that visitors paid on average only 40% of the normal price of €14 for adults and €7 for children. The higher visitor numbers more than compensated, however, for the "discount" of 60%. One suspects, though, that this effect would not be sustainable. This model was also used for a tour at a historic building. The number of visitors did not increase, but the "admission prices paid were slightly above the usual prices" [46, p. 6], which were €2 for adults and €1.50 for children. We attribute the different results of the two experiments to the differences in price levels. A test at a movie theater, whose normal price levels were similar to those of the zoo, also saw customers pay significantly less than the normal prices.

The music group Radiohead released its album "In Rainbows" online with a pay-what-you-want model. The album was downloaded over one million times, with 40% of the "buyers" paying an average price of $6 apiece [47]. Occasionally one will see a restaurant, hotel, or other service business try a similar approach. After finishing the meal or checking out, the guest pays whatever price he or she wants to. From a pricing standpoint, the seller is entirely at the buyer's mercy. In such situations, the seller may indeed see a certain number of customers pay prices that cover costs. Other customers will take advantage of the opportunity to pay little or even nothing. In contrast to zoos, museums, cinemas, or other facilities which use such models, the hotels and especially the restaurants incur variable costs which make the pay-what-you-want model much riskier. A young entrepreneur argues the opposite, though. She operates a mobile massage service at the airport in Cologne, Germany. In her experience, the customers do not take advantage of the pay-what-you-want model and pay between €1 and €2 per minute on average. She attributes this to the personal contact with the customers.

A variant of the pay-what-you-want model is variable price components which depend on customer satisfaction. The approach is occasionally used in consulting. In addition to a fixed fee, the two parties agree on a variable fee whose amount is determined by the customer's satisfaction on a pre-defined scale. In this case the supplier is also at the customer's mercy, which is why we consider such models with skepticism. But if the supplier must choose between offering an upfront discount and agreeing to a satisfaction-based variable price component, it may make sense to choose the latter option.

One can consider tipping to be another variant of the pay-what-you-want model. Normally the customers decide how much they will tip, above and beyond the formal fixed price. But there are also systems under which the tip is not truly voluntary. In most US restaurants, social customs "require" a tip of at least 15% in order to avoid a negative reaction or a protest from the wait staff. Such tips often form a significant part of the wait staff's compensation.

The platform activehours.com offers an innovative pay-what-you-want approach. The firm offers cash advances or loans against paychecks. Activehours finances the loan for a short period, and in most cases, the employer repays Activehours directly. This means that Activehours has a minimal credit risk. The difference is that it does not charge any interest or fees. Instead it says: "No fees, just tips." The model is described as follows: "Pay what you think is fair. That's right, it's all up to you. We don't have fixed fees—you can choose how much you want to pay for our service." [48] Because the cash advance (loan) is only for a short period (e.g., 1 week), even a "tip" of 1% represents an extremely high interest rate. One can also imagine that customers will want to use this service again and will therefore pay a "tip." Whether this "voluntary" pay-what-you-want model will last or face government intervention—which is currently under discussion—remains to be seen. One can interpret donations as a form of pay-what-you-want. One should not refer to a donation as a "price," however, because there is no tangible value exchange in return.

A recently published review [49] summarizes the potential benefits of a pay-what-you-want model as follows:

- Pay-what-you-want has a broad scope of application throughout industries.
- In low turnover periods, pay-what-you-want can be applied as a promotion strategy.
- Heterogeneous customer valuations of products and services can be exploited.
- Pay-what-you-want has positive effects on customer loyalty and commitment to a seller.

We see this model more critically and with a certain skepticism. One reason is that there is a fundamental difference between the pay-what-you-want and the name-your-own-price customer-driven models. In the latter model, the seller can decide whether accept or refuse the price the customer names and that decision comes before any goods or services are exchanged. Under a pay-what-you-want model, consumption can occur before payment is required or the price is set, or after payment, as an admission charge. And the seller no longer has any decision power. Pay-what-you-want offers are unconditional and put sellers at the mercy of the customers and their willingness to pay. Therefore, sellers should exercise great care with a pay-what-you-want system.

14.3.3.3 Rebate Systems

The German website billig.de is an example of a rebate system. This site refers customers to its affiliated partner shops and then receives a commission for each referral which results in a purchase. The commission varies from shop to shop. This amount is then credited to the customer's account in the form of a rebate. The online platform Shoop works on the same principle. Shoop receives a commission for each referral and passes on the full amount to customers. Shoop openly communicates that it receives a bonus payment from dealers if it makes a large enough number of referrals, that is, how the platform finances itself. One study showed that customers who receive rebates are more satisfied and cancel less often, even though they paid more to begin with [50]. The cash-back tactic we discussed in Chap. 4 can also be interpreted as a type of rebate. From the perspective of prospect theory, a customer experiences additional positive value from a rebate. Interactive price models are used more frequently in the online world than offline. This trend has by no means played out. There is room for more innovative interactive price models.

14.3.4 Pay-Per-Use

The traditional business model is straightforward: one purchases a product, pays a price, and uses the product. Under this transaction model, an airline buys jet engines for its airplanes; a logistics firm buys tires for its trucks and trailers; and a carmaker invests in a painting facility, purchases paint, and paints its cars. Leasing and renting models, as we described earlier in this chapter, abandon this traditional transaction model to some extent. Taking a needs-oriented perspective creates a totally different basis for setting prices. The needs of the customers often do not warrant owning the product; they would rather have the benefit, the performance, and the needs fulfillment that the product provides. An airline does not have to own jet engines for its aircraft. It needs thrust. Similarly, the trucking company needs the performance of the tires, and the car manufacturer needs a painted car. The user of a computer needs computational power or data availability but does not need a local server. This point of view suggests that the supplier should charge a price for the respective performance or benefit, rather than sell the product in exchange for a one-time payment. That is the basis for the innovative pay-per-use model, also known as pay-as-you-go price model. In many cases a prerequisite for such a model is new technology which allows discrete measurement of the performance aspects, allowing individual units to be priced.

Innovators in the area include the jet engine manufacturers General Electric and Rolls Royce, which offer their customers thrust instead of the jet engines themselves and charge for thrust by the hour. For a manufacturer this can mean a completely different business model as it marks the transition from a product to a service business. The company no longer sells products; it sells services. Taking this one step further, such systems create the potential for greater revenue than the previous product-based businesses. The price per hour can comprise the operation of the jet engines, their maintenance, and other services. The airline customers gain several advantages from this price model including reduced complexity, lower capital expenditure, and the elimination of fixed costs and personnel.

Michelin, the world market leader in car and truck tires, developed an innovative pay-per-use model to better capture value-to-customer. Instead of buying tires and paying for them, the customers pay a price per kilometer or mile driven. In the United States, Michelin also offers this program to public entities, e.g., for school buses. Because the number of miles driven is tracked anyway, Michelin can tap into actual data. Other tire manufacturers offer similar systems to operators of trucking or industrial vehicle fleets. Let us assume that a new tire had a performance which was 25% better than the previous model. It would be extremely difficult to charge a price that is 25% higher. As we know from psychological analyses, customers grow accustomed to price levels, which form solid price anchors over time. Tire customers are no different. Deviations from these anchors will meet resistance, even if the new products perform better. The pay-per-use model overcomes that problem. The customer pays by the mile or kilometer for use of a tire, and if the tires last 25% longer, the customer automatically pays 25% more. This model allows the seller to extract the added value to a greater degree than the traditional product-price model. The customers also benefit: the tires cost them something only when the trucks actually roll, which means the fleet is generating revenue. If demand is weak and the truck remains parked in the lots, the tires do not cost the company anything. The model also simplifies the business calculations of the truckers. They often charge their customers by the mile or kilometer, so it helps when their own variable costs (in this case, the cost of tires) are expressed in the same metric. For aircraft tires, the number of landings is used as the price metric, because the landing is what determines tire wear-and-tear.

Similarly, Dürr, the world market leader in automotive paint plants, teamed up with BASF, the world market leader in automotive paints, to offer car manufacturers a new model: charge one fixed price per car painted. This arrangement provides car manufacturers a firm basis for their own financial calculations because it transfers the price and cost risks of painting to the suppliers. It also reduces complexity and the need for capital investment. EnviroFalk, a specialist for industrial water treatment, installs its units in its customers' facilities at no cost and then charges them per cubic meter of water treated. These pay-per-use models give suppliers a cash flow they can plan on over time and also allow them to find an optimal coordination between plants/installations and the input materials. The business model, which Philips uses in cooperation with a Dutch energy utility at Amsterdam's Schiphol Airport, is similar. The airport operator does not pay for lighting installations, but rather for the required lighting, which is measured in units of lux (lumens per square meter). Philips maintains ownership of the entire installation [51].

Pay-per-use models have been put into practice in industries which would not immediately come to mind as well-suited, for example, in the insurance industry. Car insurers in several countries use the following system: a black box is installed in the customer's car, with the black box linked to a GPS system of the insurer. The customer pays by mile depending on which route the driver chooses, the time of day, and the accident risk on that route. This detailed knowledge of the customers and how they drive makes it unnecessary to have drivers with different risk profiles cross-subsidize each other [52]. Aviva, formerly Norwich Union, an insurance company in England, offered such a model, but even though it was quite popular, it was not economical because of the high technology costs. An Aviva spokesman comments on the demand for their pay-per-use model as follows: "Ultimately, we were just a bit ahead of our time" [53]. The US company Metromile offers a similar concept. It calls for the insured driver to pay a fixed monthly fee of $35 plus $0.05 per mile driven [51]. So far, this model has achieved a market share of 10% of car insurance coverage in the United States. Previous risk parameters such as age and place are replaced by truly causal risk parameters [54].

End-to-end solutions from one supplier can have a higher value for customers because they offer more assurance and more efficiency. The Australian company Orica, the global market leader in commercial explosives, offers rock quarry companies a complete solution. Orica supplies not only the explosives but also analyzes the stone formations and does the drilling and blasting itself. In this comprehensive solution, Orica provides the customer with blasted rock and charges by the ton. Because each Orica solution is customer-specific, it is hard for customers to compare prices. For Orica, revenue per customer, efficiency, and safety all increase. The customers do not have to take care of the blasting anymore. It is also harder for them to switch suppliers.

If one broadens this needs-oriented perspective, one can imagine many other opportunities for pay-per-use models. But there are certain technical prerequisites which need to be met to make such price models cost-efficient to operate. These include simple ways to measure actual usage as well as information systems which can measure and transmit usage data at low cost. For instance, there is no reason why someone needs to purchase a car or lease one at a fixed price per month. One can charge for driving—for instance, as a function of distance driven and time of day— the same way one charges for phone services or electricity. Pay-per-use or pay-per-view is also penetrating the media business. In cable television, one can charge for actual usage instead of a flat monthly rate. The Korean company HanaroTV (part of SK Broadband) quickly signed up one million customers with that kind of model. The pay-per-use model is also useful in facility management, e.g., for the operation of heating or air conditioning systems. Machines can be priced based on their actual performance rather than at fixed daily or monthly rates. Similar to the model with truck tires, such a system allows the suppliers to extract value more effectively and leads to greater overall willingness to pay.

Pay-per-use will not succeed in every situation, though. Some customers prefer to own their products outright (e.g., 24/7 availability, cleanliness), while others are willing to pay a higher bundled price so that they do not have to track their usage and expenditures constantly. At the request of a leading manufacturer, we developed a pay-per-use model for elevators in large office buildings. The initial hypothesis was that people should pay for "vertical" transportation just as they pay for "horizontal" transportation (bus, rail, taxi, etc.). There is no inherent reason why they should not. In the spirit of the pay-per-use model, the elevator manufacturer would install the units for nothing but in return would receive a long-term right to charge for elevator usage. To implement this, the tenants in the building would purchase special cards for their employees to track elevator usage or have the price model and usage tracking built into the security cards already in use in the building. This pay-per-use model allocates the cost of elevator usage appropriately and more "fairly" than the typical lump-sum models, which are incorporated either into the rent or added as a surcharge. Whoever rides more pays more. One can even differentiate the prices by floor, usage intensity, or other similar criteria. So far, this model has not seen widespread adoption. Perhaps it was too innovative and went too much against the grain of established habits. But it certainly has potential.

14.3.5 New Price Metrics

A very innovative approach is to change the measurement basis for the price. One refers to this basis as the price metric. Some of the previous cases in this chapter involve a new price metric (e.g., per mile vs. per tire), but in most of them, the company changed the business model, not just the price metric. One case from the building materials industry shows the potential that changing a price metric has. If a company sells material for wall construction, it could charge by weight (price per ton), by space (price per cubic meter), by surface area (price per square meter), or for the complete installation (price per square meter of finished wall). For each metric, the company could charge very different prices and face very different competitive relationships. For example, with one new type of concrete, a leading manufacturer's price was 40% more expensive than the competitors' with tons or cubic meters as the price metric. But with square meters as the metric, the price difference was only about 10%. Because the new blocks allowed a team to build the walls faster and more easily, the price per square meter for a finished wall conferred a price advantage of 12%. This makes it clear that the manufacturer should try to switch the price metric for these new blocks to square meters of finished wall. The problem is that it is not always easy to implement such changes to long-established metrics. The more innovative the product is or the stronger the manufacturer's market position is, the greater the chances are to convince customers that the new metric is acceptable.

Hilti is a global leader for high-performance electric power tools. Such suppliers traditionally sell their products. Hilti introduced a new system for its tools, analogous to a "fleet management" model. The customer pays a fixed monthly price for its "fleet" of Hilti tools. Hilti ensures that the customer receives the optimal set of tools for that customer's set of jobs. Hilti also takes care of everything from repairs, battery exchange, and comprehensive services. The customer can count on a predictable, fixed monthly price and can focus on its core competencies, namely, the work at the jobsite.

The rise of cloud computing has also given rise to new price metrics. Software is no longer sold on a license basis and then installed on-premise on the customer's own servers but rather offered online and on-demand for a fee. The new business model is known as Software-as-a-Service (SaaS). Microsoft's Office 365 suite is

offered as a monthly or annual subscription. The Office 365 Home Premium costs
$9.99 per month or $99.99 per year. In return the customer receives immediate
online access to the latest versions and a range of additional services. Salesforce's
Sales Cloud, the leading CRM application for managing customer contacts, leads,
and opportunities, operates under the same kind of model. The monthly price begins
at $25 for up to five users with limited functionality (SalesforceIQ CRM Starter). For
an unlimited number of users with expanded functionality, one pays $75 per user per
month (Lightning Professional). The most expensive and comprehensive version,
Lightning Unlimited, costs $300 per user per month. From these different
components, a customer can put together an online business software package
which is the ideal fit for its needs. The customer can also adjust the number of
monthly user licenses in line with its needs. The monthly price will then vary
accordingly based on the needs of the customer. Such price models are likely to
become the standard for cloud-based application software.

The price metric for car sharing services is nothing fundamentally new, but in
terms of its precision, it goes beyond the traditional model for car rentals. Zipcar,
Car2Go, and similar car sharing services charge by the minute. Furthermore, once
the base number of miles included in the rate is exceeded, a fee per mile comes into
effect. Progress in digital technology makes it possible to bill the customer on a
minute-and-mileage basis without any additional effort on the part of the customer.

The price system for Google AdWords is also based on a new price metric.
Classic media companies use reach, even though its effect on the sales volume or
image of the advertised brand remains unclear. In contrast, Goode AdWords uses a
pay-per-click system. Apparently, advertisers feel that this kind of pricing is more
closely linked to the causality of advertising effectiveness. Google has attracted a
large share of the online advertising pie.

Enercon, the global technology leader in wind energy, uses a very innovative
price metric. It describes its "Enercon Partner Concept" (EPC) as follows: "From
scheduled maintenance to security services, to unscheduled maintenance and repairs,
all eventualities are covered under one contract." The customer pays a minimum
amount based on the type of installation. That minimum fee covers, among other
things, the following services: regular maintenance, availability guarantee, and
repairs including parts, shipping, crane costs, and 24-h remote monitoring. Beyond
that the customer's payments are based on the actual annual energy yield from the
wind turbine(s). In good wind years with high yields, the customer pays more, and in
poor wind years with lower yields, the customer pays less. In order to keep the cost
burden as low as possible in the first 5 years of operation, ENERCON assumes half
of the amounts due under the EPC during this period. Starting with the sixth year of
operation, the customer pays the full amount according to the formula: Price = Sup-
plied kWh × Price per kWh [55]. This innovative offer apparently gets very high
levels of acceptance among customers. More than 85% of them sign an EPC
contract. What makes this approach stand out is how Enercon reduces its customers'
entrepreneurial risks by sharing those risks with them. An important requirement for
that commitment is that Enercon can measure the yield of the wind turbines itself.
There is no way for the customers to manipulate the data.

Alternative price metrics are also on the rise in health insurance. Certain activities with known health benefits could be incentivized through lower insurance premiums. There are many other potential ways to deploy new price metrics in the health field. Smart watches, sensors in armbands, and other forms of remote diagnosis make measurement simpler. The British health insurer AIG Direct uses body mass index (BMI) as the basis for determining monthly rates. Exemptions are made only in special cases such as people who participate in a lot of sports and whose muscle mass can therefore skew a BMI calculation [51]. Price incentives allow an insurer to reward desired behaviors and penalize detrimental behaviors [56].

The Teatreneu in Barcelona introduced a futuristic price metric—the seats in the theater were outfitted with sensors which can analyze facial expressions. The theatergoer must pay €0.30 for each laugh recognized by the sensor, up to maximum of €24 (or 80 laughs). The payment is made via cell phone. The revenue has reportedly risen by €6 per person [57]. This example may strike people as somewhat exotic, and it likely will not become the standard model for theaters in the future. But it shows what is technically possible. And does it not make sense to pay more for an enjoyable theater performance than a boring one?

Fundamentally speaking, one could call every conventional price metric into question. Let us discuss the price metric "time." Time-based price metrics are used by hotels (1 day), package tours (1 week), public transportation (1 month), museums (1 year), or craftsmen (1 h). Restaurants, however, normally use a menu-based metric, hair salons use case-by-case metric, and taxis charge on a distance-based metric. But one could imagine that restaurants, hair salons, and taxis could also use time-based metrics. If the bottleneck at a restaurant is the number of available tables, it could make more sense to charge patrons by time in order to achieve the highest possible turnover. Thinking about price metrics opens new avenues for price management.

In air travel, the price is traditionally set per person, but there is differentiation by age, status, or similar criteria. The airline Samoa Air Ltd. thought up a different price metric. It charges passengers according to their body weight. The price for a flight from Samoa to American Samoa costs $0.92/kg. Samoa has the world's third highest level of overweight people, far ahead of the United States, which makes such a price metric seems compelling. Despite initial protests, CEO Chris Langton wants to stick to the plan: "It's a pay by weight system and it's here to stay," he said [58]. The logic speaks for such a system. The weight of passengers is a true cost driver for an airline, not age or status. Why should the transport of freight be charged by weight, but not the transport of people? Some US airlines have started to demand that extremely large passengers buy two tickets on a full flight.

New technologies will increasingly make performance-based price metrics possible. As the cases described so far show, the measurement of the service delivered is crucial for pay-per-use models and new price metrics. Only if the result can be measured automatically are these models economically efficient. Software-as-a-Service (SaaS) is extending into Results-as-a-Service (RaaS), which is closer to the actual benefit the customer wants to receive (like in Teatreneu). Sensors play a critical role in this context. One can imagine in health care that the effects of pharmaceuticals, medical treatments, or other services can be measured with sensors. The prices may then be set depending on the actual efficacy or efficiency. The same can be said for industrial services related to factory automation or preventative maintenance or environmental processes. Of course, the technically measured values must be close to the value-to-customer. Only then they can be translated into price units. But that is not fundamentally different from the general problem of trying to express value-to-customer in terms of price.

14.3.6 Two-Sided Price Systems

A two-sided price system draws on revenue sources from two sides of the value chain. These are also referred to as two-sided markets. Classic examples are newspapers and magazines, who on one side charge their readers a price and on the other side generate revenue from advertisers. Two-sided price systems are also found in waste management. The waste producers pay a fee to waste management companies for removal, and the waste management companies then sell the waste to generate additional revenue. Firms which clear out buildings or houses receive a fee for their service and can resell what they have removed. Real estate agents sometimes receive a commission from buyers and sellers on the same transaction. Many online firms use two-sided systems which resemble the classic media model, i.e., a portion of revenue comes from advertising and the other portion from fees paid by users. Spotify finances its free version with advertising which the non-paying users are exposed to, while premium users pay a fee but see no advertising. Such two-sided systems work only when all parties benefit. The advertisers are interested in reaching readers, viewers, or listeners. The users appreciate having access to a medium at a lower price. Without the second revenue source, the price for the user would be significantly higher. The media company is dependent on both revenue sources in order to achieve an appropriate level of profit. The bonus program PAYBACK uses a two-sided price system for a portion of its business. In addition to fees from participating firms, the customers of the PAYBACK Visa card pay a fee of €25 starting in the second year of usage. The firm Yodlee operates an online personal finance tool for 11 of the 20 largest US banks. Yodlee is paid by the banks for this service, which gives it access to data on millions of transactions. But Yodlee sells this data to investment firms who pay an annual subscription of up to $2 million. Both revenue sources make a significant contribution to Yodlee's overall revenue [59]. The phenomenon of negative interest rates, which we will describe in greater detail below, can also lead to a two-sided price system. Financing a rental property at a negative interest rate means "the bank would pay you even as you collected rent from a tenant" [60, p. 16].

Two-sided systems offer larger degrees of freedom for pricing. One needs to decide whether to set the user price lower, in order to boost the number of users. A higher number of users brings in higher advertising revenues, which can more than compensate for the forgone contribution margin on the user side. A higher product price, in contrast, could lead to higher direct revenue but to a decrease in the number of users and lower advertising revenue.

Because of its network nature, the Internet opens up new opportunities for two-sided price systems. One of its most important abilities is to bring suppliers and customers together. Websites such as eBay, Google, and Facebook capitalize on this ability. Google also brings knowledge sources and knowledge seekers together. The participants on both sides are identifiable. Technically it would not be a problem for eBay or Alibaba to charge buyers a price and not only sellers. Google uses a one-sided price system under which only the advertisers pay. But it could be technically feasible for Google to charge the information seekers a fee. If these fees were only very tiny amounts, i.e., so-called micropayments, many users would still search via Google. The same applies to Wikipedia, which finances itself exclusively through donations and collects neither user fees nor advertising income. All in all, the Internet has a much more diverse range of potential ways than classic media to use two-sided price systems. We expect an increase in pricing innovations of that kind.

14.3.7 Negative Prices

In normal transactions, the buyer pays the seller a positive price and receives a product or service in return. With negative prices, the opposite is true. The seller pays the customer to take the product or service. At first glance it would appear that negative prices have always existed in waste disposal. But one can view these negative prices either as compensation for performing the waste disposal or conclude that the waste itself has a negative value, because getting rid of it has a cost. In most cases this applies to a by-product (e.g., chemical waste) which has no further useful value but which is an unavoidable result of producing a primary product which does have value.

Negative prices appear to be a new phenomenon. If nothing else, the frequency of their occurrence is new. Since 2009, negative prices have appeared repeatedly on the European Energy Exchange on a considerable scale. Table 14.1 shows the number of days on which negative prices occurred in the years 2009–2016.

Table 14.1 Number of days with negative electricity prices on the European Energy Exchange

Year	No. of days
2009	35
2010	18
2011	16
2012	15
2013	30
2014	28
2015	25
2016	24
2017	34

On these days, power customers paid electricity producers a (negative) price per megawatt hour. The buyer received electricity plus money. How can we explain this? Apparently one prerequisite is that at a price of zero, supply still outstrips demand. In other words, a price of zero does not create an equilibrium between supply and demand. There is an oversupply. Under such circumstances, the power companies would normally shut down production. That is not possible, however, for some forms of electricity generation, such as solar panels. Even traditional power plants have only limited flexibility to shut down and restart in response to imbalances in supply and demand. The electrical power they generate must get taken up by someone. And on some days, that happens only if the producer pays the buyer a negative price. One could speak of a "time-based by-product." In order to produce and earn a profit on days with positive prices, the producer needs to subsidize production and consumption on days with negative prices. "It is less expensive for the producers to keep their power plants online than to shut them down and restart them later" [61]. As Table 14.1 shows, negative electricity prices are not a temporary phenomenon. The opposite appears to be the case. One expert said: "the current market structure means we have the threat of negative prices becoming more frequent."

Another example for negative prices, historically speaking, are interest rates. One author describes the traditional point of view as follows: "The concept of negative interest rates was so outlandish it was not even mentioned in economics courses" [60, p. 16]. Negative interest rates were first observed in Denmark in 2012. A few years later, they had become a widespread and frequently debated topic, with the arguments sometimes taking on philosophical tones. Thomas Jordan, the president of Switzerland's central bank, said that "negative interest goes against human nature" [62, p. 29]. Countries such as Denmark, Switzerland, Germany, Finland, and Austria raised money at negative interest rates. In 2015, "the money market interest rate Euribor was calculated with a negative yield for the first time" [62]. In August 2015, the German federal government sold a 2-year bond at an interest rate of -0.25% [63]. The Swiss central bank charged an interest rate of -0.75% from its depositor banks [64]. As of 2016, there were more than €6 trillion worth of sovereign debt outstanding at negative interest rates. On a 2-year bond, Switzerland "pays" an interest of -1.14%, in Denmark the rate was -0.71%, and in Germany it was -0.29% [65]. Even private customers have not escaped the spread of negative interest rates. In October 2015 the "Alternative Bank Schweiz" (Alternative Bank of Switzerland, or ABS) became the first bank to introduce negative interest rates for private customers. For a deposit up to 100,000 Swiss francs, the depositor was charged -0.125% as interest; -0.75% was the rate for larger deposits [66]. In Germany, several banks charged negative interest rates as of 2016.

In April 2016, negative prices actually appeared for the first time in sales financing. The furniture dealer Who's Perfect offered "negative interest financing" for 24 months. The loan had an interest rate of 0%, but the buyer received 1% of the financed amount back. The financing had a negative price, albeit a slight one. That is also how Mercedes is marketing its A-Class 160 model with an effective annual interest rate of -1.26%.

But there are also loan offers at negative rates. In 2018, customers who take out loans from the online portal Check24 for €1000 only have to pay back €972.49 12 months later. This works out to an interest rate of minus 2.7%. Similarly, the comparison site Smava lends €1000 for 3 years but only asks for €923 in return [67]. In Denmark, Sweden, and Spain, private customers have received home-building loans with negative interest rates.

The economist Carl Christian von Weizsäcker speaks of "natural negative interest" as "a lasting phenomenon" [68, p. 189]. He sees the cause in the "structural oversupply of the private willingness to save vs. the private willingness to invest." With negative interest rates, the borrower not only pays no interest but receives interest from the lender, which was unthinkable in traditional banking.

If there is an oversupply of money in the market which cannot be invested even with an interest rate of zero, it can make more sense for a bank to lend the surplus money at an interest rate of -0.1% than to deposit it at the central bank at a negative interest rate of -0.2% or even -0.75% in Switzerland. When depositors are willing to make money available to banks at a negative interest rate, the bank can then lend this money at lower interest rate (absolute value) and still have a positive profit margin.

Figure 14.3 structurally illustrates the situation with positive and negative prices. We assume a price-response function of $q = 100 - 10p$, where q is the sales volume and p is the price.

At a negative price, the revenue will automatically be negative because we are multiplying a positive number (sales volume) with a negative one (price). In the

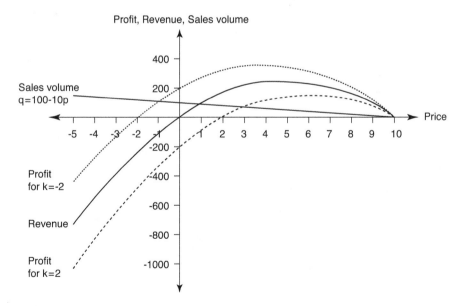

Fig. 14.3 Revenue and profit for positive and negative prices

negative price range, the revenue curve's downward slope becomes increasingly steeper. This steep drop results from a double effect. The lower the price, the greater the sales volume, i.e., both factors are larger in absolute terms, and the product of the two factors rises rapidly in absolute terms.

And what happens with profits? First, we will look at a situation in which we have positive variable unit costs of $k = 2$. For simplicity's sake we will assume that there are no fixed costs. Profit is zero when the price is 2, and the profit curve falls off in a similarly sharp fashion as the revenue curve does when prices turn negative. A price of zero yields a loss of $200, and a price of -2 results in a loss of $480. The profit curve shows how profit changes when we have variable unit costs of $k = -2$. That would correspond to the situation when banks receive money from depositors at a negative interest rate of -2% or when electricity resellers get power at negative prices.

In such cases, the profit is greater than the revenue. The profit maximum is still in the area with positive prices, in this case at a price of $4. Volume at that price is 60 units. This results in a unit contribution margin of $6, with $4 coming from the buyers as revenue and $2 from the suppliers who pay negative prices. This is a two-sided price model. The profit is $360. The firm can still earn a profit with prices between 0 and -2. The rate of decline of the profit curve is similar to those of the other profit curves when prices are negative; only the level of the curve is higher. It is theoretically possible for the profit-maximizing price to be negative. If variable unit costs were $k = -12$ in the example, the profit-optimal price would be -1, and the profit would be $1120. Nonetheless, it is highly unlikely that such a situation happens in real life.

Nowadays negative prices are still rather rare. Germany's Commerzbank is giving new customers €50. This is similar to the coupon of the same amount which METRO Cash & Carry gives to new customers. In its start-up phase, PayPal offered negative prices. Every new customer received $20 [69]. The Chinese bike rental company Mobike pays its customers for using its bikes. The goal is to attract as many customers as possible and to use their data for promotions, advertising, or localized selling [70]. Addison Lee, a big taxi company in the UK, pays customers £10 if they install its app.

There are situations across time and across products when negative prices can result. When a company introduces a new product, free samples (for instance, for a pharmaceutical product) are very common and these, of course, have a price of zero. As we showed in Chap. 6, this tactic can make sense if the price of zero stimulates unit sales in subsequent periods when the price is no longer zero and the product earns a positive contribution margin. But if one steps back and thinks about it for a moment, perhaps the acceptance of a new, previously unknown or unfamiliar product could be accelerated if the sellers pay the initial buyers a negative price instead of distributing the product at a price of "only" zero. Using a simple numerical example, we show that negative prices can be optimal under these circumstances. We consider two periods, the introductory period of a new product and the subsequent period. The goal is to maximize the total profit across both periods. The product in question is a digital product with marginal cost of zero. For

Table 14.2 Negative price with carryover

λ	p_1^*	p_2^*	π_1	π_2	Total
0.6	0	6.5	0	422.5	422.5
0.8	−0.5	7	−27.5	518	490.5
0.9	−1	8	−60	592	532

simplicity's sake we will not incorporate discounting nor will we consider fixed costs. These omissions do not affect our underlying argument.

In the first period, the price-response function is $q_1 = 50 - 10p_1$, while in the second period the function is $q_2 = 100 + \lambda * q_1 - 10p_2$, where q is the sales volume, p the price, λ the carryover coefficient, and π the profit. For various values of λ, we show the corresponding results in Table 14.2, rounded to the nearest 0.5.

With marginal costs of zero and a carryover effect, negative prices can be optimal. But the carryover coefficients must be relatively high (see Tables 7.1 and 7.2 for comparison) so that the optimal price slips into negative territory. In the era of digitalization, these conditions could certainly arise, as well as whenever marginal costs are zero. The carryover coefficients for many digital products may indeed be high, since once a customer adopts a system and is satisfied with it, he or she will remain a loyal customer.

We can use an analogous line of argument for cross-product effects. If Product A promotes sales of a highly profitable Product B, it can make sense to offer Product A at a negative price. This chain of effects lends itself to a freemium structure. The typical freemium model has a basic version with a price of zero. Why does the price floor need to be at this "arbitrary" level of zero? If the experience with the basic version really does drive conversion to the premium model, why not pay initial users or early adopters for a limited time to use the product, i.e., offer a negative price rather than a price of zero.

Another argument for using negative prices results from the anchor function which prices can have, as we discussed in Chap. 4. As mentioned above, it has often proven difficult to move away from a price of zero, especially when customers have grown accustomed to the zero price for a long period (such as for a bank account or for online information). This effect may be less severe for a negative price. In contrast to a price of zero, a negative price is not something customers would normally expect to last. They assume that it is only a matter of time before the seller charges a positive price. If this assumption is correct, it would mean that a price increase of −1 to 4 would lead to a smaller sales volume decline or loss of customers than a price increase from 0 to 4. As far as we know, this hypothesis has not yet been tested.

One should also look at the role negative prices could play in conjunction with promotions. This is especially true for new product introductions, which are often supported by large promotional budgets. That is not necessarily optimal. Depending on the relative magnitude of the price and promotion elasticities, a negative price can be more effective than advertising or similar measures. If that is true, one would be better off investing the available money in negative prices than in other marketing tools. Negative prices are still a rather rare phenomenon. Whether they will be used more often in cases of oversupply remains to be seen. Marginal costs of zero make their use more likely. But one should still be careful. One cannot rule out that certain customers exploit the negative prices without later bringing the company the sustained profits it expects.

14.3.8 Marginal Costs of Zero and the Sharing Economy

As we know from Chap. 5, marginal costs are one of the two determinants of the optimal price. According to the Amoroso-Robinson relation (Sect. 5.4.3), the profit-maximizing price results from a price elasticity-dependent markup on marginal costs. One of the special features of the Internet is that marginal costs in many cases are tending toward zero. However, the phenomenon of marginal costs at or near zero is not totally new. For software, and in some cases for pharmaceuticals and electronics, the marginal costs have been very low relative to the development costs. The same applies for the use of airline seats or hotel rooms when there is unutilized capacity. An additional guest only results in very small marginal costs. Online, though, the phenomenon of "zero marginal costs" is taking on much larger dimensions. Jeremy Rifkin [31] feels that this phenomenon is so revolutionary that in his book *The Zero Marginal Cost Society*, he even sees it leading to the "shrinking" or "eclipse" of capitalism. Taking a cue from former US Treasury Secretary Lawrence Summers, he bases his claim on the hypothesis that prices themselves are approaching the level of marginal costs. If marginal costs approach zero, prices would also approach zero, and no capitalist entrepreneur would be willing to produce goods or services at those prices any longer. Someone else must then assume that role, such as the government or a nonprofit organization. And that would be the end of capitalism.

Rifkin extends his zero-marginal-cost paradigm to many sectors of the economy [31]. One is education through so-called MOOCs or massive open online courses. Others are the energy sector (wind, solar) and the sharing economy. In the sharing economy, available capacity such as unused private rooms or cars are marketed and put to economic use instead of sitting empty or idle. There is no doubt that these phenomena—which are not totally new but which have spread like wildfire thanks to the Internet—will have significant effects on business models and price models. Some of these effects have already become reality, but the majority of them will happen in the future.

It is rare for marginal costs to be truly zero. Within his book, Rifkin correctly uses the phrasing "near-zero marginal costs" instead of the more provocative title [31]. When marginal costs are zero, as we know, the profit-maximizing price is identical to the revenue-maximizing price. At the revenue maximum, the price elasticity is -1. The Amoroso-Robinson relation maintains its validity as one approaches the revenue maximum (marginal view). We demonstrate this using the price-response function $q = 100 - 10p$ where q is the sales volume and p is the price. For unit costs of $k = 2$, the profit-maximizing price according to (5.7) is $p^* = 6$. The supplier sells 40 units. The revenue is \$240, and if we assume the fixed costs are zero, the profit is \$160. The price elasticity is -1.5, and the markup factor according to the Amoroso-Robinson relation is 3. What happens when the marginal costs drop to 0.1? The optimal price p^* falls to \$5.05 and differs only slightly from the revenue-maximizing price of \$5.00. Sales volume increases to 49.5 units, and revenue grows to \$249.98 and the profit to \$245. The price elasticity at this price is -1.0202, so that according to the Amoroso-Robinson relation (5.6), the markup factor is $-1.0202/-0.0202 = 50.5$. The calculation of $50.5 \times 0.1 = \$5.05$ confirms the optimal price. Marginal costs which are approaching zero therefore do not pose any fundamental problems to the guidelines on price decisions. The intensification of competition may result instead from the fact that the short-term lower limit for price lies at the marginal cost. Thus, when marginal cost is at or near zero, it means that the short-term lower limit for price likewise approaches zero. It should, therefore, not be surprising in the future to see extremely low prices on a more frequent basis. When marginal costs are zero, a seller which urgently needs liquidity can set its price just above marginal costs (i.e., just above zero) and still earn a contribution margin and generate cash flow.

Zero marginal costs resulting from the Internet and the sharing economy are likely to have very disruptive effects on business models, price levels, and competition. This has had a massive impact on the music industry, as we discussed at the outset of this chapter. The same is true for print media (newspapers and magazines). Book publishers and booksellers are also affected. YouTube, Netflix, and similar services form a new kind of competition for visual media such as film and television. The ability of the Internet to allow content distribution at essentially zero marginal cost has massive effects on prices. The Internet makes former intermediaries superfluous and takes away their revenue basis. Banking has changed with further radical changes to come. In contrast to conventional, manually processed transactions, digitally processed payments or securities transactions cause negligible marginal costs. The vast majority of personnel and branches will become redundant. Traditional business models which incurred significantly higher marginal costs will no longer be competitive on price and will disappear.

The effects on price and price competition from the sharing economy will be no less dramatic. The rental of unoccupied private rooms via Airbnb presents new, tough competition to hotels. The same is true for Uber and the taxi business. Apparently consumers have grown to appreciate the sharing economy, thanks to positive experiences. In a study from PwC, some 43% of the respondents said that they find it burdensome to own something and that sharing lessens that burden [71]. New players with innovative business models are entering the market all the time. On the platform zilok.com, one can borrow almost any kind of product. The commission, paid by the lending party, is based on the transaction value. The prices vary considerably. The firm BlaBlaCar, which originated in France, arranges two million ride shares per month. The BlaBlaCar prices undercut trains and even price-aggressive long-distance buses [72]. Ride sharing has historical precedents. In earlier times people would hitchhike or go through a carpooling center, but these were run more or less manually. The Internet creates a much larger ease and scale for matching someone who is already driving from A to B with someone who wants to travel that same stretch. It is logical that the extremely low prices are stimulating this demand.

The French start-up Drivy is attempting to connect customers with unused, available car capacity in another way. On average a car is in use less than 10% of the time. Drivy organizes the rental of private cars, as opposed to professional car rental. The marginal costs are low in this business as well, and in the eyes of some car owners, they may be practically zero. As a result, Drivy can follow a very aggressive price strategy. Allianz, the second largest insurers in the world, covers all rented Drivy cars with comprehensive insurance [73]. In the United States, GetAround offers a similar peer-to-peer car sharing service which also includes insurance. Lawrence Burns [74], former vice president of research and development at General Motors, estimates that such sharing economies could mean that the same level of mobility would be achieved with 80% fewer automobiles. Mobility service providers as well as car manufacturers need to equip themselves for a new form of price competition.

In the discussion of zero marginal costs, we should not forget one very important insight which Rifkin does not fully address [31]. The marginal costs define the short-term lower limit for prices. The long-term lower limit for prices is determined by the fully loaded costs, i.e., the marginal costs and the allocated fixed costs. No firm can survive in the long term solely from contribution margins; the total contribution margins must be higher than the fixed costs. That is the only way to achieve a profit. For this reason, we have difficulties accepting Rifkin's conclusions about the future of capitalism [31]. Yes, marginal costs of zero will intensify price competition, but they will not "repeal" the fundamental law that a company over time needs to collect more money than it spends.

14.3.9 Innovative Payment Systems

New payment systems will exert additional influence on price management. In recent years, in addition to credit and debit cards, a variety of systems such as PayPal, Apple Pay, Samsung Pay, Android Pay, Alipay by Alibaba, Tenpay by Tencent, WeChat Pay, and new cryptocurrencies such as bitcoin, ethereum, and others have come into existence. Surprisingly the first trial to pay through iris scanning took place in a refugee camp in Syria, where the system was tested by the World Food Program (WFP) [75].This trend is showing no signs of ending; in fact, it seems that new offerings are constantly coming on the market. Which systems will become the market standards, or compete in coexistence with other offerings, is impossible to assess at the present time. What is certain is that these new systems will influence buying behavior and willingness to pay in similar ways that checks, credit cards, and other now commonplace payment forms did in the past.

14.3.9.1 Prepaid Systems
Under prepaid systems, the consumer pays in advance of using a service or receiving a product. One can interpret this approach as a variant of advance-purchase prices.

Advance purchase discounts for events such as concerts, conferences, etc. have been a common practice for ages. With a modern prepaid system, one pays a certain amount in advance, which is usually stored on a card or on the smartphone. The consumer then uses up the stored amount over time. Another variant is the monthly prepayment, with a reconciliation at year's end based on actual usage. Prepaid cards are popular in many sectors such as cafeterias and similar services with regular repeat usage. An example is the Starbucks card, which consumers can continually reload. PAYBACK also offers a prepaid card as well as digital coupons, another form of "prepaid" which is generally meant for gifts. Prepaid cards are also increasingly offered in unusual or unexpected areas. One example is a card for private jets. This card is meant to replace the customary model of full or partial ownership in private jets (e.g., NetJets). A card for the market leader Marquis costs $100,000 for 25 flight hours [76]. But even in this segment of extreme luxury, there are special promotions. At the occasion of its 15th anniversary, PJS offered a 15-hour jet card for $71,895—all inclusive.

Prepaid models have advantages and disadvantages for both sellers and customers. Because the seller has received money in advance, the risk of nonpayment is eliminated. The seller even earns money if the customer loses a card which still has unredeemed value. A disadvantage for the seller is that the customer relationship is not as strong as under a fixed-term contract. For the customers, prepaid assures them that they will not spend more than they can afford because they have set a limit already and can track their expenditures. This is an important aspect of prepaid mobile plans for children. There can also be interesting psychological consequences arising from the time lags between payment and consumption. The negative value of paying is perhaps perceived only once, while the positive experience of consumption is experienced multiple times. Compared to concurrent payment, this situation may lead to higher consumption or induce a lower price elasticity. Based on the study we cited above [71], which stated that customers may be willing to spend more upfront in order to receive rebates later, it may make sense for a supplier to consciously set monthly prepayments at a higher amount in order to guarantee the customer a rebate at year's end [50]. Prospect theory would assert that the rebate brings an additional positive value which exceeds the negative marginal utility created by the slightly higher monthly prepayments.

Prepaid cards are especially popular in emerging countries. One reason for this is that many low-income consumers do not have bank accounts. In such countries, the vast majority of mobile telecommunications runs via prepaid systems. Prepaid shows up in unusual places in emerging markets as well. In Mexico, Zurich Insurance offers prepaid car insurance. The customers buy a card which entitles him or her to insurance for 30 days from whenever they decide to activate the card.

14.3.9.2 Bonus Systems

PAYBACK is a popular bonus system in Europe. Introduced in 2000, it now has 30 million customers. Plenti, a bonus system similar to PAYBACK, was launched in the United States in 2015. Customers collect bonus points upon making purchases in participating stores—brick-and-mortar as well as online—and can redeem these points for rewards. The discounts range from 0.5% to 4%, depending on the store. While credit card companies also offer points which customers can redeem for rewards, the functionality of the PAYBACK card is being enhanced continuously. PAYBACK and Plenti cooperate with credit card companies so that customers can use the respective card for payment as well. PAYBACK and Plenti make it possible to conduct actions which award more bonus points than usual. They can distribute e-coupons, have a prepaid function, and also a mobile app. The big difference between these bonus systems and a customer card for a single company is that PAYBACK and Plenti collect purchase data across multiple stores and sectors. This data basis lends itself ideally to data mining and comprehensive, in-depth analyses of consumer buying behavior. For this reason, PAYBACK came under close scrutiny regarding the safeguarding of personal data. In essence, PAYBACK is a discount system whose collection feature contributes to its success. The system takes advantage of many opportunities for customer interaction and will continue to develop.

14.3.9.3 Internet-Oriented Payment Systems

With well over 227 million member accounts, PayPal is the most widely used Internet-oriented payment system in the western world. The Chinese payment service Alipay has 450 million active customers, making it far larger than PayPal in that respect, but the service is regionally limited primarily to China and has only 500,000 retailers. Expansion to other countries is planned, however [77]. Founded in 1999, PayPal was acquired by eBay in 2002 and was tailored for several years to support eBay transactions before it was opened to the general market. eBay spun off PayPal in 2015. In the United States, companies which use PayPal pay 30 cents per transaction plus 2.9% of revenue. PayPal processes 15 million transactions daily. Alipay processes up to 1 billion transactions per day or 67 times as many as PayPal [78]. An important innovation PayPal launched in 2015 is one-touch payment. According to one test of the service, "companies saw higher sales figures and attracted new customers from one-touch payments" [77]. Amazon has had its highly regarded one-click ordering process for years. What makes their one-click ordering process unique is that it eliminates the explicit payment step. Uber works in a similar fashion. In contrast to a classic taxi trip, the rider exits the Uber vehicle at the end of the ride without needing to take care of payment. Even more radical is Amazon's Dash button, which allows a customer to repeat a preset order. In 2016, in its home city of Seattle, Amazon opened a test supermarket which has no checkout registers. All consumers need to shop at the "Amazon Go" store is the corresponding app on their smartphones. Sensors automatically recognize which products a shopper has taken from the shelves. When the customer is finished, he or she simply leaves the store. A short time later, Amazon deducts the amount spent from the customer's Amazon account [79]. In other words, the payment is processed digitally, just as it is on Uber. The customer receives price information in transparent form prior to purchase but does not need to "make" a payment personally. It remains unclear whether these innovations will induce changes in willingness to pay. In any case, many customers derive value from the simplification of the transaction process, which means sellers may expect some increase in willingness to pay in response.

Apple's payment system called Apple Pay can only be used in conjunction with Apple products (e.g., iPhone, iPad, and Apple Watch). Apple charges its bank partners a fee of 0.15% of the transaction amount. Apple Pay may gain considerable market share in Internet payment services, thanks to its huge customer base. Similar to Apple Pay, the newly introduced mobile Android Pay runs over near-field communication (NFC). With this launch, Alphabet sees an opportunity to penetrate further into the daily lives of users in order to capture information on buying behavior [80]. Samsung offers a similar pay service under the name Samsung Pay, which uses magnetic secure transmission (MST) technology and thus can run on 90% of all payment terminals [81]. The government of Nigeria, in cooperation with MasterCard, has developed a personal ID which can also be used as a debit card [57].

One must not forget the complex payment infrastructure behind the medium (card, smartphone) visible to the consumer. Cost, speed, and safety of payments require both complex hardware (e.g., terminals) and software. Suppliers active in these fields like Gemalto, Wirecard, Square, or G&D are hardly known to the general public but critical for the functioning and adoption of the systems.

Internet-oriented payment systems will develop beyond the pure payment function. One remaining challenge is the commercial processing of micropayments. The ability to make payments of very minimal amounts promises a vast potential for online content, entertainment, game modules, and banking services. But this potential can only be tapped when the processing of micropayments is inexpensive. Innovative payment systems can also lead to improvements with respect to the price and value aspects we discussed at the outset of this chapter. Amazon's one-click process and similar services such as PayPal provide greater convenience. Passwords and PINs will be replaced by fingerprint readers and face or iris recognition. New systems allow the integration of individualized discounts and special offers, best-price guarantees, coupons, and much more. They greatly expand the range of options and actions for price management.

14.3.9.4 Cash and Bitcoin

Fundamentally speaking, money is information and can therefore be digitized. Money in physical form is not necessary to fulfill this information function. Money in physical form does have big advantages, such as anonymity and the ability to conclude a purchase in one act. A cash payment brings the transaction process between buyer and seller to a close. If the two parties do not know each other, the transaction remains anonymous. There is no way to connect multiple purchases by one customer and thus discern purchase patterns. Payment methods such as check, wire transfer, direct debit, or credit card require additional steps to complete the transaction, and they are traceable, i.e., there is no anonymity. That last point is one reason why Harvard University economist Kenneth Rogoff [82] and others advocate the elimination of cash. They argue that if all account transactions were traceable, it would be a massive hindrance to the black market economy as well as illegal or undocumented labor. It would also be impossible to hoard cash, which means the government or the central bank could effectively manage savings and consumption behavior. Negative interest rates could compel people with money to spend it and give the economy a boost. Cash also carries security risks such as counterfeiting or theft, which creates costs.

Between 46% and 80% of all payments around the world are still made in cash. On a value basis, there are large differences between individual countries. In Germany and Austria, cash comprises over 50% of the transaction value, while in the United States, Canada, and France, cash payments make up only around a quarter of the value of all transactions [81]. In Germany, a large majority of the population opposes the elimination of cash. In a study conducted by the market research institute YouGov [83], some 74% of respondents in Germany opposed abolition of the requirement to accept cash as legal tender for any transaction. In other countries, cash is considered old-fashioned. In Sweden, a bank robber is said to have run away without completing his task because the bank no longer carried cash on hand [84]. Due to lack of demand, the Danish Central Bank decided that it will no longer print bank notes. Smaller stores and gas stations will no longer be obliged to accept cash. But admittedly, even in Denmark the money in circulation continues to grow, apparently because people are hoarding a lot of cash. This applies to Germany and Switzerland as well, where "citizens are hoarding more and more money" [85]. In Italy, cash payments exceeding €1000 are forbidden. In contrast, many emerging economies remain predominantly cash based, regardless of the transaction size. In Oman, even monthly rents, real estate purchases, and car purchases are settled using cash.

We consider the probability that cash disappears to be low. As the Russian poet Fyodor Dostoyevsky wrote, "cash is coined liberty." Should cash as we know it be forbidden, people would come up with replacements. This happened when people exchanged sea shells in the Stone Age, and it happened after World War II when people exchanged cigarettes and other objects of value. For larger payments, gold can serve as a replacement for cash. We expect that spending behavior using gold would be similar to the behavior using cash, which is less likely to be used casually or frivolously as when using a credit card. What the propagandists for the elimination of cash are really striving for would be tantamount to a nanny state for consumers with corresponding restrictions on freedom. Were gold to reappear as currency, contrary to what they desire, they may actually end up achieving the opposite effect. The interventionists' next step would then be to forbid private possession or ownership of gold.

The Internet could replace cash as we know it today, without eliminating its function. In our era, we are mostly familiar with currency issued by national governments. This was different in traditional societies, where currencies were often issued and brought into circulation by private banks. Different currencies would therefore exist in parallel. In the Internet age, private money could experience a renaissance. The most spectacular creation of such a currency is Bitcoin. "Bitcoin is an electronic currency which is created in a decentralized way over an online peer-to-peer network and encrypted on the basis of digital signatures" [86, 87]. Transactions occur when two computers connect on the Internet. The difference to conventional payments is that no central clearing function is necessary. The balances of the participants are stored in personal digital wallets. The market value of a bitcoin is governed by supply and demand. Bitcoin was described for the first time in 2008 in a white paper written by an author under the pseudonym "Satoshi Nakamoto." In 2009, the open-source bitcoin software was published [88, 89]. In the following years, the price of a bitcoin fluctuated widely.

Describing the bitcoin system in thorough detail in this chapter would be going too far. From the perspective of price management innovation, it is interesting that bitcoin closely resembles traditional cash on the one hand and gold on the other hand. The transaction is completed with the bitcoin payment, and the payment remains anonymous. The question remains open whether the cash effect, i.e., that it is less freely spent than credit card money, also applies to bitcoin. The analogy to gold lies in the fact that the number of bitcoins is limited to circa 21 million. Likewise still open is the question of whether bitcoin or another cryptocurrency like ethereum or ripple will achieve broad acceptance.

Conclusion

Throughout history there have always been innovations in price management. But they happened very infrequently and in small steps. The Internet and other new technologies have dramatically increased the innovation dynamics.

- The most direct and thus far strongest effect of the Internet is a massive increase in price transparency. Price elasticity is increasing accordingly. Price increases are generating stronger negative sales volume effects and price cuts stronger positive effects than in the past.
- Medium and long-term, the increase in value transparency may be an equally or even more important effect of the Internet. If a product receives poor reviews, price cuts will be largely ineffective, and price increases will lead to sharp drops in volume. In contrast, positive reviews lower the price elasticity on price increases and increase it for price cuts.
- Innovations in price management are driven by new business models or new technologies like sensors. In many cases, both drivers apply.
- Flat rates have achieved considerable popularity, above all in online and information technology businesses. They offer customers the advantages of limiting risk and avoiding the "taximeter" effect. From the supplier perspective, flat rates should be viewed with caution. This applies even when marginal costs are zero, because the companies may sacrifice substantial revenue potential from heavy users.
- Freemium is a very popular online price model. Establishing the boundary between the free and paid offers is difficult but critical for economic success. One variant is to finance the free part of the model, at least partially, through advertising.
- In general, the pricing of content is a major barrier. The "free culture," which characterized many online offers, is now a historical burden which is difficult to overcome. The same holds true for free competing offers. They impose a massive constraint on pricing.

(continued)

- Name-your-own-price, an interactive price model, began with big hopes which were not fulfilled. The impression remains that potential buyers are not revealing their true willingness to pay and instead are just hunting for bargains. That does not preclude that this model may undergo a renaissance.
- Pay-what-you-want is, in our view, a price model driven more by illusion than realism. It is suited solely for special situations and not a sustainable strategy.
- Pay-per-use is a price model which is penetrating more and more markets. The foundation is often sensor technology which offers a low-cost way to track performance or usage, thus making new price metrics possible. Pricing innovations with a pay-per-use model and new price metrics have a promising future.
- Two-sided price systems not only increase revenues but also expand leeway across price parameters. The Internet offers more opportunities in this regard than the traditional economy.
- Negative prices are a new phenomenon which appeared primarily in electricity markets and for interest rates. Negative prices induce a two-sided price system. In such cases, the optimal price can be negative.
- Marginal costs of zero reduce the short-term lower limit for price to zero and can lead to very aggressive price strategies. These are especially threatening to established, incumbent suppliers who operate with positive marginal costs. The use of underutilized capacity in the context of the sharing economy is an important driver behind this trend. One must still observe that the long-term lower limit for price lies at the fully loaded unit costs.
- New technologies and the Internet have given rise to numerous innovative payment systems, including cryptocurrencies such as bitcoin. These systems are likely to influence buying behavior and willingness to pay, but it is too early to fully estimate their ultimate effects right now.

We assume that the flow of innovations relevant to price management is by no means at an end. It will continue to swell. The total elimination of cash is unlikely, but an increasingly larger share of transactions are being conducted and processed digitally. Price management will remain exciting.

References

1. Barrot, C., Albers, S., Skiera, B., & Schäfers, B. (2010). Vickrey vs. eBay: Why Second-price Sealed-bid Auctions Lead to More Realistic Price-Demand Functions. *International Journal of Electronic Commerce (IJEC)*, 14(4), 7–38.
2. Coase, R. H. (1960). The Problem of Social Cost. *Journal of Law and Economics,* 3(1), 1–44.

3. Demsetz, H. (1968). The Cost of Transacting. *Quarterly Journal of Economics,* 82(1), 33–53.
4. Burstein, M. L. (1960). The Economies of Tie-In Sales. *Review of Economics and Statistics,* 42 (1), 68–73.
5. Adams, W. J., & Yellen, J. L. (1976). Commodity Bundling and the Burden of Monopoly. *Quarterly Journal of Economics,* 90(3), 475–488.
6. Oren, S. S., Smith, S. A., & Wilson, R. B. (1982). Nonlinear Tariffs in Markets with Interdependent Demand. *Marketing Science,* 57(1), 287–313.
7. Statista Inc. (2018). Apple's revenue from iTunes, software and services from 1st quarter 2013 to 1st quarter 2018 (in billion U.S. dollars). https://www.statista.com/statistics/250918/apples-revenue-from-itunes-software-and-services/. Accessed 12 March 2018.
8. Fortune (2018). Spotify Stock Goes Public, Giving the Streaming Music Giant a $30 Billion Market Cap. http://fortune.com/2018/04/03/spotify-stock-market-cap-ipo-direct-listing. Accessed 19 April 2018.
9. Bradshaw, T. & Garrahan, M. (2015, June 06). Apple Streaming Service Leaves iTunes Behind. *Financial Times,* p. 12.
10. Garrahan, M. (2015, June 10). Apple and Spotify to Face the Music. *Financial Times.* p. 12.
11. Coscarelli, J. (2016). Adele's '25' Finally Comes to Streaming Services. https://www.nytimes.com/2016/06/24/arts/music/adele-25-streaming-spotify-tidal-apple.html?_r=0. Accessed 16 January 2017.
12. Anonymous. (2015). How Much do Musicians Really Make From Spotify, iTunes and YouTube? https://www.theguardian.com/technology/2015/apr/03/how-much-musicians-make-spotify-itunes-youtube. Accessed 16 January 2017.
13. Christman, E. (2018). U.S. Music Industry Hits Highest Revenue Mark in a Decade, Fueled by Paid Subscriptions. https://www.billboard.com/articles/business/8257558/us-music-industry-2017-highest-revenue-in-decade-fueled-paid-subscriptions. Accessed 19 April 2018.
14. Goldman, D. (2014). 5 Best Apps to Find Cheap Gas. http://money.cnn.com/2014/12/29/technology/mobile/gas-price-apps/. Accessed 16 January 2017.
15. Anonymous. (2013, August 23). Deutsche vergleichen Online Preise. *Lebensmittel Zeitung,* p. 44.
16. De La Merced, M.J. (2015, July 17). Data Start-up Lands Big Name. *International New York Times,* p. 16.
17. GfK (2015). Handys sind wichtige Einkaufsbegleiter. GfK-Studie zur Nutzung von Mobiltelefonen im Geschäft. Nürnberg. http://www.gfk.com/de/news-und-events/presse/pressemitteilungen/seiten/handys-sind-wichtige-einkaufsbegleiter.aspx. Accessed 30 June 2015.
18. Anonymous. (2015, May 28). Eine Ethik für das Digitale Zeitalter. *Handelsblatt,* pp. 12–13.
19. Levine, R., Locke, C., Searls, D., & Weinberger, D. (2011). *The Cluetrain Manifesto:* 10th Anniversary Edition. New York: Basic Books.
20. Domizlaff, H. (1982). *Die Gewinnung des öffentlichen Vertrauens: Ein Lehrbuch der Markentechnik* (New Edition). Markentechnik. Hamburg: Marketing Journal.
21. Stadie, E., & Zwirglmaier, K. (2015). Neue Technologien im Preismanagement. In L. Binckebanck, & R. Elste (Ed.), Digitalisierung Im Vertrieb. Strategien Zum Einsatz neuer Technologien in Vertriebsorganisationen. Gabler, Wiesbaden, pp. 105–121.
22. Rentmeister, J., & Klein, S. (2003). Geschäftsmodelle – Ein Modebegriff auf der Waagschale. *ZfB-Ergänzungsheft,* 73(1), 17–30.
23. Stähler, P. (2001). *Geschäftsmodelle in der digitalen Ökonomie.* Lohmar: Eul.
24. Burkhart, T., Krumeich, J., Werth, D., & Loos, P. (2011). Analyzing the Business Model Concept – A Comprehensive Classification of Literature. *Proceedings of International Conference on Information Systems (ICIS),* 1–19.
25. Simon, H. (2000). Internet und Flatrates. Workshop. Bonn: Deutsche Telekom. November 20.
26. Anonymous. (2015, March 31). Rundumverpflegt in die Ferien. *Tierischer Volksfreund,* p. 8.
27. Netflix.com (2015). Wählen Sie den Plan, der Ihren Bedürfnissen am besten entspricht. https://www.netflix.com/getstarted?locale=de-DE. Accessed 7 June 2015.

28. CNBC (2018). Netflix Adds 5.3 Million Subscribers During Third Quarter, Beating Analysts' Estimates. https://www.cnbc.com/2017/10/16/netflix-q3-2017-earnings.html. Accessed 15 January 2018.
29. Garrahan, M. & Bond, S. (2015, 22 January). Jeff Bezos, the Great Disrupter who has Turned the Book Publishing and Retail Sectors on their Heads, is Shaking up Film and Newspapers, but Both Sectors will Test his Customer-First, Profit-Later Strategy. *Financial Times*, p. 9.
30. Tix, M. (2017). Strom-Flatrate ist Ladenhüter. http://www.energate-messenger.de/news/176990/strom-flatrate-ist-ladenhueter. Accessed 12 March 2018.
31. Rifkin, J. (2014). Die Null-Grenzkosten-Gesellschaft: *Das Internet der Dinge, kollaboratives Gemeingut und der Rückzug des Kapitalismus*. Frankfurt am Main: Campus.
32. Anonymous. (2015, September 01). Zu viel gehört – Digitalhändler in Amerika reduziert Hörbuch-Flatrate. *Frankfurter Allgemeine Zeitung*, p. 11.
33. Anonymous. (2013, April 03). Nicht jedes Angebot ist ein Schnäppchen. Null-Prozent-Finanzierungen werden für den Handel immer wichtiger. *General-Anzeiger Bonn*, p. 6.
34. Anonymous. (2015, April 20). Heftiger Flirt mit der App. *Frankfurter Allgemeine Zeitung*, p. 22.
35. Anonymous. (2015, January 22). Microsoft überrascht mit Computerbrille. *Frankfurter Allgemeine Zeitung*, p. 19.
36. The New York Times (2015). Choose the Times Digital Subsciption that is Best for You. http://international.nytimes.com/subscriptions/inyt/lp87JWF.html?currency=euro&adxc=277706&adxa=406556&page=homepage.nytimes.com/index.html&pos=Bar1&campaignId=4LH46. Accessed 8 June 2015.
37. Berman, S. J. (2011). *Not for Free: Revenue Strategies for a New World*. Boston: Harvard Business Review Press.
38. Zitzmann, M. (2015). Webzeitung "Mediapart" – Ein Vorbild für investigativen Journalismus. http://www.nzz.ch/feuilleton/medien/ein-vorbild-fuer-investigativen-journalismus-1.18459759. Accessed 16 January 2017.
39. Anonymous (2016). Super Mario Run reviews hit Nintendo share price. http://www.bbc.com/news/technology-38365559. Accessed 16 January 2017.
40. Shmilovici, U. (2011). The Complete Guide to Freemium Business Models. http://techcrunch.com/2011/09/04/complete-guide-freemium/. Accessed 15 July 2015.
41. Vance, A. (2015). *Elon Musk – Tesla, SpaceX and the Quest for a Fantastic Future*. New York: HarperCollins. Kindle Version: Position 2266.
42. Lambert, F. (2018). Tesla Plans Expansion of Fremont Factory Supercharging Station – Making it the Biggest in America. https://electrek.co/2018/03/01/tesla-supercharger-fremont-factory/. Accessed 16 March 2018.
43. Tesla (2017). Supercharger. https://www.tesla.com/supercharger. Accessed 16 January 2017.
44. Priceline (2015). Investor Relations. http://ir.pricelinegroup.com/index.cfm. Accessed 15 July 2015.
45. Schmidt, K. M., Spann, M., & Zeithammer, R. (2015). Pay What You Want as a Marketing Strategy in Monopolistic and Competitive Markets. *Management Science*, 61(6), 1217–1236.
46. Anonymous. (2013, March 18). Zwischen Fairness und Schnäppchenjagd. *General-Anzeiger Bonn*, p. 6.
47. Buskirk, E. van (2007, November 05). 2 out of 5 Downloaders Paid for Radiohead's "In Rainbows". *Wired Magazine*, p. 47.
48. Activehours.com (2015). https://www.activehours.com/. Accessed 18 May 2015.
49. Roggentin, A. S. & Bues, M. (2017). Pay-What-You-Want Pricing. A Structured Review on Drivers of Prices Paid by Customers. *Marketing Review St. Gallen*, 6/2017.
50. Schulz, F., Schlereth, C., Mazar, N., & Skiera, B. (2015). Advanced Payment Systems: Paying Too Much Today and Being Satisfied Tomorrow. *International Journal of Research in Marketing, 32*(3), 238–250.
51. Oldemann, O. (2015). Innovating your Price Model: Pricing for TopLine Power. Amsterdam: *Simon-Kucher & Partners*. November.

52. Friemel, K., & Malcher, I. (2006). Gewusst wie. *McKinsey Wissen,* 18, 18–25.
53. Brignall, M. (2017). Pay-as-you-go car insurance – perfect for the low mileage driver? https:// www.theguardian.com/money/2017/feb/11/pay-as-you-go-car-insurance-low-mileage-driver- cuvva-just-miles Accessed 4 December 2017.
54. Siebenbiedel, C. (2014). Revolution der KfZ-Versicherung. http://fazarchiv.faz.net/document/ showSingleDoc/FAS__SD1201401124153932?q=Revolution+der+KfZVersicherung& dosearch=new&&annr=223006&highlight=% 5CeJxzs9LisrFSUODSs8pOqwLTZalFxZnJGalFpXnpQAE7oKyBjgFQoii1LD%2BntCQzPw %2BsLiW1CEi7WcVTZgAA3wUjLg%3D%3D%5C. Accessed 15 June 2015.
55. ENERCON GmbH (2010). ENERCON Windenergieanlagen – PartnerKonzept (EPK). http:// www.enercon.de/p/downloads/Enercon_EPK_2010_deu.pdf. Accessed 26 January 2015.
56. Zuboff, S. (2015, March 23). Die Vorteile der Nachzügler. *Frankfurter Allgemeine Zeitung,* p. 15.
57. Morozov, E. (2013, November 02). Unser Leben wird umgekrempelt. *Frankfurter Allgemeine Zeitung,* p. 14.
58. Craymer, L. (2013). Weigh More, Pay More on Samoa Air. http://www.wsj.com/articles/ SB10001424127887323646604578399943583708244. Accessed 15 September 2015.
59. Hope, B. (2015, August 10). Company Tracks Bank Cards and Sells Data to Investors. *Wall Street Journal,* 10–11.
60. Stewart, J. B. (2015, April 24). Chasing a Negative Mortage-Rate. *International New York Times,* p. 16.
61. Anonymous. (2018). What are Negative Prices and how do They Occur? http://www.epexspot. com/en/company-info/basics_of_the_power_market/negative_prices. Accessed 16 March 2018.
62. Anonymous. (2015, April 25). Negativzins widerspricht nicht der menschlichen Natur. *Frankfurter Allgemeine Zeitung,* p. 29.
63. Anonymous. (2015, August 20). Negativrendite bleibt gefragt. *Frankfurter Allgemeine Zeitung,* p. 25.
64. Anonymous (2015, May 05). Großanleger erwägen Flucht ins Bargeld. *Frankfurter Allgemeine Zeitung,* p. 23.
65. Anonymous (2015, November 24). Mehr als 2 Billionen Euro Staatsanleihen mit Negativzins. *Frankfurter Allgemeine Zeitung,* p. 23.
66. Anonymous. (2015, October 23). Negative Zinsen auch für ganz normale Privatkunden. *Frankfurter Allgemeine Zeitung,* p. 23.
67. Reinhardt, D. (2018). Kredit von Smava und Check24: So viel Geld gibt es mit Minuszins. https://www.focus.de/finanzen/banken/ratenkredit/ratenkredite-von-smava-und-check24-so- viel-geld-gibt-es-mit-minuszins_id_8544941.html. Accessed 16 March 2018.
68. von Weizsäcker, C. C. (2015). *Kapitalismus in der Krise? Perspektiven der Wirtschaftspolitik,* 16(2), 189–212.
69. Veerasamy, V. (2016). PayPal's $60m Referral Program: A Legendary Growth Hack. https:// www.referralcandy.com/blog/paypal-referrals/. Accessed 12 March 2018.
70. Lee, F. (2017, March 18). Pekings Plage mit den Fahrrädern. In Chinas Hauptstadt boomt der Markt mit Leihrädern. Nutzer werden teilweise sogar bezahlt. *General Anzeiger Bonn,* p. 11.
71. Anonymous. (2015, March 26). Wer teilt was mit wem? *Frankfurter Allgemeine Zeitung,* p. 26.
72. Anonymous. (2015, April 27). Mit Vollgas zum Transportnetzwerk. *Frankfurter Allgemeine Zeitung,* p. 18.
73. Anonymous. (2015, April 28). Der Fremde in meinem Auto. *Handelsblatt,* p. 23.
74. Burns, L. (2013, May 09). A Vision of our Transport Future. *Nature,* 497, 181–182.
75. Anonymous. (2017). http://www.globaltimes.cn/content/1052839.shtml. Accessed 12 March 2018.
76. Roberts, D. (2015, April 01). The Rise of the Jet Card. *Fortune,* p. 14.

77. Chip (2015). Ein-Klick Payment mit PayPal schnell und einfach bezahlen ohne Passwort. http://business.chip.de/news/Ein-Klick-Payment-mit-PayPal-Schnell-und-einfach-bezahlen-ohne-Passwort_78753875.html. Accessed 3 May 2015.
78. Millward, S. (2016). China's Alipay just saw a record 1 billion transactions in a day. https://www.techinasia.com/alibaba-alipay-1-billion-transactions. Accessed 12 March 2018.
79. Anonymous. (2016, December 07). Amazon testet Supermarkt ohne Kassen. *Frankfurter Allgemeine Zeitung*, p. 23.
80. Barr, A. (2015, May 29). Google Unveils New Rival to Apple Pay. *Wall Street Journal*, p. 17.
81. Anonymous (2015, May). Mobiles Bezahlen – Wettkampf der Systeme. Der Handel – *Das Wirtschaftsmagazin für Handelsunternehmen*, p. 44.
82. Rogoff, K. S. (2016). *The Curse of Cash*. Princeton: Princeton University Press.
83. Anonymous. (2015, May 28). Die Deutschen wollen das Bargeld nicht aufgeben. *Frankfurter Allgemeine Zeitung*, p. 25.
84. Anonymous. (2015, May 09). Ein weiterer Schlag gegen das Bargeld. *Frankfurter Allgemeine Zeitung*, p. 31.
85. Anonymous. (2015, June 13). Bürger horten immer mehr Bargeld. *Frankfurter Allgemeine Zeitung*, p. 30.
86. bitcoin.de. (2015). Retrieved from www.bitcoin.de. Accessed 30 April 2015.
87. Nestler, F. (2015). Deutschland erkennt Bitcoins als privates Geld an. http://www.faz.net/aktuell/finanzen/devisen-rohstoffe/digitale-waehrung-deutschland-erkennt-bitcoins-als-privates-geld-an-12535059.html. Accessed 6 March 2018.
88. Nakamoto, S. (2008). Bitcoin: A Peer-to-Peer Electronic Cash System. https://bitcoin.org/bitcoin.pdf. Accessed 28 April 2014.
89. Davis, J. (2014). The Crypto-Currency: Bitcoin and its Mysterious Inventor. http://www.newyorker.com/magazine/2011/10/10/the-crypto-currency. Accessed 15 June 2015.

Acknowledgments

We express our thanks to many colleagues and co-workers for their suggestions, case examples, technical and methodological support, editing, and proofreading.

From the team at the Otto Beisheim Chair of Marketing and Commerce at the WHU—Otto Beisheim School of Management, we thank Philipp Babicky, Patricia Gräfin Kerssenbrock, Jonas Schütz, Alexander Schultze, and Sarina Steiger. Graphic artist André Zimmermann helped us prepare the figures and tables. Above all, we are very thankful to our project team leader Anna-Karina Schmitz for all of her efforts.

We offer our heartfelt thanks to numerous partners and associates from Simon-Kucher and Partners for their contributions to this book: Omar Ahmad, Kai Bandilla, Dr. Christoph Bauer, Jens Baumgarten, Thomas Beducker, Dr. Men-Andri Benz, Dr. Philip Biermann, Maximilian Biesenbach, Mark Billige, Joshua Bloom, Grigori Bokeria, Eduardo Bonet, Dr. Daniel Bornemann, Franck Brault, James Brown, Tim Brzoska, Thomas Buchholz, Hong-May Cheng, David Chung, Dr. Gunnar Clausen, Dr. Peter Colman, Martin Crépy, Björn Dahmen, Philip Daus, Dr. Sven de Labey, Juriaan Deumer, Michael Dilger, Robert Dumitrescu, Dr. Allison Dupuy, Peter Ehrhardt, Dr. Jan Engelke, Francesco Fiorese, Chuck Gammal, Frank Gehrig, Dr. Martin Gehring, Ignacio Gomez, Josh Goodman, Dr. Razmic Gregorian, Dr. Tobias Maria Günter, Jan Hämer, Dr. Thomas Haller, Eddie Hartman, Dr. Klaus Hilleke, Dimitris Hiotis, Dr. Thomas Hofmann, Florent Jacquet, Lisa Jäger, Dr. Volker Janßen, Andreas Jonason, Dirk Kars, Dr. Wei Ke, Nicholas Keppeler, Lovrenc Kessler, Gabor Kiss, Petra Knüsel, Dr. Jochen Krauss, Jörg Krütten, Dr. Eckhard Kucher, Michael Kühn, David Lee, Susan Lee, David Lefevre, Dr. Matthias Liefner, Dr. Andrea Maessen, Dr. Marc Matar, Dr. Rainer Meckes, Wolfgang Johann Mitschke, Dr. Jens Müller, Ursina Müller, Dr. Clemens Oberhammer, Onno Oldeman, Dr. Rainer Opgen-Rhein, Raf Onclin, Manuel Osorio, Christoph Petzoldt, Betty Pio, Madhavan Ramanujam, Christian Rebholz, Kornelia Reifenberg, Juan Rivera, Damien Robert, Stephen Rosen, Ricardo Rubi, Guillermo Sagnier, Nina Scharwenka, Dr. Dirk Schmidt-Gallas, Dr. Gerald Schnell, Christian Schuler, Dr. Fabian Schulz, Stephan Schurz, Othmar Schwarz, Dr. Karl-Heinz Sebastian, Deepak Sharma, David Smith, Brad Soper, Dr. Ekkehard Stadie, Heather Steinfield, Sebastian Strasmann, Jochen Strube, Dr. Silvio Strübi, Dr. Nathan Swilling, Dr. Georg Tacke, Mert Terzioglu, Dr. Enrico Trevisan, Jonathan van Spijker Baan, Marie Verdier, David Vidal, Dr. Andreas von der Gathen,

Andre Weber, Antoine Weill, Jan Weiser, Dr. Georg Wübker, and Dr. Kajetan Zwirglmaier. Administrative assistant Ingo Lier provided outstanding support.

We also owe our thanks to editors Frank Luby and Stephanie Werner of Present Tense LLC, who enhanced and polished our manuscript. Last but not least, it was always a pleasure to work with Nicholas Philipson of Springer Nature, New York, on this project. We thank him for his collaboration and for keeping this project on track.

Any errors and omissions are the sole responsibility of the authors.